MW00791864

Routledge International Handbook of Masculinity Studies

The *Routledge International Handbook of Masculinity Studies* provides a contemporary critical and scholarly overview of theorizing and research on masculinities as well as emerging ideas and areas of study that are likely to shape research and understanding of gender and men in the future.

The forty-eight chapters of the handbook take an interdisciplinary approach to a range of topics on men and masculinities related to identity, sex, sexuality, culture, aesthetics, technology and pressing social issues. The handbook's transnational lens acknowledges both the localities and global character of masculinity. A clear message in the book is the need for intersectional theorizing in dialogue with feminist, queer and sexuality studies in making sense of men and masculinities.

Written in a clear and direct style, the handbook will appeal to students, teachers and researchers in the social sciences and humanities, as well as professionals, practitioners and activists.

Lucas Gottzén is Professor at the Department of Child and Youth Studies, Stockholm University, Sweden. His research takes feminist and critical perspectives on youth, gender and sexuality, particularly focusing on young and adult men's violence. His recent books include *Av det känsligare slaget: Män och våld mot kvinnor* ('The (Un)Sensitive Kind: Men and Violence against Women', 2019), *Genus* ('Gender', 2020, with Eriksson) and *Men, Masculinities and Intimate Partner Violence* (2020, co-edited with Bjørnholt and Boonzaier).

Ulf Mellström is an anthropologist and Professor of Gender Studies at Karlstad University, Sweden. He has published extensively within the areas of masculinity studies, transport- and mobility studies, gender and technology, gender and risk, engineering studies, globalization and higher education. He is the founder and editor-in-chief of *NORMA: International Journal for Masculinity Studies*.

Tamara Shefer is Professor of Women's and Gender Studies, Faculty of Arts, University of the Western Cape, South Africa. Her scholarship has focused on intersectional gender and sexual justice, including research on critical masculinities studies. Her current work is focused on rethinking scholarship on sexualities and gender within feminist decolonial approaches. Recent co-edited books are *Engaging Youth in Activist Research and Pedagogical Praxis: Transnational and Intersectional Perspectives on Gender, Sex, and Race* (2018, with Hearn, Ratele & Boonzaier) and *Socially Just Pedagogies in Higher Education: Critical Posthumanist and New Feminist Materialist Perspectives* (2018, with Bozalek, Braidotti & Zembylas).

Routledge International Handbooks

Routledge Handbook of the Belt and Road
Edited by Cai Fang and Peter Nolan

Routledge Handbook of Language Acquisition
Edited by Jessica S. Horst and Janne von Koss Torkildsen

Routledge Handbook of Identity Studies, 2e
Edited by Anthony Elliott

Routledge International Handbook of Poverty
Edited by Bent Greve

Routledge International Handbook of New Digital Practices in Galleries, Libraries, Archives, Museums and Heritage Sites
Edited by Hannah Lewi, Wally Smith, Dirk vom Lehn and Steven Cooke

Routledge International Handbook of Human Trafficking
A Multi-Disciplinary and Applied Approach
Edited by Rochelle L. Dalla and Donna Sabella

The Routledge Handbook of Comparative Rural Policy
Edited by Matteo Vittuari, John Devlin, Marco Pagani and Thomas Johnson

Routledge International Handbook of Masculinity Studies
Edited by Lucas Gottzén, Ulf Mellström and Tamara Shefer

Routledge Handbook of European Welfare Systems, 2e
Edited by Sonja Blum, Johanna Kuhlmann and Klaus Schubert

Routledge International Handbook of Heterosexualities Studies
Edited by James Joseph Dean and Nancy L. Fischer

For more information about this series, please visit: www.routledge.com/Routledge-International-Handbooks/book-series/RIHAND

Routledge International Handbook of Masculinity Studies

Edited by Lucas Gottzén, Ulf Mellström and Tamara Shefer

EDITORIAL SECRETARY
MARINETTE GRIMBEEK

LONDON AND NEW YORK

First published 2020 by Routledge

2 Park Square, Milton Park, Abingdon, Oxon OX14 4RN
605 Third Avenue, New York, NY 10017

Routledge is an imprint of the Taylor & Francis Group, an informa business

First issued in paperback 2021

Copyright © 2020 selection and editorial matter, Lucas Gottzén, Ulf Mellström and Tamara Shefer; individual chapters, the contributors

The right of Lucas Gottzén, Ulf Mellström and Tamara Shefer to be identified as the authors of the editorial material, and of the authors for their individual chapters, has been asserted in accordance with sections 77 and 78 of the Copyright, Designs and Patents Act 1988.

All rights reserved. No part of this book may be reprinted or reproduced or utilised in any form or by any electronic, mechanical, or other means, now known or hereafter invented, including photocopying and recording, or in any information storage or retrieval system, without permission in writing from the publishers.

Notice:
Product or corporate names may be trademarks or registered trademarks, and are used only for identification and explanation without intent to infringe.

Publisher's Note

The publisher has gone to great lengths to ensure the quality of this reprint but points out that some imperfections in the original copies may be apparent.

British Library Cataloguing-in-Publication Data
A catalogue record for this book is available from the British Library

Library of Congress Cataloging-in-Publication Data
Names: Gottzén, Lucas, editor. | Mellström, Ulf, editor. | Shefer, Tamara, editor.
Title: Routledge international handbook of masculinity studies / edited by Lucas Gottzén, Ulf Mellström and Tamara Shefer.
Description: Abingdon, Oxon ; New York, NY : Routledge, 2020. |
Series: Routledge international handbooks | Includes bibliographical references and index.
Identifiers: LCCN 2019029444 (print) | LCCN 2019029445 (ebook) |
ISBN 9781138056695 (hardback) | ISBN 9781315165165 (ebook)
Subjects: LCSH: Men's studies. | Masculinity–Study and teaching.
Classification: LCC HQ1088 .R68 2020 (print) | LCC HQ1088 (ebook) |
DDC 305.31071–dc23
LC record available at https://lccn.loc.gov/2019029444
LC ebook record available at https://lccn.loc.gov/2019029445

ISBN: 978-1-138-05669-5 (hbk)
ISBN: 978-1-03-217634-5 (pbk)
DOI: 10.4324/9781315165165

Typeset in Bembo
by Swales & Willis, Exeter, Devon, UK

Contents

Contributors

Editors

Lucas Gottzén is Professor at the Department of Child and Youth Studies, Stockholm University, Sweden. His research takes feminist and critical perspectives on youth, gender and sexuality, particularly focusing on young and adult men's violence. His recent books include *Av det känsligare slaget: Män och våld mot kvinnor* ('The (Un)Sensitive Kind: Men and Violence against Women', 2019, Makadam), *Genus* ('Gender', 2020, Liber, with Eriksson) and *Men, Masculinities and Intimate Partner Violence* (forthcoming in 2020, co-edited with Bjørnholt and Boonzaier).

Ulf Mellström is an anthropologist and Professor of Gender Studies at Karlstad University, Sweden. He has published extensively within the areas of masculinity studies, transport- and mobility studies, gender and technology, gender and risk, engineering studies, globalization and higher education. He is the founder and editor-in-chief of *NORMA: International Journal for Masculinity Studies*.

Tamara Shefer is Professor of Women's and Gender Studies, Faculty of Arts, University of the Western Cape, South Africa. Her scholarship has focused on intersectional gender and sexual justice, including research on critical masculinities studies. Her current work is focused on rethinking scholarship on sexualities and gender within feminist decolonial approaches. Recent co-edited books are *Engaging Youth in Activist Research and Pedagogical Praxis: Transnational and Intersectional Perspectives on Gender, Sex, and Race* (2018, Routledge, with Hearn, Ratele & Boonzaier) and *Socially Just Pedagogies in Higher Education: Critical Posthumanist and New Feminist Materialist Perspectives* (2018, Bloomsbury, with Bozalek, Braidotti & Zembylas).

Authors

Miriam J. Abelson is Assistant Professor of Women, Gender, and Sexuality Studies at Portland State University, USA, and holds a PhD in sociology from the University of Oregon. Her research and teaching focus on masculinities, queer and transgender studies, research methods and LGBT people's lives across urban and rural spaces. Her book, *Men in Place: Trans Masculinity, Race, and Sexuality in America*, was published in 2019 (University of Minnesota Press).

Jonathan A. Allan is Professor and a Canada Research Chair in the Faculty of Arts at Brandon University, Canada. He is an editor for *Journal of Bodies, Sexualities, and Masculinities* (Berghahn Press, beginning publication in 2020) and associate editor of *Journal of Popular Romance Studies*. His book *Reading from Behind* (2016, University of Regina Press) is a study of anality and masculinity in literary and cultural theory.

Josep M. Armengol is Professor of U.S. Literature and Gender Studies at the University of Castilla–La Mancha, Spain. His research has appeared in journals such as *Signs* and *Journal of Gender Studies*, amongst others. His latest books include *Masculinities in Black and White* (Palgrave Macmillan, 2014) and *Masculinities and Literary Studies* (Routledge, 2017). He is the literary studies editor of *Men and Masculinities*. Currently he is working on aging men and masculinities.

Dag Balkmar is Associate Professor and researcher in Gender Studies, Örebro University, Sweden. His research encompasses three main areas: (1) Studies of men, masculinities, technology, risk-taking and (un)sustainable mobilities; (2) Policy, violence and intersectionality and (3) gender, organization and innovation. Recent publications include articles in *Applied Mobilities*, *Mobilities* and *Transfers: Interdisciplinary Journal of Mobility Studies*.

Rusty Barrett is Associate Professor of Linguistics at the University of Kentucky, USA. His research focuses on Mayan languages, verbal art and poetics, and language, gender and sexuality. He is the author of *From Drag Queens to Leathermen: Language, Gender, and Gay Male Subcultures* (2017, Oxford University Press) and, with Kira Hall, is co-editor of the *Oxford Handbook of Language and Sexuality* (forthcoming).

Chris Beasley is Professor in Politics (Adjunct) at the University of Adelaide, Australia, at which she founded the Fay Gale Centre for Research on Gender. Her research is in social/political theory, gender/sexuality studies and cultural politics. Her books include *The Cultural Politics of Contemporary Hollywood Film* (with Heather Brook, 2019, Manchester University Press), *Heterosexuality in Theory and Practice* (with Heather Brook and Mary Holmes, 2012, Routledge), *Gender & Sexuality* (2005, Sage) and *What is Feminism?* (1999, Sage).

Deevia Bhana is the NRF/DST South African Research Chair and Professor of Gender and Childhood Sexuality at the University of KwaZulu-Natal, South Africa. Among her recent publications are *Love, Sex and Teenage Sexual Cultures in South Africa: 16 turning 17* (2018, Routledge) and *Childhood Sexuality and AIDS Education: The Price of Innocence* (2016, Routledge).

José Blanco F. is an Associate Professor in the Department of Fashion at Dominican University in River Forest, Illinois, USA. His research focuses on dress and popular culture in the late twentieth century, with an emphasis on male fashion. He is also interested in fashion and visual culture in Latin America. José is the general editor of the award-winning encyclopaedia *Clothing and Fashion: American Fashion from Head to Toe*. With Raúl J. Vázquez-López, he has co-authored several articles and book chapters on Puerto Rican dress, costume and fashion.

Floretta Boonzaier is Professor of Psychology at the University of Cape Town, South Africa, and Co-Director of the Hub for Decolonial Feminist Psychologies in Africa. Her research and teaching are in the areas of feminist, critical, social and decolonial psychologies, with special interests in participatory and narrative methodologies and gendered and sexual violence. Her recent publications include *Engaging Youth in Activism, Research and Pedagogical Praxis: Transnational and Intersectional Perspectives on Gender, Sex and Race* (Routledge, 2018, co-edited) and *Feminist Decolonial Community Psychology* (Springer, 2019, co-edited).

Tristan Bridges is Assistant Professor of Sociology at the University of California, Santa Barbara, USA. His primary research interests have to do with transformations in contemporary gender and sexual identities and inequalities. He has studied bodybuilders, fathers' rights activists, pro-feminist men, bar regulars, and is currently collecting interviews with American couples who have "man caves" in their homes. With C.J. Pascoe, he edited *Exploring Masculinities: Identity, Inequality, Continuity and Change* (2016, Oxford University Press).

Lih Shing Chan is a Lecturer at the Department of Asian and Policy Studies, the Education University of Hong Kong. A graduate from Doshisha University, Japan, he is a multilingual researcher, with a critical approach to media sociology. He has studied media representation, Chinese-ness and youth identity. His recent work on Chinese masculinity can be found in *Men and Masculinities*.

Alex Channon is Senior Lecturer in Physical Education and Sport Studies at the University of Brighton, UK. His research on martial arts and the politics of gender has been published across a variety of academic journals. He is the co-editor of *Global Perspectives on Women in Combat Sports: Women Warriors around the World* (Palgrave Macmillan, 2015) and *Sex Integration in Sport and Physical Culture: Promises and Pitfalls* (Routledge, 2017).

Ann-Dorte Christensen is Professor of Gender and Sociology, CeMAS, Centre for Masculinity Studies, Aalborg University, Denmark. Her field of research is focused on gender, masculinity, intersectionality, everyday life, and belonging. Within masculinity studies she has been writing on hegemonic masculinity and intersectionality, masculinity ideals, masculinity risk and safety, war and masculinity, violence in left wing movements and marginalized masculinities. She is co-editor of *NORMA: International Journal for Masculinity Studies*.

Richard Collier, FAcSS, is a Professor of Law at Newcastle University, UK. He has published widely in the areas of law and gender, family law, fatherhood and legal professions and is presently writing the book *Wellbeing, Law and Society*. His previous books include *Men, Law and Gender* (2010, Routledge-Cavendish), *Fragmenting Fatherhood* (2008, Hart), *Masculinities, Crime and Criminology* (1998, Sage), *Masculinity, Law and the Family* (1995, Routledge) and *Fathers' Rights Activism and Law Reform in Comparative Perspective* (2006, Hart).

Sam de Boise is a Senior Lecturer at the School of Music, Theatre and Art at Örebro University, Sweden. His research focuses on music participation and engagement from a critical, feminist perspective, and he has written on men, affect and embodiment, and music and gender in/equalities in Sweden and the UK. His most recent book is *Men, Masculinity, Music and Emotions* (2015, Palgrave Macmillan).

Sarah Diefendorf is a Scholars Strategy Network Postdoctoral Fellow, with joint appointments in the Department of Political Science and the Department of Sociology at the University of Utah, USA. She studies conservative religious organizations and their beliefs about gender and sexuality. Her most recent work is on white evangelical sexual politics in the era of Trump. Sarah has a PhD in Sociology from the University of Washington.

Claire Duncanson is a Senior Lecturer in International Relations at the University of Edinburgh, UK. Her research interests lie at the intersection of international security and gender politics. She has published widely on military masculinities, including *Forces for Good? Military masculinities and peacebuilding in Afghanistan and Iraq* (Palgrave Macmillan, 2013). Her most recent work focuses on the need for a feminist political economy perspective on peacebuilding.

Fataneh Farahani is Associate Professor of Ethnology at the Department of Ethnology, Gender Studies and History of Religions at Stockholm University, Sweden. Her research interests and teaching experiences are shaped by gender and sexualities, postcolonial theories, diaspora and transnationalism, critical race and whiteness studies, hospitality and hostility, diverse research methodologies and processes of knowledge productions, and her recent publications include *Gender, Sexuality and Diaspora* (Routledge, 2018) and "The Racialised Knowledge Economy" (in S. Khadka, J. Davis-McEligatt, & K. Dorwick (Eds.), *Narratives of Marginalized Identities in Higher Education: Inside and Outside the Academy*, 2018, Routledge, with Thapar-Björket).

Steve Garlick is Associate Professor of Sociology at the University of Victoria, Canada. His research encompasses a range of issues concerning masculinity, sexuality, technology, bodies, new materialisms and critical social theory. He is the author of *The Nature of Masculinity: Critical Theory, New Materialisms, and Technologies of Embodiment* (UBC Press, 2016).

Miklós Hadas is Professor of Sociology and Gender Studies, Head of the Culture and Communication Doctoral School, and Co-Director of the Centre for Gender and Culture at Corvinus University of Budapest, Hungary. He is the author of numerous articles on gender and masculinity. Relying on Norbert Elias' civilization theory and process sociology, his current research interest concentrates on the transformation of Western masculinities over the past millennium.

Nils Hammarén has a PhD in Social Work and is Associate Professor of Child and Youth Studies at the University of Gothenburg, Sweden. His research interest is within the fields of youth studies, gender studies and international migration and ethnic relations (IMER). His most recent publication is *The Conundrum of Masculinity: Hegemony, Homosociality, Homophobia and Heteronormativity* (Routledge, 2017, with Chris Haywood, Thomas Johansson, Marcus Herz and Andreas Ottemo).

Chris Haywood is a Reader in Critical Masculinity Studies in the Department of Media, Culture and Heritage at Newcastle University, UK. He is interested in exploring how different conceptual deployments of masculinity shape what we know and are able to know about gender and sexuality. His recent publications include *Men, Masculinity and Contemporary Dating*, *The Conundrum of Masculinity* (2017, Routledge, co-authored) and *Marginalized Masculinities* (2017, Routledge, co-edited).

Jeff Hearn is Senior Professor, Gender Studies, Örebro University, Sweden; Professor Emeritus, Hanken School of Economics, Finland; Professor of Sociology, University of Huddersfield, UK; Professor Extraordinarius, University of South Africa; and honorary doctor in Social Sciences, Lund University, Sweden. He is co-chair, RINGS International Research Association of Institutions of Advanced Gender Studies; co-managing editor of *Routledge Advances in Feminist Studies and Intersectionality* book series; and co-editor, *NORMA: International Journal for Masculinity Studies.*

Helena Wahlström Henriksson is Professor of Gender Studies at Uppsala University, Sweden. Research interests include feminist cultural studies, masculinity studies, and kinship studies. She has published widely on parenthood and childhood in literature, for example in *New Fathers? Contemporary American Stories of Masculinity, Domesticity and Kinship* (2010, Cambridge Scholars) and "Pappahandbooks: Guidebooks for Dads in Twenty-First Century Sweden" (2016). She chairs the Swedish Network for Family and Kinship Studies.

Richard Howson is Associate Professor in the Sociology Program at the University of Wollongong, Australia. His research interests are in the areas of political sociology, masculinities studies, and migration. He is the author of *Challenging Hegemonic Masculinity* (2006, Routledge) and *A Sociology of Postmarxism* (2017, Routledge) and has co-edited the volumes *Migrant Men* (2009, Routledge), *Hegemony* (2009, Routledge) and *Engaging Men in Building Gender Equality* (2015, Cambridge Scholars).

Tobias Hübinette is Associate Professor in Intercultural Education and Senior Lecturer in Intercultural Studies and in Swedish as a Foreign Language at the Department of Language, Literature and Intercultural Studies, Karlstad University, Sweden. His research has, for example, centered on transnational adoption and transracial adoptees, Fascism and the Far Right, migration and minorities, and Swedish whiteness and Swedish race relations. Through the years he has published and been active within the fields of Korean and Asian studies, critical adoption studies and Korean adoption studies, postcolonial and cultural studies, ethnic and migration studies, and critical race and whiteness studies.

Martin Hultman is Associate Professor at Chalmers University, Sweden, and has published widely on energy, climate and environment, including "The Making of an Environmental Hero: A History of Ecomodern Masculinity, Fuel Cells and Arnold Schwarzenegger"; "A green fatwā? Climate change as a threat to the masculinity of industrial modernity"; and the books *Discourses of Global Climate Change* and *Ecological Masculinities.* Hultman leads research groups analyzing masculinities and energy, ecopreneurship and climate change denial.

Sune Qvotrup Jensen is Associate Professor of Sociology at Aalborg University, Denmark. His research interests include urban studies, subculture, criminology, radicalization, social differentiation, gender, masculinity and intersectionality. Within masculinity studies, he has written on intersectionality and hegemonic masculinity as well as ethnic minority masculinities. He currently manages a research project on masculinity and radicalization and is chairperson of CeMAS, Centre for Masculinity Studies, Aalborg University, Denmark.

Thomas Johansson, PhD, is Professor of Pedagogy at the University of Gothenburg, Sweden. He has published extensively in the fields of youth studies, urban studies, the sociology of the family, social theory and critical studies on men and masculinities. His most recent publications are *Fatherhood in Transition: Masculinity, Identity and Everyday Life* (Palgrave, 2017, with Jesper Andreasson), and *Extreme Sports – Extreme Bodies* (Palgrave Macmillan, 2018, with Jesper Andreasson).

Tristen Kade is a graduate student in sociology at Portland State University, USA. He is currently working toward his dissertation on trans masculine individuals of color and their understandings and constructions of their gendered sexualities.

Patricia Lewis is Reader in Management at the Kent Business School, University of Kent, UK. Her research on gendered entrepreneurial identity includes investigations of the masculine norm, authenticity and postfeminist entrepreneurial femininities. She has recently edited (with Yvonne Benschop and Ruth Simpson) *Postfeminism and Organization* (2017, Routledge) and has published in journals such as *Organization Studies*, *Human Relations* and *Work, Employment & Society*. She is currently joint-editor-in-chief of *Gender, Work & Organization*.

Mario Liong is Associate Professor at the College of International Relations, Ritsumeikan University, Japan. His research focuses on the critical study of men and masculinities in family and youth culture. He is the author of *Chinese Fatherhood, Gender and Family: Father Mission* (Palgrave Macmillan, 2017). His recent publications include "Walking a Tightrope on (Hetero)Sexuality" (in *Men and Masculinities*) and "Sacrifice for the Family" (in *Journal of Gender Studies*).

Madhura Lohokare is an anthropologist transitioning to be a writing pedagogue, based in the Centre for Writing Studies at O. P. Jindal University in India. Her doctoral research examined the making and unmaking of gendered masculine identities within the exclusionary geographies of caste and class in urban India. Her current research interests revolve around urban modernity and upper-caste self-making in India, inclusive writing pedagogies and methodologies to evolve a more publically engaged academic practice.

Gareth Longstaff is a Lecturer in Media and Cultural Theory at Newcastle University, UK. In his forthcoming monograph, *Celebrity and Pornography: The Psychoanalysis of Self Representation* (I.B Tauris, 2020), he engages and applies queer theory to Freudian and Lacanian psychoanalysis, the impersonality of desire and the mediated screening of subjectivity and jouissance in self-representational photography, pornography/sexual representation and digital/networked media.

Máirtín Mac an Ghaill works at Newman University, UK. With Chris Haywood, he is author of a recent collection, *Muslim Students, Education and Neoliberalism: Schooling a "Suspect" Community*. This is part of a wider interest in synthesizing a post-masculinity frame and ethnographic alternative representations of a millennial generation of young Muslim men. In so doing, this enables the reflexive self-authorization of critical narratives of local agency to emerge within conditions of globally inflected urban transformations.

Christopher R. Matthews is a Senior Lecturer at Nottingham Trent University, UK. His main area of research is within boxing, where he has conducted a variety of long-term ethnographic studies. He has also developed the notion of 'pastiche hegemony' as a contribution to masculinity theory. His current focus is on the sociology of health and well-being, the medical regulation of combat sport, experiences of concussion, and drug use in sport.

Robyn Mayes is an Associate Professor in the School of Management at Queensland University of Technology, Brisbane, Australia. Her research interests include labour migration, gender, rurality, and community. This research is grounded in empirical work which critically examines the Australian mining sector but also encompasses, more recently, work and working in the digital economy.

Terrance H. McDonald is currently a Postdoctoral Fellow at the Posthumanism Research Network (Brock University in St. Catharines, Ontario, Canada). He is the editor of *Interconnections: Journal of Posthumanism/Interconnexions: revue de posthumanisme*. His work has appeared in *Men and Masculinities*, *NORMA: International Journal of Masculinity Studies*, *Symposium: Canadian Journal of Continental Philosophy* and other venues.

Lee Monaghan is Associate Professor of Sociology, University of Limerick, Ireland, where he teaches the sociology of health and illness, social theory and the sociology of the body. Some of his books include *Bodybuilding, Drugs and Risk* (2001, Routledge), *Men and the War on Obesity* (2008, Routledge) and *Challenging Myths of Masculinity: Understanding Physical Cultures* (2014, Ashgate, with Michael Atkinson).

Andreas Ottemo is Senior Lecturer at the University of Gothenburg, Sweden. His main research interest concerns the intersections between gender, technology, and sexuality, which he currently explores in a project on geek masculinity. Similar themes are addressed in his dissertation, *Gender, body, desire, and technology: Passion and instrumentality in two technical university programs* (2015, University of Gothenburg, in Swedish). Recent publications include *The Conundrum of Masculinity: Hegemony, Homosociality, Homophobia and Heteronormativity* (2017, Routledge, co-authored).

Tal Peretz, PhD, Assistant Professor of Sociology and Women's Studies at Auburn University, USA, has engaged in and studied men's gender justice activism for over a decade. He is the co-author of *Some Men: Male Allies and the Movement to End Violence Against Women* (2015, Oxford University Press, www.somemen.org), with Michael Messner and Max Greenberg. His latest research looks at how intersecting race, class, religious and sexual identities shape men's gender-justice organizing.

Barbara Pini is a Professor in the School of Humanities, Languages and Social Sciences at Griffith University, Brisbane, Australia. Her research focuses on social inequality in rural communities. She has undertaken research which examines the intersections of gender and rurality and explored how gender and rurality are mediated by social locations such as disability, class, sexuality, youth, ethnicity and Indigeneity to create inclusions and exclusions.

Paul Pulé holds a PhD examining transitions from hegemonization to ecologization in modern Western men and masculinities. He is both activist and scholar, mentoring boys and men towards broader, deeper and wider caring masculinities while teaching on the subject at senior university levels as well. He is postdoctoral research fellow in Science, Technology and Society at Chalmers University of Technology in Sweden and is co-author of *Ecological Masculinities: Theoretical Foundations and Practical Guidance* (2018, Routledge).

Kopano Ratele is Professor in the Institute of Social and Health Sciences at the University of South Africa, Director of the South African Medical Research Council's Extra-Mural Unit on Men, Masculinity, Injury and Violence, and leads the Transdisciplinary African Psychologies Programme. His books include *There Was This Goat* (with Antjie Krog and Nosisi Mpolweni, 2009, University of KwaZulu-Natal Press), *Liberating Masculinities* (2016, HSRC Press), and *The World Looks Like This From Here* (2019, Wits University Press).

Signe Ravn is Senior Lecturer in Sociology at the University of Melbourne, Australia. She is a sociologist researching youth, risk, gender and processes of marginalization; and she has extensive experience with creative research methods. She has published her work in a range of high-ranked journals such as *Men & Masculinities*, *British Journal of Sociology of Education*, and *Sociology of Health & Illness* and recently published the co-authored book *Youth, Risk, Routine* (with T. B. Bengtsson, 2019, Routledge).

Todd W. Reeser is Professor of French and Gender, Sexuality, and Women's Studies at the University of Pittsburgh, USA. His research treats questions of gender and sexuality in early modern and contemporary Europe and of theoretical approaches to masculinity. His books include *Moderating Masculinity in Early Modern Culture* (2006, University of North Carolina Press); *Masculinities in Theory* (2010, Wiley); *Setting Plato Straight: Translating Ancient Sexuality in the Renaissance* (2016, University of Chicago Press).

Andrew (Andy) Reilly, PhD, is a Professor in the Fashion Design and Merchandising program at the University of Hawai'i, Mānoa. His research examines the intersections of gender, sexuality, and post-postmodernism in dress. His books include *Crossing Gender Boundaries: Fashion to Create, Disrupt, and Transcend* (2019, Intellect) and *Fashion, Dress, and Post-postmodernism* (2020, Bloomsbury). He is founding editor of *Critical Studies in Men's Fashion* (Intellect).

Steven Roberts is Associate Professor of Sociology, School of Social Sciences, Monash University, Australia. Steven's research on masculinity includes young men's engagement with sexting, emotionality, domestic labour, education and employment. He is editor of *Sociological Research Online*, associate editor of *Journal of Youth Studies*, and international advisory editor of *Men and Masculinities*. Recent books include *Young Working Class Men in Transition* (2018, Routledge) and *Debating Modern Masculinities* (2014, Palgrave Macmillan).

Steve Robertson is Programme Director, University of Sheffield, UK, Emeritus Professor, Leeds Beckett University, UK, and Adjunct Professor, Waterford Institute of Technology, Ireland. He is editor-in-chief of the *International Journal of Men's Social & Community Health*, mental health section editor of the *American Journal of Men's Health* and author of the seminal text *Understanding Men & Health: Masculinities, Identity and Wellbeing* (2007, McGraw-Hill).

Victoria Robinson is Professor of Sociology and Director of the Centre for Women's Studies, University of York, UK. She has published widely in the areas of sexualities, masculinities, risk and extreme sport, and feminist theory. With Diane Richardson she is co-editor of *Introducing Gender and Women's Studies* (5th ed., forthcoming, Palgrave Macmillan, 2020) and Palgrave's international series *Genders and Sexualities*.

John Scott is a Professor in the Faculty of Law at Queensland University of Technology, Australia. His primary research interests are the governance of sexual deviance, masculinity and violence, and the ecology of crime (especially crime in remote and isolated places). He is co-editor of the *International Journal for Crime, Justice and Social Democracy* and the Routledge book series Crime and Justice in Asia and Global South. His recent books include *Southern Criminology* (2019, Routledge) and *Key Concepts in Crime and Society* (2014, Sage). He also co-edited the *Handbook of Criminology and the Global South* (2018, Palgrave Macmillan) and *Male Sex Work and Society* (2014, Harrington Park).

Tim Shand is a PhD candidate at University College London's Institute for Global Health focusing on masculinities and health in Malawi. He has worked extensively in the field of health and gender equality, including leadership positions with Promundo-US, Georgetown University's Institute for Reproductive Health, and Sonke Gender Justice in South Africa. He is currently an independent consultant. Tim holds a Masters in Public Health and has published and spoken widely.

Ruth Simpson is Professor of Management at Brunel Business School, UK. Her research interests include gender and organizations, inequality and 'dirty work', and gender and careers. She has authored, co-authored, and co-edited several books including *Gendering Emotions in Organizations* (2007, Red Globe); *Men in Caring Occupations: Doing Gender Differently* (2009, Palgrave Macmillan); *Emotions and Transmigration* (2011, Palgrave Macmillan); *Dirty Work: Concepts and Identities* (2012, Palgrave Macmillan); *The Handbook in Gender and Organizations* (2014, Oxford University Press); and *Gender, Class and Occupation* (2017, Palgrave Macmillan).

Kris Southby is a Research Fellow in the Centre for Health Promotion Research at Leeds Beckett University, UK. His PhD, completed in 2014, examined the experiences of adults with learning disabilities as football fans and the impacts on social inclusion. Kris' research broadly concerns strategies to promote social inclusion for people with learning disabilities as well as issues of empowerment, identity and inclusion in health promotion more generally.

Michelle Szabo, PhD, is Professor of Environmental Studies and Sociology at Sheridan College in Oakville, Canada. She publishes and teaches on masculinities and cooking, consumer culture and sustainability, gender theory, and the sociology of food. She recently co-edited the interdisciplinary volume *Food, Masculinities and Home* (2017, Bloomsbury). Her work has also appeared in *Journal of Gender Studies*, *Women's Studies International Forum*, *Sociology*, *Food, Culture & Society*, *Journal of Consumer Culture* and *Agriculture & Human Values*.

Anna Tarrant is Senior Lecturer in Sociology at the University of Lincoln, UK. Her research interests include men and masculinities, family life, the lifecourse and methodological developments in qualitative secondary analysis. She has recently completed a Leverhulme Trust funded study, 'Men, Poverty and Lifetimes of Care' (2014–2018), which explores the family participation of men living on a low income from a lifecourse perspective.

Suruchi Thapar-Björkert is Associate Professor at the Department of Government, Uppsala University, Sweden. She researches gender, colonialism and nationalism, gendered violence, ethnicity, social capital and social exclusion, racialization and stigmatizaton of urban peripheries and also uses qualitative feminist research methodologies. She has published widely in these areas in journals such as *Ethnic and Racial Studies*, *Feminist Review*, *Feminist Theory*,

Sociological Review and *Interventions*. She is the recipient of many research awards, including the Uppsala University award (2012).

Bettina Uppenkamp is Professor of Art and Visual History at Hochschule für bildende Künste Hamburg, Germany. Her research areas include early modern art, mainly Italian painting, and gender studies related to visual representation and contemporary art. Recent publications include "(Un)zeitgemäß und subversiv? Sticken bei Annette Messager und anderen feministischen Künstlerinnen in den 1970er Jahren" (in M. Bushart & H. Haug (Eds.) and *Unzeitgemäße Techniken: Historische Narrative künstlerischer Verfahren*, 2019, Böhlau).

Taryn van Niekerk is a Scarce Skills Postdoctoral Fellow in the Department of Psychology at the University of Cape Town, South Africa. Her primary research and teaching areas include feminist poststructuralist theories of gender, critical psychological and post-colonial theories of identity, and intersectional studies on men, masculinities and intimate partner violence against women in South Africa. She has published in these related areas, including her forthcoming co-edited volume *Decolonial Feminist Community Psychology* (Springer, 2019).

Michael R. M. Ward is a Lecturer in Social Sciences at Swansea University, UK. His work centres on the performance of working-class masculinities within and beyond educational institutions. He is the author of the award-winning book *From Labouring to Learning: Working-Class Masculinities, Education and De-industrialization* (Palgrave MacMillan, 2015). Mike has held visiting scholarships in Canada, the USA, Iceland and Germany. He is the editor of *Boyhood Studies, an Interdisciplinary Journal.*

Katarzyna Wojnicka is Research Associate at the Centre for European Research at the University of Gothenburg, Sweden. She holds a doctoral degree in sociology from the Jagiellonian University in Krakow, Poland. Her research falls in the intersection of critical men and masculinities studies, gender studies, migration studies and social movements research. Her work has been published in various internationally recognized outlets such as *Palgrave Macmillan, Routledge, Men and Masculinities, Social Movement Studies* and others.

Acknowledgments

This book has taken a few years in its making and has involved a huge amount of logistical work as well as scholarly engagement. We are greatly indebted to Dr. Marinette Grimbeek, who has put in many hours of dedicated work over the last few years, not only administratively but also though sharing her intellectual and editorial expertise. We acknowledge each other as editors, knowing that we all have multiple other commitments and responsibilities yet always found the space to extend ourselves to the many layered engagements that editing a book of this nature entails. We have worked together across oceans, mostly virtually but with some embodied meetings in our different contexts, generously hosting each other in special spaces, towards a project that hopefully speaks of and is informed by an ethics of care and relationality. We appreciate and value the many authors who are represented here who engaged with a relatively lengthy process with patience and willingness to revise. Thanks to those less visible in all our lives that make it possible for such work. Thanks to the publishers for flexibility and support.

Introduction

Mapping the field of masculinity studies

Lucas Gottzén, Ulf Mellström and Tamara Shefer

How does one map a research field? How does one tell the story of a field and provide an account of the 'state of the art'? There are several tales about the research tradition that is often called Masculinity Studies or Critical Studies on Men and Masculinities.[1]

The dominant narrative of the field, often found in textbooks and reviews, is that men have been at the centre in mainstream social science and humanities scholarship for a long time, but this place has been mostly taken for granted and an 'absent presence' where they have not been studied as gendered beings. It was not until the 1970s, when feminist and gay researchers started to theorize the role of men and masculinity in society, that an explicit inquiry into men as *men* and masculinities started on a broader scale. Masculinity studies was founded by a group of primarily White, pro-feminist men in the U.S., U.K. and Australia in the 1980s – most of them social scientists and sociologists. Throughout 1990s, the research area grew considerably, developed new topics and theories and spread into a variety of social sciences and humanities disciplines, as well as to different regions of the world. Masculinity studies is today a well-established part of interdisciplinary gender research. The last decades have been characterized by an increased empirical diversity and development of new theoretical perspectives. Since the early 2000s, a growing number of masculinity scholars have integrated theoretical insights from contemporary 'third wave' feminism and its poststructuralist and postcolonial influences. Queer and sexuality studies have also been of great importance, and the study of intersections between social categories such as gender, class, ethnicity, race, embodiment and age has emerged lately. According to this story, the field was primarily developed in Anglo-American settings, but there is now scholarly work from all parts of the world, including the global South.

A second, somewhat more critical narrative emphasizes the epistemological differences between masculinity studies and gender studies in general. During the last decade, Chris Beasley has explored the relationships between different feminist and gender studies subfields and the possibilities for dialogue and engagement between them. She identifies masculinity studies as largely characterized by modernist perspectives since its influential theorists primarily present social constructionist and socialist-feminist frameworks (Beasley, 2005, 2013, 2015; see also Beasley, this volume). In contrast, since the 1980s, other major research areas in gender studies have largely embraced what she calls 'postmodern' perspectives. This is a somewhat ambiguous term for a variety of frameworks that emphasize ontological and epistemological fragmentation and fluidity and are critical to modernist understandings of universalism, objective reality, reason and humanism. While at times antagonistic, poststructuralism, discourse analysis and other 'postmodern' traditions often emphasize the constitutive role of language. Largely influenced by poststructuralism, feminist theorists have lately argued for posthumanist and new materialist epistemologies that are not anthropocentric and that subvert traditional boundaries between humans, animals, technology and matter (Alaimo & Hekman, 2008; Braidotti, 2013; Coole & Frost, 2010; Mellström, this volume). Today, poststructuralist and discursive approaches are mainstream while posthumanism and new materialism are increasingly influential within gender and sexuality studies. Beasley has an important message to masculinity studies: 'postmodern' perspectives are not necessarily better, but since masculinity studies is primarily modernist, it has difficulties communicating with the other gender studies subfields. By not jumping on the 'postmodernist' bandwagon, masculinity studies has become, or runs the risk of becoming, the 'odd man out' (Beasley, 2009).

While Beasley has primarily focused on the work of thinkers that emerged in the 1980s and early 1990s – such as Harry Brod, Raewyn Connell, Jeff Hearn, Bob Pease and John Stoltenberg – one could argue that masculinity studies still largely remains modernist in approach. This is noticeable in more recent influential contributions to the field, such as Michael Schwalbe's (2015) theory of 'manhood acts' and Eric Anderson's (2009) inclusive masculinity theory. It is also evident in the field's continued preoccupation with hegemonic masculinity theory (see Messerschmidt, 2018).

However, there is also at least a third story to tell about the field. In order to understand if and why masculinity studies may (or not) be the odd man out, we need to go back to 1987. In that year, a number of books were published in the small but emerging field that at the time primarily was called men's studies. Connell (1987) and Hearn (1987) published their monographs *Gender and Power* and *The Gender of Oppression*. Brod (1987) and Michael Kimmel (1987), respectively, edited the volumes *The Making of Masculinities: The New Men's Studies* and *Changing Men: New Directions on Men and Masculinity*. This early masculinity studies literature is perhaps not cited that much anymore but was for a long time central to the field, and its authors have since then been considered to represent what C. J. Pascoe and Tristan Bridges (2016, p. 327) have termed the 'multiple masculinities' perspective and what became 'proper' masculinity studies.

The relationship that early masculinity scholars had to poststructuralism is noteworthy. Such perspectives were barely mentioned in the books published in 1987, and several of the authors have later on been explicitly hesitant towards them. According to Michael Messner (1996), who contributed to both Brod's and Kimmel's volumes, the unwillingness to include 'theories of deconstruction' (p. 226) has partly been related to a general sociological scepticism towards the humanities. He did not want to throw out the baby with the bathwater but criticized 'deconstructionism' on epistemological and political grounds. The poststructuralist emphasis on language underestimates material and social relations, he argued, and while it may be useful to deconstruct binary categories, doing so does not provide any tools for social change. It therefore will lead to individualized and depoliticized research about men, he warned.

> As many feminists have pointed out, although it is certainly true that every woman is at least somewhat uniquely situated, a radical deconstruction of the concept *woman* could lead to a radical individualism that denies similarity of experience, thus leading to a depoliticized subject.
>
> *(Messner, 1996, p. 227)*

Some years later, Connell (2001) provided a similar account of poststructuralism in a critical discussion of Judith Butler's work that was accused of over-emphasizing fluidity and obscuring material inequality. Connell argued that Butler 'is strikingly unable to account for work, child care, institutional life, violence, resistance (except as individual choice), and material inequality' (p. 22).

Connell, Messner and other sociologists of masculinity in the 1990s and early 2000s were concerned that queer, poststructuralist and deconstructionist approaches were too idealist (in the sense of being narrowly focused on language and discourse), did not take materiality seriously and presented a voluntarist ontology where subjects were able to enact gender freely in different settings. These may obviously be reasonable concerns, but our point here is rather that while sociological masculinity researchers expressed such worries, humanities scholars argued that the very same theories in fact enabled feminist and critical analyses of men and masculinities.

The same year these books from the emerging field of masculinity studies were published, another but somewhat different book on masculinity was produced: *Men in Feminism*, edited by the literature scholars Alice Jardine and Paul Smith (1987). The book has not attracted the same attention as the other publications and is rarely cited in masculinity studies 'proper'. It is interesting to compare the epistemological stances in this anthology with the literature mentioned above. Connell, Hearn, Kimmel – but also Brod, a philosopher – all have different perspectives on men and masculinities, and they diverge in their relationship to poststructuralism. All of them did (at least at the time), however, write in a social constructionist tradition, and they were all in various ways influenced by Marxism and socialist feminism. These perspectives are also found in *Men in Feminism*, but its primary theoretical influences are, rather, continental philosophy and, particularly, poststructuralism. Contributors to Jardine and Smith's anthology (1987) make use of and discuss theorists such as Roland Barthes, Hélène Cixous, Michel Foucault, Luce Irigaray, Jacques Lacan, Teresa de Lauretis and Gayatri Chakravorty Spivak. The book even includes a transcript from a seminar with Jacques Derrida, where he discusses his term 'phallogocentrism' and deconstructs the category 'man'. Cary Nelson illustrates the general positive reception of poststructuralism in the volume when arguing that Derrida's work has 'been immensely useful for some feminists' and that he is 'about as close to being "in" feminism as any male theorist has come' (1987, p. 168). Several young scholars who contributed – including Naomi Schor, Elizabeth Weed, Stephen Heath and Rosi Braidotti – have since become pivotal in poststructuralist and new materialist gender and sexuality studies.

What is fascinating is that the approach to the critical study of men and masculinities that this volume opened up has barely been acknowledged or incorporated into masculinity scholarship. This is perhaps due to the fact that the contributing authors did not attempt to establish a field of masculinity studies; men and feminism was a temporary topic. There are also other scholars who have made major contributions to masculinity theory but that seldom are included in masculinity studies 'proper'. We come to think of Jack Halberstam (1998), who has theorized about female masculinities such as tomboys, dykes and butches; and David Eng's (2001) critical discussion of how Asian men are portrayed in literature and film. Most important is perhaps Eve Sedgwick's early and ground-breaking work on homosociality, *Between Men* (1985), as well as her later discussions about the contingent relationship between men and masculinity (e.g., Sedgwick, 1995). Todd Reeser (2015) identifies an epistemological divide between masculinity studies within the humanities and the social sciences that is highlighted in the uptake of Sedgwick's work. While she became highly influential in queer theory and humanities approaches to masculinity, she has been largely neglected in masculinity studies within the social sciences.

> While Sedgwick's ground-breaking book made its way into some contemporaneous work in social-science work in men's studies, it is rarely cited or discussed, suggesting a rather strict separation between more literary/cultural approaches and social science ones, even as Sedgwick's work resembled that of other scholars in that it aimed to incorporate both feminist and gay approaches.
>
> *(Reeser, 2015, p. 29)*

So how could we map the field of masculinity studies across the humanities–social sciences divide? Robyn Wiegman (2012) has presented three different traditions within U.S. masculinity studies since the 1980s. To start with, she identifies research on *social and historical constructions of masculinity* (similar to what Pascoe and Bridges (2016) call the 'multiple masculinities' perspective). Here she includes many of the relatively central (and primarily sociological) researchers within masculinity studies, such as Connell, Kimmel, Seidler, Hearn, Brod and Kaufman. She calls the second area of research *cultural representations of masculinity*. Here we find cultural studies scholars such as Eng, Lee Edelman and Susan Bordo. Finally, she identifies a research field she terms *masculinity without men*, which includes Halberstam but that was initiated by Gayle Rubin's (1992) essay on butch and which later has developed into trans studies. Wiegman (2012) also points out that there was an early interest in men and masculinity within black feminism, apparent in the work of Audre Lorde (1984/2007) and bell hooks (1984) as well as in the Combahee River Collective's statement (1977/1997) that 'We struggle together with Black men against racism, while we also struggle with Black men about sexism' (p. 65).

Wiegman's description is flawed since it centres on the U.S. and largely excludes the theoretical development of the field in the rest of the world; but by highlighting the humanities, a wide range of onto-epistemological stances within masculinity studies surface. If we only acknowledge sociology and social science, masculinity studies has definitely been, and perhaps still is, modernist, since social constructionism still defines such approaches. But if we see critical studies on men and masculinities as an interdisciplinary field of inquiry that also includes the humanities, it is difficult to maintain the same argument, since this tradition has never been dominated by modernism; rather, at least from the mid-1980s, poststructuralism has been pivotal when humanities scholars have studied men and masculinities. Focusing only on social sciences also reproduces a rather patriarchal version of the field. While *Men in Feminism* was a volume with many women scholars, and later influential theorists of masculinity within the humanities have been women and queers, the main narrative about masculinity studies is a story about a group of White 'founding fathers', predominantly located in the global North. But there is a risk that masculinity studies within the humanities also becomes heteronormative and masculinist. As Bruce Traister (2000) has pointed out in a critical review of masculinity scholarship within American Studies, 'To some degree, cultural "masculinity studies" has become a code term for "heterosexual masculinity studies"' (p. 275).

Towards a minor masculinity studies literature

Clare Hemmings (2011) has pointed out that gender studies scholars often present a progress narrative, in which (previous) modernist onto-epistemologies are portrayed as problematic while contemporary poststructuralist approaches are presented as creative, radical and the solution to the dilemmas of previous 'essentialist' feminist research. Within such a narrative, masculinity studies (at least in the way that it is often presented) could not only be argued to be the odd man out but also be characterized as something of a failure narrative, where the field is hopelessly behind the rest of gender studies. The field has failed to grow up and become as theoretically advanced as contemporary feminist theory. It has failed to ask the right questions and therefore has difficulties communicating with others.

In lines with the notion of narratives of progress, one could argue that during the last decade or so we may identify something of a 'third phase' (Hearn et al., 2012, p. 37) within masculinity studies, where scholars are increasingly influenced by poststructuralism, queer theory and postcolonial, posthumanist and new materialist approaches. But arguing that masculinity studies is experiencing a third phase runs the risk of reproducing the same progress narrative that Hemmings (2011) identified in gender studies generally. This story is obviously problematic, since modernist theorizing continues to be important in the field and since scholars of men and masculinities – also outside the humanities (e.g., Edley & Wetherell, 1997; Gutterman, 1994) – have embraced poststructuralist approaches for a long time. It is also problematic because modernist perspectives are far from as 'essentialist' or naïve as often portrayed by poststructuralist scholars. In fact, it is possible to re-read early masculinity scholars and show how they at times lean more towards poststructuralist approaches (Berggren, 2014). Instead of producing a new canon and new linear narratives, we want to emphasize the multiple and contradictory stories about the field. To this end, we think masculinity studies could be understood as what Gilles Deleuze and Félix Guattari (1986) have called 'minor literature', which is 'deterritorializing', collective and connects the individual and the political. Following Deleuze and Guattari, we would argue that it is crucial to search for and develop theorizing about men and masculinities from below. This theorizing is 'rhizomatic', as it avoids producing stable and hierarchical systems of thought that are like tree roots. Minor masculinity studies does not refer to 'specific literatures but the revolutionary conditions for every literature within the heart of what is called great (or established) literature' (Deleuze & Guattari, 1986, p. 18). In every single contribution there are possibilities to destabilize masculinity studies 'proper' as well as the ontology of masculinity. To do that we need modernist and poststructuralist as well as posthumanist approaches that decentres the role of Man and aims for less hierarchical ontologies.

This rhizomatic approach to masculinity studies is the very opposite of creating a canon of 'proper' research and a 'majority literature' (Deleuze & Guattari, 1986). Canon is a term that was first used in the early Church and refers to the texts deemed to be sanctioned by its leadership and which defined Christianity. Scholarly canon can be said to be a collection of privileged texts that, together with their interpretations, define the subject. Canon formation occurs by the extent to which a particular work or a particular theorist is used, how they are interpreted and by whom. There are many exclusions in canon formation. Recurrently quoting a few social theorists as *the* theory of masculinity studies obscures not only humanities traditions but also other epistemologies and ontologies – particularly knowledge from the global South as well as racialized, queer and female researchers.

This raises questions about citing practices within the field. As feminist scholars have pointed to for some time now (e.g., Haraway, 1988; Lykke, 2010), the position from where one speaks and where one carries out one's research is crucial for one's knowledge production. Paraphrasing Donna Haraway (1992), one might say that our *site* and our *sight*, but also how and whom we *cite*, are interrelated and important for what sort of knowledge is produced. It is far from evident that masculinity scholars position themselves as feminist. Even when they do, there is a risk of – and perhaps a tendency toward – creating a division between masculinity studies and other gender studies where masculinity scholars do not use, relate to or learn from feminist, queer or postcolonial theorizing. Such politics of citation work not only to reproduce inequality within masculinity studies (Bridges, 2019) but also to create a field where cis-men 'could feel sufficiently comfortable, appear as progressive and gender-equal, but without facing their own participation in maintaining patriarchy' (Forsberg, 2010, p. 4).

Another related issue regards 'travelling theories' (Said, 1982). There is a propensity to present research produced in the U.S., U.K. and Australia as 'theory', which is then 'applied' in different peripheral settings, whereas knowledge developed in the global South or in a European semi-periphery is not seen as 'theory' but, rather, as 'case studies' or empirical applications of these theories. Hegemonic masculinity has no doubt been such a 'travelling theory' concept which has been applied in many different corners of the world although originating from a specific centre of knowledge production. This is obviously tied to the economic and power relations between global centre and periphery, where some countries have far better financial possibilities to support research than others. But it also connects directly to Anglo-globalization and a global academic capitalism resting on English as the language of power in the current global food chain of research and higher education.

Let us exemplify with the current discussion about 'hybridity', which is mentioned in several chapters of this handbook. The debate revolves partly around whether hegemonic masculinity is still a relevant framework in societies characterized by increased gender equality and LGBTQ friendliness. Some argue that this indicates that 'orthodox' masculinity is losing its hegemonic power (Anderson, 2009), while others maintain that we are rather seeing the emergence of 'hybrid' masculinities that incorporate progressive elements while continuing to uphold patriarchal relations and create new gendered hierarchies albeit in more nuanced and subtle ways (Bridges & Pascoe, 2014). Our point here is not to discuss if this is the case or not but to point out that similar issues for many years have been discussed in masculinity studies in other parts of the world, such as the Nordic countries. These critical theoretical discussions have in part been developed in the Scandinavian languages (e.g., Jalmert, 1979; Liliequist, 2006) but also in English (see Christensen & Jensen, 2014; Hearn et al., 2012). Nevertheless, hybridity continues to be debated as an American or British experience, and few lessons are learned from other societies where changes in gender relations, masculinity and gender equality have been taking place for a long time. Instead, Nordic scholars use hybridity or inclusivity frameworks and apply them in their 'empirical' research (e.g., Andreasson & Johansson, 2016; Petersson & Plantin, 2019).

It seems as if hybridity is not a particularly novel phenomenon, but it has characterized masculinity politics in the global North since at least the 1970s (Jalmert, 1979). The Nordic countries have often been pointed out as exceptional with regard to gender relations. Internationally, they are in the top tier regarding gender equality and have been called a 'gender nirvana' (Zahidi, 2013). This obviously does not apply equally at all levels of society, and the changes are often contradictory, but in family policy, for instance, the involved and gender-equal father has clearly become hegemonic. Research further suggests that parental leave is not only accepted but also the norm among men from different backgrounds (e.g., Holth & Mellström, 2011; Johansson & Klinth, 2008). One problem, though, is that this notion of gender equality has been articulated through a national (and to some extent nationalist) discourse that creates an imagined community by excluding Other, in particular non-White men or nations in the global South. We could perhaps talk of an 'outsourcing of patriarchy' (Grewal, 2013), 'homonationalism' (Puar, 2007) or 'femonationalism' (Farris, 2017), where White men are presented as inherently progressive, gay friendly and gender equal, while non-White men are seen as always already embodying sexism, misogyny and homophobia and thus need to learn 'our' liberal values (Gottzén & Jonsson, 2012).

This seems to be a widespread, global issue and therefore critical for masculinity studies. As highlighted by a number of the chapters in this volume (e.g., Boonzaier & van Niekerk; Farahani & Thapar-Björkert; Lohokare; Ratele; Wojnicka), men in global Southern contexts and in minority and immigrant communities in global Northern settings are often represented as more patriarchal, sexist and homophobic than their Northern, White, middle-class counterparts (see also Farris, 2017; Haritaworn, 2015; Puar, 2007). Such binaristic discourses reflect global relations of privilege and subjugation. In South Africa, for example, notwithstanding a progressive human rights framework, including the enshrinement of gender and sexual equality, high rates of sexual, homo- and transphobia violence persist. Much of the research, policy and programmatic emphasis has been directed at poor communities, reinstating a negative construction of young Black masculinities in particular, bolstering long histories of raced and classed 'othering' discourses (see Bhana; Boonzaier & Van Niekerk; Ratele, in this volume; Bhana & Pattman, 2009; Ratele, 2014; Shefer, 2016). While there has been an established critical scholarship on men and masculinities in South Africa (as acknowledged by Hearn & Howson in this edition), closely entangled with postcolonial feminist studies, it has tended to remain localized, considered valuable only as ethnographic work rather than viewed as contributing to global scholarship and thinking. Interestingly, as with most marginal parts of the world, texts will likely flag their location in African or South African contexts in the title, which never seems a necessity by authors in global Northern centres, even when much of this work is frequently specifically located in a particular national or regional geopolitics.

These examples of the reproduction of new hierarchies in different settings calls for more nuanced knowledge production and critical scholarship on men and masculinities that is 'world-centred, rather than metropole centred' (Connell, 2014, p. 217), a call that has guided the making of this handbook.

What is new with this book?

It has been about 15 years since the foundational *Handbook of Studies on Men and Masculinities* was published (Kimmel, Hearn & Connell, 2005). Since then we have seen a range of shifts in global practices of knowledge production given the intensification of neoliberal global capitalist logics and how these have been taken up in institutions of higher education. There has been a huge growth of published academic work and shifting paradigms of scholarship both in response and in resistance to such pressures of 'fast', output-based research within a global neoliberal politics and associated planetary eco-challenges related to the dominance of a destructive human-centred planet (see Mellström; Pulé & Hultman, this volume). It is not surprising but also encouraging that this handbook captures the texture and intensity of proliferating contemporary thinking within current paradigmatic and deepening theoretical moves in gender studies and masculinity studies in particular, but arguably within critical scholarship in general. In overviewing the contents of this book, we highlight the novel contributions that are evident in the chapters in the volume. While we have attempted to include key areas of scholarship historically and currently evident in the field in order to provide a wide-ranging resource, we also acknowledge that such a project is always already incomplete and that there will always be areas omitted or less represented (some key areas for various reasons not covered in this volume include economy, financial markets and neoliberalism). This is especially the case since studies on boys, men and masculinities tend to be diversely located across disciplines and fields of study and frequently entangled in research that is not always clearly flagged as masculinity studies, as argued earlier.

A number of key themes and arguments surface within and through the handbook that arguably speak to fresh or emergent areas of scholarship and/or strengthen more marginal directions in masculinity studies. Firstly, the foregrounding of the imperative to exercise a decentring of global Northern and Western knowledge (or in whichever way we name the continued privileging of certain locations of knowledge) is a strong thread in many of the chapters. The centring of certain knowledges – particularly those located in geopolitical terrains which are more privileged as a result of legacies of coloniality and contemporary global capitalist logics – and the erasure of global Southern scholarship continued to be a challenge throughout the preparation of the volume. The norm tended to be the review of literature predominantly located in the global North with a scattering of global Southern examples, and usually as empirical contributions rather than as a resource for theoretical framing. Yet many of the authors articulate such a critique and engage in destabilizing such normative logics of dominant scholarship, pointing to 'the ethnocentrism, race blindness and lack of historical specificity of Western (and White) masculinity studies' (Farahani & Thapar-Björkett, in this volume). A significant number of the chapters contribute to the project of unravelling the way in which colonial and patriarchal relationships are reproduced in the genealogy and contemporary knowledge practices in masculinity studies (Boonzaier & van Niekerk; Farahani & Thapar-Björkett; Ratele). For example, Madhura Lohokare points to the 'irony of the possibility of the field of critical masculinity studies replicating a hegemonic masculinist pattern in the way knowledge on masculinities is produced at the global level', arguing the impetus for engaging in 'questions of *where* research on masculinities is produced and *who* produces this research.' Similarly, many acknowledge the gaps of particular knowledge in the scholarship in their areas, such as Miriam Abelson and Tristen Kade, who call for future research on trans masculinities

> to continue to expand the geographic scope of knowledge about trans masculinities and, drawing inspiration from the expanding work on transgender geography, to take serious how specific spaces and places shape trans masculinities. It is crucial to build knowledge of trans masculinities outside of major cities and beyond the U.S. and U.K. contexts.

Linked to the acknowledgement and critique of the geopolitics of masculinity studies is a related theme of engaging a transnational lens, of acknowledging both the localities and globalness of theorizing and researching men and masculinities. Hearn and Richard Howson specifically elaborate on the valuable framework of transnational masculinity studies, while many of the chapters speak to the complex global dynamics which shape, but are also shaped by, local conditions and contexts of intersectional gender. The editorship of this handbook, and indeed the many authors included, are testimony to transnational dialogue. While representing multi-layered privileges, they are also representative of diverse peripheries of those geopolitical contexts that have historically predominated in the imaginary of leading masculinity scholarship.

This theme also shapes a third emphasis of the handbook, that of theorizing intersectionality in making sense of masculinities. Many of the chapters speak to intersectional understandings and the acknowledgement of nuanced and fluid multiple contexts in their different areas of scholarship in the field, for example, rural masculinities (Pini & Mayes), gay masculinities (Barrett), trans masculinities (Abelson & Kade), gay subcultures (Barrett), disa/ability (Monaghan, Robertson & Southby), military masculinities (Duncanson), young masculinities (Bhana), fatherhood (Wahlström) and risky masculinities (Robinson), amongst others. Chapters speak to ever-re-emerging multiplicities of masculinities across fluid local and transnational context, not only in relation to hegemonic or dominant forms of masculinity in a particular time and space but indeed also disrupting the very binarism of gender. For instance, Rusty Barrett speaks of the surfacing of new forms of masculinity through the 'combination of masculine (and feminine) signs in new and unique ways', and Abelson and Kade foreground the 'troubling' of gender binarism through non-binary and genderqueer performance and identity. Indeed, in many ways this handbook provides impetus for the strengthening imperative of masculinity studies scholars 'to critically distance themselves from the very concept they have invested in so heavily' (Gottzén, this volume).

Within the emphasis on context, another key strand in the handbook is the importance of contemporary global neoliberal contexts accompanied by massive shifts in technologies of living and communication. A number of chapters speak to the way in which neoliberal capitalist market imperatives strengthen particular global and local forms of medicalization of men's bodies (Robertson & Shand) and while human-technology entanglements and advancements may offer some advantages, for example in dealing with challenges of disability for those men who can afford it, neoliberal logics also open up increased surveillance and rationalize the dispensability of many bodies and lives (Monaghan, Robertson & Southby).

Importantly, what the handbook and its chapters do is open up new areas for study, for thinking and researching boys, men and masculinities while dialoguing with more established bodies of scholarly and activist engagement around the 'glocal' project of gender justice. Chapters revisit older foundational thinking to make novel readings, such as Lucas Gottzén's chapter on Foucault, or salvage conceptual contributions from those heavily critiqued within larger gender scholarship, such as Miklos Hadas' chapter on Pierre Bourdieu. Many authors acknowledge their roots in overlapping scholarly programmatic areas, dialoguing with feminist, queer and sexuality studies as well as (pro)feminist activism. While some authors, such as Beasley, critically assess the relationship between masculinity studies and feminist scholarship, it is also notable that many of the chapters acknowledge their debt to feminist thinking, and generally the handbook represents a stronger sense of the entanglement and shared projects of these overlapping bodies of work.

Many of the chapters point to novel and emerging directions, as well as gaps that are opening up due to contemporary critique and reconceptualization and changing contexts locally and globally. Given the speeded-up nature of global knowledge production, also accompanied by ground-shifting scholarly moves over the last few decades, it is also not surprising and is indeed welcomed that the handbook includes chapters that are powerfully located in emerging epistemological and ontological turns such as queer theory, affect theory, new materialism and posthumanism and exploring their relevance for masculinity studies (e.g., Allan; Balkmar; Gottzén; Hultman & Pulé; Mellström; Ottemo; Reeser). Many authors, in reviewing the literature, also flag new questions opening up in their slice of scholarship as well as identify areas of marginality and erasure that become evident in reflecting on a particular field of study.

Of particular note, the handbook speaks to multi-, inter-, trans- and perhaps even post-disciplinary accounts of contemporary masculinity scholarship. While scholarship on masculinities has historically been predominantly located in policy-directed social sciences, as evident in earlier volumes, the current handbook has attempted to broaden the inclusion of productive terrains of knowledge on men and masculinities across and between multiple disciplines and scholarship, specifically in the arts, humanities, cultural and aesthetical scholarly endeavours and practices (e.g., Armengol; McDonald; Reilly & Duncan; Szabo; Uppenkamp) and within public, institutionalized, popular and activist spaces (Collier; Peretz). In this way, the handbook also 'troubles' or points to the strengthening critique of rigid disciplinary or other forms of siloed scholarly legacies that have shaped masculinity studies as it has other bodies of work.

Taken together, we believe that the contributions to this handbook showcase a 'minor literature' of masculinity studies that simultaneously present and destabilize masculinity studies 'proper' and the ontology of masculinity.

Overview of the book

Crafting a structure for this handbook was a creative task that is always imperfect, yet necessary in a volume with 48 chapters. We begin with a theoretical section in which theory, while addressed in many of the other chapters in other sections, more specifically speaks to the project of making theory towards rigorous critical analysis of men and masculinities. *Section 1* starts with a contextualizing chapter on the institutionalization of masculinity studies across geopolitical contexts by one of the best-known masculinity scholars globally, Hearn, also editor on the foundational handbook of this nature (Kimmel, Hearn & Connell, 2005), with co-author Howson. Beasley's chapter follows, which focuses on the creative possibilities of the dis/junctures between feminist and critical masculinities studies, which are taken forward through a dialogue clearly embedded in a long history of philosophical engagement with these bodies of work. In the third chapter, Howson and Hearn engage with a key concept in the larger body of work on masculinities over some decades – hegemonic masculinity – and extend their use below the dominant current usage of such terms in scholarship on men and masculinities. Hadas' chapter is a call to reclaim the value of Bourdieu's body of work and conceptual contributions, including and beyond *Masculine Domination*, for gender scholarship. Gottzén flags the relative marginality of Foucauldian thinking in masculinity studies to present two figures in Foucault's larger body of work, the masturbating boy and the free man in Greek and Latin antiquity, towards illustrating and arguing for key components of his conceptual framework that speak to critical masculinities studies. Jonathan Allan, arguing that queer studies and masculinities studies have worked alongside each other but often in isolation, elaborates the importance of queer theory for the field of critical masculinities because it opens up space for 'the unsaid, the non-normative, and the complexity and messiness of desire' (Allan, this volume). The imperative to acknowledge diverse minority masculinities and destabilize unitary and binary imaginaries of masculinity is taken further in chapters on intersectionality and postcolonial masculinities. Arguing that intersectionality can fill certain theoretical gaps in this scholarship, Ann-Dorte Christensen and Sune Qvortrup Jensen provide an historical overview and current implications of intersectionality followed by key principles and challenges in their use in scholarship on masculinities, while further providing two examples of such an intersectional analysis in their arguments for the value of intersectionality conceptualization. Fataneh Farahani and Suruchi Thapar-Björkert illustrate the value of a postcolonial masculinities lens for addressing gaps in the majority of contemporary masculinity studies, arguably engaged primarily with Euro-American masculinities. The next two chapters are located within transdisciplinary epistemological and ontological shifts framed within new materialism, posthumanism and the affective turn. While avoiding the well-trod path of research on masculinities and emotion, yet pursuing a conceptual clarification of affect and emotion, Reeser engages with thinking through ways to approach critical studies of men and masculinity in the light of the proliferating body of work in affect studies, with emphasis on the possibilities such work offers for reconfiguring masculinities and new ways of performing gender. Ulf Mellström's chapter offers an introduction to the posthumanist and new materialist turn in social theory through a novel mapping of its connections with masculinities studies, particularly focusing on notions of transcendence, embodiedness and connectedness to nature, materiality and corporeality.

A recurring argument in masculinity studies is that the need to pluralize men and masculinities as gendered experience and life conditions is due to context. As Sedgwick (1990/2008, p. 22) put it, 'people are different from each other'. Men do not share a single sex role, gendered identities and experiences rather vary over time, place and social position. All contributions to the volume point to this, but the chapters in *Section 2* focus particularly on intersectional power relations, experiences and subjectivities. Kopano Ratele demonstrates this basic argument in his chapter as he takes a postcolonial perspective on black masculinities and discusses some of the neglected histories and theoretical resources that are relevant to critical studies of men and masculinities. Similarly, Tobias Hübinette highlights an often-unrecognized white norm in masculinity studies and also provides analytical tools to explore white masculinities and the current masculinist white supremacy movements. Sedgwick's lesson that people are different is also exemplified in Mario Liong and Lih Shing Chan's chapter, where they problematize the homogenization of East Asian men as always embodying a 'soft' masculinity. Instead, the authors highlight historical and cultural differences between China, Japan and Korea. Masculinity studies has a long history of interest in social class, not least since early scholars were socialist or Marxist feminists. In his contribution, Mike Ward presents an exposition of this field and focuses primarily on the working class and masculinity but also points to the need for incorporating spatial perspectives in the field.

The body is pivotal for the production of different forms of masculinity. In their chapter, Steve Robertson, Lee Monaghan and Kris Southby nuance the understandings of disability by contrasting men having intellectual disabilities with the 'cyborg bodies' that are possible for some athlete men with physical disabilities. Another way to explore the relationship between masculinity and the body is trans, a growing field of research that Abelson and Kade review. Transmen and trans masculine experiences highlight that sometimes masculinity has nothing to do with (cis)men (see Sedgwick, 1995) so should not be used merely to make theoretical arguments, but it is also crucial to explore the particular challenges and conditions of trans persons in different settings.

Another dimension critical for understanding the pluralities of men and masculinities is the life course. This dimension is somewhat different others – such as race, class and sexuality – as individuals grow in and out of life phases and consequently in and out of privilege. In three different chapters, Deevia Bhana, Signe Ravn and Steven Roberts and Anna Tarrant review scholarship on childhood, youth, ageing and men and masculinities. Taken together, the authors demonstrate that although masculinity studies has been interested in men of different ages, there is an adult norm in the field where maturity and rationality is rewarded, while immaturity and dependence – which characterize the younger and older positions in the life course – are obscured.

Sex and sexuality is a central dimension of men's lives and the key focus of *Section 3*. Nils Hammarén and Thomas Johansson provide an overview of homosociality scholarship and develop a theory that differentiates between hierarchical and horizontal homosociality, as men can reproduce hierarchies but also try to create more equal relationships. Although homophobia and 'sexual prejudice' seem to be in decline in some parts of the world, Sarah Diefendorf and Tristan Bridges suggest that it is still a central part of masculinity. To understand this paradox, they propose to recognize homophobias as plural and explore both the reproduction of, and challenges to, contemporary sexual prejudice. In his chapter, Rusty Barrett discusses different gay male subcultures such as bears, circuit boys and leathermen and demonstrates how individuals construct specific social personae by combining signs that point to distinct meanings associated with gender, race, ethnicity, age etc. While Barrett takes a semiotic perspective, Steve Garlick develops an affect theory approach to masculinity and pornography in order to understand the affordances of digital pornscapes. Digitalization has not only affected men's relationship to pornography but has also contributed to new forms of relationship initiation such as speed dating, mobile romance, online dating, holiday romances and hooking-up. In his contribution, Chris Haywood points out that the changes force heterosexual men to become more reflexive about their own bodies and appearance. Another sexual area that seems to be influenced by technological changes is prostitution, where the number of male sex workers are increasing, as John Scott shows. Even though men represent a significant minority of sex workers and the majority of the ones buying sex, Scott argues that there has been a paucity of research on men and masculinities in the field.

In *Section 4* we are guided through research of how masculinities are constituted through spatial metaphors and practices, different forms of physical and imaginary mobilities and technologies of movement. The embodied dimensions of masculinity are foregrounded as key to new as well as established ways of understanding masculinities in the field. Masculinity and bodies in space and place are the main themes running through this section. Katarzyna Wojnicka shows the multidimensionality of male migrant practices and the necessity of an intersectional approach but also adds spatiality as a crucial dimension of understanding how to position male migrants in the social structure of both host and sending societies. The importance of spatiality is further emphasized by Lohokare, who develops an account of masculinity as spatially situated and argues for the need to incorporate spatiality with regard to the unequal geographies of knowledge production in studies on men and masculinities. Similarly, Barbara Pini and Robyn Mayes argue that we need to understand rural masculinities beyond their local context, and they emphasize the relational, contextual, multi-faceted and multiscalar character in symmetric or asymmetric relationship to other social categories. In the next chapter, by Ruth Simpson and Patricia Lewis, we learn about the practices of masculinity in female dominated occupations. The authors trace an increasing degree of gender flexibility on a labour market that still is characterized by a strong gender-based occupational segregation. Helena Wahlström Henriksson in her chapter introduces us to critical fatherhood scholarship, which has been a dominating research field in masculinity studies. However, she shows how fatherhood is an evasive analytical category that can be cross-fertilized with various strands of thought beyond masculinity studies as such. Moving to education and masculinity, Máirtín Mac an Ghaill argues that the field has opened to an awareness of the complexity between local and the global interconnections, which is crucial as educational settings are projections of national and international gender structures and anxieties. In his chapter, Andreas Ottemo maps the often-neglected scholarship on technology and masculinity. He proposes conceptualizing technology as a metaphorical key to understanding various forms of masculine embodiment and self as hardwired, strong, enduring and fast. In a similar fashion, Dag Balkmar focuses on masculinity, auto-mobility and car cultures, arguing that masculinity studies have much to contribute in an era in urgent need of sustainable transport and mobility systems. In the last chapter of the section, Robertson and Tim Shand guide us through a brief history of medicalization, with a focus on men and masculinities. Although medicalization has a long history in medical sociology, it was not until the early 2000s that masculinity scholars began to look into the issue.

Section 5 looks into cultural expressions and aesthetic practices of men and masculinities as gendered beings rather than the normative and taken-for-granted in various arenas such as film, media, art, literature, sports, cooking, fashion and music. In the first chapter of the section, Christopher R. Matthews and Alex Channon discuss sports as historically constituted male power and further develop the concept of 'male preserve' as an analytical tool to capture the social dynamics of masculine spaces that resist gender change. In the next chapter, Terrence H. McDonald guides us through significant methodological questions for the study of masculinities and moving images and highlights key contributions that have been formative for theory and praxis of cinematic and media representations of masculinity. Andrew Reilly and José Blanco F. show how dressing the male body is about managing and performing identity in general and masculinity in particular, and how masculinity is always at risk of being countered, ridiculed or resisted by visual means of appearance management. In her chapter, Michelle Szabo presents the emerging field of masculinities, food and cooking, demonstrating that personal food preferences are constitutive for social categories such as class, race, religion and sexuality. Sam de Boise outlines how masculinity has been represented and studied in musical texts and sounds. He also makes the link between masculinity and music's appeal and also discusses the gendering of the global music industry. In the next chapter, Josep Armengol argues that, despite a growing body of work on masculinities in literary studies, the field is still marginal, especially in comparison to the literature on women. According to Armengol, we need a radical re-vision of the way literature about men and masculinities is read, conceptualized and perceived. Bettina Uppenkamp's contribution demonstrates the enormous complexity of the concept of masculinity in art and art history. The multiplicity of traditions, perspectives and methodologies is vast, and she highlights various representations of masculinity in art, the representation of the male artist, the male gaze, nudity, racism and sexuality.

Heeding a long call within the larger body of critical masculinities studies to appreciate, study and work with the complexities and nuances of both the problems created by men and the problematic impact of their gender on themselves (e.g., Hearn, 2007), the chapters in *Section 6* flag such an emphasis over the last few decades of critical masculinities research and practice. At the same time, these chapters point to new directions where boys and men and the destabilization of gender and patriarchy may become a part of the challenge to the problems of intersectional gender and social injustices and violences and against people, non-humans and the planet. Richard Collier's chapter explores the rich offerings of contemporary work on masculinities in legal scholarship to the larger body of work on men and masculinities, and he argues that socio-legal studies have much to gain from a closer dialogue with contemporary critical studies of masculinities. Following a sign-posting of the extensive scholarship on masculinities and interpersonal violence, Floretta Boonzaier and Taryn Van Niekerk take up a de/postcolonial feminist critique of how such scholarship serves to reiterate and bolster racist and colonial stereotypes of black and African men in local and transnational research, calling for a more contextual, historical and intersectional approach to men and violence. Claire Duncanson also discusses masculinity and violence but focuses on war and military. She reviews scholarship that employs critical masculinities studies in the project of understanding militarism and war and that works towards challenging violent, militaristic masculinities as key to strategies for local and global peace. In her chapter, Victoria Robinson engages with the large and diverse literature on men as a risk to others, as well as a risk to themselves, including sexual risks, violence and extreme sports. Martin Hultman and Paul Pulé extend the focus on 'the problems that men create' to talk about systemic and material violence towards the planet and all who live on it through the damaging impact of 'manthropocentric' exploitation of planetary resources. Located within a posthumanist, new materialist turn and drawing on critical masculinities and feminist ecology, the authors provide a critical analysis of contemporary forms of masculinities that dominate in global politics and are strongly implicated in the massive ecological challenges facing us globally. The final chapter draws the handbook to a positive close with reflections on contemporary trends in local and global community-based praxis that engages men for gender justice. Tal Peretz provides a theoretical framing for this work, followed by a review of the current state of men's anti-violence and gender-justice engagements globally, elaborating on general themes in this work as well the multiple contestations, constraints and challenges in these movements and activisms, argued to present a key strategic task for scholars and activists working in these terrains.

Note

1 We want to thank Kalle Berggren for his helpful comments on an earlier draft of this chapter.

References

Alaimo, S., & Hekman, S. J. (Eds.). (2008). *Material feminisms*. Bloomington, IN: Indiana University Press.

Anderson, E. (2009). *Inclusive masculinity: The changing nature of masculinities*. London: Routledge.

Andreasson, J., & Johansson, T. (2016). Global narratives of fatherhood: Fathering and masculinity on the Internet. *International Review of Sociology*, *26*(3), 482–496.

Beasley, C. (2005). *Gender and sexuality: Critical theories, critical thinkers*. Thousand Oaks, CA: Sage.

Beasley, C. (2009). Is masculinity studies increasingly the 'odd man' out? Considering problems and possibilities in contemporary gender/sexuality thinking. In A. Biricik & J. Hearn (Eds.), *GEXcel work in progress report volume VI: Proceedings from GEXcel theme 2: Deconstructing the hegemony of men and masculinities* (pp. 173–181). Linköping: Centre of Gendering Excellence.

Beasley, C. (2013). Mind the gap? Masculinity studies and contemporary gender/sexuality thinking. *Australian Feminist Studies*, *28*(75), 108–124.

Beasley, C. (2015). Caution! Hazards ahead: Considering the potential gap between feminist thinking and men/masculinities theory and practice. *Journal of Sociology*, *51*(3), 566–581.

Berggren, K. (2014). Sticky masculinity: Post-structuralism, phenomenology and subjectivity in critical studies on men. *Men and Masculinities*, *17*(3), 231–252.

Bhana, D., & Pattman, R. (2009). Researching South African youth, gender and sexuality within the context of HIV/AIDS. *Development*, *52*(1), 68–74.

Braidotti, R. (2013). *The posthuman*. Cambridge: Polity Press.

Bridges, T. (2019). The cost of exclusionary practices in masculinity studies. *Men and Masculinities*, *22*(1), 16–33.

Bridges, T., & Pascoe, C. J. (2014). Hybrid masculinities: New directions in the sociology of men and masculinities. *Sociology Compass*, *8*(3), 246–258.

Brod, H. (Ed.). (1987). *The making of masculinities: The new men's studies*. Winchester, MA: Allen & Unwin.

Christensen, A. D., & Jensen, S. Q. (2014). Combining hegemonic masculinity and intersectionality. *NORMA: International Journal for Masculinity Studies*, *9*(1), 60–75.

Combahee River Collective. (1977/1997). A Black feminist statement. In L. Nicholson (Ed.), *The second wave: A reader in feminist theory* (pp. 63–70). New York: Routledge.

Connell, R. W. (1987). *Gender and power*. Cambridge: Polity Press.

Connell, R. W. (2001). Understanding men: Gender sociology and the new international research on masculinities. *Social Thought & Research, 24*(1/2), 13–31.

Connell, R. W. (2014). Margin becoming centre: For a world-centred rethinking of masculinities. *NORMA: International Journal for Masculinity Studies, 9*(4), 217–231.

Coole, D., & Frost, S. (Eds.). (2010). *New materialisms: Ontology, agency, and politics*. Durham, NC: Duke University Press.

Deleuze, G., & Guattari, F. (1986). *Kafka: Towards a minor literature*. Minneapolis, MN: University of Minnesota Press.

Edley, N., & Wetherell, M. (1997). Jockeying for position: The construction of masculine identities. *Discourse & Society, 8*(2), 203–217.

Eng, D. L. (2001). *Racial castration: Managing masculinity in Asian America*. Durham, NC: Duke University Press.

Farris, S. R. (2017). *In the name of women's rights: The rise of femonationalism*. Durham, NC: Duke University Press.

Forsberg. L. (2010). Masculinity studies as fetish and the need of a feminist imagination. *NORMA: Nordic Journal for Masculinity Studies, 5*(1), 1–5.

Gottzén, L., & Jonsson, R. (2012). Goda män och Andra män. In L. Gottzén & R. Jonsson (Eds.), *Andra män: Maskulinitet, normskapande och jämställdhet* (pp. 7–23). Malmö: Gleerups.

Grewal, I. (2013). Outsourcing patriarchy: Feminist encounters, transnational mediations and the crime of 'honour killings'. *International Feminist Journal of Politics, 15*(1), 1–19.

Gutterman, D. S. (1994). Postmodernism and the interrogation of masculinity. In H. Brod & M. Kaufman (Eds.), *Theorizing masculinities* (pp. 219–238). Thousand Oaks, CA: Sage.

Halberstam, J. (1998). *Female masculinity*. Durham, NC: Duke University Press.

Haraway, D. (1988). Situated knowledges: The science question in feminism and the privilege of partial perspective. *Feminist Studies, 14*(3), 575–599.

Haraway, D. (1992). The promises of monsters: A regenerative politics for inappropriate/d others. In L. Grossberg, C. Nelson & P. A. Treichler (Eds.), *Cultural studies* (pp. 295–337). New York: Routledge.

Haritaworn, J. (2015). *Queer lovers and hateful others: Regenerating violent times and places*. London: Pluto Press.

Hearn, J. (1987). *The gender of oppression: Men, masculinity and the critique of Marxism*. Brighton: Wheatsheaf.

Hearn, J. (2007). The problems boys and men create, the problems boys and men experience. In T. Shefer, K. Ratele, A. Strebel, N. Shabalala & R. Buikema (Eds.), *From boys to men: Social constructions of masculinity in contemporary society* (pp. 13–33). Cape Town: University of Capetown Press.

Hearn, J., Nordberg, M., Andersson, K., Balkmar, D., Gottzén, L., Klinth, R., Pringle, K., & Sandberg, L. (2012). Hegemonic masculinity and beyond: 40 years of research in Sweden. *Men and Masculinities, 15*(1), 31–55.

Hemmings, C. (2011). *Why stories matter: The political grammar of feminist theory*. Durham, NC: Duke University Press.

Holth, L., & Mellström, U. (2011). Revisiting engineering, masculinity and technology studies: Old structures with new openings. *International Journal of Gender, Science and Technology, 3*(2), 313–329.

hooks, b. (1984). *Feminist theory: From margin to center*. Boston, MA: South End Press.

Jalmert, L. (1979). *Små barns sociala utveckling. Kritisk granskning av forskning*. Stockholm: Stockholm University.

Jardine, A., & Smith, P. (Eds.). (1987). *Men in feminism*. New York: Routledge.

Johansson, T., & Klinth, R. (2008). Caring fathers: The ideology of gender equality and masculine positions. *Men and Masculinities, 11*(1), 42–62.

Kimmel, M. (Ed.). (1987). *Changing men: New directions in research on men and masculinity*. Thousand Oaks, CA: Sage.

Kimmel, M., Hearn, J., & Connell, R. W. (2005). *Handbook of studies on men and masculinities*. Thousand Oaks, CA: Sage.

Liliequist, J. (2006). Sexualitet. In J. Lorentzen & C. Ekenstam (Eds.), *Män i Norden: Manlighet och modernitet 1840–1940* (pp. 167–207). Hedemora: Gidlunds.

Lorde, A. (1984/2007). *Sister outsider: Essays and speeches*. Berkeley, CA: Crossing Press.

Lykke, N. (2010). *Feminist studies: A guide to intersectional theory, methodology and writing*. London: Routledge.

Messerschmidt, J. W. (2018). *Hegemonic masculinity: Formulation, reformulation, and amplification*. Lanham, MA: Rowman & Littlefield.
Messner, M. A. (1996). Studying up on sex. *Sociology of Sport Journal, 13*(3), 221–237.
Nelson, C. (1987). Men, feminism: The materiality of discourse. In A. Jardine & P. Smith (Eds.), *Men in feminism* (pp. 153–172). New York: Routledge.
Pascoe, C. J., & Bridges, T. (Eds.). (2016). *Exploring masculinities: Identity, inequality, continuity, and change*. New York: Oxford University Press.
Petersson, C. C., & Plantin, L. (2019). Breaking with norms of masculinity: Men making sense of their experience of sexual assault. *Clinical Social Work Journal*, doi: 10.1007/s10615-019-00699-y.
Puar, J. (2007). *Terrorist assemblages: Homonationalism in queer times*. Durham, NC: Duke University Press.
Ratele, K. (2014). Currents against gender transformation of South African men: Relocating marginality to the centre of research and theory of masculinities. *NORMA: International Journal for Masculinity Studies, 9*(1), 30–44.
Reeser, T. W. (2015). Concepts of masculinity and masculinity studies. In S. Horlacher (Ed.), *Configuring masculinity in theory and literary practice* (pp. 11–38). Leiden: Brill.
Rubin, G. (1992). Of catamites and kings: Reflections on butch, gender, and boundaries. In J. Nestle (Ed.), *The persistent desire: A femme-butch reader* (pp. 466–482). Boston, MA: Alyson.
Said, E. (1982). Travelling theory. *Raritan: A Quarterly Review, 1*(3), 41–67.
Schwalbe, M. (2015). *Manhood acts: Gender and the practices of domination*. New York: Routledge.
Sedgwick, E. K. (1985). *Between men: English literature and male homosocial desire*. New York: Columbia University Press.
Sedgwick, E. K. (1990/2008). *Epistemology of the closet*. Berkeley, CA: University of California Press.
Sedgwick, E. K. (1995). Gosh, Boy George, you must be awfully secure in your masculinity! In M. Berger, B. Wallis & S. Weston (Eds.), *Constructing masculinity* (pp. 11–20). New York: Routledge.
Shefer, T. (2016). Resisting the binarism of victim and agent: Critical reflections on 20 years of scholarship on young women and heterosexual practices in South African contexts. *Global Public Health, 11*(1/2), 211–223.
Traister, B. (2000). Academic Viagra: The rise of American masculinity studies. *American Quarterly, 52*(2), 274–304.
Wiegman, R. (2012). *Object lessons*. Durham, NC: Duke University Press.
Zahidi, S. (2013). The secret of the Nordic gender nirvana. *World Economic Forum*. Retrieved from www.weforum.org/agenda/2013/10/the-secret-of-the-nordic-gender-nirvana.

Part 1
Theories and perspectives

1

The institutionalization of (critical) studies on men and masculinities

Geopolitical perspectives

Jeff Hearn and Richard Howson

Introduction

Studies on men and masculinities are, in one sense, ancient. Men have studied men for centuries, though often as an 'absent presence'. Men have historically dominated the written word, in academia, research, science, histories, literature, religion and many further arenas. Often this domination has taken the shape of men writing about men, and for men, generally implicitly so. And even when men have written on and about women, this has often been largely for an audience of men. Meanwhile, for a long time, 'gender' was largely seen as a matter of and for women; men were generally seen as ungendered, natural or naturalized. This absent presence and naturalized understanding that has operated through much of history is taken up in Genevieve Lloyd's (1984) thesis on the relationship between man and reason. Thus, men and masculinity become the benchmark against which everything else about human nature is explained, and 'men' and 'masculinities' as individuals, groups or categories have typically *not* been problematized. This is now no longer the case, as exemplified in the relatively rapid growth of various kinds of studies on men and masculinities: some less critical, some more critical; some framed outside, even antagonistically to, feminist, Women's or Gender Studies, some framed within those studies.

The broad approach and framing we focus on here, namely, critical studies on men and masculinities (CSMM), highlights how the gendering, yet absent presence, of men and masculinities is located within systems and relations of gender power and domination, and how understanding this necessitates drawing on the full range of feminist and critical gender and sexuality scholarship, as part of feminist, women's and gender studies. So, while studying men and/or masculinities does not in itself guarantee criticality, CSMM foregrounds the critical impulse, unlike some other approaches to the object of study, such as those men's studies that include men's rights and some men's movement positionings.

In this chapter, we examine the *institutionalization* of explicitly gendered studies on men and masculinities, that is, the making, reproduction and change in more durable academic activities, structures and interventions. Whilst acknowledging our Anglophone bias, we seek to understand these developments within a geopolitical perspective. In this, we make some connections with policy and activism, and to substantive and theoretical developments in CSMM, but to explore those areas more fully would require two further chapters.

Naming and framing

Different studies on men and masculinities pass under a number of names, including 'men's studies', 'masculinity studies', 'critical masculinity studies', 'critical men's studies', 'male dominance studies', 'studies on men and masculinities', 'critical studies on men', or simply 'men and masculinities', or – our preferred term – 'critical studies on men and masculinities'. These different namings may seem innocent, but they are also associated with, and thus index, different orientations to men and masculinities – and indeed different ontologies, epistemologies and relationships with feminisms.

Let us start here with the term 'men's studies'. The term may seem the most obvious and innocent enough, but it is not; indeed naming can be politically dangerous. The term is used in different ways, even within the Anglophone world, as well as in other languages. Sometimes it is almost an equivalent to CSMM, especially when prefixed as *critical* men's studies. More often, 'men's studies' is ambiguous – are these studies on and about men or studies that '*belong*' to men, a form of homosocial arena, even if comprising men defined as progressive? Are 'men's studies' intended to be an equivalent, a parallel, a competitor to women's studies, or even gender studies? Are these 'men's studies' to be done critically at all and/or in relation to feminism? Sometimes, explicit, gendered studies on men and masculinities are conducted *without* reference to feminism or criticality or gender emancipation, or speak against feminism, giving men another platform to exercise their voice. Imagine if (non-critical) white studies were championed by white people against black studies. For these reasons, CSMM, conducted by women, men and further genders, as part of feminist, Women's and Gender Studies, are necessary (Hearn, 1997, 2004). CSMM encompass various orientations, including that labelled (critical) masculinity studies, even if those strands usually focus their critique more on masculinity than men. Significantly, in contrast to some 'men's studies', women have, in some parts of the world, for example, Central and Eastern Europe, been leading the development of CSMM, as part of feminist theorizing and praxis (for example, Blagojević, 2000/2005).

There are many reasons why studies on men and masculinities are developed, and these may be very often different for women, men, queer or trans people. There is a long history of women writing (critically) about men. This can be traced back to the so-called First Wave of feminism and to the voluminous writings of Second Wave feminism. Hanmer (1990) reported 54 feminist texts published by 1975 on women's lives and their relationships to men. Additionally, different feminisms have different grounds, ontologies and epistemologies for studying men, as suggested in the question, 'Can men be subjects of feminist thought?' (Harding, 1998, p. 71): becoming 'truly rational men' in line with feminist empiricism; criticizing bourgeois, sexist ideology, in line with Marxist feminism; refusing to be men, following radical feminism; becoming historically situated feminist men, as according to socialist feminism; and developing multicultural, global feminist analyses on and by men. In such various ways, some men may claim to be 'feminist', and some women may attribute 'feminist' to some men. Ironically, liberal feminists, who may have most ease in allying with men, may have the least reason to theorize men; radical feminists who may keep the most distance from men, socially and intellectually, may have a stronger motivation to analyze men, not least because subversive analyses of men as a gendered social category are part of that political and academic project. Meanwhile, Messner (1997) outlined different motivations for men to become interested in gender politics, and that would clearly include feminism and gender equality, ranging from the costs of masculinity to the recognition of difference and to the search and support for gender justice (see Egeberg Holmgren & Hearn, 2009). Furthermore, men adopt different discursive positions in relation to (other) men (Hearn, 1998).

Critical studies on men and masculinities

Critical studies on men and masculinities specifically present critical, explicitly gendered accounts, descriptions and explanations of men and masculinities in their social and societal contexts that bring them into sharper relief as objects of theory and critique. The idea that gendering men and masculinities derives from a fixed inner trait or core is problematic, even antagonistic, within CSMM; men are not to be essentialized and reified. CSMM have developed in part through critique of the (inter)personalization of gender relations and men, and specifically sex role approaches, to the completion of multiple local ethnographies, as in the 'ethnographic moment' (Connell, 1998). Key early texts include the feminist collection *On the Problem of Men* (Friedman & Sarah, 1983) and texts by gay/bisexual/straight men (Snodgrass, 1977; Tolson, 1977). There are obviously different narratives about the sub-field, for example, to what extent social science research is emphasized. For instance, a relatively early expression/intervention within the humanities occurred at sessions on men, feminism and feminist theory at the 1984 Modern Languages Association (MLA) convention, leading to the volume *Men in Feminism* (Jardine & Smith, 1987).

The 1980s saw many texts on black and minority ethnic men and masculinities that contributed to the demythologizing of racist stereotypes and discourses. Gender-subversive concerns have figured throughout, as with such questions as what is/counts as a 'man'? In developing CSMM, certain themes have been stressed that have often been in contradiction with definitions that privilege and prioritize men; as such, they have exposed and examined issues often ignored, such as local, personal, bodily/embodied or immediate/present. This has led to questions about sexuality, family, fatherhood, emotions, everyday life and so on, which in turn have attracted more attention than the 'big (socio-political) picture' (Connell, 1993).

In all of this, the development of masculinities theory from the late 1970s onwards, most famously through the work of Connell (1995) and colleagues, has been central in the institutionalization of CSMM, particularly through the employment of the concept of hegemonic masculinity, in its various interpretations, uses and critiques, including those of the hegemony of men (Hearn, 2004) and manhood acts (Schwalbe, 2014). The concepts of masculinity and masculinities have been at times difficult to define, in that they can refer variously to: practices, configurations or assemblages of practice, identities, types, structures, institutions, processes, psychodynamics, discursive and so on. A key complication is that masculinity is often linked to men and/or male bodies; sometimes, there is a separation of masculinity from men/male bodies, as in female masculinity (Halberstam, 1998); and a further critical position is that the concept of masculinity, like femininity, is to be used sparingly, if at all, in seeking to move beyond binary positions, languages and attributions.

In *Cultures of Masculinity*, Edwards (2006) outlines three phases in the development of studies on men and masculinities: a first based on the *sex role paradigm* in 1970s, in which men and masculinity were understood in relatively static, culture-bound and/or micro-sociological ways; a second emerging in the 1980s primarily out of criticism of the first, with a *more political* rationale, emphasizing power relations; and a third clearly influenced by *post-structural* theory, particularly questions of normativity, performativity and sexuality. These map somewhat onto distinctions between more liberal reformist, structural resistance and deconstructive rebellious framings and feminisms (Lorber, 2005) that suggest different approaches to changing men, men as subjects, men as objects and men's relationships to feminist, Women's Studies and Gender Studies scholarship – and thus tensions within CSMM.

These various characterizations are an over-simplification, but not a gross one. Recent years have seen further diverse influences on CSMM, from different feminist traditions, globalization, postmodernism, transgender studies, postcolonialism, queer studies and science and technology studies. Arguably, we are now witnessing a fourth phase of CSMM, with greater attention to international, comparative, supranational, global, postcolonial and transnational approaches (including migration, global inequality, war and so on), materialist-discursive, new materialist analysis and approaches and more rebellious positions on gender hegemony. There has been an important expansion of studies on or from the 'global South' (for example, Cornwall & Lindisfarne, 1994; Ouzgane & Coleman, 1998; Cleaver, 2002; Pease & Pringle, 2002; Jones, 2006; Donaldson et al., 2009; Cornwall et al., 2011, 2015; Ruspini et al., 2011; van der Gaag, 2014).

While not playing down differences between different investigative and epistemological traditions, the broad critical approach to studying men and masculinities can be characterized by:

- an *explicit and specific focus* on men and masculinities;
- taking account of *feminist, gay, queer and other critical gender and sexuality scholarship*;
- recognizing men and masculinities as *explicitly gendered*;
- understanding men and masculinities as *socially constructed, produced and reproduced*, rather than as somehow just 'naturally' one way or another;
- seeing men and masculinities as *variable and changing* across time (history) and space (culture), within societies, through life courses and biographies;
- emphasizing men's relations, albeit differentially, to *gendered power*;
- spanning both the *material and the discursive*;
- interrogating men and masculinities through *intersections with other social divisions*.

To summarize, CSMM, methodologically, emphasizes *historical, cultural, relational, materialist, anti-essentialist, de-reified and deconstructive studies on men and masculinities* and is committed to developing studies along those lines. Overall, CSMM resists the potential to re-centre men's power and moves, if only implicitly, towards the de-centring, the othering, of men, through both naming and deconstruction. Whatever the exact forms these interventions take, a material-discursive space is opened up for further critical inquiry.

Conditions of development

In terms of academic institutionalization, a geopolitics perspective is important in understanding what drives, differentially, the development of CSMM globally. Explicitly gendered critical studies on men and masculinities developed initially in 1960s and 1970s by women and men in Australia, North America and Northwest Europe. This Anglophone hegemony within CSMM is now being challenged, with increasing emphasis on the establishment of clear non-Anglophone research traditions and on the growing body of work produced and being produced across Europe, Latin America, North, South and East Asia and Southern Africa (for example, Gutmann, 2009; Vigoya, 2018; Novikova & Kambourov, 2003; Morrell, 2001; Shefer et al., 2007). Increasingly, transnational concerns across borders are on research agendas, often with attention to globalizing/glocalizing men and masculinities.

In considering what might be the conditions that are giving rise to CSMM and its diverse development, it may be useful to locate it in relation to some more general societal features. Especially important here are the geopolitical positionings of men and masculinities within the processes of globalization, neoliberalism, (post)colonialism, (post) imperialism and the structures of metropoles, semi-peripheries and peripheries or margins (Blagojević, 2009). Such positionings are often created at the intersection of class, gender and racialization, and they frequently affect and relate to power, capital accumulation, patterns of violence, migration, health and well-being, subordination and so on – which in turn affect the form and content of CSMM. In many world regions, slavery, colonialism and postcolonialism are fundamental to the framing of these studies. Closely linked to these geopolitical forces is the relative power of the market, the state, feminism and gender/sexuality politics more generally. For example, the place of the (welfare) state and gender equality in and across the Nordic region affect the construction of men and masculinities in research and policy.

Academic and intellectual traditions more generally also impact CSMM, with clear contrasts across different parts of the world (Hearn, 2000/2001), even whilst most CSMM work is against the academic mainstream. For example, in the US, there have been many studies based in role theory, psychological and social psychological approaches, culturalist theory and critical race theory. Without overstating the contrast, Western European studies on men and masculinities, for example, have taken different methodological paths, with greater influence from critical social theory, whether Frankfurt School, poststructuralist, humanistic or postcolonial. Further traditions are found in other world regions, for example, the intersections of Confucianism, communism and modernity in China and for the Chinese diaspora (Louie, 2015, 2016; see also Song & Hird, 2013; Lin et al., 2017). Interestingly, no volume adequately represents 'Asia' holistically; many volumes purporting to represent 'Asian' masculinities address specific geographical regions, countries and cultures of Asia, with marginalization of others. As Kwai-Cheung Lo (2010, pp. 26–27) writes:

> Although it is all too obvious that the concept of Asia was and still is a Western construct, I want to look at the dimension of 'Asia' as a sign. Whether it is a fully loaded entity or simply an empty signifier with no determinate meaning, Asia as a proper name always already designates its presence as opposed to its absence.

Finally in this section, while most studies have been framed nationally or locally, the increasing importance of cross-national research collaboration should be noted. This includes: extensive links across Europe, especially through European Union research and policy projects such as the 15-country CROME project (2000–2003); the five-country FOCUS – Fostering Caring Masculinities project (2005–2007); The Role of Men in Gender Equality report (2011–2012) (Scambor et al., 2013) and the IMPACT – Evaluation of European Perpetrator Programmes project (2013–2014); the International Men and Gender Equality Survey (IMAGES), beginning in 2009 and recent reporting on the Middle East and North Africa region (El Feki et al., 2017); and various global North-South collaborations, such as between Nordic countries and South Africa (Shefer et al., 2018).

For the remainder of this chapter, we focus on forms of institutionalization, before some concluding comments.

Forms of institutionalization

Across the various approaches noted, there has been a considerable growth of publications in CSMM. Since the 1970s many collective publications, research groups and centres, national and international research projects, journals and book series have appeared. Though early work was scattered, both MIT, 1979 and Kathleen Grady, Robert Brannon and Joseph Pleck produced bibliographies on men and masculinities in 1979; in 1985, Sam Femiano collated US syllabi into a mimeographed publication (Femiano, 1985) and August produced a 'men's studies' bibliography (August, 1985); and a UK-based sourcebook followed (Ford & Hearn, 1988/1989/1991). A more recent broad-ranging resource is *Manhood and Masculinity: A Global and Historical Bibliography* (Janssen, 2007). The Australia-based XY Online, a major bibliographic online resource, was created in 1992 and is now in its 20th edition.

Another important form of broad-based institutionalization is publishers' book series, including those from:

- Unwin Hyman: *Critical Studies on Men and Masculinities* 1988–1990;
- Routledge, namely, *Male Orders* 1990–95; *Critical Studies on Men and Masculinities* 1990–95; *Critical Studies of Men and Masculinities* 2016–;
- Sage: *Men and Masculinities* included 15 edited thematic volumes 1992–2002, culminating in the 500-page *Handbook of Studies on Men and Masculinities* (Kimmel et al., 2005);
- Zed, and subsequently Springer-Palgrave Macmillan: *Global Masculinities*;
- Hong Kong University Press: *Transnational Asian Masculinities*.

Routledge has published the 2000-page, 5-volume collection *Men and Masculinities* (Whitehead, 2006) and the 700-page *International Encyclopaedia of Men and Masculinities* (Flood et al., 2007) (also see Kimmel & Aronson, 2004). Large overviews have been produced in German with emphasis on the humanities (Horlacher et al., 2016). The Routledge book series launched in 1990, *Critical Studies on Men and Masculinities*, was explicitly feminist, profeminist, gay-affirmative, alive to postcolonialism and had a strong international advisory group of scholars from those directions. In contrast, the Routledge book series of virtually the same name, *Critical Studies of Men and Masculinities*, launched 2016, takes a different approach, aiming to explore how men will fit into a new and changing world; it is much more men-centred and without an international feminist presence or profeminist positioning.

Teaching in colleges and universities began sporadically from the 1970s in the US and from at least the early 1980s in Europe, including teaching for students in social work, women's studies and social sciences. Research groups and centres have been formed, partly to support undergraduate and postgraduate teaching and doctoral researchers, for example, at Bradford University from 1985 and the joint Manchester Universities Campus from 1988, both in the UK. During the 2000s, the Unit for Critical Studies in Men and Masculinities, Nottingham Trent University, UK, ran a Diploma course on men and masculinities, with a focus towards social work, violence and children. In Sweden, CSMM research groups date from 2006 in Linköping University and from 2014 at Örebro University (linked to GEXcel Centre of Excellence established 2006, and more recently the GEXcel Consortium also involving Karlstad University). In Australia at the University of Wollongong, the Centre for Research on Men and Masculinities (CROMM) was formed in 2011, with the *Engaging*

Men in Building Gender Equality conference the following year (Flood & Howson, 2015). The Center for the Study of Men and Masculinities was established in 2013 at State University of New York, Stonybrook, USA, followed by a major conference in 2015, and has begun a master's degree on men and masculinities. The Centre for Masculinity Studies (CeMAS), Aalborg University, Denmark, was established in 2016. At the University of South Africa, the Research Unit on Men and Masculinity (RUMM) has recently been established, following summer schools in 2016 and 2017.

Some centres have a more male-affirmative stance. The Men and Masculinities Center at the University of Massachusetts at Amherst, USA, supports male student success and healthy masculinities from a male positive, multicultural and pro-feminist perspective (www.umass.edu/masculinities/). At Western Illinois University, USA, The Center for the Study of Masculinities and Men's Development states

> Research is clear that men are in crisis, particularly men from underrepresented populations. However, considerable disagreement exists about how to most effectively support men's engagement and development, while maintaining focus on social justice. The Center ... aims to provide quality scholarship, advocacy, and programming that positively influences college men's development in a manner congruent with gender equity and social justice.
>
> *(www.wiu.edu/coehs/es/csmmd/)*

An activist slant is foregrounded by the Masculinities Network (M-NET), operating from the Centre for Human Rights, York University, Canada (http://rights.info.yorku.ca/m-net/). This self-represents as a community of self-identified men intent on repelling silences around violence and sexual assault by: encouraging men to take personal responsibility for their role in preventing gender-based violence; exploring and challenging how masculinities are socially constructed and expressed via reflection on gendered selves; investigating relations between masculinity, violence and rape; and working for gender-based violence prevention on campus. Extra-university activist centres include Centar E8, Serbia (http://e8.org.rs/), and the Center for Men and Masculinities Studies, Bangladesh (http://cmmsbd.net/).

To illustrate the diversity in teaching, we take some examples from Australia, where there are several university-based courses and subjects on 'men and masculinities'. At the University of Tasmania, the 'Masculinities' subject aims to uncover the meaning of masculinity and explore why it exists at all, focusing on culture and following the growth of men from boyhood to old age and taking account of class and race. Masculinity is not seen as inherent, natural or given but as linked to gender performance. The subject of 'Masculinities' at the University of Sydney takes a more strident CSMM approach with the claim that masculinity is an effect of power linked to oppression, specifically women's. Its case-study methodology suggests the social construction of masculinity through investigation of various practices that produce it and forms of representation that sustain it. The University of Wollongong's 'Men and Masculinities' subject within Sociology emphasizes men's positions in gender relations, the shifting and contested social organization of masculinities, current scholarship on gender, key concepts in masculinities theory and alternative approaches to understanding men and change. The major theme here is hegemony, leading to the critical investigation of men and masculinity's privilege, priority and possibilities for change. Less explicitly about men and masculinities are subjects run at the Australian National University and the University of Western Australia, whose objective is to understand history better. The former addresses the existence and impact of masculinity on Western History, including global exploration, imperialism and anti-colonialist reactions. The latter discusses constructions of masculinities within case studies in Europe, Australia and Asia since c. 1700.

Thus, from this brief review, there seems to be no 'natural' home for men and masculinities studies: they can just as easily be located in history as gender studies, as cultural studies or sociology. Further, if the descriptions of these subjects mean anything, then people want to study men and masculinities at university level and do so drawing broadly on feminist scholarship. However, a significant footnote is the University of South Australia example where a 'male studies' course was dramatically reformed by the university in 2014 because it was considered 'anti-feminist', due to its intellectual links to men's rights and anti-feminist groups, some of whose leaders lectured on the course. The university decided to reduce the course to two health-based subjects, with all teaching undertaken by university staff.

At another level, the development of research and teaching into the sub-field of men and masculinities has led to a small number of professorships and senior positions. The earliest we know of are a Professorship in Men's Health and a Professorship in Men, Gender and Health; both at Leeds Beckett University, UK, and both made redundant in 2017. The first generic Professorship in Critical Studies on Men and Masculinities was instituted at Linköping University, running 2006 to 2013; a Professorship in Gender and Masculinity Research, Oslo University, Norway, following initial ministerial funding, began shortly after and continues, with both based in Gender Studies. A personal chair in Masculinities Studies was awarded, now curtailed by retirement, at Curtin University, Communication and Cultural Studies Department, Australia, and a personal Readership was recently created in Critical Masculinity Studies at Newcastle University, UK.

Beyond teaching and related institutional appointments, research has been a strong driving force in the CSMM development, and important here are the developing contacts made by researchers *across* institutions that lead to and/or constitute conferences, networks and associations nationally and internationally. The American Men's Studies Association conferences, whose organization began in the 1980s, have become regular since 1993, with the 26th event held in 2018. Earlier Men and Masculinity conferences led to the *Men's Studies Newsletter*, in 1984 (Doyle & Femiano, 1999/2013). Other newsletters have included *International Association for Studies on Men Newsletter*, produced from 1993 for some years in Norway, and *Nieuwsbrief Mannenstudies* (the Netherlands) from the mid-1980s. In the UK, profeminist organizing within the British Sociological Association dates from about 1982 (Hearn et al., 1983).

An important shift in the relations between feminism, men and masculinities was the invitation from the organizers for sessions on 'Men's Responses to the Feminist Challenge: Relationships of Theory and Practice', at the 3rd International Interdisciplinary Congress on Women entitled 'Women's Worlds, Visions and Revisions' at Trinity College, Dublin, 1987. The first major international conference was in the UK in 1988, leading to the edited book *Men, Masculinities and Social Theory* (Hearn & Morgan, 1990). In 1997, the first South African conferences were held, post-apartheid. There have been five Nordic conferences since 2006, one in each of the five Nordic countries, under the auspices of the Nordic Association for Studies on Men and Masculinities. Since 2006 there have been occasional sessions on CSMM at the International Sociological Association Congresses. In Canada, the Réseau Masculinités et Société research network organizes conferences. The third in a series of conferences on 'Political Masculinities' took place at the University of Koblenz-Landau, Germany, December 2017, with a summer school in August 2018 (see Starck & Sauer, 2014). Other summer schools have been held in, for example, Denmark, Latvia and South Africa. The first international conference on men and masculinities in Turkey was at İzmir in 2014, with a second conference planned for 2016 postponed by the political situation. The 2016 'Narratives of Masculinity' conference held at Bielefeld University, Germany, was introduced as the first such international conference, though it was clearly not. Recent conferences in Latin America include 'Igualdad de género desde la perspectiva de las masculinidades,' Mexico, August 2017; 'Violencia de género y masculinidades: Desafíos en la intervención con varones que ejercen violencia basada en género,' Uruguay, November 2017; and 'Nuevas Masculinidades,' Mexico, December 2017. More specialist conferences range widely, for example, the 2017 Extreme Masculinities International Conference at the University of Vienna within the discipline of anthropology.

A further significant expression of institutionalization through publication is in the form of specialist journals, including: *American Journal of Men's Health, Boyhood Studies: An Interdisciplinary Journal, The Journal of Black Masculinity, Journal of Men's Health, Journal of Men's Health and Gender, The Journal of Men's Studies, Masculinities & Social Change, Masculinities: A Journal of Identity & Culture, Men and Masculinities, NORMA: International Journal for Masculinity Studies, Psychology of Men and Masculinity, Spectrum: A Journal on Black Men, Boyhood Studies*, and *World Journal of Men's Health.* Discontinued journals include *Culture, Society and Masculinities, Fathering, International Journal of Men's Health, Journal of Men, Masculinities and Spirituality* and *Masculinities* (US, not Turkey). Special issues have been produced in 'more general' journals since the early 1970s, for example, *Impact of Science on Society*, and *Black Scholar.* Two recently established open access journals are *Masculinities & Social Change* and *Masculinities: A Journal of Identity and Culture.* The former emerges from a lack of relevant journals in Spain and Latin America and publishes in English, Spanish, Catalan, Euskera and Galician. The latter, based in Turkey, is a 'biannual journal of interdisciplinary and critical studies of gender and masculinity . . . related to the representations of gender, particularly masculinity, formations of gendered identities, cultural, social, and aesthetic reflections of masculinity in culture and literature.'

Collaborations in the CSMM sub-field have also been driven through policy-based research, as well as national and international conferences, for example, those held under the auspices of the European Union in Örebro, Sweden 2001, Helsinki 2006, and Brussels 2012. Nordic governmental cooperation led to a Nordic Men and Gender Equality Programme 1995–2000 and a Nordic Region Coordinator for Men's Studies/CSMM at the Nordic Institute for Women's and Gender Studies (NIKK) in the late 1990s and early 2000s.

In terms of broader policy, practice and developmental work, MenEngage has now become a major global umbrella organization with more than 700 members and constituted by networks in Africa (17), the Caribbean (5), Europe (16), Latin America (10), North America (2) and South Asia (5). The second MenEngage Global Symposium in November 2014 in New Delhi attracted more than 1,200 people and 400 abstracts from 63 countries, producing the 'Delhi Declaration and Call to Action' (www.menengage dilli2014.net/delhi-declaration-and-call-to-action.html). There is a host of local and broadly progressive intervention and development projects and campaigns working on changing men and boys, with especially strong activity in Latin America, Southern Africa and South Asia (for example, Chowdhury & Al Baset, 2018).

There are also signs of some increasing overlaps and movements between policy development, NGO/INGOs, academic work and entrepreneurialism. This might in some cases entail activities ranging from some individual researchers' strenuous self-promotion, self-marketing websites and offering themselves to be conference keynotes, to small-scale consultancy on equality and welfare issues for public sector and NGO clients, through to more elaborate contractual work for international corporate businesses, thus bringing their own translations and contradictions.

Trends and implications

Overall, there has been a significant quantitative, qualitative and geographical expansion of the sub-field of CSMM. This has occurred over recent decades, from roots located in feminist, Women's Studies, Gender Studies and other disciplines. The alignment of CSMM with feminism and profeminism is an imperative feature of its epistemological frame, as is the continuing development of investigations into men and masculinities in popular consciousness and the intersubjective space between civil and political societies and/or the social and the political. This type of work brings to the fore previously neglected areas, such as men's violence, conditions for complicity/aspiration in the context of hegemony and critical policy in such areas as migration, work and health. In addition, or as a consequence of the CSMM's epistemological frame, key theoretical innovations continue to be developed, for example, around hegemony (Howson & Hearn, this volume) and challenges to privilege and absent presence within popular consciousness of 'ideal' masculinity. Studies towards global, transnational, postcolonial concerns, including cross-national and cross-language studies as well as scholarship from the global South and semi-peripheries continue to grow, elaborating the existing work and understanding at the global level. The institutionalization perspective offers evidence that the sub-field continues to grow and contributes important knowledge to the broader field of Gender Studies and feminism; notwithstanding this, the sub-field remains characterized by contestation, with strong, if uneven and shifting, links across activism, policy and theory.

References

August, E. R. (1985). *Men's studies: A selected and annotated interdisciplinary bibliography*. Littleton, CO: Libraries Unlimited.

Blagojević, M. (Ed.). (2000/2005). *Mapiranje mizoginije u Srbiji: Diskursi i prakse* [Mapping misogyny in Serbia: Discourses and practices] Volumes 1 and 2. Belgrade: AŽIN.

Blagojević, M. (2009). *Knowledge production at the semiperiphery*. Belgrade: Institut za kriminološka i sociološka istraživanja.

Chowdhury, R., & Al Baset, Z. (Eds.). (2018). *Men and feminism in India*. Abingdon: Routledge.

Cleaver, F. (Ed.). (2002). *Masculinities matter! Men, gender and development*. London: Zed.

Connell, R. (1993). The big picture: Masculinities in recent world history. *Theory and Society*, *22*(5), 597–623.

Connell, R. (1995). *Masculinities*. Cambridge: Polity.

Connell, R. (1998). Masculinities and globalization. *Men and Masculinities*, *1*(1), 3–23.

Cornwall, A., Edström, J., & Greig, A. (Eds.). (2011). *Men and development: Politicising masculinities*. London: Zed.

Cornwall, A., Kariosis, F., & Lindisfarne, N. (Eds.). (2015). *Masculinities under neoliberalism*. Chicago: University of Chicago Press.

Cornwall, A., & Lindisfarne, N. (Eds.). (1994). *Dislocating masculinity: Comparative ethnographies*. London: Routledge.

Donaldson, M., Hibbins, R., Howson, R., & Pease, B. (Eds.). (2009). *Migrant men: Critical studies of masculinities and the migration experience*. New York: Routledge.

Doyle, J. A., & Femiano, S. (1999/2013). A history of the Men's Studies Press and its association with the American Men's Studies Association. *The Journal of Men's Studies*, *21*(1), 24–33.

Edwards, T. (2006). *Cultures of masculinity*. London: Routledge.

Egeberg Holmgren, L., & Hearn, J. (2009). Framing 'men in feminism': Theoretical locations, local contexts and practical passings in men's gender-conscious positionings on gender equality and feminism. *Journal of Gender Studies, 18*(4), 403–418.

El Feki, S., Heilman, B., & Barker, G. (Eds.). (2017). *Understanding masculinities: Results from the International Men and Gender Equality Survey (IMAGES) – Middle East and North Africa.* Cairo/Washington: UN Women/Promundo-US.

Femiano, S. (Ed.). (1985). *Men's studies syllabi* (12th ed., 1996). Northampton, MA: S. Femiano.

Flood, M., Gardiner, J. K., Pease, B., & Pringle, K. (Eds.). (2007). *International encyclopedia of men and masculinities.* London: Routledge.

Flood, M., & Howson, R. (Eds.). (2015). *Engaging with men in gender equality.* Newcastle: Cambridge Scholars.

Ford, D., & Hearn, J. (1988/1989/1991). *Studying men and masculinity. A sourcebook of resources and materials.* Applied Social Studies Publication 1. Bradford, UK: University of Bradford.

Friedman, S., & Sarah, E. (Eds.). (1983). *On the problem of men: Two feminist conferences.* London: Women's Press.

Grady, K. E., Brannon, R., & Pleck, J. H. (1979). *The male sex role: A selected and annotated bibliography.* Rockville, MD: National Institute of Mental Health.

Gutmann, M. C. (Ed.). (2009). *Changing men and masculinities in Latin America.* Durham, NC: Duke University Press.

Halberstam, J. (1998). *Female masculinity.* Durham, NC: Duke University Press.

Hanmer, J. (1990). Men, power and the exploitation of women. In J. Hearn & D. Morgan (Eds.), *Men, masculinities and social theory* (pp. 21–42). London: Unwin Hyman/Routledge.

Harding, S. (1998). Can men be subjects of feminist theory? In T. Digby (Ed.), *Men doing feminism* (pp. 171–195). New York: Routledge.

Hearn, J. (1997). The implications of critical studies on men. *NORA: Nordic Journal of Women's Studies, 5*(1), 48–60.

Hearn, J. (1998). Theorizing men and men's theorizing: Men's discursive practices in theorizing men. *Theory and Society, 27*(6), 781–816.

Hearn, J. (2000/2001). Forskning om maend i fire dele af verden: USA, Australia, England og Norden, *NIKK Magasin, 1*, 7–9; Critical Studies on men in four parts of the world. *NIKK Magasin, 3*, 12–15.

Hearn, J. (2004). From hegemonic masculinity to the hegemony of men. *Feminist Theory, 5*(1), 49–72.

Hearn, J., & Morgan, D. (Eds.). (1990). *Men, masculinities and social theory.* London: Unwin Hyman/ Routledge.

Hearn, J., Morgan, D., Creighton, C., Middleton, C., Thomas, R., & Pearson, C. (1983). Changing men's sexist practice in sociology. *Network (British Sociological Association), 25*, 3.

Horlacher, S., Jansen, B., & Schwanebeck, W. (Eds.). (2016). *Männlichkeit: Ein interdisziplinäres Handbuch.* Berlin: Springer.

Janssen, D. F. (2007). *Manhood and masculinity: A global and historical bibliography.* Harriman, TN: Men's Studies Press.

Jardine, A., & Smith, P. (Eds.). (1987). *Men in feminism.* New York: Routledge.

Jones, A. (Ed.). (2006). *Men of the Global South: A reader.* London: Zed.

Kimmel, M., & Aronson, A. (Eds.). (2004). *Men and masculinities: A social, cultural and historical encyclopedia, 2 Volumes.* Santa Barbara, CA: ABC-CLIO.

Kimmel, M., Hearn, J., & Connell, R. (Eds.). (2005). *Handbook of studies on men and masculinities.* Thousand Oaks, CA: Sage.

Lin, X., Haywood, C., & Mac an Ghaill, M. (Eds.). (2017). *East Asian men: Masculinity, sexuality and desire.* Houndmills: Palgrave Macmillan.

Lloyd, G. (1984). *The man of reason: 'Male' & 'female' in Western philosophy.* London: Routledge.

Lo, K.-C. (2010). *Excess and masculinities in Asian cultural productions.* Albany, NY: State University of New York Press.

Lorber, J. (Ed.). (2005). *Gender inequality: Feminist theories and politics.* Los Angeles, CA: Roxbury.

Louie, K. (2015). *Chinese masculinities in a globalizing world.* London: Routledge.

Louie, K. (Ed.). (2016). *Changing Chinese masculinities: From imperial pillars of state to global real men.* Hong Kong: Hong Kong University Press.

Messner, M. (1997). *Politics of masculinities.* Thousand Oaks, CA: Sage.

MIT: Massachusetts Institute of Technology Humanities Library. (1979). *Men's studies bibliography* (4th ed.). Cambridge, MA: MIT.

Morrell, R. (Ed.). (2001). *Changing men in Southern Africa*. Durban/London: University of Natal Press/Zed.

Novikova, I., & Kambourov, D. (Eds.). (2003). *Men and masculinities in the global world: Integrating postsocialist perspectives*. Helsinki: Kikimora Publishers, Aleksantteri Institute.

Ouzgane, L., & Coleman, D. (1998). Postcolonial masculinities: Introduction. *Jouvert: A Journal of Postcolonial Studies*, *2*(1), 1–10.

Pease, B., & Pringle, K. (Eds.). (2002). *A man's world: Changing men's practices in a globalized world*. London: Zed.

Ruspini, E., Hearn, J., Pease, B., & Pringle, K. (Eds.). (2011). *Men and masculinities around the world*. Houndmills: Palgrave Macmillan.

Scambor, E., Wojnicka, K., & Bergmann, N. (Eds.). (2013). *Study on the role of men in gender equality*. Brussels: European Commission.

Schwalbe, M. (2014). *Manhood acts: Gender and the practices of domination*. Boulder, CO: Paradigm.

Shefer, T., Hearn, J., Ratele, K., & Boonzaier, F. (Eds.). (2018). *Engaging youth in activist research and pedagogical praxis: Transnational perspectives on gender, sex, and race*. New York: Routledge.

Shefer, T., Ratele, K., Strebel, A., Shabalala, N., & Buikema, R. (Eds.). (2007). *From boys to men: Social constructions of masculinity in contemporary society*. Cape Town: University of Cape Town Press and HSRC Press.

Snodgrass, J. (Ed.). (1977). *A Book of readings for men against sexism*. Albion, CA: Times Change Press.

Song, G., & Hird, D. (2013). *Men and masculinities in contemporary China*. Leiden: Brill.

Starck, K., & Sauer, B. (Eds.). (2014). *A man's world? Political masculinities in literature and culture*. Newcastle upon Tyne: Cambridge Scholars.

Tolson, A. (1977). *The limits of masculinity*. London: Tavistock.

van der Gaag, N. (2014). *Feminism & men*. London: Zed.

Vigoya, M. V. (2018). *Les couleurs de la masculinité: Expériences intersectionnelles et pratiques de pouvoir en Amérique du Sud*. Paris: La Découverte.

Whitehead, S. (Ed.). (2006). *Men and masculinities: Critical concepts in sociology* (Vol. 5). London: Routledge.

2

Feminism and men/masculinities scholarship

Connections, disjunctions and possibilities

Chris Beasley

Introduction

This chapter reflects upon and extends my previous analyses of the relationship between contemporary feminist and critical men/masculinities (MM) scholarship within the gender/sexuality field. These analyses considered the character of the relationship and/or highlighted the relationship by employing feminist thought in discussion of particular questions of importance within MM studies. They attended to this relationship because MM studies makes central its debt and commitment to feminist thinking. It is thus appropriate within the terms that MM scholarship sets for itself to review the implications of potential disjunctions between them for the present positioning and future directions of MM studies.

I examine the relationship between MM and feminist scholarship by concentrating on the *main theoretical* frameworks or paradigms which shape their *overall* agendas.[1] In other words, my analysis will not and cannot cover every single framework, writer or text in these two forms of scholarship but, rather, is intended to develop an analysis based upon their major trajectories. In order to give central attention to main theoretical paradigms I note the range of Feminist and MM scholarship, but sometimes concentrate on exemplary writers who have shaped and continue to shape the overall agendas of these fields. This attention to main theoretical paradigms—that is, overarching frameworks of understanding which involve ontological and epistemological considerations—does not imply that all scholars in the field of scholarship/theorising will put forward the same views. Indeed, such theoretical paradigms are not necessarily discrete or in opposition to each other and are in any case constantly mutating. Moreover, in characterising shifts in main theoretical paradigms over time and noting the prevalence of one or another, I do not intend to suggest a linear account of their development in which each as it emerges replaces the previous one,[2] or that any particular paradigm is inevitably more or less valuable. Rather, I offer a perspective which puts forward intersections between such paradigms.

In the exploration which follows, the focus is upon potentially dissonant theoretical directions taken by feminist and pro-feminist MM scholarship with the aim of offering a new conceptualisation of these disjunctions that might reveal not only potential hazards but some perhaps unexpected creative possibilities.

While I locate MM studies as one of three main subfields in the overall Gender/Sexuality field to indicate connections between MM, Feminist and Sexuality studies, in the first section I focus on the field's potential *discontents*—indicating possible barriers to dialogue and coalition. The analysis outlines the differential uptake of postmodernist/poststructuralist theoretical paradigms—hereafter described as postmodern.[3] MM theorising continues to demonstrate relatively less, and more inconsistent, engagement with postmodern perspectives as compared with feminist (or sexuality) thinking (see Beasley, 2005, 2012). This account of problematic disjunctions between feminist and MM theorising—in the light of the pro-feminist commitments of MM scholarship—turns in the second section to reflections upon the *potential advantages and creative possibilities* associated with this heterogeneity.

Connections and disjunctions: the gender/sexuality field and its theoretical discontents

This chapter begins from a recognition that the present location and future directions of MM scholarship are linked with Feminism in their co-location within the broad rubric of what I have described as the Gender/Sexuality field (Beasley, 2005). There are a number of important reasons for invoking an understanding of Feminist, MM and Sexuality studies as robustly connected subfields located within this overarching field (see Beasley, 2013). MM scholarship is feminist inspired in its initial emergence and continues to define itself in relation to a feminist sympathetic or more usually an explicitly pro-feminist perspective (Connell, 1995/2005; Flood, 1997/2002; Whitehead, 2002; Messner, 1997; Kimmel, 1992). In this context, I have argued that any attempt to entirely disengage Feminist, MM or Sexuality studies from each other would amount to an impossible dismemberment of existing linkages. It is now difficult (if not well-nigh impossible) to disaggregate the subfields.

To outline the relationship between the different subfields I have employed the methodological device of a notion of a continuum within the Gender/Sexuality field (see also Beasley, 2013, 2015), ranging from strongly modernist to strongly postmodern thinking. In this approach I have endeavoured to view modernism and postmodernism as broad theoretical trajectories located on a continuum, rather than as entirely distinct—much less necessarily oppositional.[4] The continuum shows the ways in which the feminist, MM and sexuality subfields draw upon a largely similar theoretical terrain with similar main paradigms. The subfields are not spread entirely equally across this continuum of main theoretical directions. Rather, they tend to clump differently in certain locations across the continuum and, more specifically, evince a differential uptake of modernist and postmodern paradigms.

Debate about the advantages and limits of postmodern inflected theories like Queer Theory continues to occupy feminist and sexuality studies—along with emerging associated debates about 'new materialism' (Fox & Alldred, 2018)—linking them in terms of theoretical terrain, shared key theorists (such as Judith Butler) and theoretical debates regarding gender categories/identities. However, this theoretical debate is less developed in MM studies. MM scholarship continues to draw strongly upon modernist terminologies, concepts and modes of analysis. There have, to be sure, been some theoretically oriented writings since the mid-1990s in MM studies—variously described as 'post-structuralist', 'discursive', 'material-discursive', 'Foucauldian', 'postmodern' or 'third wave' in orientation (Berggren, 2014; Edley & Wetherell, 2014; Hearn, 2014; Petersen, 2003; Whitehead, 2002; Pease, 2000; Martino, 2000)—which have developed more postmodern lines of enquiry. Nevertheless, engagement with postmodernism arose much later in MM thinking than in the feminist and sexuality subfields and still remains comparatively less usual.

While some MM scholars, especially more recently and in writings associated with the Humanities, have questioned the generally modernist frame of reference of the subfield, this questioning is well established, indeed almost 'old hat', in feminist and sexuality theorising. The differential character of the MM subfield is evident, for example, when MM writers such as Petersen and Edwards, in 2003 and 2006 respectively, refer to the 'challenge' the emergence of 'developing' trends such as postmodernism might pose for MM studies, following the crucial impact of such trends during the 1980s/90s in other areas of critical enquiry such as Feminism and Queer Theory (Edwards, 2006; Petersen, 2003). Indeed, many writings within MM studies retain significant investments in a modernist theoretical approach and especially in a Social Constructionist perspective.[5] Social Constructionism (in upper case—that is, SC) is a designated label for a particular grouping of modernist thinkers, including thinkers in the Gender/Sexuality field who have a modernist stress upon power as social structures—that is, as macro, foundational, centred and more or less determining—and are more inclined than postmodern thinkers to view power/structures negatively, in terms of oppression. SC writers assert that identities are formed by the social structuring effects of power. However, they stress historically/culturally specific *social variability and complexity* of relatively unified subjects rather than emphasising virtually unlimited fluidity per se, as postmodern thinkers are inclined to do.[6]

The prevalence of Social Constructionism as a theoretical framework within MM studies—as against in feminist and sexuality studies—highlights a seeming theoretical disjunction, a gap, between them (Beasley, 2009). This attachment is evident in the work of Raewyn Connell, whose contribution to the subfield is consistently acknowledged as continuously central by most writers within it, including those offering critical reflections (Beasley, 2005; Ford & Lyons, 2012; Morrell et al., 2012; Wetherell & Edley, 1998). Connell's ongoing pre-eminent positioning in the subfield means that her work is almost always employed in MM studies, and her conceptual apparatus, especially terms like 'hegemonic masculinity', is virtually omnipresent in that subfield (Beasley, 2005, 2012; Hearn, 2004). Her theoretical stance is by no means simply an individual contribution to MM studies but occupies a uniquely privileged position in the subfield which inflects its particular character in a substantial sense. While a number of MM writers in recent times have offered postmodern and other critiques of her work, they do not as yet shape the overall theoretical trajectory of the subfield.

While evidence of an ongoing attachment to a modernist SC theoretical stance is registered in the continuing centrality of a Connellian approach within MM scholarship, this attachment may arguably even be found in the work of those who pay attention to postmodern thought. A comparatively limited number of MM scholars invoke postmodern theory—relative to its uptake in feminist and sexuality subfields—but, additionally, I would argue that even then this is often undertaken in a way that reveals the continuing significance of modernist thinking in the MM subfield. When postmodern thinkers and theoretical concepts and terms are cited, they tend to be added on to a largely unchanged modernist foundation often associated with Connell's framework and key concepts.

I do not intend to suggest that it is impossible to draw upon both modernist and postmodern frames of reference. However, this is by no means a straightforward exercise, since they are based upon different theoretical assumptions and hence cannot be simply stuck together without explanation (Beasley, 2012). The comparatively fewer MM scholars who do refer to postmodern theorising tend not to articulate the significant difficulties attached to combining these frames of reference, let alone clarifying *how* any such combination could be undertaken. The result is frequently a certain inconsistency or even incoherence.[7]

Since the 1960s/70s, the subfields have aligned in shifting ways. While Feminism and men/masculinities scholarship once shared a very similar modernist theoretical agenda under the rubric of 'gender', this has changed. Instead, feminist and sexuality theorising have increasingly tended to move closer together in terms of awareness and uptake of postmodern agendas and in terms of overarching theoretical frameworks. Feminist and Sexuality studies are by no means entirely postmodern in their theoretical orientations, but employment of postmodern/poststructuralist thinking—or at the very least being well versed in its complexities, even if the approach is not accepted—is now virtually a given in their *theoretical* frameworks, terminologies and debates. This account of shifts in the broad theoretical directions of the two subfields is not an especially uncommon claim. A number of writers, including early commentators such as Michele Barrett and Steven Seidman, have drawn attention to the take-up of this particular theoretical 'turn' (Barrett, 1992, p. 204; Seidman, 1994). By comparison, in MM *theorising*, usage of postmodernism or knowledge of its intricacies is by no means a certainty, as has been stated by many MM scholars (e.g. Garlick, 2017; Petersen, 2003). I suggest in this context that the MM subfield appears in some ways as 'the odd man out', as anomalous in its broad comparative engagement with a modernist theoretical framework (Beasley, 2009). This is not to suggest that theorists and theoretical frameworks to be found *within* each of the subfields all have the same perspectives, or to suggest that they should have, let alone that they should all shift towards postmodernism. Rather, the issue here is that the different *theoretical* trajectories of Feminist, Sexuality and MM studies have shifted in relation to their differential uptake of postmodern perspectives. Their differential uptake is worthy of note because it has implications for the subfield's account of itself as strongly linked with Feminism and implications for dialogue and coalition between the MM and feminist subfields.

Disjunctions in theory: gender categories/identities

In earlier publications, I have demonstrated this divergence by pointing out a number of indicative points. The different *main theoretical paradigms* of feminist and MM studies can be seen when comparing *central theorists* in the three subfields (for example, differential engagement with the work of Judith Butler), different views of *power*, different understandings of *the relationship between gender and sexuality* and, relatedly, differential adherence to *gender categories/identities* (see Beasley, 2015, 2013, 2012). In this chapter, I attend to only one of these points. In relation to gender categories/identities, the well-established antagonism to the presumed limits of gender categories found in sexuality studies is also these days relatively widespread in feminist work but comparatively is not a marked feature of the MM subfield.

The 'second wave' women's movement was constituted around notions of gender identity reliant upon the notion of a shared experience of oppression (Holmes, 2011; Beasley, 1999). This identity or category politics was initially challenged by those who drew attention to differences within gender categories such as 'woman' or 'women' (see Yuval-Davis, 1991). By the mid-1990s the associated emphasis on plurality within gender categories had shifted sharply towards a critique of these identity categories under the banner of postmodern inflected analyses. In short, though at the height of the 'second wave' Feminism initially focused for the most part upon *singularity*—the singular identity category 'woman'/women, this concern shifted towards *plurality*—to multiple category groups of women enabling, for example, recognition of race (Beasley, 1999; Philips, 1996). Attention to plurality then shifted again towards notions of postmodern *fluidity* which precisely challenged adherence to gender categories and indeed the very status of these categories (Beasley, 1999). While scepticism about gender categories is less adamantly advanced in feminist work which is more practice, empirical or policy oriented, this critical stance towards gender categories is now very widespread in Feminism (Beasley, 1999).[8] By contrast, theoretical writings in MM studies commonly retain a relatively unqualified and central investment in gender identities. The instance of gender categories/identities can be employed as a concrete means to illustrate what I have described as a disjunction between feminist and MM theorising.

In this context, Raewyn Connell's key significance in MM thinking is indicative. Connell conceives power as structural, as macro oppression ('patriarchy'), imposing upon subjects to produce a hierarchical pyramid of masculine identity groupings (which closely mirrors the hierarchical arrangement of Marxian class groupings). These masculine group identities (such as 'hegemonic', 'marginalised' and 'subordinated' masculinities) are construed in largely homogeneous terms and are typically further homogenised by a reduction to actual groups of men (Connell, 1995/2005).[9] As an illustration, hegemonic masculinity is understood in terms of actual transnational businessmen who are seen as 'having' power (Beasley, 2008; Elias & Beasley, 2009). Connell's account of gendered power as oppression—that is, patriarchy—imposes upon the micro-level of subjects to produce gendered identities/beings, which in turn respond to, resist and reconstitute structure (Connell, 2000; Holmes, 2007). The gendered identities Connell outlines are largely conceived as unified and stable platforms for action, whether complicit or resistant. This form of modernist theorising concentrates on particular modes of 'being'.

Suffice it to say that postmodern thought is at odds with Connell's modernist assumption that power is structural oppression and is a property that can be owned/possessed by (gendered) subjects, as well as with Connell's conception of identity as concerned with being—that is, identity as a platform for intentional action with a cognitive social agent at the helm. Postmodern approaches to subjectivity/identity place in question modernist accounts of identities as unified stable sites for action that can be accept or throw off power. Postmodern thinkers do not focus on 'being' but rather upon 'subject positions'—that is, placement of subjects in multiple contesting discourses (e.g. Foucault, 1980; Mouffe, 1988; Skrzypiec, 2011). This refusal of any inner unity to gender identities/subjects, a refusal of notions of 'being' in favour of fluid inchoate *practices*, is associated in postmodern thinking with a focus on 'undoing' or 'troubling' gender (Butler, 2004). Postmodern approaches thus offer a substantial challenge to Connell's modernist adherence to structural power and gender categories/identities. Hence Connell's scepticism concerning postmodern agendas and thinkers such as Judith Butler is consistent with her espousal of a modernist stance (Beasley, 2009).

As noted earlier, there are some MM scholars who do engage with postmodernism. Yet this engagement remains far less common and uneasy compared with feminist work. Such uneasiness produces muddled or even incoherent modes of analysis, paradoxically reiterating the MM subfield's primarily modernist theoretical orientation. For instance, Bob Pease, a major contributor to these theoretical considerations in the MM subfield, reveals a rare awareness that his asserted adoption of a postmodern approach is rather hesitant and not all of a piece. Pease, unlike many MM writers, does explicitly acknowledge that he is attempting to bring together postmodern and modern approaches and that this endeavour is no simple exercise. While proposing that he is advancing a 'postmodern masculinity politics', Pease also notes his refusal to abandon the 'the values of modernity and Enlightenment project of human emancipation' (Pease, 2000). However, such an investment does not merely render his postmodernism 'weak', as he describes it, so much as placing it at odds with postmodernist proposals.

Similarly, while Pease stresses that not all men are the same and that 'men' is not a homogeneous grouping, such an emphasis upon the diversity of men does not represent a challenge to gender categories that would be in keeping with postmodern thinking. Rather, simply pluralising of the category 'men' is associated with the modernist Social Constructionism and is in keeping with the modernist pluralisation of the gender identities such as the concept of woman found in feminist theorising during the late 1980s/90s. Further, his acceptance of approaches which demonstrate how social agents may refuse structures is entirely in accordance with Connell's adherence to a distinction between structural power and intentional gendered subjects which presently predominates within MM thinking and is scarcely aligned with the decentred epistemology of postmodern thinking that he proposes to support (Pease, 2000). All the same, Pease's work in a number of ways offers a thoughtful engagement with postmodernism. Much of MM scholarship which attends to postmodern theorising seems more theoretically underdeveloped than this and hence more noticeably incongruent (see Beasley, 2012).

Unlike the now well-established place of postmodernism in feminist thinking and debates, this theoretical paradigm continues to have a somewhat uncertain place in MM thought. The upshot is an inclination to attach postmodern elements to a modernist frame of reference, without registering that postmodern and modernist approaches are far from straightforwardly commensurable. I would like to stress here that this problem is not confined to a few scholars or one field of social theorising, let alone to MM scholarship. Nevertheless, within the context of MM studies, the incoherence of the mixture may take the form of initial or occasional rhetorical gestures towards postmodernism, by making passing reference to major figures such as Foucault or Butler, followed by a reversion to analyses which in all other respects demonstrate a continuing adherence to modernist structural assumptions (including, among others, unqualified usage of terms like 'patriarchy' and 'oppression'), to unified agentic conceptions of the self (particularly when outlining empirical studies), and to use of Connellian concepts/terminologies concerning seemingly homogenous gendered categories/identities. By contrast with postmodern concerns regarding 'undoing' gender such that gender identities are rendered permanently open and contestable (see Seidman, 1996, p. 12), MM theorising very commonly manifests ongoing investments in identities. This is often evident in the inclination to delineate pluralised, hierarchically organised gender identities/masculinities, to develop homogenising typologies (Francis, 2010) and, relatedly, to focus upon homogenised groups of *actual* men.

Key scholars in MM thinking such as Raewyn Connell offer a very consistent and eloquent adherence to modernism, while others who invoke postmodern theorising often do so in rather partial ways. In short, MM scholarship continues, for the most part, to be comparatively less engaged by the waves of postmodern critique that have so heavily influenced other arenas of the Gender/Sexuality field, including Feminism. My concern here is not to suggest that modernist and postmodern theoretical trajectories can never be articulated, or that MM should necessarily adopt the robust critique of gender categories/identities that is familiar in much contemporary feminist theorising. Rather, I aim to raise the issue of dissonance as a matter requiring closer consideration with regard to alliance between the two subfields.

Creative possibilities

The self-definition of the MM subfield is that it is feminist inspired and inflected. Moreover, there are robust connections between the MM and feminist subfields in terms of their shared location under the rubric of the Gender/Sexuality field. In the light of these intimate alliances, it seems necessary to consider carefully the issue of disjunctions between their main theoretical trajectories. However, their heterogeneity may not simply figure as a problem, a gap, but ironically may also provide space for creative possibilities. Rather than regarding all such attempts at linking apparently dissonant forms as inevitably condemned to internal contradiction, I prefer Chantal Mouffe's espousal of the advantages of agonism rather than consensus (Mouffe, 2005; see also Skrzypiec, 2011) and the embrace of mobile theoretical uncertainties enunciated by Deleuze and Guattari (1980/1987). In the context of the attention I have given to the problem of theoretical incoherence, this might appear odd. Yet it seems to me that it is quite possible to outline difficulties attached to lumping together different theoretical trajectories without attention to their differences, while simultaneously endorsing their possibilities for interaction.

Such a bridging approach could take two forms: one involving a deliberately contingent use of gender categories differentiated as necessary within particular political practices (see Beasley, 2015); and the other entailing some use of 'strategic essentialism' regarding group categories such as gender identities. Here I consider the second possibility.

Some feminist scholars have asserted that, while *theoretically* gender identity categories must be unsettled and resisted, *in practice* use of a universalised group identity may sometimes be strategically necessary. Gayatri Spivak's work provides a widely known instance of this agenda (Butler, 1997/2013; Spivak, 1984–5/1990). The 'strategic essentialism' perspective has attracted a variety of criticism regarding its seemingly incoherent refusal and simultaneous adoption of gender categories (see Beasley, 1999; Milner & Browitt, 2002). It is possible, however, to argue that this critique rests upon an overly sharp theory/practice binary. I suggest that varying use of gender categories becomes more coherent and capable of being considered consistent when strategic essentialism is interpreted as pursuing a view of both theory and practice as bound together through an emphasis on praxis in relation to power. What I mean here is that broadly divergent use of gender categories in feminist and MM scholarship which signal disjunctions between the subfields—associated with their differential uptake of the postmodernism and its critique of these categories—can be bridged by use of a specific form of strategic essentialism connected to the character of the subfields themselves. I noted earlier that while feminist and sexuality studies provide examples of political thinking which advocate on behalf of the marginalised categories for which they speak—that is, women and non-heterosexual sexualities—MM scholarship—precisely because it is pro-feminist—does not take up the cause of the privileged category of masculinity/men. Relatedly, it can be argued that there are very good grounds regarding why much feminist theorising has taken up postmodern agendas. Located as on 'the side' of the subordinated, feminist theorists have every reason to dispute gender category limitations. By contrast, MM theorising is intent upon reminding those to whom it speaks of the privileged status of the category positioning of men/masculinity. MM scholars, unlike feminist writers, have every reason to show considerable interest in attending to gender identity. The task of offering a critique of accepted understandings of men/masculinities requires insistently drawing attention to gender category privilege.

'Strategic essentialism' might involve not foreclosing certain usages of gender categories but, rather, paying robust attention to them—that is, paying attention to those categories concerning the privileged, even as they are subjected to continuous critique—precisely in order to mount strategic responses to power and advance a shared feminist/pro-feminist agenda regarding social change. Gender categories become in this setting less a question of identities/types (modes of being) and more a means to speaking back to power. Categories of privilege may be strategically employed less as adherence to fixed conceptions of the self and more as in relationship to power, while categories of subordination may be more likely to be contested and understood as shifting/fluid. In short, paying attention to and rejection of gender categories—in theory and practice—can express different positionings in relation to power. This perspective involves a bridging approach to postmodernism/modernism theoretical paradigms and to the relationship between feminist and MM subfields, an approach organised around power and political praxis.[10]

Conclusion

Men and masculinities scholarship has self-identified as a pro-feminist approach and may also be located along with feminist and sexuality studies under the auspices of an overarching Gender/Sexuality field on the basis of many shared features. Yet these two subfields have increasingly displayed certain tensions, even divergences, signalled by their differential theoretical engagement with postmodernism. Such divergences are evident in their use of gender identities/categories. In the light of the considerable connections between the feminist and MM subfields, it seems important to reflect on these tensions. This chapter offers a new conceptualisation of disjunctions between them aimed at revealing not only potential hazards but also some perhaps unexpected creative possibilities. I note that disjunctions between them might be approached by reconceiving their differential use of gender categories/identities in ways that encourage dialogue and coalition. Such a bridging approach enables a more coherent recognition that disjunctions between feminist and MM scholarship are not necessarily cause for sorrow because they are not inevitably signs of inconsistency or division so much as they may well arise, ironically, from a shared strategic purpose.

Notes

1 This focus on *theory*, on *main* theoretical frameworks and on *overall* agendas deliberately specifies my analysis of disjunctures between MM and feminist scholarship. The analysis is not the only narrative available, nor is it about all MM theorising, let alone about the whole of MM scholarship, a point which Gottzén (2018) thoughtfully articulates (see also Introduction, this volume).
2 For example, the modernist framework of so-called 'second wave' radical feminism associated with Catherine MacKinnon has recently shown signs of rejuvenation (Bazelon, 2015).
3 I refer from this point onwards to 'postmodern' as an abbreviation embracing a range of terminologies. This condensed usage is deliberately chosen (e.g. Beasley, 2005) to enable what I see as a more inclusive analytical overview which can encompass a wide variety of usages in disparate fields including architecture, art, literature and the social sciences. The aim is to avoid the more specific theoretical and disciplinary associations of 'poststructuralism' or 'deconstruction'.
4 In this context, despite undoubted difficulties, some writers have aimed to bring into dialogue modernist and postmodern approaches or to undertake modes of analysis which might engage with both (e.g., among many others, Beasley, 2008; Beasley & Bacchi, 2007, 2012; Jackson & Scott, 2010).
5 Social Constructionism is one of the five groupings in the continuum of main theoretical paradigms evident in the Gender/Sexuality field (see Beasley, 2005, 2012).
6 Social Constructionism (upper case) as a particular theoretical direction may be distinguished from social constructionism (in lower case), which refers to a broad anti-essentialist stance or strategy and includes a whole range of perspectives from modernist to postmodern approaches (Beasley, 2012).
7 See Beasley (2012) for a more detailed account of this issue.
8 Even feminist approaches which do not accept the postmodern critique of gender identity categories such as 'women' acknowledge the widespread, almost ubiquitous uptake of that critique in feminist theorising (Gunnarsson, 2013).
9 For a related discussion, see Whitehead (2002, p. 111).

10 This approach is in keeping with the central concerns of Connell's work. While Connell addresses relationships between men/masculinities, the core of her approach is about social hierarchy between men and women (Connell & Messerschmidt, 2005). The bridging approach I have outlined brings Connell's key insights back into focus, as a modernist pathway connecting feminist and MM thinking.

References

Barrett, M. (1992). Words and things. In M. Barrett & A. Phillips (Eds.), *Destabilizing theory: Contemporary feminist debates* (pp. 201–219). Cambridge: Polity.

Bazelon, E. (2015, September 10) The return of the sex wars. *The New York Times Magazine*. Retrieved from www.nytimes.com/2015/09/13/magazine/the-return-of-the-sex-wars.html?mcubz=2.

Beasley, C. (1999). *What is feminism? An introduction to feminist theory*. London and Thousand Oaks, CA: Sage.

Beasley, C. (2005). *Gender & sexuality: Critical theories, critical thinkers*. London: Sage.

Beasley, C. (2008). Re-thinking hegemonic masculinity in a globalising world. *Men and Masculinities, 11*(1), 86–103.

Beasley, C. (2009). Is masculinity studies increasingly the 'odd man' out? Considering problems and possibilities in contemporary gender/sexuality thinking. In A. Biricik & J. Hearn (Eds.), *Deconstructing the hegemony of men and masculinities, volume VI* (pp. 173–183). Linköping & Örebro Universities, Sweden: GEXcel Centre of Gender Excellence.

Beasley, C. (2012). Problematising contemporary men/masculinities theorising: The contribution of Raewyn Connell and conceptual-terminological tensions today. *British Journal of Sociology, 63*(4), 747–765.

Beasley, C. (2013). Mind the gap? Masculinity studies and contemporary gender/sexuality thinking. *Australian Feminist Studies, 28*(75), 108–124.

Beasley, C. (2015). Caution! Hazards ahead: Considering the potential gap between feminist thinking and men/masculinities theory and practice. *Journal of Sociology, 51*(3), 566–581.

Beasley, C., & Bacchi, C. (2007). Envisaging a new politics for an ethical future: Beyond trust, care and generosity towards an ethic of social flesh. *Feminist Theory, 8*(3), 279–298.

Beasley, C., & Bacchi, C. (2012). Making politics fleshly. In A. Bletsas & C. Beasley (Eds.), *Engaging with Carol Bacchi: Strategic interventions and exchanges* (pp. 99–120). Adelaide: University of Adelaide Press.

Berggren, K. (2014). Sticky masculinity: Post-structuralism, phenomenology and subjectivity in critical studies on men and masculinities. *Men and Masculinities, 17*(3), 231–252.

Butler, J. (1997/2013). Performative acts and gender constitution: An essay in phenomenology and feminist theory. In C. R. McCann & S. Kim (Eds.), *Feminist theory reader: Local and global perspectives* (3rd ed., pp. 419–430). London and New York: Routledge.

Butler, J. (2004). *Undoing gender*. New York: Routledge.

Connell, R. (1995/2005). *Masculinities* (2nd ed.). Cambridge: Polity.

Connell, R. (2000). *The men and the boys*. Berkley, CA: University of California Press.

Connell, R., & Messerschmidt, J. (2005). Hegemonic masculinity: Rethinking the concept. *Gender and Society, 19*(6), 829–859.

Deleuze, G., & Guattari, F. (1980/1987). *A thousand plateaus: Capitalism and schizophrenia Vol. 2* (B. Massumi, Trans.). Minneapolis, MN: University of Minnesota.

Edley, N., & Wetherell, M. (2014). A discursive psychological framework for analysing men and masculinities. *Psychology of Men and Masculinity, 15*(4), 355–364.

Edwards, T. (2006). *Cultures of masculinity*. London: Routledge.

Elias, J., & Beasley, C. (2009). Hegemonic masculinity and globalization: 'Transnational business masculinities' and beyond. *Globalizations, 6*(2), 281–296.

Flood, M. (1997/2002). *Frequently asked questions about pro-feminist men and pro-feminist men's politics* (3rd ed., rev. 3 January), *XYOnline*. Retrieved from www.xyonline.net/content/frequently-asked-questions-about-pro-feminist-men-and-pro-feminist-mens-politics.

Ford, M., & Lyons, L. (2012). Introduction: Men and masculinities in Southeast Asia. In M. Ford & L. Lyons (Eds.), *Men and masculinities in Southeast Asia* (pp. 1–19). London and New York: Routledge.

Foucault, M. (1980). *Power/knowledge: Selected interviews and other writings 1972–1977*. London: Harvester Press.

Fox, N., & Alldred, P. (2018). New materialism. In P. Atkinson, S. Delamont, M. Hardy & M. Williams (Eds.), *The Sage encyclopedia of research methods*. Retrieved from www.researchgate.net/publication/320016117_New_Materialism.

Francis, B. (2010). Re/theorising gender: Female masculinity and male femininity in the classroom? *Gender and Education, 22*(5), 477–490.

Garlick, S. (2017). The return of nature: Feminism, hegemonic masculinities, and new materialisms. *Men and Masculinities, 22*(2), 380–403.

Gottzén, L. (2018). Is masculinity studies really the 'odd man out'? *NORMA: International Journal for Masculinity Studies, 13*(2), 81–85.

Gunnarsson, L. (2013). *On the ontology of love, sexuality and power: Towards a feminist-realist depth approach* (Diss.). Sweden: Örebro University.

Hearn, J. (2004). From hegemonic masculinity to the hegemony of men. *Feminist Theory, 5*(1), 49–72.

Hearn, J. (2014). Men, masculinities and the material(-)discursive. *NORMA: International Journal for Masculinity Studies, 9*(1), 5–17.

Holmes, M. (2007). *What is gender? Sociological approaches*. London and Thousand Oaks, CA: Sage.

Holmes, M. (2011). Gendered identities. In A. Elliott (Ed.), *Routledge handbook of identity studies* (pp. 186–202). Milton Park and New York: Routledge.

Jackson, S., & Scott, S. (2010). *Theorizing sexuality*. Maidenhead and New York: Open University Press/McGraw-Hill Education.

Kimmel, M. S. (1992). *Against the tide: Pro-feminist men in the U.S., 1776–1990*. Boston, MA: Beacon Press.

Martino, W. (2000). Policing masculinities: Investigating the role of homophobia and heteronormativity in the lives of adolescent boys at school. *The Journal of Men's Studies, 8*(2), 213–236.

Messner, M. (1997). *Politics of masculinities: Men in movements*. Thousand Oaks, CA: Sage.

Milner, A., & Browitt, J. (2002). *Contemporary cultural theory: An introduction* (3rd ed.). Sydney: Allen & Unwin.

Morrell, R., Jewkes, R., & Lindeggger, G. (2012). Hegemonic masculinity/masculinities in South Africa: Culture, power and gender politics. *Men and Masculinities, 15*(1), 11–30.

Mouffe, C. (1988). New political subjects: Toward a new concept of democracy. In C. Nelson & L. Grossberg (Eds.), *Marxism and the interpretation of culture* (pp. 89–104). Urbana: University of Illinois Press.

Mouffe, C. (2005). *The return of the political*. New York and London: Verso.

Pease, B. (2000). *Recreating men: Postmodern masculinity politics*. London: Sage.

Petersen, A. (2003). Some implications of recent theory for future work. *Men and Masculinities, 6*(1), 54–69.

Philips, R. (1996). Undoing an activist response: Feminism and the Australian government's domestic violence policy. *Critical Social Policy, 26*(1), 192–219.

Seidman, S. (1994). Introduction. In S. Seidman (Ed.), *The postmodern turn: New perspectives on social theory* (pp. 1–26). Cambridge: Cambridge University Press.

Seidman, S. (1996). Introduction. In S. Seidman (Ed.), *Queer theory/sociology* (pp. 1–30). Oxford: Blackwell.

Skrzypiec, L. (2011). *A radical alternative? A re-evaluation of Chantal Mouffe's radical democratic approach* (Unpublished doctoral dissertation). Australia: University of Adelaide.

Spivak, G. ((interview with E. Grosz)) (1984–5/1990). Criticism, feminism and the institution. In S. Harasym (Ed.), *The post-colonial critic: Interviews, strategies, dialogues—Gayatri Chakravorty Spivak* (pp. 1–16). London: Routledge.

Wetherell, M., & Edley, N. (1998). Gender practices: Steps in the analysis of men and masculinities. In K. Henwood, C. Griffin & A. Phoenix (Eds.), *Standpoints and differences: Essays in the practice of feminist psychology* (pp. 156–173). London: Sage.

Whitehead, S. M. (2002). *Men and masculinities: Key themes and new directions*. Cambridge: Polity.

Yuval-Davis, N. (1991). The citizenship debate: Women, ethnic processes and the state. *Feminist Review, 39*(1), 58–68.

3

Hegemony, hegemonic masculinity, and beyond

Richard Howson and Jeff Hearn

Introduction

This chapter explores two "crucially important" concepts and their relationship in critical studies of men and masculinities (CSMM): hegemony and hegemonic masculinity. Following Gramsci, hegemony always refers to a historical situation, in which power is won and held; it is not a matter of the pushing and pulling of ready-formed groupings but is partly a matter of the formation of social groupings – in this context, gender groupings (cf. Carrigan et al., 1985; Hearn, 2004). The most well cited definition of hegemonic masculinity is:

> … the configuration of gender practice which embodies the currently accepted answer to the problem of legitimacy of patriarchy, which guarantees (or is taken to guarantee) the dominant position of men and the subordination of women.
>
> *(Connell, 1995, p. 77)*

In this chapter, we do not give a step-by-step review of different approaches to the two key concepts (see Aboim et al., 2016; Connell & Messerschmidt, 2005; Hearn, 2004; Howson, 2006); rather, we develop a specific line of theorizing that locates the two concepts and seeks to go beyond their predominant current use in studying men and masculinity.

The reasons for these two concepts and their relationship being considered as crucially important draw from the centrality of critique to understanding men and masculinities (see also the chapter by Hearn and Howson in this volume), but for now an important point of departure for our analysis within a broader gendered context is the consideration of popular consciousness. This emphasis on popular consciousness underpins one, if not the most important, feature of both hegemony and hegemonic masculinity, that is, they are both considered as social constructions, and therefore neither exists because there is something essential that enables their constitution. Further, neither is ever stable and coherent, and, as such, neither can claim to be universal and/or continuing. This might *prima facie* seem counter-intuitive, given that when we reflect historically on the nature of gender it might well seem that men and masculinity have *always* enjoyed unique privileges. It surely indicates the existence of "something" essential, stable, even universal, about masculinity that enables men to act within a continuous system of gendered privilege/importance/authority that cannot and so "should" not be questioned.

This view of men and masculinity we will refer to as the *foundationalist* position. In popular consciousness and the configurations of practice that constitute the everyday life of people that in turn mark gender across the Occident today, it is the foundationalist position that holds predominance. Thus, what becomes crucial for a critical understanding of the foundationalist approach to men and masculinity, and thereby gender more broadly, is the relationship between hegemony and hegemonic masculinity, particularly how the latter informs this popular consciousness. This raises questions about why men and masculinity have come to predominance and, even more importantly, how this predominance is sustained and maintained. Further, there needs to be recognition that this popular consciousness works at the collective, social, national and then global levels that, in turn, effectively expose the social world as a gendered system.

Critical studies of men and masculinities (CSMM), as a sub-field of study, "presents critical, explicitly gendered accounts, descriptions and explanations of men and masculinities in their social contexts that bring men and masculinities into sharper relief, as objects of theory and critique" (Hearn & Howson, this volume). Pushing this understanding further, it is possible to understand CSMM as a discursive[1] space in which is contained a set of tools capable of critically exposing, examining and evaluating the social conditions that produce and sustain men and masculinity. Many of these theoretical (discursive) tools, it could be argued, were examined and developed, albeit in the nascent context of CSMM, in "Theorizing Men and Men's Theorizing" (Hearn, 1998) and have now, arguably, become part of the methodology of CSMM. However, within CSMM it is accepted that they first took form from the socio-political theoretical fundamentals that feminism provided, predominantly in the latter half of the twentieth century. As Hearn (1998, p. 783) goes on to point out:

> Although feminist theory and practice has addressed the problem of men throughout its development, the major emphasis has been on the analysis of women's experiences of the consequences of men's domination rather than the focused theorization of men. Feminist writing is not, as it is sometimes characterized, "just about women"; this is simply not the case. Feminists have always been simultaneously involved in making women visible, developing critiques of men, and making men not just visible but problematic.

So, for simplicity, and drawing from the above, the key points we focus on, which also gave rise to CSMM, concern issues around the (in)visibility of men and/or critical explorations of masculinities within gendered life, and the taken-for-grantedness of gendered/men's actions on the basis of an essentialized, and thereby privileged, masculinity. Put simply, we see CSMM as a space within which to investigate men through a critical evaluation of the masculinities that become exposed, the actions produced, and the consequences for gender relations.

Both invisibility and taken-for-grantedness have deep theoretical roots that have extended out from feminist theory more generally, into feminist-inspired masculinities theory more specifically and, in the latter case, what Hearn (2017) refers to as the most developed and cited approach in the CSMM, perhaps because of the multiple influences on and interpretations of it that include: patriarchy theory; Gramscian Marxism; gay politics; critiques of categoricalism; practice theory; psychoanalysis; structuration theory; theorizing on the body;[2]

and even pluralism (cf. Aboim, 2010). Interestingly, though, when masculinities theory is considered, there is often an immediate leap to what may be referred to as its "central pillar" (Hearn, 2017, p. 25), that is, hegemonic masculinity: a concept that resonates with many of the influences referred to above and whose definition, paraphrasing Connell (1995), exposes the embodied configurations of practice that produce and sustain legitimacy within the gendered system that, in turn, ensures the privileged position of masculinity and, thereby, men, while ensuring the de-privileging of femininity and, thereby, women. It is perhaps not hard to see why hegemonic masculinity is considered as the central pillar of the critical studies of men and masculinities, not least because it offers the beginning of an articulation about the problematic relationship between our understanding of masculinity and the practice of men with how femininity is understood as underpinning the expected practices of women. Most importantly, this articulation is developed, sustained and in some cases altered through "culture" that, in turn, produces and populates popular consciousness.

So, while the centrality of hegemonic masculinity that has developed over the past four decades emphasizes the importance of culture (notwithstanding a substantial critique; see Beasley, 2008; Flood, 2002; Hearn, 2004; Howson, 2006; Petersen, 1998) that is not disputed here. To understand it better, and in particular why and how it is enabled and sustained within culture by popular consciousness producing informal or "normative" as well as formal or "legal/legitimate" privileges, it is important to take our examination back to its grounding theory, that is, hegemony (see Howson, 2006). In so doing, hegemony opens up the context in which invisibility and taken-for-grantedness are enabled and sustained but also allows investigation into how we might then move CSMM into the theoretical beyond. So, examining and applying key features of the theory of hegemony exposes the theoretical ground upon which can be built a more nuanced insight into the hegemonic nature of popular consciousness and practices in the gendered system(s) (what will otherwise be called here "hegemony"). This is because it exposes both the ideological and material basis upon which privilege is able to obfuscate or, worse, make invisible men and masculinity while simultaneously showing how men and their actions, through our taken-for-grantedness, are legitimized. It should not be surprising then that invisibility and taken-for-grantedness are positioned, both implicitly and explicitly, within Connell's definition of hegemonic masculinity. However, hegemonic masculinity through this approach becomes more than simply a problem for the gender system. By pushing the hegemony/hegemonic masculinity synergy beyond its current articulation, it is possible to offer an important opportunity to move CSMM forward, by enabling the introduction of the concept of "empty signifier".

Hegemony and the hegemonic

In masculinities theory, it is safe to say that the use of hegemony was, and still is, predominantly an attempt to give a theoretical basis to that which is clearly set out in the definition of hegemonic masculinity, namely, the dominance of men and the subordination of women.

> What emerged from this matrix in the mid-1980s was an analogue, in gender terms, of power structure research in political sociology – focusing the spotlight on a dominant group. Hegemonic masculinity was understood as the pattern of practice (i.e., things done, not just a set of role expectations or an identity) that allowed men's dominance over women to continue.
>
> *(Connell & Messerschmidt, 2005, p. 832)*

In the context of masculinities theory, this description of hegemonic masculinity does two important things. First, it implicitly operationalizes the concept of hegemony through its reference to political sociology that in turn implies a focus on the relationship between civil society and political society or resistance and power. But here, given the emphasis on masculinity, the emphasis is more on power and less on resistance. Second and most importantly, it offers an explicit interpretation of hegemonic masculinity that links it to domination. Specifically, it states that hegemonic masculinity represents "things done", in a way that subordinates the non-material processes of expectation, meaning and identification, suggesting that these "things done" "allow" for a system of domination by men over women to exist. So how should we understand these two aspects of hegemonic masculinity in the context of the theory of hegemony? Later on the same page, Connell and Messerschmidt (2005, p. 832) offer an important clue: "[h]egemony did not mean violence, although it could be supported by force; it meant ascendancy achieved through culture, institutions, and persuasion" (cf. Hearn, 2012). Here the creation and then application of hegemony refers to processes of ascendency achieved by control of the institutions of persuasion but where violence (informal and formal) can always be operationalized (if required). The idea of hegemonic masculinity as the domination by masculinity/men over femininity/women can now be tempered, challenged even, because what is really being enabled is persuasion-based ascendency (for more detailed discussion, see Howson, 2006). This situation puts some theoretical strain on the nexus of hegemony and hegemonic masculinity because it alters, or has the potential to alter, what is meant by domination and, as a consequence, subordination. It could be argued that ascendency is an inevitable and natural process of building hegemony within a complex organic society. Further, that persuasion-based ascendency is very different to simple domination. So, then, how should hegemony be understood in this context within the CSMM?

A particularly instructive place to begin examining persuasion as a feature of hegemony is Joe Buttigieg's critique of the London School of Economics Centre for Civil Society's approach to hegemony. Buttigieg, a leading Gramscian scholar and expert on Gramsci's development of the relationship between hegemony and civil society, argues that:

> [h]egemony, as theorized by Gramsci, is not imposed; quite the opposite, the governing class achieves hegemony (i.e., becomes hegemonic) through *leadership and persuasion*, so that instead of imposing itself on the subordinate or subaltern classes, it acquires their consensus. This leadership is not exercised solely or even primarily from the seat of government, but also and much more importantly within the sphere of civil society where consensus is generated.
>
> *(Buttigieg, 2005, pp. 37–38, our emphases)*

This is a crucial intervention in understanding hegemony and for applying it to hegemonic masculinity and, more broadly, to masculinities theory. In effect, the application of hegemony means that the things done, that in turn allow men to become hegemonic, align better with the theory of hegemony when they are not representative of impositions or things demanded. Hegemony is not domination forced upon subaltern groups.[3] Rather, hegemony is achieved because there is consensus, significantly expressed in masculinities theory as *complicity*. However, this only produces a qualified, contingent, shifting and fundamentally unstable consensus. Thus, in the description given by Connell and Messerschmidt, two important ideas can be drawn out, albeit implicitly. First is the importance of aspiration as the basis of achievement. There is much value to be gained by unpacking or deconstructing this relationship, because in so doing it explicitly exposes the conditions for and processes of persuasion and, thus, complicity. Further, the achievement of hegemony is, for Buttigieg, enabled because the things done are given meaning and organized through leadership, which for Connell and Messerschmidt (2005) is implicit in the reference to "ascendency". So, to claim that a particular society or transnational society's hegemonic constitution includes hegemonic masculinity as a form of domination imposed on men and women, where domination in its taken-for-grantedness removes or ignores the important subtleties of leadership/ascendency and persuasion that have been built into the theory of hegemony, will make it difficult to make sense of masculinity in all its forms and expressions.[4] In taking up this approach, it is also instructive to include processes that lead to the development of meaning, as well as practice through leadership. Leadership, in turn, is the starting point from which persuasion is made possible and, thus, complicity and consensus are achieved. This heightens the importance of the structural nature of hegemony in which both material and non-material facets – notably, meaning, identity as well as, practice or things done – operate in synthesis. Leadership as ascendency then, holds discursive value and gives meaning to the aspirations of men (and women), and then their actions for achievement, that expose the crucial importance of persuasion and complicity in the creation and maintenance of hegemonic masculinity and hegemony:

> What distinguishes hegemony from domination is precisely the symbiotic relationship between the government (which is frequently identified with the State in mainstream political theory) and civil society, a relationship, then, that cannot be analyzed in any meaningful way if one starts with a conception of civil society as something separate from and opposed to the State. No one explained this more clearly than Gramsci in his Prison Notebooks.
>
> *(Buttigieg, 2005, pp. 37–38)*

Power structures within the gender system, as Connell and Messerschmidt point out, were in fact identified in the early research, and in so doing, the focus was placed on the conversion of power to domination and the identification of men, or more specifically men who express particular forms of masculinity, as capable of this conversion and thus positioned as the "dominant" group. In many ways, since then, the application of hegemony to hegemonic masculinity has continued this focus. However, this has been, in perhaps too many instances within CSMM, to the exclusion of the importance of the broader civil society or what Gramsci referred to as the "subaltern" and, more importantly, the synergetic nature of both groups. In both Weber and Gramsci we see that domination expresses a set of processes whereby rules are followed – not always by imposing coercion but, rather, by producing agreement within the popular consciousness of the rules. Thus, by challenging the domination emphasis and in line with the approach to hegemony set out by Buttigieg's interpretation of Gramsci's texts, the reason there is value in deconstructing the relationship between hegemonic masculinity and domination is that it enables clarity around the importance of the symbiotic relationship. In other words, it highlights the importance of the other forms of masculinity such as "complicit", "subordinate" and "marginalized", as well as femininity and, in particular, "emphasized femininity", for the continuation of the hegemonic process. This more than anything problematizes the foundationalist position meaning/identity/practice, because it exposes the radically contingent nature of hegemonic masculinity and the contingent relations of multiple masculinities.[5] So here, the term "symbiotic relationship" takes on particular importance because it indicates that, for each identity within the plurality of masculinities and femininities (see Howson, 2006), the constitution of their meaning/identity must rely on the influence of the "other" and not autonomously (or essentialistically) produced meaning/identity. The product of this networked reliance is the gender system. So again, why it is important to push hegemonic masculinity beyond the domination analogue is that by doing so it is possible to put aside the essentialism and foundationalism that enables the taken-for-grantedness of privilege and makes men visible within symbiotic networks. More importantly still, it exposes the very real enabling role of ascendency and leadership, persuasion, aspiration towards achievement, complicity, the operation of violence and coercion in the making of gendered meanings and identifications that inform and produce the configurations of practice within the hegemony.

It is fair to say that within CSMM a significant amount of research energy has been expended applying, explaining and critiquing hegemonic masculinity; notwithstanding this, the outcome is the representation of hegemonic masculinity as a static concept (see Messerschmidt, 2012). It could be argued that this has been and is because of the continued presence of domination in its articulation. While this emphasis and approach provide the tools for being able to express a clear and present dichotomy within the gender system, it is far less effective in enabling understanding of the conditions that enable hegemonic masculinity within the current gender system. In short, to understand these conditions better, there is much research value in shifting attention to complicity within the gender system.

But equally important as the move beyond the domination analogue towards leadership and complicity are two further additions. First, while consensus is the basis of the making of a hegemonic group such as, men, it is not the only force in operation. Hegemony will always involve, predominantly indirectly but directly when required, the use of coercion. In other words, the exercise of power, simply put as the ability to impose one's interests upon the other against their resistance (see Weber, 1978), is required but is not the primary force. Gramsci (1971, p. 263) put it this way, "one might say that State = political society + civil society, in other words hegemony protected by the armour of coercion." This opens up the second addition, that is, that hegemony is never created and sustained in those spaces within society where power or pure power operates as domination. For Gramsci, this is no more than the crude operation of politics. Instead, hegemony is very much a force that is enabled through power's engagement with civil society,[6] that is, the subaltern and therefore the creation of consensus. But it is always an engagement that is underwritten or protected by processes of coercion and, where necessary, violence, and it is here that political society, in Gramsci's terms or ascendant groups for Connell and Messerschmidt, play their part. So, for a group to become and operate hegemonically, it must be able to operate effectively within the nexus: the political/power and the social/subaltern. This means articulating and dispersing a legitimacy that enables the engagement and the building of consensus and complicity rather than simply imposing power as domination that ensures a crude form of subordination. The question of legitimacy, though present in the early definitions of hegemonic masculinity, has often not been highlighted in most subsequent usages and applications.

Thus the application of these few, but key, concepts within the theory of hegemony enables us to see that a hegemonic group exercises pure power not as domination but, rather, as a form of legitimized leadership as authority, and here we can define the latter as: *authority = power + legitimacy*. Moreover, applying hegemony to gender systems, in the way outlined here, means problematizing not only of the pushing and pulling of ready-formed groupings, and different kinds of masculinity, but also the taken-for-grantedness of the very categories of men and women, as in concern with the hegemony of men (Hearn, 2004). It also opens up national, societal or cultural hegemony to transnational and transsocietal problematics (cf. Connell, 2007; Hearn, 2015).

Hegemonic masculinity and beyond

In masculinities theory, hegemony grounds understandings of men and masculinity. But we argue here that there is value in a reconsideration of the concept that goes into the theoretical beyond, notwithstanding an acceptance of the points made by Connell and Messerschmidt (2005). An important caveat, though, in moving into the theoretical and practical beyond, is that while ascendency and leadership have been argued here to be important, we should not accept these as necessarily positive aspects of hegemonic masculinity – rather, that hegemonic leadership is simply a configuration of practices and meanings that enable the building of compliance based on a consensus of the rules. In the context of hegemonic masculinity this produces the taken-for-grantedness and invisibility that have become part of the nature of men and masculinities. This configuration of practices and meanings is what might be referred to, following Laclau and Mouffe (1985) and Laclau (1990), as the centre of the (material) discursive space. However, if we can understand hegemonic masculinity as the centre of a gendered discursive space, then we must also recognize that its meanings and practices have been hegemonically given through its radically contingent symbiotic relations with "the other" within the gender system, and so it is fraught with antagonisms and contestation. It is a centre that because of these conditions can only be understood in the context of that which the centre must hegemonically exclude, such as subordinate and marginalized masculinities and femininity. These excluded identifications become its radical contingent outside. They are radical because, while outside of the centre, they exert upon it a constitutive force. This is because in a discursive space no identity puts in place practices without meaning attached, and no meaning exists in and of itself with complete stability and fixity. Yet, as Messerschmidt (2012, p. 72) concludes, albeit with respect to the "character type" of hegemonic masculinity, this is predominantly how hegemonic masculinity is being applied in CSMM, that is:

> Within the core articles examined, there remains a fundamental *collective* intellectual tendency by numerous editors, reviewers, and authors "to read 'hegemonic masculinity' as a static character type, ..." [emphasis in original]

To move beyond the static ossification that pervades the application of hegemonic masculinity in CSMM, there is value, as Messerschmidt points out and following Connell, in considering moving away from the individuation of hegemonic character to exploring how all meaning and all practices are enabled, even constituted, through the relationality between identities and particularly with their radical outside. This removes whatever essentialist and individualist privileges and positions are perceived to be given by hegemonic masculinity to men, and replaces them with a more questioning approach to privilege based on the dynamics inherent to socially construction.

Crucially though, as suggested above, the relationality involved in social construction also creates antagonism, and it is this that converts a social relationship into a political relationship, thereby marking relationships between the centre and the radical other. For example, tensions between gay and straight, black and white, as well as, for example, inter-religious differences are very often converted into political antagonism. However, for hegemonic masculinity to be created in such a way that it can produce a level of compliance based on a hegemonized consensus, it is necessary that a masculinity type be able to empty itself of meanings and practices and be able to constitute and re-constitute itself to accommodate new meanings and practices that align with, but can also influence, the popular consciousness. This is while simultaneously legitimizing the application of coercion, where required, to exclude and/or marginalize others. Once included, the broader task of hegemony is to then create the perception of stability and fixedness and the desire within the mass (of men) to aspire towards that which is now given legitimacy and privilege.

In *Challenging Hegemonic Masculinity* (Howson, 2006), it was shown how, in the Australian cultural context, hegemonic masculinity defined but also stabilized itself upon the "hegemonic principles" of heterosexuality, breadwinning and aggression (a process that extends and has been highlighted in other international and transnational cultural contexts). The continued privilege received by men that allows certain character traits of hegemonic masculinity to remain taken-for-granted, and thus invisible, have their social ontological roots in the enabling of these principles. This ontological, and indeed epistemological, approach emphasizes the socio-political objective that seeks to uncover and analyse the conditions that enable hegemonic masculinity, as opposed to the ontic where the focus of analysis is simply exposing and describing specific sorts of masculinities in an attempt to classify and compare. In addition, because a specific form of masculinity/femininity can only be understood in relation to all the others, the meaning and practices attributed to any one form is not essentially given but is always in relation to meaning and practice that exist radically.

In the context of the discussion so far, there is value in revisiting our understanding of hegemonic masculinity and specifically, by bringing to it a "sociology of postmarxism" (see Howson, 2017). In this context, three issues need to be highlighted. First, it is problematic to continue applying hegemonic masculinity as domination, given that the basis of hegemony itself is marked by leadership and persuasion in the creation of complicity. Second, it is equally problematic to accept hegemonic masculinity as a stable masculinity type, because this simply moves the emphasis away from social dynamic reality to an emphasis on the individual and processes of individuation. Finally, in emphasizing the centring of hegemonic masculinity within the gender system, but also its non-essentialist nature, the radical contingent nature of its constitution is exposed, and with it antagonism. What these three issues indicate is that the very nature of the hegemony of men is far more complex than the model of patriarchal domination as universal. The hegemony of men and the hegemonic masculinity produced must negotiate a way to make non-essentialism and particularity appear as essential and universal, with the latter being the expression of the legitimate privilege enjoyed by "all" complicit men, as implied within the definition of hegemonic masculinity. To overcome these problems of particularity, which in postmarxism is referred to as organized within the logic of difference, requires movement to a logic of equivalence. Central to this movement and highlighted in the application of hegemonic masculinity within CSMM, it has been argued elsewhere (e.g. Howson, 2017) that hegemonic masculinity be considered as an "empty signifier" (see Laclau, 1996, p. 36; Howson, 2017) because, *inter alia*, this assists in addressing these key issues of complicity and in the movement from difference to equivalence through the application of concepts, such as complicity and aspiration central to the development and maintenance of the hegemony of men.

We can begin to understand what an empty signifier is by considering what appears as completely obvious. It is a signifier without a signified; representation without meaning; identity or type without content. As Laclau states, this definition also expresses a problem insofar as how there can be a disconnection between signifier and signified. The answer is because the system has inherent to it a "structural impossibility" that further is expressed as a subversion of the system (Laclau, 1996, p. 37). By structural impossibility is meant that the structure of the system, for our purposes the gender system, can never complete itself, and, as such, its own stability is impossible. This is where hegemony and its key mechanism hegemonic masculinity as an empty signifier play a most important role, because here it must create the perception of completeness and stability. However, as an empty signifier it cannot represent the purity of masculinity, because what it must constantly do is enact exclusions (the very idea of masculinities as plurality indicates that the purity of masculinity is impossible). Nor can it expose the pure difference between men and women, between masculinities and between femininities, because the structural impossibility of the system produces antagonisms (which means that, for example, the difference between gay and straight is not given by a clearly defined limit) that, in turn, express the subversion of pure difference. Rather, hegemonic masculinity as the empty signifier of a structurally impossible gender system has the task of bringing together a range of differential meanings and practices and binding them into a particular discursive formation. Just as in the process of ascending to leadership, the task is to bring together elements of gender to work together to persuade the popular consciousness of the legitimacy of its hegemonic principles as well as the exclusion and marginalization of anything that might jeopardize or not represent the these principles. So, the real privilege and authority of hegemonic masculinity as being expressed in things done is only part of the whole; by moving beyond this point, we can now understand it to be expressed not by what it does or is or is perceived to contain in terms of meanings and practices but, instead, through its instability, fluidity and, ultimately, its emptiness; in this way it can address the problems of structural impossibility and produce compliance and consensus within the whole gender system.

Concluding discussion

The emptiness of any signifier, such as hegemonic masculinity, means that it exists because a system cannot get to a point where it can complete itself and provide stability but, rather, is always open and dynamic, where the meanings and practices that constitute the discursive content must be able to be altered to protect the hegemony. Likewise for hegemony, or a hegemonic facet, the "objective" of hegemonic masculinity is to create the perception of the purity of masculine meaning and practice and, as a consequence, its authority. At this point, it is important to remind ourselves that hegemony, which is the building of authority through the exercise of power and the creation of legitimacy on the basis of the obfuscation or blocking of radical content, is not achieved on the basis of the modernist imperative for truth and progression or even more problematic domination. Rather, it is achieved predominantly on the basis of a hegemonized consensus that enables aspiration and compliance. In other words, hegemonic masculinity as the empty signifier of the gender system must indeed become the centre and the authority capable of ensuring that the majority of people continue to aspire towards certain forms of masculinity and femininity and thus must embody certain meanings and practices. However, the representation of the gender system through an empty signifier such as hegemonic masculinity does not mean that masculinity has not been achieved; rather, it is constitutively unachievable. It is perhaps why there has been much discussion about what actually constitutes hegemonic masculinity. Do we need to express it in global, transnational or national terms? Are there many hegemonic masculinities? The answer is to address these questions not ontically but, rather, ontologically, that is, by examining the conditions of the gender system such as its hegemonic principles, desire and aspiration, leadership and processes of persuasion, that in turn require consideration of hegemonic mechanisms such as the media, the family, the workplace, religion and sport. This then makes the purity and truth of masculinities secondary to the ontological or hegemonic task of persuasion and aspiration. But, most importantly, it is about exposing the processes of obfuscation of the constitutive nature of antagonism and its radically excluded content from hegemonic masculinity. In this way, it acts as the re-presentation of what is an effectively impossible masculine purity in and across gender relations.

Notes

1 We use the terms "discursive" and/or "discursive space" drawing on the postmarxist approach to discourse. A discursive space is constituted by processes of meaning construction and delivery (discursive) that connect to, influence, and cannot be separated from the material configurations of practice (extra-discursive) that consequently emerge (Laclau & Mouffe, 1985).

2 It is not always acknowledged that the earliest use of hegemonic masculinity was in the 1979 paper entitled "Men's bodies" (Connell, 1979/1983).

3 Domination can be understood to be enforced by rules, and in this context Weber (1978, p. 53) defines domination as "the probability that a command [rule] with a specific content will be obeyed by a given group of persons." This suggests that here we have exposed the nexus between power and cooperation or the basis of complicity/consensus. Rules cannot operate and be obeyed without cooperation (Howson, 2017).

4 Throughout the body of Connell's work there is a consistent recognition and in many cases development of civil society, institutions, persuasion and cultural aspects of hegemony. Yet, in the descriptions of hegemonic masculinity in both *Masculinities* and the "Rethinking Hegemonic Masculinity" article, it is domination that seems to dominate explanations of gender relations.

5 Drawing on Laclau's later work, in particular the development of the idea of "radical contingency" (see Laclau, 1990; Laclau & Mouffe, 1985), its application to masculinities theory is possible (Howson, 2017).

6 Gramsci (1971) makes a number of important revisions to how civil society had been understood. First, Gramsci separates political society, the economy and civil society, but primarily for analytical purposes. Secondly, because civil society does not include the economy, it can be described as constituted by the Church (or similar), associations, trade unions and cultural institutions. Third, civil society is key to the creation of the State (as hegemony), and so is always connected to political society.

References

Aboim, S. (2010). *Plural masculinities: The remaking of the self in private life*. Farham: Ashgate.

Aboim, S., Hearn, J., & Howson, R. (2016). Hegemonic masculinity. In G. Ritzer (Ed.), *Blackwell encyclopedia of sociology* (2nd ed.). Oxford: Wiley-Blackwell. Retrived from https://onlinelibrary.wiley.com/doi/full/10.1002/9781405165518.wbeosh022.pub2.

Beasley, C. (2008). Rethinking hegemonic masculinity in a globalizing world. *Men and Masculinities, 11*(1), 86–103.

Buttigieg, J. (2005). The contemporary discourse on civil society: A Gramscian critique. *Boundary 2, 32*(1), 33–52.

Carrigan, T, Connell, R., & Lee, J. (1985). Towards a new sociology of masculinity. *Theory and Society, 14*(5), 551–604.

Connell, R. (1979/1983). Men's bodies. In R. Connell, *Which way is up?* (pp. 17–32) Sydney: Allen & Unwin.

Connell, R. (1995). *Masculinities*. Cambridge: Polity.

Connell, R. (2007). *Southern theory: The global dynamics of knowledge in social science*. Cambridge: Polity.

Connell, R., & Messerschmidt, J. W. (2005). Hegemonic masculinity: Rethinking the concept. *Gender and Society, 19*(6), 829–859.

Flood, M. (2002). Between men and masculinity, an assessment of the term masculinity in recent scholarship on men. In S. Pearce & V. Muller (Eds.), *Manning the next millennium: Studies in masculinities* (pp. 203–215). Perth: Black Swan.

Gramsci, A. (1971). *Selections from the prison notebooks*. London: Lawrence & Wishart.

Hearn, J. (1998). Theorizing men and men's theorizing: Varieties of discursive practices in men's theorizing of men. *Theory and Society, 27*(6), 781–816.

Hearn, J. (2004). From hegemonic masculinity to the hegemony of men. *Feminist Theory, 5*(1), 49–72.

Hearn, J. (2012). A multi-faceted power analysis of men's violence to known women: From hegemonic masculinity to the hegemony of men. *Sociological Review, 60*(4), 589–610.
Hearn, J. (2015). *Men of the world: Genders, globalizations, transnational times*. London: Sage.
Hearn, J. (2017). Two challenges for critical studies on men and masculinities: The hegemony of men, and trans(national)patriarchies. *Casopis za Kritiko Znanosti: Domisljijo in novo antropologijo, 267*, 23–34.
Howson, R. (2006). *Challenging hegemonic masculinity*. London: Routledge.
Howson, R. (2017). *A sociology of postmarxism*. London: Routledge.
Laclau, E. (1990). *New reflections on the revolution of our time*. London: Verso.
Laclau, E. (1996). *Emancipation(s)*. London: Verso.
Laclau, E., & Mouffe, C. (1985). *Hegemony and socialist strategy: Towards a radical democratic politics*. London: Verso.
Messerschmidt, J. W. (2012). Engendering gendered knowledge: Assessing the academic appropriation of hegemonic masculinity. *Men and Masculinities, 15*(1), 56–76.
Petersen, A. (1998). *Unmasking the masculine: "Men" and "identity" in a sceptical age*. London: Sage.
Weber, M. (1978). *Economy and society volume one*. Berkeley, CA: University of California Press.

4

Pierre Bourdieu and the studies on men and masculinities

Miklós Hadas

Introduction

Pierre Bourdieu was the most frequently quoted sociologist around the fin-de-millennium, and today, more than 15 years after his death in 2002, his international prestige seems unquestioned. However, relative to his fame, Bourdieusian influence has been modest as far as gender studies and studies on men and masculinities are concerned. Entering the terms "Bourdieu", "gender" and "masculinity" into Google Scholar yields but a few dozen articles with titled containing these items, while thousands of titles include the "hegemonic masculinity" concept.

This chapter argues the value of Bourdieu's thinking for contemporary critical men and masculinities studies. The chapter starts with an outline of the most important positive references to Bourdieusian scholarship formulated within gender studies (including studies on men and masculinities). Next, the principal claims of *Masculine Domination*, Bourdieu's only book on masculinity, are scrutinised. This book demonstrates several virtues and limitations of Bourdieu's thinking. It is concluded that, despite the criticism directed at Bourdieu, the inclusion of a Bourdieusian conceptual framework might benefit studies on men and masculinities; by using the notions of habitus, capital, symbolic violence and social field, the plurality of masculinities can be conceptualised as a *system of relations among masculine dispositions* both within and between fields.

Positive references to Bourdieu in gender studies

In the 1990s, some authors intended to integrate key Bourdieusian categories (habitus, social field, capitals, symbolic violence) into gender studies. The first significant text was by Toril Moi, who stressed the importance of materialist approaches for feminism, emphasising that one of the chief merits of Bourdieu's theory was that "it permits the grasp of the immense variability of gender as a social factor" (Moi, 1991, p. 1035). The next influential author was Leslie McCall, who claimed that Bourdieu's work offers "a powerfully elaborate conceptual framework for understanding the role of gender in the social relations of modern capitalist society," and that his "epistemological and methodological approach to social science research parallels and enhances feminist positions on this important subject" (McCall, 1992, p. 837). Other feminist scholars have drawn constructively on Bourdieusian concepts, for example Suzanne Laberge, who referred to examples of gendered experiences in sport and argued that "the adaptation of Bourdieu's model is a potentially enriching approach" (Laberge, 1995, p. 132). Diane Reay (1997), concentrating on the situation of "classlessness", utilised the notions of habitus and field to analyse the complex emotional and psychological processes underpinning everyday social class practices in contemporary Britain. In another area of feminist research, Reay (2004) deployed the concept of "emotional capital", extending Bourdieu's concept of capitals to the realm of emotions and described the intense emotional engagement of mothers with their children's education. Also within feminist scholarship, Bridget Fowler (2003) concentrated on Bourdieu's realist theory of practice and assessed the logic of his argument on women's complicity with gender domination. Lois McNay can also be mentioned in this context. Dealing with the issues of disembodiment and disembeddedness, she claims that the "idea of habitus yields a more dynamic theory of embodiment central to a feminist understanding of gender identity"; furthermore, the "idea of the 'field' provides a more differentiated analysis of the social context in which the reflexive transformation of gender identity unfolds" (McNay, 1999, p. 95). Following McNay's line of reasoning, Julie McLeod suggests a "feminist rethinking of the relationship between gender change, habitus and social field" (McLeod, 2005, p. 11), while David Brown (2005) recommends teaching physical education from the perspective of Bourdieu's embodied sociology.

The most widely cited volume in this context was edited by Adkins and Skeggs (2004). Bev Skeggs writes in the introduction that

> Bourdieu has been particularly useful for enabling feminists to put the issue of class back onto the feminist agenda. His analysis of capitals provides a route to be mapped between the two major strands of class theory that proved mostly infertile for feminist analysis. [...] So what does Bourdieu offer? Firstly, the linking of objective structures to subjective experience (necessity and will, or structure and agency). Secondly, his metaphoric model of social space [...]. Thirdly, his methodological insights, in which reflexivity as a prerequisite to knowledge, provides us with a way of examining the positions from which we speak.
>
> *(Skeggs, 2004, pp. 20–21)*

Another oft-quoted contribution on Bourdieusian feminist work is the article by Beate Krais which, emphasising the importance of the habitus concept, demonstrates that "Bourdieu's theoretical understanding of gender as a powerful principle of social differentiation opens up new analytical perspectives for feminist sociological theory" (Krais, 2006, p. 119). Jo-Anne Dillabough also argues for "a more creative and empirical engagement with the recent work of Bourdieu", claiming that "Bourdieu's oeuvre is able to resist incomprehensibility. It stands as a highly focused, realistic and generative attempt" (Dillabough, 2004, p. 489).

As far as the more restricted field of the studies on men and masculinities is concerned, comparatively few authors use Bourdieusian terminology. One of these is Joanne Hollows (2003), who examines how a mode of domestic masculinity is negotiated in Jamie Oliver's television shows and cookbooks. Another is Tony Coles (2009), who, introducing the concept of "multiple dominant masculinities", presents a theoretical model of masculinities based on a combination of Connell's theories of hegemonic masculinity and Bourdieu's concepts of habitus, capital and fields. Analysing masculinities in the "snowboarding fiel", Holly Thorpe (2010) argues that recent feminist extensions of Bourdieu's original conceptual schema – field, capital, habitus and practice – may help reveal more nuanced conceptualisations of both masculinities and male-gendered reflexivity. Miklós Hadas intends to prove (Hadas, 2007a, 2007b, 2009) that masculine dispositions became civilised and modernised in Europe during the 18th and 19th centuries. His overriding thesis is that the drive to fight and kill the enemy was gradually extended by competitive and, later, co-operative dispositions. Following Bourdieu and Norbert Elias, Hadas argues that various existential conditions in various social fields produce different habitus, which can be transferred to diverse areas of practice. However, few renowned scholars refer to Bourdieu in studies on men and masculinities. There is no reference whatsoever in two of the early comprehensive volumes of this field (Gardiner, 2002; Haywood & Mac an Ghaill, 2003) and only one reference in another (Whitehead & Barrett, 2001), while Bourdieu is mentioned three times in a third (Adams & Savran, 2002).[1]

Bourdieu's *Masculine Domination*

The best way of illustrating the Bourdieusian impact on gender studies, and more particularly on studies on men and masculinities, is to investigate the principal statements of his only book on masculinity and its reception. *La domination Masculine* (1998) (in English: *Masculine Domination*, 2001) was one of Bourdieu's last works and became a sociological classic – even before Bourdieu's death. It had a unique appeal in France and was published in an edition of 78,000 copies in 1998, with another 30,000 copies being published four years later (these are stellar numbers for a social science publication). Within a few years, it was translated into several languages. Consequently, it can be considered one of the most popular big-picture narratives about masculinity – not only for the broader public but also for social scientists.

The central thesis of the book (which also appeared in an earlier version: Bourdieu, 1990) is that masculine domination – argued as the model of all kinds of domination – is a social institution deeply inculcated in objective social and subjective mental structures over millennia and is practically governed by the same laws in the pre-modern Kabyle society of the Mediterranean region as in Virginia Woolf's Bloomsbury circle in early 20th-century London. Its emergence is ascribed to the *libido dominandi*, i.e., the instinctive desire for domination, a sort of sense of duty based on the inner conviction that a man "owes himself" that is acquired unconsciously in the course of socialisation. This drive, or *illusio dominandi*, is constitutive of masculinity and causes men to be socially instituted to allow themselves to be caught up, like children, in all the games of domination that are socially assigned to them, of which the form par excellence is war. At the same time, men also become victims – victims of their illusion.

In this sexually determined, "sexualised and sexualising" social order of labour division, men are active mainly in the public sphere, while women in the non-public, private spheres are not oriented towards profit or power. In practice, women comprise goods of exchange in the men's games based on honour and dignity, serving in this capacity the reproduction of men's symbolic capital. Women, argues Bourdieu, are disposed to generate desirability and positive representation, both personally and for the family and community. Women are mainly in charge of ceremonies organised upon aesthetic premises (family and firm feasts, literary salons, receptions, etc.), so they may fill important positions in different cultural fields and specialise in producing differentiating symbolic distinctions. Besides, continues Bourdieu, borrowing Virginia Woolf's metaphor, they act as "flattering mirrors" in which men can view their magnified images. Ultimately, then, all women enrich the wealth of the men who possess them, although they have the perspicacity of outsiders.

Salient significance is ascribed to habitus, that is, to behavioural patterns fixed in durable dispositions, which govern human praxis at the non-conscious level. Being perceptible, these "structured, structural structures" are liable to social classification and differentiation. Bourdieu writes about "the somatisation of power relations" and formulates a thesis according to which the socially constructed biological body is also a politicised body or, more precisely, no less than "embodied politics". He refers, for instance, to elementary school education, which incorporates in the dispositions of growing generations a multitude of sexually differentiated ethical, political or even cosmological elements – e.g., teaching pupils how to hold the (masculine) right hand, how to walk, look into someone's eyes, dress, etc.

The arguments in *Masculine Domination* are supported by two types of empirical references. The book's primary source is the pre-modern Kabylian community in Algeria, where negative connotations are mainly attached to women and positive ones to men. All activities connected with the concepts "internal", "damp", "low" and "crooked" (not only child-rearing but also such dirty chores as mucking out the stable) are performed by women, as compared to the "external", "official", "straight", "dry", "tall" (etc.) activities of men. Typically enough, sexual intercourse itself is deemed "normal" and "classical" in the case where a man is above the woman, while all other sexual positions are condemned as perverted and often penalised by sanctions. The other reference is to Virginia Woolf's *To the Lighthouse*, in which the protagonist, Mr Ramsey, incorporates modern masculine dispositions based on the *libido academica*, that is, a special variation of the *libido dominandi*. An early 20th-century academic intellectual, Mr Ramsey is a man "whose words are verdicts," all whose predictions "are self-fulfilling, they make themselves true," and whose "paternal prophecy is both a forecast of science and a prediction of wisdom, which sends the future into the past," writes Bourdieu (p. 70).

The central claim of *Masculine Domination* is that

> the changes visible in conditions, in fact, conceal permanent features in the relative positions: the levelling-out of the chances of access and rates of representation should not be allowed to mask the inequalities which persist in the distribution of boys and girls among the various types of schooling and therefore among possible careers.
>
> *(Bourdieu, 2001, p. 90)*

Bourdieu uses the term "permanence in and through change" (p. 91) and claims that

> whatever their position in the social space, women have in common the fact that they are separated from men by a negative symbolic coefficient which, like skin colour for people of colour in racist societies, or any other sign of membership of a stigmatized group, negatively affects everything that they are and do, and which is the source of a systematic set of homologous differences.
>
> *(p. 93)*

Consequently, "the structure of the gaps is maintained" (p. 91) because "girls internalize, in the form of schemes of perception and appreciation not readily accessible to consciousness, the principles of the dominant vision" (Bourdieu, 2001, p. 95). In other words: "the constancy of habitus [...] is one of the most important factors in the relative constancy of the structure of the sexual division of labour" (p. 95).

Bourdieu defines the study of social institutions (church, state, school, family) that sustain continuity as the primary task of the approach to "the history of women":

> Historical research cannot limit itself to describing the transformations over time of the conditions of women, or even the relationship between the sexes in the different epoch. It must aim to establish, for each period, the state of system of agents and institutions – family, church, state, educational system, etc., which, with different weights and different means at different times, have helped to remove the relations of masculine more or less completely from history.
>
> *(pp. 82–83)*

Writing about domination and love in the postscript, Bourdieu states that some borderline cases may be exceptions to the general rule of masculine domination. Such a borderline case is "the enchanted island of love, a closed and perfectly autarkic world which is the site of a continuous series of miracles, can be snatched from the icy waters of calculation, violence and self-interest" (Bourdieu, 2001, p. 110). In the appendix, dealing with the gay and lesbian movement, he raises the following questions: "How can one stand up to a hypocritical universalism without universalising a particularism? [...] How can one prevent the conquests of the movement from ending up as a form of ghettoisation?" (Bourdieu, 2001, p. 123).

Critics on *Masculine Domination*

Contemporary studies focusing on the plurality and historical variability of masculinities take an opposite route to Bourdieu, who completely ignored previous scholarship on men and masculinities. It is therefore not surprising that several points of criticism have been raised in the 28 years since the publication of the first version of *Masculine Domination* (Bourdieu, 1990). Most of these critics find the book wanting in providing adequate empirical grounds for its claims. As stated by Wallace,

> the sole "data" that informs *Masculine Domination* comes from anthropological information about the Kabyle society (a Mediterranean ethnic group) that Bourdieu gathered in the 1960s and a reading of Virginia Woolf's *To the Lighthouse*. By comparison with the thoroughness of his previous work, *Masculine Domination* seems a brisk treatment of a subject that does not have Bourdieu's full attention. [...] Furthermore, as Terry Lovell (one of Bourdieu's most frequent and incisive critics) points out, "it is not always possible to know when [Bourdieu] is restricting his observations to the particular case of Kabyle society, when he is extending them to encompass the whole Mediterranean culture of honour/shame, including that of the modern period, and when he is offering universal generalizations."
>
> *(Wallace, 2003, p. 20)*

Undoubtedly, as Toril Moi writes, "Bourdieu's empirical data are almost exclusively from his investigations among the Kabyle people of Algeria carried on in the 1950s which he has not updated or put to self-reflection" (1991, p. 1033). This failure allows Anne Witz to accuse him of "dubious gender anthropology" (2004, p. 211). Particularly defective are his concrete references to late 20th-century developments; ignoring these undermines the author's ambition to provide a broad historical horizon. This neglect of data is unusual for Bourdieu, whose best works (e.g., Bourdieu, 1984, 1989, 1992, 1993) are characterised by a sophisticated interpretation of subtle qualitative and quantitative variables. In short, the suspicion that in this work he only collected the arguments that would substantiate his preconceived thesis is not unfounded.

Another group of critical remarks charges the author with "determinism" and "pessimism", referring to a problem often raised in the critical interpretation of the Bourdieusian oeuvre. Some critics say Bourdieu's thinking is characterised by a "hyperfunctionalist", extreme structuralism (Joas & Knöbl, 2011, p. 25). Others, more politely, opine that "the author is more at home in analysing the specificities of reproduction than those of social change" (Perrot et al., 1999, p. 209). Yet others claim that "he overemphasises the significance of order and structure" (Skeggs, 2004, p. 30), while Chambers argues that

> parts of Bourdieu's analysis also imply that it will be difficult if not impossible for us even to conceptualise radical change, for he asserts that women living under patriarchy lack the cognitive resources to do so (Bourdieu, 2001, p. 35; 2000, p. 170). Such a conclusion is problematic for it seems to rule out social change, and conflicts with the fact that change does occur, sometimes as the result of radical theorising, for example of feminists about and against patriarchy. Bourdieu's contention that change in consciousness also requires a change in the underlying social structures does have some force.
>
> *(Chambers, 2005, p. 334)*

Connell and Messerschmidt (2005) include one reference to Bourdieu in their oft-quoted article (presumably, this is the first time that Connell mentions Bourdieu in any of her publications), according to which

> in social theories of gender, there has often been a tendency toward functionalism – that is, seeing gender relations as a self-contained, self-reproducing system and explaining every element regarding its function in reproducing the whole. [...] Bourdieu's (2001) late intervention to explain masculine domination has given a new lease on life to *functionalism* [emphasis added] in gender analysis.
>
> *(Connell & Messerschmidt, 2005, p. 844)*

While appreciating the critique of functionalism in social theories of gender, Connell and Messerschmidt are incorrect when they label Bourdieu, without cogent argument, as functionalist. As is well known, Bourdieu's paradigm is a synthesis of several different traditions: the philosophy of symbolic forms, French structuralism, phenomenological sociology of knowledge, the sociologies of Durkheim, Weber and Marx – in addition, Michel Foucault and Norbert Elias also had a significant influence on his oeuvre.

According to Krais, one point of criticism among feminist scholars is that "the living conditions, practices, views and struggles of women today are not reflected at all in Bourdieu's text, which instead paints the picture of a gender order so completely doxic and closed that it seems almost totalitarian" (2006, p. 122). The roots of his pessimism lie in "his view of the perpetual reproduction of class-based inequality [that] appears to leave little prospect that things will get better" (Joas & Knöbl, 2011, p. 29). Although Bridget Fowler (the British feminist most sympathetic towards Bourdieu's theory) stresses that Bourdieu's praxis theory is not entirely deterministic, for in the final analysis people always have the possibility of reflection, she still takes the view that *Masculine Domination* cannot grasp the periods of the transformation of patriarchal structure with due subtlety and is particularly defective in its analysis of changes during capitalist modernity (Fowler, 2003).

Related criticism centres on the fact that Bourdieu fails to refer to gender studies literature. "There is something frustrating about the ease and briskness with which Bourdieu dismisses whole schools of feminist thought," argues Wallace (2003). Some critics acidly note that because of its lack of citations and ambiguous allusions, *Masculine Domination* would not pass a test in the first year of a PhD course (Mathieu, 1999). Lovell remarks that

> Julia Kristeva and Luce Irigaray share a footnote in the 1990 version in which they are summarily dismissed as essentialist – a familiar charge, but one against which defences have been mounted (Grosz, 1989; Whitford, 1991). Even this backhanded acknowledgement had disappeared by 1998. Bourdieu's lack of engagement with those who already occupy the well-tilled 'field' of gender studies is quite remarkable.
>
> *(Lovell, 2001, p. 44)*

When a prominent sociologist, who also happens to be male, almost entirely ignores the bulk of feminist and gender literature in a book on genders, and thus fails to recognise the significance of the female agent's history-forming power, several reviewers suggest that he not only represents the historical processes in a false light but also symbolically reproduces masculine domination (Lagrave, 2003). According to Beate Krais,

> to reconstruct the standpoints of others – in this case, of women – Bourdieu would have had to do a thorough reading of the feminist research, which would have meant recognizing his feminist colleagues as "equal players" in the intellectual field. [...] It is difficult to understand why Bourdieu – who in his other works emphasizes the importance of symbolic conflict and struggle – pays only cursory attention to the symbolic struggles over the gender order. [...] Apparently, it is difficult even for critical male social scientists to reflect upon their masculine position. On the other hand, critical female scientists often seem to share a similar blind spot as regards their position, and a similar hesitance to accept the contributions of male colleagues who dare enter their territory – particularly those who represent strong analytical positions – like Bourdieu.
>
> *(Krais, 2006, pp. 123–124)*

True enough: Bourdieu primarily calls feminist historiography to account as part of his larger critique of permanence, and thus rhetorically shows that he underestimates the importance of the agency of the feminist movement. As he writes,

> a history of women [...] cannot be content, for example, to record the exclusion of women from this or that occupation, this or that branch or discipline; it must also take note of and explain the reproduction of both the hierarchies (occupational, disciplinary, etc.) and of the hierarchical dispositions which they favour and which lead women to contribute to their own exclusion from the places from which they are in any case excluded.
>
> *(Bourdieu, 2001, p. 83)*

When writing of the "power of the structure" and the "symbolic negative coefficient" in *Masculine Domination*, Bourdieu expands the paradigm expressed in its most sophisticated form in *Distinction* (1984). In this earlier work he analyses the interrelations between different social classes three-dimensionally by examining: the quantity of capital possessed by the classes and class fractions; the structure of this capital (the rate of economic and cultural capitals, the re-conversion strategies between different types of capital); and the temporal changes of these two factors. In other words, in *Masculine Domination* Bourdieu replaces class with gender and replaces class habitus with gender(ed) habitus. When he discusses "the constancy of habitus" (p. 95), "the negative symbolic coefficient by which women are separated from men" (p. 93), the "permanence in and through change" (p. 91) or the "strength of the structure" (p. 102), he extends his theory about the displacement of the social structure to the displacement of the men/women relationship. Nevertheless, while *Masculine Domination* reflects on a few feminist authors, albeit minimally, it ignores the body of work on men and masculinities.

The usefulness of Bourdieu for studies on men and masculinities

No matter how problematic *Masculine Domination* is, it would be a mistake to throw out the baby with the bathwater. First and foremost, it presents us with a coherent, theoretically embedded paradigm with a lot of free valences suited for scientific analysis, which offers a well-established tool for bridging the structure-agency dichotomy. Bourdieu gives an elegant and witty examination of pre-modern Kabyle society, stressing the social embeddedness of masculine domination and its decisive structural weight. The book convincingly points to certain permanent elements of masculine domination, proving that the habitus concept might be relevant for studying symbolic domination and symbolic violence. The value of the book is further enhanced by some conceptual innovations, such as *libido dominandi* as the dispositional foundation of masculine domination, and some related categories (*libido sciendi, libido academica, illusion dominandi*).

In other words, the criticisms cited in the previous section should not prevent us from applying some of his key terms, in the hope that the inclusion of a Bourdieusian conceptual framework might benefit studies on men and masculinities on several counts. By using the notions of habitus, capital, symbolic violence and social field, the plurality of masculinities can be conceptualised as a *system of relations among masculine dispositions* both within and between fields. As is well known, fields, in the Bourdieusian sense, are social microcosms in which there is a symbolic struggle for the monopoly of the reproduction of professional knowledge, defined as capital, among experts. Capital does not exist or function except in relation to a field. Each field, like a game, can only exist if "players" who know "how to play" are involved and inclined to play. The structure of the field is determined by the positions of the players and by the overall volume and form of the capital they possess. The struggle is waged by the experts partly to convince the laity and partly to gain more favourable positions within the field.

As I have shown elsewhere, the value of Bourdieu for studies on men and masculinities lies in the notion that various existential conditions in varying social fields produce different habitus. This idea can be transferred to diverse areas of practice. Consequently, sports – duelling, fencing, hunting, horse racing, rowing, gymnastics, athletics, cycling and football – might be regarded as indicators of the changing masculine dispositional patterns of different social groups (Hadas, 2007a, 2007b, 2009). The radical innovation of the new sport of gymnastics as it emerges in Europe in the mid-19th century, for example, is manifest in converting the morally permeated collective ideal of the nation into the ideologically permeated individual ideal of the body (Hadas, 2009). When the health of their offspring becomes an aim in itself for the middle classes, this social group employs the increasingly widely used techniques of self-control and obedience in the service of envisioned long-term social mobility. By incorporating and internalising these rational and teleological elements, the steepness of the bourgeois family's mobility curve is increased, i.e., their chances of progress in the social sphere are enhanced. To put it differently, gymnastic exercises can be considered generators of revolutionary changes in the way of life: this umbrella sport is destined to create the corporeal foundation of modernity.

Authors cited earlier have all made convincing efforts to introduce a Bourdieusian conceptual framework into gender and masculinity studies. This synthesis can be achieved relatively easily because – as mentioned above – both Bourdieu and Connell focus on the symbolic relationships among qualitatively and quantitatively measurable power elements and both are interested in the relational dynamic of distinctions on a Marxist basis. Thanks to this "family resemblance", the Bourdieusian terminology can be harmonised with the theory of hegemonic masculinity.

Note

1 Some of the authors who refer to Bourdieu are Sofia Aboim (2010), Garth Stahl (2016) and Timothy Barrett (2018).

References

Aboim, S. (2010). *Plural masculinities: The remaking of the self in private life*. London: Routledge.

Adams, R., & Savran, D. (Eds.). (2002). *The masculinity studies reader*. Malden, MA: Wiley-Blackwell.

Adkins, L., & Skeggs, B. (Eds.). (2004). *Feminism after Bourdieu*. Oxford: Blackwell.

Barrett, T. (2018). Bourdieu, hysteresis, and shame: Spinal cord injury and the gendered habitus. *Men and Masculinities*, *21*(1), 35–55.

Bourdieu, P. (1984). *Distinction*. London: Routledge & Kegan Paul.

Bourdieu, P. (1989). *La noblesse d'état*. Paris: Minuit.

Bourdieu, P. (1990). La domination masculine. *Actes de la recherche en science sociales*, *84*(1), 2–31.

Bourdieu, P. (1992). *Les regles de l'art*. Paris: Seuil.

Bourdieu, P. (1993). *La misere du monde*. Paris: Seuil.

Bourdieu, P. (1998). *La domination masculine*. Paris: Seuil.

Bourdieu, P. (2001). *Masculine domination*. Cambridge: Polity Press.

Brown, D. (2005). An economy of gendered practices? Learning to teach physical education from the perspective of Pierre Bourdieu's embodied sociology. *Sport, Education and Society*, *10*(1), 3–23.

Chambers, C. (2005). Masculine domination, radical feminism and change. *Feminist Theory*, *6*(3), 325–346.

Coles, T. (2009). Negotiating the field of masculinity: The production and reproduction of multiple dominant masculinities. *Men and Masculinities*, *12*(1), 30–44.

Connell, R. W., & Messerschmidt, J. W. (2005). Hegemonic masculinity. Rethinking the concept. *Gender and Society*, *19*(6), 829–859.

Dillabough, J.-A. (2004). Class, culture and the "predicaments of masculine domination": Encountering Pierre Bourdieu. *British Journal of Sociology of Education*, *25*(4), 489–506.

Fowler, B. (2003). Reading Pierre Bourdieu's *Masculine Domination*: Notes towards an intersectional analysis of gender, culture and class. *Cultural Studies*, *17*(3/4), 468–494.

Gardiner, J. K. (Ed.). (2002). *Masculinity studies and feminist theory*. New York: Columbia University Press.

Hadas, M. (2007a). Gentlemen in competition: Athletics and masculinities in nineteenth-century Hungary. *The International Journal of the History of Sport*, *24*(4), 478–498.

Hadas, M. (2007b). Gymnastic exercises, or "work wrapped in the gown of youthful joy": Masculinities and the civilizing process in 19th century Hungary. *Journal of Social History*, *41*(1), 161–180.

Hadas, M. (2009). The rationalisation of the body: Physical education in Hungary in the nineteenth century. *History of Education*, *38*(1), 61–77.

Haywood, C., & Mac an Ghaill, M. (2003). *Men and masculinities: Theory, research and social practice*. Buckingham: Open University Press.

Hollows, J. (2003). Oliver's twist: Leisure, labour and domestic masculinity in *The Naked Chef*. *International Journal of Cultural Studies*, *6*(2), 229–248.

Joas, H., & Knöbl, W. (2011). Between structuralism and *Theory of Practice*: The cultural sociology of Pierre Bourdieu. In S. Susan & B. S. Turner (Eds.), *The legacy of Pierre Bourdieu* (pp. 1–33). London: Anthem Press.

Krais, B. (2006). Gender, sociological theory and Bourdieu's sociology of practice. *Theory, Culture & Society, 23*(6), 119–134.

Laberge, S. (1995). Toward an integration of gender into Bourdieu's concept of cultural capital. *Sociology of Sport Journal, 12*(2), 132–146.

Lagrave, R. M. (2003). La lucidité dés dominées. In P. Encrevé & R. M. Lagrave (Eds.), *Travailler avec Bourdieu* (pp. 313–329). Paris: Flammarion.

Lovell, T. (2001). Thinking feminism with and against Bourdieu. *The Sociological Review, 49*(S1), 27–41.

Mathieu, N. C. (1999). *Bourdieu et le pouvoir autohypnotique de la domination masculine.* Paris: Les temps modernes.

McCall, L. (1992). Does gender fit? Bourdieu, feminism, and conceptions of social order. *Theory and Society, 21*(6), 837–867.

McLeod, J. (2005). Feminists re-reading Bourdieu: Old debates and new questions about gender habitus and gender change. *Theory and Research in Education, 3*(1), 11–30.

McNay, L. (1999). Gender, habitus and the field: Pierre Bourdieu and the limits of reflexivity. *Theory, Culture and Society, 16*(1), 95–117.

Moi, T. (1991). Appropriating Bourdieu: Feminist theory and Pierre Bourdieu's sociology of culture. *New Literary Theory, 22*(4), 1017–1049.

Perrot, M., Sintomer, Y., Krais, B., & Duru-Bellat, M. (1999). Autour du livre de Pierre Bourdieu. *La domination masculine. Travail, genre et sociétés, 1*(1), 202–207.

Reay, D. (1997). Feminist theory, habitus, and social class: Disrupting notions of classlessness. *Women's Studies International Forum, 20*(2), 225–233.

Reay, D. (2004). Gendering Bourdieu's concepts of capitals? Emotional capital, women and social class. *Sociological Review, 5*(2 Suppl.), 57–74.

Skeggs, B. (2004). Context and background: Pierre Bourdieu's analysis of class, gender and sexuality. In L. Adkins & B. Skeggs (Eds.), *Feminism after Bourdieu* (pp. 19–34). Oxford: Blackwell.

Stahl, G. (2016). White working-class male narratives of 'loyalty to self' in discourses of aspiration. *British Journal of Sociology of Education, 37*(2), 663–683.

Thorpe, H. (2010). Bourdieu, gender reflexivity, and physical culture: A case of masculinities in the snowboarding field. *Journal of Sport and Social Issues, 34*(2), 176–214.

Wallace, M. (2003). A disconcerting brevity: Pierre Bourdieu's *Masculine Domination. Postmodern Culture, 13*(3). Retrieved from http://pmc.iath.virginia.edu/issue.503/13.3wallace.html.

Whitehead, S., & Barrett, F. (Eds.). (2001). *The masculinities reader.* Hoboken, NJ: Wiley & Sons.

Witz, A. (2004). Anamnesis and amnesis in Bourdieu's work: The case for a feminist anamnesis. In L. Adkins & B. Skeggs (Eds.), *Feminism after Bourdieu* (pp. 211–223). Oxford: Blackwell.

5

Foucault's men, or what have masturbating boys and ancient men to do with masculinity?

Lucas Gottzén

Introduction

The French philosopher Michel Foucault is without doubt one of the most cited scholars in the humanities and social sciences.[1] His theories have also been popular within feminist studies since the 1970s, although the relationship to his work has been somewhat ambivalent. Some researchers have been explicitly critical, while others were heavily influenced by him, or at least developed constructive dialogues with his work (see Diamond & Quinby, 1988; Ramazanoğlu, 1993; Taylor & Vintges, 2004). Foucault has been immensely important within sexuality studies as well, particularly in queer theory, which is much in debt to Foucault for its theoretical development (Turner, 2000).

Insights from Foucault have also featured in masculinity studies, but he seems to have a more peripheral position here than in the neighboring fields. Early masculinity scholars cited Foucault but were hardly influenced by him, and his impact in the field remains comparatively limited. Given this relative lack of uptake of Foucault within masculinity studies, it is somewhat surprising to find that he recurrently referred to men and boys. For instance, in *Discipline and Punish* (1977), he discussed the development of disciplinary power in institutions aimed at boys and young men, such as drill-schools for young army recruits and reformatories for delinquent boys. He was mostly not explicit (or perhaps even aware) about the gendered aspects of his inquiries but there is one moment, however, where he in fact is upfront about the fact that he studies gendered beings. In *The Use of Pleasure* he emphasizes that ethics in Ancient Greece was a masculine matter:

> It was an ethics for men: an ethics thought, written, and taught by men, and addressed to men – free men, obviously. A male ethics, consequently, in which women figured only as objects or, at most, as partners that one had best train, educate, and watch over when one had them under one's power, but stay away from when they were under the power of someone else (father, husband, tutor).
>
> *(Foucault, 1985, p. 22)*

Foucault's work can obviously be useful as a general humanities or social science theory and methodology about discourse, power and genealogy, or by using other concepts from his rich theoretical toolbox. I think he has more to offer critical masculinity studies, though. This passage not only provides insight into his studies on antiquity but also enables a re-reading of his larger body of work as theories about men and masculinity. But to make his scholarship relevant to masculinity theorizing, I think that we need to move somewhat beyond his work. A part of this move is to name Foucault's men as *men* (Hearn, 2004), which implies highlighting the sexual difference that is mostly taken for granted in his discourse and turning men and masculinity to an explicit object of his inquiry. To elucidate what Foucault has to offer a critical masculinities project, I look for traces of masculinity and attempt to place "the man" at the center of his theory.

Rather than applying concepts from the Foucauldian toolbox to men and masculinities, in this chapter I will therefore discuss two of the masculine figures that Foucault has presented. These two figures illustrate key components of his conceptual framework that speak to critical masculinity studies. I discuss the masturbating boy, where Foucault introduces the concepts *dispositif* (or apparatus) and biopower, and the free man in Greek and Latin antiquity, where he develops notions about the technologies of the self and the caesura of masculinity. I offer a reading of these concepts as technologies of gender that are useful to theorize men and masculinity. But first I will present a brief overview of how Foucault has been discussed within masculinity studies and feminist theory, particularly emphasizing the critique against Foucault for obscuring gendered and sexual difference.

Foucault in masculinity studies

As in many other fields of gender studies, Foucault's impact on masculinity studies is not easy to measure, as much of his theorizing has become so widespread that it is not always explicitly referenced. For instance, his conceptualization of power as multiple and omnipresent is today almost the dominant theory of power within critical scholarship. However, given that most of the early masculinity scholars within the social sciences who have become almost synonymous with the field primarily embraced modernist onto-epistemologies (see Introduction and Beasley, this volume), Foucault was either ignored or dismissed for not taking gender relations and human experience into account, as well as accused of relativism and discursive reductionism (e.g., Connell & Dowsett, 1992/2001; Hearn, 1998; Seidler, 1987). Raewyn Connell, for instance, argues that Foucault assumes that normalization strategies are always successful and dismisses his discussions of resistance as simply being "a metaphysical claim in the absence of a substantive account of the generation, articulation and historical organization of resistance" (Connell & Dowsett, 1992/2001, p. 195).

In an early and trenchant critique of Foucault and masculinity, Victor Seidler (1987) discusses Foucault's criticism of reason, desire and sexuality (see also Foxhall, 1994; Schor, 1987 for other early accounts). Seidler points out that Foucault (1967) demonstrates that the construction of reason that was paradigmatic in Renée Descartes's philosophy resulted in an exclusion of madness and insanity. However, while Foucault "offers important insights", Seidler argues that "there are limitations to his analysis, not least because of his failure to grapple with gender" (1987, p. 82). Moving beyond Foucault, Seidler argues that during the Enlightenment, reason and rationality became a central part of masculinity while nature needed to be controlled. In this rationalist tradition, feelings became dangerous, as they were inclinations that could lead men astray. Sexuality became particularly challenging, since desire posed a threat to rationality, and women embodied this danger as they attracted men sexually. This view of sexuality was not new to the Enlightenment but was also found in the early Christian church, as Foucault (1986) points out. Men, Seidler (1987) argues, have historically learned to repress desire and emotions – what Foucault has described as our "lyricism" (Huffer, 2010, p. 65) – to control themselves and dominate others.

While Seidler adds much to Foucault's analysis of madness, instead of taking Foucault's epistemology seriously and discussing how his critique of the modern subject and his theory of power can destabilize contemporary gendered norms of sexuality, he recurrently emphasizes what Foucault does not touch upon, in particular that he does not explore sexuality and gender phenomenologically. The French philosopher is accused of reducing everything to language and discourse while ignoring individual experience. Since a fundamental phenomenology is argued to be lacking, Seidler supplements with psychoanalytical theories – part of the psychologizing of the subject that Foucault in fact wants to destabilize (cf. Huffer, 2010). Seidler's (1987) use of psychoanalysis also produces a discourse about gender that is universalist, ahistorical and binary, which is in stark contrast to Foucault's genealogical method.

Not all masculinity scholars have been as critical of Foucault. Michael Kimmel (1993) refers to *The History of Sexuality* (1978) to argue that homosexual acts during the 19th century came to be seen as expressions of sexual orientation and identity. Jeff Hearn (1998) similarly acknowledges Foucault's significance for the history of sexuality but also argues that he obscures how sexuality relates to violence, sexual domination and gender relations. However, some years later, Hearn (2004) is more positive and argues that a Foucauldian focus on the microphysics of power could be combined with more "global" perspectives on power and are thus useful to Hearn's theory of the hegemony of men.

Looking beyond these scholars, we find both early and more recent examples of researchers using Foucault to inquire into men and masculinity. Many social scientists have drawn on Foucault to discuss the historical construction of male sexuality (e.g., Edwards, 1993; McCormack, 2013). Others see Foucault as the founder of discourse theory and use this perspective to explore how masculine subjectivity is produced and negotiated (e.g., Jefferson, 1994; Milani, 2014; Wetherell & Edley, 1999). Yet others have turned to Foucault (1978) to understand the intricate forms of power and resistance that characterize gender relations (e.g., Mutluer, 2011; Pease, 2000). While many have integrated Foucault with Connell's (1995) hegemonic masculinity theory (e.g., Wetherell & Edley, 1999), Richard Pringle (2005) argues that the two approaches are not easily combined as they have fundamental theoretical and ontological differences. In addition, he argues that Foucault is more useful in theorizing how power works at a bodily level than the Gramsci-inspired analyses that have dominated masculinity studies. Within the humanities, masculinity scholars have generally seemed somewhat keener to embrace Foucault (e.g., Buchbinder, 2013; Halberstam, 1998). Todd Reeser and Lewis Seifert (2008) point out that Foucault may be limited in his understanding of masculinity, especially since he does not articulate the implications of normative masculinity's anxiety about homosexual desire. Nevertheless, "he lays the groundwork for what might be called genealogies of masculinity" (p. 25).

Similar discussions about Foucault could be found in feminist and queer studies, which have ranged from explicit warnings about his theory (Moi, 1985) to fruitful dialogues (Butler, 1990). There is not enough space here to do justice to the extensive debates about Foucault in feminist and queer theory, so I will only touch upon Teresa de Lauretis' discussion in *Technologies of Gender* (1987), as she not only points out his shortcomings but also shows how we can think about gender *with* and *beyond* Foucault. By obscuring sex difference in discourses about sexuality, she argues that Foucault – like other male poststructuralists – reproduces the male norm that feminist philosophers have identified in the history of Western thinking (for a different view, see Schor, 1987). Nevertheless, he is useful for the theorizing of gender since sexuality discourses always are gender-differentiated. From a Foucauldian perspective, de Lauretis contends, gender can be seen as a technology – a "bio-medical apparati" (1987, p. 3) – that creates sex difference similarly to how sexuality can be seen as a technology that creates differences between hetero and homosexuality. Foucault's lack of interest in gender may indeed obscure sexual difference and the cultural production of men and women. Yet it is possible to read Foucault as a theory of the gendered production of sexuality, that is, as a process where masculinity and (hetero)sexuality are created simultaneously (cf. Butler, 1990), as is the case with the masturbating boy.

The masturbating boy, or what is a *dispositif*?

The "repression thesis" around masturbation starts Foucault's long-term inquiry into sexuality. He is critical of the argument presented by Herbert Marcuse (1955/1965) and others, namely that sexuality has been suppressed under Western capitalism. Rather than silence and prohibition, Foucault suggests that the 18th and 19th centuries were characterized by a discursive explosion of sex and sexuality, particularly about the masturbating boy.

In his analysis of masturbation, Foucault developed the analytical concept *dispositif*, often translated as "apparatus" in English. A dispositif includes both discursive and non-discursive elements while the "dispositif itself is the system of relations that can be established between these elements" (Foucault, 1980, p. 194). The concept highlights heterogeneity in the various practices and associations that are produced. According to Gilles Deleuze (1992), Foucault's concept involved four levels that are distinct, but intertwined: thinking, observation, subjectivation and action.

The first level relates to the science and knowledge production of sexuality, and the second concerns observation systems for controlling and monitoring sexuality. These two levels were apparent in the anxieties about masturbation. When masturbation became a widespread concern in the late 18th and early 19th centuries in European contexts, it only involved the child and the teenager's sexuality but emphasized parents' responsibility (Laqueur, 2004). Numerous pamphlets and manuals for parents were produced, as well as wax museums built, where parents should take their children to demonstrate "all the health problems someone could suffer if they masturbated" (Foucault, 2003, p. 235). Masturbation thus became a somatization of the soul; the body's state revealed the masturbator's uncontrolled desire. Masturbators were argued to spread nauseating odors, have loose teeth and gums covered with ulcers "that foretold a scorbutic degeneration" (p. 238). Masturbation was considered to be extremely widespread but also "an unknown or ignored practice that no one has spoken about" (p. 59). As a consequence, it was seen as the root of all evil and explained all sorts of diseases and conditions. When masturbating, the boy "puts his entire life at risk once and for all when he puts his hands on his sex" (p. 241).

What Foucault (2003) calls "the crusade against masturbation" was primarily directed toward the bourgeois family. The child was responsible but not to blame; instead it was the parents' fault, since they had other adults taking care of their children that could lead them astray. In particular, it was a critique and fear of the feminization of the home where female governesses and servants dominated the household. By seeking in the children compensation for their forced celibacy, these females were viewed as the cause of especially boys' unnatural and excessive sexuality. To combat masturbation, parents were urged to be more involved in their children's lives and to reorganize the family space into a place of constant monitoring.

Children had to be watched when they washed themselves, when they went to sleep and while sleeping. Parents had to keep their children's bodies close and carefully follow what they did to prevent their children from masturbating. For instance, parents were encouraged to tie the child's hands together or to sleep in the same room or, if possible, in the same bed. A variety of devices was produced to prevent boys from masturbating, such as metal corselets that allowed the boy to urinate but not touch himself.

The third level of the *dispositif* concerns which subjects are produced, and the fourth refers to the technologies used. With regard to sexuality, Foucault (2003) explores the production of the masturbating boy as a "tiny monster" but also, above all, the construction of a psychological interior. Confession became perhaps the most pivotal technique in the crusade against masturbation. Children had to confess to their families, their family physicians and to physicians specializing in sexuality. Foucault (2003) traces the relationship between masturbation and confession to the penance rituals of the Catholic Church in the 16th century, when sexual sin went from being a matter of intersubjective relations to one primarily concerning the individual's own body. The body became a bearer of desires, of self and consciousness, and masturbation became the link between the individual's body and his soul. This approach was not spread throughout the entire population but primarily in the theological seminars and universities, which were populated by young men. The role of confession spread to larger parts of the populace, first with the crusade against masturbation and then through the emerging field of psychiatry and particularly through Freudian psychoanalysis. Rather than being an issue of actual practice, sexuality became "something that must be talked about inside a ritual discourse organized around a power relationship" (Foucault, 1996, p. 164).

Although techniques of confession were used in psychoanalysis, with Freud masturbation also started to be seen as a natural experience connected to the development of the child into a "civilized" and heterosexual adult. The positive connotations of masturbation were even more emphasized with the sexual revolution of the 1960s, and it has since then increasingly been seen as an experience associated with self-esteem and an act that enables relationships to others by first appreciating oneself (Laqueur, 2004). But masturbation is not always considered positive and liberating. When linked to (heterosexual) boys, it often appears to be problematic, particularly when it occurs in the wrong place, is too frequent and requires mass-produced visual aids, that is, pornography. As Don Kulick (2006) puts it, "All shimmering recommendations that masturbation is good, positive and healthy only applies as long as the act is performed in the absence of pornography" (p. 77; my translation). Contemporary masturbation emerges as a gendered phenomenon. While girls' masturbation manifests itself as practiced only with the aid of fantasy, young men's masturbation is presented as always being conducted with visual means, and thus bad. The boy's masturbation is equated with porn consumption and said to either turn him into a sex addict or to someone who will force his girlfriend to consent to anal intercourse (Kulick, 2006).

Power is the force that brings together the different parts of the *dispositif*. In the case of masturbation, the form of power that emerged is what Foucault (2003) calls biopolitics, a new apparatus tied to the state's strategies around education and population control. Masturbation was the place where sex and biopower first became entwined as it focused on the relationship between individuals and the pleasure of their own bodies. This suggests that "biopolitical mechanisms of security operate not only above but also below the disciplining of individual masturbating bodies" (Garlick, 2016, p. 104). In this case, biopolitics seems to be situated at the level of affect. The biopolitics of masturbation that Foucault explores suggests that a mature masculinity requires having mastered childish sexual inclinations.

Masculinity then appears not primarily as a gender role or an identity but, rather, as a technology of producing sexual difference and for regulating forces of life, as attempts to control intractable sexual affect (Garlick, 2016).

The ancient man and the caesura of masculinity

One of the reasons why Foucault was interested in sexuality was that it highlights other issues, especially questions about power and subjectivity. As discussed, he showed the intricate weave of power relations created around sexuality in modernity, particularly around young masculinity. One of the differences between sexuality and the other domains that Foucault was interested in (e.g., madness, illness, death, criminality) was that the power in these other domains appeared to come from outside the subject. In the studies of sexuality, power seems more to work *through* the subject itself. Admittedly, pediatricians and therapists organized the truth discourse on masturbation, but it centered on the individual's relationship to themselves and their desires.

In his late work, Foucault developed these discussions on sexuality, confession and subjectivity through studies of Latin and Greek antiquity, primarily the classical age (about 4th century BCE) and the 1st and 2nd centuries CE (Foucault, 1985, 1986, 1988, 2018). Here we find a second Foucauldian figure that I call the Ancient man. In these studies, sexuality does not primarily regard an outside power as subjectivating the individual but as an act of self-subjectivation – the individual's relation to himself. Sexuality and, above all, its moderation become a way for the free man in antiquity to govern himself and to be able to govern others.

It has often been pointed out that Foucault identifies epochs when sexuality was freer than today. This is partly true, but he did not argue that antiquity constituted a golden age for sexual freedom, rather that it was characterized by other forms of regulation of sexuality. While distinct from the ethics we find in modern societies, homosexuality was *de facto* constituted as an ethical problem in the classical era as well. There was no explicit prohibition, for example, against the "love of boys" or extramarital affairs, but Foucault found early negative sentiments around it. Instead, what differs is the individual's relationship to such ethics. The critique of sexual practices has to be seen not primarily as prohibition but as "the elaboration and stylization of an activity in the exercise of its power and practice of its liberty" (Foucault, 1985, p. 23). In other words, it was not so much a matter of following norms and rules as it was how one is to "transform oneself into the ethical subject of one's behavior" (p. 27). Moral action is thus a kind of self-formation, a relation of the self to itself. As previously pointed out, Foucault (1986) is explicit that these ethics only regarded free men and that it was a world "very strongly marked by the central position of the male personage and by the importance accorded to the masculine role in sexual relationships" (pp. 34–35).

In the ethical stylization of the classical age, the central issue was not the boundaries between heterosexual and homosexual acts. The question was not with whom did you had sex; at least no major attention was paid to whether you had sex with a woman, boy or slave (the main prospective sex partners of a free man). The decisive factor in the so-called *aphrodisia* was, rather, who is active and who is passive in the sexual act as well as in the relationship in general (Foucault, 1985, 1986, 2018). The active and dominant partner was always attributed positive values, while a partner to a free man always had to be seen as passive, dominated and inferior. This posed no major problems with regard to women and slaves, but the boys were challenging, as a boy was expected to grow up to become a free man and sexual subject himself. This could destabilize the adult man's position and make him appear passive and, thus, feminized.

The second central issue in aphrodisia concerned pleasure. Sex was seen as fundamentally natural and good, and sexual pleasure was not evil but was qualitatively inferior to self-control. It was therefore crucial for the man to master himself. Just as he was expected to govern the household, he must "make his manly qualities prevail within himself. Self-mastery was a way of being a man with respect to oneself; that is, a way of commanding what needed commanding, of coercing what was not capable of self-direction" (Foucault, 1985, p. 82).

The issue of activity and pleasure exemplify the "principle of isomorphism" that governed sexuality in Greek antiquity. Isomorphism refers to an analogy in terms of social and financial position, meaning that "a sexual union, a physical relationship, is better when it is in accordance with the rules and principles that direct social relations" (Foucault, 2018, p. 97). This isomorphic notion of a social-sexual continuum regarded marriage as the best place for sex, but it was possible, as previously noted, to have sex outside marriage as long as the free man was superior, active and moderate.

During the first two centuries CE, the cultivation of the self was increasingly emphasized, which was partly due to (heterosexual) marriage becoming more valorized. From being seen as simply a form of cohabitation, the marital bond – particularly the emotional attachment between the couple – became idealized. If the pros and cons of marriage were deliberated previously (e.g., it was discussed whether marriage was the best way of life for philosophers), marriage now became something self-evidently good for everyone. Sex was appropriate only in marriage, and should even then be characterized by self-control, moderation and not too strong affect since the goal was procreation. The fact that marriage became the foremost place for aphrodisia also changed the man's relationship to his wife, according to Foucault (2018). They became more equal, and the man's fidelity became just as important as the wife's fidelity had always been. Somewhat paradoxically, however, the man could still have extramarital relationships.

It is in his discussions about the change in isomorphism that we perhaps find Foucault's most crucial contribution to masculinity theorizing. As mentioned above, in the previous isomorphic ideals of aphrodisia, social status was considered to directly affect sexual relations. But in the new forms of aphrodisia that developed during the 1st centuries CE, social status and sexuality were separated, and the man developed two different relationships with himself as a man:

> He will thus be a male individual inasmuch as he will have a sexual activity within this relationship. And in the social field, he will again be a man, a male, but this time his identification as a man, as male will no longer be linked to the exercise of a sexual activity, but simply to the fact that in society he actually has a status as man, a status of masculinity that excludes or is independent of the excessive of his [sexual] activity itself.
>
> *(Foucault, 2018, p. 262)*

Foucault describes this change as a "caesura of masculinity" (p. 308) in the free man's relationship to his own sex. Since the free man is seen as the hinge that secures the relationship between family and society, he needs to split his masculinity; "he has as it were two sexes: a statutory sex and a relational sex, a sex-status and a sex-activity" (p. 262). In other words, to be a man becomes an indication of status in the social field, but it no longer includes the right to, or a practicing of, sexual activity:

> [T]he new duty of fidelity and the construction of a more equal relationship between man and wife require every married citizen to dissociate "statutory" masculinity and "active" masculinity. In public he will have to govern and dominate others when he is hierarchically superior to them, but desexualizing his social relationships. On the other hand, he will have to reserve his sexual masculinity to his wife, but seeing her consent, taking care that this activity does not take the form of asymmetrical domination.
>
> *(pp. 307–308)*

This caesura of masculinity is consequential for the free man's relation to himself, as it requires him to exercise permanent self-control in marriage as well as in social life. If a man has sex with a female or male slave, he is no longer considered to be in control of himself and his desires. While earlier, self-control primarily concerned not being drawn into practices and relationships that were completely unacceptable (i.e., him being a passive partner), in this new order a general control and sexual self-mastery became pivotal.

It is, Foucault argues, in the splitting between social and sexual masculinity that the technologies of the self emerge. What previously exclusively involved the free man's actions related to others becomes actions that relate to himself. It is no longer just a matter of moderating one's actions and sexual activities "but of working on oneself, of becoming an object for oneself in such a way as to carefully assure this division and control" (Foucault, 2018, p. 285). We thus find a movement away from pleasure as a relational act to an issue of the individual's relation to his own pleasures.

Towards a Foucauldian masculinity studies

In this chapter, I have argued that Foucault is not only useful to masculinity studies as a generic theorist of discourse or power but that he also actually has something to say about masculinity itself. While Foucault did not apply a gender perspective in his inquiries into sexuality and did not theorize the production of sexual difference, he largely studied men and boys. Through emphasizing these as being masculine figures, we may rethink his work as theories of not only sexuality but also masculinity.

Nevertheless, a Foucauldian-inspired inquiry into masculinity places men's sexuality at the center of different forms of subjectivity and power such as biopolitics, which have been argued to be a dominant form of power in contemporary societies (Repo, 2016). As discussed, the development of biopolitics pivoted on the regulation of young heterosexual masculinity. The masturbating boy was obviously not the only figure that had to be normalized; homosexuals and other "deviants" have also been targets of the biopolitical apparatus. The role of masculinity in the development of modern biopolitics warrants inquiries to contemporary uses of the concept of masculinity. Today the concept – that once promised emancipation from men's biological destiny – appears to have become a global neoliberal biopower to regulate sex and optimize life. In the name of (sexual) freedom, masculinity is used to govern men through gender mainstreaming and calls to engage men and boys in gender equality that simultaneously reproduce gender binaries and sexual difference (Repo, 2016). A Foucauldian approach may help masculinity scholars to critically distance themselves from the very concept they have invested in so heavily.

Both Foucault's work on the crusade against masturbation and on the sexual ethics in antiquity highlight masculinity as a technology for controlling sexual affect. The masturbation epidemic reveals a *dispositif* that comes from the outside and works through the bourgeois family, to control the excessive sexuality of boys through practices, devices and spatial arrangements but also, through confession, the creation of an interior, a subjectivity. Ancient masculine ethics rather concerned self-discipline, which here does not mean oppressing oneself but letting a man's higher values control his lower ones. The free man must direct himself and work on his self, otherwise he will neither be able to govern his family nor be a respectable citizen.

The caesura of masculinity Foucault identifies in the 1st centuries CE suggests that control of desires and affect did not become an issue as late as in the crusade against masturbation or even in the Age of Reason, as Seidler (1987) argues. It also suggests that masculinity is not simply a matter of gender norms or following such norms of behavior or sexuality, and that patriarchal masculinity is not necessarily tied to homophobia or prohibition of same-sex relationships (which is often argued in masculinity studies). Masculinity is not even primarily an issue of gendered identity, even though it may be an outcome of productive powers. Rather, following Foucault, masculinity could be seen as both a technology of the self and a biopower where men's sexuality – with all its passions and pleasures – sometimes is to be controlled and other times to be stylized, but perhaps always moderated.

Note

1 I want to thank Sara Andersson and Fanny Edenroth Cato for their incisive comments.

References

Buchbinder, D. (2013). *Studying men and masculinities*. London: Routledge.

Butler, J. (1990). *Gender trouble: Feminism and the subversion of identity*. New York: Routledge.

Connell, R. W. (1995). *Masculinities*. Cambridge: Polity Press.

Connell, R. W., & Dowsett, G. (1992/2001). The unclean motion of the generative parts: Frameworks in Western thought on sexuality. In R. Parker & P. Aggleton (Eds.), *Culture, society and sexuality: A reader* (2nd ed., pp. 188–206). Philadelphia, PA: Temple University Press.

de Lauretis, T. (1987). *Technologies of gender: Essays on theory, film, and fiction*. Bloomington, IN: Indiana University Press.

Deleuze, G. (1992). What is a dispositif? In T. J. Armstrong (Ed.), *Michel Foucault: Philosopher* (pp. 159–168). New York: Routledge.

Diamond, I., & Quinby, L. (Eds.). (1988). *Foucault and feminism: Reflections on resistance*. Boston, MA: Northeastern University Press.

Edwards, T. (1993). *Erotics and politics: Gay male sexuality, masculinity, and feminism*. London: Routledge.

Foucault, M. (1967/2001). *Madness and civilization: A history of insanity in the Age of Reason*. London: Routledge.

Foucault, M. (1977/1995). *Discipline and punish: The birth of the prison*. New York: Vintage.

Foucault, M. (1978/1990). *The history of sexuality: An introduction, volume I*. New York: Vintage.

Foucault, M. (1980). The confession of the flesh. In C. Gordon (Ed.), *Power/knowledge: Selected interviews and other writings, 1972–1977* (pp. 194–228). New York: Pantheon.

Foucault, M. (1985/1992). *The history of sexuality, vol. 2: The use of pleasure*. London: Penguin.

Foucault, M. (1986/1988). *The history of sexuality, vol. 3: The care of the self*. New York: Vintage.

Foucault, M. (1988). Technologies of the self. In L. H. Martin, H. Gutman & P. H. Hutton (Eds.), *Technologies of the self: A seminar with Michel Foucault* (pp. 16–49). London: Tavistock.

Foucault, M. (1996). Schizo-culture: Infantile sexuality. In S. Lotringer (Ed.), *Foucault live: Collected interviews, 1961–84* (pp. 154–167). New York: Semiotext(e).

Foucault, M. (2003). *Abnormal: Lectures at the Collège de France, 1974–1975*. New York: Picador.

Foucault, M. (2018). *Subjectivity and truth: Lectures at the Collège de France, 1980–1981*. London: Palgrave Macmillan.

Foxhall, L. (1994). Pandora unbound: A feminist critique of Foucault's *History of sexuality*. In N. Lindisfarne & A. Cornwall (Eds.), *Dislocating masculinity* (pp. 133–145). London: Routledge.

Garlick, S. (2016). *The nature of masculinity: Critical theory, new materialisms, and technologies of embodiment.* Vancouver, BC: UBC Press.

Halberstam, J. (1998). *Female masculinity.* Durham, NC: Duke University Press.

Hearn, J. (1998). Theorizing men and men's theorizing: Varieties of discursive practices in men's theorizing of men. *Theory and Society, 27*(6), 781–816.

Hearn, J. (2004). From hegemonic masculinity to the hegemony of men. *Feminist Theory, 5*(1), 49–72.

Huffer, L. (2010). *Mad for Foucault: Rethinking the foundations of queer theory.* New York: Columbia University Press.

Jefferson, T. (1994). Theorising masculine subjectivity. In T. Newburn & E. A. Stanko (Eds.), *Just boys doing business? Men, masculinities and crime* (pp. 10–31). London: Routledge.

Kimmel, M. S. (1993). Sexual balkanization: Gender and sexuality as the new ethnicities. *Social Research, 60*(3), 571–587.

Kulick, D. (2006). Ensamhetens gränser: Onani och socialitet. In M. Karlsson & S. Rider (Eds.), *Den moderna ensamheten* (pp. 69–92). Stockholm/Stehag: Brutus Östlings bokförlag Symposion.

Laqueur, T. (2004). *Solitary sex: Cultural history of masturbation.* New York: Zone Books.

Marcuse, H. (1955/1965). *Eros and civilization: A philosophical inquiry into Freud.* Boston, MA: Beacon Press.

McCormack, M. (2013). *The declining significance of homophobia: How teenage boys are redefining masculinity and heterosexuality.* Oxford: Oxford University Press.

Milani, T. (2014). Queering masculinities. In S. Ehrlich, M. Meyerhoff & J. Holmes (Eds.), *The handbook of language, gender, and sexuality* (pp. 260–278). Malden, MA: Wiley-Blackwell.

Moi, T. (1985). Power, sex and subjectivity: Feminist reflections on Foucault. *Paragraph: The Journal of the Modern Critical Theory, 8*(5), 95–102.

Mutluer, N. (2011). Disposable masculinities in Istanbul. In R. L. Jackson & M. Balaji (Eds.), *Global masculinities and manhood* (pp. 74–105). Urbana: University of Illinois Press.

Pease, B. (2000). *Recreating men: Postmodern masculinity politics.* London: Sage.

Pringle, R. (2005). Masculinities, sport, and power: A critical comparison of Gramscian and Foucauldian inspired theoretical tools. *Journal of Sport and Social Issues, 29*(3), 256–278.

Ramazanoğlu, C. (Ed.). (1993). *Up against Foucault: Explorations of some tensions between Foucault and feminism.* London: Routledge.

Reeser, T. W., & Seifert, L. C. (2008). Introduction: Marking French and francophone masculinities. In T. W. Reeser & L. C. Seifert (Eds.), *Entre Hommes: French and francophone masculinities in culture and theory* (pp. 13–50). Cranbury, NJ: Associated University Press.

Repo, J. (2016). *The biopolitics of gender.* Oxford: Oxford University Press.

Schor, N. (1987). Dreaming dissymmetry: Barthes, Foucault, and sexual difference. In A. Jardine & P. Smith (Eds.), *Men in feminism* (pp. 98–110). New York: Routledge.

Seidler, V. J. (1987). Reason, desire, and male sexuality. In P. Caplan (Ed.), *The cultural construction of sexuality* (pp. 82–112). London: Tavistock.

Taylor, D., & Vintges, K. (Eds.). (2004). *Feminism and the final Foucault.* Urbana, IL: University of Illinois Press.

Turner, W. B. (2000). *A genealogy of queer theory.* Philadelphia, PA: Temple University Press.

Wetherell, M., & Edley, N. (1999). Negotiating hegemonic masculinity: Imaginary positions and psycho-discursive practices. *Feminism & Psychology, 9*(3), 335–356.

6

Queer theory and critical masculinity studies

Jonathan A. Allan

In his book *Men of the World*, Jeff Hearn, one of the architects of critical studies of men and masculinities, has defined a series of requirements that are, to his mind, essential to the critical study of men and masculinities. He writes:

> First, these studies, by recognizing men and masculinities as *explicitly gendered* rather than non-gendered, emphasize men's relations, albeit differently to *gendered power*. They have entailed a *specific* rather than an implicit or incidental, *focus* on the topic of men and masculinities, informed by *feminist, gay, queer and other critical gender scholarship*. Men and masculinities are understood as *socially constructed, produced, and reproduced* rather than as somehow just "naturally" one way or another; as *variable and changing* across time (history) and space (culture), within societies, and through life courses and biographies, spanning both the *material and the discursive* in analysis; and also in terms of the *intersections of gender and gendering with other social divisions*.
>
> *(2015, p. 8, emphasis in original)*

In this chapter, then, I want to take Hearn at his word and to think about the ways in which queer theory in particular can and should inform the critical study of men and masculinities, while also recognizing that "critical studies of men need to be carefully monitored—to avoid creating a new power base for men, and a new way of ignoring or forgetting women, feminist work and gendered power relations between men and women" (2013, p. 35).

From the outset, I think it is important to recognize that queer theory is quite different from gay theory or gay studies. Queer theory is less about an identity politic, though "queer" has become an identity politic, and more about considering "the open mesh of possibilities, gaps, overlaps, dissonances and resonances, lapses and excesses of meaning when the constituent elements of anyone's gender, of anyone's sexuality aren't made (or can't be made) to signify monolithically," to borrow the words of Sedgwick (1993, p. 8). In this rendering, then, queer theory is not wholly invested in "gay" as an identity, nor is it doing the work of "gay studies," which might work to see the gayness of a given thing or person, or work to reclaim gay histories. To be certain, queer theory benefits from the work of gay studies, but queer theory has a different agenda. Queer theory, in the words of Annamarie Jagose,

> focuses on mismatches between sex, gender and desire. For most, queer has been prominently associated with those who identify as lesbian and gay. Unknown to many, queer is in association with more than just gay and lesbian, but also cross-dressing, hermaphroditism, gender ambiguity and gender-corrective surgery.
>
> *(1996, p. 3)*

Queer theory, thus, recognizes the complexities of an intersection that accounts for gender, sex, and desire. Queer theory plays and embraces the messiness of complexity. Finally, for someone like David M. Halperin,

> queer is by definition whatever is at odds with the normal, the legitimate, the dominant. There is nothing particular to which it necessarily refers. It is an identity without an essence. "Queer" then, demarcates not a positivity, but a positionality vis-à-vis the normative.
>
> *(1995, p. 13)*

These definitions, thus, while articulating different concerns, highlight some of the elements of queer theory. Queer theory is, in a sense, oppositional insofar as it situates itself outside of the normative. Moreover, queer theory is not interested in *just* gay (and lesbian) identity politics but, rather, expands its analysis to include nearly every manifestation of sex, gender, and sexuality that imagines itself (or is imagined) to be outside of the normative.

Each of the above definitions might be considered "early" definitions insofar as they were published during the rise of queer theory. Recently, Donald E. Hall and Annamarie Jagose, in their introduction to *The Routledge Queer Studies Reader*, write,

> While arguing for the validity and significance of various marginalized sexual identities and practices—such as barebacking, bisexuality, intersex and transgender subjects, public sex cultures, pornography and sadomasochism—queer studies attempts to clear a space for thinking differently about the relations presumed to pertain between sex/gender and sex/sexuality, between sexual identities and erotic behaviors, between practices of pleasure and systems of sexual knowledge.
>
> *(2013, p. xvi)*

This definition, written in 2013, has the advantage of looking back upon the brief history of queer theory, while the earlier definitions from Halperin (1995), Sedgwick (1985), and Jagose (1996) were all written while queer theory was still being articulated and crafted in the 1990s. As such, we can see a fairly consistent interest in the so-called "non-normative," as well as shifts in critical interests between, say, the theoretical and the practical. For instance, it is one thing to speak about sexual knowledge and quite another to speak about sexual practices. In many ways, these definitions all speak implicitly, if not directly, to the study of men and masculinities. What have we not addressed in our studies because we have not been focused on "the open mesh of possibilities"; what are the "gaps" in knowledge? Indeed, this might well serve as an interesting and important methodological challenge to the field. What are we not talking about and for what reasons are we not talking about a given identity, practice, or desire?

Queer theory and critical studies of men and masculinities

As a theoretical paradigm, queer theory is, like the study of men and masculinities, about thirty years old. In 1985, for instance, we see the advent of "hegemonic masculinity" as theoretical concept articulated by Carrigan, Connell, and Lee (1985) in their agenda-setting "Toward a New Sociology of Masculinity," but, in that same year, we see the publication of Eve Kosofsky Sedgwick's equally influential and agenda-setting book *Between Men: English Literature and Male Homosocial Desire*. Looking back, today, both "hegemonic masculinity" and "homosocial desire" seem like some of the central concepts that we use without blinking, as if we already understand them, and yet they both have a particular history attached to their own theoretical alignments. There are, of course, other examples. Both *GLQ* and *Journal of Men's Studies*, two important publications, both with the goal of outlining the field, begin publishing in 1992–1993. Queer theory and studies of men and masculinities, therefore, have a history that is written alongside one another and yet, at times, a history that is seemingly written in isolation.

Queer theory, thus, is an important intervention in the field because it might allow for critical studies of men and masculinities to focus on the unsaid, the non-normative, and the complexity and messiness of desire. There are any number of works that could prove interesting to the study of men and masculinities, for instance, Judith Halberstam's agenda-setting *Female Masculinity* (1998) taught scholars of men and masculinities that perhaps the most interesting site of analysis is not men but, rather, women in a study of masculinity. Halberstam explains, "I want to look in an extended way at what happens when academic discussions of male masculinity take place to the exclusion of discussions of more wide-ranging masculinities" (1998, p. 15). What is so central and so important to Halberstam's work, then, is a recognition that "we seem to have a difficult time defining masculinity" even though,

> we as a society have little trouble in recognizing it, and indeed we spend massive amounts of time and money ratifying and supporting the versions of masculinity that we enjoy and trust.
>
> *(1998, p. 1).*

But, when confronted by "more wide-ranging masculinities," we seem to become confounded, especially when that masculinity is female masculinity, which is "far from being an imitation of maleness"; instead, "female masculinity actually affords us a glimpse of how masculinity is constructed as masculinity" (Halberstam 1998, p. 1). Halberstam argues, and in important ways, that "masculinity [...] becomes legible as masculinity where and when it leaves the white male middle-class body" (1998, p. 2). While those in the field of critical studies of men and masculinities might rebel against such a definition, let us recall the oft-cited definition of masculinity provided by Erving Goffman, and one which, if we are honest, continues to inform the field:

> In an important sense, there is only one complete unblushing male in America: a young, married, white, urban, northern, heterosexual, Protestant, father, of college education, fully employed, of good complexion, weight, and height, and a recent record in sports ... Any male who fails to qualify in any one of these ways is likely to view himself—during moments at least—as unworthy, incomplete, and inferior.
>
> *(1963, p. 128)*

Halberstam, thus, insisted that the study of masculinity move beyond its "canonical" definition and work to consider minority masculinities or rather, the masculinities contained within "the open mesh of possibilities" (Sedgwick 1993, p. 8).

Queer/ing method

Beyond the theoretical task of *Female Masculinity*, Halberstam also proposes an important methodological challenge. Too often, disciplinary studies have resided within the limits, borders, and comforts of its disciplinary traditions; as such, various cultural practices and texts have remained unstudied. Halberstam, thus, establishes a "queer methodology" which is defined as follows:

> A queer methodology, in a way, is a scavenger methodology that uses different methods to collect and produce information on subjects who have been deliberately or accidentally excluded from traditional studies of human behavior. The queer methodology attempts to combine methods that are often case as being at odds with each other, and it refuses the academic compulsion towards disciplinary coherence. Although this book [*Female Masculinity*] will be immediately recognizable as a work of cultural studies, it will not shy away from more empirical methods associated with ethnographic research.
>
> *(1998, p. 13)*

This "queer methodology" thus challenges the limits of discipline, which have, for too long, limited the kinds of studies that could be completed. Critical studies of men and masculinities, as Hearn noted, is inherently interdisciplinary, but we would do well to reflect on which disciplines we most easily draw from and which ones prove more difficult. The reasons may be merely personal, or they may be significantly more ideological and political. This queer methodology has a long and important history that continues to inform and shape debates in queer theory today. For example, Juana Maria Rodriguez's recent work adopts a similar methodology. Rodriguez argues that "traditional disciplinary boundaries become inadequate containers for subjects whose lives and utterances traverse the categories meant to contain them" (2014, p. 31). As such, when critical studies of men and masculinities contends that it is inherently interdisciplinary, it must stop and reflect upon what it means by interdisciplinary. Would our studies align with Halberstam's methodology, or would we more likely find a continued interest in and reliance upon empirical research methods?

Indeed, perhaps one of the most interesting and important interventions in queer theory has been to consider the role of the scholar-as-theorist-as-subject. This is a shift in method because it recognizes the importance of the subject completing the study, but this is not necessarily the same as autoethnography. One of the most striking examples of this may well be Tim Dean's *Unlimited Intimacy: Reflections on the Subculture of Barebacking* (2009), in which Dean positions himself as a theorist of barebacking, as well as a barebacker himself, thus braiding together the "practices of pleasure and the systems of sexual knowledge" (Hall & Jagose 2013, p. xvi). Dean's work has had a significant influence on queer theory, particularly in thinking about the relationship between theorist and sexual subject, a task that has been admirably taken up by other scholars: for instance, Mimi Schippers's recent book, *Beyond Monogamy: Polyamory and the Future of Polyqueer Sexualities* (2016). In these books, the authors are able not only to draw on a theoretical paradigm to explore practices and knowledge but also to shift the narrative surrounding empiricism and method. What might it mean to situate oneself as both the object and subject of study? Such an approach, particularly for the critical study of men and masculinities, might well prove instrumental in thinking about the position of the scholar. Hearn, for instance, has certainly tried to do some of this in his own work when reflecting on his sexuality, but unlike Schippers and Dean, for instance, he has not produced a monograph on the subject. Michael Kimmel (2001), likewise, did this in his article on deciding whether or not to circumcise his son. But neither of these scholars are actively thinking about queering the methods they use. Rather they frame these episodes as anecdotes or starting points for larger and more complicated studies. Dean, by way of contrast, is as interested in his own sexual practices as he is in the discourse surrounding barebacking. For Schippers, we see a braiding together of the polyamorous lifestyle with theory and method (recalling here, once more, Halberstam's *Female Masculinity*); for instance, she develops a "polyqueer" method, which is about the "refusal to commit [one]self to one and only one theory or methodology, and as is the case with polyamorous relationships, each perspective, theory, and method brings something unique and essential to the table" (2016, p. 28). A queer approach, then, to the study of men and masculinities might well ask how we might queer not only masculinities but also the methods that are central to how the field operates.

Queer theory and men's sexualities

In recent years, we have witnessed a sustained interest in the queerness of men's sexualities, including heterosexual men. Jane Ward's provocative *Not Gay: Sex Between Straight White Men* (2015), explores what Diamond (2008) understands as "sexual fluidity." Discussions of sexual fluidity have long focused on women's sexuality, but we are witnessing a shift in the discourse to consider men. Of course, men's sexual fluidity should not come as a surprise; after all, the *Kinsey Reports* demonstrated this:

> Homosexual activity in the human male is much more frequent than is ordinarily recognized. In the youngest unmarried group, more than a quarter of the males have some homosexual activity to the point of orgasm. The incidence among these single males rises in successive age groups until it reaches a maximum of 38.7 per cent between 36 and 40 years of age.
>
> *(Kinsey, Pomeroy, & Martin, 1948, p. 259)*

What is perhaps new in Ward's work is the braiding together of queer theory, sexuality studies, and critical studies of men and masculinities, and in so doing, Ward seeks to understand and explore the complexity of not just sexual identities but also sexual practices. In her work, Ward argues that,

> To the extent that sexual contact between straight white men is ever acknowledged, the cultural narratives that circulate around these practices typically suggest that they are *not gay* in their identitarian consequences, but are instead about building heterosexual men, strengthening hetero-masculine bonds, and strengthening the bonds of white manhood in particular.
>
> *(2015, p. 4)*

Ward then argues that her

> aim is to offer a new way to think about heterosexual subjectivity—not as the opposite or absence of homosexuality, but as its own unique mode of engaging homosexual sex, a mode characterized by pretense, disidentification, and heteronormative investments. In particular, I am going to argue that when straight white men approach homosexual sex in the right way—when they make a show of enduring it, imposing it, and repudiating it—doing so functions to bolster not only their heterosexuality, but also their masculinity and whiteness.
>
> *(2015, p. 5)*

In this way, Ward moves beyond the identity politics of, say, gay studies and embraces a queerer reading of straight men's sexualities, which may and often do act out, it would seem, sex acts that are read as gay. The data that she draws upon are empirical not in the sense of ethnography but, rather, in the sense outlined by Halberstam. Ward draws on a range of cultural texts and examples, including "saloons and tenement houses, to military barracks and fraternity clubs, and to truckstops and bathrooms" (2015, p. 47) as well as film, including a close reading of *Humpday*, through to internet pornographies that draw on hazing rituals.

In many ways, Ward's work can be read as a queer reading of Eric Anderson's work and the larger school of Inclusive Masculinity Theory, of which Anderson is chief architect. Ward describes Anderson's work as "a goldmine of information about straight male college athletes kissing, taking 'body shots' off of one another, and 'jacking each other off' during threesomes with girls and teammates" (2015, p. 13). Anderson's work has worked to demonstrate that British culture in particular, as well as American culture (the sites of his fieldwork) are undergoing a process in which homophobia is becoming less and less present, and with this we are witnessing a loosening of restrictions on how men can be men, that is, men can now, for instance, "cuddle and spoon" one another (Anderson & McCormack 2015) without fears of being homosexualized by a homophobic culture. Inclusive masculinity theory, as an approach, does not extend beyond sociological research that is ethnographic in nature, that is, its methods and theoretical claims have not been applied beyond sociology, for instance in historical studies, literary studies, or cultural studies. As such, inclusive masculinity theory poses two potential challenges: firstly, it is entirely committed to sociology; and secondly, while everything may appear queer, Anderson and the IMT school more broadly have yet to draw on queer theory to analyze and understand the sexualities under consideration. If cultures are becoming less homophobic, what then can be said of queer theory (and its role)?

Queer theory's language trouble

Queer theory, of course, is not without its critics. One of the most persistent critiques of queer theory, especially from those outside of the humanities, has been its impenetrability. Anderson, for example, has been highly critical of this aspect of queer theory (and post-structuralism) in his work. For example,

> … when I discuss poststructural concepts, I avoid the language in which most poststructuralists frame their ideas. This is because much of poststructuralist thought comes in extremely inaccessibility [*sic*] writing. [Judith] Butler (1990), for example, is so inaccessible that she commits a violent, shameful act of academic exclusion. Furthermore, post-structural inaccessibility often leads scholars to differently interpret what the author means, like preachers arguing over varying interpretations of biblical passages.
>
> *(Anderson 2009, p. 33)*

While it might be easy to sympathize with Anderson's critique of Butler, we need to be careful not to commit our own acts of violence by avoiding precise language. Butler is using precise and specific language intentionally. However, Anderson is not alone. Mark McCormack echoes Anderson's thoughts, speaking of *Gender Trouble* as "impenetrable" and describing her prose as "ponderous and elitist writing" (2012, p. 9). Of course, one is tempted to ask: why is this critique so often levelled against the humanities and social sciences, but not the pure sciences, which have developed their own disciplinary languages that may just as well be inaccessible to the lay reader? Accordingly, and importantly, we must recognize that queer theory has been critiqued for its inaccessibility, particularly at the level of prose. However, I would suggest that we have witnessed significant changes in style over the decades, because we have seen a "fine-tuning" of the theory.

Expanding the scope of analysis

While a critique of the language of queer theory is important, the stronger and perhaps more interesting critiques have been about its own claims to inclusion (a similar critique, it must be admitted, could be extended to inclusive masculinity theory). What does it mean, for instance, that queer theory is so remarkably white? This debate reached its climax at the Gay Shame Conference held at University of Michigan and organized by David M. Halperin and Valerie Traub, which in the words of David L. Eng, Judith Halberstam, and José Esteban Muñoz "was a conference that included only one queer person of color out of forty invited participants" (2005, p. 12). In "Shame and White Gay Masculinity," Halberstam begins by boldly declaring that

> the more I thought about the conference and its theme, the more I became convinced that gay shame, if used in an uncritical way, was for, by, and about the white gay men who had rejected feminism and a queer of color critique and for whom, therefore, shame was still an active rubric of identification.
>
> *(2005, p. 219)*

For Halberstam, the turn to "gay shame" was very much about a shame afforded to white gay men, and Halberstam cautiously warns that "if queer studies is to survive gay shame, and it will, we all need to move far beyond the limited scope of white gay male concerns and interests" (2005, p. 231). Hiram Perez, who was "the only invited queer person of color present" at the Gay Shame conference (Perez 2005, p. 171), argues that "queer theorizing more resolutely needs to investigate how dominant Euro-American formations of gay, lesbian, and queer cultures (not only during this era of normalization but also historically) collude with hegemonic white masculinity" (p. 179).

Queer theorists have responded to this "lack" at the Gay Shame conference and have produced a stunning body of work on queer of color critique (Ferguson 2003). *Gay Latino Studies: A Critical Reader*, for example, provides another explicit and implicit critique of the Gay Shame conference by focusing on latino studies. At the Gay Shame conference, one of the most problematic moments occurred when Ellis Hanson presented a lecture with a stream of photographs taken from the pornographic magazine *Latin Inches*, which seemingly had nothing to do with the lecture, as noted by Halberstam and Perez. This volume includes numerous chapters that ask about the state of race in queer theory, recognizing that "despite the failure of so many canonical works in queer theory to live up to their own promises to address race complexly, queer theory clearly offers something useful to theorists, as it has continued to entrench itself in the academy," which leads Michael Hames-García to "suspect that the success of queer theory actually has much to do with that failure" (2001, pp. 32–33). *Gay Latino Studies* is a significant intervention that critiques queer theory for its failures to engage with questions of race, but it does so in a way that works to challenge queer theory, to make queer theory better.

Certainly, *Gay Latino Studies* is one volume of many that explores race, as Hames-García explains that a

> ... virtual renaissance of what Roderick Ferguson calls "queer of color critique" has emerged. Any list would inevitably be incomplete but would likely include José Esteban Muñoz's *Disidentifications* (1999), José Quiroga's *Tropics of Desire* (2000), David Eng's *Racial Castration* (2001), Linda Garber's *Identity Poetics* (2001), Robert Reid-Pharr's *Black Gay Man* (2001), Ann Stoler's *Carnal Knowledge* (2002), María Lugones *Pilgrimages/Peregrinajes* (2003), Martin Manalasan's *Global Divas* (2003), Juana María Rodríguez's *Queer Latinidad* (2003), Ferguson's *Aberrations in Black* (2004), M. Jacqui Alexander's *Pedagogies of Crossing* (2005), Gayatri Gopinaths's *Impossible Desires* (2005), Dwing McBride's *Why I hate Abercrombie and Fitch* (2005), Catriona Rueda Esquibel's *With Her Machete in her Hand* (2006), and collections like David Eng's and Alice Hom's *Q & A: Queer in Asian America* (1998), Arnaldo Cruz-Malavé's and Martin Manalansan's *Queer Globalizations* (2002), and E. Patrick Johnson's and Mae G. Henderson's *Black Queer Studies* (2005).
>
> *(2001, p. 37)*

These works were all published between 1998 and 2006, and since that time we have witnessed a plethora of works that have helped to shape and reform the debates unfolding in queer theory and that have done the work of engaging with questions of race. Recent work of particular interest to scholars of men and masculinities, might include *Brown Boys and Rice Queens: Spellbinding Performance in the Asias* by Eng-Beng Lim (2013), Jeffrey Q. McCune's *Sexual Discretion: Black Masculinity and the Politics of Passing* (2014), *Queer Masculinities in Contemporary Latin American Cinema: Male Bodies and Narrative Representations* by Gustavo Subero (2014), *A View from the Bottom: Asian American Masculinity and Sexual Representation* by Tan Hoang Nguyen (2014), C. Riley Snorton's *Nobody is Supposed to Know: Black Sexuality on the Down Low* (2014), *Geisha of a Different Kind: Race and Sexuality in Gaysian America* by C. Winter Han (2015), in addition to new anthologies such as *Blacktino Queer Performance*, edited by E. Patrick Johnson and Ramón H. Rivera-Servera (2016), *No Tea, No Shade: New Writings on Black Queer Studies* edited by E. Patrick Johnson (2016), and *Queer Indigenous Studies: Critical Interpretations in Theory, Politics, and Literature*, edited by Qwo-Li Driskill, Chris Finley, Brian Joseph Gilley, and Scott Laurie Morgenson (2011).

Queer theory has continued to expand its reach; for instance, one noteworthy title is *Fat Gay Men: Girth, Mirth, and the Politics of Stigma* (2014) by Jason Whitesel, which turns our attention to the intersection of fat studies and queer theory. In this work, we find an exploration of body politics, a critique of body fascism, and a new set of questions about the desirable and sexual body. Queer theory has also sought to explore ability, particularly by way of "crip theory," as outlined in *Crip Theory: Cultural Signs of Queerness and Disability* (2006) by Robert McRuer, as well as the collection *Sex and Disability* (2012) edited by Robert McRuer and Anna Mollow. Needless to say, queer theory has, in some ways, responded to the critiques of the Gay Shame conference and started to explore the diversity of queerness, which extends well beyond the whiteness which was—and continues to be—so central to its articulation.

Global queer theory

Queer theory, moreover, has influenced debates globally. Queer approaches are at the heart of anthologies like the *Queer African Reader*, edited by Sokari Ekine and Hakima Abbas (2013). Likewise, though more explicitly concerned with sexuality, *African Sexualities: A Reader*, edited by Sylvia Tamale (2015), provides an extensive view of how queer, as well as other gender, approaches might inform the study of sexualities in Africa. Scholars have also applied queer theoretical models to questions of development in the Global South, for instance, *Women, Sexuality, and the Politics of Pleasure* (2013), edited by Susie Jolly, Andrea Cornwall, and Kate Hawkins, asks what it might mean to consider and understand how women's sexual desires play out in development (similar questions can certainly be asked of a range of identities).

Queer theory has been of interest to scholars working in Latin American studies as well. For instance, queer approaches have had a significant influence on discussions of colonization, particularly with regard to the intersection of sexualities and colonialism. Michael J. Horswell's *Decolonizing the Sodomite: Queer Tropes of Sexuality in Colonial Andean Culture* (2005), and Pete Sigal's *Infamous Desire: Male Homosexuality in Colonial Latin America* (2003) build on the legacy of Richard Trexler's *Sex and Conquest* (1995). These works explicitly consider the role and place of queer sexualities and identities in the colonization of Latin America. Recently, Zed Tortorici has organized an edited collection called *Sexuality and the Unnatural in Colonial Latin America* (2016), which sought to expand the archive of materials. Scholars working on contemporary Latin America have drawn on queer theory to interpret literary and cultural texts, such as David William Foster's pioneering work on queering Latin American literature and culture—*El ambiente nuestro: Chicano/Latino homoerotic writing* (2006), *Sexual Textualities: Essays on Queer/ing Latin American Writing* (1997), and *Argentine, Mexican and Guatemalan Photography: Feminist, Queer, and Post-Masculinist Perspectives* (2014)—through to Daniel Balderston's *El deseo enorme cicatriz luminosa: Ensayos sobre homosexualidades latinoamericanas* (2004) and José Quiroga's *Tropics of Desire: Interventions from Queer Latino America* (2000).

Conclusion

Queer theory, in spite of its imperfections, remains an important avenue for scholars of men and masculinities precisely because it affords a way of looking at gender and sexuality, particularly the "gaps" in knowledge, the things about which we choose not to speak, or do not speak about. For instance, how might we theorize and think through sexual practices like barebacking, public sex, sex between straight white men, or celibacy. All of these practices confound the expectations of critical studies of men and masculinities because they highlight the slipperiness of gender and sexuality, and yet have been very influential in queer theory. We often think we know a lot about men's sexuality, but what do we really know? How are we studying and engaging with men's experiences of sexuality? Queer theory may well afford a different way of answering that kind of a question. Queer theory offers us much when we think about the nature of patriarchy, especially in light of theories about inclusive masculinity. We can recall Sedgwick's discussion of patriarchy in *Between Men*—how does inclusive masculinity augment patriarchy? If the men are "inclusive," is that good enough?

To conclude, as should be evident, queer theory remains a theoretically rich way to explore the complexities of men and masculinities precisely because it moves the discussion away from the "hegemonic" and towards alternative practices, identities, and desires inherent to men and masculinities. Masculinities are not static, and to study the fluidity of masculinities requires a theoretical perspective that relishes the slipperiness of identity. Moreover, queer theory provides interesting and important challenges to methods and methodology. So much work in critical studies of men and masculinities is oriented towards empiricism and the human subject, but what of representations of masculinities? What about the role of the scholar as subject of research? And what about methods that defy the demands of disciplinary monogamy? Queer theory, I believe, affords important ways to reconceive of the field of critical studies of men and masculinities precisely because it calls into question the normative.

References

Anderson, E. (2009). *Inclusive masculinity: The changing nature of masculinities*. New York: Routledge.

Anderson, E., & McCormack, M. (2015). Cuddling and spooning: Heteromasculinity and homosocial tactility among student-athletes. *Men and Masculinities, 18*(2), 214–230.

Carrigan, T., Connell, B., & Lee, J. (1985). Toward a new sociology of masculinity. *Theory and Society, 14*(5), 551–604.

Dean, T. (2009). *Unlimited intimacy: Reflections on the subculture of barebacking*. Chicago, IL: University of Chicago Press.

Diamond, L. (2008). *Sexual fluidity : Understanding women's love and desire*. Cambridge, MA: Harvard University Press.

Eng, D. L., Halberstam, J., & Muñoz, J. E. (2005). What's queer about queer studies now? *Social Text, 23*(3/4)(84/85), 1–17.

Ferguson, R. A. (2003). *Aberrations in black: Towards a queer of color critique*. Minneapolis, MN: University of Minnesota Press.

Goffman, E. (1963). *Stigma*. Englewood Cliffs, NJ: Prentice Hall.

Halberstam, J. (1998). *Female masculinity*. Durham, NC: Duke University Press.

Halberstam, J. (2005). Shame and white gay masculinity. *Social Text, 23*(3–4)(84–85), 219–233.

Hall, D. E., & Jagose, A. (2013). Introduction. In D. E. Hall, A. Jagose, A. Bebell & S. Potter (eds.), *The Routledge queer studies reader* (pp. xiv–xx). New York: Routledge.

Halperin, D. M. (1995). *Saint Foucault: Towards a gay hagiography*. New York: Oxford University Press.

Hames-García, M. (2001). Queer theory revisited. In M. Hames-García & E. J. Martínez (eds.), *Gay Latino studies: A critical reader* (pp. 19–45). Durham, NC: Duke University Press.

Hearn, J. (2013). Methods and methodologies in critical studies of men and masculinities. In B. Pini & B. Pease (eds.), *Men, masculinities and methodologies* (pp. 26–38). London: Palgrave Macmillan.

Hearn, J. (2015). *Men of the world: Gender, globalizations, transnational times*. London: Sage.

Jagose, A. (1996). *Queer theory: An introduction*. New York: New York University Press.

Kimmel, M. (2001). The kindest uncut: Judaism, feminism, and my son's foreskin. *Tikkun, 16*(3), 43–48.

Kinsey, A. C., Pomeroy, W. B., & Martin, C. E. (1948). *Sexual behavior in the human male*. Bloomington, IN: Indiana University Press.

McCormack, M. (2012). *The declining significance of homophobia: How teenage boys are redefining masculinity and heterosexuality*. Oxford: Oxford University Press.

McRuer, R. (2006). *Crip theory: Cultural signs of queerness and disability*. Durham, NC: Duke University Press.

McRuer, R., & Mollow, A. (Eds.). (2012). *Sex and disability*. Durham, NC: Duke University Press.

Perez, H. (2005). You can have my brown body and eat it, too! *Social Text, 23*(3/4)(84/85), 171–191.

Rodriguez, J. M. (2014). *Sexual futures, queer gestures, and other Latina longings*. New York: New York University Press.

Schippers, M. (2016). *Beyond monogamy: Polyamory and the future of polyqueer sexualities*. New York: New York University Press.

Sedgwick, E. K. (1985). *Between men: English literature and male homosocial desire*. New York: Columbia University Press.

Sedgwick, E. K. (1993). Queer and now. In E. K. Sedgwick, *Tendencies* (pp. 1–20). Durham, NC: Duke University Press.

Ward, J. (2015). *Not gay: Sex between straight white men*. New York: New York University Press.

Whitesel, J. (2014). *Fat gay men: Girth, mirth, and the politics of stigma*. New York: New York University Press.

7

Intersectionality

Ann-Dorte Christensen and Sune Qvotrup Jensen

During the last three decades, intersectionality has had a huge influence on gender studies as a way to conceptualize and analyze structural inequalities, their multifaceted interrelations, as well as how the interplay between these structural inequalities influences people's everyday llives The number of journal articles and special issues from different parts of academia is one indicator of this so-called institutionalization of intersectionality. Intersectionality thus has been one of the most applied approaches among researchers within women's studies, cultural studies, and other interdisciplinary fields (Cho, Crenshaw, & McCall 2013; Collins 2015; Collins & Bilge 2016; Davis & Zarkov 2017; Grib & Strid 2017). In comparison, the influence of intersectionality on studies of men and masculinity has been limited. There have been no special issues and only a few titles in the leading journals within men and masculinity studies from 2007 to 2017 that include "intersectionality".

Despite the limited application to the field, intersectionality is in our view highly relevant to studies of men and masculinity. The research field for many years has had an interest in differences between men and between masculinities, oftentimes in a power perspective. The most widespread example is R.W. Connell's concept of hegemonic masculinity and the well-known distinction between *hegemonic, complicit, subordinate,* and *marginalized masculinities* (Connell 1995; Connell & Messerschmidt 2005; see also Beasley, this volume). Other examples are Wetherell and Edley's (1999) theoretical discussion of *a multiplicity of masculinities* constructed through complex, contradictory, and ambiguous processes, Anderson's use of the concept *inclusive masculinities* (2008, 2009), Bridges and Pascoe's (2014) use of the concept *hybrid masculinities*, and Messerschmidt's (2014) distinction between *hegemonic, dominant, and dominating* masculinities. Studies of men and masculinity thus share an interest in describing and explaining differences between men and between masculinities, including the social processes that shape these differences and their connections to other forms of social differentiation such as class, ethnicity, race, or sexuality. The field, however, lacks theoretical tools that can facilitate such analysis.

Intersectionality can fill this gap as it offers a well-established analytical tool suited for grasping differences among and between men, and – perhaps most importantly – how other social differences play a role in the processes that shape and condition masculinities, i.e., the ambiguities, complexities, and differences in power relations related to men and masculinities. Admittedly, some studies of men and masculinities do exist that are either implicitly (such as Frosh, Phoenix, & Pattman 2002; Ratele 2014) or explicitly (such as Staunæs 2003) intersectional.[1] Nevertheless, the potential remains unfulfilled.

In this chapter, we introduce intersectionality and provide arguments for its analytical potential for the study of men and masculinities. The chapter consists of three parts. The first part presents the history, reception, and implications of intersectionality. In the second part, we present seven basic principles and challenges of intersectional research. In order to illustrate some of the principles and challenges in relation to masculinity studies, we outline two concrete examples of intersectional analysis in the third part. Finally, in the conclusion we sum up why masculinity research could benefit from a stronger focus on intersectionality.

Intersectionality: history, reception and implications

The fundamental principle of the concept of intersectionality stresses the interaction between social categories such as gender, race/ethnicity, class, age, and sexuality (Crenshaw 1989, 1991). The term is derived from the common US English phrase "intersection" meaning *crossroads*. It has been emphasized that intersectionality has a long history related to both social movement activism in the 1960s and 1970s and academic analyses of the interplay between race, class, and gender in the US (Anthias & Yuval-Davies 1983; Collins 1989; Combahee River Collective 1977/1983; hooks 1989).

To some extent it nevertheless makes sense to argue that this mode of analysis remained unnamed until 1989, when the term "intersectionality" was coined by Kimberle Crenshaw, who in the reception has become "intersectionality's foremother" (Crenshaw 1989, 1991). It is important to emphasize that intersectional thinking predates the actual coining of the term and has its primary historical roots in US Black Feminism (Collins 2015; Collins & Bilge 2016). Intersectional thinking thus originated among black feminists in the US who put their particular situation in relation to gender and race at the analytical centre in order to challenge white middle-class women's dominance in the women's movement and black men's dominance in antiracist organizations (Collins 1993, 1998; Crenshaw 1989, 1991). The concept shares some similarities with the notion of *triple oppression*, which has been central to third-world postcolonial feminists' analyses of the combined impact of class dominance, male dominance, and racial dominance on the lives of black working-class women since the 1970s (Hendricks & Lewis 1994). This notion, however, has had relatively little influence on contemporary gender studies in the global North, illustrating that feminist theory has flowed easily from North to South or from West to East, whereas flows in other directions practically are sparse (Dongchao 2005, 2011; see also Connell 2007). It is important to acknowledge the role and inspiration of postcolonial feminist theory in the roots of intersectional thinking. But as stated by Kerner (2017), there not only is a significant overlap but also are important divergences between the two fields, because the postcolonial feminism approach to multiple inequalities is transnational and framed within North–South power relations and asymmetries (see also Mohanty 2003; Ozkazanc-Pan 2012).

Since its coining, intersectionality has been a rapidly travelling and evolving concept, which has crossed borders, continents, and contexts as well as academic disciplines, subject areas, and feminist positions. Whereas the original American debate put relatively high emphasis on structural power relations, in Europe the concept was developed within the humanities and social sciences, putting more emphasis on everyday practices and complex identities (e.g., Phoenix 2006; Staunæs 2003; Yuval-Davis 2006). In a Scandinavian context, intersectionality has also been applied in a specific critique of the predominant political and academic perspective on inequality as related to class; a perspective which has not been able to address inequalities related to ethnicity and race (de Los Reyes, Molina, & Mulinari 2005).

The travelling process has strengthened dynamism and encouraged creativity and development. But the successful travel has also raised critical questions about what has been labelled as "intersectionality's institutional incorporation" and the loss of radical critical thinking (Collins & Bilge 2016). A related debate has addressed the question of "ownership" and the contested argument that intersectionality's travel, for instance to Europe, has led to losing its origins in US Black Feminism, implying that the specific situation for women of colour has once again disappeared. As stated by Davis and Zakov, it has been "argued that the concept has been 'hijacked' to include everyone, even white heterosexual men" (2017, p. 2).

Although we acknowledge the origins of intersectionality, from our point of view the production of knowledge can never be a question of intellectual ownership. As we will return to below, bringing men and masculinity into the analytical lens is imperative if one believes that intersectionality is a characteristic of the social world rather than merely a characteristic of specific less privileged groups (Choo & Ferree 2010; Hancock 2007a, 2007b). It can furthermore be argued that the success and spread of intersectionality constitute an unprecedented acknowledgement of the intellectual strength and broader relevance of black feminist thought. In this chapter we thus encourage even further travel of intersectionality, this time to the field of men and masculinities studies which oftentimes – but not always – happens to include white heterosexual men.

Intersectionality is an open-ended and sensitizing, perhaps in some sense even incomplete, concept. According to Davis and Zarkov (2017), the conceptual openness is one of the advantages of intersectionality (see also Davis 2008). Several scholars have noted that there has always been considerable confusion about what intersectionality actually means and whether it is a theory, a concept, an approach, a methodology, or even a paradigm (Davis 2008; McCall 2005; Phoenix & Pattynama 2006). In the same vein, Collins recently addressed the definitional dilemmas of intersectionality and emphasized that the goal should not be to construct the one and only definition but more to provide a navigational tool for thinking about intersectionality (2015). Nevertheless, if addressing intersectionality is to be a meaningful endeavour it is necessary to outline some kind of shared minimum theoretical core.

The overall aim of intersectional analysis is to explore intersecting patterns between different structures of power and how people are simultaneously positioned – and position themselves – in multiple categories, such as gender, race/ethnicity, and class (Phoenix 2011; Phoenix & Pattynama 2006; Yuval-Davis 2006). The theoretical core of intersectionality could thus be the assertion that *different social categories mutually constitute each other as overall social structures as well as in creating complex identities.* Social identities are thus complex, multi-dimensional, sometimes contradictory, and conditioned by the way several different categories interact to shape our understanding of ourselves and other people's descriptions of us. The same is true for social forms of differentiation on a systemic, structural, or institutional level. Here it is argued that gender, race/ethnicity, class, etc. can be considered mutually constitutive or interlocking social systems (Andersen 2005). As stated by Collins (1998), "As opposed to examining gender, race, class, and nation, as separate systems of oppression, intersectionality explores how these systems mutually construct one another" (p. 63). On this level, the concept of intersectionality thus contains a theory of institutional interpenetration (Choo & Ferree 2010; Yuval-Davis 2011).

In other words, intersectionality claims that categories are not parallel or static, neither on an identity or everyday level nor on a structural level (Hancock 2007b). Gender, race/ethnicity, class, etc. constitute, construct, and re-construct each other and therefore cannot be analysed separately. Furthermore, this mutual constitution takes place as interplay both between different categories and between different levels of the social – and the interplay may often take paradoxical or contradictory forms.

The paradoxical and contradictory nature of social differentiation has been a crucial point for some observers who have argued that intersectionality is a too structurally biased concept which cannot do justice to contradictions and complexity. Some researchers have thus argued that the concept of *interference* is better suited. Interference refers to the merging of waves, which can be light, sound, or water. The merging can result in higher intensity, but waves can also weaken or cancel each other (Geerts & van der Tuin 2013; Mellström 2015). The argument is that interference to a higher degree than intersectionality opens up the questions of the character of interactions related to how differences are made, interact, and sometimes dissolve each other. In her analysis of the interference between disability, gender, and class, Moser (2006) has convincingly showed how the categories are turned around, showing how disability is sometimes made irrelevant and gender relevant. We acknowledge this critique, but we also think that this way of thinking about social differentiation can be included in intersectionality's core principle of mutual constitution.

What, then, does this principle of mutual constitution imply for studies of men and masculinity? Why is intersectionality important to this field of study? And how can the intersection of different categories be said to shape, form, and (co-)constitute masculinity? An intersectional perspective implies that other categories, such as race/ethnicity, class, age, and sexuality influence and shape masculinities (Choo & Ferree 2010). The meaning, experiences, and power relations related to masculinity thus vary for different ethnic groups, according to class, age, etc.

Consequently, the category of masculinity is unstable and successively altered by the intersection with other categories. As Kofoed (2005) puts it, "categories can exaggerate each other, subvert each other, or even cancel each other" (p. 44, our translation) – what some would refer to as interference. One way to think about this is that race/ethnicity, class, and sexuality can support the dominant position and male privilege of some men because it strengthens the legitimacy of their masculinity. Intersectional analysis may thus provide insight into the complex processes which advance some masculinities to the top of the hierarchy – for instance, by looking at the interplay between masculinity, whiteness, heterosexuality, and class position among the financial business elite. Likewise, masculinity can intersect with other categories in specific configurations that challenge or even subvert male privilege. It can thus be argued that race/ethnicity, class, etc. can weaken or subvert the legitimacy of some men to the extent that they are either unable to gain any form of advantage from being men or can only lay claim to a symbolic or stylistic form of (hyper) masculinity in a social situation where very little else can be claimed. In such situations, masculinity as a symbolic form and a dimension of social identity is often exaggerated, for instance through the interplay with blackness and working-classness (Christensen & Jensen 2014; Christensen & Larsen 2008). In other words, intersectionality can help us to expand our knowledge about masculinity, power, and social differentiation by grasping *both* the processes and interplays that solidify and amplify masculine privilege *and* how being a man can be a category of disempowerment and lack of privilege rather than a privileged position.

Basic principles and challenges of intersectional research

Despite diversity and variation among intersectionality scholars, it is possible to highlight some basic principles and challenges that most scholars in the field would agree are central to intersectional analysis and methodology.

First, most intersectionality scholars would agree on the importance of **multi-level analyses** that link structural differentiations and systems of oppression (Collins 1998, 2015; de

Los Reyes & Mulinari 2005) with the level of formations of complex identities and everyday life. Intersectional analysis thus implies not only an attempt to unravel the interplay of different social categories but also to grasp the interplay between the macro, the meso, and the micro level of the social world (Christensen & Jensen 2012; Winkler & Degele 2011; Yuval-Davis 2006, 2011).

Second, intersectionality is a **process-centred analytical approach** focusing on the meeting and interacting of categories (and not single categories such as, for instance, only gender or only class). For example, Choo and Ferree (2010) have argued for the need to focus on dynamic forces rather than closed and final categories, "racialization more than races, economic exploitation rather than classes, gendering and gender performance rather than genders" (p. 134; cf. Ferree 2011). One way to think of such processes is to emphasize how racialization and social marginalization, for instance, feed into social processes that are formative for specific marginal but expressive masculinities. Discursive and actual hyper-masculinization of minority men is an example of this.

Third, many intersectionality scholars would agree on the necessity of **non-additive analysis** of the interplay between social categories (de la Rey 1997; Staunæs 2003). This implies that it is not possible to simply take the effect of class, then add the effect of ethnicity, gender, etc. The combined effect of a given configuration of social categories is always qualitatively different from just the sum of the effect of each difference. The theoretical argument for this assertion is that since categories are mutually constitutive, there can be no "pure" effect of class, outside of gender and race, that can then be added to the likewise "pure" effect of other categories. In the words of Yuval-Davies "[t]here is no meaning to the notion 'black' for instance, which is not gendered or classed, no meaning to the notion of "women", which is not ethnocized and classed etc." (2007, p. 565).

Fourth, many intersectionality scholars would stress the interplay between **different forms of difference**. Although intersectionality is interested in the interplay and mutually constitutive nature of social categories, it is important to stress that the categories point to forms of social differentiation that are ontologically different and work through different social logics and mechanisms. Some categories are naturalized (people often refer to gender categories, men and woman, in a naturalized and unproblematized way), while others are euphemized or denied (such as the common denial of class even within some strands of contemporary sociology) (Yuval-Davis 2006). Furthermore, social categories are contextualized and may have different meanings according to context. In the US, for instance, race is an official statistical category, whereas in Europe and especially in Germany race is, for historical reasons, a problematic, implicit, and often euphemized category. In the US, class has mostly been used as a descriptive category, whereas European scholars have historically been more influenced by Marxist conceptions of class as a relational concept linked to power and exploitation (Collins 2015; Knapp 2005).

Fifth, some intersectionality scholars would agree with what Staunæs refers to as **the majority-inclusive approach** (2003). Staunæs thus argues that social categories are not minority issues but are, on the contrary, constituted in a relational interplay between minority and majority. In her words "[s]ocial categories do not count only for the Others, the non-powerful and the non-privileged: they also count as conditions for the more privileged and powerful people" (Staunæs 2003, p. 105) In an overlapping argument, Choo and Ferree (2010) emphasize the importance of "studying the unmarked categories where power and privilege 'cluster'" in intersectional studies (p. 133). The majority-inclusive approach provides a strong argument for bringing men, whites, heterosexual, and the middle and upper classes inside the analytical scope of intersectionality: not for the sake of privileging already-privileged groups but in order to investigate how configurations of privilege may strengthen and multiply each other. In other words, this principle runs counter to the argument about "ownership" to intersectionality and that it should focus only on women of colour.

Sixth, intersectionality scholars have to handle the fact that intersectional analysis in principle could include an indefinite number of social differences. It is oftentimes not enough, perhaps not even relevant, to focus on what Davis and Zarkov (2017) refer to as the "Big Three" (gender, race, class). Collins (2015), for instance, mentions "Race, class, gender, sexuality, age, ability, nation, ethnicity, *and similar categories of analysis*" (p. 14, emphasis added). To this list, we might add religion (Nyhagen & Halsaa 2016; Yuval-Davis 2011) and geographical locality (Faber & Nielsen 2016; Pini & Leach 2011; Valentine 2007). The list of categorical differences is in principle permanently open-ended, and researchers always run the risk of being criticized for not including the next category that could have been important. In addition, the relevance of categories might vary depending on context and research theme, but then again, categories that are not explicitly or overtly important may play an important role more implicitly, hence Matsuda's idea of "asking the other question" – i.e., asking about the possible relevance of categories that do not present themselves as obviously relevant (Davis 2008; Matsuda 1991). There is no consensus among intersectionality scholars about how to deal with this challenge of managing complexity. Some scholars maintain that empirical openness towards the concrete context is preferable. Staunæs (2004), for instance, argues against granting specific categories a-priori priority. Other scholars argue for the necessity of pre-selecting a number of strategic anchor points of analysis in order to make analysis manageable (Christensen & Jensen 2012; Ludvig 2006; McCall 2005; Phoenix 2006; Yuval-Davis 2006).

Seventh, the field of intersectionality studies is home to a multitude of scholars, with considerable variation in terms of disciplinary, geographical, and institutional affiliations. Even if the concept has undergone changes and permutations as it has travelled from context to context, it has become a kind of unifying key concept in gender studies across different positions such as structuralist, post-structuralist, and queer gender studies (see also Davis & Zarkov 2017).

Consequently, **intersectionality hosts different epistemologies**. Some scholars have been mostly interested in deconstructing and destabilizing cultural identity categories because these are seen as oppressive per se. For other scholars, categories such as class, gender, and race point to structural forms of social differentiation that are ontologically real and can be investigated empirically. In one of the most widely referenced and influential contributions to intersectionality, McCall has argued that it is possible to carry out intersectional analysis in three different ways. *The anti-categorical approach* (most often grounded in post-structuralist, deconstructivist, or radical constructivist epistemologies) aims at destabilizing categories. *The intra-categorical approach*, more realist in its epistemology, focuses on differences within one category – not in order to destabilize but to provide a more precise analysis and criticism of social injustice. *The inter-categorical approach* studies complexity, variation, and inequality by comparing different categories – oftentimes statistically and grounded in a realist philosophy of science (McCall 2005). It is thus important to stress that it is possible to study intersectionality in different ways and that different approaches to intersectionality may produce different types of important knowledge.

Intersecting masculinities

Given the relatively abstract nature of the introduction and discussion above, we will now outline two more concrete examples of areas of analysis that illustrate some of the principles and challenges in relation to masculinity studies. The argument will focus on methodological implications rather than presenting actual research findings.

The first example could be based on an anti-categorical intersectional approach focusing on, for instance, Danish public discourses about ethnic/racial minority young men. One could analyse how specific configurations of gender, age, and visible minority background (race) are equated with trouble, danger, and crime in such discourses. A non-additive point may be that youth, maleness, and ethnic minority background in combination constitute a strong sign of social trouble, which cannot be reduced to the sum of its parts (Alexander 2000). Geographical location may be an important category to include, as the stereotype of the criminal young immigrant/black man is often tied to the territorial stigmatization of specific residential areas labelled as ghettos (Wacquant 2007). In terms of "asking the other question", one might ask how class is inscribed in these public discourses oftentimes without explicit mentioning. Furthermore, one could analyse how the public trope of the "the gang" is a racialized, gendered, and classed concept and how the idea of the criminal young black man is related to the postcolonial imaginaries of the dangerous racialized other (Jensen 2010, 2011). Such an analysis would be mostly anti-categorical, as it would strive to deconstruct the discourses under scrutiny.

The second example could be about masculinity, war, and political radicalization. Following McCall's and Yuval-Davis' methodological principles, such an analysis could combine the dynamics of an intra-categorical and inter-categorical approach by focusing on both the variation between different categories (inter-categorical) and the differences within groups (intra-categorical) (McCall 2005; Yuval-Davis 2011). Investigation of war, violence, and masculinity could furthermore benefit from a multi-level intersectional approach (Christensen & Rasmussen 2017). At the macro level, focus could be on public policies, debates, and ideologies which directly or indirectly reflect gendered discourses and specific configurations framed within the intersection between masculinity, nation, religion, class, and ethnicity. This could be seen, for example, when discourses about warriors and heroes were used as a part of cultural re-masculinization of post 9/11 US politics. As Messerschmidt has shown, heroic masculinity was put on the agenda when the American president George W. Bush branded himself as a "real man" who could – and would – defend the nation against its enemies (Ducat 2004; Messerschmidt 2010). The micro level could include masculine subjectivities, processes of mobilization, and radicalization. A highly relevant example of this could be the case of extremism, radicalization, and politico-religious violence in an intersectional perspective. Recent years have seen an increase of radical Islamist violence, for instance, both in Western countries and in the global South. One might analyse how processes of intersectional marginalization, classed and racist in nature, relegate ethnic minority youth – mostly male – to the social margins from where the promises of radical Islamist ideology can be perceived as a better alternative; a vehicle for vengeance and for obtaining social status within jihadist subculture. A multidimensional, intersectional approach can then facilitate an analysis of how male subcultures that articulate resistance or opposition against social marginalization can, at the same time, reproduce or strengthen gendered and sexual hierarchies. The masculinism of some minority male countercultures may illustrate this point (Hughey 2009; Jensen 2010). In an intersectional perspective, it must therefore be emphasized that radical Islamism is oftentimes characterized by extreme versions of homophobia and misogyny as well as extreme forms of gendered violence (Necef 2016).

Conclusion

In this chapter, we have introduced and discussed intersectionality as a relevant approach for studies of men and masculinity. The concept was coined in US Black Feminism, although ways of thinking similar to the intersectional perspective is older and has existed in other parts of the world. The concept during the last three decades has travelled beyond its original context of coining. Intersectionality is in many ways an open-ended and sensitizing, perhaps in some sense even incomplete, concept. Adopting intersectionality can thus be complicated, as there are many challenges involved in designing and carrying out intersectional research, some of which we have accounted for above. But for a research field whose very *raison d'être* is grasping, describing, and explaining gendered power relations as well as differences between men and between masculinities complexity is a condition, not something to be avoided. At this point, intersectionality offers analytical tools well suited to grasping differences among and between men and – perhaps most importantly – for grasping how other social differences play a role in the social processes that shape and condition masculinities.

Note

1 In addition, the argument that taking intersectionality seriously could be productive for masculinity research is not entirely new; see, e.g., Bartholomaeus & Tarrant 2016; Berggren 2013, 2014; Christensen & Jensen 2012, 2014; Christensen & Larsen 2008; Hearn 2011, 2015; Madfis 2014; Mellström 2003, 2009; and Näre 2010.

References

Alexander, C. E. (2000). *The Asian gang: Ethnicity, identity, masculinity*. Oxford: Berg.

Andersen, M. L. (2005). Thinking about women: A quarter century's view. *Gender and Society*, *19*(4), 437–455.

Anderson, E. (2008). Inclusive masculinity in a fraternal setting. *Men and Masculinities*, *10*(5), 604–620.

Anderson, E. (2009). *Inclusive masculinity: The changing nature of masculinities*. New York: Routledge.

Anthias, F., & Yuval-Davies, N. (1983). Contextualizing feminism: Gender, ethnic and class divisions. *Feminist Review*, *15*, 62–75.

Bartholomaeus, C., & Tarrant, A. (2016). Masculinities at the margins of "middle adulthood": What a consideration of young age and old age offers masculinities theorizing. *Men and Masculinities*, *19*(4), 351–369.

Berggren, K. (2013). Degrees of intersectionality: Male rap artists in Sweden negotiating class, race and gender. *Culture Unbound: Journal of Current Cultural Research*, *5*, 89–211.

Berggren, K. (2014). *Reading rap: Feminist interventions in men and masculinity research* (Doctoral dissertation). Uppsala University, Uppsala.

Bridges, T., & Pascoe, C.J. (2014). Hybrid masculinities: New directions in the sociology of men and masculinities. *Sociology Compass*, *8*(3), 246–258.

Cho, S., Crenshaw, K., & McCall, L. (2013). Toward a field of intersectionality studies: Theory, applications, and praxis. *Signs*, *38*(4), 785–810.

Choo, H. Y., & Ferree, M. M. (2010). Practicing intersectionality in sociological research: A critical analysis of inclusions, interactions, and institutions in the study of inequalities. *Sociological Theory*, *28*(2), 129–149.

Christensen, A-D., & Jensen, S. Q. (2012). Doing intersectional analysis: Methodological implications for qualitative research. *NORA: Nordic Journal of Feminist and Gender Research*, *20*(2), 109–125.

Christensen A-D., & Jensen, S. Q. (2014). Combining hegemonic masculinity and intersectionality. *NORMA: International Journal for Masculinity Studies*, *9*(1), 60–75.

Christensen, A-D., & Larsen, J. E. (2008). Gender, class, and family: Men and gender equality in a Danish context. *Social Politics*, *15*(1), 53–78.

Christensen, A-D., & Rasmussen, P. (Eds.). (2017). *Masculinity, war and violence*. Oxon: Routledge.

Collins, P. H. (1989). The social construction of Black feminist thought. *Signs*, *14*(4), 745–773.

Collins, P. H. (1993). Toward a new vision: Race, class and gender as categories of analysis and connection. *Race, Sex and Class*, *1*(1), 25–46.

Collins, P. H. (1998). It's all in the family: Intersections of gender, race and nation. *Hypatia*, *13*(3), 62–82.

Collins, P. H. (2015). Intersectionality's definitional dilemmas. *Annual Review Sociology*, *41*, 1–20.

Collins, P. H., & Bilge, S. (2016). *Intersectionality*. Cambridge: Polity.

Combahee River Collective. (1977/1983). The Combahee River Collective statement. In B. Smith (Ed.), *Home girls: A black feminist anthology* (pp. 264–274). New York: Women of Color Press.

Connell, R. W. (1995). *Masculinities*. Cambridge: Polity.

Connell, R. W. (2007). *Southern theory: The global dynamics of knowledge in social science*. Cambridge: Polity.

Connell, R. W., & Messerschmidt, J. W. (2005). Hegemonic masculinity: Rethinking the concept. *Gender & Society, 19*(6), 829–859.

Crenshaw, K. W. (1989). Demarginalizing the intersection of race and sex: A black feminist critique of antidiscrimination doctrine, feminist theory and antiracist politics. *The University of Chicago Legal Forum, 1*, 139–167.

Crenshaw, K. W. (1991). Mapping the margins: Intersectionality, identity politics and violence against women of colour. *Stanford Law Review, 43*(6), 1241–1299.

Davis, K. (2008). Intersectionality as a buzzword: A sociology of science perspective on what makes a feminist theory successful. *Feminist Theory, 9*(1), 67–85.

Davis, K., & Zarkov, D. (2017). Retrospective on intersectionality (introduction). *European Journal of Women's Studies, 24*(4), 313–320. Virtual Special Issue: Intersectionality.

de la Rey, C. (1997). South African feminism, race and racism. *Agenda, 13*(32), 6–10.

de Los Reyes, P., Molina, I., & Mulinari, D. (Eds.). (2005). *Maktens olika förklädnader: Kön, klass och etnicitet i det postkoloniala Sverige*. Stockholm: Atlas.

de Los Reyes, P., & Mulinari, D. (2005). *Intersektionalitet*. Malmö: Liber.

Dongchao, M. (2005). Awakening again: Travelling feminism in China in the 1980s. *Women Studies International Forum, 28*(4), 274–288.

Dongchao, M. (2011). *A new approach to travelling theory, an alternative feminist methodology*. Paper presented at the Sino-Nordic Gender and Women Conference, Aalborg University, Denmark.

Ducat, S. J. (2004). *The wimp factor; Gender gaps, holy wars, and politics of anxious masculinity*. Boston: Beacon Press.

Faber, S. T., & Nielsen, H. P. (2016). *Remapping gender, place and mobility: Global confluences and local particularities in Nordic peripheries*. New York: Routledge.

Ferree, M. M. (2011). The discursive politics of feminist intersectionality. In H. Lutz, M. Vivar, & L. Supik (Eds.), *Framing intersectionality: Debates on a multi-faceted concept in gender studies* (pp. 55–65). Farnham: Ashgate.

Frosh, S., Phoenix, A., & Pattman, R. (2002). *Young masculinities*. Basingstoke: Palgrave.

Geerts, E., & van der Tuin, I. (2013). From intersectionality to interference: Feminist onto-epistemological reflections on the politics of representation. *Women's Studies International Forum, 41*(3), 171–178.

Grib, L., & Strid, S. (2017). Intersektionella gränser. *Tidskrift för genusvetenskap, 38*(3), 3–9.

Hancock, A. (2007a). Intersectionality as a normative and empirical paradigm. *Politics & Gender, 3*(2), 248–254.

Hancock, A. (2007b). When multiplication doesn't equal quick addition: Examining intersectionality as a research paradigm. *Perspectives on Politics, 5*(1), 63–79.

Hearn, J. (2011). Neglected intersectionalities in studying men: Age(ing), virtuality, transnationality. In H. Lutz, M. T. H. Vivar, & L. Supik (Eds.), *Framing intersectionality: Debates on a multi-faceted concept in gender studies* (pp. 89–104). Farnham: Ashgate.

Hearn, J. (2015). *Men of the world: Genders, globalizations, transnational times*. London: Sage.

Hendricks, C., & Lewis, D. (1994). Voices from the margins. *Agenda: Empowering Women for Gender Equity, 10*(20), 61–75.

hooks, b. (1989). *Talking back: Thinking feminist, thinking black*. Cambridge, MA: South End Press.

Hughey, M. W. (2009). Black aesthetics and Panther rhetoric: A critical decoding of black masculinity in *The Black Panther*, 1967–1980. *Critical Sociology, 35*(1), 29–56.

Jensen, S. Q. (2010). Masculinity at the margins: Othering, marginality and resistance among young marginalized ethnic minority men. *NORMA: Nordic Journal for Masculinity Studies, 5*(1), 7–26.

Jensen, S. Q. (2011). Othering, identity formation and agency. *Qualitative Studies, 2*(2), 63–78.

Kerner, I. (2017). Relations of difference: Power and inequality in intersectional and postcolonial feminist theories. *Current Sociology Review, 65*(6), 846–866.

Knapp, G-A. (2005). Race, class, gender: Reclaiming baggage in fast travelling theories. *European Journal of Women's Studies, 12*(3), 249–265.

Kofoed, J. (2005). Holddeling: Når der gøres maskulinitet og hvidhed. *Kvinder, Køn og Forskning, 14*(3), 42–52.

Ludvig, A. (2006). Differences between women? Intersecting voices in a female narrative. *European Journal of Women's Studies, 13*(3), 245–258.

Madfis, E. (2014). Triple entitlement and homicidal anger: An exploration of the intersectional identities of American mass murderers. *Men and Masculinities, 17*(1), 67–86.

Matsuda, M. J. (1991). Beside my sister, facing the enemy: Toleration, adaption and appropriation. *Stanford Law Review, 43*(6), 1183–1192.

McCall, L. (2005). The complexity of intersectionality. *Signs, 30*(3), 1771–1800.

Mellström, U. (2003). *Masculinity, power and technology: A Malaysian ethnography*. Aldershot: Ashgate.

Mellström, U. (2009). Editorial. *NORMA: Nordic Journal for Masculinity Studies, 4*(2), 113–118.

Mellström, U. (2015). Difference, complexity and (onto)epistemological challenges in masculinity studies. *NORMA: International Journal for Masculinity Studies, 10*(1), 1–4.

Messerschmidt, J. W. (2010). *Hegemonic masculinities and camouflaged politics: Unmasking the Bush dynasty at its war against Iraq*. Boulder, CO: Paradigm Publishers.

Messerschmidt, J. W. (2014). *Masculinities in the making: From the local to the global*. Lanham, MD: Rowman & Littlefield.

Mohanty, C. T. (2003). *Feminism without borders: Decolonizing theory, practicing solidarity*. Durham, NC: Duke University Press.

Moser, I. (2006). Sociotechnical practices and difference: On the interferences between disability, gender, and class. *Science, Technology & Human Values, 31*(5), 537–564.

Näre, L. (2010). Sri Lankan men working as cleaners and carers: Negotiating masculinity in Naples. *Men and Masculinities, 13*(1), 65–86.

Necef, M. (2016). If men were men then women would be women: ISIL's construction of masculinity and femininity, Center for Mellemøststudier, News Analysis May 2016.

Nyhagen L., & Halsaa, B. (2016). *Religion, gender and citizenship: Women of faith, gender equality and feminism*. London: Palgrave Macmillan.

Ozkazanc-Pan, B. (2012). Postcolonial feminist research: Challenges and complexities. *Equality, Diversity and Inclusion: An International Journal, 31*(5/6), 573–591.

Phoenix, A. (2006). Interrogating intersectionality: Productive ways of theorising multiple positioning. *Kvinder, Køn og Forskning, 15*(2/3), 21–30.

Phoenix, A. (2011). Psychosocial intersections: Contextualising the accounts of adults who grew up in visibly ethnically different households. In H. Lutz, M. Vivar, & L. Supik (Eds.), *Framing intersectionality: Debates on a multi-faceted concept in gender studies* (pp. 137–152). Farnham: Ashgate.

Phoenix, A., & Pattynama, P. (2006). Editorial: Intersectionality. *European Journal of Women's Studies, 13*(3), 187–192.

Pini, B., & Leach, B. (2011). Transformations of class and gender in the globalized countryside. In B. Pini & B. Leach (Eds.), *Reshaping gender & class in rural spaces* (pp. 1–23). Farnham: Ashgate.

Ratele, K. (2014). Currents against gender transformation of South African men: Relocating masculinity to the centre of research and theory of masculinities. *NORMA: International Journal for Masculinity Studies, 9*(1), 30–44.

Staunæs, D. (2003). Where have all the subjects gone? Bringing together the concepts of intersectionality and subjectification. *NORA: Nordic Journal of Feminist and Gender Research, 11*(2), 101–110.

Staunæs, D. (2004). *Køn, etnicitet og skoleliv*. Frederiksberg: Forlaget Samfundslitteratur.

Valentine, G. (2007). Theorizing and researching intersectionality: A challenge for feminist geography. *The Professional Geographer, 59*(1), 10–21.

Wacquant, L. J. D. (2007). Territorial stigmatization in the age of advanced marginality. *Thesis Eleven, 91*(1), 66–77.

Wetherell, M., & Edley, N. (1999). Negotiating hegemonic masculinity: Imaginary positions and psycho-discursive practices. *Feminism & Psychology, 9*(3), 335–356.

Winkler, G., & Degele, N. (2011). Intersectionality as multi-level analysis: Dealing with social inequality. *European Journal of Women's Studies, 18*(1), 51–66.

Yuval-Davis, N. (2006). Intersectionality and feminist politics. *European Journal of Women's Studies, 13*(3), 193–209.

Yuval-Davis, N. (2007). Intersectionality, citizenship and contemporary politics of belonging. *Critical Review of International, Social and Political Philosophy, 10*(4), 561–574.

Yuval-Davis, N. (2011). *The politics of belonging: Intersectional contestations*. London: Sage.

8

Postcolonial masculinities

Diverse, shifting and in flux

Fataneh Farahani and Suruchi Thapar-Björkert

> Colour is not a human or a personal reality; it is a political reality.
>
> James Baldwin (1963, p. 88)

Two seminal contributions that launched the scholarship on the discursive construction of Otherness were *The Second Sex* (1949/1989) by Simone de Beauvoir and *Black Skin, White Masks* (1952/1986) by Franz Fanon. The former emphasizes the othering process of (white) women while the latter focusses on the construction of the (masculine) racial-other. Considering the intersections of these two writers' intellectual and social circles, chronological contiguity in their integration of otherness and the widespread scandal involving *The Second Sex*, it is reasonable to believe that Fanon not only was informed but perhaps also was influenced by de Beauvoir's book, despite no citational reference to her in his book. Focusing mainly on the otherness of the racialized black man, Fanon's failure to refer to de Beauvoir can be understood as personal defiance or sexism (Adkins, 2013; Moi, 2008). It can also mean a failure to consider gender, as Fanon's racialized masculine 'other' is not scrutinized as a gendered subject. He is solely a racialized subject detached from historical and cultural contexts of class, sexuality and gender relations. In fact, women who seem integral for his theorization of 'manhood' are the subalterns on whose bodies racial politics are inscribed. Moreover, Fanon's exclusive focus on race not only disregards other power relations but also fails to consider the particularities of the processual power relations across the continuum of skin colour, sexuality, class and the ways in which these relations shape the lived experiences of men and women (Lane & Mahdi, 2013). At the same time, de Beauvoir's instrumental operationalization of the slave/woman analogy and her portrayal of women as slaves of men does not mean that she acknowledges female racial oppression. It rather demonstrates her limited conceptualization of 'woman'—which mainly includes white heterosexual middle-class woman (Gines, 2010)—her narrowness in understanding of race as involving mainly black men and her disregard of black women's racialized oppression.

Tracing this historical genealogy, our chapter evaluates three prisms: first, the race-blindness of (Western) feminist theories and their complicity in establishing essentializing cultural scripts on masculinity; second, the gender blindness and heteronormativity of (male) postcolonial theories despite their influential interventions on processes of otherization; and third, the ethnocentrism and race blindness of primarily Western (and white) masculinity studies, with a few exceptions (such as Hearn & Blagojević, 2013). We draw on a postcolonial critical masculinities framework to evaluate migrant and diasporic masculinities and to highlight local constructions of race and whiteness through two geographical sites, the UK and Sweden.

Race-blindness of (Western) feminist theories

Many postcolonial feminist authors such as Hill Collins (1990), hooks (1989), Mohanty (1984) and Spivak (1988) have emphasized that colonial discourses, like sexist discourses, are maintained by the fixity of the construct of the 'other'. By examining the discursive construction of *non-Western* women by *Western feminist* scholars, Mohanty (1984) not only challenged the false universalistic claim of *active Western women* and *passive third-world women* (Wallaschek, 2017) but also criticized the race-blindness of Western feminists. Moreover, Stoler (1999), for example, has vigilantly shown how colonial authority and racial distinctions were/are fundamentally arranged in gender terms. Therefore, women were degraded not only as Oriental/colonial subjects but also in gender-specific ways. These feminist observations draw attention to how colonial and Orientalist discourses have historically employed sexuality as a prominent signifier for (re)presenting otherness (see also Lewis, 1996; Stoler, 1999; Tamale, 2011; Yeğenoğlu, 1999), exemplified through the fascination with 'beauty behind the veil' and the eroticization of the *harem* in Orientalist texts. Oriental promiscuous femininity in the mysterious *harem* was constructed in opposition to the nonsexual, passionless, domesticated femininity of the European middle-class nuclear family (Lewis, 1996). This oppositional gendering foregrounded the binary polarization of the chaste, desexualized Christian woman in the marital home with the promiscuous morally suspect non-Christian woman, always available, in a sexualized harem. The racialized desire (Farahani, 2018) towards the exoticized oriental women and the primitivized and eroticized African women was, however, compounded with fear of racial mixture and interracial exchange (Lay, 1993). For example, during the apartheid era in South Africa, the Prohibition of Mixed Marriages Act of 1949 disallowed marriage or sexual intimacy between white people and people of other race groups and even annulled interracial marriages of South Africans that occurred outside of the country. Even though the law was repealed in 1985, interracial marriage still remains contentious (also see Stevens et al., 2013). Interracial exchange, considered a threat to the purity of nation, lead to a harnessed racial mixing by colonialists as a tool to drive a wedge between blacks and mixed-race groups and between all people of colour and whites. Through valorization of lighter-skinned mixed-race groups (pigmentocracies or shadeism), colonialists established a hierarchy that linked skin colour to economic and social class. In fact, 'groups that gained political and economic power as a result of métissage maintained their dominant position by discrimination against others who are further down the skin colour scale. This discourse continues after colonialism and remains relevant in contemporary times' (Lane & Mahdi, 2013, p. 170). Interracial relationships become further complicated when viewed through the prism of gender. While sexual relationships between white men and racialized women have historically been silently accepted, racialized (particularly black) men's relationships with white women has meant putting their lives at risk (for example the 'black peril' panics in South Africa, India, Papua New Guinea and Rhodesia). Thus the patriarchal nature of white supremacy not only ratifies the dominance of white men over racialized men but also contributes to the (partial) decrease of white women's racial privileges, if and when they enter/inhabit an interracial (intimate) relationship (Nkweto Simmonds, 1995; also see Byrne, 2006; Harman, 2010; Twine, 2000).

Like interracial issues, colonial discourses were also fraught with ambiguities. 'Colonial imperialists', as Leila Ahmed (1992) has discussed, selectively appropriated feminism to serve colonialism's civilizing mission, though this commitment to feminism was not genuine. This 'colonial feminism', according to Ahmed (1992), justified Western men's exploitation of Oriental women in the name of 'saving [the] brown women from brown men' (Spivak, 1988, p. 297; also see Khalid, 2011), while simultaneously subordinating women in their home countries. It is noteworthy that imperial women were 'complicit' in the making of the empire and supported cultural scripts on race which associated the constructs of masculinity of 'other' men as either feeble and desexualized (Asian) (Eng, 2001); heroic and revolutionary (Kurdish) (Aktürk, 2015); hypersexualized (black) and femininity as undisciplined and promiscuous (black) (Tamale, 2011); and exotic and erotic (Arab and Muslim) (Farahani, 2018; Yeğenoğlu, 1999). This historical genealogy, paradoxically, never entered the cannons of Western feminism.

Gender-blindness and heteronormativity of postcolonial theories

Generally, postcolonial studies have focussed on the consequences of identity formation from two different but interrelated directions: *the colonizer* and *the colonized* (McLeod, 2000), which arguably, like forms of racialization, were hierarchically structured yet competed with each other. For instance, while in *Orientalism* (1994) Edward Said focuses on *how* and in *what ways* the knowledge constructed by colonizers legitimizes their domination, Fanon, in *Black Skin, White Masks* (1952/1986), demonstrates the psychological impacts of colonialism on the colonized (male) subjects, who internalize the image of the self as 'other'. The colonizing project represents, for example, the 'black' man as everything the 'white' man is not, because, as Fanon explicitly declares, '[a] man was expected to behave like a man. I was expected to behave like a black man' (1986, p. 114). The consequences of the internalization of self as other result from the processes of *self-orientalization* (Tavakoli-Targhi, 2001) or incorporating 'various "essences" into the patterns of representation used to describe them', as Bakić-Hayden (1995, p. 917) suggests in the context of former Yugoslavia. This, as Fanon implies, demonstrates how the end of geographical colonialism does not necessarily mean the end of (other aspects of) colonialism.

Nonetheless, Said and Fanon's gender blindness has been challenged by feminist scholars. Refusing to construct a master narrative with a singular history of Orientalism that represents Orient as the 'Other' (the male as an ungendered subject) of the Occident, Lewis (1996) and Lowe (1991) challenged Said's Orientalism as gender-blind, monolithic and reductionist. They explained how Orientalist images of women demonstrate colonial authority and racialization through gender and class relations. By foregrounding heterogeneity, Lowe (1991) aims to open up a space 'that permit[s] the articulation of other differences—themselves incongruous and non-equivalent—not only of nation and race but also of gender, class, region, and sexual preference' (p. 29). McClintock (1995, p. 363) confronts Fanon's exclusion of gender in his understanding of the Manichean dialect, which by 'postponing a theory of gender, presumes that subjectivity itself is neutral with respect to gender'. Both men and women were actively engaged in the social production of the 'gender order' as well as hierarchies of race, culture and (hetero)sexuality, which not only came into existence through and in relation to each other but also were crucial for the development of Western industrial modernity (McClintock, 1995, p. 5).

Here it is worth mentioning that the influence of postcolonial feminist theories bridged the gaps on the race blindness of (Western) feminist theories and gender blindness of (male) postcolonial theories. Nonetheless, despite this significant bridging, postcolonial feminist developments fell short of analysing racialized men as a gendered subject and heteronormative sexuality problematically framed postcolonial conceptual development. The burgeoning of masculinity studies was the first step to study men as a gendered subject, though still through highly unraced lens.

Race-blindness of (Western) masculinities studies

The subject of men and masculinity formation has been a prevalent topic in Western academia during the last three decades (e.g., Brod & Kaufman, 1994; Connell, 1995) and has contributed, among other things, in challenging the classification of men as an ungendered category (Hearn & Pringle, 2006). Connell and Messerschmidt (2005) have argued that much of the recent focus on masculinities remains largely divorced from discussions of femininities, and since 'gender is always relational, patterns of masculinity are socially defined in contradistinction from some model (whether real or imaginary) of femininity' (p. 848). Nonetheless, there are certain contentious issues. First, studies of (Western) masculinity/masculinities have mainly examined Euro-American masculinities (Connell, 1995; Kimmel, 1987), though some are couched within localized ethnographic accounts. Second, these studies have been notably criticized for falling short due to their ethnocentrism, race-blindness, lack of historical specificity, false causality, to some extent psychologization and conceptual ambiguity (see Hearn, 2004). Where race is acknowledged, specifically in multicultural contexts, the conceptualization of, for example, 'Islamicated men' (Babayan & Najmabadi, 2008)—or, as we suggest, men who are reduced to being Muslim with a certain reading of Islam—not only predominates but moreover remains confined to constructions of 'nationalist heroes', 'oppressive and overprotective' vis-à-vis the 'equality-oriented' and 'liberated Western men' (Connell, 1995; Khosravi, 2009). These binary approaches set up truncated parameters of analysis, which leads to 'either denying that Islamic practices are necessarily oppressive or asserting that oppressive practices are not necessarily Islamic' (Kandiyoti, 1996, p. 9). Thus, while it is reductionist to accuse Islam of being exclusively accountable for repressive gendered practices, it is problematic to entirely exonerate 'Islamic doctrines', especially in communities where Islamic ideology is normative.

(Post)colonial masculinities

Postcolonial historiography re-enacts the dialogical relations between the North (with all its heterogeneities) and the 'Rest' (with all its entities and complexities), a relationship that was essential to the formation of the ethos of modernity as well as construction of modern/non-modern, progressive/primitive female or male (gendered) subject positions. By being attentive to geospatial, subject-positions and (post)colonial experiences at the margins, we can provide alternative readings of gendered agency and subjectivity and simultaneously tackle the issue of (non)representation and power (see also Morrell, 2005; Morrell & Swart, 2005). We do not see postcolonialism reductively, as marking the closure of a historical period, but as a term with which we can analyse contemporary power relations as structural continuities of colonialism (see Shohat & Stam, 2014).

Since postcolonial theory draws on anti-essentialist poststructuralism, it also pays attention to the intersecting and shifting identities generated by geographical displacement that followed the post-independence era and thus incorporates the (dis)continuities of colonialism. The theoretical edge to postcolonialism is set up to not only examine the diverse colonial periods but also scrutinize the lasting economic, political and cultural impacts of colonization now in the former colonies as well as societies of colonial power. As Stuart Hall (2001) suggests, the actual determination of the postcolonial includes both 'after colonization' and 'beyond colonization', and therefore both descriptions cannot be separated from each other (pp. 242–261). Thus, in lieu of the three inconsistencies outlined above, it becomes imperative to examine how diverse and intersecting (post)colonial masculine subject positions after/beyond colonialism are formed in relation/in response/in (dis)continuation with different types of masculine position during colonialism and vice versa through colonialism (also see Treacher Kebesh, 2013).

By here focusing on displaced men in different Western multicultural contexts together with their transnational, translocational and diasporic experiences, our deployment of displacement draws not only on the temporal and spatial shifts but also on dislocatory events and experiences which open up the possibility for new though contradictory assemblages: 'If on the one hand, they threaten identities, on the other, they are the foundation on which new identities are constituted' (Laclau, 1990, p. 39). Transnational migratory movements illuminate the complicated relationship between displacement and the construction of diasporic and transnational masculinities (and femininities). It illuminates not only the fluidity and plurality in regards to constructions of masculinities (and femininities) but also how men experience racialization differently from women. By focusing on how men's notion of masculinity resolidifies or/and (trans)forms due to the movements across national and cultural boundaries (together with the burden of haunted histories of colonialism, see Treacher Kebesh, 2013), ethnographic research on the construction of diasporic masculinities seeks to contribute to fill the gap on what is still a frequently neglected issue in existing debates. Furthermore, the importance of a gendered, raced, classed, aged generational understanding of diaspora and transnational practices is significant for grasping some of the hierarchies and intersecting forms of power that are simultaneously enacted and negotiated between as well as within different diasporic communities (Sawyer, 2008).

The receiving Western metropolitan countries process not only men and women differently but also different men differently and slot them into predetermined hierarchical racialized boxes (Muslim, Middle Eastern, East Asian, East European, African). Through a range of distinct and intersecting factors (such as race/ethnicity, skin colour, education, age, (lack of) language skill, (lack of) religiosity, occupation, looks, wealth and social and cultural capital), displaced men can (dis)relate to 'normative' white masculinity and can occupy a position of (dis)privilege. However, attributing men's (and women's) transformations and even disagreements only to geographical displacements and what is constructed as a strict dichotomized grouping of a *traditional culture* vis-à-vis *modern Western culture* and problematic division of *religious subject positions* vis-à-vis *secular subjects positions* is problematic (for more in-depth discussion see Farahani, 2018). This not only engenders a reductionist and homogenized approach to culture and religion and overrides other components of identity formation but also implicitly considers *modernization* and *Westernization* the same instead of considering modernization as a multiple and simultaneous process that takes place all over the world (see Tavakoli-Targhi, 2001).

Many people encounter the West long before coming to the West; conversely, Western people have constructed their Western-ness by constructing an Orientalist orient. This does not mean that there are no social, political and cultural differences between the countries of their origins and the 'host' environments. Nor do we suggest a lack of transformation among people who encounter 'another' culture. Nor are we unaware of the financial and social transformations of many displaced men. The objection is to focusing on the dichotomizing of the construction of difference between cultures and the chronological and linear ways of studying modernity that lead to a reductionist compartmentalizing of cultures (Farahani, 2018). The differences quite often entail boundaries that are more blurred than a simple dichotomized rationalization is capable of explaining (see also Farahani, 2012, 2013). For example, in the Swedish context, the representation of native/migrant/transnational men is filtered through an understanding of the national self-image of the *gender-equal*, 'modern, liberated and equality seeking' white Western/Swedish men (Farahani, 2012, 2013; Gottzén & Jonsson, 2012). Furthermore, the construction of masculinities of young and second-generation immigrant men through problematic discourses that tie race and ethnicity to crime, problematic and aggressive (hetero)sexuality (Hammarén, 2008; Jonsson, 2007) and radicalization by Islamic movements such as the Islamic State of Iraq and Syria (ISIS), among others, generates 'moral panic' concerning 'home-grown terrorists'; such discourses single them out as inferior in relation to their white counterparts and vilify and demonize them.

Disclocations, identifications and articulations

Diverse dislocatory experiences (Ingridsdotter, 2017; Laclau, 1990) of social, political and economic marginalization after migration place many displaced men for the first time in the position of the subordinated *other*. In her ethnographic study among Iranian-born diasporic men in Stockholm, Sydney and London, Farahani (2012, 2013), demonstrates how the local and global constructions of masculinities are related and shaped by (dis)continuities of intersecting hierarchical racial, social, class-based and rural/urban division. For instance, in Farahani's study, Iranian-homosexuals, Iranian-Kurds, Iranian-Baloch, Iranian-Azaris, Iranian-Armenians and Iranian Baha'is (not necessarily mutually exclusive groups) had already experienced discrimination due to their ethnicity, sexuality and beliefs when they lived in Iran. In contrast, Persian middle-class male heterosexual Shia Muslim subjects in Iran, belonging to the normative unracialized, unsexed, unethnicized and ungendered ethnic group, often experience being the *other* for the first time when they moved to the West.

Similar to white middle-class heterosexual men in the West, ethnically Persian heterosexual Muslim subjects, who belong to the normative and most powerful ethnic group in Iran, have the luxury of overlooking the centrality of gender, sexuality and class in shaping their lives in Iran. Yet they face different racializing practices in diaspora that mark them as non-white and non-normative. Thus, while Tehranian men often failed to understand or even recognize racism in Iran, the Kurdish, Azari and Baha'i men in this study offered detailed accounts of racist practices in Iran, as well as among Iranians in the diaspora. Paradoxically, most of the research participants were not keen on presenting themselves as subjected to racist and discriminatory practices. While many of the interviewees, particularly the first generation, have faced devaluation of their degrees and previous work experiences, they were unwilling to understand this as a sign of discrimination. Many of them lived in marginalized suburbs, their children had experienced different conflicts and problems due to their backgrounds, names, looks, accents and so on, but they were reluctant to see this as a consequence of racial discrimination. In fact, the only instance when some of the respondents acknowledged that they were the subject of racist discrimination was when they were at a family divorce court, which probably indicates that these men, who belong to the normative group in Iran, still consider power and loss of power only in relation to their wives. According to these men, the courts have blindly and prejudicially condemned them because they were Middle Eastern men and favour their wives as (victimized and subordinated) Middle Eastern women.

According to Farahani (2013), racialized migrant Iranian men's desire to present themselves as an indisputable part of a *collective (white) we* partly explains the research participants' denial of racist practices. According to these men's accounts, racism was something that happens to Africans, Arabs, Kurds and Turkish people who did not know how to adjust in this society, or not to the 'civilized we' who are middle class, well-educated Iranians (although many of them did not occupy that position). Thus the narratives of men with different ethnic backgrounds demonstrate how understandings of race are also forced to be reworked in diaspora. Iranian masculinity is linked to local constructions of race and whiteness, colonial and postcolonial process and most probably this is partly the reason behind why they refuse to see themselves as victims of discrimination. To put it bluntly, accepting racism would mean they should hand over the image of themselves as white (and thereby civilized), which is a tricky task, while denying racism provides them leeway to position themselves as higher in the existing racist hierarchies left behind, after and through, different colonial process. This also indicates not only the simultaneous existence of different masculinities but also simultaneous presence of different masculinities in each and every man. Therefore, 'even the most sovereign masculinity has to be earned, or achieved: ruling masculinities are themselves conditional, relational, subject to anxiety and destabilization' (Newell, 2009, p. 246).

Farahani's observations resonate with ethnographic work conducted by Sanghera and Thapar-Björkert (2012), who in their study on second-generation British Pakistani Muslim men in Bradford in the UK, explore how intersections of class, ethnicity, religion and gender produce a range of Pakistani Muslim masculinities, which coexist, compete and contradict. Bradford in West Yorkshire is both racially and culturally heterogeneous and is one of the most deprived areas in Britain due to processes of deindustrialization and recession during the 1970s and 1980s. Furthermore, Bradford became synonymous with the urban disturbances of 1995 and 2001 and, rather tenuously and problematically, with the 7 July 2005 (7/7) London bombings when two of the so-called 'home-grown' bombers were found to have previously lived in Bradford and all of the bombers had some connection with the county of West Yorkshire. Moral panic about Muslims and concerted attempts to explain 'why they behave the way they do' have focussed principally on Muslim men. The traditional stereotypes of Muslim men and masculinities as sexist, patriarchal and misogynistic have been supplanted by newer ones which associate them with radicalization and Islamic terrorism, which in turn have often been explained in terms of 'cultural deficit', 'cultural dysfunction' or a supposed 'clash of civilizations' (see Sanghera & Thapar-Björkert, 2012). The subsequent intensification of Islamophobia that 'reinforces the disadvantage and discrimination experienced by many Muslims' (Ansari, 2004, p. 394) has also meant that the young Muslims are resentful of having their loyalty to Britain questioned, concerned at being stereotyped as potential terrorists and indignant at the idea that they should do more to integrate into British life. Afshar et al. (2005, p. 276) note that Islamophobia has 'produced both solidarity and further tensions between generations and youths and women in the Muslim community as well as between the hosts and the Muslim communities.' Nonetheless, it is imperative to examine these masculinities as negotiated in and through specific historical and spatial contexts and in relation to other masculinities. In fact, 'meanings of masculinity [...] admit to cultural borrowing; masculinities imported from elsewhere are conflated with local ideas to produce new configurations' (Cornwall & Lindisfarne, 1994, p. 12). At times, young

Pakistani Muslim men in Bradford exhibited a 'hard' masculinity that drew on both transnational connections with an imagined Islamic, deterritorialized *umma* and more localized discourses of the 'gangsta' masculinities (gang membership), which employ an 'association between popular black identities and hegemonic ideals of masculinity such as status, "coolness" and strength' (Archer, 2003, p. 55) and which stood in sharp contrast to prior stereotypes of 'soft', 'weak' and 'effeminate' Asian masculinity. This 'hard' performative masculinity was constructed and enacted in relation to male peers, both within the ethnic group and other young men (giving them 'street cred'; see Nayak, 2003), in relation to their families and in relation to Muslim femininities. Nonetheless, this is not the only form of masculinity amongst British Pakistani Muslims although often the one that makes the media headlines. In fact, different masculinities were enacted over the course of their life, with a Muslim religious identity foregrounded as a tool for educational and career goals; to fulfil familial expectations and to draw distance from negative 'gangster'-like 'social vices' of working-class co-ethnic peers. Here the masculine identity is both religious and conformist—while religious identification provides them the moral motivation to succeed economically, it also reaffirmed normative gender roles that reinstated the male as the breadwinner and located the Muslim woman in the domestic sphere. Interestingly, adhering to a specific religious masculine identity was to counteract vilified stereotypes of Islam in the wider British society; to demonstrate a rootedness in '[one's] own culture' but also to differentiate themselves from the more narrow territorial Pakistani co-ethnic masculinities. These examples highlight not only a more heterogeneous nature of masculinities but also explore the symbolic investments made in particular subject positions in specific contexts, together with their intersection with different power relations. Furthermore, there can be a simultaneous coexistence and embodiment of different notions of masculinities by men, which are valorized in different (post)colonial contexts.

Conclusion

In this chapter, we reflect on seminal developments which have been instructive in the constitution of postcolonial masculinities—as a burgeoning critical dimension of postcolonial historiography—which arguably are (re)articulated, contested and negotiated in and through specific historical moments, spatial contexts, local/transnational discourses and in relation to other dominant/hegemonic (white) masculinities. Thus, these are not fixed and coherent but fractured by other forms of identification such as class, ethnicity, religion, sexuality, age and place.

Understanding racialized (marginalized) masculinities through postcolonial perspectives necessitates a recognition of the diversity of socio-political specificities as well as interrelationships that can display how men are (dis)privileged based on intersecting factors. By focusing on diasporic masculinities, we aim to address a lacuna in much of mainstream masculinity studies, which, with all its layers and nuances, has tended to engage mainly with Euro-American masculinities and also feminist postcolonial studies which mainly has focussed on women. We illustrate some of these salient issues by placing our narrative in and through two geopolitical positionings in transnational diasporic contexts of Sweden and the UK.

Dislocatory experiences for Iranian men and second-generation Pakistani Muslim men, both in terms of their marginality and alienation from dominant (white) discursive constructions and the impact of dislocatory events (political transformations in the country of origin and well as terrorist attacks in Western multicultural contexts which contributed to further stigmatization of Muslim racialized men), shape their everyday lives in different ways. The place of origin or the homeland continues to exert an influence on social identities in new destinations/place of habitation as men (and women) can transport aspects that shaped their identity in the homeland to the diaspora. These dislocatory experiences in (post)colonial diasporic spaces, together with the shifts in political contexts, inform the ways in which masculinities are negotiated, disrupted or operate in a state of flux.

References

Adkins, A. V. (2013). Black/feminist futures: Reading Beauvoir in *Black skin, white masks*. *South Atlantic Quarterly, 112*(4), 697–723.

Afshar, H., Aitken, R., & Franks, M. (2005). Feminisms, Islamophobia and identities. *Political Studies, 53*(2), 262–283.

Ahmed, L. (1992). *Women and gender in Islam: Historical roots of a modern debate*. New Haven: Yale University Press.

Aktürk, A. S. (2015). Female cousins and wounded masculinity: Kurdish nationalist discourse in the post-Ottoman Middle East. *Middle Eastern Studies, 52*(1), 46–59.

Ansari, H. (2004). *The infidel within: The history of Muslims in Britain, 1800 to the present*. London: C. Hurst.

Archer, L. (2003). *Race, masculinity and schooling*. Milton Keynes: Open University Press.

Babayan, K., & Najmabadi, A. (2008). *Islamicate sexualities: Translations across temporal geographies of desire*. Cambridge: Harvard University Press.

Bakić-Hayden, M. (1995). Nesting orientalisms: The case of former Yugoslavia. *Slavic Review, 54*(4), 917–931.

Baldwin, J. (1963). Down at the cross: Letter from a region in my mind. In J. Baldwin, *The fire next time* (pp. 19–89). London: Penguin.

Brod, H., & Kaufman, M. (Eds.) (1994). *Theorizing masculinities*. Thousand Oaks, CA: Sage.

Byrne, B. (2006). *White lives: The interplay of 'race', class and gender in everyday life*. London: Routledge.

Connell. R. (1995). *Masculinities*. Cambridge: Polity.

Connell, R. W., & Messerschmidt, J. (2005). Hegemonic masculinity: Rethinking the concept. *Gender and Society, 19*(6), 829–859.

Cornwall, A., & Lindisfarne, N. (1994). Dislocating masculinity: Gender, power and anthropology. In A. Cornwall & N. Lindisfarne (Eds.), *Dislocating masculinity: Comparative ethnographies* (pp. 11–47). London: Routledge.

de Beauvoir, S. (1949/1989). *The second sex*. New York: Vintage Books.

Eng, D. L. (2001). *Racial castration: Managing masculinity in Asian American*. Durham, NC: Duke University Press.

Fanon, F. (1952/1986). *Black skin, white masks*. New York: Grove.

Farahani, F. (2012). Diasporic masculinities: Reflections on gendered, raced and classed displacements. *Nordic Journal of Migration Research, 2*(2), 159–166.

Farahani, F. (2013). Racializing masculinities in different diasporic spaces: Iranian born men's navigations of race, masculinities and the politics of difference. In J. Hearn, M. Blagojević & K. Harrison (Eds.), *Rethinking transnational men: Beyond, between and within nations* (pp. 147–162). New York: Routledge.

Farahani, F. (2018). *Gender, sexuality and diaspora*. New York: Routledge.

Gines, K. T. (2010). Sartre, Beauvoir, and the race/gender analogy: A case for black feminist philosophy. In M. Davidson, K. T. Gines & D. Dale Marcano (Eds.), *Convergences: Black feminism and continental philosophy* (pp. 35–51). Albany, NY: State University of New York Press.

Gottzén, L., & Jonsson, R. (Eds.). (2012). *Andra män: Maskulinitet, normskapande och jämställdhet*. Malmö: Gleerups.

Hall, S. (2001). When was 'the post-colonial'? Thinking at the limit. In I. Chambers & L. Curti (Eds.), *The post-colonial question: Common skies, divided horizons* (pp. 242–261). London: Routledge.

Hammarén, N. (2008). *Förorten i huvudet: Unga män, om kön och sexualitet i det nya Sverige*. Stockholm: Atlas.

Harman, V. (2010). Experiences of racism and the changing nature of white privilege among lone white mothers of mixed-parentage children in the UK. *Ethnic and Racial Studies, 33*(2), 176–194.

Hearn, J. (2004). From hegemonic masculinity to the hegemony of men. *Feminist Theory, 5*(1), 97–120.

Hearn, J., & Blagojević, M. (2013). Introducing and rethinking transnational men. In J. Hearn, M. Blagojević & K. Harrison (Eds.), *Rethinking transnational men: Beyond, between and within nations* (pp. 1–24). New York: Routledge.

Hearn, J., & Pringle, K. with members of Critical Research on Men in Europe. (2006). *European perspectives on men and masculinities*. Houndmills: Palgrave Macmillan.

Hill Collins, P. (1990). *Black feminist thought: Knowledge, consciousness, and the politics of empowerment*. Boston, MA: Unwin Hyman.

hooks, b. (1989). *Talking back: Thinking feminist, thinking black*. Toronto: Between the Lines.

Ingridsdotter, J. (2017). *The promises of the free world: Postsocialist experience in Argentina and the making of migrants, race, and coloniality*. Huddinge: Södertörns högskola.

Jonsson, R. (2007). *Blatte betyder kompis: Om maskulinitet och sprak i en högstadieskola*. Stockholm: Ordfront.

Kandiyoti, D. (1996). Contemporary feminist scholarship and Middle East studies. In D. Kandiyoti (Ed.), *Gendering the Middle East: Emerging perspectives* (pp. 1–27). Syracuse, NY: Syracuse University Press.

Khalid, M. (2011). Gender, orientalism and representations of the 'other' in the War on Terror. *Global Change, Peace and Security, 23*(1), 15–29.

Khosravi, S. (2009). Displaced masculinity: Gender and ethnicity among Iranian men in Sweden. *Iranian Studies, 42*(4), 591–609.

Kimmel, M. (1987). *Changing men: New directions in the study of men and masculinity*. Newbury Park, CA: Sage.

Laclau, E. (1990). *New reflections on the revolution of our time*. London: Verso.

Lane, L., & Mahdi, H. (2013). Fanon revisited: Race, gender and coloniality vis-a-vis skin colour. In R. E. Hall (Ed.), *The melanin millennium: Skin color as 21st century international discourse* (pp. 169–181). New York: Springer.

Lay, K. J. (1993). Sexual racism: A legacy of slavery. *National Black Law Journal, 13*(1–2), 165–183.

Lewis, R. (1996). *Gendering orientalism. Race, femininity and representation*. New York: Routledge.

Lowe, L. (1991). *Critical terrains: French and British orientalisms*. Ithaca, NY: Cornell University Press.

McClintock, A. (1995).'No longer in a future heaven': Gender, race, and nationalism. In A. McClintock, A. Mufti & E. Shohat (Eds.), *Dangerous liaisons: Gender, nation, and postcolonial perspective* (pp. 89–112). Minneapolis: University of Minnesota Press.

McLeod, J. (2000). *Beginning postcolonialism*. Manchester: Manchester University Press.

Mohanty, C. T. (1984). Under Western eyes: Feminist scholarship and colonial discourses. *Boundary 2, 12*(3), 333–358.

Moi, T. (2008). *Simone de Beauvoir: The making of an intellectual woman*. Oxford: Oxford University Press.

Morrell, R. (2005). Men, movements and gender transformations in South African Studies. *Journal of South African Studies, 24*(4), 605–630.

Morrell, R., & Swart, S. (2005). Men in the world: Postcolonial perspectives on masculinity. In M. S. Kimmel, J. Hearn & R. W. Connell (Eds.), *Handbook of studies on men and masculinities* (pp. 90–113). Thousand Oaks, CA: Sage.

Nayak, A. (2003). 'Boyz to men': Masculinities, schooling and labour transitions in de-industrial times. *Educational Review, 55*(2), 147–159.

Newell, S. (2009). Postcolonial masculinities and the politics of visibility. *Journal of Postcolonial Writing, 45*(3), 243–250.

Nkweto Simmonds, F. (1995). Love in black and white. In L. Pearce & J. Stacey (Eds.), *Romance revisited* (pp. 210–222). London: Lawrence & Wishart.

Said, Edward. (1994). *Orientalism*. New York: Vintage Books.

Sanghera, G. S., & Thapar-Björkert, S. (2012). 'Let's talk about ... men': Young British Pakistani Muslim women's narratives about co-ethnic men in 'postcolonial' Bradford. *International Journal of Postcolonial Studies, 14*(4), 591–612.

Sawyer, L. (2008). Engendering 'race' in calls for diasporic communities in Sweden. *Feminist Review, 90*, 87–105.

Shohat, E., & Stam, R. (2014). *Unthinking Eurocentrism: Multiculturalism and the media*. London: Routledge.

Spivak, G. (1988). Can the subaltern speak? In C. Nelson & L. Grossberg (Eds.), *Marxism and the interpretation of culture* (pp. 271–313). Basingstoke: Macmillan.

Stevens, G., Duncan, N., & Hook, D. (Eds.). (2013). *Race, memory and the apartheid archive: Towards a transformative psychosocial praxis*. London: Palgrave Macmillan.

Stoler, A. L. (1999). *Race and the education of desire: Foucault's history of sexuality and the colonial order of things*. Durham, NC: Duke University Press.

Tamale, S. (2011). *African sexualities: A reader*. Cape Town & Dakar: Pambazuka Press.

Tavakoli-Targhi, M. (2001). *Refashioning Iran: Orientalism, Occidentalism and historiography*. New York: Palgrave Macmillan.

Treacher Kebesh, A. (2013). *Postcolonial masculinities: Emotions, histories and ethics*. London: Routledge.

Twine, F. W. (2000). Bearing blackness in Britain: The meaning of racial difference for white birth mothers of African-descent children. In H. Ragoné & F. Twine (Eds.), *Ideologies and technologies of motherhood: Race, class, sexuality and gender* (pp. 79–110). New York: Routledge.

Wallaschek, S. (2017). In dialogue: Postcolonial theory and intersectionality. *Momentum Quarterly*, *4*(4), 218–232.

Yeğenoğlu, M. (1999). *Colonial fantasies: Toward a feminist reading of orientalism*. Cambridge: Cambridge University Press.

9

Approaching affective masculinities

Todd W. Reeser

What does or can "affect" do to masculinity? The widespread "affective turn"—which Patricia Clough (2007) described as "a new configuration of bodies, technology, and matter instigating a shift in thought in critical theory" (p. 2)—has allowed gender studies scholars to shift beyond language-focused theoretical approaches to gender. Affect studies has emerged in part through and with feminist and queer studies, but masculinity has not significantly factored into this work. As a result, this chapter offers ways to approach critical studies of men and masculinity in light of affect studies. The goal is to offer gender studies scholars approaches to include and to adapt in their own work. The relationship between masculinity and "emotion" is not taken up, as the topic has been covered in gender studies scholarship now for many years, even as affect's relationship to emotions will remain a central concern. It is not possible to cover all elements of the large body of work in affect studies, and because affect itself is a slippery concept, it is not possible to nail down with precision what it means. The focus is on how affect—alone or along with emotion—can transform normative or hegemonic masculinity and on how it can reify or reaffirm gender normativity or hegemony. Affect's lack of fixity is part of the reason that it can reconfigure masculinities that purport or attempt to be stable and unchanging, thereby adding another model to movement-centered models of masculinities (see Reeser, 2009).

Affect and emotion in dialogue

Affect and emotion are not the same thing: while affect is pre-personal, emotion is primarily culturally coded. In a certain cultural context, a man may learn that he should not feel afraid, and when he talks about his emotion, he may use discursive conventions that he has been taught, essentially citing others who have spoken about similar emotions. He may imitate the words of his father or of an action-movie hero. Or, an inexpressive male may have learned that he should not express emotions in the first place, meaning that he has learned to avoid discourse on the topic. He may have learned that some emotions (e.g., anger) are acceptable for a man to express while others are not and may be coded as feminine. Relationships to emotions are crucial to the construction of masculinity, but by the time a male subject expresses an emotion (or not), something more visceral and more intense has already taken place. He has been affected by a force outside himself that he has not yet put into words, and his body already may have had a physical reaction that has been transformed into a discursive expression of emotion. One contribution of affect as analytic lens, then, is to factor in the role of the body in questions related to an individual's feeling and thereby take the role of intensity seriously. If a homophobic, sexist, white supremacist expresses his anger about gay rights, feminism, and anti-racism to another man, for instance, he may have already responded viscerally and physically to a situation related to these cultural movements. An expression of anger—because he has learned it—may not directly reflect the affective reaction but may function as a kind of retroactive justification for what he decided he was experiencing, not necessarily corresponding to what he was experiencing at the time. If he calls in to a right-wing talk radio show with an affective reaction to feminism that he has not yet put into language himself, the host of that show may explain in language what he is supposedly feeling, creating his emotion on his behalf. In cases such as these, emotions "capture" and stabilize ineffable and hard-to-pin-down affect, putting it into culturally recognizable discourse.

As influential theorist Brian Massumi puts it in a well-known phrasing about capturing affect, an emotion is "the sociolinguistic fixing of the quality of an experience which is from that point onward defined as personal ... the conventional, consensual point of insertion of intensity into semantically and semiotically formed progressions ... It is intensity owned and recognized" (2002, p. 28). Affect may be a problem for normative or hegemonic masculinity because it reveals that a male body is not in full control, since affect affects it in unpredictable ways. Massumi writes: "actually existing, structured things live in and through that which escapes them. Their autonomy is the autonomy of affect" (2002, p. 35). The autonomy of affect may dismantle a man's perception of his own autonomy or self-control if he does not want to live through what escapes him. Lacking control over himself may imply that he cannot assert control or power over others. His visceral reaction to feminism may be an issue for him because it implies his inability to influence the gendered situation. It may also be a problem that, as Massumi writes, "there is no cultural-theoretical vocabulary specific to affect" (2002, p. 27), meaning that a male subject may sense that he cannot use words to contain, control, and capture an affect which remains linguistically autonomous, outside his discursive control.

Affective subjectivities

Because affect is pre-personal and does something to a body before the articulation of what one thinks is happening, it may seem nonexistent. That seeming absence does not mean that it is not possible to express affect at all, however: the man who says that he was so angry that he could feel the blood pumping in his veins is expressing an affective reaction of corporeal intensity. Labeling something "visceral" or "beyond words" suggests affect. But affect can only be expressed retroactively, as something over and in the past, and the inability to describe affect can itself be described. A literary passage can express an affective moment, but it does so with words and may rely on describing the corporality or the inexpressibility of the experience. A film, video, or photo may depict a certain male character having a nonverbal, corporeal reaction that a viewer can sense by sight. In other words, the nondiscursive nature of affect does not mean that people will not try to represent the nondiscursivity using discourse or visual means and by extension relations between gender and affective representation.

Affect and emotion do not have to be entirely separate, however, but may function as a chain, with one leading to the other. Affect can be considered in its relation to nonaffective moments over the course of time and not simply in a single moment. Using the term "affective practice" to describe a combination of affective elements, Margaret Wetherell is critical of Massumi's idea of the autonomy of affect: for her, characteristics of affect are one element in a chain of actions and reactions in potential dialogue with discourse or captures. There are not, she writes, "discrete and separable elements that are ordered or put together but an integrated and organic unfolding and weaving" (2012, p. 89). Clare Hemmings uses the term "affective cycles," which "form *patterns* that are subject to reflective or political, rather than momentary or arbitrary judgement" and which we should imagine "not as a series of repeated moments—body-affect-emotion" but as "an ongoing, incrementally altering chain—body-affect-emotion-affect-body-doubling back upon the body" (2005, p. 564, emphasis in original). For scholars like Wetherell and Hemmings, such practices or such cycles contain nonlinear oscillations of affect and emotion, of autonomy and capture, of the difficult-to-articulate and the culturally coded, or of the visceral and the noncorporeal.

A scholar might consider how masculinity relates not simply to affect but also to certain kinds of cycles or patterns, or how certain affect-emotion chains recur in culture and come to constitute or buttress masculinity. The example above about a sexist man calling in to a radio show could serve as one example. An affect may be turned into an emotion, but when that cycle recurs over and over and becomes culturally legible, the cycle may become a two-part brand of sexist masculinity beyond one individual's experience. That dyadic cycle may lead to another affective moment based in visceral rage provoked by emotional capture, adding another element to the cycle and becoming culturally legible by virtue of its repetition. Or, a man affected by affect may go on to focus exclusively on its capture, essentially forgetting that he had an affective reaction in the first place. Forgetting affect may itself be part of how masculinity functions: the articulation of anger may be a way for him to justify his lack of control as his heart pumps and he feels rage in his body that has the potential to cause loss of masculine self-control. But in such cases, it is the full unfolding that should be imagined as constituting masculinity, not one affect or one emotion in itself. At the same time, such movement-based patterns may not be culturally legible or recurring but, rather, "organic" and unpredictable. Talking about fear in culturally coded terms may be so constraining that it leads to an affective reaction because of the discursive constraint of the emotion, or not talking about feeling afraid may actually produce an intense, visceral reaction instead of taming affect.

Affect's pre-personal nature is an important element to consider. Theorists Gilles Deleuze and Félix Guattari describe affects as "nonsubjectified," or as beyond subjectivity (1987, p. 262). If a sexist man's affect, during the moment that it takes place, lies beyond gender subjectivity because it lacks the language necessary to convey gender, concerns about missing, lost, or absent masculinity in that moment may influence him to express more extreme masculinity to recuperate his perceived lack of masculinity. Conversely, nonsubjectification has the potential to transform a male subject, affecting and decomposing his masculinity. The intensity of affect may revamp his gender, moving him out of normative or hegemonic masculinity for a moment.

In some circumstances, the nonsubjective characteristics of affect may dismantle masculinity for the longer term, shocking it into change. Affect can be a becoming, a movement into a new way of performing gender instead of a movement backward in a conservative mode of stasis. Gregory Seigworth and Melissa Gregg define the power of affect as "a body's *capacity* to affect and to be affected" (2010, p. 2, their emphasis), meaning that a male body's gender subjectivity can be affected and reconfigured by external forces that cannot be known or predicted in advance. Theorist Michael Hardt argues that "the production of affects, subjectivities, and forms of life present an enormous potential for autonomous circuits of valorization, and perhaps for liberation" (1999, p. 100). This potential liberation would be from, among other things, "patriarchal order" (p. 100). The not-knowing what a male body can be or become offers the capacity to free male bodies and those held under a sexist regime from the patriarchal stasis that requires that male bodies remain the same and not be put into movement. The Swedish film *Force Majeure* could be taken to exemplify this kind of gender transformation. In this film, the normative main character Tomas has a breakdown in front of his wife and children that is coded as extremely affective. After the scene, his normative gender is reconfigured substantially, in part because it is shown to be performative and because his wife has increased agency (Reeser, 2017b).

Another way to consider the transformative power of affect is to answer yes to the question asked by Jasbir Puar: "is it the case that there is something queer about affect, that affect is queer unto itself, always already a defiance of identity registers, amenable to queer critique?" (2007, p. 207). The results of affect may queer normative masculinity, leaving it not discrete but in movement or leaving it not fully heteronormative. The constraints of homophobia may create an intense affect for a heterosexual man who goes swimming with his heterosexual male friend but also feels joy being with him, such that the experience of affect has a queer element to it. Or such a man may relish affect because he appreciates the experience of queerness that moves him out of normativity. He may seek to go swimming again to relive that affect. It is also possible that affect's potential to queer masculinity may lead this man cover up, hide, or dominate affect, as best he can. In such a case, the seeming invisibility of affect reaffirms his masculinity if he views the success of stoic masculinity as a reaffirmation of nonqueer masculinity. The man who feels joy swimming with his male friend may work extra hard to keep any affect from emerging or from being visible to his friend, not simply because of homophobia or anxiety of same-sex love but because of the queer potential of affect itself.

Instead of taking affect as autonomous, it is also possible to consider affect in terms articulated by Raymond Williams, who famously coined the phrase "structure of feeling." Art and literature are special places to find a structure of feeling, which, "because it is at the very edge of semantic availability, has many of the characteristics of a pre-formation, until specific articulations—new semantic figures—are discovered in material practice" (Williams, 1977, p. 134). When an affect is not really recognizable and does not fit easily into some predetermined category, it may be a pre-formation not yet categorizable or able to be filed away and forgotten. As Williams defines structure of feeling, it is "a social experience which is still in process, often indeed not yet recognized as social but taken to be private, idiosyncratic, and even isolating" (1977, p. 132). An affect–emotion dyad may gesture toward a gendered relationship that is not yet part of culture in a way that is widely legible. The affect that a heterosexual man experiences with his friend at the swimming pool may not be fully affective because it contains some linguistic elements. He may be able to describe some elements of his experience but in an incomplete way. That proximity to language may suggest that there is an emerging cultural relationship between men on the horizon not yet put into language, not captured by terms such as "friendship" or "love." There may not be, as of yet, a way to explain their relationship in culturally legible terms, but that kind of interaction may be in the process of becoming culturally legible, and the affective relationship may one day be signified in emotional terms.

Leaky affect

What I have been discussing so far suggests two options: that affect reconfigures masculinity or that dominating affect reifies and restabilizes masculinity. There is, however, a third possibility, what I might call "leaky affect," in which affect affects a male body but only to a limited extent. A male subject may be partially affected in a given circumstance but remain in an intermediary position between domination and full loss of subjectivity. This type of affective quasi-capture points to a release valve model of masculinity, in which a force with the potential to upend masculinity is permitted to release some pressure so that the whole system of masculinity is not obliterated. Kenneth Lonergan's American film *Manchester by the Sea* (2016) emblematizes this form of affective masculinity. The main character Lee has suffered through his children's death earlier in his life, and in the film's narrative, his brother dies and he becomes the unwilling legal guardian of his adolescent nephew. Much of the film revolves around the question of whether he can work through his past in order to take on the responsibility for his nephew in the present. From an affective point of view, the exchanges between him and his nephew are neither full of, nor devoid of, affect; and his expression of visceral pain from his children's death is neither fully contained nor fully released. He may seem very stoic generally, but at moments he looks slightly affected by his past or by love for his nephew. The film represents the leakiness in the opening scenes of the film as Lee, who works as a handyman, fixes a leaky toilet out of which water is dripping through a stopper. The scene conveys that what is leaking is Lee himself as his past is not stopped but drips out and affects him.

Reading masculinity may entail locating elements of a seemingly stoic or unemotional masculinity when affect leaks. Such leakiness may be visible on the body, in small expressions that reveal affect in ways or in moments that are hard to locate. Sam de Boise and Jeff Hearn suggest that language and emotions do not have to be the only element of interviews that ethnographers focus on when doing work on masculinity and emotions: "Visible indicators in interviews—such as averting one's gaze during topics, blushing, tension or irritation at certain questions, smiling when discussing a particular subject—could all be considered indicators of affective response which require classification and interpretation" (2017, p. 12). A normative man being interviewed about gender may respond affectively in one way, but then move on to respond emotionally and linguistically in another way, leaving someone else the task of determining what the affect might be or what the affective cycle or pattern might be as affect becomes affective expression which in turn becomes discursive.

The masculinity of affect

Deleuze and Guattari write that affect is "man's nonhuman becoming" and that a man may become woman as he reaches "a zone of indetermination" that "precedes [his] natural differentiation" (1994, p. 173). Affect can be coded as feminine, rendering a normative man feminized because, for instance, he lacks, or is perceived to lack, the autonomy or power to resist or because he is controlled by an alien force and not by himself. In contrast, the representation of affect may be masculinized because the sheer force or energy of affect may be taken as a kind of masculine phenomenon. Deleuze and Guattari, in a key articulation of affect, define it in militaristic terms: "Affect is the active discharge of emotion, the counterattack ... Affects are projectiles just like weapons ... Weapons are affects and affects weapons" (1987, p. 400). The force or power of affects may affect a normative man violently, and that force or violence may in fact reconfigure masculinity after victory in a kind of battle between affect and masculinity. The whole problem of the film *Force Majeure* begins when Tomas runs away from his wife and two young children on the terrace of a ski lodge while having lunch because an avalanche comes dangerously close to the table. But if affect is highlighted as the center of the film, the avalanche allegorizes the masculinity of affect, a sign of what is to come later on. This example suggests that one element of studying affective masculinity is to consider not simply how affect itself may change gender but also how affective representation operates *as* masculinity. The affect of masculinity as well as the masculinity of affect can be studied.

There is an important caveat that needs to be taken into account in imagining affect as asubjective. As scholars have discussed in critiques of affect, coding affect as outside identity risks reinscribing a male norm. Clare Hemmings writes that "affective rewriting … ignor[es] the counter-hegemonic contributions of postcolonial and feminist theorists, only thereby positioning affect as 'the answer' to contemporary problems of cultural theory" (2005, p. 548; see also Pedwell & Whitehead, 2012). Taking affect as liberatory risks ignoring other ways in which hegemonic masculinity is dismantled. For Deborah Thien, affect theory reproduces the gendered division reason/emotion with a new binary opposition:

> The jettisoning of the term "emotion" in favour of the term "affect" seems compelled by an underlying revisiting … of the binary trope of emotion as negatively positioned in opposition to reason, as objectionably soft and implicitly feminized. In this conceptual positioning, these transhuman geographies re-draw yet again not only the demarcation between masculinist reason and feminized emotion, but also the false distinction between "personal" and "political" which feminist scholars have extensively critiqued.
>
> *(2005, p. 452)*

Affect, Thien suggests, is assumed to be outside the political because it is taken as intensively personal, though it should not be separated from the political nor coded as unmarked or masculine. What I have called the masculinity of affect may reinscribe a gender binary, with emotion as feminized and affect as the agential and masculine element of the opposition. What if the autonomy or freedom characterizing affect is itself a reinscription of the supposed freedom of the normative male subject from political constraint and subjectivity? Taking affect as outside language may have the result of rendering it implicitly masculine, taking gender studies backwards to an unmarked universalism that is actually male but not explicitly coded as such.

A second risk is that the autonomy of affect, as standing alone and not subject to language, permits it to become justification for sexism or for other hegemonies. In his article on men's rights movements in North America, Jonathan Allan considers affect as potentially outside reason and thus necessarily self-evident and beyond critique:

> the declaring of affect is a remarkably powerful declaration precisely because it cannot be denied, that is, by turning to affect the men's rights activists do not need to prove the truth of their claims because their affects—the feeling that it is true—trump the veracity of the thing causing the feeling.
>
> *(2016, p. 27)*

When taken as outside culture and thus as true, affect may allow for gender hegemonies to be conveniently forgotten, and that supposed blank slate may be used for other ends that privilege men and masculinity in new ways.

Transmitting affective masculinity

Affect positions the body in a broad swath of forces as a given body receives and then passes on affect. As Seigworth and Gregg note, "affect marks a body's belonging to a world of encounters" (2010, p. 2). Affective energies or intensities may transmit from another source that may or may not be human through a male body into another human or non-human body, a phenomenon that Teresa Brennan terms "the transmission of affect" (2004). The energy of a gay man's drag performance may pass into a normative heterosexual male body, affecting it in ways predicated not on homophobia or transphobia but on a new gender subjectivity that may be hard to characterize at all. Or, the violent energy of a football match in a stadium or on television may be transmitted to a male body in a way that renders him violent. He may in turn transmit that affect to other bodies. In such cases, the transmission of affect may be experienced as disrupting masculine autonomy or as intensifying the masculinity of a male body.

Affect does not have to simply be related to what a single body undergoes but may define the relationship or encounter between people. In a difficult-to-handle exchange between two or more people, it may suggest the recognition of subjectivities new to the perceiver in a given situation, including one's own. If, for example, a heterosexual cisgender man asks a transwoman out on a date and then she tells him that she is transgender, an intensely awkward affect lingering silently in the air may be the impetus for a recognition on his part of a gendered subjectivity that he may not have previously seen as involved in his dating life. In this way, affect can open up new gendered configurations or relations for the man who is not invested in maintaining heterosexual masculinity as stable and who is willing to let himself be affected in new ways. This man may undo what dating means for him or what his heterosexuality or his masculinity means. He may question what it means to be "a woman." But the same awkward affect may also, conversely, lead to the covering up of difference and be taken as an excuse to move on and to forget that intense moment when he did not know what to do or say. This hypothetical man may simply excuse himself and remain firmly within his fixed definitions of gender and sexual subjectivity, on guard to keep the same situation from ever arising in the future. Instead of opening up new gendered possibilities, the articulation of awkward affect may eclipse them and offer carte blanche to ignore them.

Such affective moments not only arise in daily life but also can be invented or staged for the very same reasons. Creating lingering affects that do not get resolved or that do not get immediately resolved can be a representational strategy to invite those who witness the affect to call attention to the potentiality of gender and to think about or experience gender in new ways. Ineffable moments of visceral potentiality can have the effect of revisioning masculinity away from its normativity or its hegemony, of putting it into motion, or of queering it. The notion that with and through affect, we do not know what a body can do, or that affect opens up potentialities, has important implications for masculinity studies. On the one hand, affective representations can be lingering moments that aim to influence the stasis and boundedness of normative masculinity, opening it up to new configurations through specific affects such as awkwardness (Reeser, 2017a). Creating affects of this kind can be what Massumi calls "a pragmatic politics of the in-between," which opens up the potential for the recognition of new forms of relating (2015, p. 18). Such a political gesture is not an identity politics but a relational mode of transformation. On the other hand, however, affect may be evoked and allowed to circulate, but then dominated by ending its movement or transmission. One way to assert masculinity is to go through a bipartite process in which affect is evoked in order to be contained. The international TV prank show *Awkward Jokers* is one example of a cultural representation in which normative men aim to create for other men very awkward public affects that have to be dominated, and the domination of awkwardness is tied to asserting or maintaining normative masculinity and not becoming feminized or queer. Those revisionary moments may be temporary, contained, and evoked only to be effaced, serving to reinforce the normativity of masculinity in a more pernicious way than without them (Reeser, 2017a).

Reading the ambiguity of affect

It may not always be possible to determine whether masculinity is affected and opened up to new possibilities, whether it is closed off, or whether it is queered or re-rendered normative. In particular, it may be a viewer's own hermeneutic or way of seeing masculinity that creates the narrative of masculinity. The slipperiness of affect may permit slipperiness in how affective masculinity is read and understood, opening up an interpretive space of confusion or ambiguity. In other cases, ambiguity around affect may be the focus of the representation of masculinity. As an example, I might cite US photographer Richard Renaldi's book *Touching Strangers* (2014), a collection of photos in which two perfect strangers are invited to pose for the camera as they touch. By virtue of the subject matter, the photos all stand in some inherent relationship to awkward affect: two strangers being asked to touch, and pose for the camera, is inherently awkward and may look this way to the viewer. The photos themselves capture a moment in time in which two strangers are forced to relate to each other. Some of the photos convey a visible image of comfort in strangeness that brings people together across divides of visible forms of identity such as race/ethnicity, religion, age, or able-bodiedness. But in other cases, it is unclear what the momentary affect is or how it has come about, particularly when two male bodies are touching each other. In one photo, a thin man of color in a green tank top touches a larger white man wearing a cowboy hat, with an American flag in the background (Renaldi, 2014, p. 11). The difficulty of the touch is palpable but not discursive, and the viewer may consider why. Their awkwardness is not overcome, but the intersubjective affect calls attention to the affect of male–male relations as invented and open-ended if viewers craft a narrative about the image based on the details that strike them. One viewer may invent a narrative about homophobia, another about repressed attraction, another about geography, another about race, etc. Because the photos invite a story on the part of the viewer, the image of masculinity has many possible discursive outcomes, allowing for any number of gender configurations to jump out of the frame. It is the hermeneutic open-endedness that permits multiple narratives around masculinity to emerge, driving home that discursive captures are necessarily interpretive and do not reflect an essence about masculinity. But as I have suggested in this chapter, open-endedness is only one characteristic of the relationship between masculinity and affect, and scholars should be on guard to constantly seek out the multiplicity of ways in which affect functions vis-à-vis masculinity, never assuming that it takes only one form.

References

Allan, J. A. (2016). Phallic affect, or why men's rights activists have feelings. *Men and Masculinities, 19*(1), 22–41.

Brennan, T. (2004). *The transmission of affect*. Ithaca, NY: Cornell University Press.

Clough, P. T. (Ed.). (2007). *The affective turn: Theorizing the social*. Durham, NC: Duke University Press.

de Boise, S., & Hearn, J. (2017). Are men getting more emotional? Critical sociological perspectives on men, masculinities and emotions. *The Sociological Review, 65*(4), 779–796.

Deleuze, G., & Guattari, F. (1987). *A thousand plateaus: Capitalism and schizophrenia* (B. Massumi Trans.). Minneapolis, MN: University of Minnesota Press.

Deleuze, G., & Guattari, F. (1994). Percept, affect, and concept. In Deleuze & Guattari, *What is philosophy?* (H. Tomlinson & G. Burchell Trans.). New York: Columbia University Press.

Hardt, M. (1999). Affective labor. *Boundary 2*, *26*(2), 89–100.
Hemmings, C. (2005). Invoking affect: Cultural theory and the ontological turn. *Cultural Studies*, *19*(5), 548–567.
Massumi, B. (2002). *Parables for the virtual: Movement, affect, sensation*. Durham, NC: Duke University Press.
Massumi, B. (2015). *Politics of affect*. Cambridge: Polity.
Pedwell, C., & Whitehead, A. (2012). Affecting feminism: Questions of feeling in feminist theory. *Feminist Theory*, *13*(2), 115–129.
Puar, J. K. (2007). *Terrorist assemblages: Homonationalism in queer times*. Durham, NC: Duke University Press.
Reeser, T. W. (2009). *Masculinities in theory*. Malden, MA: Wiley-Blackwell.
Reeser, T. W. (2017a). Producing awkwardness: Affective labour and masculinity in popular culture. *Mosaic: An Interdisciplinary Critical Journal*, *50*(4), 51–69.
Reeser, T. W. (2017b). Theorizing the masculinity of affect. In J. M. Armengol, M. Bosch-Vilarrubias, À. Carabí, & T. Requena-Pelegrí (Eds.), *Masculinities and literary studies: Intersections and new directions* (pp. 109–119). New York: Routledge.
Renaldi, R. (2014). *Touching strangers*. New York: Aperture.
Seigworth, G. J., & Gregg, M. (2010). An inventory of shimmers. In M. Gregg & G. J. Seigworth (Eds.), *The affect theory reader* (pp. 1–25). Durham, NC: Duke University Press.
Thien, D. (2005). After or beyond feeling? A consideration of affect and emotion in geography. *Area*, *37*(4), 450–454.
Wetherell, M. (2012). *Affect and emotion: A new social science understanding*. Los Angeles, CA: Sage.
Williams, R. (1977). *Marxism and literature*. Oxford: Oxford University Press.

10

Masculinity studies and posthumanism

Ulf Mellström

Introduction

This chapter maps some of the connections between a posthumanist turn in the social sciences and the humanities in relation to masculinity studies. It is a large and vague task that by necessity is an inherently interdisciplinary one, looming around binaries like nature–culture; human–non-human; machinic–somatic; materiality–organic. This chapter overviews how posthumanism and new materialism have been taken up in masculinity studies. Under the three headings of "Transcendence", "Man plus metaphors" and "Posthumanism and new materialism in masculinity studies" it is demonstrated how masculinity can and has been theorised and studied in relation to different entanglements of human–non-human; machinic–somatic; culture–nature; material–organic. It is further shown how a cyborgic paradigm has been truly important for the conceptual as well as biological evolution of Man and masculinity. In addition, it is also shown that the emancipatory promise of an egalitarian posthuman ontology is ambivalent in relation to masculinity and a future posthumanity by selective readings but focuses on how posthumanist thinking has been absorbed into or taken up in studies of men and masculinities. It is a reading situated in my background in science and technology studies (STS), anthropology in combination with gender studies and in particular feminist technology studies.

In the field of feminist new materialism, there are few texts that explicitly problematise masculinity in ontological terms or that have masculinity as their central focus. So, mapping the texts that engage more deeply with issues of masculinity is a manageable task, but if we extend the assignment to mapping the question of how Man is entangled with nature, culture, materiality and corporeality in knowledge production, it is not. We then rather cut to the core of how masculinity is the "gender of no gender" or the normative node of what it means to be (hu)man, or how the social sciences uncritically have presumed a masculine subject when examining (hu)man conditions, or how a knowledgeable subject has been presumed and required to be a man in science or politics. This is key, of course, as the ontological politics and epistemological practices of many forms of new materialisms is to displace (hu)man exceptionalism (Alaimo, 2016), to displace the central role of Man and to decentre the masculine subject as such. Corporeal and materialist ethics and politics consequently take us toward entanglements, intimacies, dependence upon nature, culture and materiality. My focus is first on showing how such entanglements are and have been constitutive for masculinity through the idea of transcendence. Second, I focus on the many metaphors for various forms of masculinity that are emerging to describe embodiedness and connectedness to nature, materiality and corporeality. My third aim is to engage with the sparse but important literature in masculinity studies that critically anchors masculinity in new materialism and posthumanism.[1]

Transcendence

In the spirit of Simone de Beauvoir (1993/1949), my understanding of transcendence refers to different forms of bodily transgression. As de Beauvoir pointed out, transcendence is an ontological state that has been closely connected with masculinity in contrast to the immanence of an embodied trapped femininity. If, as a starting point, we take how masculine identity has been connected to materiality and how the very idea of Man is connected to transcendence and transgressing the (hu)man flesh, the best metaphor we possibly can find is the cyborg (see also Robertson, Monaghan & Southby, this volume). For the purpose of this chapter, I believe it works as an encompassing term for a self-regulating system that combines and transcends the organic and the artificial, the machinic and the non-machinic and that has been so characteristic for the conceptual as well as biological evolution of Man and masculinity. Although the term itself originates from a 1960 article by Clynes and Kline, melding cybernetic and organic into cyborg, the conceptualisation has been paramount to describe the fusion between (hu)man and machine. It is as specific and general as tool and machine, but just as important to portray a politics of the body in historical accounts as well as portraying our contemporary "Zeitgeist". As the prolific cyborg theorist Chris Hables Gray points out, "Cyborgs were a dream long before there were even machines" (2000, p. 4).

Through religious "engineering", (hu)mankind has nourished the idea of human–non human creatures in myths, cosmologies, tales and stories of all kinds. Hindi and Taoist mythology, for example, has been dominated by gods and goddesses and creatures of all sorts that transgress borders between the (hu)man, the worlds of animals, gods and machinic creatures. In many non-western cosmologies, the idea of a sharp mind–body and/or nature–culture dualism is not applicable, which of course opens up for a myriad of forms of existence that involve organic and non-human components and most often extend into the mundane practices of everyday life. For instance, in my own work among mechanics in the Chinese-Malaysian diaspora of Penang, Malaysia (Mellström, 2003), I documented how tools and material objects are part of the concept of a person, or what makes up personhood in itself in a Taoist-Confucian cosmology. The idea of a "self" has, in the ontology of the local folk beliefs, a polar relationship with "others". Following from this is that each particular is a consequence of every other and determined by every other particular. (Hu)man existence is then constitutive in relation to "others" and incorporates an extensive idea of subjectivity where the "self" is a subject, that constantly is constituted and re-constituted in relation to "others" and networks of "others", including machines as "others". The mechanics embody "others" in the form of tools and machines, and such an embodiment of machines is a constitutive part of their sense of masculine entitlement as well as deeply grounded in a belief system that is inherently transgressive with regard to anything that we label human or non-human.

The cyborgic idea is a leitmotif that runs deep throughout the history of religion, art, science and technology in the Western as well as the non-Western world, and a crucial drive in this leitmotif is the male desire of transcendence. This desire of transcendence has been invested in and nurtured through, for instance, religious, mythological and technical fantasy creatures such as automatons, golems, robots etc. A characteristic feature of these artefacts and creatures has been their prosthetic capacity with an inherent Janus face. Historically, as well as in relation to the future of masculinity, this points in two different directions: destructiveness and emancipatory hopes of transcendence through cyborgisation. In combination, cyborgs are thus political technologies and ambivalent creatures. The Janus face of such political technologies, for instance are outlined by Donna Haraway (1997, p. 135):

> From one perspective, a cyborg world is about the final imposition of a grid of control on the planet, about the final abstraction embodied in a Star Wars apocalypse waged in the name of defence. From another perspective, a cyborg world might be about lived social and bodily realities in which people are not afraid of their joint kinship with animals and machines, not afraid of permanently partial identities and contradictory standpoints. The political struggle is to see from both perspectives at once.

Her symbolic appropriation of the concept was crystallised in her famous sentence "I'd rather be a cyborg than a goddess", in the just as famous "Cyborg manifesto" (Haraway, 1985). In many ways, this was a turning point for a feminist intervention into a conceptual and experiential world which until then had been almost totally dominated by male bodies and a masculine discursive space. Although she would hardly use the term "posthuman" (see, for instance, Haraway, 2016), Haraway nonetheless opened up an emancipatory space for a posthuman understanding and symbolic appropriation of technological intimacy as entanglement, reciprocity, proximity and affinity with vibrant materialities that has become the key component of feminist, critical posthumanism and new materialism (Alaimo, 2016; Barad, 2007; Braidotti, 2013). Despite her own reluctance regarding the posthumanist label, Haraway is increasingly being honoured for being a "prophet" of the posthuman era and having developed a wider understanding of diverse forms of ontological hybridity; "In critical terms, the posthuman is the progeny of the cyborg" (Ferrando, 2015, p. 275). This ethico-onto-epistemological (Barad, 2007) grounding of new materialism is slowly moving into masculinity studies.

There are many different arenas in which we can trace how masculinity has been constructed through and entangled with intimacy, corporeality, technology connected through a desire for transcendence with a particular focus on the fusion of masculinity and the machinic. From a perspective of a cyborg-epistemology formulated as "thesis, anti-thesis, synthesis, prosthesis" (Gray, 2001, p. 189), one could argue that a history of masculinity in a Western context and beyond is intrinsically linked to transcendence and cyborgisation and intimacy with technological artefacts in particular. The destructive character of such cyborgic entanglements can be traced in various forms of military masculinities, for instance,. Entanglements of the machinic in the military is a long-standing theme with many strands of thought in relation to hybrid imaginations of power and pleasure, eroticism, lust, submission, penetration etcetera. Lewis Mumford (1946) argued that the very first machine was an army consisting of men and their weapons as the moving parts. He pointed to how weaponry and the disciplining of individual bodies/soldiers into cleanly working parts, and the military's fostering of automation, have contributed to an ideal of masculinity which has formed endless generations of men. In addition, it has also formed many postwar generations of prosthetic and disabled men (Neumann, 2010).

Consequently, it is also from the experience of warfare and military practices where cyborgian ideals have been articulated long before Clynes and Kline coined the term "cyborg". The pre-cyborgian history is full of automatons, golems, homunculi etc. A desire for and fantasy of human transcendence is a common feature for these hybrid creatures. In premodern history, different forms of automatons are without exception connected to different religious pursuits trying to transgress life in its limited organic corporeal form. However, it is in the 19th and 20th centuries that automatons have become an important part of military machineries and imaginaries, although the dream of the invulnerable and indestructible machinic man probably goes back to the dawn of Man. The mechanisation of war and the cyborgisation of Man go hand in hand with industrialism and "scientific management". The machinalisation of mankind that Nietzsche wrote about was also a machinalisation of war in the name of industrial efficiency and technical rationality (McGinn, 1980). The idea of Man multiplied by machinery is thus a central theme throughout modernity, ideologically as well as in different forms of embodied expressions of masculinity. This is what Gray (2001) calls "Man Plus".

The long-lived dream of the prosthetic integration of masculinity and weaponry has had many sad moments in history. Such a truly vitalistic moment of possible transcendence is described by Klaus Theweleit (1980) in his two-volume *Männerphantasien* [Male Fantasies], where he examines the biopolitics of the German Freikorps during WWI. Theweleit portrays the emergence of a new type of man, one with a deeply erotic and ambivalent relationship with mechanisation. This is a man whose physique had been machinalised, his psyche eliminated – or in part displaced into his body armour. It is a deeply affective relationship that in the words of Theweleit, interpreting the work of Ernst Jünger, performs a self-mechanised masculinity "whose instinctual energies have been smoothly and frictionlessly transformed into functions of his steel body" (Theweleit, 1980, p. 162). This machinalised man with a mechanised psyche and steel body is expected to devote his life to the machinic. "Yes the machine is beautiful: its beauty is self-evident to anyone who lives life in all its fullness and power. We must imbue the machine with our own inner qualities" (Theweleit, 1980, p. 197). In return, the soldier will reach "a higher and deeper satisfaction" (p. 197). The ideological and performative function of this self-mechanisation, which Jünger held as the ultimate ideal for the soldier man, is evident. It would motivate him to bear the burdens of a dreadful existence in the trenches, to find a higher motive in the hopelessness of an endless war. The ultimate goal of affective explosion is, according to Theweleit: "The crucial impulse behind the regeneration of the machine seems to be its desire for release – and release is achieved when the totality-machine and its components explode in battle" (p. 155).

The writings of Ernst Jünger interpreted by Theweleit is a figuration where mechanisation, intimacy and the body are tightly entangled and which has since become a psychological profile and ideal for generations of military masculinities, both in a modern and postmodern sense. The integrated man-machine ontologies have been accentuated since. Or as Gray (2000, p. 281) has it: "This long standing incestuous relationship between war, men, and machines may well have finally birthed the psychological reality of cyborgs in the hell of 1917".

Besides the destructive and fatalistic character of a prosthetic integration of masculinity and weaponry, there are numerous ways of conceptualising a prosthetic paradigm of Man and masculinity in relation to materiality, nature and technology. This could go in many different directions. In classic palaeontological archaeology and human palaeontology, it is the very definition of what it means to be (a) man. For instance, in the work *Man the Tool-Maker*, Oakley (1960, p. 1) claims in the characteristic universal tone of the time: "Man is a social animal, distinguished by "culture": by the ability to make tools and communicate ideas". To be a tool-making animal is also, according to Oakley, what gives Man the possibility to transcend the incompleteness of human life. In classic palaeontological archaeology and human palaeontology, the very definition of Man indicates a posthuman meaning in a deeply ontological sense of the word. Man is inevitably connected to an extension, attribute, artefact or tool, substituting for the incompleteness of Man alone. If we extend the argument into sexual difference theory, it is possible to interpret the Man plus along a deeply gendered differentiation of two sexes:

> since the little man that the little girl is, must become a man minus certain attributes whose paradigm is morphological – attributes capable of determining, of assuring, the reproduction-specularisation of the same. A man minus the possibility of (re)presenting oneself as a man=a normal woman.
>
> *(Irigaray, 1985, p. 27)*

The ontological primacy of sexuality, drawing on a core assumption of Freud, is here foregrounded as a version of man plus versus man minus. These are but two examples of how a prosthetic integration or an attribute are foundational in different tenets for thinking around a posthuman masculine subjectivity.

Man plus metaphors

As masculinity studies has grown rapidly since the 2000s, we have increasingly seen how new, more or less evocative metaphors are being used to discuss masculinity in connection to materiality and nature. Obviously, this seems to reflect men's and masculinities social and cultural practices with regard to different occupations, transport systems, industries, technologies and ecology.

In gender, transport and mobility studies there is a certain liking for using metaphors that multiply masculinity in relation to engines, vehicles and closely related metaphors. Redshaw (2018) differentiates between *combustion masculinity* and *hydraulic masculinity*. She defines the former as a form of masculinity with "the bursting, spurting speed and power indicating high performance [...] Combustion, or fire power, is explosive and associated with violent excitement, agitation, or discontent. It requires ignition or rapid oxidation and the constant burning of fuel" (p. 89). Drawing on the work of the theorist of speed, Paul Virilio, she conceptualises combustion masculinity as the power to penetrate as well as the power to destroy. Combustion power is a force capable of great destruction and is both the source of power and an expression of power. It is an archaic form of masculinity linked to violence, risky behaviour, speed and acceleration. As such it connects to an old masculine love affair with automobile technology and car cultures. This is a love affair based on a gendered and affective economy of speed, pleasure and embodiment and something that has been truly constitutive for various forms of masculinity in the age of late industrialism (Balkmar & Mellström, 2018). Redshaw argues that the ultimate symbol of combustion masculinity is the race-car driver. She identifies the lonesome road warrior with a high propensity for risk-taking as the most popular and established image in car advertising. Redshaw (2018) also discusses hydraulic masculinity as an alternative image related to vehicles and the future of driverless cars. Most machines rely on hydraulic power to function, and this is a power that uses pressurised liquid for flexible, controlled and accurate operations. Redshaw sees a transformation to a hydraulic masculinity as a necessary if we are to meet the many challenges of climate change and the congestion of car-intensive societies as well as the need for more energy-efficient forms of mobility and transport. Furthermore, in relation to the anticipated future of automated vehicles and driverless cars on our roads, Redshaw argues that such a transition will not be possible if combustion masculinity remains the dominant model of how we imagine future systems of automobility in the Western world and beyond. This implies a transformation from a combustion masculinity to a hydraulic masculinity.

In a similar vein, Balkmar and Joelsson (2010) have theorised vehicles as an integrated part of the male body and masculine subjectivity. Drawing on a posthuman understanding in feminist science and technology studies, they suggest the figuration of *the bionic man* as a way to conceptualise a man plus ontology; that is, how cars and other vehicles are extensions of the (male) body. The idea of the bionic man is further closely linked to the concept of *auto-eroticism* as a way for understanding the profound embodied and emotional relationship between men, technologies of movement and risk-taking. Balkmar and Joelsson argue that the emotional aspects of driving need to be regarded as vital and crucial aspects when studying men's risk-taking in traffic space (see also Balkmar, 2012, 2014, this volume; Balkmar & Mellström, 2018; Joelsson, 2013, 2014). In addition, Balkmar (2014) has also suggested another metaphor for a man plus ontology in masculinity studies, namely modifier masculinity. Balkmar uses queer theory to discuss how the modified stylish but less powerful plastic rockets (in contrast to old muscle cars, Amcars), may undermine symbolic links between men, masculinity and power in a modifier community. According to Balkmar, these plastic rockets produce a "productive insecurity" – a queer potentiality that puts normative masculinity at risk.

Another closely related metaphor is what Stacy Alaimo labels *carbon heavy masculinities*. Alaimo's work emanates from feminist new materialism, queer theory, feminist science studies, environmental studies and cultural studies rather than masculinity studies per se (2016). Nonetheless, she identifies those kinds of "masculinities of impenetrability and aggressive consumption and, in another domain, the universalising modes of detached scientific vision" (p. 94). Alaimo cuts to the core of the question framing this chapter: the implicit question of her work is whether the masculine subject has never been detached but rather embodied all along. Has it always been inscripted with the machines, means of production, means of power deeply engraved in the material-semioticness of the world, nature and ecology? This may seem obvious but is still crucial to point out, as masculinity studies are recurrently seen as the "odd man out" (Beasley, 2009; Introduction, this volume; Garlick, 2016; Gottzén, 2018) with regard to contemporary theorising in gender studies in general and feminist theory in particular. This is, of course, questionable. Hearn, for instance (2014, 2015), has always been concerned with the materiality of men and has long been advocating a material (-)discursive perspective stemming from a wide range of materialisms. This involves "materialism as including (productive) labour/work, biological reproduction, housework, violence, sexuality, bodily generativity/degeneration, and culture/ideology/discourse" (Hearn, 2014, p. 5). Still, Alaimo's implied questions point to the emergence of a renewed and deeper engagement with the connection between masculinity, materiality, nature and technology. Characteristic of this kind of work is often their man plus point of departure, both in terms of how they theorise nature and embodiment but also in relation to affect and complexity theory (see, for instance, Reeser & Gottzén, 2018).

The work of Anshelm and Hultman (2015) and Hultman and Pulé (2018, this volume) are prime examples of how current work in masculinity studies incorporates a deeper engagement with nature, culture and systems of ecology. Hultman and his colleagues have in different constellations coined metaphors that systematically investigate relationships between nature, ecology, energy production, consumption, industrialism, modernity and different configurations of masculinity. In Hultman and Anshelm's work, they have looked into, for instance, the relationship between climate scepticism and the masculinity of industrial modernity. In their 2014 article "A green fatwā? Climate change as a threat to the masculinity of industrial modernity", they show how a small group of climate sceptics in Sweden, consisting of elderly men with influential positions in academia or large private companies, are evoking dystopic imaginaries and catastrophe scenarios with regard to a climate friendly political agenda. They also show how these climate sceptics were part of an industrialist core and how their lives and careers are deeply invested in a belief in rationality and instrumentality draped in a language of scientific positivism. This is parallel to what Bryld and Lykke (2000) have termed a "cult of ratio".

Hultman and Anshelm (2017; Anshelm & Hultman, 2015) contrast this masculinity of industrial modernity to an ecomodern masculinity, with an in-depth recognition of environmental problems that at the same time supports policies and technologies that conserve the structures of climate-destroying systems. Another configuration discussed by Hultman and Pulé (2018, this volume) is *ecological masculinities*, which considers the insights and limitations of masculinities politics, deep ecology, ecological feminism (especially contemporary developments of queer ecology) and feminist care theory and encourages scholarly masculinities inquiries and practises towards "broader care for the glocal commons" (Hultman & Pulé, this volume). The urgent contemporary concerns for the role of masculinity in the rapid climate change we are witnessing are also observed in the collected volumes by Cenamor and Brandt, *Ecomasculinities: Negotiating Male Gender Identity in U.S. Fiction* (2019), Enarson and Pease, *Men, Masculinities and Disaster* (2016) and McGregor and Seymour's special issue on "Men and Nature: Hegemonic Masculinities and Environmental Change" (2017). These important volumes indicate a growing field in masculinity studies grounded in posthumanism and new materialism, although not explicitly labelling themselves as such.

Posthumanism and new materialism in masculinity studies

Reeser and Gottzén (2018, p. 149) argue that "we need to understand affective masculinities as not only embodied expression regulated by gendered emotions regimes but *also* as the action potential of human and non-human bodies". Drawing on well-known work by Deleuze (1988) and Massumi (2002), they further argue that male bodies exist in networks where affect is channelled through non-discursive and charged materialities. Gendered affect is consequently to be understood as a dynamic interplay channelled between technologies, linguistic expressions, embodied gestures and discursive structures. Reeser and Gottzén's special issue on masculinity and affect (2018) is a productive example of how the distinctions human–non-human, machinic–somatic and material–organic are being problematised in contemporary masculinity studies. As much as Reeser and Gottzén help to invent a subfield in masculinity studies, they are also inviting an ontological politics in masculinity studies that troubles old gendered baselines like rationality–irrationality, abstract–concrete, etc. As we are moving in the direction of affective and embodied studies of men and masculinities, these baselines are in much need of being revised. de Boise and Hearn (2017, p. 789) also point in such a direction as they argue: "Existing research on men, masculinities and emotions veers uneasily between biological determinism – suggesting that emotions are inherent but 'hidden' – and constructionist determinism".

de Boise and Hearn (2017) advocate for the necessity of widening the field of masculinity studies and incorporating feminist, material-discursive approaches in order to avoid biological essentialist approaches as well as approaches determined by social constructionism. I have also (Mellström, 2016, p. 2) worked along those lines using the theoretical framework of Barad and argued that "diffraction and interference could provide a methodologically fine-tuned way to open up the open-endedness of becoming as a material-discursive practice in masculinity studies". Harrison and Olofsson (2016) are similarly inspired by the work of Karen Barad as they apply her concept of intra-action in a reading of the prosthetic relationship between the members of a local fire brigade in Sweden and their tools, as well as the organisational dynamics that forge this relationship. Harrison and Olofsson point to how Barad's work has been useful within feminist theories, while there have been few attempts to investigate how her work can benefit critical studies of men and masculinities. A somewhat different study that opened for asking deeply grounded ontological questions in masculinity studies is Schyfter's (2009) sociophilosophical investigation of motorcycle riders in Costa Rica. Besides being a welcomed empirical non-Western contribution, Schyfter develops the concept of entangled ontologies as an analytic lens that highlights the dependence and close connection that characterise the ontological constitution of artefacts, subjects and bodies in social life in relation to masculinity. Drawing on a rich tradition in philosophy, sociology of technology, new materialism and feminist technology studies, Schyfter contributes to an intriguing theoretical advancement in masculinity studies through the intersection of an eclectic set of perspectives.

In certain ways Schyfter's work, with its focus on entangled ontologies, foreshadows that of Steve Garlick (2016). Garlick's work is, to my knowledge, the most comprehensive compilation of thoughts that combine masculinity studies with new materialism. Garlick (2016, p. 5) formulates a "critical theory of masculinity *as a technology*". His ambitious project is to construct a theory of masculinity "that emphasises the extent to which masculinities may be conceived of as technologies for the control of nature" (p. 6). In Garlick's attempt to renew masculinity studies, he revisits a number of theorists such as Latour, Giddens, Connell, Adorno etc., taking up various elements of their frameworks to theorise masculinity in terms of new materialism, including theories of affect, biopolitics and complexity. His definition of masculinity as

> a technology of embodiment that limits the potentials of men's bodies to affect and to be affected and that produces habitual ways of being oriented toward the dispelling of ontological security through achieving and maintaining control or domination over nature and one's world
>
> (*p. 96*)

clearly opens up for conceptualising a deeply posthuman future that houses intertwined and open-ended materialities of ecology, technology and corporeality in relation to masculinity.

Conclusion

The conclusion for a chapter on posthumanism and masculinity seems to leave us with the essential question "Where does the posthuman condition leave men and masculinity?" (Matthews, 2018, p. 86, paraphrasing Braidotti, 2013). Matthews argues that posthumanism is fundamentally a postphallocentrism and the ultimate death of Man. As we currently are witnessing a time where ecologies and different hypermaterialities are "speaking back" to the human subject and possibly undermining the hierarchical exclusivity of Man, the urgency of redefining masculinity is no doubt a pressing concern. However, the relationship between masculinity, masculinity studies and posthumanism is complex. The promise of an emancipatory and egalitarian posthuman ontology is, in comparison to much feminist and posthumanist theorising, less clear in relation to masculinity and a future posthumanity. As I have tried to demonstrate in this chapter, masculinity has a long history of wishful transcendence by merging different forms of organic and non-organic materiality. It is an enduring theme throughout modernity and post-modernity, and long before that. However, it always comes in the Janus face of destruction vis-a-vis creation. The special masculine hubris of transcending (hu)man life via technology and materiality is a gigantic challenge for any future posthumanism. The modern Prometheus unbound (Shelley, 1818/1999) has, throughout industrialism and modernity, almost exclusively been an ambivalent one-sex "monster". Any attempt to appropriate and transform the baselines of such an onto-epistemology will meet resistance. The ethos of posthumanism is thus asking a lot (Braidotti, 2013), but why not?

Note

1 "Posthumanism" is an umbrella term that refers to a variety of movements and schools of thought. In this chapter, I focus on posthumanism as an ontology that problematises what it means to be human in an era characterised by an increased potential for technohybrid bodily transgressions, ecological awareness, fluidity of gender and sexual relations, a heightened awareness of human-animal relations and equality between species. My reading of different work includes an awareness of the larger onto-ethico-epistemological turn we observe in the social sciences and humanities but is primarily related to posthumanism and feminist new materialism, rather than transhumanism, antihumanism and metahumanism (for differences and relations, see, for instance, Ferrando, 2013).

References

Alaimo, S. (2016). *Exposed: Environmental politics and pleasures in posthuman times*. Minneapolis, MN: University of Minnesota Press.

Anshelm, J., & Hultman, M. (2015). *Discourses of global climate change: Apocalyptic framing and political antagonisms*. Abingdon: Routledge.

Balkmar, D. (2012). *On men and cars: An ethnographic study of gendered, risky and dangerous relations* (Doctoral dissertation). Linköping University, Linköping.

Balkmar, D. (2014). Negotiating the "plastic rocket": Masculinity, car styling and performance in the Swedish modified car community. *NORMA: International Journal for Masculinity Studies*, *9*(3), 166–177.

Balkmar, D., & Joelsson, T. (2010). Den bioniske mannen på autoeroriska äventyr: Mäns risktagande i trafikrummet. *NORMA: Nordic Journal for Masculinity Studies*, *5*(1), 27–44.

Balkmar, D., & Mellström, U. (2018). Masculinity and autonomous vehicles: A degendered or resegregated future system of automobility?. *Transfers*, *8*(1), 44–63.

Barad, K. M. (2007). *Meeting the universe halfway: Quantum physics and the entanglement of matter and meaning*. Durham, NC: Duke University Press.

Beasley, C. (2009). Is masculinity studies increasingly the "odd man" out? Considering problems and possibilities in contemporary gender/sexuality thinking. In A. Biricik & J. Hearn (Eds.), *Deconstructing the hegemony of men and masculinities, Vol. VI* (pp. 173–183). Linköping & Örebro Universities. Linköping, Sweden: GEXcel Centre of Gender Excellence.

Braidotti, R. (2013). *The posthuman*. Cambridge: Polity.

Bryld, M., & Lykke, N. (2000). *Cosmodolphins: Feminist cultural studies of technology, animals and the sacred*. London: Sed.

Cenamor, R., & Brandt, S. L. (Eds.). (2019). *Ecomasculinities: Negotiating male gender identity in U.S. Fiction*. New York: Lexington Books.

Clynes, M. E. & Kline, N. S. (1960). Cyborgs and space. *Astronautics*, *5*(9), 26–27, 74–76.

de Beauvoir, S. D. (1993/1949). *The second sex*. London: Campbell.

de Boise, S., & Hearn, J. (2017). Are men getting more emotional? Critical sociological perspectives on men, masculinities and emotions. *The Sociological Review*, *65*(4), 779–796.

Deleuze, G. (1988). *Spinoza: Practical philosophy*. San Francisco, CA: City Lights Books.

Enarson, E., & Pease, B. (Eds.). (2016). *Men, masculinities and disaster*. London: Routledge.

Ferrando, F. (2013). Posthumanism, transhumanism, antihumanism, metahumanism, and new materialisms: Differences and relations. *Existenz: An International Journal in Philosophy, Religion, Politics, and the Arts*, *8*(2), 26–32.

Ferrando, F. (2015). Of posthuman born: Gender, utopia and the posthuman in films and TV. In M. Hauskeller, M. Carbonell & C. D. Philbeck (Eds.) *The Palgrave handbook of posthumanism in film and television* (pp. 269–278). Houndmills: Palgrave Macmillan.

Garlick, S. (2016). *The nature of masculinity: Critical theory, new materialisms and technologies of embodiment*. Vancouver: University of British Columbia Press.

Gottzén, L. (2018). Is masculinity studies really the odd man out? *NORMA: International Journal for Masculinity Studies, 13*(2), 81–85.

Gray, C. H. (2000). Enhanced cyborgs and the construction of the future masculine. *Science as Culture, 9*(3), 277–301.

Gray, C. H. (2001). *Cyborg citizen: Politics in the posthuman age*. London: Routledge.

Haraway, D. J. (1985). A manifesto for cyborgs: Science, technology and socialist feminism in the 1980s. *Socialist Review, 80*, 65–107.

Haraway, D. J. (1997). *Modest_Witness@Second_Millennium.FemaleMan©_Meets_OncoMouse: Feminism and technoscience*. New York: Routledge.

Haraway, D. J. (2016). *Staying with the trouble: Making kin in the Chthulucene*. Durham, NC: Duke University Press.

Harrison, K., & Olofsson, J. (2016). Becoming a fire-fighter: On the intra-active relationship between fire-fighters and their tools. *NORMA: International Journal for Masculinity Studies, 11*(3), 158–173.

Hearn, J. (2014). Men, masculinities and the material(-)discursive. *NORMA: International Journal for Masculinity Studies, 9*(1), 5–17.

Hearn, J. (2015). *Men of the world: Genders, globalisations, transnational times*. Los Angeles, CA: Sage.

Hultman, M., & Anshelm, J. (2017). Masculinities of climate change. Exploring examples of industrial, ecomodern and ecological masculinities in the age of anthropocene. In M. Cohen (Ed.) *Climate change and gender in rich countries* (pp. 19–34). London: Routledge.

Hultman, M. & Pulé, P. M. (2018). *Ecological masculinities: Theoretical foundations and practical guidance*. Milton Park: Routledge.

Irigaray, L. (1985). *Speculum of the other woman*. Ithaca, NY: Cornell University Press.

Joelsson, T. (2013). *Space and sensibility: Young men's risk-taking with motor vehicles* (Doctoral disseration). Linköping University, Linköping.

Joelsson, T. (2014). Careless men, careless masculinities? Understanding young men's risk-taking with motor vehicles as violations. *NORMA: International Journal for Masculinity Studies, 9*(3), 191–204.

Massumi, B. (2002). *Parables for the virtual: Movement, affect, sensation*. Durham, NC: Duke University Press.

Matthews, M. (2018). *Ex machina* and the fate of posthuman masculinity: The technical death of man. *Journal of Posthuman Studies, 2*(1), 86–104.

McGinn, R. E. (1980). Nietzsche on technology. *Journal of the History of Ideas, 41*(4), 679–691.

McGregor, S., & Seymour, N. (Eds.) (2017), Men and nature: Hegemonic masculinities and environmental change [Special issue]. *RCC Perspectives 4*. DOI: 10.5282/rcc/7977.

Mellström, U. (2003). *Masculinity, power and technology: A Malaysian ethnography*. Aldershot: Ashgate.

Mellström, U. (2016). From a hegemonic politics of masculinity to an ontological politics of intimacy and vulnerability? Ways of imagining through Karen Barad's work. *Rhisomes: Cultural Studies in Emerging Knowledge, 30*. DOI: 10.20415/rhis/030.e07.

Mumford, L. (1946). *Technics and civilisation*. Chicago, IL: University of Chicago Press.

Neumann, B. (2010). Being prosthetic in the First World War and Weimar Germany. *Body & Society, 16*(3), 93–126.

Oakley, K. P. (1960). *Man the tool-maker*. Chicago, IL: University of Chicago Press.

Redshaw, S. (2018). Combustion, hydraulic, and other forms of masculinity: An essay exploring dominant values and representations of the driver in driverless technology. *Transfers: Interdisciplinary Journal of Mobility Studies, 8*(1), 86–103.

Reeser, T. W., & Gottzén, L. (2018). Masculinity and affect: New possibilities, new agendas. *NORMA: International Journal for Masculinity Studies, 13*(3/4), 145–157.

Schyfter, P. (2009). *Entangled ontologies: A sociophilosophical analysis of technological artefacts, subjects, and bodies*. (PhD thesis) University of Edinburgh, Edinburgh.

Shelley, M. (1818/1999). *Frankenstein, or, the modern Prometheus*. New York: Modern Library.

Theweleit, K. (1980). *Männerphantasien*. Reinbek bei Hamburg: Rowolth.

Part 2
Identities and intersectionalities

11

African and black men and masculinities[1]

Kopano Ratele

"Toussaint was a whole man."

(James, 1938/1989, p. 290)

In the play *Toussaint L'Ouverture: The Story of the Only Successful Slave Revolt in History*, the Afro-Trinidadian historian, novelist, essayist and playwright C. L. R. James (1936/1992) offers what appears to be a simple point but turns out be a terrifically significant insight that seems to have great import in reading and undertaking and teaching studies on men and masculinity, not only African. It is an insight from which I derive the concept of *non-men*—a vital conceptual resource for *thinking with* in this chapter. James' insight pivots around a document. The vital document, a copy of the Constitution of Saint Domingue, now Haiti, which had declared itself a free state, was sent by General Toussaint, the leader of the Haitian revolution, to General Napoleon Bonaparte. On receiving the Constitution, Napoleon had this to say: "This is the most outrageous document that has ever come into my hands. We shall put these impertinent blacks in their place" (James, 1936/1992, p. 91).

For readers unfamiliar with the history of the coming into being of Haiti, James creates his play from the facts of slavery and the colonisation of this Caribbean island and the long struggles of the slaves to emancipate themselves. Elsewhere James writes, "The history of the West Indies is governed by two factors, the sugar plantation and Negro slavery. [...] Whenever the sugar plantation and slavery existed, they imposed a pattern" (James, 1938/1989, p. 391). In the fictionalised transatlantic encounter between Toussaint and Napoleon, we do not only witness a bloody political fight for power between two male generals. We catch a glimpse about the question of the human.

It is true, of course, as James says—or rather repeats—in *The Black Jacobins* that "war is a continuation of politics by other means" (1938/1989, p. 296), and the confrontation between General Toussaint and General Bonaparte was the ultimate confrontation: a savage war. What takes place between the two was men's age-old fight for power and against oppression. At stake was the slave's will to freedom and the master's devotion to enslave the other. The slave-master goes to war to assert his conquest. The enslaved man fights to cast off his chains.

Yet what transpires between Toussaint and Napoleon is about something else as well. This other thing is much more fundamental than war, however cruel and gory that war is; something that goes to the very idea of the human. It may be that this distinctive thing is as important as the fact of war in studies on black *and* white men, African and European; it may be the thing that needs to be given more weight than it usually is in masculinity studies. That thing is a fact peculiar to slavery and colonisation: the human/non-human split that constructs some men as men and others as males; one man as a man and the othered, although biologically male, as something else but not quite a man.

In this chapter, while the focus is on studies on African and black men and masculinities, attention is also drawn to work that brings onto the field some neglected histories and theoretical resources. A crucial issue this chapter does not deal with (but which is taken up in the introduction to this volume and the chapter by Jeff Hearn and Richard Howson) is precisely the boundaries, trajectory, and horizons of the field of men and masculinities. Does the field of men and masculinities include only research that regards itself, or is regarded by the authorities in the field, or is regarded by a sizable number as work on men and masculinities? What of works such as W. E. B. Du Bois' *The Souls of Black Folk* (1903/2015)? What of Richard Wright's (1937/2000) stomach-turning record in *Black Boy*? What is the place of Frantz Fanon's (1952/1967, p. 231) cry that "the disaster and inhumanity of the white man lie in the fact that somewhere he has killed man"; Ali Mazrui's (1974) article on political culture that is clearly on warrior masculinity; or Steve Biko's (1978, p. 28) anguish that "the type of black man we have today has lost his manhood"? I submit these works as part of the multiversal histories and resources within the field of studies on masculinities, certainly studies on African and black men. Whereas Western feminism and women's liberation movements are often regarded as guarantors of global Northern critical studies of men and masculinities, these other works indicate that conceptual resources to make legible African and black men and masculinities have to be sought also in the long struggles against slavery and colonialism and their aftermath; with coloniality, racism, apartheid and Jim Crow; and for freedom, civil rights and the liberation of black peoples. Keeping these historical and more contemporary facts and their transgenerational effects in mind, I will draw out from the literature and introduce three salient ideas useful in reading, conceptualising, and researching: *coloniality*, *non-men* and *blackgenders*.

Men, masculinity, and the peculiarity of the situation of coloniality

To write about African men, or black men (or Asian men, Latin American men and all men who are located at the peripheries, margins, outside, or beneath the world) is to engage in what the Black Caribbean Africana philosopher Lewis Gordon (2007, p. 121) calls "explicit adjectival techniques of appearance." These are men without a firm historical place in Western colonial scholarly and political thought, and as such have to be *named* to be recognisable. Only white, rich and middle-class heterosexual men have enjoyed the privilege of referring to themselves and being referred to without recourse to adjectives. Things are changing, but not always in the direction of justice, more freedom and deeper equality among all men. Things are changing, but only because of ongoing critique against the Western colonial racist patriarchal centre.

To study African men or black men adequately, to interpret their stories as complex, whole human stories, one cannot but appreciate the peculiarity of the situation of coloniality. It is a peculiarity composed of three parts:

(1) A radical difference exists between these two beings, a difference introduced by colonialism and slavery. The effects of this difference—coloniality—persist across generations.
(2) Drawing on the war between Toussaint and Napoleon, only one of the two is a whole human and thus a man in the proper sense. The "Other" being has up to this point been property. A man is not property. In other words, this human "male-thing" is not a man but a non-man; man only in appearance; a human male who expresses what is here called non-masculinity.
(3) The property wants "itself" and other ex-non-humans to be recognised as humans as the man proper. The real man, who represents the humans and imperial Europe and its ideas of man/human, is outraged and will marshal the forces of the French state to deny the former slaves their freedom and claim to human/manhood.

A focus on coloniality ushers in three closely related theses. First, the fight against slavery and determination to enslave others was more than a fight for power; it ultimately was about what Europeans (who would come to be defined as white in colonial racial ideology) came to think about "the human." In this fight, the black cannot be human in the eyes of the white. Attempts to understand black masculinities that fail to consider the acts of men and ideologies of manhood against the dark historical trauma of colonialism, slavery, apartheid and global racism may inadvertently reproduce coloniality of masculinity categories. The reproduction of coloniality of categories of masculinities (and femininity) refers not only to the need to historicise masculinity studies in world context but also in approaching masculinity within the contemporary milieu of racism, global apartheid and the death that has accompanied the attempts by black and African men to migrate to Europe. The historicisation of masculinity as power itself challenges those studies that tend to focus on power among marginalised black and African men. A need therefore exists for decolonising work and decolonial approaches to the very category of men, the very language and concepts we use to think of masculinity. With the former I intend to focus on, for example, politics and economics of colonisation, with questions such as oppression, liberation, self-determination, recognition, reparation, identity and resource distribution; with the latter I refer to diverse epistemological, conceptual and theoretical positions that concern themselves with coloniality (e.g., Grosfoguel, 2011; Lugones, 2007; Maldonado-Torres, 2011; Ndlovu-Gatsheni, 2018; Quijano, 2000).

Second, the global black struggle for recognition for *being* and the revolt against *non-being* is true for slave women too. The struggle to be seen as a human being and the refusal for the condition of the non-human applies to ex-non-men and ex-non-women. As such, while we are focused on the slave/non-man, of course the slave master and mistress also refuse recognition of humanity to the slave/non-woman. Like the non-man, the slave/non-woman is not human but *a thing*. Her body is not hers. She cannot be raped by the master. Her children can be taken away from her. They are born slaves. All this flows from the fact that she is property. Blackness- and Africanness-centralising masculinity studies cannot but be struggles for *blackgender* legibility. *Blackgender* suggest that black men and women are always already raced and gendered at once. Put differently, African and black men are not allowed to be universal men, but always black, particular, localised and never representative of humanity. *Blackgender* signals to the links between European colonialism and slavery on the one hand and, on the other, contemporary ways of thinking about gender and race. It is common cause that, depending on the social forces at the time, Europeans sought to conquer, possess, control and exploit the lands and labour of Africans, Amerindians and other non-European people. The relationship of dominance of white men and masculinity over black men and masculinity to conquest, possession, control and exploitation of lands and bodies did not end with slavery and colonialism. This relationship is one to keep in political activism, research, teaching and work with African and black men and masculinities—and to all men and masculinity generally.

The third thesis concerns *dehumanisation*—of the facticity, following Frantz Fanon, of some subjects/objects as things, as non-men and non-women. "My turn to state an equation," Aimé Césaire (1955/1972, p. 42), writes: "colonization = thingification." Dehumanisation, thingification, the making of some men and women as non-men and non-women, is constituted through Europe's imperial drive, the transatlantic slave trade, colonialism and their afterlives. Being less than human, to restate the point, *being a thing*, the slave is not a man but some*thing* that resembles one only in form. The point here is that the enslaved non-man and non-woman are *not* human. This state is repeatedly, daily, paternalistically or cruelly asserted by violence—against body and mind and space. The slave is the embodiment of powerlessness *par excellence*. In the wake of slavery and colonialism, whose effects are observable in the present era in the wanton shooting and mass incarceration of darker men in the US or their unmourned death trying to cross into Europe, how do masculinity studies understand these subjects/objects and current facts and struggles of men and manhood? If masculinity is also *a place*, as Raewyn Connell (1995) has noted, what is the place of the non-man in critical studies of men? On the whole, studies of men and masculinity have been shy to fully integrate coloniality in shaping contemporary colonialised gendered social orders, not only in Africa and the black diaspora but also, of course, in Europe, the Americas and Australasia. Indeed, the idea of some men as coming out of a dehumanised past and its enduring associations as non-men seriously complicates critical masculinity studies. Thinking about the idea of hegemony, one might ask, in what world is a non-man hegemonic?

The place of non-men in masculinity studies

What is the place, assuming there is one or many such places, of African and black non-men in a field that unwittingly or consciously puts masculinity on the same place as coloniality, where the latter means the epochal force that sought to deny these men masculinity and, indeed, deny that they are human at all? Coloniality is here taken to refer to that form of power inaugurated by slavery, colonialism and world order founded on the idea of some human beings as fungible property. Concerned with the level of culture as distinct from, for instance, being, knowledge, or gender (although culture is entwined with each of these), Kevin Mulcahy (2010, p. 155) regards coloniality as

> an experience involving dominating influence by a stronger power over a subject state. However, this is not just a matter of external governance or economic dependency, but of a cultural dominance and epistemic power that creates an asymmetrical relationship between the "center" and the "periphery", between the ruling "hegemon" and the marginalized "other".

In the same vein as Nelson Maldonado-Torres (2007, 2011), Sabelo Ndlovu-Gatsheni (2018, p. 43) offers a more straightforward description: "the persistence of colonialism beyond dismantlement of its direct administrative structures." Ramón Grosfoguel (2011) states that coloniality is the entanglement of heterarchies of "domination and exploitation where the racial/ethnic hierarchy of the European/non-European divide transversally reconfigures all of the other global power structures [...] where racism becomes the organizing principle that structures all of the multiple hierarchies of the world-system" (p. 11). We cannot turn away from the persisting effects of colonialism in men's lives and its differentiated impact on the lives of those who would be white and those who are signified as black. African and black men are subjects entangled in heterarchies of historical and contemporary domination/subordination. Their gendered lives are inextricably co-constituted by racism. Following Maria Lugones (2010), then, we can only speak of masculinity, the socially constructed gender, as opposed to maleness, with regards to those men who are regarded as having assumed civilisation. African and blacks (males) cannot be men under coloniality. How shall we study non-men in studies of men?

One need not be a specialist on the history of transatlantic slave trade, slavery or colonialism to recognise the impact of these historical facts on men's lives. One simply has to avail oneself to historical archives on slavery and coloniality (inadequate as they often are) and literature (which can offer generative possibilities). Research on men's power and violence has remained partial by excluding the significance of slavery and colonialism on men's power and violence. Slavery and colonialism were not footnotes in the history of masculinity. They were decisive in the making of modernity and modern gender relations. Slavery and colonial rule fundamentally reconfigured masculinities in not only the colonies but also in the metropole. They shaped how we come to reflect on gendered racialisation and racialised genders. The effects are still with us. As an example, the afterlives of slavery and colonialism are visible in the lack of empathy for violence and injury against some men's lives in contemporary times. Thus, research on men's power and violent masculinities that ignores or minimises the history of slavery and colonialism can only give a distorted, at best partial, picture as compared to an account that gives full recognition of the afterlife of slavery as productive of different men/non-men and women/non-women in gender orders. Ta-Nehisi Coates (2015), talking about some of the effects of slavery on black bodies, says:

> Here is what I would like for you to know: In America, it is traditional to destroy the black body—*it is heritage*. Enslavement was not merely the antiseptic borrowing of labor—it is not so easy to get a human being to commit their body against its own elemental interest. And so enslavement must be casual wrath and random manglings, the gashing of heads and brains blown out over the river as the body seeks to escape. It must be rape so regular as to be industrial.
>
> *(p. 103)*

Centralising coloniality in masculinity studies

There is, surprisingly, not a considerable library of works within critical studies on men and masculinities that centralises slavery and colonialism. But that does not mean there are no attempts at all which grapple, with varying levels of success, with the issue (e.g., Adu-Poku, 2004; Bowleg, 2004; Ferber, 2007; Gallego, 2009, 2014; Jacob, 2005; Sinha, 1995). For example, William Pinar (2001) makes a commonplace observation when he states that being enslaved meant a totalising subjugation of black men, which should be taken to mean that black men under slavery were oppressed not only in economic and political terms but also, for instance, as regards education, movement, family-making, gender and sexuality. Enslaved men were also under the control of white women, not just white men. Samuel Adu-Poku (2004) simply observes that "colonisation played a major role in the subversion of traditional gender roles and relations in many African societies" (p. 259). He also supports Pinar's general sentiment when he notes that "because some white women benefit from the exploitation of black people and, historically, because they have been inheritors of colonial gain, white feminism is linked to the perpetuation of racial oppression" (p. 267). Lisa Bowleg (2004) writes that black masculinity in the United States cannot be isolated from the socio-historical context of slavery which fostered the link between economic power and white slave-owning men's idealised masculinity while at the same time denying access to this form of masculinity to black men.

Given that slavery and colonialism were epochal systems of oppression, how can researchers in masculinities studies explain men's lives against the slow-death project that is slavery and colonialism that inaugurate colonial capitalist modernity? Enveloped in this question is the contention that coloniality has been somewhat minimised, treated as equal or even secondary to masculinity, if sometimes altogether brushed aside in studies on masculinities in theorising not just contemporaneous men under slavery but also those men who hundreds of years later have been "(dis)*placed"* in the world by slave-master privilege and slave abjection.

The facts of enslavement, slow death, dehumanisation and the drive to conquer in those who enjoyed the benefits of dominating others are inadequately accounted for by theories of gender hegemony in critical studies of men. The best accounts of the effects of enslaved men and the trauma slavery deposited in subsequent generations appear to lie outside of the field of masculinity studies as it currently looks (although I am uncertain what the boundaries of the field are or if masculinities is in fact a field). If this is the case, that there are inadequate accounts of slavery in enslaved men and slave-masters' lives in critical masculinity studies, perhaps there is need to expand the boundaries of these studies to incorporate works that focus on the facts.

The political-economic mission to enslave, to colonise, to dominate others, is central to the colonial paradigm, imperialism and the racial hierarchisation of humans. The colonial mission to subjugate perdured in neo-colonialism, racism, Jim Crow, apartheid and the current global capitalist modernity. What, then, is the proper weight to be accorded to this persisting fact of human enslavement, meaning dehumanisation and infrahumanisation, in explaining how we consider men and in how men conceive of themselves and "others"?

There have been great efforts to explain some men's lives in the blinding light of slavery. These efforts, however, as indicated, often lie outside of what is commonly thought of as critical masculinities studies. Mention has been made of African American intellectual W. E. B. Du Bois (1903/2015), who wrote of how black men, classed by slavery with the ox, "welcomed freedom with a cry" (p. 103) and how white men had fought desperately to deny their slaves emancipation. Through the character of Toussaint L'Ouverture, James (1936/1992, p. 77) writes that "as soon they came here and saw only black men from Africa were slaves, and because they were black could be nothing else but slaves, one thought became dominant in their minds—freedom!" Frantz Fanon, the Martinican psychiatrist turned Algerian revolutionary, stated that "a man was expected to behave like a man. I was expected to behave like a black man—or at least a nigger" (1952/1967, p. 86). The African American novelist and essayist James Baldwin, in a letter to his nephew, wrote: "They have had to believe for many years, and for innumerable reasons, that black men are inferior to white men" (Baldwin, 1962, p. 5). Written on the hundredth anniversary of the Emancipation in the United States, its date is as significant as its contents. South African black consciousness movement political leader Steve Biko said, "all in all the black man has become a shell, a shadow of man, completely defeated, drowning in his own misery, a slave, and ox bearing the yoke of oppression with sheepish timidity" (1978, p. 29). The black feminist bell hooks (2004, p. 3) writes:

> When we read annals of history, the autobiographical writings of free and enslaved black men, it is revealed that initially black males did not see themselves as sharing the same standpoint as white men about the nature of masculinity. Transplanted African

> men, even those coming from communities where sex roles shaped the division of labor, where the status of men was different and most times higher than that of women, had to be taught to equate their higher status as men with the right to dominate women, they had to be taught patriarchal masculinity. They had to be taught that it was acceptable to use violence to establish patriarchal power. The gender politics of slavery and white-supremacist domination of free black men was the school where black men from different African tribes, with different languages and value systems, learned in the "new world", patriarchal masculinity.

Biko, Du Bois, Fanon, hooks, James, Mazrui and Wright are just some of the figures among numerous others whose thought deserves attention in thinking about black and African masculinities, certainly, but perhaps even more so in thinking about power from below, in thinking about non-black and non-African men from beneath.

From the works of these figures, alongside the writings on slavery, colonialism and racism, it is apparent that the struggle for freedom from slavocratic, colonial and racist domination has to be a key theme in accounts of black and African men and masculinities, indeed all men and masculinities studies. However, among the intellectual resources typically reflected in critical studies on men and masculinities, the preponderance of which are published in the global North, considerations of coloniality and men's aspirations for freedom from oppression (in contrast to men's will to oppress), aspirations to be regarded as men, is precisely what tends to be missing. Coloniality is treated as one among other variables instead of being regarded as fundamental as gender. The coloniality of the category of masculinity inaugurated by slavery and the racist order is, in other words, not given its due weight.

Property, not men

What makes the document that Napoleon received from Hispaniola so outrageous? The slave who demands recognition for his humanity, his body, his freedom, is outrageous. I suggest that James is deliberate in using the word *blacks* instead of *men*. Property cannot declare itself free of its owner. Hence, the slave must be put in his place—below the master's house, in the slave quarter, outside the circle of humans. In *Between the World and Me*, a beautiful letter to his son, Coates (2015, p. 106) writes: "It is truly horrible to understand yourself as the essential below of your country." Is it not odd that we as researchers of masculinity are more often led to focus not on powerful institutions and powerful men at the top but precisely those below?

The slave has to have some recognition that his quiescence is essential to the order. But instead of being in society, he is the constitutive abjection below society. The epitome of dehumanisation, the slave cannot feel pain, is undeserving of all that comes with human freedom. Pain is for humans. Human freedom is, per definition, for humans.

A little more needs to be said about the idea of non-women and non-men's bodies as uninjurable, as integral to slave trading and enslavement. Injurability is a notion that deserves thinking about in studies of violence. The perceived uninjurability of some bodies is one of the afterlives of slavery and colonialism. Studies indicate that people believe that blacks feel less pain than whites (e.g., Trawalter, Hoffman & Waytz, 2012). This is particularly the case for black men. Other research points out that black men are dehumanised, or infrahumanised. Dehumanisation and infrahumanisation (i.e., one group seeing another group as less human than itself) of black men is associated with the callousness and brutality against black men. Phillip Atiba Goff and his associates (2008, p. 292) quote US Chief Justice

Roger Brooke Taney: "The Black man has no rights which the White man is bound to respect. … He may justly and lawfully be reduced to slavery […] and treated as an ordinary article of traffic and merchandise (*Dred Scott v. Sandford*, 1856)." Goff and colleagues (2008, p. 292) then observe that:

> the United States has a shameful history of dehumanizing Black Americans. As quoted above, Chief Justice Taney states clearly what many 19th century U.S. citizens believed: that Blacks were inherently inferior to Whites and therefore could be justifiably subjugated. In fact, the very first article of the U.S. Constitution declares that, when determining state populations, "all other persons"—by which it meant enslaved Africans—should be counted as three fifths of a human being.

Dehumanisation flows from moral exclusion. Moral exclusion enables the slave, the oppressed, the other or the black to be "perceived as outside the boundary in which moral values, rules, and considerations of fairness apply" (Opotow, 1990, p. 1). Once morally excluded, you do not matter, your whole life does not matter, you can be raped, maimed and murdered, and anything that is done to you is permissible.

Upon laying his eyes on Toussaint's future *empire*—the slave mimics the master, down to the violence and language—Christopher Columbus termed it "La Perle des Antilles" (Pearl of the Caribbean). The wars that would follow a few centuries later were precisely because Hispaniola was a pearl. It became a very profitable slave colony for the Europeans. All of the profit came from trading in slaves and slave labour.

Landing on present-day Haiti and the Dominican Republic on December 5, 1492, Columbus *named* the island La Isla Española (The Spanish Island). Such naming, it might need pointing out, was a common element of European colonisation. For 5,000 years, the island had been home to the Arawaks, other indigenous peoples of present-day South America, and all of those would be called the Taino (2015). Between 1492 and 1531 the indigenous population was cut down to about 3,000. Over eighty percent of the population had perished, worked to death in the mines and cotton fields, killed if they revolted, died from European disease like smallpox or committed suicide to escape the cruelty of their new masters. It was because of the annihilation of the Amerindians that the European settlers began importing African slaves in 1503.

Whereas the earlier revolts had been brutally crushed, beginning with a revolt commencing in August 1791, the slaves would eventually successfully overcome. They destroyed most of the white plantations. They murdered many whites. They forced the surviving whites to flee the island. A decade on, in 1801, after bloody years of fighting the slaves declared themselves free, and Toussaint came to rule the island of Hispaniola. His power was short-lived. A free black republic on an island surrounded by the white slavocratic world was simply incomprehensible. There is no white empathy with the condition of the slave/ex-slave. The slave/ex-slave who demands freedom has to be put back in his place. The slave must be whipped until he learns to act *against* a human being's most elemental instinct—to be free; *against* the human instinct to be free from hunger, free from oppression by another, free to choose how and when to offer his labour, free to govern him- or herself. When the slave rebels, he must be subdued. If he is does not submit, he must be killed. If the slave escapes, he must be captured and tortured until he asks for mercy and the mind learns to totally succumb. There is no place for free black republicans in a world where the slave is the black. This is profoundly significant in meditating on masculinities: the African man and woman is forced into being a slave, and the slave becomes the black—the non-man and non-woman. There is, then, no place for women and men like these—free black people—in the "New World."

If masculinity is a place in gender relations, what is the place of slave non-men and slave nonmasculinity in masculinity studies? There is *a no-place* for these non-men and non-women, except *below*, on the margins, outside. It follows then that there cannot be real human empathy for the slave in a slave society, no empathy for black non-men within the colonial order. The idea of a place of free or equal black men in masculinity studies makes no sense, just as the idea of a free black men was a threat to the very idea of whiteness, not merely white patriarchal supremacy. Along with the attention to power and violence and other important issues, one other critical task for masculinity studies is to think non-men into (new) men so as to enrich global masculinity studies. To think non-men is to think of constitutive outside (of) masculinities; to properly consider the idea of study nonmasculinity constitutive of masculinity.

Conclusion

This chapter has sought to draw attention within studies of men to the minimisation, and sometimes blindness, to the historical and persisting effects of slavery and coloniality in general on some men's lives and their relationships to the world, themselves and others. It has suggested that the avoidance of or indifference to the aftermath of slavery and to coloniality limits our research, theory, politics and pedagogy related to all men, masculinities and gender. Opening up to the transgenerational effects of slavery and to coloniality in masculinity studies enables, among several outcomes, the generation of work that speaks to how some men have been, and may still be, engaged in the struggle of being seen as human, in the struggle to move from a position of non-men to that of being men. In that way, opening up studies of men and masculinities enables us to be creative and reparative in our critiques and not only suspicious.

Notes

1 A note about the terms "African" and "black." The focus of this chapter is on African and black men and masculinities. There is overlap between African men and black men. However, there are obvious divergences. African men can be black, and black men can be African. But there are men born in Africa who are not identified as black. Examples include men in North African countries like Tunisia, Morocco and Libya, and white men in South Africa and Zimbabwe. There are, contrastingly, phenotypically dark-skinned men who have were born in Colombia, India, Japan, New Zealand and the United Kingdom. They may have a distant genetic relationship with Africa, but neither they nor several generations of their progenitors ever set foot in Africa. "Black" is a much broader category than "African." "Black" also conveys more consciously political overtones compared to "African," bringing under its signification those people who are not identified or excluded from whiteness in racist political systems. What this means is that while African and black men are interchangeably used in this chapter to indicate an overlapping category of men, the distinction is vital and should not be minimised.

References

Adu-Poku, S. (2004). Envisioning (Black) male feminism: A cross-cultural perspective. In P. F. Murphy (Ed.), *Feminism and masculinities* (pp. 255–271). Oxford: Oxford University Press.

Baldwin, J. (1962/1993). *The fire next time*. New York: Vintage.

Biko, S. (1978). *I write what I like: A selection of his writings*. Randburg: Ravan Press.
Bowleg, L. (2004). Love, sex, and masculinity in sociocultural context HIV concerns and condom use among African American men in heterosexual relationships. *Men and Masculinities*, 7(2), 166–186.
Césaire, A. (1955/1972). *Discourse on colonialism*. New York: Monthly Review.
Coates, T. (2015). *Between the world and me*. New York: Spiegel & Grau.
Connell R. W. (1995). *Masculinities*. Cambridge: Polity.
Du Bois, W. E. B. (1903/2015). *The souls of black folk*. New York: Routledge.
Fanon, F. (1952/1967). *Black skins, white masks*. New York: Grove Press.
Ferber, A. L. (2007). The construction of black masculinity: White supremacy now and then. *Journal of Sport & Social Issues*, *31*(1), 11–24.
Gallego, M. (2009). "What does it mean to be a man?": Codes of black masculinity in Toni Morrison's paradise and love. *Revista de Estudios Norteamericanos*, *14*, 49–65.
Gallego, M. (2014). Progressive masculinities: Envisioning alternative models for Black manhood in Toni Morrison's novels. In Á. Carabí & J. Armengol (Eds.), *Alternative masculinities for a changing world* (pp. 161–173). New York: Palgrave Macmillan.
Goff, P.A., Eberhardt, J. L., Williams, M.J., & Jackson, M.C. (2008). Not yet human: Implicit knowledge, historical dehumanization, and contemporary consequences. *Journal of Personality and Social Psychology*, *94*(2), 292–306.
Gordon, L. R. (2007). Problematic people and epistemic decolonization: Toward the postcolonial in Africana political thought. In N. Persram (Ed.), *Postcolonialism and political theory* (pp. 121–142). Landham, MD: Lexington Books.
Grosfoguel, R. (2011). Decolonizing post-colonial studies and paradigms of political-economy: Transmodernity, decolonial thinking, and global coloniality. *Transmodernity: Journal of Peripheral Cultural Production of the Luso-Hispanic World*, *1*(1). Retrieved from https://escholarship.org/uc/item/21k6t3fq.
hooks, b. (2004). *We real cool: Black men and masculinity*. New York: Routledge.
Jacob, W. C. (2005). The masculine subject of colonialism: The Egyptian loss of the Sudan. In L. Ouzgane, & R. Morrell (Eds.), *African masculinities: Men in Africa from the late nineteenth century to the present* (pp. 153–169). New York: Palgrave Macmillan.
James, C. L. R. (1936/1992). The Black Jacobins. In A. Grimshaw (Ed.), *The C. L. R. James reader* (pp. 67–111). Oxford: Blackwell.
James, C. L. R. (1938/1989). *The Black Jacobins: Toussaint L'Ouverture and the San Domingo revolution*. New York: Vintage.
Lugones, M. (2007). Heterosexualism and the colonial/modern gender system. *Hypatia*, *22*(1), 186–219.
Lugones, M. (2010). Toward a decolonial feminism. *Hypatia*, *25*(4), 742–759.
Maldonado-Torres, N. (2007). On the coloniality of being: Contributions to the development of a concept. *Cultural Studies*, *21*(2/3), 240–270.
Maldonado-Torres, N. (2011). Thinking through the decolonial turn: Post-continental interventions in theory, philosophy, and critique—An introduction. *Transmodernity: Journal of Peripheral Cultural Production of the Luso-Hispanic World*, *1*(2), 1–15. Retrieved from https://escholarship.org/uc/item/59w8j02x.
Mazrui, A. A. (1974). Phallic symbols in politics and war: an African perspective. *Journal of African Studies*, *1*(1), 40–69.
Mulcahy, K. V. (2010). Coloniality, identity and cultural policy. In J. P. Singh (Ed.), *International cultural policies and power* (pp. 155–165). London: Palgrave Macmillan.
Ndlovu-Gatsheni, S. J. (2018). *Epistemic freedom in Africa: Deprovincialization and decolonization*. New York: Routledge.
Opotow, S. (1990). Moral exclusion and injustice: An introduction. *Journal of Social Issues*, *46*(1), 1–20.
Pinar, W. F. (2001). Black men: You don't even know who I am. *Counterpoints*, *163*, 855–938.
Quijano, A. (2000). Coloniality of power and eurocentrism in Latin America. *International Sociology*, *15*(2), 215–232.
Sinha, M. (1995). *Colonial masculinity: The "manly Englishman" and the "effeminate Bengali" in the late 19th century*. Manchester: Manchester University Press.
Taino. (2015, November 12). *New World Encyclopedia*. Retrieved from: www.newworldencyclopedia.org/p/index.php?title=Taino&oldid=991941.
Trawalter S., Hoffman K. M., & Waytz, A. (2012). Racial bias in perceptions of others' pain. *PLoS One*, 7(11), e48546.
Wright, R. (1937/2000). *Black boy: A record of childhood and youth*. London: Vintage.

12
White masculinity

Tobias Hübinette

It is doubtless a truism that for several consecutive centuries (and until quite recently), being white principally meant being a white man, while being a human being and belonging to "mankind" likewise mainly meant being a man. Until quite recently, many, but not all, white men equally wielded enormous and extraordinary power over the planet, humanity and practically all other living beings, in spite of always having been a numerically small minority on earth. Thus there are numerous parallels between the entities, properties, categories, assemblages and concepts of whiteness and masculinity. The research fields of critical studies on men and masculinities (CSMM), or simply masculinity studies, and critical whiteness studies (CWS) and critical whiteness theory, or simply whiteness studies, have even coincided to such an extent that their foundational texts were published during the same period: Raewyn Connell's *Masculinities* (1995) and Richard Dyer's *White* (1997) are but two of the most well-known and already canonical references, both of which also bear rather self-explanatory titles.

It is probably not a coincidence that masculinity studies and whiteness studies were both products of the post-Cold War climate of the 1990s. Men's studies and masculinity studies developed from women's studies and gender studies and from the men's movement of the 1970s and 1980s, while the field of whiteness studies and critical whiteness theory had its origins in Marxism, women's studies and gender studies, as well as in the antiracist movement of the same decades as the men's movement. Both these movements were at the time dominated by white men, and both fields were products of new post-1968 social movements and the New Left. Furthermore, both fields were originally part of the social constructionist wave of the 1980s and were also influenced by poststructuralism and the linguistic turn, although perhaps not to the extent as certain subfields within gender studies. Ever since the foundational years of the 1990s, in both cases, there has always been a strong relationship to queer theory and critical race theory, which is also reflected in the research interests and topics of several studies from these fields (Frankenberg, 1993; Halberstam, 2005; Morrison, 1992; Roediger, 1991; Ward, 2015).

Further, both fields are also unabashedly emancipatory and progressive in the sense that they consciously aim for and strive to uncover, deconstruct and decentre the not always so obvious privileges of males and whites, respectively. This is done not least through the ethics of critical self-reflection, as the two fields are also principally populated by male researchers and white researchers, respectively (Epstein, 1998; Lund & Carr, 2012; Lundström, 2014; Messner, 2011; Pease, 2004, 2010; Steyn & Conway, 2010). The fact that masculinity studies and whiteness studies both emerged in the 1990s is probably also related to the ever increasingly gender-equal and multiracial Western world resulting from second-wave feminism, postcolonial immigration and globalisation, all of which finally made both males and whites visible – and in particular, perhaps, their historically inherited and ingrained privileges.

However, while the field of masculinity studies tends to concentrate on white men (although there are also studies of non-white and non-Western men), the field of whiteness studies by comparison instead tends to decentre white men, so that white women are just as often the focus of research in whiteness studies as are white men. One reason for this difference might well be that whiteness studies also had founding mothers in addition to founding fathers like Richard Dyer, such as Peggy McIntosh (1988) and Ruth Frankenberg (1993), while most of the founders of masculinity studies were white men. Whiteness studies therefore could potentially contribute to developing masculinity studies when it comes to unveiling and disrupting taken-for-granted norms, as whiteness sometimes seems to be a rather unproblematised norm for many masculinity studies researchers. Recently there has also been a discernible and productive trend to try to bring the two fields together, as for example in the works of Michael Kimmel (2013) and in studies on the far right, which is very much a white men's movement in practically every Western country where it exists.

Finally, both fields originated and developed in the English-speaking world and mainly in the post-civil rights US, and partly in the post-imperial UK, thereafter becoming more or less institutionalised in the US, in the UK, in Australia and in Canada – and to a perhaps lesser extent in South Africa and New Zealand. In these countries, research centres and institutes, courses and programmes and academic associations and journals are today well established, and symposia and conferences take place regularly. Here, however, the parallels between the two fields cease. The field of masculinity studies has been able to gain quite a strong foothold outside of Anglophone academia, for example in the Nordic countries as well as in several Western European countries. Whiteness studies, in contrast, with very few exceptions, has not been institutionalised outside of the Anglo-American world. This is probably due to the reluctance towards researching race in general in German- and French-speaking academic contexts and even more so in the Nordic countries, with Sweden as perhaps the most extreme example (Hübinette & Pripp, 2017).

Given all these above-mentioned parallels, and the fact that the two fields were formed during the same time period, in the same countries and within the context of the new social and political movements that followed the 1960s and 1970s, it is surprising that only a limited number of studies focusing specifically and explicitly on white masculinity have been published since the 1990s. There are, however, some studies that preceded the formation of masculinity studies and whiteness studies and that in practice almost exclusively studied white men, but without operationalising the concept of white masculinity. Many if not most of those early studies derive from the late colonial and postcolonial periods and include titles such as Gustav Jahoda's *White Man* from 1961, Julia Blackburn's *The White Men* from 1979 and Ashis Nandy's *The Intimate Enemy* from 1983. Even if none of these operationalised the concepts of masculinity and whiteness, and even less so white masculinity, they all addressed white men in colonial and non-white settings and made white men the objects of study by labelling them as white men, thereby making them visible and, consequently, also arguably vulnerable. This is also the goal and sometimes almost the *raison d'être* of both masculinity studies and whiteness studies.

It is therefore no coincidence that one of the earliest studies making use of the concept of white masculinity, Morrell's (1996) "Forging a Ruling Race", focuses on white men in a colonial context. The issues of both whiteness and masculinity become glaringly apparent in geographical places and in racial spaces where whites were/are the minority and where white men have historically been far more numerous than white women. Morell looks into the introduction and reception of rugby in the British South African colony of Natal, arguing that the sport played an important part in the identity building of white male settlers who felt a need to foster a white British identity in a geographically distant colony as well as bolster their masculinity in a region where they were demographically outnumbered by the mighty Zulu nation, which at times even had defeated them in combat.

Aldrich's (2003) *Colonialism and homosexuality* is yet another historical study set in the overseas colonies. Although it does not make use of the concept of white masculinity explicitly, it is clearly about white men. Aldrich specifically focuses on white non-heterosexual men who may well have been overrepresented as explorers, visitors and settlers in the mainly British colonies in the Americas, Africa, Asia and Oceania, especially during the era of high imperialism. At that time, many of them felt that they had much more sexual freedom in the colonies and in the company of non-white and non-Christian indigenous people than in Europe itself.

Colley's (2002) *Captives* is yet another encyclopedic historical treatise based on extensive archival research and set in the British colonies. It principally deals with white men, but again without making use of the term "white masculinity". Colley surveys the thousands of white, mainly British, men who were captured by indigenous and non-Christian people and who were, for example, soldiers, diplomats, scholars, settlers and tradesmen. Colley looks at how they interacted with their captors: some were adopted and stayed with their captors for life, while others returned after some years and wrote books about their experiences as white men who had lived with and among non-white natives in a non-European setting.

Two more recent white masculinity studies set in the Global South are Conway's (2008) "Contesting the Masculine State" and Gillen's (2016) "Rethinking Whiteness and Masculinity in Geography". Conway explores how white and mainly Afrikaans-speaking men, who refused to perform compulsory military service in South Africa in the 1980s, challenged a heavily militarised white settler state which idealised the hypermasculinised so-called *grensvegter* [border fighter] who combatted Angolan and Cuban soldiers and took part in South Africa's Cold War conflicts with its neighbouring countries. Gillen's study covers his own research trips to Vietnam and consists of a critical (self-)reflection on white male researchers who conduct fieldwork in Vietnam, and indirectly also in other postcolonial countries in the Global South. Such researchers are sometimes able to exercise enormous power as well as to access both information and informants in very privileged ways, which may include intimate and sexual ways, as white men in most postcolonial and non-white contexts are associated with status, wealth and future opportunities compared to indigenous men. Gillen ends his study by calling on other white men who are conducting research in the Global South to become aware of the enormous interventionist and disruptive power white masculinity still wields in the postcolonial present:

> As critical geographers it is our responsibility to "write the world" in ways that assess racism and sexism and provide alternative paths in order to imagine a more just and inclusive world. As important as this responsibility is, it should not be restricted to certain limited geographical areas because we will unwittingly be insulting the task we have outlined: masculinity and whiteness play out outside of the spaces of our backyards, in languages other than English and Romance languages, and in ways that do not reflect

> some of the now standard issues surrounding positionality and reflexivity that exist when conducting research at home.
>
> *(Gillen, 2016, p. 599)*

The vast majority of studies on white masculinity in a contemporary Western context are from the US or the UK, while some are from Western European and Nordic countries. To begin with, one type of research seems to tend to view white men as still powerful, while another type of research tends to regard white men as not being so powerful anymore – instead of appearing to be invisible and invulnerable, they have become highly visible and vulnerable. In these latter studies, white masculinity is seen above all as currently in crisis. As mentioned above, both masculinity studies and whiteness studies were from the beginning quite strongly embedded within the social constructionist wave of the 1980s and 1990s. Therefore, most of these studies can be said to take a sociological approach, while there are also studies on white masculinity taking a more humanities and cultural studies approach (more on these below). While the latter studies mostly examine the position of white men in the former colonies and in the Global South, the former studies often examine white working-class and lower middle-class men in post-industrial England, or white men in connection to the far right in, for example, the US, Norway or Finland (Eriksson, 2013; Hughey, 2012a, 2012c; Kimmel, 2013; Nayak, 2003, 2006; Norocel et al., 2018; Svendsen, 2015). There is also, interestingly enough, a growing body of work on white antiracists and white antiracism, both of which tend to be represented by white men, although not exclusively (Hughey, 2012a; Hübinette & Lundström, 2014; Spanierman & Cabrera, 2015; Wekker, 2016).

Although he did not coin the notion, the idea that white masculinity is in crisis has in particular been connected to and developed by Michael Kimmel in his 2013 monograph *Angry White Men*, which came out in an expanded, updated and revised version in 2017 in connection with the rise of the Tea Party movement and President Trump's victory in the presidential election of 2016. At the same time, it is important to remind that the idea of a masculinity in crisis, which the Tea Party movement and similar Conservative and far right political movements in many other Western countries have both voiced and capitalised on, has in various versions been on the agenda at least since the 19th century, and this is something which Kimmel also has pointed out and asked us to be wary of already in his book *Manhood in America* (Kimmel, 2006). In other words, Kimmel makes use of the notion of a masculinity in crisis as a theoretical concept and as a critical tool, and for him as well as others, this means that a seemingly growing number of white men perceive that they are losing power to women as well as to minorities.

Kimmel argues that many white men in the US are not just suffering from white male rage but are fuelled by what he calls "aggrieved entitlement", described as "the sense that those benefits to which you believed yourself entitled have been snatched away from you by unseen forces larger and more powerful" (Kimmel, 2013, p. 18). According to Kimmel, those "forces" are, for at least the angry white American men that he has interviewed, above all minorities – sometimes also including Jews, women and LGBTQ people – who, according to them, are to "blame" for the feelings of aggrieved entitlement among so many white American men. Kimmel's concept has been useful to understand the growth of the far right in both the US and in Europe as well as the phenomenon of mass shootings in the US, which Kimmel also relates to feelings of aggrieved entitlement among a certain segment of white American boys and men (Kalish & Kimmel, 2010; Kimmel, 2013; Vito, Admire, & Hughes, 2018).

Another concept which comes from the recent and increasing coming together of masculinity studies and whiteness studies is Hughey's (2010, 2012a) term "hegemonic whiteness", which originally comes from Connell's theory of hegemonic masculinity. Although Lewis (2004) coined the expression in the first place, Hughey has developed the concept theoretically, arguing that it works "(1) through positioning those marked as 'white' as essentially different from and superior to those marked as 'non-white', and (2) through marginalizing practices of 'being white' that fail to exemplify dominant ideals" (Hughey, 2010, p. 1290). The theory of white hegemonic masculinity comes from his own ethnographic study among white antiracists and white nationalists in the US who, in spite of being ideological enemies, share many white American privileges and white American perspectives, not least in relation to non-white Americans. Although the concept is useful in understanding how whiteness has evolved and become hegemonic in a certain national context, at the same time it has pitfalls similar to Connell's hegemonic masculinity theory, as it also tends to flatten out and homogenise all whites regardless of background and position.

Other areas of research wherein white men have been highlighted in the contemporary era of the crisis of white masculinity are studies of extreme sports, survivalism and the so-called prepper culture, all of which seem to be mainly practised and populated by white men who are seemingly trying to resurrect almost superhuman and superhero-like ideals of whiteness which, according to John Preston, can be likened to prosthetic qualities (Kusz, 2007; Preston, 2010; Yochim, 2010). Another subfield of white masculinity studies focuses on the sometimes but not always antagonistic and fragile relationships and encounters between white and non-white men. As with most studies on white masculinity, this research area is principally US based and also mainly looks at white and black American men (Bucholtz, 1999; Hughey, 2012b). Yet another subfield – also American and closely related to the research on encounters between white and black American men – looks at white masculinity in the South in relation to ideas of Southern gallantry and chivalry (Plath & Lussana, 2009; Pugh, 2013; Watts, 2008).

Lastly, with regards to studies of white masculinity in the humanities, ever since Richard Dyer's monograph *White*, studies on white men on screen, in films and in visual culture in general have continuously been published. One of these is Hamilton Carroll's *Affirmative Reaction* from 2011, which argues that American white masculinity as it is played out in titles like *The Deer Hunter* (1978), *Falling Down* (1993), *8 Mile* (2002) and *Gran Torino* (2008) has always been in crisis, although these moments of crisis have been understood differently over the years. In relation to the contemporary US, which is rapidly developing into a majority minority demographic make-up with whites no longer in the majority but instead the biggest of many minorities, white masculinity has not only become increasingly visible according to Carroll but also has been able to redefine itself as a marginalised category. This notion is present in the rhetoric of reversed racism or reversed sexism and the idea of white men having become the new oppressed minority.

A similar argument is presented in an early literary study by Robinson (1999), *Marked Men*, which looks at a selected number of works written by white American male authors – such as John Updike's *Rabbit Redux* (1971), Philip Roth's *My Life as a Man* (1974) and Pat Conroy's *The Prince of Tides* (1986) – to be able to dissect how post-1968 American whiteness has been formed, negotiated and reformulated in the post-civil rights US and at the time of the so-called culture wars. Savran (1998), Abbott (2002), Rose (2014) and Engles (2018) are other scholars coming from the field of cultural studies and critical theory and who study images, depictions and representations of white men in cinema, literature and other cultural productions.

To sum up, it is quite probable that "the era of unquestioned and unchallenged male entitlement is over", as Kimmel (2013, p. xii) has somewhat dramatically put it. Faludi

(1999) already observed this new development in her acclaimed book *Stiffed*, although she did not focus only on white men but looked at working-class men in general. Arguably, however, both Kimmel and Faludi mainly refer to white men and not the least as "working-class men" often in practice means white working-class men, and especially young white men in the US, in Europe and in the West in general, who are nowadays also being statistically outperformed by not just young white women but also, to a growing extent, by young minority women and in certain Western countries even by certain groups of young minority men such as Asian men (Frey, 2014). The number of academic studies explicitly operationalising the concept of white masculinity, however, is still quite limited – meaning that it would not be fully correct to say that research on white masculinity is a booming field at the moment, even though there are many studies researching white men as such or working-class men in general.

Notwithstanding, white masculinity studies is a research field which clearly has a future, not least given that white men are increasingly voting for far-right and right-wing populist parties, presidents, leaders and movements in almost every Western country and to such a disproportionate extent that this may well be called a white men's movement and perhaps even described as the last stand of white masculinity as we have known it so far (Eriksson, 2017; Hughey, 2012c; Keskinen, 2018; Svendsen, 2015). This means that critical studies of white masculinity already is and also will be highly relevant. Having existed as coherent but quite separate research fields for about a generation or 30 years by now, masculinity studies and whiteness studies have come together more and more during recent years, with theories on aggrieved entitlement and hegemonic whiteness as some of the most representative examples. All this points to a promising future for further exploring, researching and theorising white masculinity, as continuing gender equality and increasing racial diversity are at the time of writing slowly but steadily changing the lives of white men forever.

References

Abbott, M. E. (2002). *The street was mine: White masculinity in hardboiled fiction and film noir*. New York, NY: Palgrave Macmillan.

Aldrich, R. (2003). *Colonialism and homosexuality*. London: Routledge.

Blackburn, J. (1979). *The white men: The first response of Aboriginal peoples to the white man*. London: HarperCollins.

Bucholtz, M. (1999). You da man: Narrating the racial other in the production of white masculinity. *Journal of Sociolinguistics*, *3*(3/4), 443–460.

Carroll, H. (2011). *Affirmative reaction: New formations of white masculinity*. Durham, NC: Duke University Press.

Colley, Linda. (2002). *Captives: Britain, empire and the world, 1600–1850*. London: Jonathan Cape.

Connell, R. W. (1995). *Masculinities*. Berkeley, CA: University of California Press.

Conway D. (2008). Contesting the masculine state. White male war resisters in apartheid. In South Africa. In J. L. Parpart & M. Zalewski (Eds.), *Rethinking the man question: Sex, gender and violence in international relations* (pp. 127–142). London: Zed Books.

Dyer, R. (1997). *White: Essays on race and culture*. London: Routledge.

Engles, T. (2018). *White male nostalgia in contemporary North American literature*. Cham: Palgrave Macmillan.

Epstein, D. (1998). Marked men: Whiteness and masculinity. *Agenda*, *37*, 49–59.

Eriksson, M. (2013). Wronged white men: The performativity of hate in feminist narratives about anti-feminism in Sweden. *NORA: Nordic Journal of Feminist and Gender Research*, *21*(4), 249–263.

Eriksson, M. (2017). Breivik and I: Affective encounters with "failed" masculinity in stories about rightwing terrorism. *NORMA: International Journal for Masculinity Studies*, *12*(3/4), 1–14.

Faludi, S. (1999). *Stiffed: The betrayal of the American man*. New York, NY: William Morrow.

Frankenberg, R. (1993). *White women, race matters: The social construction of whiteness*. Minneapolis, MN: University of Minnesota Press.

Frey, W. H. (2014). *Diversity explosion: How new racial demographics are remaking America*. Washington, DC: Brookings Institution Press.

Gillen, J. (2016). Rethinking whiteness and masculinity in geography: Drinking alcohol in the field in Vietnam. *Antipode, 48*(3), 584–602.

Halberstam, J. (2005). Shame and white gay masculinity. *Social Text, 23*(3/4), 219–233.

Hübinette, T., & Lundström, C. (2014). Three phases of hegemonic whiteness: Understanding racial temporalities in Sweden. *Social Identities: Journal for the Study of Race, Nation and Culture, 14*(6), 423–437.

Hübinette, T., & Pripp, O. (2017). Etnicitet, ras och vithet. In J. Gunnarsson Payne & M. Öhlander (Eds.), *Tillämpad kulturteori* (pp. 293–317). Lund: Studentlitteratur.

Hughey, M. W. (2010). The (dis)similarities of white racial identities: The conceptual framework of "hegemonic whiteness". *Ethnic and Racial Studies, 33*(8), 1289–1309.

Hughey, M. W. (2012a). *White bound: Nationalists, antiracists, and the shared meanings of race*. Stanford, CA: Stanford University Press.

Hughey, M. W. (2012b). Black guys and white guise: The discursive construction of white masculinity. *Journal of Contemporary Ethnography, 41*(1), 95–124.

Hughey, M. W. (2012c). Show me your papers! Obama's birth and the whiteness of belonging. *Qualitative Sociology, 35*(2), 163–181.

Jahoda, G. (1961). *White man: A study of the attitudes of Africans to Europeans in Ghana before independence*. London: Oxford University Press.

Kalish, R., & Kimmel, M. (2010). Suicide by mass murder: Masculinity, aggrieved entitlement, and rampage school shootings. *Health Sociology Review, 19*(4), 451–464.

Keskinen, S. (2018). The "crisis" of white hegemony, neonationalist femininities and antiracist feminism. *Women's Studies International Forum, 68*, 157–163.

Kimmel, M. (2006). *Manhood in America: A cultural history* (2nd ed.). New York: Oxford University Press.

Kimmel, M. (2013). *Angry white men: American masculinity at the end of an era*. New York, NY: Nation Books.

Kusz, K. (2007). *Revolt of the white athlete: Race, media and the emergence of extreme athletes in America*. New York, NY: Peter Lang.

Lewis, A. (2004). What group? Studying whites and whiteness in the era of colorblindness. *Sociological Theory, 22*(4), 623–646.

Lund, D. E., & Carr, P. R. (2012). Disrupting white privilege in teacher education. In P. C. Gorski, K. Zenkov, N. Osei-Kofi & J. Sapp (Eds.), *Cultivating social justice teachers: How teacher educators have helped students overcome cognitive bottlenecks and learn critical social justice concepts* (pp. 108–125). Sterling, VA: Stylus.

Lundström, C. (2014). *White migrations: Gender, whiteness and privilege in transnational migration*. Basingstoke: Palgrave Macmillan.

McIntosh, P. (1988). White privilege: Unpacking the invisible knapsack. *Peace and Freedom Magazine*, July/ August, 10–12.

Messner, M. A. (2011). The privilege of teaching about privilege. *Sociological Perspectives, 54*(1), 3–13.

Morrell, R. (1996). Forging a ruling race: Rugby and white masculinity in colonial Natal, c. 1870–1910. In J. R. Nauright & T. J. L. Chandler (Eds.), *Making men: Rugby and masculine identity* (pp. 91–120). London: Frank Cass.

Morrison, T. (1992). *Playing in the dark: Whiteness and the literary imagination*. Cambridge, Mass.: Harvard University Press.

Nandy, Ashis. (1983). *The intimate enemy: Loss and recovery of self under colonialism*. Delhi: Oxford University Press.

Nayak, A. (2003). Last of the "real Geordies"? White masculinities and the subcultural response to deindustrialisation. *Environment and Planning D: Society and Space, 21*(1), 7–25.

Nayak, A. (2006). Displaced masculinities: Chavs, youth and class in the post-industrial city. *Sociology, 40*(5), 813–831.

Norocel, O. C., Saresma, T., Lähdesmäki, T., & Ruotsalainen, M. (2018). Discursive constructions of white Nordic masculinities in right-wing populist media. *Men and Masculinities*, 1097184X18780459.

Pease, B. (2004). Decentring white men: Critical reflections on masculinity and white studies. In A. Moreton-Robinson (Ed.), *Whitening race: Essays in social and cultural criticism* (pp. 119–130). Canberra: Aboriginal Studies Press.

Pease, B. (2010). *Undoing privilege: Unearned advantage in a divided world*. London: Zed Books.

Plath, L., & Lussana, S. (Eds.). (2009). *Black and white masculinity in the American South, 1800–2000*. Newcastle upon Tyne: Cambridge Scholars.
Preston, J. (2010). Prosthetic white hyper-masculinities and "disaster education". *Ethnicities, 10*(3), 331–343.
Pugh, T. (2013). *Queer chivalry: Medievalism and the myth of white masculinity in Southern literature*. Baton Rouge, LA: Louisiana State University Press.
Robinson, S. (1999). *Marked men: White masculinity in crisis*. New York, NY: Columbia University Press.
Roediger, D. R. (1991). *The wages of whiteness: Race and the making of the American working class*. London: Verso.
Rose, S. (2014). *Abolishing white masculinity from Mark Twain to hiphop: Crises in whiteness*. Lanham, MD: Lexington Books.
Savran, D. (1998). *Taking it like a man: White masculinity, masochism, and contemporary American culture*. Princeton, NJ: Princeton University Press.
Spanierman, L. B., & Cabrera, N. L. (2015). The emotions of white racism and antiracism. In V. Watson, D. Howard-Wagner & L. Spanierman (Eds.), *Unveiling whiteness in the twenty-first century: Global manifestations, transdisciplinary interventions* (pp. 9–28). Lanham, MD: Lexington Books.
Steyn, M., & Conway, D. (2010). Introduction. Intersecting whiteness, interdisciplinary debates. *Ethnicities, 10*(3), 283–291.
Svendsen, S. H. B. (2015). Feeling at loss: Affect, whiteness and masculinity in the immediate aftermath of Norway's terror. In R. Andreassen & K. Vitus (Eds.), *Affectivity and race: Studies from Nordic contexts* (pp. 133–150). Burlington, VT: Ashgate.
Vito, C., Admire, A., & Hughes, E. (2018). Masculinity, aggrieved entitlement, and violence: Considering the Isla Vista mass shooting. *NORMA: International Journal for Masculinity Studies, 13*(2), 86–102.
Ward, J. (2015). *Not gay: Sex between straight white men*. New York, NY: New York University Press.
Watts, T. (Ed.). (2008). *White masculinity in the recent South*. Baton Rouge. LA: Louisiana State University Press.
Wekker, G. (2016). *White innocence: Paradoxes of colonialism and race*. Durham, NC: Duke University Press.
Yochim, E. C. (2010). *Skate life: Re-imagining white masculinity*. Ann Arbor, MI: University of Michigan Press.

13

Men and masculinities in contemporary East Asia

Continuities, changes, and challenges

Mario Liong and Lih Shing Chan

The shared cultural heritage of East Asian societies has resulted in similar constructions of masculinities in both premodern and contemporary periods. Confucianism and neo-Confucianism—which promote a distinct sexual division of labour and the subordination of women, tolerance of homosexuality between men (Taga, 2005a), and the acceptance (or even hegemony) of literary, cultural qualities in manhood (Louie, 2012)—were distinctive in the Chinese, Japanese, and Korean cultures of the premodern period. Today, these shared cultural traditions continue to have varying impacts on the construction and popularity of the "beautiful man" in East Asia. This gentle, non-aggressive, and even effeminate "soft masculinity" is characteristic of East Asian media and cultural products (Louie, 2012). Nevertheless, the different social, economic, cultural, and political trajectories that each East Asian society has followed result in different practices and representations of manhood.

In this chapter, we mainly review the existing academic works related to men and masculinities in each East Asian society in order to outline current knowledge about East Asian men and masculinities. However, we acknowledge that there is a body of literature discussing masculinities among East Asian men living in other regions of the world. As readers may also be interested in these studies, we discuss them briefly in the last section.

China, Hong Kong, and Taiwan

In addition to the insightful and ground-breaking concept of *wen-wu* used in theorizing Chinese masculinities (Louie, 2002), scholars have mapped out the impacts of the immense socio-political and economic transformations of Chinese societies on the construction of Chinese masculinities. Moreover, both popular culture and the virtual world have played crucial roles in bringing about new, alternative forms of masculine subjectivities and practices.

Political, economic, and sexual subjectivity

Socio-political circumstances have had a strong influence on the construction of masculinities in China. In the Maoist era, the strong state influence on personal lives and on recreating gender created a sense of castration among men, who felt their virility was being lost (Zhang, 2011). In post-Mao China, a cultural politics of "remasculinization" emerged in reaction to the gender-equality discourse of the Maoist era and the "inferiority complex" towards Western culture (Song, 2010, p. 408). In the 1980s, the works of male intellectuals reflected their desire for power (Zhong, 2000), and rock music expressed the yearning to recover repressed manhood through a rebellious attitude and political resistance to the state (Baranovitch, 2003). However, with the June 4th Tiananmen Square Massacre in 1989, in which the communist regime dispatched troops to kill demonstrators who were demanding democratic political reform, not only was the democratic movement in China brutally truncated but also the effort to reassert masculinity was suppressed. Baranovitch (2003) suggests that commonly recognized effeminate qualities such as loyalty, submissiveness, and obedience towards the state were restored via political oppression, resulting in a softer image of men in China during the 1990s and into the millennium.

Similarly, the economic and political turmoil in Hong Kong were found to have impacted the construction and practice of masculinities. At the turn of the 21st century, the handover of the sovereignty of Hong Kong from Britain to China and the economic downturn triggered by the Asian financial crisis induced a sense of despair about the future of the city. This frustration was reflected as a crisis of masculinity in Hong Kong cinema (Pang, 2002). In recent years, the failure of the political struggle for universal suffrage has also induced a subservient attitude to the authority of Beijing (Ho, Jackson, & Kong, 2018), a conflict of masculinities between young and middle-aged men (Liong & Ho, 2019), and a consumerist lifestyle (Kong, 2011) among heterosexual and gay men, respectively. Only with the 2019 protest against the extradition bill in which protestors demonstrated the use of force, such as charging into the Legislative Council building and escalating conflict with the police (Lee, 2019), did we witness a change in protest masculinities.

The economic success of China following its market economic reform has largely determined the construction of masculinity. Material possession and consuming power have become the criteria on which a man's social standing is judged (Kolbjørnsen, 2012). However, possessing wealth alone is not enough to garner top status in the masculine hierarchy. Embodying Confucian morality and self-cultivation, knowledge of fashion and grooming, the consumption of luxury items, and living a lavish lifestyle define the hegemonic masculinities of contemporary China (Hird, 2017; Kolbjørnsen, 2012; Zurndorfer, 2016). In Taiwan, although metrosexuality and consumerism are prevalent in men's fashion magazines (Shiau, 2013), this media representation—rather than being hegemonic—paradoxically empowers Taiwanese boys who adopt a "feminized" masculinity (Yang, 2014).

China and Taiwan also demonstrate different ideas about sexuality. The economic miracle of China turned the "castration anxiety" of the 1980s on its head. Sexual potency is now a way to define "real manhood" (Zheng, 2009). Chinese business and political elites demonstrate their masculinity with the ability to attract beautiful women who serve them like kings (Osburg, 2013), whereas working-class men uphold their masculine dignity by keeping mistresses and providing for them (Xiao, 2011). In contrast, although businessmen in Taiwan visit hostess clubs to build closer business relationships through drinking and sexual seduction of female hostesses (Boretz, 2004), this "flower drinking" practice is a way for these middle- and upper-class men to demonstrate their superiority through self-restraint, i.e., by controlling their lust and indulgence in drinking (Bedford & Hwang, 2011). While in mainland China being single is often regarded as a failure (Lin, 2017) and adult children continue to submit themselves to their parents' strong expectations of marriage (Deng, 2014), young professional men in Taiwan tend to see marriage as a personal choice that should be based on romantic attraction rather than a standard life path that every man should follow (Chen & Mac an Ghaill, 2017).

Masculinities in popular culture

In the midst of the social inequality created by the widening of the wealth gap, a new resistant form of masculinity, *diaosi*, was constructed in China's online community. This self-mocking label is used by young men in general to refer to themselves when they do not have "wealthy parents, powerful *guanxi* (connections), good looks" and therefore cannot measure up to the successful male image of "tall, rich, and handsome" (Best, 2014, pp. 20–21). Those who come from less affluent families or the rural areas embrace the label of *diaosi* to cynically challenge China's hard-to-achieve masculine standards (Szablewicz, 2014) and unequal social structure (Kan, 2013).

Other new forms of masculinity have also emerged from the media and virtual culture in recent years. The media image of delicate men begging softly to women for love is prevalent in China; it has become a source of romantic and sexual fantasy for women and a source of role models and ideals that men imitate (Baranovitch, 2003). Stay-at-home fathers are celebrated by the print media in Hong Kong because they sacrifice their careers for their children (Liong, 2017). *Zhainan*, young men who stay home playing video games and surfing the Internet, are portrayed as potentially desirable romantic partners in some Chinese web essays and mass media because they are naïve, simple, passive in love, and morally upright (Song & Hird, 2013). In response to the pervasive sexualized media culture and the demand for self-control over their sexuality, young men in Hong Kong are "performatively vigilant"—active and strategic in their use of the available discursive resources as they position themselves in different social relationships to avoid being associated with stigmatized lustful masculinity (Liong & Chan, 2018).

Japan

Men's studies in Japan mainly focus on the impact of the gender division of labour on Japanese men. Japan has historically been a developed country that restricts women from applying their abilities and career potential in the workplace (Economist, 2014). This rigid gender structure not only restricts women but also impacts men in situations where conventional masculinity is challenged or does not fit in. After the burst of the Japanese economic bubble, social issues surrounding Japanese manhood raised concerns and prompted academic inquiries into divorce among male retirees (Itô, 1993), the rising suicide rate, and death by overwork among men (Kashima, 1993); the Japanese male was thus problematized as a significant subject in gender studies.

In his pioneering work on men's studies in Japan, Itô (1996) pinpoints that Japanese men are just as affected by patriarchal norms and gender conventions as women. Following this line of thought, Kasuga (1999) examines how occupational division impacts Japanese men's career development, especially in occupations that are unconventional for men, such as nursing and care work. Taga's (2005b, 2010) studies on the role of fathers in parenting and family education take a further step and illustrate how Japanese fathers negotiate the gender structure. This gender order not only structures Japanese manhood but also is manifested in the construction of the epitome of Japanese masculine subjectivity: the salaryman (white-collar employees in corporations).

Economic and sexual subjectivity

Economic power is definitive in Japanese manhood. As Japan's main economic labour force, the corporate figure of the salaryman and the corporate environment that encapsulates him have attracted much scholarly attention. Early studies (e.g., Allison, 1994; Kelly, 1986; Plath, 1964; Vogel, 1971) focused on the social construction of this new middle class and how corporate ideology extended to the personal lives of these salarymen, who serve as the breadwinner of the household. Dasgupta (2000, 2003) further argues that the salaryman model is a form of hegemonic masculinity, not only because the national-capitalist system upholds these stable, middle-class, and heterosexual values but also because popular culture and the media continue to reproduce corporate masculinity as the idealized yet normative masculinity.

Apart from economic power, the hegemony of the salaryman also lies in its heteronormativity. Japan remains a largely heterosexist society in which unchallenged heterosexuality determines sexual standards, marital relationships, and family configurations in Japanese men's lives (Taga, 2003). In corporate settings, bonding with colleagues or clients involves patronizing hostess clubs after work hours (Allison, 1994). According to Satoru Itô (2001), the illusion of Japanese society being tolerant of male homosexuality stems from historical homosocial settings underpinned by patriarchy. McLelland (2003) also notes that the representation of homosexuality in Japanese media does not provide a realistic or accurate depiction of gay people's lives. Under such social conditions, homosexuality, as a non-conforming sexual identity and form of expression, stands out as a challenge to the conventional notion of masculinity.

Masculinities in popular culture

Apart from work and career, existing literature has also explored the construction of Japanese masculinity in sports and leisure activities. Masculine embodiment in sports has been reproduced through physical education at schools, as seen in the disciplining of the body and the ideology of winning-at-all-costs (*shôrishijô shugi*) in sports competitions (Sekiguchi, 2001). This type of sports masculinity is constructed differently from those of Western culture. Using rugby teams at Japanese schools as a case study, Light (2003) discovered that, as opposed to the rugby cultures in Australia and New Zealand that condone violence as the expression of hyper-masculinity, Japanese rugby players tend to internalize and favour self-control as the marker of masculinity. Light (2003) suggests that combined with endurance and loyalty, Japanese masculinity in sports resembles the virtues of *wu* (warrior), which is one of the idealized binary forms of Chinese masculinity (Louie, 2003). In addition, the masculinities expected and demanded in sports are part of athletes' everyday lives. For example, the self-monitoring of the sumo wrestler's body is extended to their clothing and hairdo in public places so that they continue to live up to the masculine image of sumo (Kawano, 2013).

Given that Japanese masculinity is constituted based on the life course of work and career (as embodied by the salaryman), Japanese men who are perceived to indulge in leisure activities or hobbies are deemed to be deviating from the masculine ideal. Such is the derogatory label of *otaku* in Japan. Galbraith (2015) looked into the history of this term's emergence in the 1980s and the social anxiety surrounding the subculture of otaku, which stems from a man's "failed" manhood. If we move away from the hegemonic reading of otaku, this masculinity can be understood as a response of younger men to contemporary socio-economic conditions in Japan. For example, Tsuji (2009) suggests that the emergence of the railway and train "maniac" (*tetsudô mania*) after the burst of the economic bubbles was not simply the romance of Japanese men towards their childhood memories but, more importantly, was a manifestation of male anxiety in response to the restructuring of the post-bubble economy. Additionally, railway and train fandom is a site where male participants can perform their manhood through homosocial interaction (Ukai, 1999).

The representation of Japanese masculinity in media and popular culture has become more diverse, but, rather than encouraging alternative masculinities, it is a phenomenon stemming from the consumerist nature of the cultural industry. The creation of *herbivore men*, which seems to contest the conventional image of masculinity, is creating a new buzz in which the media appeal to the public through sensationalization (Charlebois, 2015). Japanese fashion magazines for men may suggest a change in the construction of masculinity but are largely channels for promoting fashion and beauty products under a consumption-oriented ideology. An analysis of these magazines found that they lack a concrete discourse about gender diversity and fluidity, and a large proportion of the content goes to advertisements and product placements (Tsuji, 2013). Similarly, based on the conventional operation of the media, men's magazines were found to reproduce the hegemonic representation of masculinity through sexualized content (Seo, 2001).

Korea

The majority of published work in English about Korean men and masculinities examines militarized masculinity and media representations of masculinity in K-pop and popular TV shows. Similar to the *wen-wu* dyad in pre-modern China (see Louie, 2002), Korea's premodern society also structured its masculinities using the framework of a class hierarchy. Fighting prowess was the accepted masculinity among commoners, whereas self-control, ritual norms, and moral goals are the standards of scholar-class masculinity (Tikhonov, 2007). These two forms of masculinity co-exist in contemporary Korean society under the influence of the political situation and popular culture.

Militarized subjectivity

Men's fighting prowess was emphasized in Korea as a nationalist response to the country's colonial history and the political tension in the region. At the turn of the 20th century, sporting masculinity in the form of self-discipline and morality, as defined in Confucianism, was revived and encouraged as a patriotic response to the imperialist invasion by Japan (Tikhonov, 2007). After the Korean War, the state promoted the ideal of militarized masculinity, aiming to remasculinize the nation (Lee, 2009). The Park Chung Hee regime (1961–79) created the ideal male citizen subject as a warrior fighting for the glory of the nation both in war and in the economy, thus limiting the definition of Korean masculinity to protecting and providing (Han & Ling, 1998). Therefore Park (2016) identifies two masculinities that perpetuate men's dominance in the nation: first, the militarized masculinity that normalizes and naturalizes able-bodied men as superior and worthy citizens in protecting the nation; and second, the neoliberal masculinity that encourages men's pursuit of wealth and political power.

Militarized masculinity has become so hegemonic in Korea that men who object to conscription are considered cowards or as irresponsible, even though these conscientious objectors dare to be imprisoned (Kwon, 2013). The heterosexist military organization is a site for maintaining the hierarchy of masculinity and subordinating men who do not embody hegemonic masculinity. For example, gay men feel they are discriminated against in the military (Kwon, 2013), and higher-ranking members of the military sexually abuse lower-ranking men to demonstrate power and control (Kwon, Lee, Kim, & Kim, 2007). Therefore, Park (2016) argues that these hegemonic masculinities have become obstacles to envisioning a transformation of the patriarchal structure in the country.

Masculinities in popular culture

Masculinities represented in Korean popular culture offer a different picture from the hypermasculine model described above. Scholars suggest that the representation of masculinity in Korean popular culture is hybridized, consisting of multiple and overlapping masculinities. K-pop idols are typically divided between "flower boys" (*kkonminam*), who generally have pretty faces, slim bodies, and a feminine look, and "beast idols" (*jimseungdol*), who have muscular and tough bodies (Anderson, 2014). Interestingly, however, both types of men involve androgynous, well-groomed, metrosexual masculine images. Members of the same boys' group can even demonstrate different masculinities to suit their respective persona in different media outlets and programmes. Some group members embody the "cool" guy masculinity, whereas some perform the soft, effeminate, and cute (*aegyo*) masculinity (Manietta, 2010). Oh (2017) attributes this metrosexual masculine representation in Korean popular culture to the rise of the consumption power of women and girls. Female fans who now assume a more dominant position in media consumption fantasize and desire this type of metrosexual masculine body image in erotic performance.

In particular, the appearance and popularity of *kkonminam* attracted much scholarly attention because it departs from the hypermasculine militarized masculinity. Apart from being well-groomed, good-looking, and fashionable, kkonminam are caring, sensitive, and emotionally expressive (Elfving-Hwang, 2011). The idea has much in common with *bishōnen* (beautiful young men) in Japan and *dushili'nan* (city beautiful men) in China (Louie, 2012). Some scholars suggest that this preference reflects the continual influence of Confucian *wen* masculinity (*seonbi* in Korean) in contemporary times (Jung, 2011).

In her book *Korean Masculinities and Transcultural Consumption*, Jung (2011) argues that Korean masculinities in popular culture are not limited to soft masculinity but are actually taken to a more global level through *mugukjeok* (non-nationality) or *chogukjeok* (transnationality) construction to attract wider audience and fan bases in Asia. A hybrid and transcultural form of masculinity that consists of the odourless global element (e.g., well-toned muscles) and the national component (e.g., kkonminam) has resulted. A typical example is Rain, who is physically well built with tanned muscles but is also cute-looking and well groomed (Lee, 2014). Within this hybrid and transcultural model of masculinity, even the tough and beast-like *jimseungdol* participate in cross-dressing and perform feminized soft masculinity in game shows or reality shows, reflecting the flexible and strategic nature of this media-manufactured masculinity (Jung, 2011).

However, hybridized masculinity does not necessarily mean a shift towards gender equality or diversity. Elfving-Hwang (2011) argues that the kkonminam masculine representation reinforces the conventional gender order to a greater extent than it subverts it, because the kkonminam characters in TV dramas are not only physically glamorous but also rich and powerful, whereas the female characters are simply ordinary. This gender setting is designed to provide fantasy for female audiences and has the effect of reinforcing the existing power differential between women and men (Elfving-Hwang, 2011). In practice, men remain privileged by keeping their jobs more easily than women in times of economic downturn (Maliangkay, 2013), and women continue to be expected to prioritize housework and childcare over labour force participation (Kim, Park, Kwon, & Koo, 2005; Kim, 2006).

East Asian masculinities in other societies

The minority status of East Asian men and masculinities in host societies, as well as the strategies they use to counteract stigma and seek acceptance, are common themes in studies of East Asian men living abroad (Louie, 2014). In particular, under the hegemonic Western masculine discourse, Asian men are typically stigmatized (Kong, 2012; Shek, 2007). Consenting to the hegemony, Asian men in these countries employ various strategies to assert their masculinity, from redefining their masculinities and compensating for their stigmatized ethnicity (Chen, 1999; Chow, 2008; Hibbins, 2006) to asserting their masculinity by dominating women (Chua & Fujino, 1999). Some Korean men chose to emigrate from the West and "go back" to Korea to escape their marginalized identities and take advantage of their overseas status in South Korea (Suh, 2017).

East Asian men are subordinated not only in Western societies but also in other Asian countries. For example, Mellström (2003) reveals that in response to the constraining and disciplining Malaysian state that treated Chinese as second-class citizens, Penang-born Chinese Malaysian working-class men asserted their masculinity through the embodiment of the mastery of machinery. Non-heterosexual Asian men encounter even more stereotypes due to their sexuality (Kumashiro, 1999). They also develop their own strategies, depending on their capital and social background, to address the hegemony (Hibbins, 2006; Kong, 2011).

Conclusion

Given the similarities and intense interactions and exchanges among East Asian societies, we agree with Taga (2005a) that more comparative studies concerning East Asian men and masculinities are needed. Although more than ten years have passed since the publication of Taga's (2005a) chapter, few additional comparative studies have been conducted. As globalizing forces increase in the East Asian region, the conditions and mechanisms for the emergence of change in masculinities and men's practices need to be mapped. Furthermore, studies about the impact of transnational culture and migration on East Asian men and masculinities are crucial to understanding the transformation of gender. More importantly, collaborations between men and masculinity scholars studying East Asia are valuable in examining the underlying processes that construct and maintain the hegemony of men in this socio-cultural context (e.g., Hearn, 2004, 2012, 2014). We need more research to debunk how men as a social category are normalized and naturalized by the gender system, are created and reproduced by everyday and institutional practices, and are supported by different women's practices (Hearn, 2012). Without theorization of the hegemony of East Asian men and masculinities, our understanding of men's domination and oppression will not be complete.

References

Allison, A. (1994). *Nightwork: Sexuality, pleasure, and corporate masculinity in a Tokyo hostess club*. Chicago, IL: University of Chicago Press.

Anderson, C. S. (2014). That's my man! Overlapping masculinities in Korean popular music. In Y. Kuwahara (Ed.), *The Korean wave: Korean popular culture in global context* (pp. 117–131). Basingstoke: Palgrave Macmillan.

Baranovitch, N. (2003). *China's new voices: Popular music, ethnicity, gender, and politics, 1978–1997*. Berkeley, CA: University of California Press.

Bedford, O., & Hwang, S. (2011). Flower drinking and masculinity in Taiwan. *Journal of Sex Research, 48*(1), 82–92.

Best, K. (2014). Diaosi: China's "loser" phenomenon. *On Politics*, 7(1), 20–31.

Boretz, A. (2004). Carousing and masculinity: The cultural production of gender in Taiwan. In C. Farris, A. Lee & M. Rubinstein (Eds.), *Women in the new Taiwan: Gender roles and gender consciousness in a changing society* (pp. 171–198). New York: M.E. Sharpe.

Charlebois, J. (2015). Herbivore masculinity: Opposition or accommodation to hegemonic masculinity?. In S. A. Jackson (Ed.), *Routledge international handbook of race, class, and gender* (pp. 117–127). London: Routledge.

Chen, A. S. (1999). Lives at the center of the periphery, lives at the periphery of the center. *Gender & Society, 13*(5), 584–607.

Chen, B., & Mac an Ghaill, M. (2017). Negotiating family/filial responsibilities: Reflexivity, tradition, and Taiwanese (younger) professional men. In X. Lin, C. Haywood & M. Mac an Ghaill (Eds.), *East Asian men: Masculinity, sexuality and desire* (pp. 51–67). London: Palgrave Macmillan.

Chow, Y. F. (2008). Martial arts films and Dutch–Chinese masculinities: Smaller is better. *China Information, 22*(2), 331–359.

Chua, P., & Fujino, D. (1999). Negotiating new Asian-American masculinities: Attitudes and gender expectations. *The Journal of Men's Studies*, 7(3), 391–413.

Dasgupta, R. (2000). Performing masculinities? The 'salaryman' at work and play. *Japanese Studies, 20*(2), 189–200.

Dasgupta, R. (2003). Creating corporate warriors: The "salaryman" and masculinity in Japan. In K. Louie & M. Low (Eds.), *Asian masculinities: The meaning and practice of manhood in China and Japan* (pp. 118–133). London: Routledge.

Deng, X. H. (2014). Zhongguo nanxing xing gong zuo zhe de xing bie xie shang. In J. M. Huang (Ed.), *Dakai nanxing: Yanggang qigai de bianzou* (pp. 110–126). Hong Kong: Chung Wah Book & Roundtable Synergy Books.

The Economist. (2014, March 29). Japanese women and work: Holding back half the nation. Retrieved from www.economist.com/news/briefing/21599763-womens-lowly-status-japanese-workplace-has-barely-improved-decades-and-country.

Elfving-Hwang, J. (2011). *Not so soft after all: Kkonminam masculinities in contemporary South Korean popular culture*. Paper presented at the 7th Korean Studies Association of Australasia Biennial Conference.

Galbraith, P. W. (2015). Otaku research and anxiety about failed men. In P. W. Galbraith, T. H. Kam, & B. Kamm (Eds.), *Debating otaku in contemporary Japan: Historical perspectives and new horizons* (pp. 21–34). London: Bloomsbury Academic.

Han, J., & Ling, L. (1998). Authoritarianism in the hypermasculinized state: Hybridity, patriarchy, and capitalism in Korea. *International Studies Quarterly, 42*(1), 53–78.

Hearn, J. (2004). From hegemonic masculinity to the hegemony of men. *Feminist Theory, 5*(1), 49–72.

Hearn, J. (2012). A multi-faceted power analysis of men's violence to known women: From hegemonic masculinity to the hegemony of men. *The Sociological Review, 60*(4), 589–610.

Hearn, J. (2014). Men, masculinities and the material(-)discursive. *NORMA: International Journal for Masculinity Studies, 9*(1), 5–17.

Hibbins, R. (2006). Sexuality and constructions of gender identity among Chinese male migrants in Australia. *Asian Studies Review, 30*(3), 289–303.

Hird, D. (2017). In league with gentlemen: Junzi masculinity and the Chinese nation in cultural nationalist discourses. *Asia Pacific Perspectives, 15*(1), 14–35.

Ho, P. S. Y., Jackson, S., & Kong, S. S. (2018). Speaking against silence: Finding a voice in Hong Kong Chinese families through the umbrella movement. *Sociology, 52*(5), 966–982.

Itô, K. (1993). *Otokorashisa no yukue: Dansei-bunka no bunka-shakai-gaku* [Where are men going? Cultural sociology of masculine culture]. Tokyo: Shinyôsha.

Itô, K. (1996). *Danseigaku nyûmon* [An introduction to men's studies]. Tokyo: Sakuhinsha.

Itô, S. (2001). Dansei keisei to dôseiai keno [The construction of men and homophobia]. In H. Asai, S. Itô, & Y. Murase (Eds.), *Nihon no otoko ha dokokara kite, doko e iku no ka* [Where did the Japanese men come from, and where do they go to] (pp. 222–233). Tokyo: Seiunsha.

Jung, S. (2011). *Korean masculinities and transcultural consumption: Yonsama, Rain, Oldboy, K-pop idols*. Hong Kong: Hong Kong University Press.

Kan, K. (2013). The new "lost generation": Inequality and discontent among Chinese youth. *China Perspectives, 2*, 67–73.

Kashima, T. (1993). *Otoko no zahyôjiku: Kigyô kara katei shakai e*. [The configuration of men: From business to home and society]. Tokyo: Iwanami Shoten.

Kasuga, K. (1999). Dansei Keawaakaa no kanôsei [The possibility of men as careworkers]. In Y. Nishikawa & M. Ogino (Eds.), Danseiron: Kyôdô kenkyû [Men's studies: Collaborative research] (pp. 76–93). Kyoto: Jinbun Shoin.

Kawano, S. (2013). Rikishi no yosooi to masukyuriniti [Sumo wrestlers' dressing and masculinity]. *Osaka Shoin Women's College Research Bulletin*, *3*, 147–158.

Kelly, W. W. (1986). Rationalization and nostalgia: Cultural dynamics of new middle-class Japan. *American Ethnologist*, *13*(4), 603–618.

Kim, N. Y. (2006). "Patriarchy is so third world": Korean immigrant women and "migrating" white Western masculinity. *Social Problems*, *53*(4), 519–536.

Kim, U., Park, Y., Kwon, Y., & Koo, J. (2005). Values of children, parent–child relationship, and social change in Korea: Indigenous, cultural, and psychological analysis. *Applied Psychology*, *54*(3), 338–354.

Kolbjørnsen, T. S. (2012). *Who's the man? An exploration of contemporary Chinese urban middle class men's expressions of masculinity* (MA thesis). University of Oslo.

Kong, T. S. K. (2011). *Chinese male homosexualities: Memba, tongzhi and golden boy*. Oxon: Routledge.

Kong, T. S. K. (2012). Chinese male bodies: A transnational study of masculinity and sexuality. In B. S. Turner (Ed.), *The Routledge handbook of the body* (pp. 289–306). Oxon: Routledge.

Kumashiro, K. K. (1999). Supplementing normalcy and otherness: Queer Asian American men reflect on stereotypes, identity, and oppression. *International Journal of Qualitative Studies in Education*, *12*(5), 491–508.

Kwon, I. (2013). Gender, feminism and masculinity in anti-militarism: Focusing on the conscientious objection movement in South Korea. *International Feminist Journal of Politics*, *15*(2), 213–233.

Kwon, I., Lee, D., Kim, E., & Kim, H. (2007). Sexual violence among men in the military in South Korea. *Journal of Interpersonal Violence*, *22*(8), 1024–1042.

Lee, J. (2009). Surrogate military, subimperialism, and masculinity: South Korea in the Vietnam war, 1965–73. *Positions*, *17*(3), 655–682.

Lee, F. L. F. (2019, July). The anti-extradition bill protests and the democracy movement in Hong Kong. #AsiaNow. Retrieved from www.asian-studies.org/asia-now/entryid/234/the-anti-extradition-bill-protests-and-the-democracy-movement-in-hong-kong.

Lee, N. J. Y. (2014). Pop-orientalism and the Asian star body: Rain and the transnational Hollywood action movie. In W. Leung, & A. Willis (Eds.), *East Asian film stars* (pp. 35–48). New York: Palgrave Macmillan.

Light, R. (2003). Sport and the construction of masculinity in the Japanese education system. In K. Louie & M. Low (Eds.), *Asian masculinities: The meaning and practice of manhood in China and Japan* (pp. 107–124). London: Routledge.

Lin, X. (2017). Single male rural-urban migrant workers and the negotiation of masculinity in China. In X. Lin, C. Haywood & M. Mac an Ghaill (Eds.), *East Asian men: Masculinity, sexuality and desire* (pp. 13–30). London: Palgrave Macmillan.

Liong, M. (2017). Sacrifice for the family: Representation and practice of stay-at-home fathers in the intersection of masculinity and class in Hong Kong. *Journal of Gender Studies*, *26*(4), 402–417.

Liong, M., & Chan, L. S. (2018). Walking a tightrope on (hetero)sexuality: Performatively vigilant masculine subjectivity in response to sexualized culture. *Men and Masculinities* (advance online publication), 1097184X17753267.

Liong, M., & Ho, P. S. Y. (2019). Men in upheaval: Integrating Hong Kong politics and critical studies of men and masculinities. *Gender, Place & Culture*, *26*(7–9), 1081–1093.

Louie, K. (2002). *Theorising Chinese masculinity: Society and gender in China*. Cambridge: Cambridge University Press.

Louie, K. (2003). Chinese, Japanese and global masculine identities. In K. Louie, & M. Low (Eds.), *Asian masculinities: The meaning and practice of manhood in China and Japan* (pp. 1–15). London: RoutledgeCurzon.

Louie, K. (2012). Popular culture and masculinity ideals in East Asia, with special reference to China. *The Journal of Asian Studies*, *71*(4), 929–943.

Louie, K. (2014). Chinese masculinity studies in the twenty-first century: Westernizing, Easternizing and globalizing wen and wu. *NORMA: International Journal for Masculinity Studies*, *9*(1), 18–29.

Maliangkay, R. (2013). Catering to the female gaze: The semiotics of masculinity in Korean advertising. *Situations*, 7(1), 43–61.

Manietta, J. B. (2010). *Transnational masculinities: The distributive performativity of gender in Korean boy bands* (MA thesis). Missouri State University.

McLelland, M. (2003). Gay men, masculinity and the media in Japan. In K. Louie & M. Low (Eds.), *Asian masculinities: The meaning and practice of manhood in China and Japan* (pp. 67–86). London: Routledge.

Mellström, U. (2003). *Masculinity, power and technology: A Malaysian ethnography*. Farnham: Ashgate.

Oh, C. (2017). "Cinderella" in reverse: Eroticizing bodily labor of sympathetic men in K-pop dance practice video. In X. Lin, C. Haywood & M. Mac an Ghaill (Eds.), *East Asian men: Masculinity, sexuality and desire* (pp. 123–141). London: Palgrave Macmillan.

Osburg, J. (2013). *Anxious wealth: Money and morality among China's new rich*. Stanford, CA: Stanford University Press.

Pang, L. (2002). Masculinity in crisis: Films of Milkyway image and post-1997 Hong Kong cinema. *Feminist Media Studies*, 2(3), 325–340.

Park, Y. (2016). The crucible of sexual violence: Militarized masculinities and the abjection of life in post-crisis, neoliberal South Korea. *Feminist Studies*, *42*(1), 17–40.

Plath, D. (1964). *The afterhours: Modern Japan and the search for enjoyment*. Berkeley, CA: University of California Press.

Sekiguchis, H. (2001). Taiku supôtsu ni okeru "otokorashisa" [Manhood in physical education and sports]. In H. Asai, S. Itô, & Y. Murase (Eds.), *Nihon no otoko ha dokokara kite, doko e iku no ka* [Where did the Japanese men come from, and where do they go to] (pp. 204–221). Tokyo: Seiunsha.

Seo, T. (2001). Masu media ni miru danseizô [The portrait of man from the mass media perspective]. In H. Asai, S. Itô, & Y. Murase (Eds.), *Nihon no otoko ha dokokara kite, doko e iku no ka* [Where did the Japanese men come from, and where do they go to] (pp. 150–169). Tokyo: Seiunsha.

Shek, Y. L. (2007). Asian American masculinity: A review of the literature. *The Journal of Men's Studies*, *14*(3), 379–391.

Shiau, H. (2013). Consumption and masculinity: A case study of GQ magazine covers in Taiwan. In A. Y. H. Fung (Ed.), *Asian popular culture: The global (dis)continuity* (pp. 94–110). Oxon: Routledge.

Song, G. (2010). Chinese masculinities revisited: Male images in contemporary television drama serials. *Modern China*, *36*(4), 404–434.

Song, G., & Hird, D. (2013). *Men and masculinities in contemporary China*. Leiden: Brill.

Suh, S. C. (2017). Negotiating masculinity across borders: A transnational examination of Korean American masculinities. *Men and Masculinities*, *20*(3), 317–344.

Szablewicz, M. (2014). The "losers" of China's internet: Memes as 'structures of feeling' for disillusioned young netizens. *China Information*, *28*(2), 259–275.

Taga, F. (2003). Rethinking male socialisation: Life histories of Japanese male youth. In K. Louie & M. Low (Eds.), *Asian masculinities: The meaning and practice of manhood in China and Japan* (pp. 137–155). London: Routledge.

Taga, F. (2005a). East Asian masculinities. In M. S. Kimmel, J. Hearn & R. W. Connell (Eds.), *Handbook of studies on men and masculinities* (pp. 129–140). Thousand Oaks, CA: Sage.

Taga, F. (2005b). Seibetsu yakuwari bungyô ga hiteisareru nakade no chichioya yakuwari [The role of fatherhood denied by the gender division]. *Fôramu gendai shakaigaku [Contemporary Sociology Forum]*, *4*, 48–56.

Taga, F. (2010). Chichioya no kateikyôiku" gensetsu to kaisô jendaa kôzô no henka [The discourse of father's family education and the structural change of class and gender]. *Kyôiku kagaku seminarii [Education Science Seminary]*, *14*, 1–15.

Tikhonov, V. (2007). Masculinizing the nation: Gender ideologies in traditional Korea and in the 1890s–1900s Korean enlightenment discourse. *The Journal of Asian Studies*, *66*(4), 1029–1065.

Tsuji, I. (2009). Naze tetsudô ha "otoko no roman" ni natta no ka [Why did railways become the romance of a man]. In S. Miyadai, I. Tsuji & T. Okai (Eds.), *Otokorashisa no kairaku: Popyuraa bunka kara mita sono jittai* [The pleasure of manhood: Reality from the popular culture perspective] (pp. 219–246). Tokyo: Keisou shobou.

Tsuji, I. (2013). Zasshi ni egakareta "otokorashisa" no henyô: Dansei Fasshonshi no naiyô bunseki kara [The transformation of manliness as represented in magazines: A content analysis of male fashion magazines]. *Jinbun Gakuhô*, *467*, 27–66.

Ukai, M. (1999). Tetsudô mania kôgengaku [The social phenomena of railway and train maniac]. In Y. Nishikawa & M. Ogino (Eds.), *Danseiron: Kyôdô kenkyû* [Men's studies: Collaborative research] (96–124). Kyoto: Jinbun Shoin.

Vogel, E. F. (1971). *Japan's new middle class: The salary man and his family in a Tokyo suburb*. Berkeley, CA: University of California Press.

Xiao, S. (2011). The "second-wife" phenomenon and the relational construction of class-coded masculinities in contemporary China. *Men and Masculinities*, *14*(5), 607–627.

Yang, H. (2014). Flower boys on campus: Performing and practicing masculinity. *Journal of Gender Studies*, *23*, 391–408.

Zhang, X. (2011). Masculinities in crisis? An emerging debate on men and boys in contemporary China. In E. Ruspini, J. Hearn, B. Pease & K. Pringle (Eds.), *Men and masculinities around the world: Transforming men's practices* (pp. 191–203). New York: Palgrave Macmillan.

Zheng, T. (2009). *Red lights: The lives of sex workers in postsocialist China*. Minneapolis, MN: University of Minnesota Press.

Zhong, X. (2000). *Masculinity besieged? Issues of modernity and male subjectivity in Chinese literature of the late twentieth century*. Durham, NC: Duke University Press.

Zurndorfer, H. (2016). Polygamy and masculinity in China: Past and present. In K. Louie (Ed.), *Changing Chinese masculinities: From imperial pillars of state to global real men* (pp. 13–33). Hong Kong: Hong Kong University Press.

14

Disability, embodiment and masculinities

A complex matrix

Steve Robertson, Lee Monaghan and Kris Southby

Introduction

It has previously been suggested that femininity and disability are mutually reinforcing, as both are similarly constructed as marginalised identities within hegemonic able-bodied patriarchies. In contrast, masculinity and disability are said to exist in a state of conflict: the elements of strength, stamina, authority and potency associated with hegemonic masculinity practices are considered antithetical to the experiences and representations of men with impairments (Shuttleworth, Wedgwood & Wilson, 2012). Within Western culture, the Cartesian split between (male) mind and (female) body reinforces a view that men's bodies are expected to (naturally) function well, without overt attention, and are therefore simultaneously dissociated from their identity whilst being an integral part of it. The gender identity options open to men with impairments are seemingly left as 'failed', 'spoiled' or in need of reformulation. However, as Moser (2006) suggests, interactions of difference such as disability and gender are more complex and can interact to support and reinforce but also to challenge and undermine each other.

Within this chapter, we outline the historical development of scholarly work on masculinities and disability, paying attention to conceptual shifts in thinking on this relationship. We consider what some (Hearn et al., 2012)[1] have called 'third wave' conceptualisations of masculinities, linking these to ongoing theorising within disability studies and particularly discussions about social and relational models of disability. We consider work on masculinities and learning impairment, in addition to 'cyborg bodies' and gender, as useful examples to explore how this recent thinking in both masculinities and disability studies can inform each other. We conclude by considering how the above can help situate thinking around disabled masculinities within the wider neoliberal context. We do this recognising that concepts such as 'hegemonic masculinity' and neoliberalism are themselves open to interrogation and refinement (Connell & Messerschmidt, 2005; Monaghan, Bombak & Rich, 2018; Robertson, Gough & Robinson, 2017).

Historical emergence of masculinities and disability

Since the 1980s, feminist work has noted how gender has often been invisible and how the experiences of disabled men have been taken as representative of all disabled experience (e.g., Morris, 1993). Simultaneously, key disability studies writers were recognising that little research explored the lived experiences of disabled men (Shakespeare, 1996, 1999). Shakespeare (1996) helps unpack this paradox by suggesting that women, researching through predominantly feminist approaches, tended to explore the personal aspects of sexuality, relationships and identity, whereas men often focused on employment, housing and more material social issues. This, he says, reproduced the public (realm of the male)–private (realm of the female) split, leading to an under-representation of disabled men's lived experiences.

Accounts of men's personal experiences of impairment and links to 'masculinity' began to emerge with autoethnographic pieces (e.g., Kriegel, 1998; Murphy, 1987; Zola, 1982) highlighting the difficulties some men had in negotiating a gendered identity, usually following acquired physical impairment. These accounts tended to focus on an 'embattled identity'; the struggles men had in meeting society's (and their own) conflicting expectations of what it is to be male. However, such accounts also showed how aspects of masculinity could assist in surviving the experience of becoming impaired:

> Be a man! An old battered idea that has not fared well. Like all clichés, it embarrasses. Yet clichés spring from the cultures that give them life, and to the idea of what it meant to be a man in 1944 I owe my survival.
>
> *(Kriegel, 1998, p. 5)*

Whilst such work is important in highlighting how 'disability' is a gendered issue for men, it risks reproducing an overly individualised focus on how men 'handle' the experience of impairment. Critical questions lay dormant regarding cultural representations of 'disability' and 'masculinity', the structural embedding of these representations and how this embedding is responsible for contributing to and generating such identity conflict (Robertson & Smith, 2013). From a historical view, these ideas are not necessarily new. For example, Neumann (2010) highlights the cultural ideals attached of a new type of prosthetic man and the changing construction of disability following World War I.

Other work countered this individualising trend. Oliver, Zarb, Silver, Moore and Salisbury's (1988) research into men's experiences following spinal cord injury (SCI) proposed a social adjustment model where social context was crucial to understanding the consequences and experiences of impairment. In doing so, it developed links between men's experience and the wider social context, showing how structural (material) issues were significant in shaping such experience. Similarly, Gerschick and Miller (1995) helped theorise masculinities and disability in ways that explored individual experience in relation to the wider gender order. They identify three main coping strategies in the (re)negotiation of gendered identity: *reliance*, where on-going effort is made to fulfil traditional/hegemonic ideals; *reformulation*, where hegemonic ideals are redefined in new ways and; *rejection*, where hegemonic masculinity ideals are renounced, inverted and downplayed. Gerschick (1998) later shifted emphasis, opting for a model with two strategies: compliance with or resistance to societal norms of hegemonic masculinity. For Gerschick, rejection and/or resistance – the construction of 'counter-hegemonic alternatives' (1998, p. 208) – represent the approaches that provide men with impairments the best opportunity for escaping gender domination.

By the late 1990s, debate was taking place within disability studies about the limitations of both individualised *and* social models of disability. The former was seen to run the risk of slippage into biomedical 'personal tragedy' models, whilst many (pro-)feminist disability scholars were highlighting the limitations of the social model in exploring the socially integrated nature of the personal effects of impairment for an individual (Robertson & Smith, 2013; Thomas, 2007). A significant outcome of this debate was a desire to extend the social model of disability into questions of culture, representation and meaning to help understand how personal 'impairment effects' (Thomas, 2004, 2007) differ, both quantitatively and qualitatively, not only between disabled men and women but also between different groups of disabled men. As Shuttleworth et al. (2012) and Barrett (2014) highlight, early work on masculinities and disability often presented 'disability' as a generic category rather than focusing on how masculinities intersect differently with varying types of impairment.

More recently, work has developed that recognises the importance of understanding the plurality of 'masculinities' and their intersections with diverse 'disabilities' (Hickey-Moody, 2015). Smith (2013) offers a nuanced account attentive to heterogeneity by drawing on Connell's (1995) relational theory of gender and Thomas' (2007) relational theory of disability to examine men's varied understanding of health several years after acquiring a SCI. He notes how the men felt they *should* care about health, and this was partly a result of the materiality of impaired bodies that require daily health work. However, such concern could put masculinities at risk when health is generally constructed as a feminine domain. These men therefore also stated that whilst they cared about their health, they did not care *too* much (see also Robertson, 2007), and this enabled them to accrue masculine capital and uphold their masculine identity. Smith (2013) further highlighted how the men upheld gendered identities by performing resilience; by demonstrating an ability to positively adapt to adversity or risk. Resilience was about recovering quickly if illness or health problems arose but was also a resource for gaining masculine capital and upholding masculinities. By drawing on masculine signifiers – like strength and control – resilience became a resource for legitimating not caring about health too much and therefore a way of 'doing' masculinity.

Work on men with Duchenne Muscular Dystrophy (DMD) also illuminates how masculinities intersect differently with different types of impairment. Drawing from Connell and Bourdieu, Gibson, Young, Upshur and McKeever (2007) reveal that in certain social fields, men with DMD adapted masculine signifiers such as strength, intelligence, leadership and autonomy. The men gave accounts of providing high levels of emotional support to family members, eschewing notions of stoicism whilst conforming to notions of (male) mental resilience. In different contexts, the men aligned even more directly with hegemonic forms of masculinity. In the education field, some participants recalled intimidating younger, emotionally or cognitively weaker boys through physical violence or verbal aggression. These acts represented a source, at least in their view, of 'positive' gendered capital helping them sustain a dominant position among other disabled persons. The men thus reproduced masculine capital whilst engaging in practices that contributed to transforming these meanings. Such issues are not limited to developed world contexts. In South Africa, for example, Lipenga (2014) reveals how men with various disabilities reconstruct their gendered self by reintegrating themselves within a dominant grid of masculinity while simultaneously reformulating some aspects of hegemonic norms.

However, Gibson et al. (2007) also suggest that these men with DMD rarely questioned dominant masculinity structures or consciously attempted to create spaces for alternate forms of masculinity. Whilst they claimed power in some fields, within the larger social space they remained profoundly marginalised. For example, they were marginalised through the inaccessibility of the built environment and the ways their visible bodily differences were negatively marked. This marginalisation was embodied, and was simultaneously experienced as troubling, but also 'normal' such that 'an embodied reality for men with DMD whereby they come to "believe" that the margin is (more or less, and with some exceptions in particular fields) where they belong' (p. 514).

Third-wave masculinities and disability

Much of the work above draws on Connell's (1995) relational model of masculinities. Here gender is understood as sets of relationships between men and women but is also about relationships *amongst* men and *amongst* women: masculinities are a part of, not distinct from, the larger system of relationships that Connell terms the 'gender order'. Such conceptualisation avoids casting masculinity as consisting of traits or characteristics that men possess to a greater or lesser extent. Instead, masculinities are recognised as diverse processes of arranging and 'doing' social practices that operate in individual and collective settings; what Connell (1995) terms 'configurations of practice' within and between which men move. These configurations are hierarchical, consisting of hegemonic masculinity practices to which other masculinity practices are complicit, subordinated or marginalised. Such theorising opens up opportunities for seeing power relations within the gender order as a nexus that also operates along other identity axes such as sexuality, ethnicity, disability etc.

There are many critiques of Connell's original formulation of masculinities and, in particular, hegemonic masculinities. It is not our intention to consider such critiques here.[2] Rather, we consider aspects of third-wave conceptualisations of gender/masculinities (Hearn et al., 2012) – specifically Inclusive Masculinity Theory and 'hybrid masculinities' – that are said to move beyond early formulations of hegemonic masculinity and how these relate to work on disability.

Inclusive Masculinity Theory (IMT) (Anderson, 2009; Anderson & McGuire, 2010) was conceived when considering empirical data suggesting that an increasing number of young straight men were rejecting homophobia, were more emotionally open, more tactile and more open to gay peer friendships (Anderson & McCormack, 2018). Anderson and colleagues were reluctant to explain these changes as a simple cultural shift in decreasing homophobia; many of these open expressions of masculinity practices also occur in cultures where homophobia is still present. Instead, Anderson (2009) introduced the concept of homohysteria – defined as the fear of being socially perceived as gay.

IMT argues that within cultures with reduced homohysteria, Connell's theorising of masculinities being hierarchical with certain practices being hegemonic begins to collapse. Rather, diverse forms of masculinity practices, such as subordinated and marginalised practices, become more evenly esteemed and valued and 'femininity' in men less stigmatised (Anderson, 2009). IMT is optimistic about the changes in masculinities and gender practices, seeing this as a trend likely to continue.

Little work has yet been done considering what IMT can offer to understanding the heterogeneous experiences of men with varying impairments. Anderson and Kian (2012) completed a case-study media analysis of an American football player withdrawing from a game after experiencing concussion, links this partly to a softening of masculinity and concludes that 'major sport media are beginning to support the notion of health over a masculine warrior narrative' (p. 152). This seems rather sparse evidence on which to base such a conclusion. Barrett (2014) points to the possibilities of applying IMT to the disability studies field but rightly notes: 'the question of whether the posited emergence of a 'softer' masculinity, less invested in the tropes of domination, aggression, and inequality, is also promoting the social inclusion of disabled men requires further exploration' (p. 52).

Whilst IMT suggests a radical rupture in gender and masculinity practices, some scholars take a different view. Demetriou (2001) and Bridges and Pascoe (2014) agree that change has and is taking place but differ from IMT in the extent to which they think this has happened and the reasons for it. They suggest that changes toward more emotionally open and inclusive masculinity practices are more reconfiguration than radical rupture.

Demetriou (2001) argues for a move away from the dualism found in Connell's work between hegemonic and non-hegemonic masculinities, instead proposing the concept of a 'hegemonic masculine bloc' which recognises masculinity practices as being in a constant process of negotiation, translation, hybridisation and reconfiguration. As with IMT, this suggests that subordinated and marginalised masculinity practices previously presented as passive within Connell's framework play a more active role in the (re)production of the gender order. Rather than seeing masculine power as 'a closed, coherent, and unified totality' (Demetriou, 2001, p. 355) that stands in opposition to women's rights and homosexuality, the hegemonic 'masculine bloc' incorporates aspects of these, thereby making itself appear less threatening and more egalitarian. In hybridising hegemonic practices with marginalised or subordinated practices, the hegemonic masculine bloc masks and subtly obfuscates the way that patriarchal power and privilege are maintained.

Whilst agreeing with IMT theorists that the assimilation of previously marginalised or subordinated masculinity practices that blur social and symbolic boundaries is now widespread, those conceptualising masculinities as a 'hegemonic masculinities bloc' challenge the reasons for this. They also question the extent of this in terms of material rather than stylistic change and whether such change represents a genuine challenge to existing systems of power and inequality.

Concepts of hybrid masculinities and the 'masculine bloc' have rarely been linked to the disability studies field (or vice versa). We suggest such linking would be productive. It would allow challenge to notions that polarise 'disabled masculinity' as *either* compliant with *or* resistant to hegemonic practices. It can provide useful ways to understand how social models of disability can be linked to the individual impact of impairment – what Thomas (2012) has termed 'psycho-emotional disablism'. In doing so, it helps exploration of the complex patterns of privilege and disadvantage that disabled men negotiate – highlighted well in Gibson and colleagues' (2007) work on young men with DMD discussed earlier. It also helps explain the enduring nature of gendered/ableist power dynamics. For example, work on disabled identity in relationships suggests that whilst men in the study engaged in alternative (non-hegemonic) masculinities, the emotion work required to do so was 'indicative of the oppressive and inherent inequalities of ableist culture' (Liddiard, 2014, p. 125).

The following sections address two emerging areas: masculinity and intellectual disability; and 'cyborg bodies' and masculinities.

Masculinity and intellectual disability

The interaction between intellectual disability and masculinity has largely remained overlooked (Charnock, 2013; Shuttleworth et al., 2012), and male-specific issues for those with intellectual impairments have been mostly excluded in policy and practice discourses (Wilson, Parmenter, Stancliffe, Shuttleworth & Parker, 2010). In general, men and boys with an intellectual disability have a complex relationship with 'masculinity'. Whilst traditional hegemonic masculine ideals are something that many men and boys with an intellectual disability strive to achieve (Cwirynkalo, Borowska-Beszta & Bartnikowska, 2016), research presents a picture of diminished masculinity outside of mainstream life.

People with an intellectual disability often have limited opportunities to develop a sense of (gendered) identity, typically because of cognitive functioning, limited access to domains of life where identity formation typically occurs (i.e., work, leisure, family) or a combination of these. Whilst these men and boys may be able to engage in hegemonic masculinity practices through relative displays of strength and autonomy within disability-specific or 'sheltered' settings (e.g., supported housing, special schools), this is often not transferable to 'mainstream' settings. Charnock (2013) found that boys' opportunities to practice their developing masculinity were limited and restricted. They often talked about their struggles when attempts to project their (male) identities *as boys* resulted in the uncovering of their difference and vulnerability. Ideas of 'normalisation' suggest that people with an intellectual disability be supported to live ordinary lives alongside their non-disabled peers, including that services provide opportunities to practice 'normal' (hegemonic) masculinity. Björnsdóttir, Stefánsdóttir and Stefánsdóttir (2017) found that many homes and assisted housing units offered 'male' activities (e.g., bowling) to men and 'female' activities (e.g., shopping trips) for women. However, people with an intellectual disability are often viewed as vulnerable or helpless 'eternal children' who lack, or do not need, a gender identity (Björnsdóttir et al., 2017). In such circumstances, rather than being understood as displays of masculinity, acts of sexuality, strength, independence or assertiveness are often problematised and actively discouraged (Wilson et al., 2010).

It is necessary to construct alternative discourses of masculinity for men and boys with intellectual disabilities that take greater account of intersectionality and interaction between cultural, social, political, economic, ethnic and gender values (Björnsdóttir et al., 2017; Cwirynkalo et al., 2016; Shuttleworth et al., 2012). Wilson's (2009) concept of 'conditionally masculine' helps here. Drawn from ethnographic research in group homes for young men with significant cognitive impairments, Wilson (2009) recognises that masculinity is, for these men, not a dichotomous position but a changeable construct on a continuum. None of the participants engaged in 'mainstream' activities, and so their masculinity was constructed by this disability-specific reality; conditional masculinity therefore recognises the limitations of disability upon expressing masculinity but not upon being masculine. Similarly, in Southby's (2013) exploration of football fandom for adults with an intellectual disability, one sees how male participants, to greater or lesser extents, performed different versions of the male ritual of supporting a football club in different settings (e.g., home, football stadium, college, public house) within limitations imposed by their personal social context, including their impairment.

'Cyborg bodies' and masculinities

While disability commonly implies marginality and subordination within the contemporary gender order, there are alternative and sometimes fantastic visions and imaginaries. The cyborg (an organic-machine hybrid), for example, is a mainstay of popular culture, with *Robocop* serving as an obvious science fiction representation *qua* 'powerful male warrior' (Featherstone, 1999, p. 2). Within the social sciences, discussion of the cyborg is commonly traced to Haraway's writings (1985, 1991), which challenge antagonistic dualisms in the social construction of devalued and dominated 'others'. The cyborg has promise in terms of the re-imaging of oppression, suggesting a posthuman or transhuman world wherein human frailty, vulnerability and even mortality are overcome. Yet the cyborg is also implicated in the reproduction of masculine domination, capitalist neoliberal relations, wastefulness and toxicity (Hickey-Moody, 2015).

The cyborgian athlete is often socially constructed as a new type of hero. Various scholars discussed issues of disability and embodiment following the London 2012 Paralympic Games. Tamari (2017) focuses on Pistorius (among others) to examine the ways in which Paralympian cyborgs are implicated in the reproduction of a 'prosthetic aesthetic'. This aesthetic is defined as a 'cultural sensitivity' to body image that oscillates between a sense of attractiveness/'coolness' to abjection. This is attributed to the melding of inorganic (dead) matter with organic lived bodies creating feelings of both fascination and revulsion. In a similar vein, Swartz and Watermeyer (2008) demonstrate how the case of Pistorius breaks entrenched boundaries and lays bare core concerns in society about disability and the body.

Pistorius is taken for special consideration given the immense public and media attention given to him. As a double amputee, Pistorius, facilitated by his position as a white (privileged) male in the South African context, transformed himself into the 'Blade Runner' who sported '"spectacular biomechanical" carbon fibre prosthetic limbs' (Tamari, 2017, p. 26) which enabled him to compete against able-bodied athletes in the 2012 Olympics. As Hickey-Moody (2015) contends, this is very much a competitive homosocial process that enabled Pistorius (even if unconsciously) to attempt 'to recuperate his gendered identity from emasculating discourses of disability' (p. 139). However, in light of the highly publicised murder trial that eventually saw the formerly 'great athlete' and 'man' (rather than 'disabled person') convicted as a criminal, Tamari (2017) refers to a move 'from the fascinating heroic body with prosthetic legs to the vulnerable flesh of a criminal body without prostheses' (p. 47). Tamari therefore also highlights the ambivalent feelings and paradoxes generated by prosthetic bodies.

Focusing on 'the cyborg soldier', writers such as Masters (2005) and Satheaswaran (2016) sensitise us to the ways in which technology and masculinity are imbued with complex and contradictory meanings that include but exceed the positive values ascribed to the 'superhuman' and resilient machine-man coupling. While Masters (2005) seeks to address ethical issues as they pertain to militarised (white, heterosexual) masculinities, and the significance of advanced hard-edged technology, Satheaswaran (2016) specifically analyses what the cyborg means in relation to *disability* and masculinity (through reference to a formerly able-bodied US soldier who was fitted with a prosthetic leg after detonating a landmine and who then 'bravely' returned to two tours of duty in Iraq). Both authors highlight the tensions in hegemonic constructions of masculinity in militarised settings insofar as deployable male bodies must be 'fit', 'disciplined' and cap-*able* of serving their duties to the nation-state whilst risking their health.

While becoming a cyborg soldier might allow disabled combatants to re-enter hegemonic masculinity and trump any sense of 'personal tragedy', Satheaswaran (2016) underscores the degree to which this is underpinned by processes of dehumanization: cyborgs *qua* state property are more or less useful things that should be able to inflict and endure immense pain. If they are not up to the job then they can be terminated: these re-enabled, or even technologically enhanced, bodies are embroiled in political economies that are performative, violent and toxic. As with Paralympian cyborgs, they fit well with neoliberal logics and configurations of bodily reflexive practice wherein the 'self-made man' must be constituted and re-constituted if he is to succeed within a competitive (marketised) world. Accordingly, we would suggest that any understanding of 'inclusion' or 'inclusive masculinity', in this instance, is a chimera that belies how gendered power and technology are implicated in corrosive practices, hierarchies and an extractive/exploitative global economy.

Conclusion

This chapter provides an overview of the current field of masculinities and disabilities scholarship, moving beyond early work which suggested somewhat homogenising notions of personal tragedy and/or failed/spoiled identity. Following Moser (2006), we suggest that interactions of disability and gender are complex and interact not only to support and reinforce but also to challenge and undermine each other. After Traustadóttir (2006), we therefore suggest a perspective which recognises a 'matrix of dominance' in the study of disability and gender that facilitates consideration of the multiple layers of advantage and disadvantage experienced by men with various impairments.

Drawing on advanced relational models of gender (particularly those exploring hybrid masculinities) and disability (that emphasise material as well as psycho-emotional components) provides a conceptual model, supported by empirical evidence, which best illuminates the 'masculinities/disabilities nexus'. We offer this suggestion while retaining a critical eye on gendered power. A reflexive approach to such theorising helps us to understand, for example, how the young men in Gibson and colleagues' (2007) work on DMD would engage in counter-hegemonic practices when practically necessary but, where possible, would engage in hegemonic practices to accrue masculine capital within their micro-context.

Within this matrix of dominance, we continue to see hierarchies at work relating to diverse forms of impairment and tied to the politics of disposability. Where forms of physical impairment occur that might be 'fixed' or 'enhanced' by construction of a human-technology cyborg, a form of gendered identity may be made available that avoids emasculating discourses of disability. Of course, such technologies and their utility are context specific, as seen, for example, when they generate fascination in athletic and military domains. Furthermore, advanced prosthetic technology is likely to be only available to 'well placed' (ethnically, socio-economically and geographically favoured) bodies that are afforded the potentialities of competitive, 'carbon fibre masculinities' (Hickey-Moody, 2015). However, within neoliberal economies, such cyborg bodies, like all bodies, are only useful if/whilst they can play a role in sustaining existing (gendered, ableist) socio-economic power dynamics and the trans-national capitalist class. This critique does not depend on viewing neoliberalism as an explanatory catch-all, but, in line with Monaghan et al.'s (2018) work, we would suggest that the concept remains indispensable when seeking to interrogate bodily matters, including disability, at the present historical juncture. The greater surveillance accorded to the bodies of men (and women) with physical impairments leaves them more visible and therefore more likely to be quickly and readily dispensed with when such usefulness is no longer recognised. Neoliberal-driven policies around welfare to work and the conflicting impact of these on those with impairment have been well documented in many countries – including the UK (Owen & Harris, 2012) and Australia (Soldatic & Chapman, 2010) – and it is anticipated that the logics of neoliberalism will be antithetical to anybody positioned as a 'drain' on the system.

For men with intellectual impairment, no such cyborg identities are yet available, and their utility to the neoliberal enterprise seems minimal, with some studies showing as few as 6.6% of people with intellectual impairment being in paid employment (McGlinchey, McCallion, Burke, Carroll & McCarron, 2013). To this extent, the structural constraints experienced by men with physical impairment, and the limited representational and material value attached to them, is heavily compounded for men with intellectual impairment; indeed, their place (subordination, marginalisation) within the matrix of dominance seems particularly stark.

Many issues remain to be explored as research and theorising on masculinities and disabilities continues. Of particular importance and interest seem empirical questions around how men's experiences of varied impairments differ in their relationship to the gender order at micro, meso and macro levels, with the latter seeking ambitiously to take a comparative approach to global/ised dynamics and processes wherein forms of masculine (dis)abled embodiment are co-constituted by intersecting power relations (such as those relating to class, ethnicity, age, sexuality and nationhood). Theoretical questions also remain regarding the ways that gender-relational – and disability-relational – models can be further integrated to help adequately design and analyse such empirical studies.

Notes

1 Whilst Hearn et al. (2012) discuss this in relation to masculinities theorising in Sweden, at a broad level we see clear similarities in masculinities theorising across the global north.
2 Indeed, Connell and Messerschmidt (2005) themselves provide an excellent examination and consideration of many of these early critiques

References

Anderson, E. (2009). *Inclusive masculinity: The changing nature of masculinities*. London: Routledge.

Anderson, E., & Kian, E. M. (2012). Examining media contestation of masculinity and head trauma in the National Football League. *Men and Masculinities, 15*(2), 152–173.

Anderson, E., & McCormack, M. (2018). Inclusive masculinity theory: Overview, reflection and refinement. *Journal of Gender Studies, 27*(5), 547–561.

Anderson, E., & McGuire, R. (2010). Inclusive masculinity theory and the gendered politics of men's rugby. *Journal of Gender Studies, 19*(3), 249–261.

Barrett, T. (2014). Disabled masculinities: A review and suggestions for further research. *Masculinities & Social Change, 3*(1), 36–61.

Björnsdóttir, K., Stefánsdóttir, Á., & Stefánsdóttir, G. V. (2017). People with intellectual disabilities negotiate autonomy, gender and sexuality. *Sexuality and Disability, 35*(3), 295–311.

Bridges, T., & Pascoe, C. J. (2014). Hybrid masculinities: New directions in the sociology of men and masculinities. *Sociology Compass, 8*(3), 246–258.

Charnock, D. (2013). *'You've seen us!' Masculinities in the lives of boys with intellectual disability* (Doctoral dissertation). University of Nottingham, UK.

Connell, R. W. (1995). *Masculinities*. Cambridge: Polity.

Connell, R. W., & Messerschmidt, J. W. (2005). Hegemonic masculinity: Rethinking the concept. *Gender & Society, 19*(6), 829–859.

Cwirynkalo, K., Borowska-Beszta, B., & Bartnikowska, U. (2016). Masculinity and intellectual disability: A review of theoretical concepts and research. *International Journal of Psycho-Educational Sciences, 5*(2), 35–49.

Demetriou, D. Z. (2001). Connell's concept of hegemonic masculinity: A critique. *Theory & Society, 30*(3), 337–361.

Featherstone, M. (1999). Body modification: An introduction. *Body & Society, 5*(2/3), 1–13.

Gerschick, T. J. (1998). Sisyphus in a wheelchair: Men with physical disabilities confront gender domination. In J. O'Brien & J. Howard (Eds.), *Everyday inequalities: Critical inquiries* (pp.189–211). Malden, MA: Blackwell.

Gerschick, T. J., & Miller, A. S. (1995). Coming to terms: Masculinity and physical disability. In D. Sabo & D. F. Gordon *Men's health and illness: Gender, power and the body* (pp. 183–204) London: Sage.

Gibson, B. E., Young, N. L., Upshur, R. E., & McKeever, P. (2007). Men on the margin: A Bourdieusian examination of living into adulthood with muscular dystrophy. *Social Science & Medicine, 65*(3), 505–517.

Haraway, D. (1985). Manifesto for cyborgs: Science, technology, and socialist feminism in the 1980s. *Socialist Review, 80*, 65–108.

Haraway D. (1991). *Simians, cyborgs and women: The reinvention of nature*. London: Free Association Books.

Hearn, J., Nordberg, M., Andersson, K., Balkmar, D., Gottzén, L., Klinth, R., ... & Sandberg, L. (2012). Hegemonic masculinity and beyond: 40 years of research in Sweden. *Men and Masculinities, 15*(1), 31–55.

Hickey-Moody, A. (2015). Carbon fibre masculinity: Disability and gendered surfaces in late modernity. *Angelaki: Journal of the Theoretical Humanities, 20*(1), 139–153.

Kriegel, L. (1998). *Flying solo: Reimagining manhood, courage and loss.* Boston, MA: Beacon Press.

Liddiard, K. (2014). The work of disabled identities in intimate relationships. *Disability & Society, 29*(1), 115–128.

Lipenga, K. J. (2014). Disability and masculinity in South African autosomatography. *African Journal of Disability, 3*(1), 1–9.

Masters, C. (2005). Bodies of technology: Cyborg soldiers and militarized masculinities. *International Feminist Journal of Politics,* 7(1), 112–132.

McGlinchey, E., McCallion, P., Burke, E., Carroll, R., & McCarron, M. (2013). Exploring the issue of employment for adults with an intellectual disability in Ireland. *Journal of Applied Research in Intellectual Disabilities, 26*(4), 335–343.

Monaghan, L. F., Bombak, A. E., & Rich, E. (2018). Obesity, neoliberalism and epidemic psychology: Critical commentary and alternative approaches to public health. *Critical Public Health, 28*(5), 498–508.

Morris, J. (1993). Gender and disability. In J. Swain, V. Finkelstein, S. French & M. Oliver (Eds.), *Disabling barriers: Enabling environments* (pp. 85–92). London: Sage.

Moser, I. (2006). Sociotechnical practices and difference: On the interferences between disability, gender, and class. *Science, Technology, & Human Values, 31*(5), 537–564.

Murphy, R. (1987). *The body silent.* London: Phoenix House.

Neumann, B. (2010). Being prosthetic in the First World War and Weimar Germany. *Body & Society, 16*(3), 93–126.

Oliver, M., Zarb, G., Silver, J., Moore, M., & Salisbury, V. (1988). *Walking into darkness: The experience of spinal cord injury.* London: Macmillan Press.

Owen, R., & Harris, S. P. (2012). 'No rights without responsibilities': Disability rights and neoliberal reform under new labour. *Disability Studies Quarterly, 32*(3). http://dsq-sds.org/article/view/3283.

Robertson, S. (2007). *Understanding men and health: Masculinities, identity and wellbeing.* Buckingham: Open University Press.

Robertson, S., Gough, B., & Robinson, M. (2017). Masculinities and health inequalities within neoliberal economies. In C. Walker & S. Roberts (Eds.), *Masculinity, labour, and neoliberalism: Working-class men in international perspective* (pp. 311–334). Basingstoke: Palgrave Macmillan.

Robertson, S., & Smith, B. (2013).Men, masculinities and disability. In J. Swain, S. French, C. Barnes & C. Thomas (Eds.), *Disabling barriers: Enabling environments* (3rd ed., pp. 78–84). London: Sage.

Satheaswaran, Y. (2016). The 'cyborg soldier': A real-life version of Captain America? An analysis of disability and masculinity in a military context. *Knots: An Undergraduate Journal of Disability Studies, 2* https://jps.library.utoronto.ca/index.php/knots/article/view/27027.

Shakespeare, T. (1996). Power and prejudice: Issues of gender, sexuality and disability. In L. Barton (Ed.), *Disability and society: Emerging issues and insights* (pp. 191–214). Harlow: Longman.

Shakespeare, T. (1999). When is a man not a man? When he's disabled. In J. Wild (Ed.), *Working with men for change* (pp. 58–69). London: UCL Press.

Shuttleworth, R., Wedgwood, N., & Wilson, N. (2012). The dilemma of disabled masculinity. *Men and Masculinities, 15*(2), 174–194.

Smith, B. (2013). Disability, sport and men's narratives of health: A qualitative study. *Health Psychology, 32*(1), 110–119.

Soldatic, K., & Chapman, A. (2010). Surviving the assault? The Australian disability movement and the neoliberal workfare state. *Social Movement Studies, 9*(2), 139–154.

Southby, K. (2013). Social inclusion through football fandom: Opportunities for learning-disabled people. *Sport in Society, 16*(10), 1386–1403.

Swartz, L., & Watermeyer, B. (2008). Cyborg anxiety: Oscar Pistorius and the boundaries of what it means to be human. *Disability & Society, 23*(2), 187–190.

Tamari, T. (2017). Body image and prosthetic aesthetics: Disability, technology and Paralympic culture. *Body & Society, 23*(2), 25–56.

Thomas, C. (2004). How is disability understood? An examination of sociological approaches. *Disability & Society, 19*(6), 569–583.

Thomas, C. (2007). *Sociologies of disability and illness: Contested ideas in disability studies and medical sociology*. Basingstoke: Palgrave Macmillan.

Thomas, C. (2012). Theorising disability and chronic illness: Where next for perspectives in medical sociology? *Social Theory & Health*, *10*(3), 209–228.

Traustadóttir, R. (2006). Disability and gender: Introduction to the special issue. *Scandinavian Journal of Disability Research*, *8*(2/3), 81–84.

Wilson, N. (2009). *'Conditionally sexual': Constructing the sexual health needs of men and teenage boys with a moderate to profound intellectual disability* (Doctoral dissertation). University of Sydney, Australia.

Wilson, N. J., Parmenter, T. R., Stancliffe, R. J., Shuttleworth, R. P., & Parker, D. (2010). A masculine perspective of gendered topics in the research literature on males and females with intellectual disability. *Journal of Intellectual & Developmental Disability*, *35*(1), 1–8.

Zola, I. (1982). *Missing pieces: A chronicle of living with a disability*. Philadelphia, PA: Temple University Press.

15 Trans masculinities

Miriam J. Abelson and Tristen Kade

Early work on trans masculinities (Cromwell, 1999; Devor, 1997; Green, 2005; Rubin, 2003; Vidal-Ortiz, 2002; Wickman, 2003) provided key insights into the lives of trans men but, as noted by Gottzén and Straube (2016), often did not engage specifically with the literature and theories of masculinity studies. Overall, the field of men and masculinities evidences a cisgender and biologically essentialist bias, rarely including trans men as men or trans masculine people as central subjects in the field. Exceptions include Ekins and King's (2005) chapter on "transgendering" and brief mentions of trans masculine people by Schrock and Schwalbe (2009). A special issue of *NORMA* on trans masculinities (Gottzén & Straube, 2016) and works such as Heinz's (2016) analysis of trans masculinity and discourse hopefully signal more explicit attention to the intersections of transgender and masculinities studies. For now, this chapter focuses on broadly reviewing the existing research on trans masculinities and trans men, men who are assigned female at birth.

Trans masculinities

"Trans masculine" refers to people who were assigned "female" at birth and who identify as men or with some other masculine coded subjectivity (Edelman & Zimman, 2014), such as tomboy, masculine of center, stud or aggressive (AG), butch, drag king, or nonbinary. All of these identities are similar in that they attempt to describe individuals who reject certain notions of female/feminine embodiment and may embrace male/masculine embodiment or presentation (Bailey, 2014; Halberstam, 2012; Kuper, Wright, & Mustanski, 2014; Lane-Steele, 2011; Moore, 2006). Rather than flattening the differences between different trans masculinities, we seek to illustrate the nuances of various trans masculine enactments, embodiments, and identifications. Our broad definition of trans masculinity includes people who would not describe themselves as transgender, thus we also use the term "female masculinities" at times (e.g., Halberstam, 1998a). While we focus on people assigned female at birth, there are certainly transgender individuals who were assigned male at birth who are women or nonbinary but identify with and do masculinities, such as butch trans women (Rossiter, 2016). Gender identities and practices are constantly evolving and contested, and this review is necessarily incomplete.

While the terms "trans men" and "trans masculine" have been legible since at least the 1990s, people who were assigned as female at birth have been living masculine lives and as socially recognized as men for far longer, including female-assigned people working and living as men during the California Gold Rush of the 19th century (Sears, 2008) and trans men living ordinary lives in small cities and rural areas of the United States in the early 20th century (Skidmore, 2017). Further, historical figures, such as the U.S. civil rights and feminist activist Pauli Murray, are newly being recognized by scholars and activists as trans masculine individuals (e.g., Fisher, 2016). Thus, trans masculinities are not new phenomena, even if recent media and scholarly attention makes them appear as such.

Each of the trans and female masculinities in this chapter reflects specific spatial and cultural understandings of gender and sexuality. Much of the research on trans masculinities and thus most of the work reviewed below reflects the white, Western, and often Anglophone contexts in which they emerged. Critics have long pointed out that dominant white Western-centric understandings of transgender, especially when relying on notions of gender and sexuality as separate entities, are ethnocentric and erase racial and cultural epistemologies (Roen, 2001; Valentine, 2007). Place-specific knowledge is crucial to resist Westernized notions of trans and female masculinities. For example, dress codes in places such as Indonesia—whether in educational, religious, or work settings—might put further strain or open up possibilities for trans masculine people's expressions of gendered selves (Gordon & Pratama, 2017). Tomboi identities in other parts of Indonesia might function similarly to trans masculinity but may perhaps have fluid and changing meanings and practices in their everyday contexts (Blackwood, 2009). Gender variance among female-assigned ethnic minorities in Vietnam also rely on local cultural meanings rather than Western transgender discourses (Nguyen, 2016). Newer work in other interdisciplinary fields such as black studies shows promise in generating knowledge about trans masculinities that start with race-specific understandings rather than applying them on top of gendered analyses (Jaime, 2017; Snorton, 2009). Work such as this can better attend to the dangers of framing the lives of sexual and gender minorities in ways that reinforce dominant colonial and white supremacist notions of the masculinities in those places. For example, in the South African context, narratives that construct trans men and lesbians only as victims of ubiquitous violence show a one-dimensional view of their lives and reconstructs Black South African townships as inherently criminal and less civilized due to Black masculinist violence (Imma, 2017). Indeed, examples of transgender and queer activism across African contexts better illustrate the complexities of everyday life and resistance to transphobia as it is intertwined with colonialism and heterosexism (Ekine & Abbas, 2013; Le Roux, 2012). In one example, this means a transgender bathroom politics in South Africa that seeks not just to degender public sex-segregated bathrooms but also to decolonialize access to sanitation through an intersectional analysis of race, class, gender, and disability (Patel, 2017). These more nuanced depictions can generate knowledge about the variety of trans masculine lives without reproducing colonial and white supremacist framings of spaces that are supposedly "backward" and only intolerant of non-normative genders.

There are a variety of female masculinities and trans masculinities that challenge the idea that masculinity is only the domain of men. Stud, aggressive (AG), and masculine of center (MOC) are trans masculinities or female masculinities originating in Black and other U.S. communities of color (Bailey, 2014). Studs and AGs are assigned female at birth and usually do not identify as men but embody certain Black masculine working class traits, such as clothing styles, dialect, performance and demeanors that reference stereotypical street, rap, and gangster culture (Bailey, 2014; Halberstam, 2012; Kuper et al., 2014; Lane-Steele, 2011; Moore, 2006; Walcott, 2009). These racialized, classed, and sexualized masculinities replicate the protest masculinities associated with Black cisgender men. Studs may utilize protest masculinities as a broader survival strategy in a white supremacist culture and to shield themselves from sexism, racism, and homophobia within Black communities (Lane-Steele, 2011). At the same time, these individuals often (re)produce heteronormative cultural scripts in sexual and romantic relationships. The term "masculine of center," coined by B. Cole of the Brown Boi Project, emerged as an umbrella term for masculine-identified people to come together in political movement-building and collective transformation regardless of class and sexual identities (Bailey, 2014). Similar to and perhaps overlapping with masculine-of-center identities, butches are assigned female at birth but embody masculinity in a particularly queer way (Halberstam, 1998b), though nonbinary people, trans men, and trans women can identify as butch. In the 1990s a series of dialogues addressed "Butch/FTM (female to male transgender) border wars" in an attempt to understand the crossings, tensions, and possible coalitions between female-identified butches, trans butches, trans men, and other trans masculine people (Halberstam, 1998b; Halberstam & Hale, 1998; Hale, 1998a).[1] A wider variety of trans masculine identities gained new visibility in this time period, and these dialogues served as a way to explore the relationship between the different groups that often inhabited the same communities or spaces, as well for individuals to explore possibilities for their own gender identities. The dialogues reflected efforts to work out strains within transgender and queer communities over belonging and collective identity, as well as to locate similarities or shared aims that had potential to be the basis of political solidarity. Butches still thrive in many queer communities today alongside various nonbinary and trans masculine identities, despite fears (sometimes expressed in transphobic ways) that butches are "disappearing" in favor of newer transgender identities (Manion, 2014; Stein, 2018). In addition, trans masculine people may also identify as nonbinary or genderqueer to express a gender that is between binary gender notions of man/woman or even outside of these binaries altogether (Davy, 2019; Risman, 2018; Roen, 2002). Functioning somewhat differently than the tomboi in the Indonesian context, tomboy is a common term in the U.S., U.K. and Canada to refer to a girl who prefers activities, toys, and attires typically reserved for boys (Abate, 2011; Halberstam, 1998a). Although tomboy is both a well-known cultural concept and embodied phenomenon in Western cultures, scholarly work on tomboys is still limited (Carr, 2007; Craig & LaCroix, 2011; Hall, 2008).

Drag performance and culture often focuses on drag queens, but in the 1980s and 1990s a drag king culture emerged in several U.S. cities (Shapiro, 2007; Wickman, 2003). Drag troupes can both pose political challenges to beliefs about gender and sexuality and also allow members to imagine other ways of being gendered in their everyday lives; to try on, practice, and enact a variety of masculinities. Although many troupes have members who identify as genderqueer, non-binary, or otherwise as trans masculine, an individual who comes out as a trans man and seeks to medically transition may find themself on the outside of a formerly supportive drag community (Rogers, 2018; Shapiro, 2007).

Trans men are a diverse group of men, who were assigned female at birth and access various aspects of social, medical, and legal gender transition. Western research on trans men tends to focus on understanding masculine embodiment (Rubin, 2003), gender recognition in interactions (Dozier, 2005; Schilt & Westbrook, 2009; Williams, Weinberg, & Rosenberger, 2013), disclosure with partners and families (Hines, 2006; Kade, 2016), and workplace experiences (Connell, 2010; Schilt, 2010). Trans men adopt a range of masculinities and there is nothing inherent in trans men or a transgender identity that leads to adopting a particular masculine style (Abelson, 2019; Green, 2005; Rubin, 2003; Schilt, 2010; Vidal-Ortiz, 2002). Trans men who are recognized as men by others can receive patriarchal dividends if their practices align with normative masculinities, like any other man in a shared social position (Abelson, 2016b; Rubin, 2003; Schilt, 2010). Being read as white and heterosexual by others may further these advantages, but these "privileges" are not a primary motivation for trans men to transition (Abelson, 2014; Connell, 2010; de Vries, 2015; Schilt, 2010). Like other men, trans men face pressures to assimilate to normative local masculinities especially as intertwined with compulsory heterosexuality, though trans men further in transition report less need to defend their masculinity (Dozier, 2005; Kłonkowska, 2018; Schilt, 2010).

Transitions, bodies, and sexualities

Bodies are crucial sites where masculinity materializes. Some trans men remake their bodies through medical interventions to better reflect their sense of self as well as ensure their social recognition as men or masculine. The use of hormones, such as testosterone, and chest reconstruction surgery are the most common interventions that trans men access as part of medical transitions (Dozier, 2005; Rubin, 2003; Stein, 2018). Trans men also seek out, though less frequently, procedures such as hysterectomies and various genital surgeries. The lack of popularity of genital reconstruction surgeries both reflects a decentering by some trans men of normative connections between the size and function of men's penises, as well as the expense and common results of procedures such as phalloplasty (Johnson, 2016; Latham, 2016; Schilt & Windsor, 2014). Strong pressures from medical and psychiatric providers and institutions, as well as from other transgender people, often push trans men to access biomedical aspects of transition to both achieve proper masculinity and legitimacy as a transgender person (Catalano, 2015; Johnson, 2016). In order to manage the stigma of being labeled with a psychiatric condition, trans men variously submit to, manipulate, or resist in their interactions with therapists and other medical providers (Windsor, 2018). Along with these normative pressures related to transition, trans men often report that their most frequent experiences of violence and discrimination occur in healthcare contexts, whether they are there for transition-related care or unrelated medical needs (Abelson, 2019; Gordon & Pratama, 2017).

Bodily changes due to testosterone and chest reconstruction, especially in regard to visible secondary sex characteristics, allow for trans men to be reliably recognized by others as men in everyday interactions. This appears to be true even in the face of other bodily markers that might contradict this reading, such as one of Dozier's (2005) interviewees whose full beard made for recognition as a man despite him being nine months pregnant. At the same time, men's bodies can also be resignified within transgender and queer communities such that the idea of men or masculine people as menstruators or as pregnant becomes unremarkable (Chrisler et al., 2016). When spaces such as fertility clinics direct their services to heterosexual, cisgender, and often white couples, trans men can experience discomfort and exclusion (Epstein, 2018). Trans men also engage in physical exercise, another form of reshaping the body, to achieve particular masculine bodily ideals (Farber, 2017). Though physical transition can make for feelings of gendered betweenness, being recognizably gendered shifts how more masculine and feminine aspects of presentation are read by others—altering privileges that might be associated with being read as a white man (Nordmarken, 2014).

Sexual domains are key sites where trans men and trans masculine people develop, work out, and expand their masculine identities, practices, and subjectivities (Rubin, 2003; Vidal-Ortiz, 2002). Their experiences in these realms certainly show the complex interconnections of "gendered sexualities" (Tewksbury & Gagné, 2002). Queer sexual encounters with women and other men can both provide evidence of discomfort from being read by others as a woman and affirmation of themselves as men and of their masculinity (Rubin, 2003; Ward, 2010). Some trans men and trans masculine people use gender play in BDSM spaces as platforms to try on and come to their masculine identities (Bauer, 2016; Hale, 1997).

Further, trans masculinity is available in these spaces to queer individuals who do not necessarily identify as men or masculine in their everyday lives (Bauer, 2016). In another example, pornographic representations can create a space for renarrating trans, queer, brown, and kinky sexualities away from dominant frames (Steinbock, 2014).

Gender transitions, particularly hormone therapy and other aspects of physical transition, can shift trans masculine people's sexual behaviors and desires, though this might not signal an actual change in sexual orientation for all trans masculine people (Dozier, 2005; Pfeffer, 2017). Some trans men interviewed by Rubin (2003) reported an increased sexual drive overall, while others experienced no increase. Schilt and Windsor (2014, p. 739) found that as trans men's gendered embodiments shifted with physical transition, so too did their "sexual habitus" or "the relationship between embodiment, desires, practices, and identity." Changes to sexuality, including an increased desire for casual sex and the intensity of orgasms, can act as evidence for some trans men of their masculinity as men (Williams et al., 2013). Through the process of narrating their manhood or themselves as male in autobiographical writing, trans men pull together or assemble multiple sexual practices that materialize their maleness (Latham, 2016).

Bodies, particularly genitals, can both facilitate and interfere with narrating masculinity, but most trans men can get past what may seem like a material obstacle. Some men and trans masculine people subscribe to anxieties shared by many cisgender men about the size and functionality of penises over the life course, and others transform dominant notions of sexuality that center around a normative penis that is either "naturally occurring" or surgically constructed. In this way, trans men challenge the notion that a penis is necessary to fully access manhood (Schilt & Windsor, 2014). Edelman and Zimman (2014) find that rather than reproduce narratives of their "unaltered genitalia" as shameful or undesirable, trans men resignify these parts as desirable "boycunts" and "bonus holes," which are assets in homoerotic sexual exchanges. All of these narratives of sexuality and embodiment challenge the expectations for trans people's sexualities that are embedded in normative psychiatric diagnoses, but at times they also reinforce other dominant notions of masculinity and sexuality (Latham, 2016). These themes of embodiment and sexuality both illustrate the importance of bodies and exemplify Dozier's point that "particular body characteristics are not important in themselves but become important because of social interpretation" (2005, p. 300).

Relations to others

Beyond strictly sexual domains, trans men's transitions lead to changes in their relations to others in most settings. For example, extensive research about trans men in employment settings—such as Schilt's (2010) study of trans men across a range of workplaces, which convincingly establishes some of the mechanisms through which gender inequality is continually produced—shows that trans men often are treated as "just one of the guys" upon transitioning at work. Dozier's (2019) study of masculine females at work suggests that masculinity itself is valued in many workplaces, even if masculine females experience misgendering and harassment based on their gender presentation. In everyday public spaces, trans men of color, particularly Black and Latinx[2] men, find that they receive more negative attention from police and other authorities upon transitioning and being recognized as men (Abelson, 2019; de Vries, 2015). Thus, social interactions in specific social contexts may influence their masculinities.

These changing social relations are most evident in shifts in partnerships with women and trans masculine people's relationships with feminist politics. The shifting social gender identities and embodiments of a trans man's transition can highlight the relational nature of gender, as well as sexuality. Most scholarship on transgender partnerships focuses on relationships between transgender men and cisgender women, especially on the gender labor that women partners perform (Joslin-Roher & Wheeler, 2009; Pfeffer, 2010, 2017; Ward, 2010). This gender labor includes both gendered labor in the home and also the emotional work of witnessing nurturing, fulfilling, and authenticating that validates their trans partner's gender identity (Ward, 2010). Further, queer cisgender women who are partnered with trans men often have to negotiate their own sexual identity in regard to their partner's transitioning gender and sexual identities, especially when they are (mis)recognized as heterosexual (Joslin-Roher & Wheeler, 2009; Pfeffer, 2014).

Transition can also mean political realignments with women and feminist politics, and there are a number of important works that have laid out the terrain of the engagement between trans masculine people and feminism (Hale, 1998b; Matebeni, 2009; Noble, 2006; Ziegler, 2012). Like most groups of men, some trans men identify as feminists and others do not. As men and as trans people, trans men have particularly complicated relationships to feminist movements, especially in light of experiences with transphobic and trans exclusionary feminists (Hines, 2005). Trans men who engage in feminist organizing and want to challenge existing gender relations are limited by narrow organizational definitions of feminism as only serving heterosexual cisgender women (Matebeni, 2009). When trans men understand feminism as a singular, rigid political view, they are more likely to reject feminism as outdated and too narrow. If they see feminism as varied and multiple, they are more likely to embrace a feminist identity and politics (Abelson, 2016a). Trans men's engagements with and resistance to feminism provide important lessons for trans and cis feminists who are interested in building broader movements.

Conclusion

As scholarship on trans masculinities continues to expand at a rapid rate, we highlight a few directions for the field as it moves forward. First, future research needs to continue to expand the geographic scope of knowledge about trans masculinities and, drawing inspiration from the expanding work on transgender geography, take seriously how specific spaces and places shape trans masculinities. It is crucial to build knowledge of trans masculinities outside of major cities and beyond the U.S. and U.K. contexts. Second, more work is needed that goes beyond investigating the links between gender and sexuality but utilizes an intersectional analysis of how race, class, ability, citizenship, and other interlocking aspects of difference connect to trans masculinities. Expanding this analysis does not just mean including more diverse samples of trans men, though that is a worthy goal, but rather means focus on how these intersecting social categories affect all trans masculinities and trans masculine people, even white, middle-class, U.S. trans men. Finally, studies that examine men and masculinities more broadly should include transgender men as a subgroup of men and not see trans men as always a group that is fundamentally different from cisgender men. Trans men may have different childhood experiences than cisgender men, but cisgender versus transgender is not always the most useful analytic distinction, since there is so much within-group difference among cis men and trans men as groups. Indeed, race, class, or ability might be the defining difference rather than a cis/trans divide in a given context. Addressing geographic limitations, expanding intersectional analyses, and incorporating trans men as men promises fruitful insights for growing understandings of trans masculinities and crucial opportunities to expand the field of critical men and masculinities studies overall.

Notes

1 See Pfeffer (2017) for a comprehensive overview and deeper context for these debates.
2 This spelling is an attempt at a more gender expansive and encompassing term than Latino or other variations. See Vidal-Ortiz and Martínez (2018) for a comprehensive discussion.

References

Abate, M. A. (2011). Introduction: Special issue on tomboys and tomboyism. *Journal of Lesbian Studies, 15*(4), 407–411.

Abelson, M. J. (2014). Dangerous privilege: Trans men, masculinities, and changing perceptions of safety. *Sociological Forum, 29*(3), 549–570.

Abelson, M. J. (2016a). Trans men engaging, reforming, and resisting feminisms. *TSQ: Transgender Studies Quarterly, 3*(1/2), 15–21.

Abelson, M. J. (2016b). "You aren't from around here": Race, masculinity, and rural transgender men. *Gender, Place & Culture, 23*(11), 1535–1546.

Abelson, M. J. (2019). *Men in place: Trans masculinity, race, and sexuality in America*. Minneapolis, MN: University of Minnesota Press.

Bailey, V. (2014). Brown bois. *TSQ: Transgender Studies Quarterly, 1*(1/2), 45–47.

Bauer, R. (2016). Desiring masculinities while desiring to question masculinity? How embodied masculinities are renegotiated in les-bi-trans-queer BDSM practices. *NORMA: International Journal for Masculinity Studies, 11*(4), 237–254.

Blackwood, E. (2009). Trans identities and contingent masculinities: Being tombois in everyday practice. *Feminist Studies, 35*(3), 454–480.

Carr, C. L. (2007). Where have all the tomboys gone? Women's accounts of gender in adolescence. *Sex Roles, 56*(7), 439–448.

Catalano, D. C. J. (2015). "Trans enough?" The pressures trans men negotiate in higher education. *TSQ: Transgender Studies Quarterly, 2*(3), 411–430.

Chrisler, J. C., Gorman, J. A., Manion, J., Murgo, M., Barney, A., Adams-Clark, A., ... McGrath, M. (2016). Queer periods: Attitudes toward and experiences with menstruation in the masculine of centre and transgender community. *Culture, Health & Sexuality, 18*(11), 1238–1250.

Connell, C. (2010). Doing, undoing, or redoing gender? Learning from the workplace experiences of transpeople. *Gender & Society, 24*(1), 31–55.

Craig, T., & LaCroix, J. (2011). Tomboy as protective identity. *Journal of Lesbian Studies, 15*(4), 450–465.

Cromwell, J. (1999). *Transmen and FTMs: Identities, bodies, genders, and sexualities*. Chicago, IL: University of Illinois Press.

Davy, Z. (2019). Genderqueer(ing): "On this side of the world against which it protests." *Sexualities, 22* (1/2), 80–96.

de Vries, K. M. (2015). Transgender people of color at the center: Conceptualizing a new intersectional model. *Ethnicities, 15*(1), 3–27.

Devor, A. (1997). *FTM: Female to male transsexuals in society*. Bloomington, IN: Indiana University Press.

Dozier, R. (2005). Beards, breasts, and bodies: Doing sex in a gendered world. *Gender & Society, 19*(3), 297–316.

Dozier, R. (2019). "You look like a dude, dude": Masculine females undoing gender in the workplace. *Journal of Homosexuality, 66*(9), 1219–1237.

Edelman, E. A., & Zimman, L. (2014). Boycunts and bonus holes: Trans men's bodies, neoliberalism, and the sexual productivity of genitals. *Journal of Homosexuality, 61*(5), 673–690.

Ekine, S., & Abbas, H. (Eds.). (2013). *Queer African reader*. Nairobi: Pambazuka Press.

Ekins, R., & King, D. (2005). Transgendering, men, and masculinities. In M. S. Kimmel, J. Hearn & R. W. Connell (Eds.), *Handbook of studies on men & masculinities* (pp. 379–394). Thousand Oaks, CA: Sage.

Epstein, R. (2018). Space invaders: Queer and trans bodies in fertility clinics. *Sexualities, 21*(7), 1039–1058.

Farber, R. (2017). "Transing" fitness and remapping transgender male masculinity in online message boards. *Journal of Gender Studies, 26*(3), 254–268.

Fisher, S. D. E. (2016). Pauli Murray's Peter Panic: Perspectives from the margins of gender and race in Jim Crow America. *TSQ: Transgender Studies Quarterly, 3*(1/2), 95–103.

Gordon, D., & Pratama, M. P. (2017). Mapping discrimination experienced by Indonesian trans* FtM persons. *Journal of Homosexuality, 64*(9), 1283–1303.

Gottzén, L., & Straube, W. (Eds.). (2016). Trans masculinities [Special Issue]. *NORMA: International Journal for Masculinity Studies*, *11*(4), 217–224.
Green, J. (2005). Part of the package: Ideas of masculinity among male-identified transpeople. *Men and Masculinities*, 7(3), 291–299.
Halberstam, J. (1998a). *Female masculinity*. Durham, NC: Duke University Press.
Halberstam, J. (1998b). Transgender butch: Butch/FTM border wars and the masculine continuum. *GLQ: A Journal of Lesbian and Gay Studies*, *4*(2), 287–310.
Halberstam, J. (2012). Global female masculinities. *Sexualities*, *15*(3/4), 336–354.
Halberstam, J., & Hale, C. J. (1998). Butch/Ftm Border Wars. *GLQ: A Journal of Lesbian & Gay Studies*, *4*(2), 283–285.
Hale, C. J. (1997). Leatherdyke boys and their daddies: How to have sex without women or men. *Social Text*, *15*(52/53), 223–236.
Hale, C. J. (1998a). Consuming the living, dis(re)membering the dead in the butch/Ftm borderlands. *GLQ: A Journal of Lesbian and Gay Studies*, *4*(2), 311–348.
Hale, C. J. (1998b). Tracing a ghostly memory in my throat: Reflections on ftm feminist voice and agency. In T. Digby (Ed.), *Men doing feminism* (pp. 99–129). New York: Routledge.
Hall, J. M. (2008). Tomboys: meanings, marginalization, and misunderstandings. *Issues in Mental Health Nursing*, *29*(6), 555–565.
Heinz, M. (2016). *Entering transmasculinity: The inevitability of discourse*. Bristol: Intellect.
Hines, S. (2005). "I am a Feminist but …": Transgender men and women and feminism. In J. Reger (Ed.), *Different wavelengths: Studies of the contemporary women's movement* (pp. 57–77). New York, NY: Routledge.
Hines, S. (2006). Intimate transitions: Transgender practices of partnering and parenting. *Sociology*, *40*(2), 353–371.
Imma, Z. (2017). (Re)visualizing Black lesbian lives, (trans)masculinity, and township space in the documentary work of Zanele Muholi. *Journal of Lesbian Studies*, *21*(2), 219–241.
Jaime, K. (2017). "Chasing rainbows": Black cracker and queer, trans Afrofuturity. *TSQ: Transgender Studies Quarterly*, *4*(2), 208–218.
Johnson, A. H. (2016). Transnormativity: A new concept and its validation through documentary film about transgender men. *Sociological Inquiry*, *86*(4), 465–491.
Joslin-Roher, E., & Wheeler, D. P. (2009). Partners in transition: The transition experience of lesbian, bisexual, and queer identified partners of transgender men. *Journal of Gay & Lesbian Social Services*, *21*(1), 30–48.
Kade, T. (2016). *Passing with care: When and how transmen disclose their gender identity* (Thesis). Department of Sociology, University of New Orleans, Louisiana.
Kłonkowska, A. M. (2018). Masculinity: Assigned–reassigned–socially constructed: The social reception of trans masculinity in Poland. *Men and Masculinities*, *21*(2), 210–229.
Kuper, L. E., Wright, L., & Mustanski, B. (2014). Stud identity among female-born youth of color: Joint conceptualizations of gender variance and same-sex sexuality. *Journal of Homosexuality*, *61*(5), 714–731.
Lane-Steele, L. (2011). Studs and protest-hypermasculinity: The tomboyism within black lesbian female masculinity. *Journal of Lesbian Studies*, *15*(4), 480–492.
Latham, J. R. (2016). Trans men's sexual narrative-practices: Introducing STS to trans and sexuality studies. *Sexualities*, *19*(3), 347–368.
Le Roux, G. (2012). Proudly African and transgender. *Women: A Cultural Review*, *23*(1), 79–95.
Manion, J. (2014). Transbutch. *TSQ: Transgender Studies Quarterly*, *1*(1/2), 230–232.
Matebeni, Z. (2009). Feminizing lesbians, degendering transgender men: A model for building lesbian feminist thinkers and leaders in Africa? *Souls*, *11*(3), 347–354.
Moore, M. R. (2006). Lipstick or timberlands? Meanings of gender presentation in black lesbian communities. *Signs: Journal of Women in Culture and Society*, *32*(1), 113–139.
Nguyen, H. T. (2016). Navigating identity, ethnicity and politics: A case study of gender variance in the Central Highlands of Vietnam. *NORMA: International Journal for Masculinity Studies*, *11*(4), 255–269.
Noble, B. (2006). *Sons of the movement: FtMs risking incoherence on a post-queer cultural landscape*. Toronto: Women's Press.
Nordmarken, S. (2014). Becoming ever more monstrous: Feeling transgender in-betweenness. *Qualitative Inquiry*, *20*(1), 37–50.
Patel, N. (2017). Violent cistems: Trans experiences of bathroom space. *Agenda*, *31*(1), 51–63.

Pfeffer, C. A. (2010). "Women's work"? Women partners of transgender men doing housework and emotion work. *Journal of Marriage and Family, 72*(1), 165–183.

Pfeffer, C. A. (2014). "I don't like passing as a straight woman": Queer negotiations of identity and social group membership. *American Journal of Sociology, 120*(1), 1–44.

Pfeffer, C. A. (2017). *Queering families: The postmodern partnerships of cisgender women and transgender men*. New York: Oxford University Press.

Risman, B. J. (2018). *Where the millennials will take us: A new generation wrestles with the gender structure*. New York: Oxford University Press.

Roen, K. (2001). Transgender theory and embodiment: The risk of racial marginalisation. *Journal of Gender Studies, 10*(3), 253–263.

Roen, K. (2002). "Either/or" and "both/neither": Discursive tensions in transgender politics. *Signs: Journal of Women in Culture and Society, 27*(2), 501–522.

Rogers, B. A. (2018). Drag as a resource: Trans* and nonbinary individuals in the Southeastern United States. *Gender & Society, 32*(6), 889–910.

Rossiter, H. (2016). She's always a woman: Butch lesbian trans women in the lesbian community. *Journal of Lesbian Studies, 20*(1), 87–96.

Rubin, H. (2003). *Self-made men: Identity and embodiment among transsexual men*. Nashville, TN: Vanderbilt University Press.

Schilt, K. (2010). *Just one of the guys? Transgender men and the persistence of gender inequality*. Chicago, IL: The University of Chicago Press.

Schilt, K., & Westbrook, L. (2009). Doing gender, doing heteronormativity: "Gender normals", transgender people, and the social maintenance of heterosexuality. *Gender & Society, 23*(4), 440–464.

Schilt, K., & Windsor, E. (2014). The sexual habitus of transgender men: Negotiating sexuality through gender. *Journal of Homosexuality, 61*(5), 732–748.

Schrock, D., & Schwalbe, M. (2009). Men, masculinity, and manhood acts. *Annual Review of Sociology, 35*, 277–295.

Sears, C. (2008). All that glitters: Trans-ing California's gold rush migrations. *GLQ: A Journal of Lesbian and Gay Studies, 14*(2/3), 383–402.

Shapiro, E. (2007). Drag kinging and the transformation of gender identities. *Gender and Society, 21*(2), 250–271.

Skidmore, E. (2017). *True sex: The lives of trans men at the turn of the twentieth century*. New York: New York University Press.

Snorton, C. R. (2009). "A new hope": The psychic life of passing. *Hypatia, 24*(3), 77–92.

Stein, A. (2018). *Unbound: Transgender men and the remaking of identity*. New York: Pantheon.

Steinbock, E. (2014). On the affective force of "nasty love". *Journal of Homosexuality, 61*(5), 749–765.

Tewksbury, R., & Gagné, P. (Eds.). (2002). *Gendered sexualities*. Amsterdam: JAI.

Valentine, D. (2007). *Imagining transgender: An ethnography of a category*. Durham, NC: Duke University Press.

Vidal-Ortiz, S. (2002). Queering sexuality and doing gender: Transgender men's identification with gender and sexuality. In P. Gagne & R. Tewksbury (Eds.), *Gendered sexualities* (pp. 181–233). Amsterdam: JAI.

Vidal-Ortiz, S., & Martínez, J. (2018). Latinx thoughts: Latinidad with an X. *Latino Studies, 16*(3), 384–395.

Walcott, R. (2009). Reconstructing manhood; or, the drag of black masculinity. *Small Axe: A Caribbean Journal of Criticism, 13*(1), 75–89.

Ward, J. (2010). Gender labor: Transmen, femmes, and collective work of transgression. *Sexualities, 13*(2), 236–254.

Wickman, J. (2003). Masculinity and female bodies. *NORA: Nordic Journal of Feminist and Gender Research, 11*(1), 40–54.

Williams, C. J., Weinberg, M. S., & Rosenberger, J. G. (2013). Trans men: Embodiments, identities, and sexualities. *Sociological Forum, 28*(4), 719–741.

Windsor, E. J. (2018). Golden ticket therapy: Stigma management among trans men. In O. Gozlan (Ed.), *Current critical debates in the field of transsexual studies* (131–144). New York: Routledge.

Ziegler, K. R. (2012). How my past as a black woman informs my black male feminist perspective today. Retrieved January 26, 2015, from http://blackademic.com/how-my-past-as-a-black-woman-informs-my-black-male-feminist-perspective-today/.

16

'Little boys'

The significance of early childhood in the making of masculinities

Deevia Bhana

Introduction

Masculinities are a lifelong project and constructed over time within a gendered system of power. School-based research in early childhood studies and masculinity studies has partially illuminated the ways in which power operates in the making of junior masculinity (Keddie, 2003). During early childhood, little boys, under the age of ten, are also active in the production of masculinities as they encounter a gendered system of power. In this encounter, boys are not passive dupes of power but actively produce relations of domination where femininity, non-hetero and non-binary sexualities are subordinated. Notwithstanding the wide application of masculinity in research with men and older boys, the focus on young boys, under ten years old, is subdued. Long-standing discourses based on cognitive and biological development suggest that the time and age of early childhood development may be inimical to the production of gendered and sexualised identities. In contesting the stronghold of conventional discourses in early childhood, feminists and critical masculinities scholars have drawn on poststructuralism and Connell's (2005) theorisation of masculinities to illuminate how boys and men are active within a gendered system of power even when young. The construction of masculinities in early childhood is not a static experience but diverse, fluid and inflected by social, racial, political and economic systems of power across local and global contexts. Boys' encounters in the gendered system of power are negotiated; gender patterns are accommodated and contested. This chapter argues for a more collaborative approach to the study of little boys in early childhood in which boys' appropriation of, or struggle with, gender is raised. Feminist poststructural researchers illuminate these possibilities as they engage with early childhood studies and masculinities. Building these theoretical and interdisciplinary approaches aids the understanding of the fluidity and changing forms of masculinity and helps in developing forms of interventions that are more age relevant than hitherto.

'Little boys: tomorrow's macho lads'

Questions about children under the age of ten, in early childhood,[1] seldom feature in research and interventions that target men and boys in the work towards gender equality

(Bartholomaeus, 2013; Keddie, 2003; MacNaughton, 2000; Yelland, 1998). Whilst efforts to engage men and boys to promote sexual health and wellbeing and address violence are growing on a global scale (Barker et al., 2012), the overwhelming bulk of this research fails to consider younger boys and the construction of junior masculinity in early childhood. Indeed, the demarcation of boys and their ages in questions of masculinity are central problems that remain undeveloped and under-theorised in childhood studies. Too often little boys are ignored in masculinity studies, and early childhood studies do not give sufficient attention to gender and masculinities (Bartholomaeus & Senkevics, 2015; Renold, 2005). For some commentators, gender might be far too abstract for young children and may collide with traditional notions of early childhood development (Tobin, 1997; Yelland, 1998). Discursive constructions around age and gender have in part constrained the collaboration between childhood studies and masculinity studies. Historically, there has been a problematic relationship between feminist and childhood studies, with feminists reluctant to conflate the study of women with that of children (Thorne, 1987). Masculinity scholars too have failed to give adequate attention to boys in early childhood (Connolly, 2004; Renold, 2005; Swain, 2006).

Popular understandings of early childhood derive from developmental psychology and traditional socialisation theory. Such theorising suggests that children's investment in gender/sexual identities is only relevant when it concerns biological or cognitive development (James et al., 1998). These dominant models of identity based on gender binaries continue to frame junior masculinity as natural, innocent and an expected part of early childhood development. These theoretical assumptions are restrictive and leave patterns of masculinity unproblematised whilst supporting the formation of 'tomorrow's macho lads' based on the disparagement of feminine, non-hetero and non-binary sexualities (Bartholomaeus & Riggs, 2017). However, as this chapter claims, it is useful to think about boys and junior masculinity in early childhood outside of dominant models of identity.

Evidence from scholars suggests the need for and the value in addressing little boys at the intersection of childhood studies and masculinity studies (Bartholomaeus, 2013; Swain, 2006). MacNaughton (2000) and other poststructural feminists (Bartholomaeus, 2013; Paechter, 2007) usefully point out that one of the consequences of using simple theoretical frames is that the complexity of gender power relations in early childhood is naturalised based on common idioms such as 'boys will be boys'. Moreover, the dynamic nature of masculinity and the social and cultural embeddedness of gender are simplified by dominant theorising based on essentialist models of identity. As noted by Bartholomaeus and Senkevics (2015), feminist poststructuralists' and Connell's (2005) theories of masculinities have worked well to critique the dominance of developmental psychology and essentialism in early childhood. Poststructuralist approaches understand power as fluid and produced in discourse. Masculinity, as Connell (2005) elucidates, is a lifelong project. It is shaped by the encounters that people have within social and cultural systems. Masculinity is a configuration of practice associated with the social position of men and boys, and it changes over time (Connell, 2005). Following this line of thinking, masculinity is not fixed but is open to change depending on particular circumstances. Gender is fluid. Powerful institutions such as the school and families, however, regulate and put pressure upon boys and girls to act in appropriate ways. In this chapter, it is suggested that little boys are shaping up, into 'tomorrow's macho lads', by assembling masculinity around violence underpinned by the subordination of the feminine and non-hetero/non-binary sexualities (Keddie, 2003, p. 289). Whilst boys are not dupes of institutional power and do reject the dominant 'boy code' (Pollack, 1999), the pressure to perform masculinity based on rigid notions of domination and violence persists (Swain, 2006).

Junior masculinity is inextricably linked to sexuality. Sexuality, like gender, cannot be essentialised into biological constructs but is historical and cultural (Parker, 2009). Whilst the dominant assumption of masculinity is based on heterosexuality (Connell, 2005), masculinity is socially produced and functions in the interests of compulsory heterosexuality (Butler, 1993). Even when little, boys negotiate, reproduce and regulate gender, sexuality and hegemonic masculinity (Bhana, 2016; Connolly, 2004; Swain, 2006). Hegemonic masculinity is an exalted form of identity based on gender hierarchies, compulsory heterosexuality (Renold, 2005) and the subjugation of the feminine. Aggression, violence, physical strength, sporty conduct, toughness and heterosexuality are often key markers of hegemonic masculinity in certain historical contexts, although not limited to hegemonic masculinity (Hearn et al., 2012). These patterns in early childhood support and are supported by gendered relations of power as attested by feminist poststructuralist scholars (Bhana, 2016; Keddie, 2003; Paechter, 2007). Addressing problematic versions of masculinities amongst boys under the age of ten is vital if we are to understand the operation of power, the formation of gender hierarchies, inequalities and change.

Recognising this caveat, a developing body of educational research has provided more in-depth focus on little boys, under the age of 10 years (Bartholomaeus, 2013; Bhana, 2016; Epstein et al., 2001; Francis, 1998; Haavind, 2005; Renold, 2005; Robinson, 2013; Swain, 2006). By focusing on boys as they associate with sport (Swain, 2006), produce sexuality (Renold, 2005; Robinson, 2013; Tobin, 1997) and navigate violent gendered relations (Bhana, 2016; Keddie, 2003), this developing body of research attempts to portray boys as actively engaged in the production and reproduction of masculinities. By engaging with these issues from a collaborative interdisciplinary approach, the interpretation of early childhood as fixed to biological and cognitive development is destabilised. Whilst masculinity is constructed in many different institutions, such as families and communities, this chapter focuses on school-based research that has been significant in providing a theoretical framing to understand how boys become active gendered agents in shaping and recreating their worlds rather than simply governed by age and stage of development (Swain, 2006). Due attention to the early formation of masculinities – or junior masculinities – is required if we are to understand and address gender-inequitable conduct which is harmful to girls and other boys and which undermines boys' own wellbeing. Renold (2005) refers to junior sexualities in relation to boys and girls in the final year of primary schooling and argues for addressing gender, sexuality and age in the construction of identity. Similarly, I here use the term "junior masculinities" to refer to young boys under ten to argue for addressing the specific formation of masculinity in relation to age. Thus, attention to young boys in early childhood has the potential to provide insight into the negotiation of masculinity and to offer a far more nuanced way to theorise early childhood and masculinity. The convergence between early childhood studies and masculinity studies can illuminate boys' negotiation of identity at an age and stage that is often ignored and unacknowledged in the life-long project of gender.

'Early' childhood studies intersecting with masculinity studies

> ... though gender has been a central dimension for some of the key researchers in the field ... so far childhood scholars in general cannot be said to engage deeply with gender studies.
>
> *Eriksson (2007, p. 62)*

Several scholars have argued that early childhood studies and gender/masculinity studies can complement each other (Bartholomaeus & Senkevics, 2015; Bhana, 2016; Blaise, 2005; Connolly, 2004; Davies, 1993; Renold, 2005; Thorne, 1993). Notwithstanding this argument, childhood scholars do not engage deeply with gender, and gender scholars do not engage deeply with early childhood studies (MacNaughton, 2000). Indeed, the relative lack of take-up of hegemonic notions of masculinity when it concerns little boys in early childhood is quite striking, given the expansive field of masculinities more generally (Connell, 2005, 2012). Part of the reason for the lack of collaboration between masculinities and early childhood studies is the way in which early childhood has been configured as a fixed cycle in human development (James et al., 1998; Mayall, 2000).

Developmental psychology and traditional socialisation theories (James et al., 1998) have historically dominated the study of children and childhood (Mayall, 2000). Developmental psychology upholds a version of the child informed by addressing children as adults in the making (James et al., 1998; Mayall, 2000; Thorne, 1993). Rather than seeing children as part of the social world and as subjects, developmental psychology purports that children are objects who move within a predefined pattern of development toward adult status. This process is regarded as natural and an unavoidable path towards maturation. The assumptions of these theories are based on a child's immature status. This logic suggests that children are incapable of and incompetent in making sense of gender and sexuality because of biological and cognitive immaturity.

Traditional socialisation theory suggests that children learn about their roles from adults and the society in which they live. In other words, children's futures are determined by their social worlds (Thorne, 1993). Socialisation theory thus suggests that a child can achieve competence through a future orientated socialising process. There are several pitfalls in both developmental psychology and socialisation theory. In these theories, the child is an incompetent object and a miniature version of an adult – not fully human and also not a subject. There is little opportunity within such theorisation for individuals to engage with the social world, and neither is there any suggestion of children's ability to protest and act as agents based on a complex interaction between self and the social. Thus, if children are seen to be future orientated and maturation is expected according to fixed and naturalised stages of development, masculinity in early childhood is erased (MacNaughton, 2000) and mainly irrelevant. The dominance of developmental psychology and traditional notions of socialisation theory might explain the relative absence of research in the field of gender and early childhood studies and the preservation of the child as relatively incompetent and dependent.

In the 1980s and 1990s the new sociology of childhood provided alternate theorisation about children (James et al., 1998). Objecting to developmental psychology and traditional notions of socialisation theory of boys (and girls), the 'new' social studies of childhood rejected the view of children as passive objects determined by the social world and the adults around them. As noted by Ryan (2008), the 'new' social study of childhood conceptualises childhood as a political and cultural construct where children are active subjects rather than dupes of power as theorised by developmental and socialisation theory. Whilst Ryan (2008) disputes the newness of the conceptualisation of childhood by drawing on historical accounts of children's agency, childhood studies expanded to reconceptualise children as active subjects with the ability to exercise agency, in their own right (Mayall, 2000). Arguing against children's dependent status, the 'new' social study of childhood conceived of children as competent social actors operating within social, cultural and political structures (Mayall, 2000). This expanded view of childhood as approached by feminist poststructural scholars (Bartholomaeus, 2013; MacNaughton, 2000; Paechter, 2007) meant that issues around gender/sexuality could be analysed as part of children's competency within a social world rather than from development psychology or traditional versions of socialisation. The focus on children as actors was important in shedding the taken for granted assumptions about the fixity of childhood and the marginalisation of gender as an active part of the process of growing up. The new sociology of childhood has contributed theoretically to thinking about early childhood as a social construction. Childhood is seen as fluid and operates within and alongside broader structures of political, economic and cultural settings (James et al., 1998).

Connell (2005) suggests that hegemonic masculinity is a configuration of gender practices which legitimise patriarchy and the dominant position of men. Hegemony does not imply absolute power. Rather, as Connell and Messerschmidt (2005) indicate, hegemonic masculinity is fluid, can be disrupted and does not exist in a finite form. From a young age, little boys negotiate masculinity in a range of social contexts. These contexts, underlined by race, class, sexuality, gender and age relations, are shaped as boys shape their masculinities. Of key importance is that masculinity cannot be seen as a 'catch all' (Haywood & Mac an Ghaill, 2013) phrase to explain how boys make sense of their social worlds. Whilst patriarchy continues to have effects for dominant gender ideologies, there are variations based on social and cultural context. However, essentialist logic brushes away these variations and assumes that boys with too much masculinity will be violent whilst boys who have less masculinity will be vulnerable and subordinated. Masculinity under this rubric is simplistically positioned as based on binary differences between boys and girls. The problem with essentialism is that the social and cultural location is concealed whilst persistently addressing boys within binary and biological constructs.

Indeed, the enduring problems and dominance in theorising boys within essentialist biological definitions remain despite the gains made from childhood studies. For instance, issues about boys and masculinities in education and childhood studies often draw from mainstream controversies that cohere around gender gaps in school performance and the supposed feminisation of education (David, 2016). There are concerns about boys supposedly lagging behind girls and girls outperforming boys academically (Connolly, 2004; Martino & Pallotta-Chiarolli, 2003; Paechter, 2007). The feminisation of education has produced arguments that suggest that boys are the new victims of schooling. As Martino and Rezai-Rashti (2012) suggest, essentialist arguments indicate that boys are marginalised because of feminist reforms in education. Feminism, it is argued (Weaver-Hightower, 2008), has produced girls' academic successes and is supposedly the reason for the 'boy problem' and boys' low levels of academic attainment. Brain structure and testosterone-induced aggression based on biological essentialism explain why boys lag behind (Connolly, 2004). Considering boys as naturally laddish and driven by testosterone, however, perpetuates laddishness and reproduces the very conduct that is blamed for boys' problems at school (Connolly, 2004). Moreover, addressing boys as naturally laddish fails to address the diversity and plurality of experience in relation to social specificities, local inflections, race, age, class and gender. Indeed, addressing boys as victims of feminist success reproduces gender binaries and masks the significance of social contexts and cultural location in the construction of masculinity while undermining feminist challenges to patriarchy. Thus, what is a missing from popular discussions in early childhood is a focus on the social construction of masculinities, as Bartholomaeus and Senkevics (2015, p. 1) confirm:

> Generally, when gender is mentioned in the sociology of childhood, it tends to be fleeting, in binary terms, and/or is not discussed in relation to feminist gender theories. In this sense, gender is often reduced to a list of differences between boys and girls with no further exploration of how these differences are constructed or what they mean to children. Therefore, what is actually missing is a critical standpoint that accounts for the social construction of gender and the influence of gender relations and hierarchies among children.

A crucial gain from the new sociology of childhood is that boys are active producers of their social world. Children shape and are shaped by their social circumstances and not simply determined by these conditions (James et al., 1998). Accordingly, children are competent gendered actors who act, create, accommodate and contribute to their social worlds as the social world has effects on the way they shape their relations. Thus, little boys produce gender, are active agents and should be recognised as such rather than simplistically positioned within gender binaries and essentialist logic. Working from the new sociology of childhood studies, scholars have used feminist poststructural perspectives and queer theorising to argue that masculinity is discursively produced and shows potential for change. As Connell (2012, p. 1676) indicates, 'poststructuralist theory has been brilliantly successful as a critique of gender essentialism'. Influenced by the work of Davies (1993), Thorne (1993), Walkerdine (1990) and MacNaughton (2000), early poststructural feminists show that gender is an active part of early childhood. Taking a cue from these scholars, Keddie (2003) in Australia finds that boys even at six years of age already have invested in domination as an appropriate way of being boy. Boys produce and reproduce gender norms. They subvert discursive norms and can shift positions, but they are also under constant pressure to be seen as 'real boys' – where the real expression of boyhood is based on violence, aggression, heterosexual desires and the subordination of alternative genders and sexualities. However, despite the recognition that early childhood is key to the formation of masculine identities, research attention remains focused within the phase of teenage years and older boys (Haywood & Mac an Ghaill, 2013).

Approaching little boys in early childhood: critical masculinities and feminist poststructural possibilities

Most of the research with boys under ten has been conducted in the West, with scholarship based in the UK (Francis, 1998; Renold, 2005), Australia (Davies, 1993; Keddie, 2003) and the US (Blaise, 2005; Thorne, 1993). Thorne's (1993) empirical study in the US has made major contributions to the ways in which children's play is simultaneously gendered. Play is a significant site through which masculinities are produced in early childhood. Thorne shows how play is not a frivolous activity but an important site for 'borderwork', where children use play to separate from each other in terms of gender binaries but also come together and break boundaries as they play together. Gender both shapes and restricts how children play. Thorne's (1993) research has been critical in establishing how boys play games based on separating from girls but also play together in games such as kiss-kiss chase, involving boys and girls chasing each other whilst embedded within heterosexual expectations. Games such as kiss-kiss chase break down gender boundaries and show boys' active investment in heterosexuality whilst claiming power over girls. Similarly, Davies (1993) shows how four-year-olds police gender boundaries and work to reproduce gender categories based on who could play in the home corner. Indeed, boys produce masculinity based on dominant gender norms and have a far more complex relationship with the gendered system of power which can replicate gender binaries but also are open to challenges as they contest the naturalisation of gender and sexuality.

Drawing on such ideas, Renold (2005) and Swain (2006) in the UK and Bhana (2016) in South Africa show how heterosexuality is a key marker of gender play. Even at age seven and eight, boys are already investing in boyfriend-girlfriend relationships as they break down the borderwork that creates gender binaries (Bhana, 2016; Connolly, 2004; Renold, 2005). Researchers have observed the complex process through which heterosexual play and the performance of heterosexuality by little boys must be negotiated against understandings of gender, age and masculinity (Bhana, 2016; Renold, 2005). Little boys produce masculinity in ways that create strong binaries between boys and girls, as being too close to girls could result in the repudiation of masculinity. This is not the same for older boys, where closeness to girls is a marker of heterosexual success. Little boys struggle to give meaning to their masculinities within the specific age expectations whilst also producing heterosexuality. Plummer and Geofroy's (2010) study in the Caribbean suggests that this negotiation means that boys often produce hypermasculinity to ensure status and power. Hypermasculinity is often conceptualised as exacerbated enactment of manhood and is considered to be the ultimate way of earning power. The expression of hypermasculinity involves the denigration of femininity and alternate sexuality and is misogynistic. Boys' engagement with risky sexual conduct, crime and violence are often expressions of hypermasculinity (Paechter, 2007; Renold, 2005).

Playground cultures are critical spaces through which boys construct masculinity. During play, homophobic insults are common against boys who appear to lack the expectations of hegemonic ideals (Bhana & Mayeza, 2019). Play is significant in the production of sporty masculinities. A number of researchers have found how bodily strength and sporting skill demarcate hegemonic forms of masculinity (Bhana, 2016; Swain, 2006; Renold, 2005). Having a 'six pack', muscles and body are key to the formation of junior masculinity, and boys actively put pressure on others and themselves to fulfil the elusive ideal. Renold (2005) shows how boys who rejected soccer were mocked and teased as being effeminate and gay. Swain's (2006) work in the UK also confirms how playing soccer is key to masculinity formation. As Mayeza's (2018) study in South Africa suggests, the school playground may reflect fun and games, but it is a significant site through which boys learn what it means to have an appropriate gender and sexuality. Swain's (2006) research with nine- and ten-year-old boys in the UK similarly shows how crying, working with girls, playing games considered to be 'soft' or lacking sporting skills may lead to disparagement and the questioning of masculinity. Thus, even when little, boys are learning about the pressures associated with the performance of masculinity. For instance, boys who played with girls could be labelled 'barbies' (Swain, 2006).

The local settings set the limits for how masculinity is constructed and is shaped by contextual factors including race and class (Connell, 2012). In the South, Bhana (2016) finds that South African boys, under the age of ten and in conditions of economic marginalisation, produce toxic forms of masculinity based on violence and aggression where the fight for food is underlined by gender battles. Boys who are tough and strong are able to use their power and their bodies to fight for food. The formation of toxic masculinity, even when young, reflects the broader social and economic system, especially in a context where gender ideologies are based on the repudiation of women and girls (Bhana, 2016). The study of boys in early childhood, under conditions marked by economic and social distress, creates certain problems especially in postcolonial contexts like South Africa. Firstly, black boys in poverty are uniformly positioned as violent. Rather than addressing the social and cultural systems of power, violence becomes associated with black masculinity. These essentialist notions of masculinity must be rejected, as Bhana (2016) contends, suggesting that the evidence of peaceable masculinities in the same context must be raised as important ways to understand the formation of junior masculinity. At the same time, another problem emerges with a focus on poverty. Instead of seeing boys as agents in such contexts, there is a tendency to frame boys as passive within the larger structural inequalities. As Connell (2005, p. 116) suggests, 'the claim to power that is central in hegemonic masculinity is constantly negated by economic and cultural weaknesses'. Boys are indeed active agents and produce masculinity in different contexts and under different circumstances. Race, class and context must be at the centre of analysis in the study of masculinities in early childhood.

Conclusion

Against dominant conceptualisations of little boys functioning within ages and stages of development, this chapter has argued that a collaborative approach between early childhood studies and masculinity studies may yield important theoretical insights about the construction of junior masculinities. To date, the scarce mention of boys under ten and the lack of theorising about junior masculinity is surprising. Early childhood scholars should more strongly resist the reliance on essentialist thinking in order to understand the operation of power within a gendered system that little boys encounter on a daily basis. Masculinity studies can no longer ignore age relations and little boys' construction of masculinity in their own right. The study of little boys could emphasise the contingency and vulnerability of masculinity. Gender and age interact, and the transitive character of childhood suggests that masculinity is always changing and unstable. Despite the merit of working with little boys, the lack of collaboration between masculinity studies and early childhood studies remains. To approach little boys from a perspective that takes interest in and values gender, sexuality and relations of power, childhood studies needs to consider masculinities and, accordingly, masculinities studies needs to consider early childhood studies and the construction of age relations as a significant arena of concern and intervention. There is a need to go beyond school-based research to explore how little boys navigate families, communities, religion and other institutions. A collaborative approach is a necessary step in working towards practical interventions.

Acknowledgement

This work was supported by the South African Research Chairs Initiative of the Department of Science and Technology, Republic of South Africa and the National Research Foundation of South Africa [grant number 98407].

Note

1 Early childhood often refers to children from birth to eight years old (UNICEF, 2009), although many countries include children up to nine years old in the definition of early childhood.

References

Barker, G., Greene, M., Nascimento, M., Segundo, M., Ricardo, C., Taylor, A., & Kato, J. (2012). *Men who care: A multi-country qualitative study of men in non-traditional caregiving roles*. Washington, DC & Rio de Janeiro: International Center for Research on Women (ICRW) & Instituto Promundo.

Bartholomaeus, C. (2013). Colluding with or challenging hegemonic masculinity? Examining primary school boys' plural gender practices. *Australian Feminist Studies*, *28*(77), 279–293.

Bartholomaeus, C., & Riggs, D. (2017). *Transgender people and education*. New York: Palgrave Macmillan.

Bartholomaeus, C., & Senkevics, A. S. (2015). Accounting for gender in the sociology of childhood: Reflections from research in Australia and Brazil. *Sage Open*, *5*(2), 1–9.

Bhana, D. (2016). *Perspectives on children and young people: Gender and childhood sexuality in primary schools*. Singapore: Springer.

Bhana, D., & Mayeza, E. (2019). 'Cheese boys' resisting and negotiating violent hegemonic masculinity in primary school. *NORMA: International Journal for Masculinity Studies*, *14*(1), 3–17.

Blaise, M. (2005). *Playing it straight: Uncovering gender discourses in the early childhood classroom*. London & New York: Routledge.

Butler, J. (1993). *Bodies that matter: On the discursive limits of 'sex'*. New York: Routledge.

Connell, R. (2005). *Masculinities* (2nd ed.). Sydney: Allen & Unwin.

Connell, R. (2012). Gender, health and theory: Conceptualizing the issue, in local and world perspective. *Social Science & Medicine*, *74*(11), 1675–1683.

Connell, R., & Messerschmidt, J. W. (2005). Hegemonic masculinity: Rethinking the concept. *Gender & Society, 19*(6), 829–859.

Connolly, P. (2004). *Boys and schooling in the early years.* London: Routledge Falmer.

David, M. (2016). *Feminist manifesto for Education.* Cambridge: Polity Press.

Davies, B. (1993). *Shards of glass: Children reading and writing beyond gendered identities.* St. Leonards, NSW: Allen & Unwin.

Epstein, D., Kehily, M. J., Mac an Ghaill, M., & Redman, P. (2001). Girls and boys come out to play: Making masculinities and femininities in primary playgrounds. *Men and Masculinities, 4*(2), 158–172.

Eriksson, M. (2007). Childhood studies. In Flood, M., Gardiner, J. K., Pease, B., & Pringle K. (Eds.), *International encyclopaedia of men and masculinities* (pp. 60–63). Abingdon, Oxon: Routledge.

Francis, B. (1998). *Power plays: Primary school children's constructions of gender, power, and adult work.* Stoke on Trent: Trentham Books.

Haavind, H. (2005). Book review: Towards a multifaceted understanding of children as social participants. *Childhood, 12*(1), 139–152.

Haywood, C., & Mac an Ghaill, M. (2013). *Education and masculinities: Social, cultural and global transformations.* London: Routledge.

Hearn, J., Nordberg, M., Andersson, K., Balkmar, D., Gottzén, L., Klinth, R., & Sandberg, L. (2012). Hegemonic masculinity and beyond: 40 years of research in Sweden. *Men and Masculinities, 15*(1), 31–55.

James, A., Jenks, C., & Prout, A. (1998). *Theorizing childhood.* Cambridge: Polity Press.

Keddie, A. (2003). Little boys: Tomorrow's macho lads. *Discourse: Studies in the Cultural Politics of Education, 24*(3), 289–306.

MacNaughton, G. (2000). *Re-thinking gender in early childhood education.* Sydney: Allen & Unwin.

Martino, W., & Pallotta-Chiarolli, M. (2003). *So what's a boy? Addressing issues of masculinity and schooling.* Maidenhead: Open University Press.

Martino, W., & Rezai-Rashti, G. (2012). *Gender, race, and the politics of role modelling: The influence of male teachers.* New York: Routledge.

Mayall, B. (2000). The sociology of childhood in relation to children's rights. *The International Journal of Children's Rights, 8*(3), 243–259.

Mayeza, E. (2018). 'Charmer boys' and 'cream girls': How primary school children construct themselves as heterosexual subjects through football. *Discourse: Studies in the Cultural Politics of Education, 39*(1), 128–141.

Paechter, C. F. (2007). *Being boys, being girls: Learning masculinities and femininities.* Maidenhead: Open University Press.

Parker, R. (2009). Sexuality, culture and society: Shifting paradigms in sexuality research. *Culture, Health & Sexuality, 11*(3), 251–266.

Plummer, D., & Geofroy, S. (2010). When bad is cool: Violence and crime as a rite of passage into manhood. *Caribbean Review of Gender Studies, 4*, 1–17.

Pollack, W. S. (1999). *Real boys: Rescuing our sons from the myths of boyhood.* New York: Henry Holt & Company.

Renold, E. (2005). *Girls, boys and junior sexualities: Exploring children's gender and sexual relations in the primary school.* London: Routledge Falmer.

Robinson, K. (2013). *Innocence, knowledge and the construction of childhood: The contradictory nature of sexuality and censorship in children's contemporary lives.* New York: Routledge.

Ryan, P. J. (2008). How new is the 'new' social study of childhood? The myth of a paradigm shift. *Journal of Interdisciplinary History, 38*(4), 553–576.

Swain, J. (2006). Reflections on patterns of masculinity in school settings. *Men and Masculinities, 8*(3), 331–349.

Thorne, B. (1987). Re-visioning women and social change: Where are the children? *Gender & Society, 1*(1), 85–109.

Thorne, B. (1993). *Gender play: Boys and girls in school.* Buckingham: Open University Press.

Tobin, J. (1997). *Making a place for pleasure in early childhood education.* New Haven, CT: Yale University Press.

UNICEF. (2009). *The state of the world's children 2010: Child rights.* New York: UNICEF.

Walkerdine, V. (1990). *Schoolgirl fictions.* London: Verso.

Weaver-Hightower, M. B. (2008). An ecology metaphor for educational policy analysis: A call to complexity. *Educational Researcher, 37*(3), 153–167.

Yelland, N. (1998). *Gender in early childhood.* London & New York: Routledge.

17

Young masculinities

Masculinities in youth studies

Signe Ravn and Steven Roberts

Introduction

This chapter provides an overview of how men and masculinities have featured in the field of youth studies historically and more recently. First we briefly sketch out what characterised research on young people's lives during the emergence of the field. We next consider how young men are represented in contemporary media and how youth scholars have reacted to these representations and highlight the field's more recent research agendas. The chapter concludes by briefly discussing whether young people can be seen as being at the forefront in terms of changes in gender relations and gendered identities and whether youth studies, by implication, is a frontier for identifying social change.

Masculinities and youth studies in historical perspective

Similar to other research fields, for instance criminology (Lander, Ravn & Jon, 2014), youth studies emerged as a fairly gender-blind field; 'youth' largely equated to young men, but without explicit acknowledgment of this. Speaking of an emergent field is somewhat an exaggeration, as social research on young people's lives primarily took place within two separate streams, one focusing on transitions from education to the labour market and the other focusing on youth cultures and consumption, with little dialogue between the two (France & Roberts, 2017).

In youth transitions research, much attention was paid to how education systems prepared young men for economic participation and the changing demands of the time. Key studies on school-to-work transitions included UK-based research by Roberts (1968) and Ashton (1973). Roberts rejected ideas of 'occupational choice', instead proposing that understandings of 'opportunity structures' were necessary to adequately theorise transitions. Ashton maintained this theme in his efforts to explain how social context – the complex of experiences at home and in school – intertwined to produce relatively limited career options. In both cases, the predominant focus was on working-class young men. This focus extended to studies documenting the finer-grained detail of young men's experience of these transitions. Seminal here is Willis' (1977) ethnography on how working-class boys 'learn to labour' as a result of the educational system reproducing social inequalities. Willis emphasised that young men 'partially penetrated' the myth of meritocracy but also that their 'cross-valorisation of manual labour with the social superiority of masculinity' (Willis, 1977, p. 148) facilitated their entry into the bottom of the labour market and thus reproduces the very basis of capitalist relations.

In studies of youth cultures, scholars, particularly those associated with the University of Birmingham's interdisciplinary Centre for Contemporary Cultural Studies (CCCS), studied what they described as 'subcultures' – so-called spectacular expressions, such as those exhibited by the Teddy boys, Mods, Rockers, punks etc. (see e.g., Hall & Jefferson, 1976; Hebdige, 1979). Building on and moving beyond the Chicago School's tradition of theorising youth *delinquency* as resulting from social ecology (e.g., Empey, 1967), the emphasis here was to trouble notions of delinquency and deviance through focusing on working-class youths' style, music, substance use and acts of consumption. Such subcultural practices were theorised as providing opportunities to express one's identity but also as permitting symbolic distancing from middle-class young people and the parental generation (Hebdige, 1979). Importantly, these expressions were theorised as a collective system of resistance and as real, symbolic or ritualistic attempts to challenge and influence hegemonic power relations. Similar patterns were observed in the 'bodgies' and 'widgies' of mid-century Australia, denoting working-class teen boys and girls whose particular style was perceived by the media as 'social boils on the body of society' (Sturma, 1992, p. 129). One critical point raised by later scholars is the apparent homogeneity of 'youth' as a group in depictions by the subcultures approaches – the Chicago School as well as the CCCS (Weinzierl & Muggleton, 2003). This has been complicated by scholars, not least by scholars from the Global South, where structures such as 'race' have been noted as significant drivers of subcultural expressions. This is clear in Mooney's (2005) discussion of South African 'ducktails', for instance: white young men whose particularised styling challenged hegemonic norms of adults but whose racist violence towards black youth perpetuated racialised hegemonic power relations.

What becomes clear is that, largely, the norms in both 'youth' transitions and 'youth' cultures were being set by the study of young men as an unmarked category. This started changing with Angela McRobbie's (1978) poignant critique, which problematised how much of the subcultural analysis of the 1970s was characterised by male CCCS researchers researching young men. Women and girls, for McRobbie, were discussed merely as appendages, with gender significantly lacking recognition as a structural constraint that profoundly affected life chances and lifestyles. Similar contestation was offered by Christine Griffin (1985) in her research on British young women's school-to-work transitions. These critiques were pivotal in producing a stronger awareness of gender in youth research. They also appeared at a time when wider academic attention was beginning to focus more strongly on men as gendered beings, and they gave rise to the emergence of critical masculinities studies (Roberts, 2018).

Contemporary representations of young men and masculinities

Young men – like all young people – are often represented as being both *at risk* (as a result of contemporary social and economic changes) and also *a risk* (to themselves and others). One dominant narrative about young men, depicting them 'at risk', is what is known as the 'masculinity-in-crisis' narrative. The narrative's current iteration insists that declines in heavy industry, rising unemployment, declining marriage rates, women's increasing workforce participation and boys' relative educational underachievement combine to ensure that (young) men are the disadvantaged social group. This positions masculinity as in crisis, and men as losers in contemporary societies. These representations abound in media discussions of gender differences in educational attainment and university attendance, as well as in pop psychology books (Roberts, 2018). However, rather than being an especially novel concern, the 'masculinity-in-crisis' narrative has a long history. Academics in history and literary studies, among others, have pinpointed an array of historical periods where masculinity appears to have been 'in crisis' (Roberts, 2018), including times even prior to the rise of the women's movement or even the establishment of industrial capitalism. Many contemporary anxieties emerged at the onset of what is sometimes described as the 'post industrial' age during the 1980s. Furthermore, the mid-1990s offered a significant 'moment' that has shaped the discourse of crisis for over two decades: at this point, girls started to educationally outperform boys for the first time, leading to discernible shifts in political and research attention centred on the relationship between gender and academic attainment (see, e.g., Arnot, David & Weiner, 1996 on the UK; Martino, 1999 on Australia).

Contemporary research on youth and masculinities has critically engaged with the 'crisis' narrative. Researchers have disrupted and problematised the idea that 'boys lose out to girls' (e.g., Francis, 2010; Mac an Ghaill, 1996). This kind of concern has been revealed to be predicated on a mourning of the passing of male privileges, over and above celebrating – or even understanding – girls' progress (Griffin, 2000). Beyond the education realm, researchers have long noted that worldwide economic inequalities, in relation to wages and positions of power, make claims that men are somehow in crisis entirely untenable (Roberts, 2018). That men continue to disproportionately hold positions of power and unequal shares of material wealth, but simultaneously are more likely to academically underachieve and more likely to be unemployed, throws up a key insight: if indeed there is any kind of crisis, it is not of all men and of masculinity in total. In youth studies, then, there has been a push towards understanding which men and boys might be at risk – and why. This has meant emphasising that, despite the way it is portrayed in the popular press, gender has a smaller impact than social class or 'race' in education (Roberts, 2012). This is well captured by Ward (2014, p. 53), who usefully notes that any 'crisis of school to successful adult futures may not really be linked to a "crisis" of masculinity at all, but more to one of social class inequality'. In addition, scholars have argued that local geographies must be taken into account when seeking to understand the tensions brought about by social change that inform how working-class boys manage their masculinity in particular contexts (e.g., Andersson & Beckman, 2018; Ward, 2015).

A second dominant narrative in contemporary representations of masculinity relates to young men as risky subjects (see also Robinson, this volume), posing a risk to themselves but also to their surroundings. This narrative too is prevalent both in media representations and also some academic research, often depicting young men's engagement in various practices as specific, gendered social problems that call for intervention. For instance, Ringrose, Harvey, Gill & Livingstone (2013) have shown how the media depict young men as 'predatory and over-sexed' in relation to sexting practices, and Lumsden has illustrated how the representation of 'boy racers' in Scotland as 'reckless, irresponsible, and anti-social driving, young motorists' (2009, 2.2) took the form of a moral panic (see also Balkmar, 2012). In less dramatic terms, research and numerous statistics show how boys and young men are over-represented in crime (Lander et al., 2014; Messerschmidt, 2013) and drug and alcohol use across Europe (EMCDDA, 2017) and in Australia (Livingston, 2015). Young men's alcohol consumption in particular has also been linked to violence in public spaces (Tomsen, 1997), most recently in the media coverage of what is termed the 'king hit' or 'coward punch'.

Youth scholars have engaged critically with these perspectives by giving voice to young men's own understandings of and the cultural meanings associated with such practices, and by emphasising how these are informed by broader socio-cultural norms and structural patterns. For instance, Ravn (2018) studied how young Danish men negotiate the boundaries between legitimate and illegitimate physical aggression and concluded that, while acting outright violently or aggressively was seen by most as illegitimate, being *incapable* of a violent reaction in cases where friends or girlfriends were being targeted was an equally illegitimate performance of masculine identity. Similarly, Bengtsson (2016) has analysed the gendered performances of young people in secure-care institutions in Denmark; instead of seeing hypermasculinity as an identity performance pertaining to single individuals, she analyses this as a dominant institutional frame, in a Goffmanian sense, that guides all gender performances, regardless of the young person's gender. In relation to young men's car culture, Tanja Joelsson and Dag Balkmar have, in their two separate ethnographic studies, researched car modifiers and 'greasers' in Sweden to investigate how the young men, and the few women, involved in this youth culture engage with their cars on a day-to-day basis (Balkmar & Joelsson, 2013; see also Balkmar, 2012; Joelsson, 2014). They unpack the stereotype of the 'young, male risk-taker' by showing how a sense of control is central to their practices, and how these practices furthermore must be understood in relation to their specific geographical context; as a way of making something happen in an otherwise 'boring place' and thereby escape the label of being 'boring people' (Balkmar & Joelsson, 2013, p. 198). And finally, more recently, a growing body of research has investigated young people's engagement in sexting practices to unpack the negative and moralising representations of this phenomenon. In their study of 35 teenagers in London, UK, Harvey et al. (2013) approached sexting as a matter of gaining recognition and getting 'ratings' amongst one's peers. Most recently, Roberts and Ravn (2019) have investigated young Australian men's own perceptions of and experiences with sexting practices, finding that trust and consent were seen as pivotal in 'appropriate' sexting practices, at the same time as consent was rarely explicit and there was a clear transactional and strategic undertone to these practices.

Emerging agendas

Today, studies on young men and masculinities are moving in a couple of directions. In addition to the strands of research mentioned above, new avenues of research are emerging, and one such avenue is research on young men's body images and body work. Apart from a few notable exceptions, the body has not been given much attention in youth studies historically (Coffey & Watson, 2015). One example of earlier work in this field is Mary-Jane Kehily's (2001) writing on the construction of young men's sexual identities in schools, in which she pays explicit attention to the embodied dimensions of the dominant, heterosexual masculinities that are forged through school processes. In a similar vein, Louisa Allen (2013) has explored young men's sexual embodiment and the manifestations of male sexualities in schools. What characterises the current wave of research on the body is an engagement with newer theoretical developments in feminist research as well as theories on affect and new materialisms to go 'beyond discourse' (Ringrose, 2011). In this perspective, youth subjectivities are produced not *only* through discourse but *also* through the body; through embodied experiences; and key questions posed are 'what the body can do' (cf. Ringrose et al., 2013) and which affects it produces.

Taking this to youth sociology, researchers have started to explore young people's embodied identities, their body image and body work practices (Coffey, 2016). This is key to understanding how young (masculine as well as feminine) subjectivities are formed and expressed through work on the body, for instance through aesthetic modifications or dieting and exercising practices. In the age of austerity, being fit can be seen as an alternative means of creating and ascribing value to one's self to an extent where 'fit is the new rich' (Hakim, 2015). While body work traditionally was and still is seen as a feminine practice, that both young men and women engage in body work indicates that young men are increasingly concerned about their body image (Coffey, 2013). The ideal body image is still highly gendered, though, and in Coffey's study, the ideal body image for men was seen as being muscular and as requiring body work in the form of weight-lifting and generally staying 'fit'. Furthermore, drawing on young Danish men's perceptions of steroid use, Ravn and Coffey (2016) explored how body images and embodied subjectivities produce certain affects and how some images – such as the steroid user – are met with disgust and seen as lacking 'taste'. Such affects were central in understanding the predominantly negative attitudes to steroids as constituting an illegitimate way of achieving a muscular body. Finally, the prominence of bodies and embodiment in visual, digital cultures is also a topic for contemporary research. While much of this have tended to focus on young women, boys and young men's bodies in the digital space are also attracting attention. As previously mentioned, Harvey et al. (2013) have explored young boys' sexting practices, while Enguix and Gómez-Narváez (2017) have investigated how different body parts are made visible or indeed invisible in young men's selfies on Grindr and Instagram.

Another emerging agenda is concerned with men's performances and expressions of gender and positive changes in the nature of masculinities. This entails efforts to move beyond a sole focus on problematic and/or discriminatory enactments of traditional or hegemonic forms of masculinity. This strand of research focusing on positive developments has been captured *primarily* (but not solely; see, e.g., Elliott's (2016) exposition of 'caring masculinities') through the lens of Anderson's (2009) Inclusive Masculinity Theory (IMT) (see also Robertson, Monaghan & Southby, this volume). Key to Anderson's (2009) theorising is that hegemonic, or what he refers to as orthodox, forms of masculinity are becoming less prominent among young men in Western societies characterised by decreasing (but not entirely diminished, cf. Pascoe, 2005) levels of cultural homophobia and homohysteria; the fear of being perceived as gay. In such conditions, rather than relying only, or even mostly, upon modes of masculinity that emphasise heterosexuality, distance from femininity, misogyny and emotional constraint, a wider repertoire of behaviours and attitudes is now available and increasingly legitimised as appropriate for and by young men.

Anderson's proposition has been underpinned by vast amounts of empirical research, particularly from the UK. One central site is sports, with Channon and Matthews' (2015) study of declining homophobia and homohysteric sentiments in mixed martial arts, Roberts, Anderson and Magrath's (2017) study of an English Premier League football club youth team and Murray and White's (2015) study of Australian 'contact sports', aligning strongly with Anderson's (2014) work on a wide array of sporting men. Educational spaces too have been noted as sites of softer performances and pro-gay attitudes, with McCormack's (2012) ethnography of three UK schools being especially compelling. Anderson and McCormack (2015) have also observed a considerable amount of cuddling and 'spooning' between heterosexual university men in the UK and the US, and while numerically less obvious, a significant minority of young men were found to engage in such practices, including kissing on the lips, in a study of Australian university students (Drummond, Filiault, Anderson & Jeffries, 2015). Emotional performances are also apparent in YouTube gaming, where micro celebrity gamers are found to incorporate more sensitive versions of masculinity in interactions with one another on screen, but also with their viewers 'via the screen' (Maloney, Roberts & Caruso, 2018). This body of research leads McCormack and Anderson (2014) to assert that significant numbers of young heterosexual males are engaging in homosocial relationships characterised by a series of important traits: 1) social inclusion of gay male peers; 2) embrace of once-feminised artifacts; 3) increased emotional intimacy; 4) increased physical tactility; 5) erosion of the one-time rule of homosexuality; and 6) eschewing violence.

There are some complexities to these ideas. For instance, Gough, Hall and Seymour-Smith's (2014) work on men's use of online make-up tutorials, Gottzén and Kremer-Sadlik's (2012) exploration of fatherhood practices as they apply to kids' sporting arenas and Ralph and Roberts's (2018) research of Australian men's homosociality all specify the co-existence of inclusivity and hegemonic forms of masculinity. IMT has been subject to further critique, in some ways connected to these findings. Ingram and Waller (2014, p. 40) position IMT as being overly 'optimistic', insisting that Anderson misrepresents a 'postmodern co-existence of multiple male cultures that entail no relationship of power' (p. 39). This concern regarding unaltered power relations, as well as the implications for transformed or hybridised forms of masculinity, is also taken up further in the wider literature (e.g. O'Neill, 2015).

Discussion

Some scholars have suggested that studying young people's lives provides an opportunity for studying new trends and social changes, as young people are seen to be the first ones to experience the consequences of changing economies and labour markets, social policies, new family forms etc. (Furlong, 2013). 'Youth' can even become a metaphor for 'the future', with young people coming to represent future hopes and dreams for a place (Coffey et al., 2018). Further, young people are sometimes depicted as being more progressive than older generations, implying that 'eventually' society will change for the better. IMT is one case in point, suggesting that more progressive attitudes in men-to-men relations and gender relations in general are prevailing amongst young men and implying that this is a generational shift which paves the way for more inclusive masculinities in the future. While a more systematic exploration of whether this is the case across different segments of society, e.g., across social class and ethnicity, is still needed to be able to assess the extent of such changes, IMT does take an optimistic approach to future relations between young men.

However, this does not imply that young people are necessarily more progressive concerning gender relations on the whole. Indeed, some studies suggest that more traditional or gender-stereotypical perceptions remain, both with regard to the nature of and roles within romantic relationships and in their attitudes to (gender-based) violence (McCarry, 2010; Ravn, 2018; Sundaram, 2015). In that sense, young masculinities might be more inclusive towards other men, but less so with regard to women. It is important to be aware of and scrutinise these patterns and to ground this in young men's everyday lives and conditions as well as the broader social and cultural contexts in which these lives unfold. It is also important to think through – and research – whether some seemingly more progressive behaviour might be an effect of age; will young men retain these attitudes as they get older? Finally, it is important to focus on how gendered performances and relations look beyond the Global North. For instance, some researchers suggest the emergence of a 'pan-Asian soft masculinity' (Louie, 2012, p. 930; see also Jung, 2010 and Liong and Chan in this volume), but the extent and cultural specificity of this is unclear.

The question of age and 'maturing out' is also relevant to consider with regard to the subcultural practices on which the 'at risk' narrative focuses. While this seems to be the case at the population level with some practices such as drug use, other practices, such as sexting and engagements with digital (visual) culture in general, might be aspects of current 'youth' culture that will stay with young people into later stages of life and, in that sense, may be harbingers of the future, as MacDonald (2009) has suggested. As Hodkinson argues, we need a more nuanced approach to people's engagements with subcultural phenomena over the life course other than a 'refusal to grow up' (Hodkinson, 2013), and as part of that we need to investigate what then constitutes youth culture in changing times.

References

Allen, L. (2013). Boys as sexy bodies: Picturing young men's sexual embodiment at school. *Men and Masculinities, 16*(3), 347–365.

Anderson, E. (2009). *Inclusive masculinity: The changing nature of masculinities*. London: Routledge.

Anderson, E. (2014). *21st century jocks: Sporting men and contemporary heterosexuality*. Basingstoke: Palgrave Macmillan.

Anderson, E., & McCormack, M. (2015). Cuddling and spooning: Heteromasculinity and homosocial tactility among student-athletes. *Men and Masculinities, 18*(2), 214–230.

Andersson, Å., & Beckman, A. (2018). Young working-class men without jobs: Reimagining work and masculinity in postindustrial Sweden. In C. Walker & S. Roberts (Eds.), *Masculinity, labour, and neoliberalism* (pp. 101–123). London: Palgrave Macmillan.

Arnot, M., David, M., & Weiner, G. (1996). Educational reform, gender equality and school cultures. In B. R. Cosin & M. Hales (Eds.), *Families, education, and social differences* (pp. 132–148). London: Routledge.

Ashton, D. N. (1973). The transition from school to work: Notes on the development of different frames of reference among young male workers. *Sociological Review, 21*(1), 101–125.

Balkmar, D. (2012). *On men and cars: An ethnographic study of gendered, risky and dangerous relations* (Doctoral dissertation). Linköping: Linköping University.

Balkmar, D., & Joelsson, T. (2013). The dangerous other? Towards a contextual approach to men's risk-taking with motor vehicles. In I. Lander, S. Ravn. & N. Jon (Eds.), *Masculinities in the criminological field: Control, vulnerability and risk-taking* (pp. 187–202). Farnham: Ashgate.

Bengtsson, T. (2016). Performing hypermasculinity: Experiences with confined young offenders. *Men and Masculinities, 19*(4), 410–428.

Channon, A., & Matthews, C. R. (2015). 'It is what it is': Masculinity, homosexuality, and inclusive discourse in mixed martial arts. *Journal of Homosexuality, 62*(7), 936–956.

Coffey, J. (2013). Bodies, body work and gender: Exploring a Deleuzian approach. *Journal of Gender Studies, 22*(1), 3–16.

Coffey, J. (2016). *Body work: Youth, gender and health*. London: Routledge.

Coffey, J., Threadgold, S., Farrugia, D., Sherval, M., Hanley, J., Askew, M., & Askland, H. (2018). 'If you lose your youth, you lose your heart and your future': Affective figures of youth in community tensions surrounding a proposed Coal Seam Gas project. *Sociologia Ruralis, 58*(3), 665–683.

Coffey, J., & Watson, J. (2015). Bodies: Corporeality and embodiment in childhood and youth studies. In J. Wyn & H. Cahill (Eds.), *Handbook of children and youth studies* (pp. 185–200). New York: Springer.

Drummond, M. J., Filiault, S. M., Anderson, E., & Jeffries, D. (2015). Homosocial intimacy among Australian undergraduate men. *Journal of Sociology, 51*(3), 643–656.

Elliott, K. (2016). Caring masculinities: Theorizing an emerging concept. *Men and masculinities, 19*(3), 240–259.

EMCDDA. (2017). *European drug report 2017: Trends and developments*. Lisbon: EMCDDA. Retrieved from www.emcdda.europa.eu/system/files/publications/4541/TDAT17001ENN.pdf.

Empey, L. T. (1967). Delinquency theory and recent research. *Journal of Research in Crime and Delinquency, 4*(1), 28–42.

Enguix, B., & Gómez-Narváez, E. (2017). Masculine bodies, selfies, and the (re)configurations of intimacy. *Men and Masculinities, 21*(1), 112–130.

France, A., & Roberts, S. (2017). *Youth and social class*. London: Palgrave Macmillan.

Francis, B. (2010). Re/theorising gender: Female masculinity and male femininity in the classroom?. *Gender and Education, 22*(5), 477–490.

Furlong, A. (2013). *Youth studies: An introduction*. London: Routledge.

Gottzén, L., & Kremer-Sadlik, T. (2012). Fatherhood and youth sports: A balancing act between care and expectations. *Gender & Society, 26*(4), 639–664.

Gough, B., Hall, M., & Seymour-Smith, S. (2014). Straight guys do wear make-up: Contemporary masculinities and investment in appearance. In S. Roberts (Ed.), *Debating modern masculinities: Change, continuity, crisis?* (pp. 106–124). London: Palgrave Pivot.

Griffin, C. (1985). *Typical girls: Young women from school to the full-time job market*. London: Routledge & Kegan Paul.

Griffin, C. (2000). Discourses of crisis and loss: Analysing the 'boys' underachievement' debate. *Journal of Youth Studies, 3*(2), 167–188.

Hakim, J. (2015). 'Fit is the new rich': Male embodiment in the age of austerity. *Soundings: A Journal of Politics and Culture, 61*, 84–94.

Hall, S., & Jefferson, T. (Eds.). (1976). *Resistance through rituals: Youth subcultures in post-war Britain*. London: Hutchinson.

Harvey, L., Ringrose, J., & Gill, R. (2013). Swagger, ratings and masculinity: Theorising the circulation of social and cultural value in teenage boys' digital peer networks. *Sociological Research Online, 18*(4), 1–11.

Hebdige, D. (1979). *Subculture: The meaning of style*. New York: Methuen & Co.

Hodkinson, P. (2013). Spectacular youth cultures and ageing: Beyond refusing to grow up. *Sociology Compass*, 7(1), 13–22.

Ingram, N., & Waller, R. (2014). Degrees of masculinity: Working and middle-class undergraduate students' constructions of masculine identities. In S. Roberts (Ed.), *Debating modern masculinities: Change, continuity, crisis?* (pp. 35–51). London: Palgrave Pivot.

Joelsson, T. (2014). Careless men, careless masculinities? Understanding young men's risk-taking with motor vehicles as violations. *NORMA: International Journal for Masculinity Studies, 9*(3), 191–204.

Jung, S. (2010). *Korean masculinities and transcultural consumption*. Hong Kong: Hong Kong University Press.

Kehily, M-J. (2001). Bodies in school: Young men, embodiment, and heterosexual masculinities. *Men and Masculinities, 4*(2), 173–185.

Lander, I., Ravn, S., & Jon, N. (Eds). (2014). *Masculinities in the criminological field: Control, vulnerability and risk-taking*. Farnham: Ashgate.

Livingston, M. (2015). *Understanding recent trends in Australian alcohol consumption*. Canberra: Foundation for Alcohol Research & Education.

Louie, K. (2012). Popular culture and masculinity ideals in East Asia, with special reference to China. *The Journal of Asian Studies, 71*(4), 929–943.

Lumsden, K. (2009). 'Do we look like boy racers?': The role of the folk devil in contemporary moral panics. *Sociological Research Online, 14*, 1.

Mac an Ghaill, M. (1996). *Understanding masculinities: Social relations and cultural arenas*. Maidenhead: McGraw-Hill Education.

MacDonald, R. (2009). Precarious work: Risk, choice and poverty traps. In A. Furling (Ed.), *Handbook of youth and young adulthood: New perspectives and agendas* (pp. 167–175). London: Routledge.

Maloney, M., Roberts, S., & Caruso, A. (2018). 'Mmm … I love it, bro!': Performances of masculinity in YouTube gaming. *New Media & Society, 20*(5), 1697–1714.

Martino, W. (1999). Disruptive moments in the education of boys: Debating populist discourses on boys, schooling and masculinities. *Discourse: Studies in the Cultural Politics of Education, 20*(2), 289–294.

McCarry, M. (2010). Becoming a 'proper man': Young people's attitudes about interpersonal violence and perceptions of gender. *Gender and Education, 22*(1), 17–30.

McCormack, M. (2012). *The declining significance of homophobia*. Oxford: Oxford University Press.

McCormack, M., & Anderson, E. (2014). The influence of declining homophobia on men's gender in the United States: An argument for the study of homohysteria. *Sex Roles, 71*(3/4), 109–120.

McRobbie, A. (1978). Working class girls and the culture of femininity. In Women's Studies Group, *Women take issue: Aspects of women's subordination* (pp. 96–108). Birmingham: Centre for Contemporary Cultural Studies.

Messerschmidt, J. (2013). *Crime as structured action: Doing masculinity, class, sexuality and crime*. Lanham, MD: Rowman & Littlefield.

Mooney, K. (2005). Identi*ties* in the ducktail youth subculture in post-World-War-Two South Africa. *Journal of Youth Studies, 8*(1), 41–57.

Murray, A., & White, A. (2015). Twelve not so angry men: Inclusive masculinities in Australian contact sports. *International Review for the Sociology of Sport, 52*(5), 536–550.

O'Neill, R. (2015). Whither critical masculinity studies? Notes on inclusive masculinity theory, postfeminism, and sexual politics. *Men and Masculinities, 18*(1), 100–120.

Pascoe, C. J. (2005). "Dude, you are a fag": Adolescent masculinity and the fag discourse. *Sexualities, 8*(3), 329–346.

Ralph, B., & Roberts, S. (2018). One small step for man: Change and continuities in homosocial expression and enactment among young Australian men. *Men and Masculinities*, doi: 10.1177/1097184X18777776.

Ravn, S. (2018). 'I would never start a fight but …': Young masculinities, perceptions of violence, and symbolic boundary work in focus groups. *Men and Masculinities, 21*(2), 291–309.

Ravn, S., & Coffey, J. (2016). 'Steroids, it's so much an identity thing!': Perceptions of steroid use, risk and masculine body image. *Journal of Youth Studies, 19*(1), 87–102.

Ringrose, J. (2011). Beyond discourse? Using Deleuze and Guattari's schizoanalysis to explore affective assemblages, heterosexually striated space, and lines of flight online and at school. *Educational Philosophy and Theory, 43*(6), 598–618.

Ringrose, J., Harvey, L., Gill, R., & Livingstone, S. (2013). Teen girls, sexual double standards and 'sexting': Gendered value in digital image exchange. *Feminist Theory, 14*(3), 305–323.

Roberts, K. (1968). The entry into employment: An approach towards a general theory. *The Sociological Review, 16*(2), 165–182.

Roberts, S. (2012). 'I just got on with it': The educational experiences of ordinary, yet overlooked, boys. *British Journal of Sociology of Education, 33*(2), 203–221.

Roberts, S. (2018). *Young working class men in transition*. London: Routledge.

Roberts, S., Anderson, E., & Magrath, R. (2017). Continuity, change and complexity in the performance of masculinity among elite young footballers in England. *The British Journal of Sociology, 68*(2), 336–357.

Roberts, S., & Ravn, S. (2019). 'Towards a sociological understanding of sexting as a social practice: A case study of university undergraduate men'. *Sociology*. Early online publication at https://doi.org/10.1177/0038038519864239.

Sturma, M. (1992). The politics of dancing: When rock'n'roll came to Australia. *Journal of Popular Culture, 25*(4), 123–138.

Sundaram, V. (2015, January 6). Gender stereotypes make teenagers more accepting of violence. *The Conversation*. Retrieved from https://theconversation.com/gender-stereotypes-make-teenagers-more-accepting-of-violence-33505.

Tomsen, S. (1997). A top night: Social protest, masculinity and the culture of drinking violence. *British Journal of Criminology, 37*(1), 90–102.

Ward, M. R. M. (2014). 'We're different from everyone else': Contradictory working-class masculinities in contemporary Britain. In S. Roberts (Ed.), *Debating modern masculinities: Change, continuity, crisis?* (pp. 52–69). Basingstoke: Palgrave Macmillan.

Ward, M. R. M. (2015). The chameleonisation of masculinity: Jimmy's multiple performances of a working-class self. *Masculinities & Social Change, 4*(3), 215–240.

Weinzierl, R., & Muggleton, D. (2003). What is 'post-subcultural studies' anyway? In D. Muggleton & R. Weinzierl (Eds.), *The post-subcultures reader* (pp. 3–23). Oxford: Berg.

Willis, P. E. (1977). *Learning to labour: How working class kids get working class jobs*. New York: Columbia University Press.

18

"Maturing" theories of ageing masculinities and the diverse identity work of older men in later life

Anna Tarrant

Introduction

The writing of this chapter marks just over a decade since the empirical study of older men was described by Thomson (2006, p. 624) as "in its infancy" and by van Den Hoonard (2007) as a topic "whose time has come". At this time, the double marginalisation and absence of older men, their identities and lived experiences within a broader, interdisciplinary critical scholarship theorising both men and masculinities and ageing, was recognised. Calls to establish more focused theoretical and empirical attention to older men's lives emerged from work that emphasised the significance of the intersections of gender and age relations in the later lives of women and from the acknowledgement that, like older women, men too are gendered subjects (Arber, Davidson, & Ginn, 2003; Calasanti, 2004; van Den Hoonard, 2007). Since then, a modest and increasingly coherent interdisciplinary literature has addressed men's experiences of ageing as a gendered process, refining theories of ageing masculinities that better explain some of the contestations of older men's identities as they are enacted and experienced in a diverse range of arenas of social life. Qualitative researchers in particular have explored a considerably wider range of issues and substantive topics linked to older men's experiences and identities than was evident ten years ago.

This chapter charts and synthesises key theoretical and empirical contributions to this literature. It does so both to establish and enrich knowledge of the complexities of the gendered and diverse lives of older and ageing men and to make a case for the value of insights in age and ageing studies to developments in masculinities studies. Particular attention is given to the burgeoning international and interdisciplinary literature exploring both ageing and masculinities as socially constructed. The chapter begins by highlighting the early, and arguably ongoing, ageism that characterised both men and masculinities and ageing studies and that rendered older men less visible. Identification of older men's absence was nonetheless the catalyst for further research about older men *as men* and greater theoretical engagement with age and gender relations, underpinning more complex conceptualisations of ageing masculinities. These developments are outlined, followed by consideration of the key arenas in which older men's identities have been empirically studied and examined. Particular attention is paid to representations of older men; their health and social and sexual relationships; and their geographies.

Troubling the invisibility of older men

In 2004, Emslie, Hunt and O'Brien provided an early overview of factors leading to the relative lack of engagement by social researchers with older men's gendered lives. Citing Thomson (1994), they highlight that the elderly population in general was treated by gerontologists as a homogenous group; that old age had become feminised and synonymous with women; and that socially constructed images of older men portrayed them as asexual and without gender. Notwithstanding the focused attention on the gendered lives and experiences of older women by gerontologists (Arber et al., 2003; Calasanti, 2004), men's studies, critically described as (young) men's studies by Calasanti and King (2005), also traditionally concentrated on younger and middle-aged men. According to them "studies of manhood neglect the old just as social gerontology avoids theorizing masculinity" (Calasanti & King, 2005, p. 3).

Prompted by the relative absence of older men as empirical subjects from both men's studies and gerontology, and by calls to better theorise gender and age relations, there have been efforts to reframe older men as subjects that have gender. This stimulated a more established theoretical and empirical literature considering diversity in older men's identities, experiences and roles; and the complex relationship between gender, ageing and other social locations and divisions. Parallel developments in theories of men and masculinities have also prompted advances in conceptualizations of ageing masculinities. Taken together, consideration of the relationships between both masculinities and ageing has enhanced the contributions of both masculinity theory and ageing studies.

Theorising ageing masculinities

Acknowledgement that older men have been absent from existing research about men and about elderly populations has coincided with, and contributed to, much greater theoretical sophistication about the gendered lives of older men and about conceptualisations of ageing masculinities. There is consensus across the literature about older men that their perceptions of both masculinity and ageing matter to them as they make sense of their evolving identities in later life. Indeed, older men's identities are subject to cultural norms of both ageing and masculinity, albeit in a context where cultural scripts for, and images of, older men are limited and limiting (Eman, 2009; Hurd Clarke, Bennett, & Liu, 2014; Spector-Mersel, 2006). Scholars therefore have examined how older men reconcile their increasing age with masculinity and negotiate societal expectations about both. This is a complex task, especially given that theoretically, both age and masculinity are understood to be plural, dynamic and socially constructed, signifying diversity in performances of ageing masculinities.

Connell's theory of multiple masculinities has remained powerful within explanations about how men make sense of their identities in later life, not least because her framework of gender relations emphasises the plurality of masculinities, gendered identities and practices over time, as well as the structural relations of power between them. These are reflected in a hierarchy of dominance, subordination and marginalisation (Connell, 1995).

As a central concept in Connell's hierarchy of masculinities, hegemonic masculinity has been prolific. It is frequently referred to and has directed much research about men and masculinities (Beasley, 2008), including about older men. Hegemonic masculinities represent culturally exalted ideals or exemplars of masculinity and male identity (Connell, 1995; Connell & Messerschmidt, 2005), although, as Calasanti (2004) argues, these are not achievable by many men or even necessarily representative. Indeed, hegemonic masculinities typically valorise and promote youth and youthfulness, suggesting that older men occupy a tenuous position to them (Bartholomeaus & Tarrant, 2016). Yet critique of the concept, by Connell and Messerschmidt (2005) and others, suggests that hegemonic masculinity should not be considered a fixed, transhistorical concept; instead, it is "constituted by an amalgam of practices, values and meanings and realised in particular places and contexts" (Hopkins & Noble, 2009, p. 813). Hegemonic masculinity has therefore been described as inadequate for capturing the complexities of ageing (Jackson, 2016).

Recognition that older men make sense of their identities in particular historical and social contexts is therefore important, not least because it draws attention to the ways in which patriarchal societies privilege older men relative to women (Jackson, 2016) but also because it reveals how cultural constructions and ideals about ageing shift and influence relationships between younger and older people as well. By way of example, in the consumer-driven culture characteristic of many Western societies, grey hair, as an early sign of ageing, may be interpreted as a sign of maturity and authority in men in ways that it is not for women (Twigg, 2004). As explored later in the chapter, however, loss of mobility, libido and/or income is less acceptable (Calasanti & King, 2005). While older men will always be seen as successful, particularly in relation to women, this is only the case if not compared directly to young and middle-aged men (Eman, 2009).

The above examples indicate the complex and often contradictory interplay of age and ageing with masculinities, and older men's paradoxical positioning within interrelations of sexism and ageism that simultaneously privilege and disadvantage them. On the one hand, recognition of these interlocking systems of (in)equality highlight the variety of ways old age can make men more dependent, particularly in societies where independence is valorised (Hearn, 2011). On the other, however, later life might also be offset by the accumulation of wealth and power across the lifecourse, especially financially. Such a position demonstrates that older men's relative ability to resist ageism is linked to the privilege of accumulating resources, as well as to class position. Ageing masculinities therefore coexist with and intersect with other social differences and divisions such as sexuality, race/ethnicity and class (Slevin & Linneman, 2009) and, as Hearn (2007, p. 74) argues, are "sources of gender power for some men at least and sources of relatively less power or lack of power for other men".

The following section considers some of these complexities with reference to a number of empirical studies that have focused on a range of social contexts and arenas in which men construct and make sense of their identities as part of the ageing process. Together, these literatures highlight that – regardless of declining health, physical and/or sexual power and financial independence – notions of appropriate maleness remain significant (Davidson, 2013). This increasingly diverse literature has examined a range of overlapping themes, issues and contexts, contributing to a body of knowledge about the gendered dynamics of later life for older men and about ageing as a gendered process. Broadly conceived, this includes, but is not limited to, representations of older men in consumer culture and linked concerns about older men's physical and mental health and support needs; their social relationships and sexual lives; and their experiences of and transitions through a range of social arenas and spaces.

Representations of older men, "successful ageing" and health

A central empirical focus upon which theorisations of ageing masculinities initially emerged focused on (limited) representations of older men within the consumer culture and the promotion of "successful ageing". Early work by Calasanti and King (2005) highlighted the inherently ageist mass-marketisation of "successful ageing" as it targets older men with money. According to them, the anti-ageing industry promotes ageist stereotypes in advertisements that portray idealised ageing masculinities, constructed in relation to positive traits such as affluence, competition, health and youthfulness. As Calasanti and King argue, while well-meaning in the portrayal of ageing in a positive light, the directive for older men to remain active is both ageist and largely ignorant of the realities of working-class life for older men. These findings are largely supported by more recent research by Hurd Clarke et al. (2014). Their study, based on an analysis of portrayals of older men in advertisements and interest stories in six North American magazines, indicates that where older men are present, they are predominantly represented as powerful and experienced, healthy and happy. For Hurd Clarke et al. (2014), these representations reinforce the notion that the only way to maintain an acceptable ageing masculinity is to forestall fragility and to remain compliant with the "ageing youth culture" of the Third Age (Higgs & McGowan, as cited by Hurd Clarke et al., 2014).

While ageist and cultural constructions that accompany ageing in Western societies are significant, the ageing of the physical body (and related health concerns) is nonetheless inevitable (Drummond, 2011). Accordingly, Milligan et al. (2013) have argued that the state of older men's health increasingly needs to be recognised as a distinct public health challenge. They suggest, for example, that the causes of ongoing rates of high mortality for men could be classified as either avoidable or treatable. Indeed, previous research explains that higher rates of mortality and morbidity in men are linked to high-risk behaviours that align with hegemonic masculinity (McVittie & Willock, 2006). Stereotypes about men also mean that they are expected to be independent, especially in the context of their health and health-seeking behaviour (Smith, Braunack-Mayer, Wittert, & Warin, 2007). Oliffe et al. (2013) have also developed the men's health literature by exploring when and why older men might experience depression. In particular, they highlight the relationship between depression and anticipated and actual transitions to retirement from employment. Their study found that approaching retirement can pre-empt men's estrangement from the masculine imperative to earn and can result in identity crises for some older men.

Suicide is also a growing and pertinent problem among this population, linked to a range of complex social factors including a lack of focused welfare services (e.g., Leigh-Hunt, Eaton, Ward, & Hollingworth, 2010; Ruxton, 2006), poor social capital, disengagement from wider social relationships later in life (Davidson, Daly, & Arber, 2003; Ruxton, 2006) and social isolation and depression. More recent work has examined how a more coordinated response from statutory services might be developed in order to respond to what is a complex array of factors that, in combination, make older men more vulnerable and absent them from accessing and receiving adequate support (Milligan, 2009; Milligan & Morbey, 2016). Milligan et al.'s (2013, p. 4) work on the Men in Sheds initiative is an exception that has expanded in recent years to aid in improving "men's physical, emotional, social and spiritual health and well-being".

Older men's social and sexual relationships

The Men in Shed's initiative just described is an intervention designed to address the notable problems of social isolation and loneliness experienced by older men. Such concerns are linked to the dominant notion that men are more likely to lack meaningful social relationships in later life. Indeed, much of the early research about older men as an empirical population has focused on their health and relationships in contexts of loss, bereavement and widowhood (Bennett, 2007; van Den Hoonard, 2007). This research has explicated the profound emotional impacts of bereavement on older men's sense of self and manhood (Smith et al., 2007), highlighting the strategies men employ to negotiate the challenging emotions of grief and loss while also trying to preserve and also reconstruct masculinity (Bennett, 2007). An even more recent focus on older men highlights the impacts of ageing without children, either on a voluntary or involuntary basis (Dykstra, 2009; Hadley, 2018). Until very recently, men's experiences of childlessness, linked to global population ageing and declining fertility, have also been overlooked. Yet, as Hadley's (2018) recent semi-autobiographical study of involuntary childlessness demonstrates, men employ a range of strategies to ensure their social connectedness later in life and in the context of otherwise non-normative childbearing trajectories. This includes forging non-biological relationships that he describes as "fictive grandfatherhood", premised on the performances of the grandfather-grandchild relationship with unrelated young people (Hadley, 2018).

The emphasis on men's disconnectedness from social relationships has in part contributed to wider assumptions that older men's social relationships are problematic. However, Sorensen and Poland (2016) have usefully employed photo elicitation to reveal the informal relationships older men enjoy and value when living alone. Their focus on the everyday social interactions of sixteen men aged over 75 provided key insights into the significance of their "fleeting encounters" with other people that they either regularly viewed from the safety of their homes or met with when out in the community. A growing and notable literature has also offered rich insights into men's caregiving practices and responsibilities later in the life-course. There are two main strands of research in this regard, including the roles and identities of grandfathers (Mann, Tarrant, & Leeson, 2016; Tarrant, 2016a, 2016b; Buchanan & Rotkirch, 2017) and men who become caregivers for their spouses (Milligan, 2009; Milligan & Morbey, 2016). This research has demonstrated how caregiving, viewed culturally as a feminised activity, impacts an older men's sense of self. As in other arenas of their later lives, men negotiate dominant masculine ideologies in relation to these roles. In research about grandfathers, the paradoxes and complexities of ageing as a man are apparent. While retired men in particular describe having more time to engage in practices of hands-on care for their grandchildren than they did for their own children when they were employed, they also describe the continuation of a gendered division of labour in which women are linked to domesticity and men to leisure time and activities (Scraton & Holland, 2006; Tarrant, 2012, 2013, 2016a, 2016b).

Recent research about later-life sexuality has also provided insights into older men's sexual relationships and intimacies, demonstrating the ways in which older men's sexuality is affected by ageing and highlighting tensions inherent in representations of their sexuality, where they are constructed as either sexually deviant or asexual. Linn Sandberg's research has made important contributions in this regard (Sandberg, 2013, 2016). Based on qualitative interviews with Swedish heterosexual men (aged 67–87) about their narratives of later-life sexuality, her work unpicks the ways in which older men emphasise their intimate lives and practices of intimacy, in order to retain a heterosexual orientation throughout the ageing process and to navigate binary discourses of "asexual old age" and "sexy seniors" (Sandberg, 2013; see also 2016). Similarly, in exploring older men's sexual desires, she problematises the narrow focus on men's sexual activities and declining function, examining instead how men make sense of the continuation of sexual desire in relation to traditional masculinity discourses and those of successful ageing (Sandberg, 2016).

Geographies of older men

Finally, emerging research is considering the key spaces in which older men construct, and confront, the ageing process and their identities. This has ranged from interests in men's loss of employment and associated social engagements in public life, to the intimate and private spaces of the body and the home. It is widely recognised that spaces of employment are key arenas in which men invest their identities as men throughout the lifecourse. Indeed, retirement and the segregation of older people, especially men, from public life was deemed in early research by sociological commentators to be the key problem of old age from a gendered perspective (Russell, 2007). Studies of retirement, including consideration of the ways in which men define their experiences as retired men, demonstrates how they renegotiate their identities using class-based masculinities during this particular life transition (also see Thomson & Barnes Langendoerfer, 2016 for review). As described earlier, for some older men, the anticipated and actual transition to retirement can provoke an identity crisis, accompanied by mental ill health such as depression, particularly where men rely solely on their work identity to uphold their masculine identity (Oliffe et al., 2013). Responses to retirement are also classed, meaning that the transition is likely to be less problematic for men engaged in industries where men have been able to accumulate wealth, retire with less debt and develop more transient views of culture (Drummond, 2011).

Social geographical research has also demonstrated tensions in the literature about men's retirement and leisure experiences. Research with older men in urban Mexico found that class-based masculinities can disadvantage older men in their retirement transitions (Varley & Blasco, 2000), making them feel "out of place" in the domestic arena, which has become associated with and constructed as the domain of their wives and female partners. However, older men may also benefit from distinct continuities in domestic gendered divisions of labour between grandmothers and grandfathers. Attention to older men's carescapes (Bowlby, McKie, Gregory, & MacPherson, 2011) has revealed how the paradoxical processes of sexism and ageism operate spatially. My own research about grandfathers, for example, demonstrates how the private spaces of grandfathering open up new opportunities for caring expressions of masculinity (Tarrant, 2013). In some public spaces such as the school playground, however, their ageing bodies and assumed heterosexuality are also viewed with caution.

The body also has significance, both to being a man (e.g., Connell, 1995) and to constructions and experiences of ageing. Strength and control over the male body, as well as success in maintaining well-being in old age, are valorised in contemporary Western societies and are representative of successful ageing. Yet, as Coles and Vassarotti (2012) argue, when men age, the body weakens and becomes more susceptible to injury and illness. This either advantages or disadvantages older men. Thus, researchers have examined how older men experience their bodies in relation to cultural discourses of ageing and masculinities. There are, however, specific arenas in which some men are able to maintain control over their physical prowess in later life. Phoenix's (2010) research about ageing bodybuilders found that they promoted their ability to maintain physical prowess via bodybuilding and the performances of "scripts" linked to Western hegemonic masculinity. This is supported by a small body of international literature exploring how older men draw on discourses relating to sports and athleticism in order to make sense of their changing identities (Agnew & Drummond, 2015; Eman, 2009; Wheaton, 2017).

Conclusions

This chapter has explored what continues to be a fertile conceptual and empirical terrain concerned with the complexities of older men's lives as gendered subjects. Focus on older men as empirical subjects has underpinned greater theoretical sophistication, advancing the fields of both ageing and masculinities, and has highlighted the various identities, practices, arenas and social circumstances in which men draw upon ideas and tropes about manhood in order to make sense of otherwise individualised processes of ageing. Indeed, the synthesis of this wider corpus of work lends weight to assertions that, just as we think about masculinities in the plural, we also need to consider the variety of life*courses* experienced by older men that produce ever increasingly diverse experiences of later life (e.g., Hearn, 2007). The synthesis of this body of work lends further weight to assertions that older men "do" gender in different ways and that old age and processes of ageing cause men to re-evaluate their attitudes towards gender and manhood (Emslie et al., 2004). Attention to the relationship between age, ageing and masculinities has also been significant in ensuring developments in masculinity theory. Masculinity studies is very much in need of age and ageing studies, not least because it facilitates analyses of the politics *within* masculinities (Roberts, 2018) and advocates a temporal, processual orientation towards understandings of them.

What is evident is that older men renegotiate new ideals linked to masculinity and ageing in a context where traditional imperatives and stereotypes remain remarkably durable. Qualitative social researchers are well placed, and have the opportunity to further examine, the complexities of processes of ageing for older men and to consider how older men as gendered subjects might be better supported in later life in a diverse range of contexts. The memory work book by Jeff Hearn and colleagues perhaps represents a new emergent phase in critical studies of men and masculinities (CSMM), whereby the first generation of masculinity scholars are starting to explore their own experiences of masculinities and ageing (Hearn et al., 2016). Another way forward is to shift focus away from Western societies. In 2003, Knodel and Ofstedal asked "where are the [older] men" in the developing world? Despite posing this important question so long ago, little research since has sought to address what is a clear evidence gap in knowledge about older men's lives in majority world contexts.

References

Agnew, D., & Drummond, M. J. (2015). Always a footballer? The reconstruction of masculine identity following retirement from elite Australian football. *Qualitative Research in Sport, Exercise and Health*, 7(1), 68–87.

Arber, S., Davidson, K., & Ginn, J. (2003). *Gender and ageing: Changing roles and relationships*. Maidenhead: Open University Press.

Bartholomeaus, C., & Tarrant, A. (2016). Masculinities at the margins of "middle adulthood": What a consideration of young age and old age offers masculinities theorizing. *Men and Masculinities*, *19*(4), 351–369.

Beasley, C. (2008). Re-thinking hegemonic masculinity in a globalising world. *Men and Masculinities*, *11*(1), 86–103.

Bennett, K. (2007). "No sissy stuff": Towards a theory of masculinity and emotional expression in older widowed men. *Journal of Aging Studies*, *21*(4), 347–356.

Bowlby, S., McKie, L., Gregory, D., & MacPherson, I. (2011). *Interdependency and care across the lifecourse*. Oxon: Routledge.

Buchanan, A., & Rotkirch, A. (2017). *Grandfathers: Global perspectives*. Basingstoke: Palgrave Macmillan.

Calasanti, T. (2004). Feminist gerontology and old men. *Journals of Gerontology, Series B: Social Sciences*, *59*(6), 305–314.

Calasanti, T., & King, N. (2005). Firming the floppy penis: Age, class and gender relations in the lives of old men. *Men and Masculinities*, *8*(1), 3–23.

Coles, T., & Vassarotti, T. (2012). Ageing and identity: Dilemmas for men. *Journal of Religion, Spirituality and Aging, 24*(1/2), 30–41.

Connell, R. (1995). *Masculinities*. Berkeley, CA: University of California Press.

Connell, R., & Messerschmidt, J. (2005). Hegemonic masculinity: Rethinking the concept. *Gender & Society, 19*(6), 829–859.

Davidson, K. (2013). Home alone: Exploring social networks of older divorced and never married men. In A. Tarrant & J. Watts (Eds.), *Studies of ageing masculinities: Still in their infancy?* (pp. 6–19). London: Open University Press.

Davidson, K., Daly, T., & Arber, S. (2003). Older men, social integration and organisation activities. *Social Policy and Society, 2*(2), 81–89.

Drummond, M. (2011). Age and ageing. In M. Flood, J. Kegan Gardiner, B. Pease & B. Pringle (Eds.), *International encyclopedia of men and masculinities* (pp. 10–13). Oxon: Routledge.

Dykstra, P. A. (2009). Childless old age. In P. Uhlenberg (Ed.), *International handbook of population ageing* (pp. 671–690). Houten: Springer.

Eman, J. (2009). Constructing successful old-age masculinities amongst athletes. *NORMA: Nordic Journal for Masculinity Studies, 6*(1), 46–58.

Emslie, C., Hunt, K., O'Brien, R. (2004). Masculinities in older men: A qualitative study in the west of Scotland. *The Journal of Men's Studies, 12*(3), 207–226.

Hadley, R. A. (2018). "I'm missing out and I think I have something to give": Experiences of older involuntarily childless men. *Working with Older People, 22*(2), 83–92.

Hearn, J. (2007). From older men to boys: Masculinity theory and the life course(s). *NORMA: Nordic Journal for Masculinity Studies, 2*(2), 79–84.

Hearn, J. (2011). Neglected intersectionalities in studying men: Age/ing, virtuality, transnationality. In M. T. Herrera Vivar & H. Lutz (Eds.), *Framing intersectionality: Debates on a multi-faceted concept in gender studies* (pp. 89–104). Farnham: Ashgate.

Hearn, J., Barber, R., Blake, V., Jackson, D., Johnson, R., Luczynski, Z., & McEwan, D. (2016). *Men's stories for a change: Ageing men remember*. Champaign, IL: Common Ground.

Hopkins, P., & Noble, G. (2009). Masculinities in place: Situated identities, relations and intersectionality. *Social & Cultural Geography, 10*(8), 811–819.

Hurd Clarke, L., Bennett, E. V., & Liu, C. (2014). Aging and masculinity: Portrayals in men's magazines. *Journal of Ageing Studies, 31*, 26–33.

Jackson, D. (2016). *Exploring aging masculinities: The body, sexuality and social lives*. Basingstoke: Palgrave Macmillan.

Knodel, J., & Ofstedal, M-B. (2003). Gender and aging in the developing world: Where are the men?. *Population and Development Review, 29*(4), 677–698.

Leigh-Hunt, N., Eaton, V., Ward, C., Hollingworth, L., & Womack, J. (2010). *Audit of suicides & undetermined deaths in Leeds 2008–2010*. Leeds: Leeds City Council, NHS Airedale, Bradford & Leeds.

Mann, R., Tarrant, A., & Leeson, G. (2016). Grandfatherhood: Shifting masculinities in later life. *Sociology, 50*(3), 594–610.

McVittie, C., & Willock, J. (2006). "You can't fight windmills": How older men do health, ill health and masculinities. *Qualitative Health Research, 16*(6), 788–801.

Milligan, C. (2009). *There's no place like home: Place and care in an ageing society*. Farnham: Ashgate.

Milligan, C., Dowrick, C., Payne, S., Hanratty, B., Neary, D., Irwin, P., & Richardson, D. (2013). *Men's sheds and other gendered interventions for older men: Improving health and wellbeing through social activity: A systematic review and scoping of the evidence base*. Lancaster: Lancaster University Centre for Ageing Research.

Milligan, C., & Morbey, H. (2016). Care, coping and identity: Older men's experiences of spousal caregiving. *Journal of Aging Studies, 38*, 105–114.

Oliffe, J. L., Rasmussen, B., Bottorff, J. L., Kelly, M. T., Galdas, P. M., Phinney, A., & Ogrodniczuk, J. S. (2013). Masculinities, work and retirement among older men who experience depression. *Qualitative Health Research, 21*(12), 1626–1637.

Phoenix, C. (2010). Autophotography in aging studies: Exploring issues of identity construction in mature bodybuilders. *Journal of Aging Studies, 24*(3), 167–180.

Roberts, S. (2018). Domestic labour, masculinity and social change: Insights from working-class young men's transitions to adulthood. *Journal of Gender Studies, 27*(3), 274–287.

Russell, C. (2007). What do older men and women want: Gender differences in the "lived experiences" of ageing. *Current Sociology, 55*(2), 173–192.

Ruxton, S. (2006). *Working with older men: A review of age concern services*. London: Age Concern England.

Sandberg, L. (2013). Just feeling a naked man close to you: Men, sexuality and intimacy in later life. *Sexualities, 16*(3/4), 261–282.

Sandberg, L. (2016). In lust we trust? Masculinity and sexual desire in later life. *Men and Masculinities, 19*(2), 192–208.

Scraton, S., & Holland, S. (2006). Grandfatherhood and leisure. *Leisure Studies, 25*(2), 233–250.

Slevin, K. F., & Linneman, T. J. (2009). Old gay men's bodies and masculinities. *Men and Masculinities, 12*(4), 483–507.

Smith, J. A., Braunack-Mayer, A., Wittert, G., & Warin, M. (2007). "I've been independent for so damn long!": Independence, masculinity and aging in a help seeking context. *Journal of Aging Studies, 21*, 325–335.

Sorensen, P., & Poland, F. (2016). Positioning older men's social interactions: A visual exploration of the space between acquaintanceship and strangerhood. *Families, Relationships and Societies, 4*(3), 503–512.

Spector-Mersel, G. (2006). Never-ending stories: Western hegemonic masculinity scripts. *Journal of Gender Studies, 15*(1), 67–82.

Tarrant, A. (2012). Grandfathering: The construction of new identities and masculinities. In S. Arber & V. Timonen (Eds.), *Contemporary grandparenting: Changing family relationships in global contexts* (pp. 200–221). Bristol: Policy Press.

Tarrant, A. (2013). Grandfathering as spatio-temporal practice: Conceptualizing performances of ageing masculinities in contemporary familial carescapes. *Social and Cultural Geography, 14*(2), 192–210.

Tarrant, A. (2016a). Domestic ageing masculinities and grandfathering. In A. Gorman-Murray & P. Hopkins (Eds.), *Masculinities and place* (pp. 241–254). London: Ashgate.

Tarrant, A. (2016b). The spatial and gendered politics of displaying family: Exploring material cultures in grandfathers' homes. *Gender, Place and Culture, 23*(7), 969–982.

Thomson, E. H., Jr. (1994). Older men as invisible men in contemporary society. In E. H. Thomson (Ed.), *Older men's lives* (pp. 1–21). Thousand Oaks, CA: Sage.

Thomson, E. H., Jr. (2006). Images of old men's masculinity: Still a man? *Sex Roles, 55*(9/10), 633–648.

Thomson, E. H., Jr., & Barnes Langendoerfer, K. (2016). Older men's blueprint for "being a man". *Men and Masculinities, 19*(2), 119–147.

Twigg, J. (2004). The body, gender, and age: Feminist insights in social gerontology. *Journal of Aging Studies, 18*(1), 59–73.

van Den Hoonard, D. (2007). Aging and masculinity: A topic whose time has come. *Journal of Aging Studies, 21*, 277–280.

Varley, A., & Blasco, M. (2000). Exiled to the home: Masculinity and ageing in urban Mexico. In C. Jackson (Ed.), *Men at work: Labour, masculinities, development* (pp. 115–138). London: Routledge.

Wheaton, B. (2017). Surfing through the life-course: Silver surfers' negotiation of ageing. *Annals of Leisure Research, 10*(1), 96–116.

19

Men, masculinities and social class

Michael R. M. Ward

Introduction

In the late 20th and early 21st centuries there have been massive societal shifts in economic and gender relations, which I would argue are tied to processes of de-industrialization and neoliberal governance (Adkins, 2000; Nayak, 2006; Ward, 2015; Weis, 2004). These shifts have resulted in fragmented rites of passage for men, which have led to arguments that men are suffering an apparent "crisis of masculinity" (Faludi, 1999) or that there is currently a "war" on men raging (Tarrant et al., 2015). This "crisis" thesis has attracted criticism from some gender scholars, and, furthermore, there are arguments that this current "crisis" has a much older legacy (see Connell, 1995; Roberts, 2012). Yet, despite these contrasting arguments, what is clear is that radical social change has occurred which impacts negatively on some groups of men more so than others (McDowell, 2012; Ward et al., 2017) and that this is a global problem (Edström, Hassink, Shahrokh & Stern, 2015; Kulkarni & Jain, 2019).

Within this changing global context, studies of men and masculinities, particularly in the northern hemisphere, have had to negotiate a highly charged context of backlash politics, which has shaped a particular agenda around gender. A central feature in this "crisis" discourse is the "loss of essential masculinity" or "loss of manhood," which has led to theorists expressing concern that some scholars are using a rhetoric of loss to justify, rather than explain, certain identity practices (Bridges & Pascoe, 2014; Gilbert & Gilbert, 1998). In fact, the rhetoric of "masculinities in crisis" has been fiercely refuted with a call for more criticality regarding how "modern masculinities operate, how they are expressed and performed and what consequences follow as a corollary" (Roberts, 2013, p. 3).

Within critical studies of men and masculinities, there exists historic and significant work seeking to answer questions regarding the relationship between theories of masculinities and theories of social class. Indeed, Morgan (2005, p. 166) asks researchers of masculinity:

> If, as the class and gender debates suggested, class had been fairly strongly linked to themes of men and masculinity, were there links between changes in the gender order and changes in the position of class within the analysis of social structures?

Researchers from a range of discipline backgrounds have capitalized on a plethora of theories and approaches to understand how masculinities are constructed and experienced in reference to social class. This chapter explores the recent scholarship on the intersection of masculinity and social class to understand the theoretical underpinnings of, as well as illustrate how scholars have used, various theories together to elicit new understandings.

In discussing how identities are experienced and lived, Prins (2006, p. 278) contends that "gender is always lived in the modalities of ethnicity and class, nationality in the modalities of gender and race, and class in the modalities of gender and nationality." This intersectional thinking remains a fascinating provocation, and, to this end, I argue that we should move beyond understanding classed masculinities as what Morgan (2005) has labelled either the "masculinities of class" or "the class of masculinity." To accomplish this, I do not seek to present an exhaustive analysis of the role of social class in masculinity studies. Instead, I first define the broad trends shaping both masculinity studies and class studies. The chapter then focuses on where the intersection between class and masculinity has been most salient, specifically in research on working-class masculinities. Following this, I highlight the work of geographers of masculinity who have drawn significant attention to how local contexts shape classed masculinities. The chapter concludes with tentative arguments regarding how classed masculine subjectivities are constructed through values and meanings and how these meanings are intertwined with specific geographical contexts and lived experiences. In addition, I draw attention to significant gaps in the study of classed masculine subjectivities and suggest new directions.

Theories of masculinities and social class

Researchers theorizing masculinities work within a field where there exists "a range of language, terminology and typologies of different types of masculinities and the particular qualities or attributes associated with these" (Gorman-Murray & Hopkins, 2014, pp. 5–6). For the most part, masculinity scholars agree that masculinities are socially constructed, highly relational, and deeply contextual. According to Gilbert and Gilbert (1998, p. 46):

> Becoming a man is a matter of constructing oneself in and being constructed by the available ways of being male in a particular society. It is a matter of negotiating the various discourses of femininity and masculinity available in our culture, those powerful sets of meaning and practices which we must draw on to participate in our culture and to establish who we are.

Masculine identities are, in this sense, actively constructed and developed in everyday actions and practices within institutions such as families, sports, schools, and employment (Connell, 1995). Despite the different perspectives and theoretical frameworks adopted in contemporary masculinity studies (e.g., hegemonic, inclusive masculinity theory (IMT), post-humanism and affect theory, post-structural, Foucauldian, Bourdieusian, etc.), each perspective holds social power as significant in the formation of masculine identities (Connell & Messerschmidt, 2005). For scholars in critical studies of masculinities, gender is both a conscious and unconscious performance, part of a project towards understanding one's identity individually and in relation to the identities of others as "social practice" (West & Zimmerman, 1987). Aboim (2010) argues for the plurality of masculinities, drawing our attention to the plurality of power relations – how gender intersects with other forms of power and is constituted out of interaction between structure and agents.

For the purposes of this discussion (and despite the multiple theoretical perspectives adopted in men and masculinities studies), it should be stressed that masculinity is never conceptualized as fixed; instead, masculinity is flexible (being formed and reformed over time) and constantly being influenced, in relation to what Gorman-Murray and Hopkins (2014, p. 6) call the "broader social order." In terms of gender theory, masculinities, like femininities, are tied to the meanings that society has made in political, economic, and cultural terms.

Theorizing social class in a similar way has also come to be seen and deployed from a variety of perspectives. While largely utilized to understand social differences and practices in society, it remains grounded within a Marxist capitalist framework which largely associates class with employment and exploitation. Marxism historically, with its attention to proletariat suffering, was a common structuralist theoretical framework for exploring resistant and rebellious working-class males, though it continues to face criticisms for being too focused on economic factors and reductionist (Hall & Jefferson, 1975). As interest in Marxist and Weberian readings of class declined in the post war period, the last half of the 20th century saw a shift towards quantitative and positivist methodologies to explore class (Goldthorpe, 1996). These approaches, which primarily concerned the development and testing of class schemas, mainly defined class in terms of employment. This was followed by work on rational-choice models and the study of intra-class differences (Goldthorpe, 1998). However, more recent scholarship on class theory adopts a broader stance, incorporating a wide range of identity practices strongly influenced by Bourdieusian concepts, specifically in regards to symbolic domination and the internalization of class (Bourdieu, 1984). This shift led to a deeper theorizing of class as a matter of unequal recognition, respectability, pathologization, and exploitation alongside the unequal distribution of economic resources (Reay, 2005; Savage, 2015). Social class is not merely economic; it is, rather, a part of our lifestyle composition, being continuously created and maintained (Skeggs, 2004). As Reay (2017, p. 6) puts it when reflecting on the class landscape of her own working-class childhood in the 1950s and 60s, "class and the many images that surrounded it were routinely used to place ourselves and others, not just in relation to the labour market, but socially." Discussions concerning social class bring about feelings of self-worth as well as "injustice and moral evaluation" (Sayer, 2002, Section 1.4); or, as Bottero (2009) asserts, social class is "always about invidious comparison, and when people talk about 'class' their accounts often shift easily from social description, to social evaluation, to social abuse" (p. 10).

Therefore, social class today is theorized not simply as an individual's access to financial, cultural, and social resources but also in terms of how those resources or capital are valued by others (and created through processes of classification and judgement) (see Skeggs, 2004). Theories of class as cultural and individualized arguably revised older Marxist conceptions of class as collective and oppositional; furthermore, these new theories embraced intersectional axes of difference such as gender, ethnicity, disability, and sexuality. Understanding these recent developments in theories of social class is important for scholars of masculinities because, as Gorman-Murray and Hopkins (2014, p. 6) argue, "masculinities are continuously reconstructed in and through these social and material relations." While the Marxist framework is still useful, especially in exploring class stratification as associated with late industrial and capitalist societies, current theories of class compel us to consider class as lived experience, tied closely to status and distinction. Arguably, this potentially opens up new avenues of exploration for how classed masculinities are constructed and practised.

Thus far, this chapter has highlighted the main approaches researchers have taken when theorizing how masculinities and classed identities are constructed and experienced. To understand the theoretical junctures of both domains, I now focus on working-class masculinities, where the operationalization of these theories has arguably been most salient in critical masculinity studies.

Scholarship on working-class masculinities

Many of the early masculinity scholars discussed class and its intersections with masculinity (e.g., Connell, 1987; Hearn, 1987). Both Connell and Hearn saw men as a "gender class" and argued that power differences existed between groups of men which were to some extent understood as class-based. However, when it comes to working-class masculinities, other work, which was born out of radical youth cultural studies in the UK during the 1970s, has become more synonymous with the field. The seminal ethnographic work of Willis's (1977), *Learning to Labour: How Working-Class Kids Get Working-Class Jobs*, highlighted working-class young men as agentic, active in their resistance to formal schooling but still tied to a life of industrial work. While gender theory is largely non-existent in Willis's work, the central thesis of the ethnography is that it is primarily the working-class "lad" culture which contributes to and reaffirms their disengagement from education. Reflecting back to his research, Willis (2004, p. 173) persuasively argues that

> Through the mediations of the counterschool culture, 'the lads' of *Learning to Labor*, for instance, *penetrate* the individualism and meritocracy of the school with a group logic that shows that certification and testing will never shift the whole working-class, only inflate the currency of qualifications and legitimize middle-class privilege.

Through the lad culture, the socially validated aspects of masculinity (physicality/practicality, toughness, collectivism, territoriality/exclusion, hedonism and opposition to authority) function as the primary influence on the young men's "meaning-making," "positions" and "relationships" (Willis, 2004, p. 170). In sociological studies of masculinity, while Willis has become highly influential, there has arguably been an overemphasis on working-class masculinities (Delamont, 2000), and some male authors have been accused of almost worshipping behaviors associated with hypermasculinity (see Ingram, 2009; Skeggs, 1992; Ward, 2015 for a critique). At the same time, more recent research, such as that conducted by Shows and Gerstel (2009), shows different fathering practices between professional and working-class models of masculinity. This suggests that, in many cases, working-class men are more inclined to be "undoing gender" and subverting oppressively traditional gender roles by "participating in the daily routines of 'private fatherhood'" where upper middle-class fathers perform only "public fatherhood" by attending children's events and contributing financially (Shows & Gerstel, 2009, p. 162).

Given the seminal work of Willis, more recent research on working-class masculinities has concentrated on how masculinities are realized when working-class occupations are no longer available (Kenway, Kraak & Hickey-Moody, 2006; Nayak, 2003; Ward, 2015; Winlow, 2001). Undeniably in post-industrial times, the historic infrastructures of respectable employment, which have functioned as traditional bases of white male power, "have eroded rapidly" (Weis, 1990, p. 6). Working-class men today are required to negotiate their identities in the transition from boyhood to manhood around rapidly changing economic structures and discourses of aspiration (Ingram, 2018; Ward, 2015; Winlow, 2001). For example, in place of respectable working-class employment, we have seen the steady rise of service-level positions, which require working-class men to "learn to serve" (McDowell, 2003) in the low-paid, low-skilled "McJob" industry (Bottero, 2009, p. 9).

Kenway and Kraack (2004, p. 107) claim that the "crisis of masculinity" is felt more harshly by the working-class male whose "reproduction of working-class masculinity has been ruptured" and who, to varying degrees, may find it more difficult to adapt. In terms of adaptation, Macleod (2009) found different ethnic learner identities responded differently to a changing economic climate and conceptions of the American Dream. For MacLeod the African-American "brothers" in his ethnographic study on youth culture conducted in a US inner city did not consider meritocracy to be a myth, and, as a result, the young men he spoke to often blamed themselves when they did not achieve academically. This contrasts greatly from his other cohort, the (mostly) white "Hallway Hangers," who located their failure in the complex amalgam of agency and unequal societal structures. Similarly, in the UK, Nayak (2006) also illustrates how post-industrial challenges impact on young men and shows how a group of white working-class males were poorly equipped to adapt to the reality of post-industrialism and its dramatic changes.

These post-industrial challenges also appear to impact on young and educated, but unemployed, men, in the northern Indian city of Meerut. Jeffrey (2010) describes a sense of being left behind and spending days merely "passing time" that also, paradoxically, appears to be a "means through which young men could build youthful solidarities, sometimes across caste and class boundaries" (p. 465). In considering the ways in which these researchers of class and masculinity approach the study of how masculinities are experienced and constructed in various contexts globally, it is clear that the significance of post-industrialism, specifically how masculinity is constructed in relation to education and the labour market, cannot be overlooked. More importantly, how is this framed by the efforts of men to preserve traditional identity practices in the face of economic uncertainty? Furthermore, we also see how young men search for new forms of respectability and authenticity (Dolby, Dimitriadis & Willis, 2004; McDowell, 2003; Ward, 2015).

Compared to historic scholarship on working-class boys (Humphries, 1981; Willis, 1977), researchers today have used theory to show how working-class masculinities are fragmented and complex (Jeffrey & McDowell, 2004; Kenway, Kraak & Hickey-Moody, 2006; McDowell, 2012; Ward, 2015). However, what remains persistent, *despite* or *because of* rapid economic change and globalization, is the peer group as the primary site for identity construction and where a certain dominant form of masculinity is displayed and policed (Clarke, Hall, Jefferson & Roberts, 1975; Frosh, Phoenix & Pattman, 2002; Hall, 1975; Jeffrey, 2010; Kehily & Nayak, 1997). It has been documented that working-class males often draw on certain historically validated dispositions, such as social cohesion and social solidarity (through a legacy of union action and community involvement), to confirm their gendered, classed, and ethnic subjectivities inside and outside of schooling (Mac an Ghaill, 1994; Pye, Haywood & Mac an Ghaill, 1996; Stenning, 2005; Ward, 2015). This focus on solidarity and communal involvement also encompasses what Gerstel (2011) notes to be the greater value and reliance placed on extended family ties among working class people, including men, because "helping others with practical matters and receiving help from them is a *class-based* strategy for survival" (p. 5). However, in contrast, recent arguments have drawn attention to how working-class masculinities may be influenced by more recent theories of social class beyond the financial, cultural, and social resources (Roberts, 2012).

While contemporary scholarship of working-class masculinities has seen the influence of more recent theories of social class as linked to respectability and pathologization (Ward, 2015), there is still significant attention to the importance of employment – or lack thereof.

Lately we have seen a budding interest in scholarly work focused on the relationship between masculinities and neoliberalism (Cornwall, Karioris & Lindisfarne, 2016; Kulkarni & Jain, 2019; Walker & Roberts, 2017). Embedded in neoliberalism are the tenets of competition and risk that require agents to perform their individuality to become successful. Neoliberalism attempts to erase issues of social identities, instead positioning agents as equal players where they "come to understand themselves as responsible for the production of a self" (Burke, 2007, p. 414). However, while neoliberalism works to erase intersectional identity categories, employment – and aspirations toward employment – remains a fundamentally gendered process. Regardless of socio-economic status, cultural background, or country of origin, the role of the masculine "breadwinner" continues to have tremendous salience for the identity construction of young men entering adulthood (McDowell, 2003; Ward et al., 2017). I suggest that the historic study of working-class males and post-industrialization is essential to understanding how theory has been operationalized in exploring the intersection between masculinities and classed identities. Broadening the scope beyond the class stratification associated with industrial and capitalist societies that has heavily influenced studies of working-class masculinities, I now focus on new place-based approaches to theorizing classed masculinities, or geographies of masculinities, which demonstrate the various ways in which class and masculinity are realized in specific contexts.

Geographies of masculinity: the importance of place in theories of masculinities and social class

The interconnectedness of place, classed identities, and masculinities remains a significant aspect of critical studies on men and masculinities (McDowell, 2003; Morris, 2012; Ward, 2015). Despite the onset of globalization, there still arguably exist "acceptable" and "unacceptable" forms of masculinities tied to specific contexts and locales. This aligns with the ways in which social class is constructed in reference to place, where, as Dowling (2009) summarizes, class is "a theorization that needs to be context-specific" (p. 835). Since the early 2000s, there has been a steady increase in research about geographies of masculinities contributing significantly to understanding how theory is operationalized to understand the intersection between social class and masculinities (Berg & Longhurst, 2003; van Hoven & Hörschelmann, 2005). A key focus of this scholarship has been on understanding:

> the ways in which gender relations change over time and how younger men may no longer be able to fit quite so comfortably into categories of understanding that are now somewhat dated given their contemporary experiences of gender relations.
>
> *(Gorman-Murray & Hopkins, 2014, p. 3)*

This "uncomfortability" with(in) gendered categories tied to place and space is important, directly linking back to wider questions concerning the fragmentation of gendered and classed identities (Roberts, 2013).

In geographies of masculinity, scholarship addresses "the spatial dimensions of masculinity" (Hopkins & Noble, 2009, p. 812) as well as the spatial conceptualizations of masculinities (Gorman-Murray & Hopkins, 2014; van Hoven & Hörschelmann, 2005; Nayak, 2006; Ward et al., 2017). Within studies examining the intersection of class and masculinity, the shift toward geographies of masculinities explores how specific spaces shape the very nature of the experience of masculinity and, furthermore, how it potentially articulates "other key dimensions of social relations" (Hopkins & Noble, 2009, p. 814). For example, van Hoven and Hopkins contend (2009, p. 492) that place and masculinities speak at different levels from the local (work, home, and leisure) to the global (nationhood, legal, and cultural contexts). Understandably, a key focus of the masculinity and place scholarship has been on how young men simultaneously construct and contest their masculine identities. Nayak (2006) demonstrates how masculinities are influenced by space, where identities could be "'toned down' or 'played up' according to time, place and context" (p. 821). While the men who practise these masculinities may feel strong affiliations for their immediate locales, increasingly they are not tied to these places and – through forms of technology and social media – they are exposed to a wider variety of masculinity practices. Archer and Yamashita's (2003) study of inner-city masculinities in London demonstrated how boys' dialogues "combined globalized and localized discourses that cross-cut ethnic and national groupings" (p. 120). Masculinity researchers must therefore be reflexive, paying close attention to both embodied and local habits and cultures as well as the global flows in order to establish nuanced analyses. It is clear that contemporary structures of class are increasingly moving away from the means of production at the local level and becoming much more global than ever before.

Conclusion

In this chapter, I have highlighted both the historic trends and current state of the field regarding studies of men, masculinities, and social class. While theories of masculinities and theories of class shift, this chapter has emphasized how the socially constructed and highly relational nature of the formation of masculinities persists, specifically in how masculinities are constructed and experienced in reference to social class. Looking across the last half century, we see how men – as well as their performance of masculinities – have responded to change, where men construct their identities in relation to their conceptions of risk and insecurity. This risk could be in terms of employment but also can stem from other areas.

In reviewing international scholarship, which explores how masculinities are constructed and experienced in reference to social class, I have noted a persistent phenomenon in research on masculinity and social class, which is how men often find ways to distance themselves from class. Men, typically males from working-class backgrounds, often claim that they see people and society in general as open and equal, as opposed to shaped by disparate inequalities (Ingram, 2018; Macleod, 2009).

As we attempt to move beyond understanding classed masculinities as either what Morgan (2005) has labelled the "masculinities of class" or "the class of masculinity," there appears to be a significant lack of substantial research on masculinities in middle-class and elite settings. I would argue that a deeper analysis concerning how theories of masculinities and theories of social class can be combined would entail broadening the scope of the research to include men from all social backgrounds in order to understand how power works across class and how masculinities are realized across class. There needs to be more critical scholarship exploring masculinities and mobilities, whether in terms of upward/downward social mobility or moving across regions or nation-states for employment purposes (Kulkarni & Jain, 2019).

References

Aboim, S. (2010). *Plural masculinities*. Farnham: Ashgate.

Adkins, L. (2000). Objects of innovation: Post-occupational reflexivity and re-traditionalisations of gender. In S. Ahmed, J. Kilby, C. Lury, M. McNeil, & B. Skeggs (Eds.), *Transformations: Thinking through feminism* (pp. 259–273). London: Routledge.

Archer, L., & H. Yamashita. (2003). Theorising inner-city masculinities: "Race," class, gender and education. *Gender and Education, 15*(2), 115–132.

Berg, L. D., & R. Longhurst. (2003). Placing masculinities and geography. *Gender, Place and Culture, 10*(4), 351–360.

Bottero, W. (2009). Class in the 21st century. In K. P. Sveinsson (Eds.), *Who cares about the white working class?* (pp. 7–15). London: Runnymede Trust.

Bourdieu, P. (1984). *Distinction: A social critique of the judgement of taste.* Oxon: Routledge.

Bridges, T., & C. J. Pascoe. (2014). Hybrid masculinities: New directions in the sociology of men and masculinities. *Sociology Compass, 8*(3), 246–258.

Burke, P. (2007). Men accessing education: Masculinities, identifications and widening participation. *British Journal of Sociology of Education, 28*(4), 411–424.

Clarke, J., S. Hall, T. Jefferson, & B. Roberts. (1975). Subcultures, cultures and class. In S. Hall & T. Jefferson (Eds.), *Resistance through rituals* (pp. 1–79). London: Hutchinson & Co.

Connell, R. (1987). *Gender and power: Society, the person, and sexual politics.* Stanford, CA: Stanford University Press.

Connell, R. (1995). *Masculinities.* Cambridge: Polity.

Connell, R., & J. W. Messerschmidt. (2005). Hegemonic masculinity: Rethinking the concept. *Gender & Society, 19*(6), 829–859.

Cornwall, A., F. Karioris, & N. Lindisfarne. (2016). *Masculinities under neoliberalism.* London: Zed Books.

Delamont, S. (2000). The anomalous beasts: Hooligans and the sociology of education. *Sociology, 34*(1), 95–111.

Dolby, N., G. Dimitriadis, & P. Willis. (Eds). (2004). *Learning to labor in new times.* New York & London: RoutledgeFalmer.

Dowling, R. (2009). Geographies of identity: Landscapes of class. *Progress in Human Geography, 33*(6), 833–839.

Edström, J., A. Hassink, T. Shahrokh, & E. Stern (Eds). (2015). *Engendering men: A collaborative review of evidence on men and boys in social change and gender equality.* EMERGE evidence review Promundo-US & Sonke Gender Justice & the Institute of Development Studies (IDS). Retrieved on April 10, 2018 from http://promundoglobal.org/resources/engendering-men-evidence-review/.

Faludi, S. (1999). *Stiffed: The betrayal of the American man.* New York: Perennial.

Frosh, S., A. Phoenix, & R. Pattman. (2002). *Young masculinities.* New York: Palgrave Macmillan.

Gerstel, N. (2011). Rethinking families and community: The colour, class, and centrality of extended kin ties. *Sociological Forum, 26*(1), 1–20.

Gilbert, R., & P. Gilbert. (1998). *Masculinity goes to school.* London: Routledge.

Goldthorpe, J. H. (1996). Class analysis and the reorientation of class theory: The case of persisting differentials in educational attainment. *The British Journal of Sociology, 47*(3), 481–505.

Goldthorpe, J. H. (1998). Rational action theory for sociology. *The British Journal of Sociology, 49* (2), 167–192.

Gorman-Murray, A., & P. Hopkins. (2014). Introduction: Masculinities and place. In A. Gorman-Murray, and P. Hopkins (Eds.), *Masculinities and place* (pp. 1–24). London: Ashgate.

Hall, S. & Jefferson, T. (Eds). (1975). *Resistance through rituals: Youth subcultures in post-war Britain.* London: Routledge.

Hearn, J. (1987). *Gender of oppression: Men, masculinity and the critique of Marxism.* New York: St Martin's Press.

Hopkins, P., & G. Noble. (2009). Masculinities in place: Situated identities, relations and intersectionality. *Social & Cultural Geography, 10*(8), 811–819.

Humphries, S. (1981). *Hooligans or rebels? An oral history of working-class childhood and youth 1889–1939.* Oxford: Basil Blackwell.

Ingram, N. (2009). Working-class boys, educational success and the misrecognition of working class culture. *British Journal of Sociology of Education, 30*(4), 421–434.

Ingram, N. (2018). *Working-class boys and educational success: Teenage identities, masculinities and urban schooling.* Basingstoke: Palgrave Macmillan.

Jeffrey, C. (2010). Timepass: Youth, class, and time among unemployed young men in India. *American Ethnologist, 37*(3), 465–481.

Jeffrey, C., & L. McDowell. (2004). Youth in a comparative perspective: Global change, local lives. *Youth & Society, 36*(2), 131–142.

Kehily, M. J., & A. Nayak. (1997). "Lads and laughter": Humour and the production of heterosexual hierarchies. *Gender and Education, 9*(1), 69–88.

Kenway, J., & A. Kraack. (2004). Reordering work and destabilizing masculinity. In N. Dolby, G. Dimitriadis, & P. Willis (Eds.), *Learning to labor in new times* (pp. 95–109). New York: RoutledgeFalmer.

Kenway, J., A. Kraak, & A. Hickey-Moody. (2006). *Masculinity beyond the metropolis*. Basingstoke: Palgrave Macmillan.

Kulkarni, M., & R. Jain. (Eds.). (2019). *Global masculinities: Interrogations and reconstructions*. Oxon: Routledge.

Mac an Ghaill, M. (1994). *The making of men: Masculinities, sexualities and schooling*. Buckingham: Open University Press.

Macleod, J. (2009). *Ain't no makin' it: Aspirations and attainment in a low-income neighborhood*. Boulder, CO: Westview Press.

McDowell, L. (2003). *Redundant masculinities? Employment change and white working class youth*. Malden, MA: Blackwell.

McDowell, L. (2012). Post-crisis, post-ford and post-gender? Youth identities in an era of austerity. *Journal of Youth Studies, 15*(5), 573–590.

Morgan, D. (2005). Class and masculinity. In M. Kimmel, J. Hearn, & R. W. Connell (Eds.), *Handbook of studies on men & masculinities* (pp. 165–177). Thousand Oaks, CA: Sage.

Morris, E. (2012). *Learning the hard way: Masculinity, place, and the gender gap in education*. New Brunswick, NJ: Rutgers University Press.

Nayak, A. (2003). *Race, place and globalization: Youth cultures in a changing world*. Oxford: Berg.

Nayak, A. (2006). Displaced masculinities: Chavs, youth and class in the post-industrial city. *Sociology, 40*(5), 813–831.

Prins, B. (2006). Narrative accounts of origins: A blind spot in the intersectional approach? *European Journal of Women's Studies, 13*(3), 277–290.

Pye, D., C. Haywood, & M. Mac an Ghaill. (1996). The training state, de-industrialisation and the production of white working-class trainee identities. *International Studies in Sociology of Education, 6*(2), 133–146.

Reay, D. (2005). Beyond consciousness? The psychic landscape of social class. *Sociology, 39*(5), 911–928.

Reay, D. (2017). *Miseducation, inequality, education and the working classes*. Bristol: Policy.

Roberts, S. (2012). Boys will be boys. Won't they? Change and continuities in contemporary young working-class masculinities. *Sociology, 47*(4), 671–686.

Roberts, S. (Eds.). (2013). *Debating modern masculinities: Change, continuity, crisis?* London: Palgrave Pivot.

Savage, M. (2015). *Social class in the 21st century*. London: Penguin.

Sayer, A. (2002). What are you worth? Why class is an embarrassing subject. *Sociological Research Online, 7*(3), 1–17.

Shows, C., & N. Gerstel. (2009). Fathering, class, and gender. *Gender & Society, 23*(2), 161–187.

Skeggs, B. (1992). Paul Willis, *Learning to Labour*. In M. Barker & A. Beezer (Eds.), *Reading into cultural studies* (pp. 181–196). London: Routledge.

Skeggs, B. (2004). *Class, self, culture*. London: Routledge.

Stenning, A. (2005). Where is the post-socialist working class? Working-class lives in the spaces of (post-) socialism. *Sociology, 39*(5), 983–999.

Tarrant, A., G. Terry, M. R. M. Ward, S. Ruxton, M. Robb, & B. Featherstone. (2015). Are male role models really the solution? Interrogating the "war on boys" through the lens of the "male role model" discourse. *Boyhood Studies, 8*(1), 60–83.

van Hoven, B., & P. Hopkins. (2009). Masculinities. In R. Kitchin & N. Thrift (Eds.), *International encyclopedia of human geography* (pp. 492–495). Oxford: Elsevier.

van Hoven, B., & K. Hörschelmann. (2005). Introduction: From geographies of men to geographies of women and back again. In B. van Hoven & K. Hörschelmann (Eds.), *Spaces of masculinities* (pp. 1–16). London: Routledge.

Walker, C., & S. Roberts. (Eds.). (2017). *Masculinity, labour and neoliberalism: Working class men in international perspective*. London: Palgrave Macmillan.

Ward, M. R. M. (2015). *From labouring to learning: Working-class masculinities, education and de-industrialization*. Basingstoke: Palgrave Macmillan.

Ward, M. R. M., A. Tarrant, G. Terry, M. Robb, B. Featherstone, & S. Ruxton. (2017). Doing gender locally: The importance of "place" in understanding young men's masculinities in the male role model debate. *Sociological Review, 65*(4), 797–815.

Weis, L. (1990). *Working class without work*. New York: Routledge.

Weis, L. (2004). Revisiting a 1980s "moment of critique": Class, gender and the new economy. In N. Dolby, G. Dimitriadis, & P. Willis (Eds.), *Learning to labor in new times* (pp. 111–132). New York: RoutledgeFalmer.

West, C., & D. Zimmerman. (1987). Doing gender. *Gender & Society, 1*(2), 125–151.

Willis, P. (1977). *Learning to labour: How working class kids get working class jobs*. New York: Columbia University Press.

Willis, P. (2004). Twenty-five years on: Old book, new times. In N. Dolby, G. Dimitriadis, & P. Willis (Eds.), *Learning to labor in new times* (pp. 167–196). New York: RoutledgeFalmer.

Winlow, S. (2001). *Badfellas: Crime, tradition and new masculinities*. Oxford: Berg.

Part 3
Sex and sexualities

20

The transformation of homosociality

Nils Hammarén and Thomas Johansson

Introduction

The concept of *homosociality* describes social bonds between persons of the same sex. It is often used in studies on men and masculinities, there defined as a mechanism and social dynamic that explains the maintenance of hegemonic masculinity and how men, through their friendships and intimate collaborations with other men, maintain and defend the gender order and patriarchy (Bird, 1996; Lipman-Blumen, 1976). However, this common and somewhat overexploited use of the concept tends to simplify and reduce homosociality to an almost descriptive term that is used to show how men bond and defend their privileges. In this chapter, we aim to explore, unpack and re-define the concept of homosociality, especially male homosocial relations. We explore different aspects of homosociality and analyse how these characteristics relate to each other. We are especially interested in developing and emphasizing the contradictory aspects of the concept, pointing both towards a defence of hegemonic masculinity and towards a silent and slow process that might undermine or reconstruct this power structure (Buschmeyer & Lengensdorf, 2016).

Historically, same-sex friendships between men, and manly love, was allowed and sometimes also celebrated. In the late nineteenth century, a distinction between heterosexual and homosexual relationships was drawn, making male intimacy and friendship more complicated (Nardi, 1992). A complex, refined and dynamic view on homosociality is found in Eve Kosofsky Sedgwick's classic study *Between Men* (1985). Instead of using the concept merely as a tool to analyse social bonds and power relations between men, Sedgwick discusses the historically changing relation between different types of desire and intimate relationships between men.

Sedgwick develops an interesting and useful theory of gender and masculinity. Her main thesis is that a continuous relation is radically disrupted and gradually turned into a discontinuous relation of male homosocial and homosexual bonds, whereas there is a much more continuous relation between female homosocial and homosexual bonds. The discontinuity between male homosociality and homosexuality results in male homosocial relationships being a form of "male bonding", which is characterized by homosocial desire and intimacy, as well as homosexual panic. Homosocial desire refers to men turning their attention to other men, and homosexual panic refers to the fear of this attention gliding over into homosexual desire. In an attempt to emphasize heterosexuality, fear or hatred of homosexuals and misogynist language are developed.

In many ways, Sedgwick has set the agenda for studies on homosociality. At least three different types of readings and interpretations of the concept have evolved. We will discuss these understandings in what follows. *First*, as pointed out above, the concept is often used to analyse how men, through their relationships and social bonds with other men, construct power blocs and protect male territory and privilege. *Second*, there is a whole body of literature that pursues queer readings of homosociality and explores the underlying continuum of desires and relations. *Finally*, there is a growing body of literature on female homosociality that presents a somewhat different picture of the phenomenon in question. This literature connects in part to Sedgwick's arguments, but there are also some significant developments, for example the questioning of Sedgwick's thesis on the asymmetry between male and female homosociality.

Hegemonic homosociality

There is a massive body of literature on the homosocial ordering of men's relations (Bird, 1996; Flood, 2008; Hamrén, 2007; Lindgren, 1996; Mac an Ghaill, 1994; Messner, 2001). In this category of research, we have a number of classic studies, for example Paul Willis' study *Learning to Labour* (1977) about a group of working-class boys (the lads) who, in their informal group, make not behaving well, that is, not behaving according to middle-class ideology, the honourable thing to do. In his classic study of how young men are socialized into masculinity, Willis shows how contempt for the other (e.g., young women, "geeks" and immigrants) helps to keep the group together. The teenage working-class boys' revolt involves not only a struggle against the predominant culture at the school but also development of a fragile feeling of superiority.

Another example of and angle on these male-to-male relationships can be found in Michael Flood's (2008) article on how bonds between young men also shape their relationships with women and form their sexual attitudes and behaviour. In his interviews with young men aged eighteen to twenty-six at a military university, there were many examples of how friendship between men builds on and involves fantasies and experiences of having sex with women, as well as sharing memories of collective sexual harassments and sexual encounters. Women become a kind of currency men use to improve their ranking on the masculine social scale. According to Flood, homosociality refers first and foremost to nonsexual and same-sex bonds, involving quite high degrees of homophobia. However, Flood concludes, it is also possible to read and understand this externalized homophobia as a sign of underlying homoerotic desires.

Another much-discussed issue in relation to homosociality is the proposed lack of intimacy in men's friendship relations. Homosociality is often seen as being based on and formed through competition and exclusion. Recent research has put forward another and more complex image of masculinity and friendship. In an article exploring the "stag night", the premarital ritual involving a man who is soon to be married and his friends celebrating the coming wedding, there is evidence of certain changes in men's relationships. Thurnell-Read (2012) conducted participant observations with eight separate stag-tour groups. The observations confirmed a picture of male participants actively working to maintain and develop their friendship bonds. These groups of men were striving for group cohesion, togetherness and intimacy rather than interpersonal competition and the creation of male hierarchies. Even though this phenomenon can be seen as a part of a kind of *hegemonic homosociality*, that is, a societally legitimized and normalized homosociality, there are also traces of changes and re-definitions of masculinity.

Although there is a growing body of literature that brings forward more nuanced images of masculinity, thus stretching and extending the concept of homosociality in order to investigate potential changes in or redefinitions of hegemonic masculinity (Anderson, 2008, 2009), there is also an extensive body of work that reproduces the image of homosociality as a mechanism that supports and reinforces rather stereotypic images of masculinity (Bird, 1996; Gilmartin, 2007; Kiesling, 2005; Snyder, 2007).

Homoeroticism and homosociality

In November 1994, the *metrosexual* male was identified and described by the cultural critic Mark Simpson (Coad, 2008). This market segment consisted of young, urban, white, middle-class men – consumers and young narcissistic men preoccupied with looks, style and image. In the 1990s, these men and this phenomenon indicated a crisis in masculinity, a closer relationship between homo and hetero men and a general movement towards a new masculinity.

However, views on and interpretations of this phenomenon vary. Shugart (2008) argues that metrosexual masculinity defines and casts homosociality as a kind of universal male solidarity. Instead of pointing towards a new masculinity, and a more sensitive and inclusive masculinity (Anderson, 2008), metrosexuality reorganized homosociality in order to define homosexual men as different from both women and heterosexual men. According to Shugart (2008), the main result of this movement is a highly commercialized masculinity and a strengthening of normative masculinity.

To understand and position the whole discussion of a new masculinity, and the potential erasure of the boundaries between heterosexuality and homosexuality, we have to return to Sedgwick. Her definition of homosociality is characterized by a triangular structure, in which men have bonds with other men and women serve as the conduits through which these bonds are expressed. However, this triangle may portray as rivalry what is actually an attraction between men. The argument and the idea that there is an underlying continuum between different kinds of male homosocial desires draw out a potential arena for research on the fragile boundaries and lines between different masculinities and hetero-/homosexuality.

Henning Bech's (1997) ideas fit into this way of approaching homosociality. He identifies something he calls *absent homosexuality*. He writes: "The mode of being of absent homosexuality can only be comprehended in its relation to the other pole in the modern form of male-male eroticism, i.e. the homosexuals, in its simultaneous connection to and demarcation from them" (p. 84). He describes absent homosexuality as a ghost-like character, present but absent, desired and denied, known and unknown. Using examples from the cinema, Bech uncovers the hidden narratives of homosexual desire (cf. Ward, 2015). This idea of an absent homosexuality that structures society and men's lifestyles and desires has certain similarities with Judith Butler's idea of melancholia and identity. In *The Psychic Life of Power* (1997), Butler argues that heterosexuality naturalizes itself by insisting on the Otherness of homosexuality. Then heterosexual identity is based on a melancholic incorporation of the love that it disavows. According to Butler, the man who "insists upon the coherence of his heterosexuality will claim that he never loved another man, and hence never lost another man" (p. 139).

The idea of a homoerotic continuum has inspired several cultural analyses. What is often found is a blurred boundary and distinction between homosociality and homoeroticism. There is a complex and dynamic relationship between, for example, legitimate culture and underground print culture. Janes (2012) studied a leading British educational magazine for children (1962–1982) and found queer subtexts and a manifold of expressions of homoerotic desire in these magazines. Janes argues that it is not surprising to find a homoerotic space in writings produced by men for boys. The interplay between homophobia and close homosocial and homoerotic bonds between men created in fiction, but also in schools and in the military, can be seen as evidence for the thesis of a continuum of desires. Cultural analysis shows how fragile and anxiety-ridden the indistinctness that marks homosociality is, and it points towards the continuous boundary work being done to uphold and defend the heterosexual order (Brady, 2012). Thus, even though we have an underlying stream of homosocial desire, there are also constant attempts to suppress and rein in these streams in the heterosexual and normative order (Halberstam, 2002).

The gender continuum and female homosociality

The suggested continuum between female friendship, feminist solidarity and same-sex desire has great support in the literature. But there is also a growing critique of this way of approaching female homosociality. Sedgwick put forward a thesis on the asymmetry between male and female homosociality. She argues that male homosociality is first and foremost fashioned through the exchange of women and the consolidation of men's power in society, whereas for women this sharp cleavage between homosociality and homosexuality is not that distinct, clear and stable. According to Binhammer (2006), this is a somewhat idyllic and perhaps even naive image of women's relationships. She argues that women in many ways circulate in and are permeated by the same capitalist economy and system as men are. Women's bonds are created not outside the dominant sexual economy but as a part of it. Women's relationships are therefore not by definition and automatically a challenge to hegemonic masculinity.

Henriette Gunkel (2009) discusses and analyses the *mummy-baby* relationship in South African schools. Briefly, this is a culturally specific form of female same-sex intimacy, although similar forms are found in, for example, British boarding schools. An older girl at the school helps the newcomers, the younger girls, and provides them with emotional support. Sometimes this relationship develops into sexual encounters and relationships. Although this is taking place in a highly policed and homophobic environment, this particular form of relationship seems to exist alongside the sexuality apparatus, and seems to be accepted. The point here is that homosociality needs to be theorized and understood in different ways depending on the national and socio-cultural context.

In contrast to this study of accepted but highly policed sexual relations between women, Griffin (2000) argues that all young women in the West have to deal with the accusation of being a lesbian. This accusation also affects all women, albeit in different ways and with different effects. Griffin calls for research that is open to aspects of female friendship that are coloured and permeated by desire, fantasies and a passion for same-sex relationships. This type of friendship is immediately drawn into the naturalized model of compulsory heterosexual relationships and the pressure of "getting a man". According to Hammarén (2008), concepts of love and intimacy are feminized. In his study on identity constructions among young men in multicultural suburbs, female intimate relationships are understood as expressions of friendship and heterosexuality. Young women who kiss, hold hands and hug each other are considered not lesbians but, rather, women involved in normalized feminine heterosexual behaviour. Lesbians are therefore made invisible and are ignored. According to a heteronormative order and male gaze, women's intimate relations are understood as friendship or a sexual display aimed at heterosexual men.

There is clearly a lack of research exploring female friendships as something other than desexualized relationships. Therefore, sexual minority women's relations are not explored and researched (Arseneau & Fassinger, 2006). There is also a paucity of literature on friendships between black and white women, for example (Granger, 2002), or cross-racial friendships in general. There is obviously a need to study and problematize the idea of a continuous relation between female homosocial and homosexual bonds and friendships e.g., Marcus, 2007). The whole idea of a sharp contrast between how this works in a male versus a female spectrum of desire and relations seem to be the result of a polarized view on gender and identity (Johansson, 2007).

Towards a theory of homosociality

We will now introduce the distinction between *vertical/hierarchical* and *horizontal homosociality*. Hierarchical homosociality is similar to and has already been described as a means of strengthening power and of creating close homosocial bonds in order to maintain and defend hegemony. Although this description is primarily used to talk about men's friendships and exchange of means and valuable cultural and social capital, it is also possible to frame and investigate women's relationships using this concept. We will not argue that this concept and the idea of a vertical and hierarchical homosociality are totally gender neutral. Horizontal homosociality is similar to what was earlier described as female homosociality. This concept is used to point towards relationships between, for example, men – relationships that are based on emotional closeness, intimacy and a non-profitable form of friendship. There are, clearly, no absolute boundaries between these two approaches to homosociality. Aspects of hierarchical homosociality in horizontal relations and vice versa might be present, but making a distinction between them and discussing them separately makes it easier to analyse different aspects of the concept and highlight different implications. As discussions of vertical homosociality are more common in the literature, we will now turn our attention towards horizontal homosociality.

In popular culture, the concepts of *bromance* (which combines the words *brother* and *romance*) and *womance* (combining *woman* and *romance*) have been introduced, discussed and debated. Dave Carnie is credited with coining the term as editor of the skateboard magazine *Big Brother* in the 1990s to refer to relationships that develop between skaters who spent a great deal of time together (DeAngelis, 2014). Bromance and womance refer to close and intimate non-sexual and homosocial relationships between two (or more) men or women. Womance is similar to the above-mentioned concept of female homosociality; bromance, however, differs from traditional understandings of male homosocial relations and does not necessarily fit within the construct of masculinity found in some masculinity theories focusing on competition and hierarchies. Bromance emphasizes love, exclusive friendship and intimacy that are not premised on competition and the often described "shoulder-to-shoulder" friendship, e.g., watching football, playing golf or training for a marathon together. Bromances provide a space for intimate male friendship (Chen, 2012), even though studies also show that male friendships might include utilitarian aspects – desire, rivalry and self-interest – pointing towards a less idealized picture and in contrast to bromance (Bray, 2003).

According to Chen (2012), bromances comprise three general constitutive elements: they are restricted to men; they are asexual; and they are locations for intimacy, love and affection between men. They are also described as a complicated love and affection shared by *straight* males. The "bro" aspect of bromance may perhaps emphasize heteronormativity, as well as homophobia, indicating that it is not gay because it is between men. The focus on heterosexual men, however, seems to differ. Bromances or homosocial relationships between gay men or between a straight man and a gay man are quite rare but do exist (Nardi, 2001). Bromances imply intimacy that slips between the boundaries of sexual and non-sexual relationships.

Today we can witness men having close and intimate relationships with their friends, not least as represented in media and films (Chen, 2012). Examples of *womances* in popular culture seem to be more exceptional, although the film *Thelma and Louise* (1991) is sometimes said to be one. The terms "bromance" and "womance" are often used to refer to two heterosexual partners, although there have been celebrity male gay–straight bromances (also called homomances or hobromances). We are not suggesting that bromances and womances are similar. The popular concept of bromance, unlike the concept of womance, is perhaps a reflection of the different values assigned to male and female friendships. Additionally, while *Thelma and Louise*, for example, is about fighting misogyny and male abuse, many bromances are about how men make highly enjoyable friendships and focus on each other. Consequently, there would seem to be an underlying power relation between the concepts.

Intersected power relations

In constructions of homosocial relations, some differences between people are marked and some may be obscured. For example, the assertion of gender may overlook sexualities, age, "race" or local differences. Often the literature on homosociality has a quite one-dimensional focus. Theories of the intersections between sexuality, class, ethnicity, age and gender are seldom used to elaborate critical perspectives on these issues (Collins, 1998; McCall, 2005; Mohanty, 1998; Tayler, Hines & Casey, 2010). These social and cultural categories influence the individual at the same time and constitute flexible and often complex processes of belongings and power relations. For example, being male, heterosexual, middle class and of the majority ethnic population can be considered as occupying a hegemonic position, in contrast to being a female, working-class lesbian (Connell, 1995). However, these positions are very much contextual and situated, resulting in complex and sometimes ambiguous social relationships. Consequently, an intersectional approach involves locating individuals within these dynamics and examining how people become subjected to a plurality of changing variables.

Oware (2011), doing research on homosociality and black masculinity in rap music, claims, like several other scholars, that hip hop and especially gangsta rap music reflects a stereotypical black masculine aesthetic. Yet, unpacking the idea of hegemonic black masculinity, Oware claims that there are also progressive ways that male rappers express themselves towards friends and loved ones. Specifically discussing homosocial relations among black male rappers, Oware points out that, since prior research on hip hop has documented the harmful aspects of black masculinity, the potentially empowering, vulnerable, emotional and caring homosocial interactions between black male rappers he found in his research have been overlooked. Because many black males are marginalized in American society, they face a different relationship to hegemonic masculinity. "[B]lack masculinity, in general, must be understood to parallel *and* transgress hegemonic masculinity" (Oware, 2011, p. 33).

Homosocial relations are often described in relation to white men, heterosexuality and shared activities, such as games, playing musical instruments, watching movies, sport activities and drinking (Messner, 2001). However, relating to intersectionality, homosociality does not necessarily imply, for example, either heterosexuality or homosexuality, and these relations might also entail emotional sharing. While the concept of homosociality (and bromance) has often been applied to relations between straight men, mixed gay–straight or gay–gay non-sexual relationships between men *or* women could just as well be defined as homosocial (Nardi, 2001).

Bromances are said to maintain heteronormative hierarchies, as only heterosexuals can have a bromance (Chen, 2012). This particular boundary reflects the phenomenon of "straight panic", in which individuals experience anxiety about how others perceive their sexuality and thus feel a need to confirm their heterosexuality. However, because men in bromances are often identified in society as heterosexuals, they can have intimate friendships without risking being misperceived as gay. At the same time, bromances are a source of subordination, encouraging men to stay within rigid boundaries of sexuality norms. Bromances are also described as restraining the pool of intimate friends men can have: gay men are excluded, and consequently the culture reinforces homophobia and subordination of the gay community (Chen, 2012).

Yet friendships between gay men and the development of networks and neighbourhoods legitimize alternative forms of masculinity, thereby challenging hegemonic masculinities. In his study on the politics of friendship in the gay social movement, Nardi (2001) claims that gay friendships have the potential to produce communities, reinforce gay identity and effect socio-political change on a larger scale. The gay community helps members find meaning and dignity in a society that is trying to impose a hegemonic male order. The friendships between gay men serve to create a sense of belonging and thus help sustain a sense of "gay identity". Obviously, gay men do not automatically pose a challenge to male hegemony. They do not necessarily resist notions that, for example, men are superior to and should dominate women. However, they may undermine traditional aspects of hegemonic masculinity in that heteronormativity is questioned and homosexuality is made visible (Mills, 2001).

Even though Chen (2012) characterizes bromances as maintaining heteronormativity, she claim that bromances are a starting point for deconstructing homophobia and represent a queering of heterosexual male friendship. Consequently, they open up space for men to experience intimacy outside the heterosexual pairings, which may also lead to a dismantling of compulsory heterosexuality. Furthermore, and contrary to Chen, situating bromances in mixed gay–straight or gay–gay intimate non-sexual relationships might deconstruct homophobia and contest heterosexist norms even more (Rumens, 2011, 2012).

Conclusions

There is a clear and growing body of literature that brings forward more nuanced images of masculinity, thus stretching and extending the concept of homosociality in order to investigate possible reconstructions of hegemonic masculinity (Anderson, 2008, 2009). The overall picture from the research, however, promotes the notion that homosociality clearly is a part and extension of hegemony, thus serving to always reconstruct and safeguard male interests and power. However, changes in masculinity – for example, the construction of horizontal homosociality, in which emotional closeness, intimacy and a non-profitable form of friendship are developed – are not necessarily a sign of a strengthening of patriarchy, as many discussions on hegemonic masculinity suggest. In accordance with a post-structuralist reading, questioning certain categories, definitions and ways of approaching gender, power and power relations, our proposal is that we not predetermine the agents of change and instead remain open to the possibility of discovering potential movements towards a redefined hegemony that contains the seeds of utopian visions of the gender order (Kimmel, Hearn & Connell, 2005; Whitehead, 2002).

To some degree, the discussion in this chapter has contributed to such a break. We have both implicitly tried to raise the question of whether all hegemonies are equally bad and more explicitly tried to discern how different masculinities correspond to and underpin different ways of articulating hegemonic masculinity. One way of reading this chapter is also to understand it as pointing towards how elements historically related to women are articulated with masculinity as well. As the gender order slowly changes and loosens up, thus re-articulating hegemony, homosociality may take other forms, and friendships may not only relate to same-sex relations but also to heterosocial forms of friendship and intimate non-sexual relations (Karioris, 2016; Rumens, 2011, 2012). Consequently, sexual orientation would not be the basic principle for friendship, and rigid boundaries between friendships and romantic relationships would not be necessary (Chen, 2012). Of course, we acknowledge that articulating intimacy and emotional closeness with masculinity may not lead to a complete disruption of masculinity. It might, however, point to a potential reconfiguration of hegemonic masculinity that is not a priori and necessarily privileged in relation to femininity. Finally, situating homosociality in an intersectional framework develops, emphasizes and makes visible the inconsistent and ambiguous aspects of homosociality, focusing not only on straight men but also on women and different sexual positions and "races". Using this approach further allows us to point toward a defence of a post-structural framing of hegemonic masculinity by referring to vertical/hierarchical homosociality and toward a potential and slow process of rearticulating hegemony by referring to horizontal homosociality.

References

Anderson, E. (2008). Inclusive masculinity in a fraternal setting. *Men and Masculinities*, *10*(5), 604–620.

Anderson, E. (2009). *Inclusive masculinities: The changing nature of masculinity*. London: Routledge.

Arseneau, J. R., & R. E. Fassinger. (2006). Challenge and promise. The study of bisexual women's friendships. *Journal of Bisexuality*, *6*(3), 69–90.

Bech, H. (1997). *When men meet: Homosexuality and modernity*. Cambridge: Polity.

Binhammer, K. (2006). Female homosociality and the exchange of men: Mary Robinson's Walsingham. *Women's Studies*, *35*(3), 221–240.

Bird, S. R. (1996). Welcome to the men's club: Homosociality and the maintenance of hegemonic masculinity. *Gender & Society*, *10*(2), 120–132.

Brady, A. (2012). The transgendered Kiwi: Homosocial desire and 'New Zealand identity'. *Sexualities*, *15*(3/4), 355–372.

Bray, A. (2003). *The friend*. Chicago, IL: University of Chicago Press.

Buschmeyer, A., & D. Lengensdorf. (2016). The differentiation of masculinity as a challenge for the concept of hegemonic masculinity. *NORMA: International Journal for Masculinity Studies*, *11*(3), 190–207.

Butler, J. (1997). *The psychic life of power*. Stanford, CA: Stanford University Press.

Chen, E. J. (2012). Caught in a bad bromance. *Texas Journal of Women and the Law*, *21*(2), 241–266.

Coad, D. (2008). *The metrosexual: Gender, sexuality, and sport*. Albany, NY: State University of New York Press.

Collins, P. H. (1998). It's all in the family: Intersections of gender, race and nation. *Hypatia*, *13*(3), 62–82.

Connell, R. (1995). *Masculinities*. Cambridge: Polity.

DeAngelis, M. (Ed.). (2014). *Reading the bromance: Homosocial relationships in film and television*. Detroit, MI: Wayne State University Press.

Flood, M. (2008). Men, sex, and homosociality: How bonds between men shape their sexual relations with women. *Men and Masculinities, 10*(3), 339–359.
Gilmartin, S. K. (2007). Crafting heterosexual masculine identities on campus. *Men and Masculinities, 9*(4), 530–539.
Granger, D. (2002). Friendship between black and white women. *American Behavioural Scientist, 45*(8), 1208–1213.
Griffin, C. (2000). Absence that matter: Constructions of sexuality in studies of young women's friendship. *Feminism & Psychology, 10*(2), 227–245.
Gunkel, H. (2009). "What's identity got to do with it?": Rethinking intimacy and homosociality in contemporary South Africa. *NORA: Nordic Journal of Feminist and Gender Research, 17*(3), 206–221.
Halberstam, J. (2002). The good, the bad, and the ugly: Men, women, and masculinity. In Kegan Gardiner, J. (Ed.), *Masculinity studies and feminist theory: New directions* (344–367). New York: Columbia University Press.
Hammarén, N. (2008). *Förorten i huvudet: Unga män om kön och sexualitet i det nya Sverige*. Stockholm: Atlas.
Hamrén, R. (2007). *Vi är bara några kompisar som träffas ibland: Rotary som en manlig arena (Doctoral dissertation)*. Linköping: Linköping University.
Janes, D. (2012). Homosociality and homoeroticism in the leading British educational magazine for children, *Look and Learn* (1962–1982). *Continuum: Journal of Media and Cultural Studies, 26*(6), 897–910.
Johansson, T. (2007). *The transformation of sexuality: Gender and identity in contemporary youth culture*. Farnham: Ashgate.
Karioris, F. G. (2016). *Between class and friendship: Homosociality in an all-male residence hall in the US* (Doctoral dissertation). Budapest: Central European University.
Kiesling, S. F. (2005). Homosocial desire in men's talk: Balancing and re-creating cultural discourses of masculinity. *Language & Society, 34*(5), 695–726.
Kimmel, M. S., J. Hearn, & R. W. Connell. (Eds.). (2005). *Handbook of studies on men & masculinities*. London: Sage.
Lindgren, G. (1996). Broderskapets logik. *Kvinnovetenskaplig Tidskrift, 17*(1), 4–14.
Lipman-Blumen, J. (1976). Toward a homosocial theory of sex roles: An explanation of the sex segregation of social institutions. *Signs, 1*(3), 15–31.
Mac an Ghaill, M. (1994). *The making of men: Masculinities, sexualities and schooling*. Buckingham: Open University Press.
Marcus, S. (2007). *Between women: Friendship, desire, and marriage in Victorian England*. Princeton, NJ: Princeton University Press.
McCall, L. (2005). The complexity of intersectionality. *Signs, 30*(3), 1771–1800.
Messner, M. (2001). Friendship, intimacy and sexuality. In Whitehead, S. M. & F. J. Barrett (Eds.), *The masculinities reader* (253–265). Cambridge: Polity.
Mills, M. (2001). *Challenging violence in schools: An issue of masculinities*. Buckingham & Philadelphia: Open University Press.
Mohanty, C. T. (1998). Under western eyes: Feminist scholarship and colonial discourses. *Feminist Review, 30*, 61–88.
Nardi, P. M. (1992). "Seamless souls": An introduction to men's friendships. In Nardi, P. M. (Ed.), *Men's friendship* (pp. 1–14). London: Sage.
Nardi, P. M. (2001). "A vicarious sense of belonging": The politics of friendship and gay social movements, communities and neighbourhoods. In Whitehead, S. M. & F. J. Barrett (Eds.), *The masculinities reader* (288–306). Cambridge: Polity.
Oware, M. (2011). Brotherly love: Homosociality and black masculinity in gangsta rap music. *Journal of African American Studies, 15*(1), 22–39.
Rumens, N. (2011). *Queer company: The role and meaning of friendship in gay men's work lives*. Farnham: Ashgate.
Rumens, N. (2012). Queering cross-sex friendships: An analysis of gay and bisexual men's workplace friendships with heterosexual women. *Human Relations, 65*(8), 955–978.
Sedgwick, E. K. (1985). *Between men: English literature and homosocial desire*. New York: Columbia University Press.
Shugart, H. (2008). Managing masculinities: The metrosexual moment. *Communication and Critical/Cultural Studies, 5*(3), 280–300.

Snyder, M. (2007). Crisis of masculinity: Homosocial desire and homosexual panic in the critical cold war narratives of Mailer and Coover. *Critique: Studies in Contemporary Fiction, 48*(3), 250–277.

Tayler, Y., S. Hines, & M. E. Casey. (Eds.). (2010). *Theorizing intersectionality and sexuality.* London: Palgrave MacMillan.

Thurnell-Read, T. (2012). What happens on tour: The premarital stag tour, homosocial bonding, and male friendship. *Men and Masculinities, 15*(3), 249–270.

Ward, J. (2015). *Not gay: Sex between straight white men.* New York: New York University Press.

Whitehead, S. M. (2002). *Men and masculinities.* Cambridge: Polity.

Willis, P. (1977). *Learning to labour: How working-class kids get working class jobs.* London: Saxon House.

21
Masculinity and homoeroticism

Gareth Longstaff

Introduction

The relationship between men, masculinities and homoeroticism has emerged through tensions that circulate around cultural norms, hegemonic power relations, socio-political structures and, perhaps most potently, how desire between men is articulated, represented and embodied. If sexual desire is concerned with the eroticisation of sexual meaning and not sexual personhood, then homoeroticism potentially underpins *all* male-to-male relations because it relies on the construction and manifestation of desire through a powerful alliance of homo *and* heterosexuality. In this way, homoerotic desire can be differentiated from homosexual and heterosexual "sexuality" or the act of sex between men, because it is formed through an irregular distribution of homosocial, homosexual and, perhaps most problematically, homophobic ties. Here these paradoxical connections which weave the social, sexual and phobic desires of men together inform and invigorate the homoerotic. The aim of this chapter is to explore how these issues operate via a compound of discursive, theoretical and cultural ideas. In turn, it will also examine how the construction of homoerotic desire through a range of romantic, narcissistic and effeminate practices demands re-evaluation and reconceptualization in a range of contemporary settings. These include neo-liberal and consumer-defined society, pornography, social media and non-Western contexts.

Homoeroticism needs to be understood as a shifting discursive construct that has the potential to negotiate and negate socio-sexual restrictions that exist between men so that an "underlying continuum between different kinds of male homosocial desires open up [...] the fragile boundaries and lines between different masculinities and hetero/homosexuality" (Hammarén & Johansson, 2014, p. 4). This mixture of desires suggests that the indistinct nodes between heterosexuality, homosexuality, homosociality and homophobia are the foundation of homoeroticism, yet, as Alan Sinfield (1994) suggests, "social codes and signals [always] feed back into psychic realities; [therefore] we should [always] expect a complex interaction between representation and desire" (p. 46).

An incongruent and divergent series of identifications between men may move contemporary studies of masculinity and sexuality towards a way of renovating how "heterosexual homo-eroticism" and "homosexual homo-eroticism" might be expressed. If, as Richard Dyer suggests "Homoeroticism tends to stress libidinal attraction without sexual expression" (2002, p. 3), it has the capacity to yield "a higher affectivity" (p. 4), which points towards homosocial relations between men as more open, fluid and queer. Yet the homosocial always has the capacity to trigger the homoerotic, so that these affective modes of attraction and intimacy operate both as a way of "accommodating libidinal attraction between men, by giving it expression while simultaneously limiting and containing it" (p. 4). This may be the setting where the protocols and ethics previously associated with men identifying as either gay or straight are unpacked and renegotiated to energise a field of erotics where homo and hetero masculinity are destabilised by an erotics of *all* masculine desire that precedes male sex and masculine sexuality per se. In this setting, new ways to express and acknowledge homoerotic desire might make it possible to undo and reassemble normative structures allied to the regulated performativity of cisgender masculinity and sexuality.

Discourses and theories of homoeroticism

The construction of homoeroticism and its relationship to masculinity has emerged through an amalgamation of discursive, ideological, visual and cultural frameworks. The development of homoeroticism links with the construction of homosexuality and Michel Foucault's assertion that the homosexual as "a personage, a past, a case history, and a childhood" (1998, p. 43) develops during the nineteenth century via a repressively perverse and homophobic apparatus of "psychiatry, jurisprudence, and literature" (p. 101). Nevertheless, at the same time there also emerged a "reverse discourse" that allowed homosexuality to "speak in [on] its own behalf [...] often in the same vocabulary, using the same categories by which it was medically disqualified" (Foucault, 1998, p. 101). Furthermore, Foucault's intervention recognises how sexualised discourses shift and are transformed over time. Similar to the cultural construction of homosexuality, the production of homoeroticism has both positioned and problematised its meaning and interpretation *as* "homoeroticism". These tensions form "contradictory discourses within the same strategy [...] implanted in bodies" (p. 102) or an "analytical visible, and permanent reality" (p. 44). In this way, homoeroticism functions through simultaneously visible *and* invisible, dominant *and* subordinate layers of discourse, with features that remain both comprehensible and mysterious.

If we think of homoeroticism and the rhetoric of images and texts that have been produced around it, we see that it is forcefully related to a combination of homosexual and heterosexual masculinity. Here a central ambiguity forms in relation to homosexuality which suggests that the heterosexual and heteronormative discourses responsible for the oppression of homosexuals simultaneously cultivate the conditions for homo/gay desire. In turn, these go some way to underpinning the construction and emergence of homoeroticism as a discourse that relies upon the abstruse formation and exchange of heterosexual *and* homosexual desires, affinities and emotional bonds. Along these lines, some of the epistemologies often allied to homoeroticism rely upon distinctly heterosexist and/or hyper masculine tropes, the social control of masculinity and, in some cases, how the crossing-points of discrimination and desire inform the politics of homoeroticism between men.

Jonathan Katz (1996) suggests that by using Foucault and understanding these tensions we need to re-engage with heterosexuality and "focus [...] on the ways eroticism is produced, now and in the past, noting how social-sexual systems control individuals and populations" (p. 171). In this way heterosexuality as both a term and a concept reinforces a "sexed eroticism as specifically 'heterosexual' within a specifically 'heterosexual' society"

(p. 181), thus forcing the construction of homosexuality to take the strain of its own sexual desire because "heterosexuality *just is*" (p. 181). Lee Edelman's suggestion that the homosexual male "is distinctively and *legibly* marked" (1994, p. 7), working on the basis of "a determining relationship to textuality and the legibility of signs", indicates that for any "body" or object to signify and/or embody homoeroticism it needs to be understood in terms of "the hierarchizing imperative of the hetero/homo binary" (1994, p. xvi). Yet this binary also generates the potential to "affirm numerous communal understandings and cultural practices that have arisen in various social contexts" (Edelman, 1994, p. xvi). As a result, and as homo- and heterosexual men construct and assimilate identities in relation to one another, asymmetrical desires form in the space between both; this is where the politics of the erotic occur.

In her work *Between Men: English Literature and Male Homosocial Desire* (1985) Eve Kosofsky Sedgwick identifies homosocial desire as marked out by "discriminations and paradoxes" (p. 1). On the one hand, these are formed through oxymoronic patterns of "male friendship, mentorship, [and] rivalry" and on the other they exist in an "orbit of the 'desire' of the erotic" (Sedgwick, 1985, p. 1). Sedgwick claims that this forms a fragmented "continuum" of the homosocial and the homosexual where "visibility for men [...] is radically disrupted" (p. 2). Homoeroticism and its alliance to desire is threaded through this disruptive continuum, and this in itself marks the ways in which a "homoerotic desire" is both analogous and distinct from homosocial, homosexual and heterosexual relations. Taking her lead from Foucault, Sedgwick recognises that whilst the asymmetry of socio-erotic bonds between men are also "characterised by intense homophobia, fear and hatred of homosexuality" (1985, p. 1) they are also prompted by desire as an "affective social force" (p. 1) which shapes and sustains that relationship. This platitude can be seen in the way that the male homo/hetero relationship has been binarised and formed through creative and representational work over time. For instance, the huge range of images allied to hyper-hetero masculinities is buttressed by, and operates through, homoerotic tropes. This can be seen in all-male settings or situations riven by the tensions of homoerotic and homophobic tendencies between men. The metaphors and metonymies that have reinforced the public school, the sports team, the changing room, prison and army all capture an aspect of this, and it is in these regulated homosocial spaces that the allure and charge of homoerotic desire and same-sex sexual contact is never far away.

The alignment of same-sex desire to the discourse of the erotic also opens up the possibility that homoeroticism has the potential to move us away from the essential politics of gender and sexual identity towards a more open range of identifications. This also has the capacity to reposition gendered and sexual relations beyond the discourses that underpin them – for example, *men who have sex with men* articulates a particular sexual activity but does not confine the sex act to a sexual identity – in this way the homoerotic and its alliance to desire opens up a flexible way to both negotiate and negate sexual and social control. As Gregory Woods also observes, "homoeroticism is not the exclusive preserve of [...] a small minority you believe homosexual men to be" (1987, p. 1). Rather, and most crucially, it is "a major, self-referential part of male sexuality as a whole" (p. 1). In this way homoerotic discourses of communication, representation and consumption do not just apply to a distinctly gay male reading or gaze; rather, homoeroticism underpins all kinds of men and masculinities. More so, homoeroticism is an aspect of how all gendered and sexual relationships are articulated and at its root is a means of identification which is located "at the very centre of the mainstream" (Woods, 1987, p. 1).

Homoerotic bonds are entrenched and provoked through situational, structural and hierarchical settings. Here, hegemonic configurations and ideological rules that serve to regulate and position men together also allow homoerotic desires to develop. The demarcated "all male" settings which are categorised and upheld through cisgender conformity are where homoeroticism thrives. As before, these include a reiterative range of settings such as the university dorm or fraternity house, army barracks, gym changing room, public toilet and rugby pitch or wrestling ring. Yet within these homosocial spaces the reinforcement of gender norms, patriarchal positions and hegemony create the foundation for bodily intimacy, emotional transparency and affective modes of same-sex desire via a socio-erotic dynamic. Positioning these tensions also points to how homoeroticism has been constructed and expressed through associated discourses of the erotic and/or modes of erotic signification connected to narcissism, romance and effeminacy amongst men.

Homoerotic contexts: narcissism, romance and effeminacy

These key modes of narcissism, romance and effeminacy are useful when contextualising and historicising homoeroticism. In literature, art and media, the signification and textuality of homoeroticism – as well as the homosocial bonds that underpin masculinity and homoeroticism – often rely on a mixture of these discourses. In "On Narcissism: An Introduction", Sigmund Freud (1914) suggests that the relationship between processes of personal self-identification with the "same" gender may be dualistically expressed as homosexual/narcissistic love. This love for the same gender and/or for the self is expressed through narcissistic conflicts and tensions which influence eroticism. In this complex setting where love, sex and desire transect self and other, we also find that "*narcissistic eroticism* (autoeroticism or homoeroticism) and *sexual eroticism* (hetero-eroticism) converge" (Bergeret, 2002, p. 351). For example, autoeroticism and the transient satisfaction that the male subject feels during a process such as masturbation are experienced as a personal pleasure, both embodied and experienced through the gendered body of that subject. That is, an erotic pleasure experienced as intimate and intensely self-referential to the male subject. The notion that an erotic love or desire for the same gender can be also be allied to a love for the subject's own gendered and sexed body (in this case the masculine and the phallus) also positions narcissistic identification as one that occurs through a paradox of self-pleasuring, self-anxiety and "otherness". These differing mechanisms allied to the homosexual narcissist that Freud is alluding to might also be understood in dialogue with the work of his contemporary Sandor Ferenczi (1953), who proposes that it may be "preferable to use the term '*homoeroticism*' in order to take into account in a more precise way the affective and relational functioning of the subjects in question" (p. 352) – in this case, men. For Ferenczi, homoerotic relations between subjects presented "a truly inter-mediary structural state" (p. 354) combined and riven by sexual, social and emotional impulses and the drive of a narcissistic libido. If we think of narcissistic eroticism as a synergy of these subjective and object-led desires, we find that this continuum of homoeroticism functions as both the "prototype of pleasure, [with] inhibition its banishment" (Arundale, 2017, p. 114) and thus opens up an arena where homoerotic desire is "not explained through a defensive (dis)identification with a particular 'masculinity identity' but instead embedded in a process of de-subjectification" (Haywood, 2018, p. 592). The permutation of homoeroticism and narcissism places emphasis on the ways in which sexual *and* social experiences hold the potential to de-subjectify and thus queer desire and identities. In this way, the possibilities that come from both individual and mutual forms of homoeroticism form a nexus of libidinal repression, sublimated desire and affective pleasure which may then be negotiated and enacted as romantic attachment.

Homoerotic and romantic subtexts in literature are the main way that Sedgwick theorises homosociality. For her, the key features of homosocial bonding and homoerotic exchange are the potentials for same-sex male romance and how this is situated and understood in relation to femininity. Romantic fantasy and idealisation converge around the aches and yearnings for the male other and are formed somewhere between erotic desire and sexual anxiety, yet this does not necessarily need to be coherently gendered or framed through a hetero or homosexual axis of identity and identification. How a writer such as E. M. Forster "invented a kind of narration that powerfully expresses male homoerotic desire while shrewdly maintaining the veneer of heterosexual convention" (Markley, 2001, p. 268) can be seen in novels such as *Maurice*. Here romance functions as an "eroticised site of opposition to modernity" (Alderson, 2000, p. 40) in both the male relationships and the "naturalistic eroticism" (p. 40) allied to the broader romanticisation of pre-WWI England and the Edwardian period. The nostalgic eroticisation of youth, the boy or the transient perfection of adolescence also features as a way for homoerotic romance to operate. As a textual and visual construction of youth, passivity and purity, this runs right through the vast cultural discourse of homoeroticism. In Western literature and poetry, this juxtaposition of the romantic with the homoerotic predominantly appears in the work of figures such as Walt Whitman, Oscar Wilde, A. E. Housman's *A Shropshire Lad*, Thomas Mann's *Death in Venice*, Hart Crane, Jean Genet, Paul Monette, Edmund White and Alan Hollinghurst. We see it in the photography of Baron Wilhelm von Gloeden, George Platt Lynes, or Bruce Weber and in films like *The History Boys*, *Call Me by Your Name* and *Moonlight*. Non-Western examples are also key in terms of how romance and homoeroticism might be resituated and contextualised. Films such *Happy Together*, *The Wound* and *Tropical Malady* as well as the written work of Abdellah Taïa, Shyam Selvadurai and Saleem Haddad use themes of erotic desire and romance between men to frame the politics of cultural geographies beyond Europe and the USA. In many of these examples, a "disavowal within autoerotic discourses [...] that stress the boy or adolescent rather than the mature, socially empowered or responsible male" (Marshall, 2000, p. 89) becomes a key feature and semiotic marker of homoerotic representation.

A key site where this kind of representation is located in the image of the "bathing boy", the bathing boy poem and the activities of bathing and swimming. Here, settings where voyeurism, nudity, physicality and play converge are often key and are also overlain with allusions to Grecian, Arcadian and Utopian ideals. It is in these kinds of settings that the aesthetics and ideologies allied to homoeroticism coalesce and thrive. Building on the narcissistic and romantic tendencies embedded in homoeroticism, we also see that other more nuanced features emerge which intertwine gendered and sexual modes of identification and representation. One of the most reiterative is effeminacy and the alliance of aesthetic beauty to masculinity, which is then connected to attributes such as "dissoluteness, effeteness, softness, preciousness, [and] excess" (Sinfield, 1994, p. 39). For example, images of the youthful, beautiful and often androgynous "boy" are embedded in the history of homoerotic poetry, literature and painting where homosocial bonds and idealised discourses of beauty are once more expressed through an amalgamation of Arcadian and pastoral boyishness. Sinfield claims that, as an ideological construct, homosexual effeminacy is "founded in misogyny" and stigmatised with "the feminine" – which is perceived as weak [and] ineffectual" (p. 26). Yet, and as he also crucially points out, the construction of effeminacy has always "overlapped unevenly with same-sex passion", and "by no means did it constitute its essence; indeed, it had no essence" (p. 41).

Effeminacy might be more readily allied to the pathology of a deviant or abnormal homosexual as seen in Foucault. Paradoxically, the effeminisation of gay masculinity as an erotic trigger or tool in something like gay pornography is rare; here, gay male desire is geared towards an ideological model of sexual arousal that assumes a cathexis and fantasy of hetero-normativity. "Straightness", hyper-masculinity and discourses of heteronormative and/or homosocial bonding such as sport, the army or the prison repeatedly function as the key ideological triggers of gay male arousal. On the one hand, the history and discourse of homosexuality and effeminacy are inseparable, yet on the other they remain caught in a tryst of normative and phobic attitudes towards the perceived patterns of kinship, power and desire between men and eroticism. Effeminacy is a way for homoerotic desire to both renegotiate and regress into essential and reductive binaries; in this instance, gay/straight and the tensions between homophobia and homoeroticism. Michael Kimmel (2001) suggests that just as "homophobia is a central organising principal of our cultural definition of manhood" (p. 277) which enacts and instils itself through silencing, shame, violence and fear, it is also underpinned by a level of fascination, allure and desire that is triggered and encapsulated by homoeroticism. More so, effeminacy acts through a "split vision" (p. 276) or double bind; on the one hand it offers up a potentially dissident and subversive way for the erotic politics of sameness to occur between men, and on the other it allows heterosexual men to maintain heterosexist and patriarchal dominance over a perceived or ideological gay other.

In *Masculinity, Class and Same Sex Desire in Industrial England, 1895–1957*, Helen Smith (2015) uses oral history testimonies to claim that in this specific period and setting there was "an absence of the language of sexuality in the vocabulary of working-class men" (p. 154). It was through the non-appearance of terms such as homosexual – which could "categorise, pathologise or politicise" (p. 157) – that sex between men flourished. Here the opportunities and variables around the construction of a male-to-male sexual relationship correlates with how discourses of romance, effeminacy and, more broadly, homoeroticism were displaced. As Smith argues, for these men and within this setting "the option to have sex with other men was part of the normal range of ways in which they could express their sexual desires and urges" (p. 157). Just as these ambiguities have generated ways of seeing and constructing homoeroticism and masculinity, they also have framed this relationship as one that always relies upon representational, cultural and mediated context. As these historical homoerotic constructs merge with new formations and expressions of masculinity, the potentiality of homoerotic desire and different ways of articulating, embodying and rejecting it also emerge.

Homoeroticism: potentials and possibilities

Pornography is a setting where the "mythology of homosexual desire" (Mercer, 2004, p. 156) is expressed as something that relies upon homoerotic spaces, contexts and encounters. In this way, the sexually explicit representation of men in pornography is foregrounded through a combination of homosocial and homoerotic tensions. Time and again these are also based on the subversion and appropriation of heterosexual and hyper-masculine sexual stereotypes engaged in sexual and/or erotic exchange. John Mercer in *Gay Pornography: Representations of Sexuality and Masculinity* (2017) frames this kind of tension in relation to the models, patterns and themes in gay porn. Here the identities and identifications that run through gay porn correspond to homoerotic modes of desire seen elsewhere in other masculine and socio-cultural contexts. For instance, the erotic and at times effeminised idealisations aligned to men who perform pornographic types such as "the Boy-Next-Door", "Twink" and "the youthful and/or beautiful boy" are regularly connected to hyper-masculine types such as the "Jock", "Bear", "Daddy" and Leatherman. In turn, the production of these types and the sex acts that they perform rely upon the homoerotic encounter and/or situation to energise the porn scene. The potentially limitless range of sexual practices in gay porn are also textured by modes of sexual exchange that depend on an erotic interchange between both homo and hetero masculinity. In many of these instances, the aspiration to reiterate, embody or encapsulate heterosexuality also occurs through the signification and homoeroticisation of a "straight" identification or a "straight-acting" other. Sport, fraternity and brotherhood also inform the citations allied to "bro-mance" relationships or the gay-for-pay porn actor (Escoffier, 2003) who performs homosexuality as an entrepreneurial way to earn money and fame. In addition, the issue of homoerotic representations and identifications suggest that homoeroticism ideologically dominates the production and consumption of gay pornography and, more recently, digital, socially networked and self-representational media.

The commodification and representational politics of the self on social media relies upon modes of display and spectatorship that could also be framed through discourses of homoeroticism and fashion. Concepts and contexts which emerged in the 1990s, such as "metrosexuality" (Simpson, 1994), align to this way of "*men looking at men looking at men*" and how this is underpinned by styles of dress and performative constructions allied to gender and sexuality. In this context of fashion, the complex politics of men looking at one another is reinforced by an index of desire that positions "men as visual commodities" (Edwards, 1997, p. 117) embedded in an auto-erotic and homoerotic relationship with themselves and each other. Discursive and cultural accounts of fashion, masculinity and sexuality connect homosocial processes to homoerotic alliances through dress. In this way, dress allows men to embody and fashion themselves as an object of homoerotic desire for other men to observe and assimilate. Homoeroticism is also reliant on techniques of dress that overlay the boundaries of gay and straight male desire. For instance, the appropriation, adaptation and subversion of straight male dress and self-presentation vis-à-vis gay men relies upon the homoeroticisation of clothing that connects to working-class men, army men, sailors, athletes and construction workers. The rhetoric of homoerotic imagery in the work of artists like Tom of Finland, photographers such as Bruce Weber and via the contemporary remit and influence of gay pornography both constructs and exploits this. Hyper-masculine, heteronormative and homoerotic alliances converge through fashion and ways of dressing to simultaneously capture and recast masculinity as a gendered and sexual identity and/or identification.

This way of men reshaping or restyling modes of homoeroticism has also found a place in homosocial settings and practices where hegemonic masculinities and homophobia dominate. Contentious ideas such as inclusive masculinity (Anderson, 2009) and/or the premise that homophobic discourses are in decline (McCormack, 2012; Anderson & McCormack, 2018) attempt to prove that social rituals and erotic potentials amongst men are no longer grounded in homophobic or heteronormative structures. Yet, in both Anderson and McCormack's work, this exists within a highly restricted and privileged framework. The empirical and conceptual evidence for this is from fieldwork amongst young, predominantly white and educated men in the US and UK who are exposed to, and exploit, the situational pleasures that frat-houses, sex parties, sports teams and changing rooms trigger and amplify. If inclusivity and a move away from the obstructive taxonomies of homo-sex and hetero-sex allow these men ways to both erotically explore and contest their own bodies and desires, they do so reductively. This is due to the fact that homophobia and hyper-hegemony always lurk and expedite homoerotic encounters. This work proliferates the idea that men who experiment with their own assumed heterosexuality by kissing, jacking off and fucking other men as and when they want are somehow representative of masculinity per se.

In this context, Laud Humphreys' work (1970) is particularly well known for recognising that impersonal sex between men in American public bathrooms (known as tearooms) paradoxically involved "a minority of [men] who[m] are active in the homosexual subculture" as well as "a large group [...] who have no homosexual identity at all" (p. 11). In these often silent and transient spaces, gay and straight identities understood through sexual identity and/or personality have the capacity to disintegrate and impersonalise themselves.

In *Not Gay: Sex Between Straight White Men* (2015), Jane Ward states that she uses "the terms 'heterosexual', 'hetero-erotic', 'hetero-cultural', 'hetero-masculine' and 'heteronormative' to describe sex between men [...] as a way of signalling the culture of heterosexuality shaping these homosexual encounters" (p. 37). In these socio-sexual/socio-erotic alliances between straight men, we also find that homoeroticism props up how hetero-normativity and heterosexism attempt to contain the power and potency of erotic desire between these men. Ward drills even deeper into these issues to explore the erotic meaning of masculine desire in "straight men's homosexual encounters" (p. 154) as defined through sexual "violence, repulsion, and humiliation" (p. 153). This is encapsulated in US college initiations or "hazing" rituals which exploit homosocial, sexual and erotically charged encounters between straight white frat-men. Here the identarian politics of homo and heterosexuality are recalibrated through the male-to-male erotic encounter which often verges on the abject, humiliating and shameful. Via the hazing, ritual terms such as "hetero-flexibility" (Ward, 2015, p. 7) and "hetero-exceptionalism" (p. 99) emerge to map out a discriminatory aspect of erotic desire and sexual pleasure that seeks "to protect and justify the homosexual behaviour of heterosexuals" whilst "sustaining an underclass of queer outsiders subject to violence and discrimination" (p. 99). In this setting, both the precursors of "homo" and "hetero" seem to require an elision or re-definition and thus a re-reading of sexual fluidity, sexual accidentalism, random encounters and situational homosexuality. In turn, sex between "straight" men, masculine inclusivity and the ostensible weakening of homophobia also seem to claim that these kinds of activities are proof of how the renegotiating of white men's social rituals and bodies might help us to unpack the complex intersectional problems of heterosexism, violence and racism. More so, this also forces the colonialised politics of homoerotic desire to seek out new formations of homoeroticism and masculinity beyond white Westernised geographies.

Conclusion

In a contemporary framework, homoeroticism and its relationship to masculinity are more complex and paradoxical than ever before. The formation of collective and subjective modes of experience via online, globalised, neo-liberal and consumerist ideologies have energised men into finding new ways to articulate desire. Methods and tools of self-representational autonomy, embodiment and mediated intimacy force homoeroticism into settings which are increasingly transnational, transgressive, subversive and perhaps ultimately queer. Accounts of this kind of male-to-male eroticism are captured in work such as that of Thomas Hendriks (2016), which examines the dual use of mobile phone SIM cards to facilitate homoerotic desire and networks of sexual versatility in the urban Congo. In this context, Congolese men strategically construct and develop "erotic subject positions and emergent sexual identities that, together, constitute [...] 'this world' (of men who have sex with men)" and what Hendriks conceptualises as a "*homoerotic economy*" (p. 231). Here we find ways of negotiating homoerotic desire in the Congolese micro-geographies of Kinshasa and Kisangani that are not comparable or even compatible with Western practices. The setting of these cities cultivates "a gendered constellation of interrelated erotic categories" that rely upon a specific yet "contradictory homoerotic economy that reflects broader societal changes and shifting urban gender dynamics, while simultaneously reproducing *and* inverting dominant erotic ideologies" both inside and outside of Congolese context (Hendriks, 2016, p. 231). Edited collections such as Wieringa and Sivori's *The Sexual History of the Global South* (2013) also reveal the scope of research that is emerging through "cross-cultural and trans-disciplinary conversations" (p. viii) whereby established discourses of desire, sexuality and eroticism are unravelled and repositioned in new geographical, socioeconomic and political ways. Concepts such as homonationalism from Jasbir Puar's *Terrorist Assemblages* (2007) cleave through the ambivalence and ambiguity that US acts of racist and homophobic torture at sites like Abu Ghraib capture and force us to rethink how homoerotic and homophobic desires are abjectly and violently linked. Jeffrey McCune's work (2008) on black masculinities and his examination of the "the down low" (DL) as a way for black men who have sex with other men to renegotiate and "dis-identify with normative descriptors of sexuality" (p. 298) also point towards a more liminal, decentred and trans-cultural level of experience. It may be that whilst homoeroticism continues to affirm it also undoes the constraints of pathologising and categorising men through their gendered and sexualised identities. The erotic yields a potential for incongruent trajectories of desire that gender and sexuality paradoxically rely upon but can never attain. In this way homoeroticism which moves beyond a coherent view of masculinity is perhaps the only way to grasp some of the enigmatic potential that eroticism between men contains.

References

Alderson, D. (2000). Desire as nostalgia: The novels of Alan Hollinghurst. In D. Alderson & L. Anderson (Eds.), *Territories of desire in queer culture* (pp. 29–49). Manchester: University of Manchester Press.

Anderson, E. (2009). *Inclusive masculinity: The changing nature of masculinities*. London: Routledge.

Anderson, E., & McCormack, M. (2018) Inclusive masculinity theory: Overview, reflection and refinement. *Journal of Gender Studies*, *27*(5), 547–561.

Arundale, J. (2017). *Identity, narcissism, and the other: Object relations and their obstacles*. London: Karnac.

Bergeret, J. (2002) Homosexuality or homoeroticism? "Narcissistic eroticism". *The International Journal of Psychoanalysis*, *83*(2), 351–362.

Dyer, R. (2002). *The culture of queers*. London & New York: Routledge.

Edelman, L. (1994). *Homographesis: Essays in gay literary and cultural theory*. London: Routledge.

Edwards, T. (1997). *Men in the mirror: Men's fashion, masculinity and consumer society*. London: Cassell.

Escoffier, J. (2003) Gay-for-pay: Straight men and the making of gay pornography. *Qualitative Sociology*, *26*(4), 531–555.

Ferenczi, S. (1953). *First contributions to psychoanalysis*. London: Hogarth.

Foucault, M. (1998). *The history of sexuality, vol. 1: The will to knowledge*. London: Penguin.

Freud, S. (1914). *On narcissism: An introduction*. London: Karnac.

Hammarén, N., & Johansson, T. (2014) Homosociality: In between power and intimacy. *SAGE Open*, *4*(1), 1–11.

Haywood, C. (2018) "Leaving masculinity at the car door": Dogging, de-subjectification and the pursuit of pleasure. *Sexualities*, *21*(4), 587–604.

Hendriks, T. (2016) SIM cards of desire: Sexual versatility and the male homoerotic economy in urban Congo. *American Ethnologist*, *43*(2), 230–242.

Humphreys, L. (1970). *Tearoom trade: Impersonal sex in public places*. New Brunswick & London: Aldine Transaction.

Katz, J. (1996). *The invention of heterosexuality*. New York: Plume Books.

Kimmel, M. (2001). Masculinity as homophobia: Fear, shame and silence in the construction of gender identity. In S. M. Whitehead & F. J. Barrett (Eds.), *The masculinities reader* (pp. 266–288). Oxford: Polity.

Markley, A. A. (2001) E. M. Forster's reconfigured gaze and the creation of a homoerotic subjectivity. *Twentieth Century Literature*, 47(2), 268–292.
Marshall, B. (2000). The national-popular and comparative gay identities: Cyril Collards's *Les Nuits fauves*. In D. Alderson & L. Anderson (Eds.), *Territories of desire in queer culture* (pp. 84–96). Manchester: University of Manchester Press.
McCormack, M. (2012). *The declining significance of homophobia: How teenage boys are redefining masculinity and heterosexuality*. Oxford: Oxford University Press.
McCune, J. Q. (2008) "Out" in the club: The down low, hip hop and the architexture of black masculinity. *Text and Performance Quarterly*, *28*(3), 298–314.
Mercer, J. (2004) In the slammer: The myth of the prison in American gay pornographic video. *Journal of Homosexuality*, 47(3), 151–166.
Mercer, J. (2017). *Gay pornography: Representations of sexuality and masculinity*. London: I. B. Tauris.
Puar, J. (2007). *Terrorist assemblages: Homonationalism in queer times*. Durham, NC: Duke University Press.
Sedgwick, E. K. (1985). *Between men: English literature and male homosocial desire*. New York: Columbia University Press.
Simpson, M. (1994). *Male impersonators: Men performing masculinity*. London: Cassell.
Sinfield, A. (1994). *The Wilde century*. New York: Columbia University Press.
Smith, H. (2015). *Masculinity, class and same sex desire in industrial England, 1895–1957*. Basingstoke: Palgrave Macmillan.
Ward, J. (2015). *Not gay: Sex between straight white men*. New York: New York University Press.
Wieringa, S., & Sivori, H. (Eds.).(2013).*The sexual history of the Global South*. London: Zed Books.
Woods, G. (1987). *Articulate flesh: Male homoeroticism and modern poetry*. New Haven, CT: Yale University Press.

22

The shifting relationship between masculinity and homophobia

Sarah Diefendorf and Tristan Bridges

Introduction

Feminist social scientific research has long examined the relationship between masculinity and sexual prejudice. Sexual prejudice refers to negative attitudes based on sexual orientation. (Herek 2000). Homophobia is a common form of sexual prejudice. Men's consistently higher levels of sexual prejudice have been documented with a variety of different methods and measures. These findings helped establish early theories that sexual prejudice is gendered. In part, homophobia is an enactment of masculinity.

Over the last couple decades, however, a methodological paradox has emerged. Survey research has discovered a steady decline in sexual prejudice on most measures. This shift is unprecedented and might suggest that the relationship between masculinity and homophobia is either weakening or in decline. Nonetheless, most qualitative research continues to find that enactments of sexual prejudice and inequality remain key components of masculinity. Different measures are producing data that disagree.

In this chapter, we summarize this body of theory and research, arguing that, rather than asking which method is correct, we need to need to understand that the relationship between masculinity and homophobia is changing. The research and theory we summarize here demonstrate that the processes through which inequalities are maintained have transformed. They have shifted in ways that make some inequalities less easily recognizable but not necessarily any less effective.

The gender of sexual prejudice

Scholarship on gender and sexual prejudice in the 1970s and 1980s established the connection quantitatively. Surveys incorporating measures of sexual prejudice all came to a similar conclusion: men seemed to harbor *more* sexual prejudice than women (Herek 1986; Lehne 1976). Sexual prejudice is correlated with characteristics beyond gender. But within each category (e.g., age, political party; education; religion), men are more supportive of sexual prejudice than women. As Herek wrote, 'heterosexual masculinity [is] a culturally constructed identity, and ... expressing hostility toward gay people enhances such an identity'

(1986, p. 563). A great deal of research supports this premise. Indeed, gender differences in sexual prejudice are magnified when questions ask specifically about gay *men*.

The social psychologist Mary Kite conducted a series of meta-analyses throughout the 1980s and 1990s, discovering patterns across studies in the gendered nature of sexual prejudice. Her early work showed that sexual prejudice had declined over time but that the gender gap had increased (Kite 1984). Kite offered two explanations: (1) homophobic sentiments had become more gendered over time; and/or (2) studies started using more refined measures, allowing scholars to capture sexual prejudice more accurately. Later, Kite and Whitley (1996) performed a larger meta-analysis examining different measures: prejudice toward same-sex oriented people, sexual behavior, and rights. And while Kite and Whitley (1996) found men to be more supportive of sexual prejudice toward gay people (men in particular) and same-sex sexual behaviors, they did not find gendered differences in support for gay rights, though subsequent survey research does document less support for gay rights among men (e.g., Herek 2002; Pew Research Center 2017; Schwartz 2010). And meta-analyses continued to show that on virtually every measure, men exhibit more sexual prejudice than do women (LaMar & Kite 1998).

The connection between masculinity and sexual prejudice has also been established cross-culturally. Figure 22.1 summarizes gender differences in sexual prejudice from the World Values Survey's most recent survey of societies around the world. Individuals rate 'homosexuality' on a 1–10 scale (where 1 is 'never justifiable' and 10 is 'always justifiable'). Figure 22.1 shows that men continue to express *more* sexual prejudice than women in the majority of societies. Thus, while homophobia contains elements specific to nation and cultural context, it can also be understood as something that is gendered and on a virtually global scale.

Jasbir Puar (2007) has been critical of the ways that nationalist ideologies and gender and sexual minorities are linked via a process she calls 'homonationalism,' wherein narratives about a 'tolerant' West are mobilized to support claims of a U.S. sexual exceptionalism in contrast to the 'perversely racialized bodies of pathologized nationalities' (2007, p. 51). Puar (2013) argues that homophobia is part of a global process that transcends national boundaries. Here we use Figure 22.1 to illustrate the cross-cultural constancy of sexual prejudice as gendered.

Importantly, research on attitudinal differences between men and women has consistently found a relationship between gender and sexual prejudice. And theoretical work connecting masculinity to homophobia built on these empirical findings.

Theorizing the relationship between masculinity and homophobia

Carrigan, Connell, and Lee's (1985) early work theorizing masculinities argued that homophobia, sexual prejudice, and the subordination of gay men helped justify and produce what they labeled 'hegemonic masculinity' (see also Connell 1987, 1995). In fact, historical research on masculinity has found that the category is often constructed over time against what Mosse (1996) referred to as 'countertypes'. Constructions of masculinity routinely rely on images, stereotypes, and archetypes of countertypes. Mosse shows how Jews and gay men were relied on throughout history across Europe in constructing idealized notions of manhood. So too has historical research in the U.S. documented this process. Indeed, as Chauncey (1994) shows, around the turn of the twentieth century, *exclusive* sexual desires for women began to be framed as an integral component of manhood. A distinctly *heterosexual* masculinity did not exist prior to homophobia; rather, homophobia and masculinity as

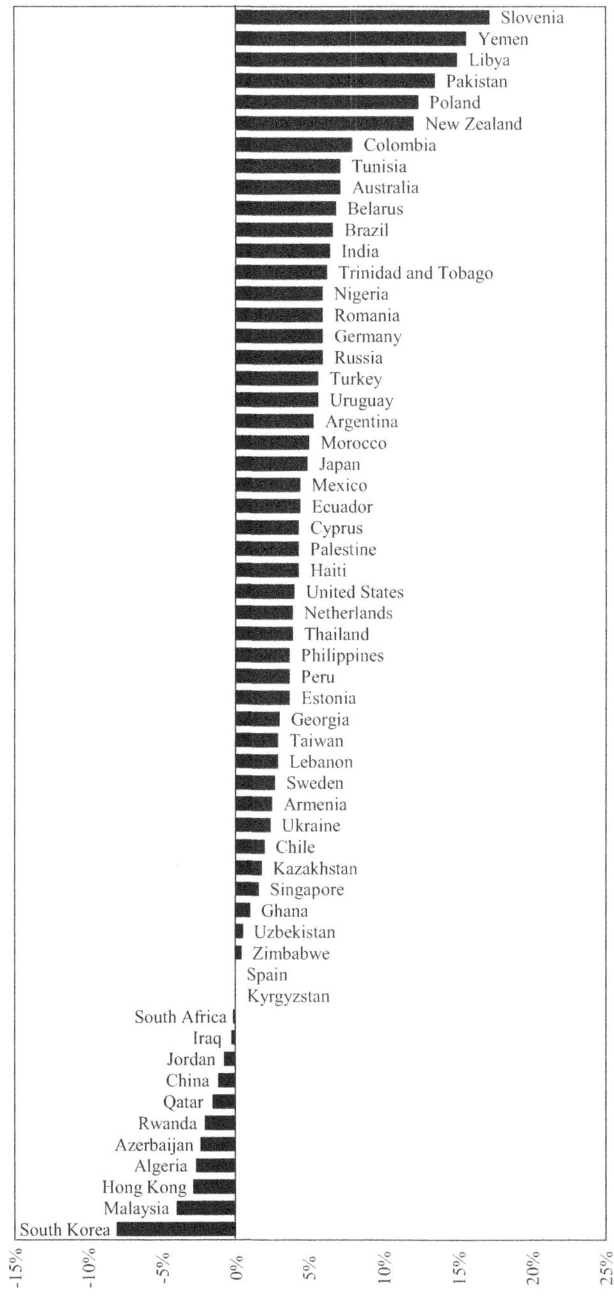

Figure 22.1 Present differences in men vs. women claiming that homosexuality is 'never justifiable' by country, 2010–2014.
Source: World Values Survey, 2010–2014.

heterosexual were historically constructed alongside one another (Connell 1992, 1995; Greenberg 1988; Katz 1990).

Raewyn Connell's (1987, 1995) theory of gender relations relied on this historical work alongside psychoanalytic and feminist theorizing about gender and the empirical work addressed above. Connell used gay masculinity as an illustration of a configuration of gender practice she calls 'subordinate masculinity'. She saw subordinate masculinities as—like countertypes—playing a critical role in the production of gender hegemony. It is through the processes of subordination, marginalization, and complicity, Connell argued, that hegemonic masculinity achieves ideological dominance that justifies a patriarchal status quo. Thus, for Connell, gay men are not the only form of subordinated masculinity, but they occupied among the most visible forms (see also Chen 1999).

Lipman-Blumen (1976) argued that homophobia will always be linked to masculinity in societies defined by gender segregation and homosociality—it works to differentiate *social* from *sexual* interactions. And Britton (1990) showed that support for institutionalized forms of sex segregation is highly correlated with sexual prejudice and that men are more supportive than are women. Building on this, Kimmel (1994) theorized masculinity as a performance produced by men *for* other men and motivated by fear of other men. Adding to psychoanalytic theories of gender, Kimmel argues that this fear of other men leads to shame and silence and that heterosexism, sexism, and racism are reproduced, in part, by this fear.

Pascoe (2005, 2007) further theorized this relationship. She conducted an ethnographic study of masculinity in a U.S. high school, examining young boys' uses of the term 'fag' in their interactions. She discovered that homophobia operates as a form of gender policing among boys and men. Pascoe's theory of what she calls 'fag discourse' focuses on the interactional and institutional levels of analysis, distinguishing her approach from Kimmel's (1994) psychoanalytic theory. She builds on the idea that homophobia is about more than sexual prejudice, demonstrating how teens engage in sexually prejudiced interactions in ways that simultaneously uphold gendered and racialized forms of inequality, a relationship that has been documented globally (e.g., Boellstorff 2004; Costa, Peroni, Bandiera & Nardi, 2013b; Dasgupta 2017; Kehily & Nayak 1997; Lancaster 1994; Ratele 2014; Verduzco & Sánchez 2011).

Indeed, Pascoe argues that 'homophobia' is the wrong term to describe the connections described in this chapter, and she proposes 'fag discourse' instead. She argues that research relying on 'homophobia' had overlooked the gendered and racialized nature of 'fag' as a sexual slur (Corbett 2001; Plummer 2001). More than homophobia, Pascoe (2007) theorizes 'fag discourse' as a disciplinary discourse through which boys and men regulate each other's behavior under the guise of playful interactions. She also showed that fag discourse carries racialized meanings and consequences, thereby joining other scholars who show that homophobia is not a racially neutral phenomenon (e.g., Connell 2016; King 2004). In interaction, Pascoe showed how masculinity is produced through fag discourse but also through a process that happens in tandem, which she calls 'compulsive heterosexuality' (Pascoe 2007). 'Fag discourse' operates as a form of gendered 'repudiation', but this process requires discourses of confirmation as well. And alongside fag discourse, Pascoe also identified sex talk among boys that worked to eroticize boys' and men's dominance over girls and women. This gendered form of dominance worked to *confirm* masculine identities. But, like fag discourse, it only worked momentarily, within interactions. Thus, Pascoe (2007) theorized masculinity and gender inequality as reproduced through the dialectical relationship between routine interactional enactments of repudiation (fag discourse) and confirmation (compulsive heterosexuality).

The connection between masculinity and homophobia has been documented across an impressive collection of institutional settings and spaces, including schools (e.g., Connell 2016; Pascoe 2007), families (e.g., Averett 2016; Bucher 2014; Kane 2006, 2012), religious communities (e.g., Diefendorf 2015; Ezren 2006), workplaces (e.g., Barber 2016; Paap 2006), online interactions (Moloney & Love 2018; Pascoe & Diefendorf 2019), and globally (e.g., Boellstorff 2004; Costa, Peroni, Bandiera & Nardi, 2013b; Dasgupta 2017; Epprecht 2013; Flood & Hamilton 2005; Lancaster 1994; M'baye 2013; Ratele 2014; Verduzco & Sánchez 2011). Here, however, is where scholars have confronted a methodological paradox. Opinion polls and representative surveys have charted important shifts in support for sexual equality in many nations, while homosexual sex and relationship are criminalized in other parts of the world. Thus there exist both losses and gains toward sexual equality on this front in different parts of the world. Despite these stark distinctions, however, surveys of LGBTQ people around the world continue to document widespread experiences of prejudice, harassment, discrimination, and violence even in societies sometimes labeled more sexually 'tolerant' (e.g., Berggren 2012; Boellstorff 2004; Bridges & Pascoe 2014; Walters 2014). Thus, while opinion polls suggest people have become more supportive of LGBTQ people, research on the lived experiences of gender and sexual minorities is inconsistent with this shift. Making sense of this apparent paradox is an important question that requires more research. We discuss this in more detail below and rely on the U.S. as a primary example, with discussions of how similar processes are occurring in other nations as well.

Shifts in gendered enactments of homophobia

We have seen recent shifts along diverse measures of sexual inequality across the globe. Scholars debate how these shifts are related to the relationship between masculinity and homophobia. In the United States, smaller numbers of Americans claim they would be upset to learn that their child identified as gay or lesbian.[1] Americans have dramatically changed their opinions about same-sex marriage. Germany, the country with the largest population in Western Europe, recently became the 15th European nation to legalize gay marriage (Lipka 2017). In September 2018, India's supreme court decriminalized homosexual sex. Data like these are sometimes interpreted optimistically, and in other cases, following Suzanna Walters (2014), more cautiously labeled as indications of 'sexual tolerance'.

Different scholars have accounted for this apparent decline in sexual prejudice and homophobia in different ways, accounting for change by citing: processes of secularization (Hicks & Lee 2006; Hooghe & Meeusen 2013); changes in etiological beliefs about sexuality (Lewis 2009; Tygart 2000); a weakening relationship between AIDS and homosexuality (Ruel & Campbell 2006); increases in physical and emotional closeness among heterosexual men (Anderson 2009; Anderson & McCormack 2015; McCormack 2012); increasing numbers of 'out' gay men and lesbians (Altemeyer 2002; Seidman 2002); advances in civil liberties, increases in the GDP of a country (LaMontagne et al. 2018); and, in the United States, liberalization more generally (Brooks 2000; Loftus 2001).[2] From this perspective, sexual prejudice appears to be on the decline.

The material bases on which sexual inequalities are institutionalized have shifted dramatically in recent history. Many societies around the world now have legislation surrounding same-sex marriage, sexual discrimination in workplaces and schools, and hate crimes. Whether these shifts are illustrations of the demise of cultural homophobia is a more difficult question to answer, but an increasingly important one. Durable systems of social inequality tend to transform as the foundations upon which they were reproduced are challenged and called into question (e.g., Bridges & Pascoe 2014, 2018; Demetriou 2001; Tilly 1999; Walters 2014). Thus, rather than uncritically claiming that homophobia is either in decline or has declined, more scholarship has sought to analyze and evaluate how it has changed (e.g., Baker 2005; Bridges 2014; de Boise 2015; Pascoe 2005, 2007; Ward 2008, 2015).

One way we can better understand how and why the relationship between masculinity can appear to be simultaneously eroding and expanding is to more carefully consider the various measurements and measurement tactics that different scholars employ. This should prompt a consideration of how homophobia and sexual prejudice and discrimination ought to be measured, as well as whether shifts in gender and sexual inequality require new measurements.

For instance, Anderson (2009) and McCormack's (2012) work documents physical, quasi-sexual, and emotional closeness between heterosexual men and use these data to argue that these interactions are face-value evidence of a declining significance of homophobia. Their work frames the relationship between masculinity and homophobia as largely attitudinal and interpersonal. The interpersonal can be a site in which one works to demonstrate that they are not homophobic, which is the focus of much work in this vein. However, interpersonal interactions are often sites in which inequalities are reproduced in somewhat hidden or surprising ways (Bridges & Pascoe 2014).

Other work suggests that we must look at multiple levels of the social world to understand and contextualize homophobia. Ward (2015) documents a long history of heterosexual men touching, kissing, and sometimes having sex before and throughout the twentieth century. But beyond this, Ward is interested in better understanding the *meanings* associated with the sexual fluidity of some straight men. Among her discoveries, Ward summarizes a collection of logics she collectively refers to as 'hetero-exceptionalism' that work as discursive alibis, situating heterosexual men's same-sex sexual interactions and encounters as consistent with both masculinity and heterosexuality (see also Carrillo & Hoffman 2018; Silva 2017). Ward's work highlights the larger systems and meanings in which these interpersonal interactions exist.

As Connell suggests, homophobia is made up of a set of social practices; homophobia is not just an attitude (1995). Interpersonal enactments of sexual inequality are an important element of the relationship between masculinity and homophobia, but they are not the only element (e.g., Bridges & Pascoe 2016; Bryant & Vidal-Ortiz 2008; Mishel 2016; Murray 2009; Pascoe & Bridges 2018; Tilcsik 2011).

New research designs, methods, and measures

Today, shifts in interpersonal enactments of sexual inequality must be understood alongside a multi-dimensional relationship between masculinity and homophobia. We must also recognize that, when scholars discuss the contemporary relationship between masculinity and homophobia, they are not always talking about the same thing. For example, one recent review finds that between 1993 and 2010, 47 different approaches to measure homophobia were used (Costa, Bandeira & Nardi, 2013a). In an effort to get at this problem, and offer insights into new directions for both questions and research, we turn to two strands of work: one that seeks to further refine measurements of homophobia; and another that highlights the enduring relationship between masculinity and homophobia through experimental design. Together, this work suggests new understandings of the relationship between masculinity and homophobia alongside dramatic shifts in public support for sexual inequality.

Recent scholarship disentangles support for sexual equality from support for the less apparent forms of inequality that confer informal sets of privileges upon heterosexual people and interactions. Relying on a survey experiment with nationally representative data in the U.S., Doan, Loehr & Miller (2014) examine the ways that Americans distinguish between what they refer to as 'formal rights' and 'informal privileges' in attitudes toward same-sex couples. The authors find that heterosexual Americans are far more supportive of formal rights for sexual minorities, such as marriage and partnership benefits, than they are of informal privileges for same-sex couples, such as support for public displays of affection.

In a related study, Doan, Miller, and Loehr (2015) were interested in Americans' attitudes about love in different types of romantic couples. Gay couples, they found, were viewed as less loving than both heterosexual and lesbian couples. Indeed, lesbian couples and heterosexual couples were perceived as equally loving in their sample. And these different perceptions of how loving heterosexual, gay, and lesbian relationships illustrate important gendered forms of sexual inequality. This work highlights the importance of identifying what the authors call 'informal privileges'—aspects of inequalities often more difficult to measure and that might not be illustrated on representative surveys primarily concerned with formal rights and social recognition (Doan, Loehr & Miller, 2014).

This research is consistent with a body of scholarship on 'modern prejudice' that works to sustain a diverse collection of social inequalities based on race (e.g., Bobo 1999; Bonilla-Silva 2003) and gender (e.g., Benokratis & Feagin 1995; Jackman 1994). As institutional and legal supports for inequality are challenged, the maintenance of durable forms of inequality at the level of *interaction* becomes even more pertinent as among the chief social mechanisms through which durable social inequalities endure.

Additionally, experimental research has also discovered that the relationship between masculinity and homophobia may persist despite the appearance of change. A great deal of this work relies on theories of social identity arguing that people will both attempt to maintain identities that are deeply held or associated with social status or esteem (e.g., Stets & Burke 2000), but also that people are motivated to act in specific ways to protect deeply held identities if they perceive them to be 'threatened' (e.g., Burke & Stets 2009). When esteemed or deeply held social identities are threatened, people respond not simply by compensating, but by *over*compensating in their attempts to recover the identity. We can learn a great deal about the various ingredients understood to comprise identities by examining what people turn to when those identities are called into question. Simply put, what masculinity 'is' is often on dramatic display when we see how men respond to their masculinities being challenged.

For example, research has documented patterned reactions when men have their masculinity experimentally 'threatened' or called into question. Some men are more likely to espouse attitudes supportive of sexual coercion and violence (Munsch & Willer 2012); some are more supportive of war and violence, are more supportive of male supremacist statements, and are more likely to express prejudice toward both homosexuality and gay men (Willer, Rogalin, Conlon & Wojnowicz, 2013). While these study designs employ atypical conditions under which men respond, others interview young men on their reported experiences of masculinity threat and still find that men's narratives implicitly call for the subordination of women and other men (Munsch & Gruys 2018).

Other recent experimental research has also discovered that men's heterosexuality is an identity easily lost when men engage in sexual activity with other men. Using a series of survey experiments, Mize & Manago (2018) discovered that a description of a single same-sex sexual encounter leads individuals to question the sexual orientation of a heterosexual man to a far greater extent than a heterosexual woman when described similarly. That is, when men are described as engaging in sexual activity that does not align with a heterosexual orientation, they are more likely to be understood to be gay. The authors account for these findings with what they refer to as men's *precarious sexuality*, further supporting the notion that there is a gendered component to our understandings of heterosexuality and sexual practice and prejudice.

This body of scholarship underscores the need to consider the various ways we can seek to understand the connections between masculinity and homophobia and 'modern prejudice', even in the wake of what sometimes appear to be massive shifts in public opinion. The relationship between masculinity and homophobia is multi-faceted, and we must attend to its multiple dimensions when assessing shifts and declaring 'change'.

Conclusion

A great deal of scholarship treats the relationship between masculinity and homophobia as though it can or should only be measured in a single way. Scholars who study the relationship between masculinity and homophobia should remember Connell's (1987, 1995) multidimensional understanding of the various ways this relationship can exist. Further, scholars should work to carefully scrutinize the variety of methodological tools that we use to measure the shifting relationship between masculinity and homophobia. Finally, scholars should continue to engage with theoretical and empirical work demonstrating that as durable forms of inequality shift, decline, and are called into question, we need theories able to capture the meanings and consequences associated with these transformations (e.g., Bridges 2014; Bridges & Pascoe 2014, 2018; Connell 1987, 1995; Demetriou 2001; Pascoe & Bridges 2018).

The relationship between masculinity and homophobia is not a social artifact of the past. In order to appreciate the endurance of this relationship, however, scholars must recognize and appreciate homophobias as plural. This appreciation will require more research and a diversity of theories that ask how different homophobias are connected to masculinity in distinct ways with distinct consequences. The tasks moving forward are not only to ask if and how masculinities are related to homophobia but to also consider what forms of homophobia are being perpetuated and how. This will require the recognition that inequalities related to gender and sexuality are often simultaneously being challenged *and* reproduced.

Notes

1 While parents do say they would not be upset to learn their child identified as gay or lesbian, big data research relying on Google searches associated with parental anxieties surrounding their children's same-sex sexual identities suggests that parents are more concerned about gay sons than lesbian daughters (Mishel & Caudillo 2017).

2 Despite this scholarship, it is also true that the U.S. is among the nations that have seen a re-emergence of the Global Right. Indeed, alongside as well as in reaction to liberalizing trends on various issues (sexual equality among them), a global backlash has occurred which portends that notions of 'progress' are premature on many issues related to gender and sexual inequality (e.g., Graff, Kapur & Walters, 2019).

References

Altemeyer, B. (2002). Changes in attitudes toward homosexuals. *Journal of Homosexuality, 42*(2), 63–75.

Anderson, E. (2009). *Inclusive masculinity: The changing nature of masculinities*. London: Routledge.

Anderson, E., & McCormack, M. (2015). Cuddling and spooning: Heteromasculinity and homosocial tactility among student-athletes. *Men and Masculinities, 18*(2), 214–230.

Averett, K. H. (2016). The gender buffet: LGBTQ parents resisting heteronormativity. *Gender & Society, 30*(2), 189–212.

Baker, P. (2005). *Public discourses of gay men*. London: Routledge.

Barber, K. (2016). *Styling masculinity: Gender, class, and inequality in the men's grooming industry*. New Brunswick, NJ: Rutgers University Press.

Benokratis, N. V., & Feagin, J. R. (1995). *Modern sexism*. Upper Sadle River, NJ: Prentice Hall.

Berggren, K. (2012). 'No homo': Straight inoculations and the queering of masculinity in Swedish hip hop. *NORMA: International Journal for Masculinity Studies*, 7(1), 50–66.

Bobo, L. (1999). Prejudice as group position. *Journal of Social Issues, 55*(3), 445–472.

Boellstorff, T. (2004). The emergence of political homophobia in Indonesia: Masculinity and national belonging. *Ethnos, 69*(4), 465–486.

Bonilla-Silva, E. (2003). *Racism without racists*. Lanham, MD: Rowman & Littlefield.

Bridges, T. (2014). A very 'gay' straight? Hybrid masculinities, sexual aesthetics, and the changing relationship between masculinity and homophobia. *Gender & Society, 28*(1), 58–82.

Bridges, T., & Pascoe, C. J. (2014). Hybrid masculinities: New directions in the sociology of men and masculinities. *Sociology Compass, 8*(3), 246–258.

Bridges, T., & Pascoe, C. J. (2016). Masculinities and post-homophobias? In C. J. Pascoe & T. Bridges (eds.), *Exploring masculinities* (pp. 412–423). New York: Oxford University Press.

Bridges, T., & Pascoe, C. J. (2018). On the elasticity of gender hegemony. In J. Messerschmidt, M. Messner, R. Connell & P. Yancey Martin (eds.), *Gender reckonings* (pp. 254–274). New York: New York University Press.

Britton, D. (1990). Homophobia and homosociality. *The Sociological Quarterly, 31*(3), 423–439.

Brooks, C. (2000). Civil rights liberalism and the suppression of a republican political realignment in the United States, 1972–1996. *American Sociological Review, 65*(4), 483–505.

Bryant, K., & Vidal-Ortiz, S. (2008). Introduction to retheorizing homophobias. *Sexualities, 11*(4), 387–396.

Bucher, J. (2014). 'But he can't be gay': The relationship between masculinity and homophobia in father-son relationships. *The Journal of Men's Studies, 22*(3), 222–237.

Burke, P. J., & Stets, J. E. (2009). *Identity theory*. New York: Oxford University Press.

Carrigan, T., Connell, R., & Lee, J. (1985). Toward a new sociology of masculinity. *Theory and Society, 14*(5), 551–604.

Carrillo, H., & Hoffman, A. (2018). 'Straight with a pinch of bi': The construction of heterosexuality as an elastic category among adult US men. *Sexualities, 21*(1/2), 90–108.

Chauncey, G. (1994). *Gay New York*. New York: Basic Books.

Chen, A. (1999). Lives at the center of the periphery, lives at the periphery of the center: Chinese American masculinities and bargaining with hegemony. *Gender & Society, 13*(5), 584–607.

Connell, C. (2016). Contesting racialized discourses of homophobia. *Sociological Forum, 31*(3), 599–618.

Connell, R. (1987). *Gender and power*. Stanford, CA: Stanford University Press.

Connell, R. (1992). A very straight gay: Masculinity, homosexual experience, and the dynamics of gender. *American Sociological Review, 57*(6), 735–751.

Connell, R. (1995). *Masculinities*. Stanford, CA: Stanford University Press.

Corbett, K. (2001). Faggot = loser. *Studies in Gender and Sexuality, 2*(1), 3–28.

Costa, A. B., Bandeira, D. R., & Nardi, H. C. (2013a). Systematic review of instruments measuring homophobia and related constructs. *Journal of Applied Social Psychology, 43*(6), 1324–1332.

Costa, A. B., Peroni, R. O., Bandiera, D. R., & Nardi, H. C. (2013b). Homophobia or sexism? A systematic review of prejudice against nonheterosexual orientation in Brazil. *International Journal of Psychology, 48*(5), 900–909.

Dasgupta, R. K. (2017). *Digital queer cultures in India: Politics, intimacies and belonging*. London: Routledge.

de Boise, S. (2015). I'm not homophobic, 'I've got gay friends': Evaluating the validity of inclusive masculinity. *Men and Masculinities, 18*(3), 318–339.

Demetriou, D. (2001). Connell's concept of hegemonic masculinity: A critique. *Theory and Society, 30*(3), 337–361.

Diefendorf, S. (2015). After the wedding night: Sexual abstinence and masculinities over the life course. *Gender & Society, 29*(5), 647–669.

Doan, L., Loehr, A., & Miller, L. R. (2014). Formal rights and informal privileges for same-sex couples: Evidence from a national survey experiment. *American Sociological Review, 79*(6), 1172–1195.

Doan, L., Miller, L. R., & Loehr, A. (2015). The power of love: The role of emotional attributions and standards in heterosexuals' attitudes toward lesbian and gay couples. *Social Forces, 94*(1), 401–425.

Epprecht, M. (2013). *Sexuality and social justice in Africa: Rethinking homophobia and forging resistance.* London: Zed Books.

Ezren, T. (2006). *Straight to Jesus.* Berkeley, CA: University of California Press.

Flood, M., & Hamilton, C. (2005). Mapping homophobia in Australia. Australia Institute Webpaper, pp. 1–15. Retrieved from www.glhv.org.au/files/aust_inst_homophobia_paper.pdf.

Graff, A., Kapur, R., & Walters, S. D. (2019). Introduction: Gender and the rise of the global right. *Signs, 44*(3), 541–560.

Greenberg, D. (1988). *The construction of homosexuality.* Chicago, IL: University of Chicago Press.

Herek, G. (1986). On heterosexual masculinity. *American Behavioral Scientist, 29*(5), 563–577.

Herek, G. (2000). The psychology of sexual prejudice. *Current Directions in Psychological Science, 9*(1), 19–22.

Herek, G. (2002). Gender gaps in public opinion about lesbians and gay men. *Public Opinion Quarterly, 66*(1), 40–66.

Hicks, G., & Lee, T. (2006). Public attitudes toward gays and lesbians. *Journal of Homosexuality, 51*(2), 57–77.

Hooghe, M., & Meeusen, C. (2013). Is same-sex marriage legislation related to attitudes toward homosexuality? *Sexuality Research and Social Policy, 10*(4), 258–268.

Jackman, M. (1994). *The velvet glove: Paternalism and conflict in gender, class and race.* Berkeley, CA: University of California Press.

Kane, E. (2006). 'No way my boys are going to be like that!': Parents' responses to children's gender nonconformity. *Gender & Society, 20*(2), 149–176.

Kane, E. (2012). *The gender trap: Parents and the pitfalls of raising boys and girls.* New York: New York University Press.

Katz, J. N. (1990). The invention of heterosexuality. *Socialist Review, 20,* 7–34.

Kehily, M. J., & Nayak, A. (1997). 'Lads and laughter': Humor and the production of heterosexual hierarchies. *Gender & Education, 9*(1), 69–88.

Kimmel, M. S. (1994). Masculinity as homophobia. In H. Brod & M. Kaufman (eds.), *Theorizing masculinities* (pp. 119–141). Thousand Oaks, CA: Sage.

King, J. L. (2004). *On the down low: A journey into the lives of straight black men who sleep with men.* New York: Broadway Books.

Kite, M. E. (1984). Sex differences in attitudes toward homosexuals: A meta-analytic review. *Journal of Homosexuality, 10*(1/2), 69–81.

Kite, M. E., & Whitley, B. E., Jr. (1996). Sex difference in attitudes toward homosexual persons, behaviors, and civil rights: A meta-analysis. *Personality and Social Psychology Bulletin, 22*(4), 336–353.

LaMar, L., & Kite, M. E. (1998). Sex differences in attitudes toward gay men and lesbians: A multidimensional perspective. *The Journal of Sex Research, 35*(2), 189–196.

LaMontagne, E., d'Elbée, M., Ross, M. W., Carroll, A., Plessis, A. D., & Loures, L. (2018). A socioecological measurement of homophobia for all countries and its public health impact. *European Journal of Public Health, 28*(5), 967–972.

Lancaster, R. (1994). *Life is hard: Danger, machismo, and the intimacy of power in Nicaragua.* Berkeley, CA: University of California Press.

Lehne, G. K. (1976). Homophobia among men. In D. David & R. Brannon (eds.), *The forty-nine percent majority: The male sex role* (pp. 68–88). Reading, MA: Addison-Wesley.

Lewis, G. B. (2009). Does believing homosexuality is innate increase support for gay rights? *Policy Studies Journal, 37*(4), 669–693.

Lipka, M. L. (2017). Where Europe stands on gay marriage and civil unions. *Pew Research Center, Fact Tank.* Retrieved from www.pewresearch.org/fact-tank/2017/06/30/where-europe-stands-on-gay-marriage-and-civil-unions/...

Lipman-Blumen, J. (1976). Toward a homosocial theory of sex roles: An explanation of the sex segregation of social institutions. *Signs, 1*(3), 15–31.

Loftus, J. (2001). America's liberalization in attitudes toward homosexuality, 1973–1998. *American Sociological Review, 66*(5), 762–782.

M'baye, B. (2013). The origins of Senegalese homophobia. *African Studies Review, 56*(2), 109–128.

McCormack, M. (2012). *The declining significance of homophobia: How teenage boys are redefining masculinity and heterosexuality.* New York: Oxford University Press.

Mishel, E. (2016). Discrimination against queer women in the U.S. workforce: A résumé audit study. *Socius: Sociological Research for a Dynamic World, 2,* 1–13.

Mishel, E., & Caudillo, M. L. (2017, November 8). Google searches show more worry over gay men and boys than over gay women and girls. *Contexts*. Retrieved from https://contexts.org/blog/google-searches-show-more-worry-over-gay-men-and-boys-than-over-gay-women-and-girls/.

Mize, T. D., & Manago, B. (2018). Precarious sexuality: How men and women are differentially categorized for similar sexual behavior. *American Sociological Review*, *83*(2), 305–330.

Moloney, M. E., & Love, T. P. (2018). Assessing online misogyny: Perspectives from sociology and feminist media studies. *Sociology Compass*, *12*(5), e12577.

Mosse, G. L. (1996). *The image of man*. New York: Oxford University Press.

Munsch, C., & Gruys, K. (2018). What threatens, defines: Tracing the symbolic boundaries of contemporary masculinity. *Sex Roles*, *79*(7/8), 375–392.

Munsch, C., & Willer, R. (2012). The role of gender identity threat in perceptions of date rape and sexual coercion. *Violence Against Women*, *18*(10), 1125–1146.

Murray, D. A. B. (2009). *Homophobias*. Durham, NC: Duke University Press.

Paap, K. (2006). *Working construction: Why white working-class men put themselves—And the labor movement—In harm's way*. Ithaca, NY: IRL Press.

Pascoe, C. J. (2005). 'Dude, you're a fag': Adolescent masculinity and the fag discourses. *Sexualities*, *8*(3), 329–346.

Pascoe, C. J. (2007). *Dude, you're a fag: Masculinity and sexuality in high school*. Berkeley, CA: University of California Press.

Pascoe, C. J., & Bridges, T. (2018). Fag discourse in a post-homophobic era. In D. B. Grusky & J. Hill (Eds.), *Inequality in the 21st century* (pp. 352–358). Boulder, CO: Westview Press.

Pascoe, C. J., & Diefendorf, S. (2019). No homo: Gendered dimensions of homophobic epithets online. *Sex Roles*, *80*(3/4), 123–136.

Pew Research Center. (2017, June 26). Changing attitudes on gay marriage: Public opinion on same-sex marriage. *Pew Research Center, Religion & Public Life*. Retrieved from www.pewforum.org/fact-sheet/changing-attitudes-on-gay-marriage/.

Plummer, D. C. (2001). The quest for modern manhood. *Journal of Adolescence*, *24*(1), 15–23.

Puar, J. (2007). *Terrorist assemblages*. Durham, NC: Duke University Press.

Puar, J. (2013). Rethinking homonationalism. *International Journal of Middle East Studies*, *45*(2), 336–339.

Ratele, K. (2014). Hegemonic African masculinities and men's heterosexual lives. *African Studies Review*, *57*(2), 115–130.

Ruel, E., & Campbell, R. T. (2006). Homophobia and HIV/AIDS: Attitude change in the face of an epidemic. *Social Forces*, *84*(4), 2167–2178.

Schwartz, J. (2010). Investigating differences in public support for gay rights issues. *Journal of Homosexuality*, *57*(6), 748–759.

Seidman, S. (2002). *Beyond the closet*. New York: Routledge.

Silva, T. (2017). Bud-sex: Constructing normative masculinity among rural straight men that have sex with men. *Gender & Society*, *31*(1), 51–73.

Stets, J. E., & Burke, P. J. (2000). Identity theory and social identity theory. *Social Psychology Quarterly*, *63*(3), 224–237.

Tilcsik, A. (2011). Pride and prejudice: Employment discrimination against openly gay men in the United States. *American Journal of Sociology*, *117*(2), 586–626.

Tilly, C. (1999). *Durable inequality*. Berkeley, CA: University of California Press.

Tygart, C. E. (2000). Genetic causation Attribution and public support of gay rights. *International Journal of Public Opinion Research*, *12*(3), 259–275.

Verduzco, I. L., & Sánchez, T. E. R. (2011). La homofobia y su relación con la masculinidad hegemónica en México. *Revista Puertorriqueña De Psicología*, *22*(1), 101–121.

Walters, S. (2014). *The tolerance trap: How God, genes, and good intentions are sabotaging gay*. New York: New York University Press.

Ward, J. (2008). Dude-sex: White masculinities and 'authentic' heterosexuality among dudes who have sex with dudes. *Sexualities*, *11*(4), 414–434.

Ward, J. (2015). *Not gay: Sex between straight white men*. New York: New York University Press.

Willer, R., Rogalin, C., Conlon, B., & Wojnowicz, M. (2013). Overdoing gender: A test of the masculine overcompensation thesis. *American Journal of Sociology*, *118*(4), 980–1022.

23

Multiple forms of masculinity in gay male subcultures

Rusty Barrett

Introduction

Connell's (1995) view of masculinities as multiple and complex originally presumed a fairly uniform hegemonic form of masculinity that was hierarchically positioned above various other forms of masculinity. Given the centrality of heterosexuality to normative understandings of masculinity, gay male masculinities naturally fell on the lowest rung of the masculinity hierarchy. Since Connell's original use of the idea, understandings of hegemonic masculinity have shifted to account for more horizontal relationships between different forms of masculinity and to address issues such as globalization, embodiment, and gender activism (Connell & Messerschmidt, 2005). Even so, gay male forms of masculinity are typically understood as appropriating or mimicking hegemonic heterosexual models of masculinity (Clarkson, 2006; Ravenhill & de Visser, 2017). While many gay men certainly accept and adopt heterosexual models of gender, the situation is often more complex than simply "appropriation". The appropriation model diminishes the actual agency of gay men in the development of distinctly gay expressions of masculinity and fails to capture the complexities involved in the formation of gay male masculinities.

In the period before World War II, European and American gay cultures involved styles that challenged normative masculinity, often involving direct displays of femininity (see Chauncey, 1994). The latter half of the twentieth century saw a move toward much more diversity in ways of expressing gay identity. In particular, subcultures that emerged around expressions of masculinity came to dominate gay culture. While one might assume that lesbians would turn to femininity at the same time, lesbian culture during this period also came to generally reject expressions of femininity (on female masculinity, see Halberstam, 1998). Research before the 1960s focused on the idea of a single "gay subculture" in opposition to straight culture. With the rise of more masculine-oriented gay identities, more and more masculine-oriented gay subcultures have emerged. There have been studies of a number of these, including research on men who meet for sex in public restrooms (Humphreys, 1970), gay skinheads (Healy, 1996), "clones" in the urban 1970s (Levine, 1998), gay gym culture (Alvarez, 2008), African American men on the "down low" (McCune, 2014), and gay gang members (Panfil, 2017).

This chapter uses gay male subcultures to outline an approach to masculinity based in semiotics and sociocultural linguistics. Within this approach, individuals construct specific social personae by creating a *bricolage* (Eckert, 2008; Hebdige, 1979; Lévi-Strauss, 1966) of distinct meanings associated with gender. These meanings are attached with specific "signs", including ways of speaking, gestures, clothing, and so on. We all construct gendered personae using signs associated with both masculinity and femininity in addition to signs that are largely independent of gendered meanings (such as nodding one's head to mean "yes"). These combinations of signs create gender through *performativity* (Austin, 1962; Butler, 1990, 1993).

Performativity allows language to enact forms of social change (including the construction of social personae). Most utterances attempt to describe the world in ways that can be true or false: *I am sleepy*, *Scott is such an asshole*, *Today is February 31st*, and so on. In contrast to such *referential utterances*, the class of *performative utterances* includes those that cause some change in the world (Austin, 1962). Peformatives are utterances like *I now pronounce you husband and wife* or *I sentence you to life in prison*. Unlike referential utterances, performatives cannot be described as being true or false. Rather, they either succeed or fail in making the expected change. Whether or not a performative succeeds depends on elements of the context matching prior cases where the performative succeeded. In other words, for a performative to work, the speaker, setting, context, and so on must be the same as prior successful utterances of the performative. For example, the speaker must have the authority to sentence people to prison (for example), and the utterance must occur in the proper setting (such as in court).

This association between utterances and expected contexts can be described in terms of *indexicality* (Ochs, 1992, 1996; Silverstein, 2003). In addition to referential meanings (the "dictionary" meaning that an utterance conveys), all utterances also convey *indexical meanings* that link utterances with expectations about the contexts in which they might occur (Ochs, 1992; Silverstein, 1992, 1998). Two utterances may share a referential meaning but have very different indexical meanings. Consider the two sentences: *I am in agreement that your suggestion is the proper way to proceed* and *Yaaas, hunty! That's exactly what we got to do!* They both "mean" (referentially) the "same thing", but we have very different ideas about what types of people might say each utterance and in what situations each might be used. The different *ways* we can say "the same thing" allow us to convey information about how we see ourselves, who we think we are talking to, and how we understand the interaction we are experiencing. Just as with legal sentencing or marriage pronouncements, whether or not any given indexical meaning "succeeds" depends on a listener's recognition of some prior case where the indexical meaning also succeeded. So, for example, in the sentences above, if one did not recognize *yaaas* or *hunty* as conveying a given social meaning, the words would fail in conveying the social identity of the speaker (or the relationship between speaker and listener). However, for listeners who have heard these words before, they are likely to evoke associations with Black women in the United States or with gay men (who have appropriated the form).

A word like *hunty* (a portmanteau of *honey* and *cunt*) conveys more than just the identity of the speaker who uses the word; it also lets us know that the speaker assumes the listener will recognize the word and that the relationship between speaker and listener is marked by the solidarity and intimacy between very close friends. These are all indexical meanings associated with the word that require recognition of some prior use of the word. Such indexical meanings are associated with every aspect of our lives. Participation in particular activities, various ways of speaking, gestures, facial expressions, physical movements, clothing, and hairstyles all index various aspects of our social identities. Individuals bring these various indexical "signs" together to construct a unique social persona with a distinctive way of expressing a particular gendered identity. While this bricolage of indexical signs may be unique to a given individual, the social personae we produce are limited by the fact that listeners must recognize the indexical meanings we exploit. Forms of social normativity emerge from the fact that there is a limited set of recognizable links between a sign and the contexts in which it might be expected to occur. Challenging normative indexical meanings associated with any specific sign may be difficult or impossible; it is much easier to challenge norms for combining various indexical meanings (expectations of how signs ought to be combined within the bricolage). For example, the combination of *yaas* and *hunty* is expected (normative) because the two signs point to the same social meanings. A combination like *yaas dude* would be non-normative because the two forms index unrelated identities (with *dude* indexing a white heterosexual masculinity that does not "fit" with the identity indexed by *yaas*).

Using this approach of analyzing combinations of indexical meanings, this chapter reviews ethnographic research on gay male subcultures to demonstrate the ways in which masculinities may be multiple and complex due to the ways in which various signs are combined. While many gay subcultures marginalize displays of femininity, they often have distinct and contradictory ways of understanding and expressing masculinity. These forms of masculinity all involve unique ways of selecting and combining signs that might otherwise index straight forms of masculinity. The chapter presents examples from three specific subcultures: leathermen (involved in BDSM and leather clubs), circuit boys (who regularly attend dance parties in different cities), and bears (an identity based on being heavyset and hairy). While the men who participate in each subculture identify as "gay men" and the members of all of these subcultures in the United States are overwhelmingly white cisgender men, the forms of masculinity they associate with gay identity differ widely across the three subcultures.

Each of these three subcultures has become global to some extent. Often, the spread of subcultures to new areas has correlated with efforts to market specific cities (or neighborhoods) as destinations for gay tourism. Thus, places like Cape Town (Visser, 2003), Sydney (Markwell, 2002), or Mexico City's *Zona Rosa* (Islas Vela, 2013) all have clubs, bars, or events marketed to leathermen, circuit boys, and bears. The globalization of these subcultures involves a local reworking of the indexical signs association with a given identity. Leathermen and circuit boys tend to reproduce the same stylistic norms across regions (see, for example, McCormick, 2018, on leather subculture in South Africa). In contrast, the norms for indexing bear identity show more variation across areas. Thus the aesthetics of Argentine bears, Mexican bears, Brazilian bears, and American bears all index masculinity but do so through distinct associations with social class.

Leathermen

The forms of masculinity associated with leather subculture (Baldwin, 1993; Barrett, 2017; Hennen, 2008; Rubin, 1997, 2000; Townsend, 2004), combine the rebellious, unrestrained masculinity associated with a motorcycle gang member with the highly disciplined and regulated masculinity associated with military institutions or law enforcement. While these two forms of masculinity may seem contradictory, they are both central to leatherman masculinity, and their combination serves to distinguish leathermen from both.

Contemporary leatherman subculture emerged in the years immediately following World War II among gay military personnel who had served overseas during the war (Baldwin, 1993; Rubin, 1997, 2000). Men who first experienced homosexuality in military contexts found the prevailing association between gay male identity and femininity too constraining. These men began to form motorcycle clubs as part of the larger trend of "rebel" biker culture in the 1950s. While biker culture provided a space for gay men to socialize, many maintained the regulated, disciplined, and hierarchical social practices associated with their shared military background. This militaristic regulation is combined with the non-normative sexual practices associated with BDSM (bondage-domination/sado-masochism).

Within this early leather culture, the behaviors of "tops" and "bottoms" were highly regulated. Within BDSM culture, the identities of "top" or "bottom" do not necessarily refer to roles in sexual intercourse but indicate the role one takes in BDSM scripts (with the "bottom" being the dominated partner). Within early leather subculture, the roles of top and bottom were indexed through specific ways of dressing and interacting. Only tops were expected to wear leather caps, and touching another man's cap was strictly forbidden. In contrast, bottoms either went without hats or wore baseball caps. Bottoms who were partnered wore locked collars to mark them as "slaves" (with their top partner possessing the key to the collar) and were expected to walk five steps behind their partner while never looking other men in the eye (Baldwin, 1993). Additional ways of indexing sexual practices emerged through wearing keys on one's hip or bandanas in a back pocket. Keys or bandanas worn on the right indexed identity as a bottom while the left indexed a top. The specific color of the bandana indexed the sexual practices that interested an individual, such as fisting, water sports, or other fetishes (Barrett, 2017). While leather culture historically centered around gay bars, many leathermen refrain from drinking alcohol (or drink lightly) because being drunk dulls the sensations associated with BDSM sex.

While leatherman culture is marked by regimented rules of interaction, dress, and highly structured sexual relationships, it also involves participating in sexual practices (such as fisting or water sports) that index unrestrained sexuality and dressing in ways similar to motorcycle gangs to convey a rebellious and anti-normative masculinity. While the individual signs in leatherman culture tend to be indexically linked to hegemonic forms of masculinity, the signs are combined in ways that do not align with their use by heterosexual men. Within hegemonic heterosexual discourse, the regimented masculinity of the military and the rebel masculinity of the biker conflict with one another. However, in leatherman subculture, signs associated with these two types of masculinity are combined in unique ways that produce a distinctly gay form of masculinity.

Leatherman culture also incorporates ways of interacting specific to gay male culture, such as the interactional patterns associated with "cruising" and the use of sexual banter and "camp" forms of humor (Harvey, 2000). Given this unique constellation of signs indexing different ways of being "masculine", the complexity of leatherman identity is lost if one views leatherman identity as "counter-hegemonic" or as a case of mimicking straight masculinity. As forms of appropriation are always partial, it is often the case that we can gain deeper insight by giving attention to the specific ways in which markers of (various forms of masculinity) are combined.

Circuit boys

Circuit boys are gay men who regularly travel to different cities to attend large dance parties (similar to raves). In contrast to leathermen, circuit boys (Alvarez, 2008; Barrett, 2017; Lewis & Ross, 1995; Weems, 2008) construct masculinity through athleticism, drug use, risk-taking, and competition (especially competition for sexual partners). As with leathermen, circuit boy masculinity is highly normative and combines highly disciplined social practices with comparatively unrestrained and rebellious behaviors.

Within gay culture, the term "circuit" emerged in reference to specific routes for cruising (for sexual partners) in larger cities (Levine, 1998). In the 1970s, smaller American cities (like Columbus or Atlanta) began hosting large dance parties to attract gay tourists. In the late 1980s and 1990s, more and more parties began to be held as fundraisers for HIV/AIDS charities. As the schedule of these parties solidified, a "circuit" or party attendance emerged, leading to the term "circuit party". By the year 2000, there was at least one circuit party every weekend of the year, with parties occurring not only in the US but also all over the world (Barrett, 2017; Weems, 2008). Critics have focused on the prevalence of drugs like GHB, crystal methamphetamine, or ketamine at party events, where overdoses are fairly common. Although there are still regular circuit parties, they have waned since the height of their popularity in the 1990s.

Masculinity among "circuit boys" is built around competition. The competitive nature of circuit parties involves physical appearance, knowledge of music, dancing skills, access to drugs, sexual conquests, and wittiness and skills in producing forms of camp humor (Barrett, 2017). The competitive nature of circuit culture produces a group of elite members who are typically imagined as white and wealthy men who can afford to travel to a different party every weekend (see Signorile, 1997). It is possible, however, for working-class men to enter into the elite members of circuit culture, through sexual attractiveness, dancing skills, or access to drugs.

The competitive sexual market drives circuit boys to maintain rigid workout routines similar to those of models or professional athletes. They typically dress in athletic wear and track shoes (useful for hours of dancing) or go shirtless with loose fitting jeans. While these signs index a disciplined masculinity associated with physical fitness, they are combined with all-night partying and drug use associated with a more reckless "frat boy" type of masculinity.[1] Signs that index these contradictory forms of straight masculinity are combined with practices that index a gay male identity, such as an interest in dancing and the use of camp humor (Barrett, 2017; Harvey, 2000).

Some practices associated with circuit identities simultaneously index multiple forms of masculinity. For example, beer or other alcoholic beverages are often unavailable at circuit parties, where many participants carry bottled water with them (or keep a bottle in their back pocket). Refraining from alcohol and carrying a bottle of water at all times index the commitment to fitness associated with circuit athleticism. However, circuit boys put their drugs (particularly GHB) in their water bottles, so that they are regularly drinking water not to maintain health but to ingest drugs. Setting the bottle down runs the risk of someone else walking away with your drugs and "ruining your buzz". This is an example of the way in which interpretation may depend on whether or not one recognizes prior performative uses of a sign. An outsider might assume that a circuit boy is drinking water because he is an athlete and wants to stay hydrated while dancing, while circuit insiders know that the water bottle is just for taking drugs.

As with leathermen, circuit masculinity involves the combination of signs associated with different and even contradictory forms of hegemonic straight masculinity. Given that the performative construction of masculinity is limited by a restricted number of signs one can use to index gender, distinct types of masculinity emerge not from appropriating or mimicking straight masculinity but, rather, through the combination of masculine (and feminine) signs in new and unique ways.

Bears

Bear subculture focuses on gay men who are heavyset and/or hairy (Barrett, 2017; Hennen, 2008; Suresha, 2002; Wright, 1997, 2001). As a subculture, bears emerged in the late 1980s and 1990s in the United States. Although early bears were primarily located in Northern California, the subculture spread quickly through mailing lists on the emerging internet. Since then, bear subculture has spread globally, with unique forms of bear identity emerging in different global contexts.

In contrast to the highly regimented and regulated forms of masculinity found with leathermen and circuit boys, bear masculinity in the United States is stereotypically imagined as natural and effortless (despite being constructed in the same ways as any other form of masculinity). Although bears typically view their gender expression as "natural" compared to other forms of gay male masculinity, their critics typically argue that bears simply mimic straight forms of masculinity (Harris, 1997). Although early bears emphasized the "naturalness" of their form of masculinity, bear understandings of gender were widely discussed and deeply considered, drawing heavily on feminist writings about body image. The emphasis on naturalness contributes to the essentialization of bear identity, and men may be described as bears regardless of whether or not they identify as part of the subculture. The idea that one is naturally a bear is common in early bear discourse, and many bears commonly discuss feeling ostracized and uncomfortable in gay male social settings until they "came out" as bears.

Early bear masculinity in the United States appropriated widely from working-class Southern forms of masculinity. Although (white cisgender heterosexual) working-class Southern men are stereotyped as usually being heavyset, their masculinity is never in question. In contrast, gay culture has traditionally marginalized larger men as being overly effeminate (for lacking the physical strength associated with masculinity). In appropriating signs that are indexically associated with working-class men in the South, bears are able to link overweight bodies with masculine attributes such as drinking beer, following American football, camping, or wearing collared shirts with the sleeves cut off (Barrett, 2017). As bear identity has spread to become a global phenomenon, the distinct form of masculinity associated with bears has varied across different cultural context. For example, while bear culture in the United States exploits styles associated with working-class men, in Mexico, *oso* style primarily indexes middle-class ("business casual") masculinity. In contrast, *ursos* in Brazil orient more towards a working-class aesthetic more like that found in the United States (see Diniz, 2017).

Because bears in the United States developed a style founded on working-class masculinity, some argue that bears simply mimic heterosexual norms of masculinity while others praise bears for challenging views of gay men as inherently effeminate (see Barrett, 2017). These opposing views have spread as bear identity has become global. For example, Benavides-Meriño (2016) criticizes bear culture in Chile for reproducing heterosexual masculinity, while Blázquez and Liarte Tiloca (2013) praise bears in Argentina for challenging stereotypes of gay men as effeminate. Both views presume that bear masculinity is entirely founded in heterosexual masculinity. These perspectives also miss the full complex understandings of gender within bear culture, which is much more accepting of gay male effeminacy compared to leathermen or circuit boys. Although bear culture appropriates widely from Southern U.S. working-class culture, the signs that are appropriated do not all index masculine identities. Among bears, activities such as knitting, crafting, and sharing recipes occur alongside activities like camping or watching sports on television. Bears also exploit signs that, while indexing Southern working-class identity, are largely neutral in terms of marking gender. For example, early bears listened to country music and incorporated elements of

Appalachian English into their writing (Barrett, 2017). Describing bear gender expression as "straight masculinity" erases the complexity of the ways in which gender (and non-gendered) signs are combined to construct a distinct bear identity.

Conclusion

Each of these three subcultures has a unique form of gender expression that could more generally be called "gay masculinity". However, each subcultural masculinity is quite distinct, despite the fact that members of all three groups would identify themselves as "gay men". In all cases, the norms for conveying specific subcultural forms of masculinity involve creating indexical links with different "types" of masculinity. Leathermen combine the regimented militaristic discipline of the military with the rebellious lawless masculinity of motorcycle gangs. Circuit boys like the disciplined controlled masculinity of professional athletes with a reckless partying persona closer to the masculinity associated with college fraternities. Bears appropriate widely from Southern working-class culture but combine signs that index masculinity with other signs that may convey femininity or may not be associated with gender at all. In all three cases, the unique pattern of masculinity is produced through an innovative way of combining indexical signs associated with gender more broadly.

These distinct forms of masculinity permeate subcultural practices ranging from personal style to sexual behavior. For example, leathermen and circuit boys both tend to engage in sexual interactions at a specific preset time, while bears expect sex to occur spontaneously. These patterns correspond to understandings of masculinity as disciplined (among leathermen and circuit boys) or as something which occurs naturally (among bears). In the same way, patterns of consumption align with subcultural views of masculinity. Leathermen may drink beer in moderate amounts, but circuit boys refrain from beer entirely (both because it might dull the sensations of drug use and because it contains so many calories). In contrast, beer is central to bear identity and is always available at bear events. In North American culture, beer is generally associated with working-class men, thus reinforcing the link between class and masculinity found elsewhere in bear culture.

Similarly, ways of dressing and forms of body modification may also index understandings of gender specific to each subculture. An example is the removal of body hair. Circuit boys generally remove all body hair (often by waxing), leaving only small tufts of pubic and underarm hair. The hairless male body makes it easier to see muscle definition and serves to index the masculinity associated with athletes, bodybuilders, male models, and porn actors. In contrast, body hair is highly valued among bears. Bears typically view the removal of body hair as "unnatural" and feminine, never shaving their body hair and often wearing beards to emphasize their "natural" masculinity. For leathermen, shaving or removing body hair is not linked to gender in the same ways, so that some leathermen shave their bodies like "musclemen" and others grow beards or mustaches more reminiscent of the "biker" side of leatherman masculinity. Thus the same sign (a waxed chest, for example) may index masculinity, femininity, or neither. The actual gendered meaning of the sign is only recognizable once that sign is combined with other signs with their own gendered indexical meanings.

Local understandings of masculinity even influence the ways that participants in different subcultures imagine themselves as forming a specific type of community. Circuit boys call themselves a *tribe*, and bears refer to themselves as a *brotherhood*, while leathermen see themselves as forming a "leather *nation*". These different ways of imagining community index the normative forms of masculinity associated with subcultural identities. For circuit boys, the concept of a "tribe" indexes the primal sexuality, experimentation with drugs, and strict adherence to ritual associated with the social persona of a circuit elite. The bear "brotherhood" conveys solidarity (as brothers) while indexing working-class masculinity by mirroring the use of "brotherhood" by labor unions such as the *International Brotherhood of Teamsters Chauffeurs, Warehousemen and Helpers of America*. For leathermen, the idea of a "nation" indexes the political unity and patriotism associated with the militaristic and disciplined side of leatherman masculinity. These distinct ways of describing their collective identities index the unique ways in which each subculture understands masculinity as an aspect of gay male identity.

While it is certainly reasonable to talk about forms of masculinity with broad terms such as "hegemonic masculinity" or "gay male masculinity", it is important to recognize the range of masculinities within such categories. Any individual's gender expression involves the combination of multiple signs, most of which are linked to specific indexical meanings associated with gender. These signs can be ways of speaking, manners of dress and personal style, or participation in particular activities. Because gender is conveyed through these combinations of signs, the gendered meaning of any given sign is only interpretable in relation to the other co-occurring gendered signs. Cowboy boots might be "masculine" in isolation, but when combined with a sequined evening gown and a wig, their ability to convey a masculine identity is greatly diminished. While each of the gay male subcultures considered here exploits forms of masculinity that are also associated with heterosexual men, they also combine signs associated with straight masculinity in new ways that create distinct innovative gay masculinities.

Note

1 A "frat boy" refers to members of college fraternities in the United States. Frat boys are stereotyped as carefree wealthy white young men who are primarily interested in throwing parties and drinking heavily.

References

Alvarez, E. (2008). *Muscle boys: Gay gym culture*. New York: Routledge.

Austin, J. L. (1962). *How to do things with words*. Oxford: Clarendon.

Baldwin, G. (1993). *Ties that bind: SM/leather/fetish/erotic style: Issues, commentaries and advice*. Los Angeles, CA: Daedalus.

Barrett, R. (2017). *From drag queens to leathermen: Language, gender, and gay male subcultures*. New York: Oxford University Press.

Benavides-Meriño, D. (2016). Osos, conceptualizando sus masculinidades en Santiago de Chile. *Revista de Psicología: Universidad de Cile*, *25*(2), 1–18.

Blázquez, G., & Liarte Tiloca, A. (2013). *Osos, locas y chongos: Masculinidades homosexuales en Córdoba*. Paper presented at the XXIX Congreso de la Asociación Latinoamericana de Sociología. Santiago, Chile. Retrieved from http://actacientifica.servicioit.cl/biblioteca/gt/GT11/GT11_BlazquezGLiarteA.pdf.

Butler, J. (1990). *Gender trouble: Feminism and the subversion of identity*. New York: Routledge.

Butler, J. (1993). *Bodies that matter: On the discursive limits of "sex"*. New York: Routledge.

Chauncey, G. (1994). *Gay New York: Gender, urban culture, and the makings of the gay male world, 1890–1940*. New York: Basic Books.

Clarkson, J. (2006). "Everyday Joe" versus "pissy, bitchy, queens": Gay masculinity on StraightActing.com. *The Journal of Men's Studies*, *14*(2), 191–207.

Connell, R. W. (1995). *Masculinities: Knowledge, power and social change*. Berkeley, CA: University of California Press.

Connell, R. W., & Messerschmidt, J. W. (2005). Hegemonic masculinity: Rethinking the concept. *Gender & Society*, *19*(6), 829–859.

Diniz, A. H. T. (2017). *Os corpos dos ursos: Uma ethnografia do Meio Ursino Paulistano* (Master's thesis). Instituto de Filosofia e Ciências Humanas, Universidade Estadual de Campinas, Brazil.

Eckert, P. (2008). Variation and the indexical field. *Journal of Sociolinguistics, 12*(4), 453–476.
Halberstam, J. (1998). *Female masculinity*. Durham, NC: Duke University Press.
Harris, D. (1997). *The rise and fall of gay culture*. New York: Hyperion.
Harvey, K. (2000). Describing camp talk: Language/pragmatics/politics. *Language and Literature, 9*(3), 240–260.
Healy, M. (1996). *Gay skins: Class, masculinity, and queer appropriation*. New York: Cassell.
Hebdige, D. (1979). *Subculture: The meaning of style*. London: Methuen.
Hennen, P. (2008). *Faeries, bears and leathermen: Men in community queering the masculine*. Chicago, IL: University of Chicago Press.
Humphreys, L. (1970). *Tearoom trade: Impersonal sex in public places*. Chicago, IL: Aldine.
Islas Vela, D. R. (2013). *Zona Rosa como territorio queer: Entre la empresarialiad, el consume y el cresol de identidades gay* (Licenciate thesis). Universidad Autónoma Metropolitana, Unidad Iztapalapa.
Levine, M. (1998). *Gay macho: The life and death of the gay clone*. Ed. Michael Kimmel. New York: New York University Press.
Lévi-Strauss, C. (1966). *The savage mind*. Chicago, IL: University of Chicago Press.
Lewis, L. A., & Ross, M. W. (1995). *A select body: The gay dance party subculture and the HIV/AIDS pandemic*. London: Cassell.
Markwell, K. (2002). Mardis Gras tourism and the construction of Sydney as an international gay and lesbian city. *GLQ, 8*(1/2), 81–99.
McCormick, T. L. (2018). Gay leathermen in South Africa: An exploratory study. *Agenda: Empowering Women for Gender Equity, 32*(3), 74–86.
McCune, J. Q., Jr. (2014). *Sexual discretion: Black masculinity and the politics of passing*. Chicago, IL: University of Chicago Press.
Ochs, E. (1992). Indexing gender. In A. Duranti & C. Goodwin (Eds.), *Rethinking context* (pp. 335–358). Cambridge: Cambridge University Press.
Ochs, E. (1996). Linguistic resources for socializing humanity. In C. Coodwin & S. Levinson (Eds.), *Rethinking linguistic relativity* (pp. 407–437). Cambridge: Cambridge University Press.
Panfil, V. R. (2017). *The gang's all queer: The lives of gay gang members*. New York, NY: New York University Press.
Ravenhill, J. P., & de Visser, R. O. (2017). "There are too many gay categories now": Discursive constructions of gay masculinity. *Psychology of Men & Masculinity, 18*(4), 321–330.
Rubin, G. (1997). Elegy for the valley of the kings: AIDS and the leather community in San Francisco, 1981–1996. In M. Levine, P. Nardi & J. Gagnon (Eds.), *In changing times: Gay men and lesbians encounter HIV/AIDS* (pp. 101–143). Chicago: University of Chicago Press.
Rubin, G. (2000). Sites, settlements and urban sex: Archaeology and the study of gay leathermen in San Francisco, 1955–1995. In R. A. Schmidt & B. L. Voss (Eds.), *Archaeologies of sexuality* (pp. 62–88). New York: Routledge.
Signorile, M. (1997). *Life outside—The Signorile report on gay men: Sex, drugs, muscles, and the passages of life*. New York: Harper Collins.
Silverstein, M. (1992). Metapragmatic discourse and metapragmatic function. In J. Lucy (Ed.), *Reflexive language* (pp. 33–58). Cambridge: Cambridge University Press.
Silverstein, M. (1998). The uses and utility of ideology: A commentary. In B. B. Schieffelin, K. A. Woolard & P. V. Kroskrity (Eds.), *Language ideologies: Practice and theory* (pp. 123–145). New York: Oxford University Press.
Silverstein, M. (2003). Indexical order and the dialectics of sociolinguistic life. *Language and Communication, 23*(3/4), 193–229.
Suresha, R. J. (2002). *Bears on bears: Interviews and discussions*. New York: Alyson.
Townsend, L. (2004). *The leatherman's handbook: Silver jubilee edition*. Beverly Hills, CA: L.T. Publications.
Visser, G. (2003). Gay men, leisure space and South African cities: The case of Cape Town. *Geoforum, 34*(1), 123–137.
Weems, M. (2008). *The fierce tribe: Masculine identity and performance in the circuit*. Logan, UT: Utah State University Press.
Wright, L. (Ed.). (1997). *The bear book: Readings in the history and evolution of a gay male subculture*. New York: Harrington Park Press.
Wright, L. (Ed.). (2001). *The bear book II: Further readings in the history and evolution of a gay male subculture*. New York: Harrington Park Press.

24

Sexual affects

Masculinity and online pornographies

Steve Garlick

The emergence of the internet as a site for sexual expression and representation over the past twenty years has led to the global expansion of pornography. The 1970s and 1980s saw much debate over pornography as feminists and many masculinity researchers developed critiques of the genre that emphasized gendered inequalities of power. After the apparent exhaustion of those debates and a subsequent period of relative latency, the topic has re-emerged as a contentious issue in gender and sexual politics. In the interim period, however, pornography has changed. Technology has always been important to the evolution of pornography, and new online pornographies have proliferated in diverse forms as digital technologies of production, distribution, and reception increasingly shape contemporary sexual experiences. Pornography is now part of a global technological ecosystem, and the forms of masculinity embedded within it have the potential to influence gender relations far from their points of production. Contemporary pornographies are also increasingly indistinct from other forms of popular culture, thus requiring new ways of thinking about the place of pornography in social relations.

This chapter briefly reviews older debates on pornography – focusing mainly on the contributions of masculinity scholars – before taking up the question of how we should best approach the study of online pornographies today. I discuss contemporary work on pornography and masculinity and highlight its strengths, gaps, and points of intersection with feminist perspectives on the topic. I then consider how online pornographies differ from older forms and why they call for a different research approach. Central to the argument of the chapter is the claim that masculinity studies must engage with theories of affect if it is to adequately respond to the challenge of understanding the stakes of gender politics in online pornographies.

The emergence of debates over pornography

If conceived simply in terms of explicit sexual representations, pornography might be said to be as old as recorded human history. However, the emergence of what is conventionally understand as pornography in most of the world today can be traced back to nineteenth-century Europe. Lynn Hunt (1993) argues that the beginnings of a genre of sexual representation resembling contemporary pornography first emerged alongside print culture in the sixteenth century. These texts and images were initially formulated mainly as forms of social or religious criticism that rejected conventional moralities, but then came to take on a more political tone in the eighteenth century. Hunt notes that this early modern literature is marked by a "preponderance of female narrators" (usually prostitutes) who were "most often portrayed as independent, determined, financially successful and scornful of the new ideals of female virtue and domesticity" (p. 38) rather than simply as sexual objects of masculine desire. The historical evidence suggests that the early nineteenth century was the crucial period for defining modern pornography as we now know it (Kendrick 1987). At this time, sexual representations lost their overtly subversive qualities, and the peculiar character of modern pornography began to take shape around the pleasures that men took in the explicit display of women's bodies (Hunt 1993, p. 42). Moral concerns over pornography at this time did not focus on gender relations, however. Walter Kendrick (1987) points out that attempts to censor, control, or eliminate pornography were driven by "the urge to regulate the behavior of those who seem to threaten the social order" (p. 235). The working classes, as well as colonized and racialized others, were considered to be closer to nature and therefore more susceptible to the disruptive affective forces unleashed by explicit sexual representations.

It was in the 1970s and 1980s, alongside the rise of second-wave feminism, that debates over pornography assumed an important place in Western gender politics. A substantial literature was generated, dominated by the work of Andrea Dworkin (1981) and Catherine MacKinnon (1987), around the contention that pornography was a form of discrimination and violence against women. Masculinity studies were less developed at this time, but some scholars did turn their attention to pornography. Most notable was the collection *Men Confront Pornography*, edited by Michael Kimmel (1990). Kimmel's introductory essay followed Dworkin's and MacKinnon's line of argument in asserting that pornography should be understood as gendered speech that takes place between men. His position emphasized that it is not sexual pleasure but, rather, men's sense of themselves as men that is at stake. For Kimmel, porn is important because it transmits messages to young men about the relationship between sexuality and masculinity. As a part of societies in which sexism is pervasive, pornography reflects men's anger against women, and it serves as a site in which masculinity may be recuperated through fantasies of sexual domination.

Many masculinity scholars adopted the feminist critique of pornography at this time. Prominent among them was John Stoltenberg (1990), whose book *Refusing to Be a Man* contained several essays stridently denouncing pornography. For Stoltenberg, the promoters and defenders of porn confused the issues of sexual freedom and sexual justice. He argued that the so-called sexual freedoms displayed in pornography were in fact premised on sexual injustice, male superiority, and the oppression of women, and that what was being consumed was in fact eroticized domination and subordination. In effect, pornography was part of a feedback loop through which a sexually unjust society represented and affirmed itself. As Stoltenberg (1990) described it, "pornography *institutionalizes* the sexuality that both embodies and enacts male supremacy" (pp. 112–113). Notably, he also includes gay male pornography within the ambit of male supremacist sexuality, arguing that it "also contains frequent derogatory references to women, or to feminized males" (p. 115). For Stoltenberg, both straight and gay porn idealize a form of masculinity that is unable to acknowledge women as equals.

Polemic accounts such as Stoltenberg's characterized pornography in very one-dimensional terms. However, not all early work on this topic was lacking in nuance. Harry Brod's (1990) essay "Eros thanatized: Pornography and sexuality," for example, analyzed some of the more ambivalent aspects of men's interactions with pornography. Arguing that pornography is the product of capitalist culture, Brod (1990) claimed that "the same forces that objectify women work to restrict and limit male sexuality as well. … The male performance principle has herein moved from the workplace to the bedroom" (p. 197). From this perspective, the consumption of porn does not necessarily serve as a salve for men's anger against women, or as an affirmation of male supremacy, but can in fact alienate men from unrealized capacities of their own bodies and lives. For Brod, pornography, along with its misrepresentation of women, poses problems for men, exacerbating tensions and discomforts rather than dispelling them. Insightfully, he observes that pornographic representations of sexuality may actually have the paradoxical effect of lessening the intensity of desire – of fostering a desire for stasis – rather than contributing to the development of the life-affirming and creative power of Eros. Central here is Brod's (1990) claim that pornography "obliterates specific differences among people in order to achieve a standard uniformity in objects of desire" (p. 194). As I have argued in more detail elsewhere (Garlick 2010, 2011), these ideas anticipate the emergence of online pornographic websites with their elaborate classificatory schemas that collapse differences even as they seemingly multiple them.

Contemporary debates on pornography

Pornography was a flashpoint issue for second-wave feminism throughout the 1970s and 1980s. By the end of the latter decade, however, the debate seemed to be reaching a point of exhaustion. Linda Williams's (1989) *Hard Core* signalled the emergence of a new approach to the study of pornography as both a genre of film and a legitimate form of popular culture. The book fostered a range of new work on pornography associated both with what is sometimes referred to as "sex-positive" feminism and with approaches that decentred gender politics in order to explore other aspects of the genre. Most notably, the advent of the internet and the growth of online pornographies has provided a significant stimulus to new work in this area. Strident anti-porn feminism has re-emerged as a force (Boyle 2010; Dines 2010; Long 2012), which has been countered with defences of the value of pornography (Jacobs 2007; McNair 2013) alongside more nuanced feminist analyses of the relationship between heteroporn and violence (Purcell 2012). Moreover, such discussions are not limited to the Global North, and feminists from the Global South have debated the significance of pornography in societies where gender norms and the expression of women's sexualities are contested in different forms, especially in contexts marked more visibly by concerns over HIV transmission (Artz 2012). Scholarship on gay porn has also expanded as its importance to the validation of gay desires has been increasingly recognized (Maddison 2017), as has the growing range of gay masculinities on offer (Mercer 2017). Other scholars have documented the increasing erosion of the boundaries between pornography and mainstream culture (Attwood 2009; Paasonen, Nikunen & Saarenmaa 2007) and this has led to the emergence of new perspectives on the production, distribution, and consumption of sexual materials.

With regard to contemporary masculinity studies, there has been research into the question of the impact of the pervasive character of pornographies on young men's formative sexual experiences and their relationships with women. Michael Flood (2007, 2010)) has demonstrated that there are gendered patterns of consumption whereby young men in Western countries view pornography with much greater frequency than young women. Given the possibility that this exposure forms a significant source of information about sexuality and "may intensify boys' investment in problematic constructions of gender and sexuality" (2007, p. 57), Flood (2010) calls for "pornography education" wherein boys are taught the critical media literacy skills that will enable them to resist sexist elements of pornographic representations (p. 177). What is of particular concern for Flood (2010) is that "'meta-analysis' finds consistent evidence that exposure to or consumption of pornography is related to male sexual aggression against women" (p. 175). Similarly, Walter DeKeseredy (2015) notes that pornography is often used as a tool to facilitate violence against women in domestic spaces. Although noting that "real world" research on the link between pornography and violence is sparse, DeKeseredy (2015) argues that "there is ample evidence showing that porn is a key risk factor associated with a myriad of abusive experiences in the lives of many adult and young women" (p. 11). Relatedly, the phenomenon of "revenge pornography", or the non-consensual sharing of explicit sexual images, has recently attracted critical attention (Hall & Hearn 2017).

A critical perspective on pornography is also present in Michael Kimmel's more recent work. In *Guyland: The Perilous World where Boys Become Men*, Kimmel (2008) devotes considerable attention to analyzing how pornography fits into the stage of extended adolescence that many young men in Western cultures increasingly find themselves inhabiting. For Kimmel, Guyland is a homosocial space in which young men struggle to live up to unattainable ideals of masculinity. Within this environment, one of the main avenues for proving manhood is the assertion of heterosexuality through the sexual conquest of women. Consequently, porn is appealing to young men as it provides them with access to a fantasy world in which women are always compliant with their desires. In the world of porn, men never need to take no for an answer, and, for Kimmel, the troubling aspects of this situation are that "the sexual fantasies of many young men become more revenge fantasies than erotic ones" (p. 175). Pornography, from this perspective, is used by young men to bond together against women, and it reflects a problematic sense of entitlement and privilege – especially that of white, middle-class men.

Generally speaking, it is anti-porn feminism that is still the predominant influence on masculinity studies in this area. This is reflected in the most sustained treatment of the topic: Robert Jensen's (2007) *Getting Off: Pornography and the End of Masculinity*. Jensen argues that mainstream heterosexual pornography holds a mirror up to conventional masculinity and allows us to see how the men who consume it view women. He points to the sexual violence and cruelty that characterizes a significant amount of contemporary porn as evidence that there are serious problems with predominant definitions of masculinity today. His work follows the path laid out by anti-porn feminism and draws inspiration from the work of Dworkin (1981) in particular. For Jensen, porn is misogyny and props up patriarchy. He notes that the sexual acts depicted in mainstream heterosexual pornography have become progressively more extreme over recent decades, and the appearance of acts such as "ass to mouth" sequences are taken to be indicative of the fact that men want to view sexual images in which women are degraded, treated cruelly, and suffer pain (pp. 59–61). Such claims are surely important to consider, yet Jensen's focus is quite narrow. His almost exclusive emphasis on interpreting porn in terms of violent or aggressive representations leaves little space for acknowledging partiality, complexity, or the underdetermined play of affect within pornographic experiences. Moreover, while Jensen recognizes that the internet has revolutionized the distribution of pornography, he does not consider whether this technology might be more than simply a means of expanding the delivery of an existing product. In contrast, the next section suggests that research on masculinity and contemporary pornographies needs to pay more attention to the ways in which the latter are being reshaped by online environments and digital technologies.

Online pornographies

Pornography has always been closely linked with developments in technology – most notably, the printing press, photography, film, and video – and digital technologies and the internet exert their own influence. Notably, online pornographies are increasingly disseminated via "tube" sites that make it easy for users to post and watch pornographic videos. The success of YouTube.com, founded in 2005, provided impetus for this type of porn site. YouTube, which serves as a distribution platform rather than as a provider of content, is widely viewed as exemplary of the participatory culture associated with Web 2.0. Its success quickly spawned pornographic imitators that, like YouTube itself, often began as independent ventures only to eventually become part of larger commercial and multinational corporate entities. In its shift online, porn has become a global business, and it is often difficult to trace ownership of popular tube sites such as xvideos.com, which may be registered in and operate out of different countries. One of the biggest players in this arena is the Luxembourg-domiciled corporation MindGeek, which owns and runs a number of the most popular online porn sites such as YouPorn.com, RedTube.com, PornHub.com, Tube8.com, and XTube .com. These sites form a linked network, and the effect is to create an impression of abundance, diversity, and choice. All of the sites emphasize that they are "free" and serve the needs of their "community", but they actually offer a mixture of (mostly short) free content and "premium" content, such as high-definition videos or live cams that require payment.

"Tube" sites are often taken to represent the democratizing potential of the internet. Indeed, one of the most interesting features of these sites is the way that different types of pornography occupy the same space. Clips of mainstream heteroporn, which often serve as advertising for commercial porn sites, sit side by side with diverse amateur productions – both those that require payment to access and others that are given away freely to others. Numerous commentators have suggested that the combination of affordable digital-recording devices and tube sites has made possible the creation of new alternative pornographies, which diversifies the range of body types represented in porn and enables independent sex workers to earn more money in a less exploitative environment, often working out of their own homes (Attwood 2007; Jacobs 2007; Lehman 2006; McNair 2002). Critics, however, have argued that most amateur porn on tube sites merely ends up reproducing the conservative gender ideologies associated with commercial heteroporn (van Doorn 2010). In a study of XTube.com, Sharif Mowlabocus (2010) notes the diversity of sexualities, bodies, and personalities evident on the site, as well as the direct connections that it fosters between members, but he is sceptical about the prospects of this leading to a reorganizing of the power relationships that characterize the porn industry. For Mowlabocus, new online modes of distribution demand increased productivity, constant availability, and forms of immaterial labour that leave independent sex workers in the same precarious position as flexible labourers at the lower reaches of the capitalist system (p. 83).

To further appreciate the specificities of contemporary online pornographies, however, it is necessary to recognize that the experience of watching a particular video clip is shaped by the technical structure and organization of a website. On the homepage of most pornographic tube sites, users are immediately presented with an array of options. There are thumbnails of recently posted video clips, along with advertisements for pay sites, and usually the invitation to "browse by category". An array of video clips is presented, each classified in a way that calls up desires for specific types of (usually) women, body parts, or sexual experience. When users arrive on a selected page within a website, they are offered an experience that is not simply one of watching a pornographic video clip. Indeed, the ostensible object of interest usually occupies less than half of the screen and is often slower to load than the other components around it. Instead of what was initially desired, the viewer's eye is drawn to advertising panels that run along the bottom and down the side of the screen. Within them, images move rapidly, colours are oversaturated, poses are striking, penises and breasts are oversized, and a hyperreal context is generated that frames the content of the video clip itself. This multimodal context shapes how users interact with and experience the pornographic videos they select to view. Tube sites especially are designed to undermine the (normatively male) viewer's satisfaction with the sexual representations on offer in the free video clips. Although no two viewers will experience a particular video clip in exactly the same way, each is positioned in a structurally similar relation to their ostensible object of desire. Although the homepage promises to endow the user with control via the ability to call up precisely the sexual object that will satisfy any desire, the experience of moving farther into a site undercuts this initial expectation.

Perhaps most importantly, as I have argued in more detail elsewhere (Garlick 2016, pp. 134–146), many of the ads on tube sites promise a "more real" experience that is to be found elsewhere. Ads often promise women "in your area" who want to "meet up for sex tonight" or women "available now" on live cams, all apparently accessible simply by clicking through the link. These messages activate what is arguably the underlying tension in the relationship between masculinity and online pornography – one which is generated by the ambivalence and ongoing ambiguity around the cultural status of masturbation. At least in the Western world, the central act toward which all pornographies lead cannot be easily detached from its historical legacy as the site of moral panics (Laqueur 2003). The question that lurks behind the desire on which online pornographies feed is whether it is really possible to be a man, to dwell securely in the masculine, while sitting and masturbating in front of a computer. Real sex is always elsewhere, and the design of online tube sites seem intended to activate and then profit from this tension.

Pornographic affects

Feminist interventions into debates over pornography, especially in North America, have often revolved around the issue of free speech. With some exceptions (Mason-Grant 2004), this has meant downplaying the material and embodied dimensions of the phenomenon. However, the overdetermined, multimodal production of meaning that characterizes many pornographic websites does not operate in a way that can be straightforwardly translated into a discursive mode. Rather, these are spaces where we can glimpse the indeterminate role of affect in the embodied circuit of pornographic production, distribution, and consumption. Indeed, as Natalie Purcell (2012) has noted, online pornographies are increasingly invested in the reality and authenticity of "intense physical and emotional experiences" (p. 156). That pornography operates via the circulation of affect might seem obvious insofar as it is immediately felt or registered by the body, yet its theorization in these terms is relatively recent and coincides with the emergence of online pornographies. Technology is a part of the pornographic ecosystem that generates and circulates affects, and recent work on online pornographies has begun to develop analytic frames that account for the workings of affect.

The concept of "affect" broadly refers to the dynamic entwining of power and energetic bodily matter prior to or in excess of discursive subjectivity. The most sophisticated discussion of affect in contemporary pornographies is to be found in Susanna Paasonen's *Carnal Resonance: Affect and Online Pornography* (2011). For Paasonen, porn is both semiotic, with representations that must be deciphered, and material insofar as it offers embodied intensities and affects. Because the latter are continually in excess of the former, critical and textual analyses of gender ideology or signification will always miss something important. As she puts it, pornography "tries to mediate the sensory and to attach the viewing body to its affective loop: in porn, bodies move and move the bodies of those watching" (p. 2).

Paasonen uses the term "resonance" to capture the interactive, visceral processing of affect in the reception of online pornographies. Here, affects are sensations and intensities that traverse bodies and that depend upon a complex ecosystem of producers, users, technologies, representations, capital, and labour. Affects can be nonlinear, unpredictable, ambivalent, and ambiguous; hence, for Paasonen, it is not a matter of being pro- or anti-porn but of trying to trace the diverse movements and attachments that pornographic affects enable.

Paasonen draws out the complicated intertwining of affective resonances with discursive attitudes of critique, resistance, or recognition in responses to online pornographies. In particular, her analysis of solitary porn users highlights the affective dynamic of arousal, desire, shame, and disgust that often accompanies masturbation in Western cultures. This affective dynamic reinforces the sense of ambiguity that attaches itself to masculinity in the pornographic domain, although Paasonen herself does not pursue questions related to gender. She acknowledges that the generic conventions of heteroporn are shaped by gender, especially the perspectives and pleasures of heterosexual men, yet she eschews any critical analysis of masculinity or gender relations. Instead, Paasonen continually characterizes critical questions concerning gender as being limited to issues of representation, identity, and ideology, which are said to hypostatize the processes at work in porn and to impose a fixed meaning on them from the outside. Drawing on Eve Sedgwick (2003), Paasonen's (2011) contention is that "in a paranoid reading, we will always 'know' that this is what pornography is and what it does; it will always be sexist, racist, classist, ageist, and ableist" (p. 243). However, I suggest that what needs to be asked here is whether all critical attention to gender in relation to pornography does indeed fall into the category of paranoid reading, or whether it might enter into issues related to affect in a different way.

Paasonen's work might be said to be a mirror opposite of Jensen's and of other studies that are dismissive of pornography as straightforwardly corrupted by masculine domination. Instead, I suggest that what is required moving forward are critical analyses of gender and pornography that encompass the always present indeterminacies of affect. A starting point might be found in Jensen's (2007) claim that it is important to recognize "how central the concept of control – of women by men – is to pornography" (p. 114). Paradoxically, however, Jensen also notes that women in the fantasy world of pornography always want sex and, if they do not immediately realize this fact, they can easily be persuaded because "it is their nature" as women (pp. 56–57). Taken together, these claims suggest that men's control appears to be less about violence than about the ability to call forth what is allegedly inherent to women's nature. Indeed, it is the link between control and nature that I suggest lies at the centre of a more productive engagement between masculinity studies and studies of affect in online pornographies. Insofar as affect concerns bodily potentials and capacities, it necessarily concerns corporeal natural forces, their susceptibility to domination, and their capacities for resistance and self-organization. It also concerns control. As Paasonen (2011) puts it, "affect points to uncontrollability in our encounters with porn – to a rupture between gut reactions and the fantasy of self-control" (p. 24). Within the pornographic experience, embodied nature becomes a site of contestation between the flow of affect and control of both oneself and others.

Pornographic affect calls us back to our embodiment as physical beings within a complex natural-social-technological ecology. It evokes an awareness of our status as a part of nature, subject to forces beyond our own control. Thus it is difficult to see how gender, as a technology of sex/nature, could not be a relevant dimension of the analysis. Gender, within the modern pornographic era, is the conceptual apparatus of sex. It enframes sexual desires and brings them to order. More specifically, we might note that fantasies of self-control are not gender-neutral. The imaginary position from which one exerts control over the world, including self-control, is normatively the masculine position.

The domination and control of nature, however, can never be complete, not only because affect will always escape but also because the feminine objects of the pornographic imagination must maintain a degree of agency for the fantasy to work. Women's imputed "natural" desire for the penis and semen, as the source of their pleasure, displaces the troubling features of men's need for sex and sustains the illusion of masculine control, yet without placing the full weight of this challenge on men. At the same time, however, as pornographic affects challenge participants' control of their bodies and of their sexual experiences, it undoes the ontological security that gender provides to individuals by assigning them a place in the social order. This reinforces the sense in which pornography carries an ambivalent charge for masculinity. The propagation of sexual affect is both an opportunity to establish masculinity through bodily control as well as a threat to the structure and institution of masculine dominance.

References

Artz, L. (2012). "Porn norms": A South African feminist conversation about pornography. *Agenda, 26,* (3), 8–18.

Attwood, F. (2007). No money shot? Commerce, pornography and new sex taste cultures. *Sexualities, 10,* (4), 441–456.

Attwood, F. (Ed.). (2009). *Mainstreaming sex: The sexualization of western culture.* New York: I. B. Tauris.

Boyle, K. (2010). *Everyday pornography.* New York: Routledge.

Brod, H. (1990). Eros thanatized: Pornography and male sexuality. In M. Kimmel (ed.), *Men confront pornography* (pp. 190–209). New York: Crown.

DeKeseredy, W. (2015). Critical criminological understandings of adult pornography and woman abuse: New progressive directions in research and theory. *International Journal for Crime, Justice and Social Democracy, 4,* (4), 4–21.

Dines, G. (2010). *Pornland: How porn has hijacked our sexuality.* Boston, MA: Beacon Press.

Dworkin, A. (1981). *Pornography: Men possessing women.* New York: Putnam.

Flood, M. (2007). Exposure to pornography among youth in Australia. *Journal of Sociology, 43,* (1), 45–60.

Flood, M. (2010). Young men using pornography. In K. Boyle (ed.), *Everyday pornography* (pp. 164–178). New York: Routledge.

Garlick, S. (2010). Taking control of sex? Hegemonic masculinity, technology, and internet pornography. *Men and Masculinities, 12,* (5), 597–614.

Garlick, S. (2011). A new sexual revolution? Critical theory, pornography, and the internet. *Canadian Review of Sociology, 48,* (3), 221–239.

Garlick, S. (2016). *The nature of masculinity: Critical theory, new materialisms, and technologies of embodiment.* Vancouver: UBC Press.

Hall, M., & Hearn, J. (2017). *Revenge pornography: Gender, sexualities and motivations.* New York: Routledge.

Hunt, L. (1993). Introduction: Obscenity and the origins of modernity, 1500–1800. In L. Hunt (ed.), *The invention of pornography: Obscenity and the origins of modernity, 1500–1800* (pp. 9–45). New York: Zone Books.

Jacobs, K. (2007). *Netporn: DIY web culture and sexual politics.* Plymouth: Rowman & Littlefield.

Jensen, R. (2007). *Getting off: Pornography and the end of masculinity.* Cambridge, MA: South End Press.

Kendrick, W. M. (1987). *The secret museum: Pornography in modern culture.* New York: Viking.

Kimmel, M. (Ed.). (1990). *Men confront pornography.* New York: Crown.

Kimmel, M. (2008). *Guyland: The perilous world where boys become men.* New York: Harper.

Laqueur, T. W. (2003). *Solitary sex: A cultural history of masturbation.* New York: Zone Books.

Lehman, P. (2006). Introduction: "A dirty little secret" – Why teach and study pornography. In P. Lehman (Ed.), *Pornography: Film and culture* (pp. 1–20). New Brunswick, NJ: Rutgers University Press.

Long, J. (2012). *Anti-porn: The resurgence of anti-porn feminism.* New York: Zed Books.

MacKinnon, C. A. (1987). *Feminism unmodified: Discourses on life and law*. Cambridge, MA: Harvard University Press.
Maddison, S. (2017). Comradeship of cock? Gay porn and the entrepreneurial voyeur. *Porn Studies, 4*, (2), 139–156.
Mason-Grant, J. (2004). *Pornography embodied: From speech to sexual practice*. Lanham, MD: Rowman & Littlefield.
McNair, B. (2002). *Striptease culture: Sex, media and the democratization of desire*. New York: Routledge.
McNair, B. (2013). *Porno? Chic! How pornography changed the world and made it a better place*. New York: Routledge.
Mercer, J. (2017). *Gay pornography: Representations of sexuality and masculinity*. New York: I. B. Tauris.
Mowlabocus, S. (2010). Porn 2.0? Technology, social practice, and the new online porn industry. In F. Attwood (ed.), *Porn.com: Making sense of online pornography* (pp. 69–87). New York: Peter Lang.
Paasonen, S. (2011). *Carnal resonance: Affect and online pornography*. Cambridge, MA: MIT Press.
Paasonen, S., Nikunen, K., & Saarenmaa, L. (Eds.). (2007). *Pornification: Sex and sexuality in media culture*. New York: Berg.
Purcell, N. (2012). *Violence and the pornographic imaginary: The politics of sex, gender, and aggression in hardcore pornography*. New York: Routledge.
Sedgwick, E. K. (2003). *Touching feeling: Affect, pedagogy, performativity*. Durham, NC: Duke University Press.
Stoltenberg, J. (1990). *Refusing to be a man: Essays on sex and justice*. New York: Penguin.
van Doorn, N. (2010). Keeping it real: User-generated pornography, gender reification, and visual pleasure. *Convergence: The International Journal of Research into New Media Technologies, 16*, (4), 411–430.
Williams, L. (1989). *Hard core: Power, pleasure, and the frenzy of the visible*. Berkeley, CA: University of California Press.

25

Exploring men, masculinity and contemporary dating practices

Chris Haywood

Introduction

At present, traditional forms of dating – such as introductions by family and friends, meetings in bars and clubs and encounters in everyday work and social life – are being accompanied by new forms of relationship initiation such as speed dating, mobile romance, online dating, holiday romances and hooking-up. As a result, there has been a move away from taken-for-granted scripts and rituals of masculinity and femininity, to a moment of gendered uncertainty where the 'rules of the dating game' have become less clear and predictable (Massa, 2012). There is the suggestion that such changes in dating scripts are having a positive impact on women, lesbian and gay communities and young people (Bauermeister, Ventuneac, Pingel & Parsons, 2012; Gomez, 2010). In India, for example, the online space of dating has given women more safety when forming romantic relationships with men (Chakraborty, 2012). However, we remain highly dependent upon media narratives that offer contradictory accounts of men's responses to contemporary dating practices. On the one hand, such narratives claim that new forms of dating are providing men with the opportunity to be more caring and sensitive. On the other, such accounts suggest that there is a 'menaissance' – a cultural moment where 'post-sensitive' men are responding to change by drawing upon traditional masculine tropes such as emotional stoicism and toughness. To explore men, masculinity and dating, this chapter provides a short summary of dating and history, followed by a consideration of gender, dating and power. The chapter ends by suggesting that new dating contexts are producing emergent masculinities.

Dating has become a very flexible term; it is used to capture a diverse range of interpersonal encounters, such as one-off romantic encounters, or to describe an ongoing relationship. For example, Poitras and Lavoie (1995, p. 300) suggest that 'dating relationships cover the spectrum of experiences ranging from one-night stands and short-term encounters to relationships that are long-lasting and stable over time, excluding cohabitation'. More recently, Chorney and Morris (2008, p. 226) define dating as 'a dyadic interaction that focuses on participation in mutually rewarding activities that may increase the likelihood of future interaction, emotional commitment and/or sexual intimacy'. We do, though, have to be careful about the assumptions that underpin dating. For example, within Egyptian communities, males and females meeting alone is often not tolerated (Jyrkiäinen & Bisset, 2016). Dating is also highly heteronormative, as it is often assumed to be a heterosexual practice. Macapagal, Greene, Rivera and Mustanski (2015) suggest that gay and lesbian communities have difficulty negotiating dates because dating requires a disclosure of sexuality. Alongside this, it is often assumed that heterosexuals date, whereas gays and lesbians 'hook up'. However, Prestage et al.'s (2015) online survey of 2562 gay and bisexual men who had primary regular partners revealed that they had met such partners through both online gay dating websites and non-dating websites. In the context of 'race'/ethnicity, inter-racial dating is seen to provoke familial opposition, hostility from friends and disapproval from strangers (Schoepflin, 2009). More specifically, Zhang and Allen (2019) suggest that 'race'/ ethnicity is gendered, with 'racialized' masculinity, such as effeminate Asian American men, inflecting dominant notions of attractiveness. Therefore it is important to acknowledge that dating as a concept is informed by a range of social and cultural ascriptions.

A history of men and dating

One of the starting points for understanding men, masculinity and dating is to consider dating practices as gendered relationship scripts. O'Hara (2002) argues that, during the late Middle Ages in Western Europe, relationship initiation was a highly structured yet complex process that involved decision making that was informed by community, parental and individual choices. Family life, it is argued, was practised through a traditional patriarchy reflecting an older patriarchal order, where 'authority over the family is vested in the elder males, or male. He, the father, makes the decisions which control the family's work, purchases, marriages' (Ehrenreich & English, 1979, p. 9). At this time, it is suggested that relationship initiation and the resulting marriage were primarily concerned with the economic stability of a tightly knit insular community. Although some contest this, suggesting that men and women did fall in love both heterosexually and homosexually, generally the expression of desires was restricted and articulated through structured rituals (Gillis, 1985). However, throughout the 15th and 16th centuries, relationship initiation rituals began to develop and appeared to loosen bounded structures. One such ritual was that of 'night courting' or 'bundling'. This involved young men and women sharing a bed within the same house as their parents. There were, however, a number of protocols that were put in place, such as no undressing from the waist downwards. In some instances, a wooden board would be set up between the couple in the bed. Shorter (1975) suggests that the main purpose of the visit was to talk and 'assess' the viability of the potential partner.

A more recent form of relationship initiation was that of 'calling'. During the 18th and 19th centuries, Bailey (1989) suggests, callers would appear at a woman's door with the hope of being permitted to come into the house to visit. Gift-giving and the leaving of calling cards were therefore very public displays of romantic intention; but they were also, it is argued, an attempt by men to control a relationship. If the man's calling ritual was rejected by the woman or the woman's family, the woman's hesitancy and secrecy became evidence of her lack of emotion or of an absence of romantic love (Eustace, 2001). The implication was that men did not fail at courting; rather, women were to blame for not being able to respond appropriately to the situation. Bailey (1989) suggests that with the onset of the 20th century, dating moved from domestic spaces to the public sphere. Compulsory schooling, increasing opportunities for work and the emergence of mass media began to create gendered scripts of relationship initiation. This period of 'dating' became governed by particular forms of media-led etiquette that 'told men "how" to be men and women "how" to be women. It also provided a way to demonstrate to others, through conforming to gender-appropriate behaviour, that one *was* a man, or *one* was a woman' (Bailey, 1989, p. 98). The rules of dating were infused with ways of ensuring the accepted gendered roles: men were expected to pay for meals, open doors for women, take the lead in asking for dates and demonstrate greater knowledge whilst on the date. Bailey suggests that this promotion of gendered ideals articulated through dating etiquette often created impossible pressures for men and women. At the same time, it was important for men and women to demonstrate to their peers that they were aspiring to these norms. Thus, in Bailey's account, masculinity becomes something that is achieved through the aspiration and demonstration of a gendered etiquette that requires men to be dominant, in control and, importantly, aware of the expectations that are placed upon them.

More recently, Bulcroft, Bulcroft, Bradley and Simpson (2000) suggest that since the 1960s there has been a breakdown in formal dating traditions and conventions. An increase in personal choice, individual responsibility and risk management has resulted in the increased popularity of personal ads, technological dating services and romance experts. Importantly, rather than following prescriptive gendered expectations, dating scripts are being framed through consumption and convenience. Within the consumerization and marketization of the relationship experience as an individuality, there is a neoliberal emphasis on choice and on individual responsibility for relationship choices. Furthermore, fast choices, of effortless proportions, become the norm where the speed of ideal relationship delivery becomes of key importance (Tomlinson, 2007). Heino, Ellison and Gibbs (2010) highlight how the metaphors that are employed in online dating circulate as consumer practices and have resulted in 'Relationshopping'. More specifically, dating becomes shaped by notions of shopping, branding and marketing, with men and women increasingly developing an emotional literacy that focuses on instantaneous, ready-made relationship solutions (Bauman, 2003). Illouz (2013) argues that dating has become increasingly intellectualized, with potential partners being subjected to evaluation through metrics; people are transformed into measurable attributes. As a result, people are ranked and compared, creating a reflexive consciousness that is 'derived from the economic sphere, thus interfering with more intuitive or epiphanic modes of knowledge' (Illouz, 2013, p. 181).

Gender, dating and power

Eaton and Rose (2011) argue that, despite the historical changes in dating such as those highlighted above, traditional patterns of gendered behaviour persist: 'Men were expected to initiate, plan, and pay for dates and to initiate sexual contact, whereas women were supposed to be alluring, facilitate the conversation, and limit sexual activity' (p. 862; see also Bartoli & Clark, 2006). Furthermore, it is argued that this symmetrical model of men as proactive and women as reactive is characteristic of the ways that dating is gendered. A 'chivalrous' approach to dating has been documented by Lever, Frederick and Hertz (2015), whose secondary analysis of 17,607 unmarried heterosexual men and women in the USA highlighted that the majority of men continue to pay for dates. The implication is that gender roles and dating scripts have changed very little and that gender stereotypes, and the unequal power relations that underpin them, are enduring. Furthermore, men's dating success is often culturally coded as evidence of being a 'real man'. According to Seal and Ehrhardt (2003), the result of this stereotypical positioning of men and women is that it enables men to control women. More specifically, as Bouffard and Bouffard (2011, p. 4) argue, 'These gendered expectations include male control and female dependence, obedience, and sexual access'.

Michael Kimmel (2008) suggests that a more recent dating phenomenon, 'hooking up', is a practice that primarily benefits young men, not only because it enables men to engage in intimate relationships without any emotional 'work' but also because it becomes a mechanism whereby young men can communicate with other men in order to secure their masculine status with other men. In the context of college campuses in the USA, 'hooking up' reinforces and celebrates traditional masculine scripts of men's penetration, sexual conquest and homosocial status (Kalish & Kimmel, 2011, p. 138). In short, it is argued that dating and its more contemporary forms mirror a broader organization of social relationships that depend upon a dyadic 'complementary' and unequal gender positioning in dating encounters.

Some researchers in the USA also suggest that men experience a 'threatened masculinity thesis' as women are assumed to be achieving greater gender equality (Hunt, Gonsalkorale & Murray, 2013). This approach argues that men are under threat from women are re-claiming their masculinities. One way of reclaiming masculinity in dating scenarios has included the use of violence. Masculinity is viewed by some as contributing to control, manipulation and violence within romantic relationships. Date rape, for example, has been explained as a consequence of the fulfilling of gendered expectations, where men are expected to control the nature of the sexual interaction as part of the broader control element of dating (Lynch, Jewell, Golding & Kembel, 2017). In response to women agreeing to go on a date, it is suggested that rape in the dating context is understood by the perpetrators as an entitlement. With dating violence – 'physical, sexual, or psychological aggression in intimate relationships' – documented as pervasive within US college campuses by McDermott, Cheng, Lopez, McKelvey and Bateman (2017), understanding the interplay between dating and masculinity is crucial. If men are expected to pay for a date, they are deemed to want something in return. This sexual exchange thesis (Basow & Minieri, 2011) posits that romantic encounters, by their very nature, become contractual with an expectation or entitlement to sex. However, such entitlement has been claimed as part of a 'natural' link between men and their claim to women's bodies. For example, 'incels' (involuntary celibates) blame women for their sexual disenfranchisement, using sexual violence and rape as legitimate ways to rightfully claim what is theirs (Jacobson, 2018). Such a position resonates with Lankster's (2019) research with more than 260 South African young men, where seven out of eight focus groups indicated that if a woman asked them to stop during heterosexual intercourse, they would pressure her to continue. It should be added that date rape is under-reported by victims due to self-blame and an enduring belief that sexual coercion is acceptable within the context of intimate relationships (Russo, 2000). Rape in this scenario was about men's right to continue. In Tanzania, Kenny (2019) argues that the cultural value placed on men as seducer blurs the boundary between seducer and rapist. In Peru, intimate partner violence is often framed as a consequence of love and jealousy; masculinity in this case being a demonstration of men's emotional investment in relationships (Ventura-León, Caycho-Rodríguez, Barboza-Palomino, Aparco & Rodas, 2018).

Entitlement is also seen to be linked to the recent trend of men using seduction coaches or pick-up artists (PUAs) to develop their romantic or sexual success. These coaches or PUAs often encourage men who feel inadequate or incompetent to adopt a 'hegemonic maleness' to gain more 'power, respect and sexual potency' when initiating relationships with women (Cosma & Gurevich, 2018, p. 88). PUAs often work with the idea that if men demonstrate their 'inner' masculinity, then this will appeal to women's innate 'femininity'. As a result, many of the self-help programmes and courses aim to draw out the 'already there' natural masculinity and teach men to reconnect with their inner selves; a self with which a feminized society has caused them to lose touch. Rachel O'Neill (2018), in her work on seduction coaches, succinctly highlights, through Raewyn Connell's work, how successfully demonstrating masculinity is 'to fuck women' (Connell, 2000, p. 102). The use of skills and techniques to cultivate a representation of masculinity can also be seen in recent online romance scams, where masculinities are being performed with the sole intention of extorting money or goods. Men use fake profiles to cultivate an intimacy, which over time deepens to false expressions of love. It is at this point that scammers often ask for money to resolve a crisis such as medical expenses or to buy flight tickets to visit the victim. In an analysis of 18 male and 19 female fraudster online profiles, Kopp, Layton, Sillitoe and Gondal (2015) found that the majority of fraudsters tended to emphasize their wealth, loyalty and respect. Importantly, they suggest that male fraudsters attempt to promote a profile of a 'perfect male partner who might share exactly the same female-related interests and hobbies' (p. 210) such as cooking or romantic dancing. The researchers also found that men tended to emphasize their religiosity as a means to represent themselves as trustworthy and moral. It appears that the fraudsters' aim is to present the image of a 'man' whose desirability becomes key to unlocking the victim's trust.

Another means of restoring masculinity in dating contexts has been through organized romantic encounters. It is suggested that the presumed erosion of masculine power in a feminized world has contributed to the emergence of 'romance tours'. For example, the romance tourism industry provides organized tours for men in the USA or the UK to the Global South, where their economic privilege gives them access to different forms of intimacy. Meszaros (2018) explores the role of such tours and finds that men paid for them because their masculine status and their attractiveness, in Western contexts, has been eroded by the Feminist movement and female emancipation in the workplace. Furthermore, Meszaros argues that romance tours promote access to femininities that are obedient and submissive. Men participating in such tours would also racialize their desire by highlighting how the women in different countries were part of racialized hierarchies of desire. For example, Filipina women were appraised for their conservative dress, in contrast to the sexy clothes and curvaceousness of Colombian women. As such, paying for tours to the Global South provides a space for men to recuperate their desirability, primarily through economic status, to form relationships with women who display a racialized passive femininity. In a similar way, Davidson (2001), in her work on Thailand, links the changing nature of gender equality in Western contexts to the rise in 'sex tourism'. Davidson suggests that the city of Pattaya in Thailand becomes a 'macho theme park' where men engage in activities such as drinking beer, riding motorbikes and employing sex workers. Of key importance for Davidson is that the holiday becomes a context where masculinities are made by men who adopt a self-understanding characterized by unrestrained conquest. Interestingly, the expression of masculinity by these men was through the deployment of a civilized/uncivilized binary in which women as the racialized 'Other' sustained men's sexual hegemony. This led to one man asking, 'What good is heroically fucking 18-year olds while your contemporaries feed pigeons in the park if nobody of equal worth recognizes this mark of your distinction?' (Davidson, 2001, p. 16). Underpinning men's pursuit of sex tourism, according to Davidson, is the way that the loss of traditional masculine privilege in Western society is producing in these sex tourists a crisis of masculinity. Men who participate in sex tourism are doing so in order to reclaim a gendered status that has been lost.

New dating practices/new masculinities

If the above section suggested that new dating practices are reinforcing traditional gendered inequalities, then this section suggests that the fracturing of traditional dating scripts is requiring men to increase their reflection on their masculinities and their dating practices. For example, in an empirically grounded study that examined older men's experiences of intimacy, Duncan and Dowsett's (2010) interviews with heterosexual and gay men suggested that men were demonstrating 'greater levels of reflexivity on the part of individuals with regard to questions of intimacy and sex' (p. 58). Although they do not claim that traditional forms of masculinity have disappeared, they do argue that traditional masculinities are being renegotiated as men attempt to develop meaningful intimate relationships with their partners. The focus on men's increasing reflexivity informs Wang's (2012) research on Internet daters in Taiwan. Wang argues that Internet dating is inherently reflexive in that it enables a number of masculine 'fronts' to be articulated as users present themselves in order to appeal to a desirable other. Although such sites provided a platform for the expression of traditional Taiwanese masculinities that were based on traditional patriarchal gender roles, alternative masculinities were also being presented. Using Foucault's notion of heterotopia, Wang argues that online dating sites give men the opportunity to display alternative fragile, tender and vulnerable masculinities. It is argued that a combination of anonymity and a lack of male-on-male policing enables 'disclosure of real, counter-hegemonic male selves' (Wang, 2012, p. 496). Wang's work is important in that it shifts the focus on men and dating from that of masculinities as being informed by homosociality or the objectification of women to a situation where a desirable other is the key dynamic in the presentation of masculinities.

The emphasis of Wang's work is that new forms of dating practices are reconfiguring men's subjectivities. In the context of gay online dating, Davis, Hart, Bolding, Sherr and Elford (2006) highlight the importance of depicting the self in a way that establishes desirability, to create an appeal to potential dates. In their work on London gay men presenting themselves through Internet-based communication, they found that men would present themselves in ways that would prove most attractive to other men whom they desired. Therefore, the emergence of online dating, mobile romance and digital 'hook-ups' requires men to make their masculinities not simply through what they do *with* their bodies (i.e., occupational or social status) but also by the work they do *on* their bodies (Haywood & Mac an Ghaill, 2011). According to Haywood (2018a), it is this focus on the body that is the basis for an emergent masculinity that is underpinned by a self-reflexive anxiety. In his research on young men and their use of Tinder, he found that the requirement for men to display themselves, either through profile pictures or an accompanying bio, exposed men to the immediate judgement of others. In response, men attempted to portray themselves through pictures of themselves playing sports, with family and with friends (not when they were drunk), and in restaurants; with the underpinning idea of trying to convey a down-to-earth and honest personality. More specifically, they found it important that their profiles gave the impression that they were a 'decent lad', 'not being a dick' or being 'an idiot or a dozer'. Importantly, the use of digital representations feeds young men's anxieties as it exposes their dependency upon the desire of the (imagined) other. As Jefferson (1994, p. 12) has pointed out in relation to men's subjectivity, 'It is almost as if to succeed in love one has to fail as a man'.

The rise of digital media as platforms for dating may not only be creating the possibilities for new masculinities to emerge; it may also be shaping what we understand as masculinity. For example, Jane Ward (2015) discusses the practice of straight men advertising for sex with other straight men on Craigslist. She argues that men maintain their heterosexual identities by framing sex through codes of homosociality of friendship, hanging or chilling out and rejecting romantic or gay cultural tropes. Similarly, Reynolds (2015) highlights how men seeking to have sex with men reinforced their heterosexual masculinity by seeking 'buds' and 'no homos'. In his research on Chaturbate – an online dating forum that involves straight-identified men garnering the attention of gay men – Cover (2015) highlights how straight-identified men adopt anal self-penetration and incorporate it into their heterosexual masculinities. In this way, men are able to engage in same-sex activities while continuing to identify with a heterosexual masculinity. A similar claim is made by Scoats, Joseph and Anderson's (2018) research on MMF threesomes. They suggest that there is more willingness among young men to engage in same-sex practices as part of an MMF threesome. In this instance, Scoats et al. attribute the expanded boundaries of heterosexuality to a collapse in the one-time rule of homosexuality, which sees a disconnection of masculinity from homophobia (see also Branfman, Stiritz & Anderson, 2018). The implication here is that new platforms for the expression of intimacy are enabling the boundaries of heterosexual masculinity to become flexible.

It is intriguing that current approaches to the reconfiguration of intimacy only alter the parameters of masculinity and not masculinity itself. As new forms of relationship initiation emerge, it is argued that not only are masculinities being reconfigured but also men are engaging in practices where new forms of gendered subjectivity are emerging that are not dependent on a concept of masculinity (Floyd, 2011). In work on heterosexual sex clubs, Haywood (2018b) argues that men are using spaces to pursue a gendered subjectivity that is not confined to 'masculinity'. The darkroom in sex clubs is a space where men and women visit to engage in anonymous, recreational sex. In the darkroom, not only are the visual cues for relationship initiation suspended; the scripts and expectations that underpin gender practices are also discarded. In the context of the gay club, Richters (2007, p. 287) argues that 'the darkroom is a world of sensation, of touch, smell, taste. Its ideals and values and, crucially, its interactional rules, are different from those of the visible world'. In the heterosexual darkroom, men not only suspend their subjective understanding of masculinity but also reject sexuality identity categories such as heterosexuality, homosexuality and bisexuality. As a result, eroticized intimate encounters take place that are not premised on masculine heterosexual scripts. Instead intimacy becomes cohered through 'bodies and pleasures' (Foucault, 1990), as men seek a qualitative different erotic experience that is not dependant on gender identities or sexualities. This process of de-subjectification suggests the possibility that new forms of relationship initiation may not simply be extending the parameters of masculinity but may in turn question masculinity as being a key part of men's gendered identities.

Conclusion

If dating had previously contained templates about being a good man that were dependent on traditional masculine tropes, contemporary problems associated with dating may have produced more complex masculinities. Some of the issues surrounding dating may result from broader social and cultural changes that are redefining what it means to be a man or a woman. In the dating context, scripts that designated 'rules of the dating game' based on traditional gender roles may be prompting men to restore or recover more traditional masculinities. Alternatively, we have also seen that the emergence of new ways of developing intimate relationships is problematizing the relevance of 'dating' as an adequate term. Furthermore, new practices of intimacy are also questioning whether men are making their gendered selves through masculinities. It is becoming increasingly apparent that as strategies for the development of new intimacies emerge, men are increasingly being asked to reflect on their role as men. Some men, in order to navigate these intimacies, appear to be re-invoking traditional tropes of masculinity connected to circuits of gendered inequality. At the same time, other men appear to be developing new ways of being men, with such ways of being challenging the very notion of what it means to be a man.

References

Bailey, B. L. (1989). *From front porch to back seat: Courtship in twentieth-century America*. Baltimore, MA: Johns Hopkins University Press.

Bartoli, A. M., & Clark, M. D. (2006). The dating game: Similarities and differences in dating scripts among college students. *Sexuality & Culture, 10*(4), 54–80.

Basow, S. A., & Minieri, A. (2011). 'You owe me': Effects of date cost, who pays, participant gender, and rape myth beliefs on perceptions of rape. *Journal of Interpersonal Violence, 26*(3), 479–497.

Bauermeister, J. A., Ventuneac, A., Pingel, E., & Parsons, J. T. (2012). Spectrums of love: Examining the relationship between romantic motivations and sexual risk among young gay and bisexual men. *AIDS and Behavior, 16*(6), 1549–1559.

Bauman, Z. (2003). *Liquid love: On the frailty of human bonds*. Cambridge: Polity.

Bouffard, L. A., & Bouffard, J. A. (2011). Understanding men's perceptions of risks and rewards in a date rape scenario. *International Journal of Offender Therapy and Comparative Criminology, 55*(4), 626–645.

Branfman, J., Stiritz, S., & Anderson, E. (2018). Relaxing the straight male anus: Decreasing homohysteria around anal eroticism. *Sexualities, 21*(1–2), 109–127.

Bulcroft, R., Bulcroft, K., Bradley, K., & Simpson, C. (2000). The management and production of risk in romantic relationships: A postmodern paradox. *Journal of Family History, 25*(1), 63–92.

Chakraborty, K. (2012). Virtual mate-seeking in the urban slums of Kolkata, India. *South Asian Popular Culture, 10*(2), 197–216.

Chorney, D. B., & Morris, T. L. (2008). The changing face of dating anxiety: Issues in assessment with special populations. *Clinical Psychology: Science and Practice, 15*(3), 224–238.

Connell, R. (2000). *The men and the boys*. Cambridge: Polity.

Cosma, S., & Gurevich, M. (2018). (Re)producing the 'natural man' in men's online advice media: Achieving masculinity through embodied and mental mastery. *Psychology & Sexuality, 9*(1), 86–97.

Cover, R. (2015). Visual heteromasculinities online: Beyond binaries and sexual normativities in camera chat forums. *Men and Masculinities, 18*(2), 159–175.

Davidson, J. O. C. (2001). The sex tourist, the expatriate, his ex-wife and her "other": The politics of loss, difference and desire. *Sexualities, 4*(1), 5–24.

Davis, M., Hart, G., Bolding, G., Sherr, L., & Elford, J. (2006). E-dating, identity and HIV prevention: Theorising sexualities, risk and network society. *Sociology of Health & Illness, 28*(4), 457–478.

Duncan, D., & Dowsett, G. W. (2010). 'There's no teleology to it; it's just about the spirit of play': Men, intimacy, and 'LATE' modernity. *The Journal of Men's Studies, 18*(1), 45–62.

Eaton, A. A., & Rose, S. (2011). Has dating become more egalitarian? A 35 year review using Sex Roles. *Sex Roles, 64*(11/12), 843–862.

Ehrenreich, B., & English, D. (1979). *For her own good: Two centuries of the experts' advice to women*. New York: Anchor.

Eustace, N. (2001). "The cornerstone of a copious work": Love and power in eighteenth-century courtship. *Journal of Social History, 34*(3), 517–546.

Floyd, K. (2011). Masculinity inside out: The biopolitical lessons of transgender and intersex studies. In S. Horlache (Ed.), *Constructions of masculinity in British literature from the Middle Ages to the present* (pp. 33–51). New York: Palgrave Macmillan.

Foucault, M. (1990). *The history of sexuality: An introduction, vol. I*. New York: Vintage.

Gillis, J. R. (1985). *For better, for worse: British marriages, 1600 to the present*. Oxford: Oxford University Press.

Gomez, A. G. (2010). Competing narratives, gender and threaded identity in cyberspace. *Journal of Gender Studies, 19*(1), 27–42.

Haywood, C. (2018a). *Men, masculinity and contemporary dating*. Basingstoke: Palgrave.

Haywood, C. (2018b) *Displacing conventional dynamics of gender and sexuality: Sex clubs, dark rooms and the 'loss of masculinity'*. Paper presented at the University of Flensburg, Germany, November 20.

Haywood, C., & Mac an Ghaill, M. (2011). Postmodern sexualities. In S. Sim (Ed.), *Companion to postmodernism* (3rd ed.) (pp. 50–61). London: Routledge.

Heino, R. D., Ellison, N. B., & Gibbs, J. L. (2010). Relationshopping: Investigating the market metaphor in online dating. *Journal of Social and Personal Relationships, 27*(4), 427–447.

Hunt, C. J., Gonsalkorale, K., & Murray, S. B. (2013). Threatened masculinity and muscularity: An experimental examination of multiple aspects of muscularity in men. *Body Image, 10*(3), 290–299.

Illouz, E. (2013). *Why love hurts: A sociological explanation*. Cambridge: Polity.

Jacobson, E. (2018). Performing and resisting toxic masculinities on sports news comment boards. In B. J. Guzzetti, T. W. Bean, & J. Dunkerly-Bean (Eds.), *Literacies, sexualities, and gender: Understanding identities from preschool to adulthood* (pp. 169–182). New York: Routledge.
Jefferson, T. (1994). Theorising masculine subjectivity. In T. Newburn & E. A. Stanko (Eds.), *Just boys doing business? Men, masculinities and crime* (pp. 10–31). London: Routledge.
Jyrkiäinen, S., & Bisset, B. (2016). Great expectations, uncertain futures: Urban and online encounters with youth, love and marriage in Egypt. *AnthropoChildren, 6*, 1–21.
Kalish, R., & Kimmel, M. (2011). Hooking up: Hot hetero sex or the new numb normative? *Australian Feminist Studies, 26*(67), 137–151.
Kenny, E. (2019). Narrating rape: An ethnographic case-study of non-consensual sexual debut in Tanzania. *Journal of Aggression, Maltreatment & Trauma, 28*(1), 106–125.
Kimmel, M. (2008). *Guyland: The perilous world where boys become men. Understanding the critical years between 16 and 26.* New York: HarperCollins.
Kopp, C., Layton, R., Sillitoe, J., & Gondal, I. (2015). The role of love stories in romance scams: A qualitative analysis of fraudulent profiles. *International Journal of Cyber Criminology, 9*(2), 205–217.
Lankster, N. M. (2019). Chap chat: Gender relations and perceptions of rape amongst adolescent males in South Africa. *Journal of Feminist Family Therapy, 31*(2/3), 129–143).
Lever, J., Frederick, D. A., & Hertz, R. (2015). Who pays for dates? Following versus challenging gender norms. *Sage Open, 5*(4), 1–14.
Lynch, K. R., Jewell, J. A., Golding, J. M., & Kembel, H. B. (2017).Associations between sexual behavior norm beliefs in relationships and intimate partner rape judgments. *Violence Against Women, 23*(4), 426–451.
Macapagal, K., Greene, G. J., Rivera, Z., & Mustanski, B. (2015). 'The best is always yet to come': Relationship stages and processes among young LGBT couples. *Journal of Family Psychology, 29*(3), 309–320.
Massa, J. (2012). *The gaggle: How to find love in the post-dating world.* New York: Simon & Schuster.
McDermott, R. C., Cheng, H.-L., Lopez, F. G., McKelvey, D., & Bateman, L. S. (2017). Dominance orientations and psychological aggression in college student relationships: A test of an attachment theory-guided model. *Psychology of Violence*, 7(4), 508–520.
Meszaros, J. (2018). Race, space, and agency in the international introduction industry: How American men perceive women's agency in Colombia, Ukraine and the Philippines. *Gender, Place & Culture, 25*(2), 268–287.
O'Hara, D. (2002). *Courtship and constraint: Rethinking the making of marriage in Tudor England.* Manchester: Manchester University Press.
O'Neill, R. (2018). *Seduction: Men, masculinity and mediated intimacy.* Cambridge: Polity.
Poitras, M., & Lavoie, F. (1995). A study of the prevalence of sexual coercion in adolescent heterosexual dating relationships in a Quebec sample. *Violence and Victims, 10*(4), 299–313.
Prestage, G., Bavinton, B., Grierson, J., Down, I., Keen, P., Bradley, J., & Duncan, D. (2015). Online dating among Australian gay and bisexual men: Romance or hooking up? *AIDS and Behavior, 19*(10), 1905–1913.
Reynolds, C. (2015). 'I am super straight and I prefer you be too': Constructions of heterosexual masculinity in online personal ads for 'Straight' men seeking sex with men. *Journal of Communication Inquiry, 39*(3), 213–231.
Richters, J. (2007). Through a hole in a wall: Setting and interaction in sex-on-premises venues. *Sexualities, 10*(3), 275–297.
Russo, L. (2000). Date rape: A hidden crime. *Trends and Issues in Crime and Criminal Justice/Australian Institute of Criminology, 157*, 1–6.
Schoepflin, T. (2009). Perspectives of interracial dating at a predominantly white university. *Sociological Spectrum, 29*(3), 346–370.
Scoats, R., Joseph, L. J., & Anderson, E. (2018). 'I don't mind watching him cum': Heterosexual men, threesomes, and the erosion of the one-time rule of homosexuality. *Sexualities, 21*(1/2), 30–48.
Seal, D. W., & Ehrhardt, A. A. (2003). Masculinity and urban men: Perceived scripts for courtship, romantic, and sexual interactions with women. *Culture, Health & Sexuality, 5*(4), 295–319.
Shorter, E. (1975). *The making of the modern family.* New York: Basic Books.
Tomlinson, J. (2007). *The culture of speed: The coming of immediacy.* Los Angeles, CA: Sage.

Ventura-León, J., Caycho-Rodríguez, T., Barboza-Palomino, M., Aparco, V., & Rodas, N. (2018). Evidence of validity and factorial invariance of a brief jealousy scale in Peruvian university students. *Journal of Educational Psychology-Propositos Y Representaciones*, *6*(2), 153–179.

Wang, Y. J. (2012). Internet dating sites as heterotopias of gender performance: A case study of Taiwanese heterosexual male daters. *International Journal of Cultural Studies*, *15*(5), 485–500.

Ward, J. (2015). *Not gay: Sex between straight white men*. New York: New York University Press.

Zhang, J., & Allen, K. R. (2019) Constructions of masculinity and the perception of interracial relationships among young male Chinese international students and scholars in the United States. *Journal of Family Issues*, *40*(3), 340–362.

26

Masculinities and sex workers

John Scott

Introduction

Sex work is a highly gendered activity and is the archetypal form of female deviance. Masculinity has been largely invisible in popular and scholarly accounts of sex work. Dennis' (2008) meta-analysis of contemporary research on the global sex trade found that men and boys are rarely cited and that two-thirds of research conflated the term 'prostitute' with a feminine persona. However, people of diverse gender are also involved in the sex industry. Indeed, only recently has sex been considered work, having been known by the more familiar and derogatory term 'prostitution' and having been historically subject to a range of social controls. This chapter distinguishes sex work from human trafficking. While human trafficking is coercive and a human rights abuse, sex work is understood here to involve consensual relations between adult persons. The distinction is an important one to make, so that anti-trafficking resources are not misapplied to sex workers. When sex work is conflated with trafficking, sex workers can be driven underground and denied proper access to legal, social and health services.

Selling and purchasing sex are stigmatised activities in terms of social and sexual identities, as reflected in the criminalisation of prostitution and activities associated with it throughout much of the world. The recent preference to describe the sale of sexual services as work reflects efforts by advocates to normalise the sex industry and to bridge the gulf that separates commercial and intimate sexual relations. As discussed below, this gulf is not unique to the global north but is evident in a wide range of cultural contexts.

Regardless of place and period, supply in sex industries has been largely female and demand largely male. Although they are the largest group involved in prostitution, clients have tended to remain invisible in public discourses surrounding prostitution. This noted, male, transsexual and transgender sex workers service a predominantly male clientele. Because participants in this exchange are of often of the same gender, male sex workers have been difficult to conceptualise in economic and gender theories of sexual exchange (Edlund & Korn, 2002). Sex work has been variously approached as oppressive, with exploitation, subjugation and violence as intrinsic aspects; as empowering, with human agency and the potential for mutual gain to both parties; and as variable, acknowledging that sex work holds the potential for 'a constellation of occupational arrangements, power relations and worker experiences' (Weitzer, 2009, p. 215).

Shifting conceptions of masculinity and sex work

The population of sex workers and their clients is largely unknown, due to the stigma associated with sex work and its legal status. While it is a very small sector of the overall market, heterosexual male sex services may be increasing in popularity due to greater social and economic freedom for women and increasing objectification of male bodies and masculinity (MacPhail, Scott & Minichiello, 2015). There is also evidence to suggest that changing social mores, technological change, migration and economic restructuring (including increased materialism and consumption) may give greater visibility to male sex workers, if not increase supply and demand for male sex workers on a global scale (Kong, 2014; Niccolai, 2014). Sex tourism for both men and women has been one aspect of this global growth (Mitchell, 2010; Padila, 2007).

Despite this, numbers of male clients of sex workers worldwide remains relatively high. Figures for female sex workers suggest that between 7–18% of men have bought sexual services in the US (Weitzer, 2000), 16% in Australia (Rissel, Richters, Grulich, de Visser & Smith, 2003), and between 4.3–25% of men in the United Kingdom (Brooks-Gordon, 2006). In the Global South, it is estimated that about 10% of men exchange money for sex in any given year (Carael, Slaymaker, Lyerla & Sarkar, 2006).

The relative lack of attention to men involved in sex work might be explained by smaller numbers of male sex workers, but male sex work has been consistently present in most societies, and, at particular historical junctures, numbers of male prostitutes have been relatively high. Historical evidence indicates that in pre-modern times, same-sex commercial sexual relations frequently occurred in major global metropolitan centres (Friedman, 2014). Elsewhere in the world, different constructs of same-sex desire meant that male sex work was largely invisible; however, this status was disrupted by social changes brought about by colonialism and modernity (e.g., Kong, 2014). Evidence is only recently emerging that male sex workers may form a majority of sex workers in some contexts outside of the Global North. For example, male sex workers may comprise two-thirds of all sex workers in Pakistan (van Winjingaarden & Iqbal, 2015, p. 147). Transsexual and transgender sex workers also represent a relatively small populations, despite transsexual and transgender people being disproportionately represented in the sex industry owing to employment discrimination, familial rejection and housing discrimination. In some cultural contexts, intersex, transsexual and transgender sex workers may present a sizable portion of the overall sex market and experience relatively high demand in terms of local or tourist markets. Examples include the *travestis* of Brazil, Thailand's *kathoey* and India's *hijras* (Ryan, 2006).

It is impossible to understand how sex work is structured and organised without appreciating the social and political organisation of space as a gendered construct. Sex work was made a social problem in modernity because new social controls emerged which restricted the movement and visibility of gendered bodies within new spatial contexts. For example, 'public' spaces were increasingly masculinised, and open displays of sexual promiscuity were highly restricted. During the modern period, female sex work came to be a metaphor for urban disintegration and disorganisation. Early criminologists and sexologists came to represent female street prostitutes as masculine in manner and appearance. Gendered constructs of space were therefore important to the way in which both female and male sex work were presented and regulated as social problems in modernity. While female street workers were considered a largely criminal population, male street workers were often presented as requiring welfare or medical interventions (Scott, 2011). In this way, the regulation of prostitution inverted common practices for managing gendered deviance.

For example, masculine association with public space has been important in informing understandings of male sex work. Early research predominantly adopted a dichotomous understanding of the male sex worker. Male sex workers were assumed to be either homosexual or heterosexual. Early researchers correlated non-masculine behaviour, appearance and mannerisms with homosexuality and hyper-masculine characteristics with heterosexuality. Notably, the hustler was presented as a heterosexual with a hyper-masculine appearance and traits (Scott, 2003a). In this way, those who worked in public spaces were typically represented as masculine and heterosexual. In contrast, males who worked in private spaces were represented as effeminate and homosexual (Scott, 2003a). Public sex workers were subject to greater scrutiny because of their visibility and also because they were more readily institutionalised as delinquents, providing ready access to researchers. This schema is also highly problematic when considering the varied ways in which masculinities are enacted and experienced globally. In most Latin American societies, the straight/gay dichotomy does not speak to how men experience their sexuality. Rather, machismo and notions of sexual activity and passivity associated with it are important in structuring commercial sexual encounters (see Minichiello, Dune, Disogra & Mariño, 2014).

Historically, research around female sex work has focused on the sex workers themselves and has largely ignored clients. Feminist research has shifted the focus. There have been several attempts to define and label men who hire female sex workers. Research has broadly defined motivations for clients in terms of seeking intimacy, physical sensation and sexual gratification, risk taking, sexual diversity or to exert power over women (Vanwesenbeeck, de Graaf, Van Zessen & Straver, 1993). Research has also presented contradictory accounts of female sex-work clients, with some research arguing that men who pay for sex are distinct from other men, showing a tendency to more pathological or problematic behaviours, such as violence (Farley et al., 2011). This is highlighted by a recent American study that explored the oppressive side of sex work via a client base that appeared to be largely driven by sensation seeking and the desire to exert power over women. When compared to a sample of men who did not hire FSW, those who did were found to have higher rates of criminal activity, lower levels of empathy towards sex workers, an increased likelihood of rape and a normalised attitude towards sex work (Farley et al., 2011). From this, the authors concluded that sex work contributes to an increased likelihood of violence against women (see also Monto & Hotaling, 2001).

Other research indicates that men who buy sex do not differ from other men in terms of key demographic characteristics (Caldwell, 2014; Horswill & Weitzer, 2018). Research has noted the transposition of traditional courtship behaviour to commercial sex encounters. This, sometimes referred to as a 'girlfriend experience', highlights the potential for transactions to extend beyond the physical to include the emotional as well (Earle & Sharp, 2008; Sanders, 2008). In spite of how research may categorise men and their motivations, there are arguments against the normalisation of sex work which caution against treating male sexual drives as biological and not subject to socially mediating controls (Huysamen & Boonzaier, 2015; Monto, 2004).

In recent decades the proportion of young men involved in prostitution who also identify as gay has increased in societies of the Global North, especially where homosexuality or sex work have been decriminalised (Ross, Crisp, Månsson & Hawkes, 2012). Elsewhere in the world, male sex workers are more likely to be engaging in survival sex and to identify as straight (Oosthuizen, 2000; Mitchell, 2010; Phua, Ciambrone & Vazquez, 2009) or a two tier structure exists between public/straight sex workers and private/gay escorts (Ozbay, 2015). This is not universal, however, and in China most male sex workers identify as gay (Kong, 2014). Shifting discourses concerning masculinity and a decline in stigma surrounding prostitution have seen recent research present a more sympathetic view of male sex work clients and sex workers (Horswill & Weitzer, 2018).

Research focused specifically on male escorts, a group often ignored in early research, has allowed for economic disadvantage and social exploitation to be questioned as root causes of male sex work, and an occupational perspective on male work has developed. Male sex work is mostly considered as a rational, financially motivated career choice taken by adult males (Minichiello, Scott & Callander, 2013). These developments have allowed for a move away from pathological paradigms of male sex work and an occupational health and safety approach to develop in understanding male sex work (Ross et al., 2012). However, these shifts have not been universal. For example, in China homosexuality might be relatively acceptable in discrete contexts, but commercial sex is frowned upon by the media and regulated by authorities. Public sex workers, referred to as 'money boys', are considered a criminal sub-population who require stricter government control. Even China's gay community has reacted adversely to male sex work, considering it an 'improper' expression of a gay identity because of its commercialism, which brings the gay community into disrepute (Jeffreys, 2007; Kong, 2014). Similarly, research from southern and eastern Africa suggests that men who have sex with men are likely to have female sex partners and engage in sex work as a means of survival (see Boyce & Isaacs, 2014).

Postmodern understandings of masculinity and sex work

Stigma has been used by a number of researchers to show how male sex workers and sex-work clients create strategies that distance the self from the deviant aspects of their career and accomplish and preserve masculinities. Gaffney and Beverley (2001), for example, have argued that male sex workers are less likely to take on submissive roles for their clients due to hegemonic or misogynistic social constructs of masculinity. Salamon (1989) found that negative portrayals of clients by prostitutes were strategies employed by sex workers to negotiate their own perceived deviant status. Similarly, early research found masculinity informed the types of services provided and the nature of the relationship with the client (e.g., Reiss, 1961). In terms of masculinity, Earle and Sharp (2008) found that paying for sex may damage male self-esteem, especially with regard to hegemonic masculinity. The association of male sex work with prostitution and homosexuality has produced a double stigma for male sex workers and their clients to manage. The mixing of commercial and sexual relations is also considered immoral in diverse cultural contexts (e.g., Kong, 2014; Niccolai, 2014).

Despite the residual stigma, however, there is much evidence to indicate that commercial sex has been increasingly normalised in a number of global contexts, which is reflected in drives to legalise or decriminalise sex work and related offences. This noted, commercial sex remains highly stigmatised in many nations and regions throughout the world (see Aggleton & Parker, 2015). In some cases, commercial sex may be tolerated while homosexuality is criminalised (Ozbay, 2015).

The rise of online escorting has transformed the structure and organisation of sex work. There is evidence that male sex workers may be more likely than their female or transgender counterparts to work online, with the vast majority of male sex workers operating independently as online escorts (Cunningham & Kendall, 2011). The internet has brought what was previously considered a deviant and solitary behaviour into a public forum, being utilised widely by sex workers to promote to a wider socio-demographic audience and becoming a new sex work venue with a less restricted reach than traditional methods of marketing

(Holt & Blevins, 2007; Parsons, Koken & Bimbi, 2007). This noted, men traditionally have been less likely to work for agencies or brothels and less reliant on third parties, for example pimps. For sex work in wealthy nations of the Global North, there appears to be a significant decrease in the number of street sex workers, which has coincided with the expansion of new technologies such as the mobile phone and internet (MacPhail et al., 2015). This noted, this shift has not been universal, and street workers remain a sizable population in regions experiencing economic restructuring, high levels of internal migration and economic disadvantage (e.g., Allman & Bozhinov, 2015; Koken, Bimbi, Parsons & Halkitis, 2004; Uy, Parsons, Bimbi, Koken & Halkitis, 2004).

The internet has also driven the globalisation of male sex work, giving visibility to sex work in varied geographic spaces. Dennis (2008) has argued that the core of research on sex work has been dominated by the core states, these being the colonial powers of Western Europe and auxiliaries, with the periphery of sub-Saharan Africa, east and southern Asia and the Middle East largely ignored. Until very recently, for example, there were few accounts of male sex work in Muslim majority nations (see Ozbay, 2015) or former Eastern-bloc states (see Niccolai, 2014). Aggleton's collection of essays, *Men Who Sell Sex* (1999), was the first attempt to present a global account of male sex work. Recent collections which have adopted a global perspective include Minichiello and Scott (2014) and Aggleton and Parker (2015).

Global perspectives on male sex work have drawn attention to how distinct local articulations of masculinity inform the structure, organisation, understanding and experience of male sex work. Mitchell (2010), for example, documents Brazil's 'Michês' – straight street workers – who service gay tourists through the lens of Latino masculinities. Michês are an aspirational group who are engaged with consumerist society and are motivated to be socially mobile. Moscheta, McNamee and Santos (2013) examine discursive strategies used to limit stigma in Brazil. Many strategies draw on elements of masculinity and emphasise utilitarian or commercial motivations for sex work. Hodge (2005) examined male sex work through Cuba's shift from a revolutionary to (post)socialist society. He shows how street workers (who refer to themselves as 'pingueros') reproduce revolutionary nationalism and traditional Cuban masculinities but are also a criminalised population, whose sexual and material desires are linked to a global capitalist market. Alcano (2011) provides a vivid account of how masculinity is uniquely constructed, enacted and reproduced in a Southeast Asian setting. While research in southern and eastern Africa suggests that most male sex work is conducted for 'survival', research has also indicated that the motivation to provide sexual services can be specifically for exploring same-sex desire and escaping family pressure to marry, given a lack of legal opportunities to express sexuality (Boyce & Isaacs, 2014, 303).

Health and safety

Sex workers may suffer from a range of general health problems associated with poor eating habits, lack of sleep, inadequate accommodation, substance abuse and physical and psychological stress. But such health issues are rarely the focus of research; most research is more intent on protecting the general public from 'risks' embodied by sex workers, rather than addressing risks to sex workers posed by the general public or employment conditions. There is also little acknowledgement that sex workers might be endangered by public attitudes or legal regulations which perpetuate homophobic or misogynistic behaviour by stigmatising sex work and driving sex workers and their clients underground (Jamel, 2011).

Sex workers of diverse gender are subject to various forms of interpersonal violence from male clients. Numerous studies of sex work have found that men and women working in public spaces or in groups are more at risk for violence than those working in private spaces (Hubbard, 1999; Niccolai, 2014). For example, between 1990 and 2003, 87 street workers were murdered in the UK (Kinnell, 2008). This may be a result of an increased ability to screen clients and the fact that workers were aware of possibility of dangers and took appropriate precautions. Also, a sense of camaraderie among male sex workers and their clients' desire for anonymity may assist to prevent violence (Minichiello et al., 1999). Examples of violence towards sex workers can include rape, robbery, police harassment, violence and, most commonly, sexual assault (Liguori & Aggleton, 1999; Richter & Isaacs, 2015). In contrast to female sex workers, who are subject to misogynistic abuse, male sex workers can be subject to victimisation by homophobes, including police (Minichiello et al., 2013). This context may be created in part due to masculine notions of sexuality and dominant and marginalised forms of men's sexualities. Research also suggests that violence may vary regionally and be linked to specific localised constructs of masculinity (Richter & Isaacs, 2015). The recent acknowledgement that many clients of male sex workers may identify as heterosexual (Scott, 2003b) is highly significant in that stigma may prevent such men from reporting experiences of interpersonal violence.

A public-health paradigm has driven much of the research on sex work, and this has directed its main focus on sex workers and their behaviour as opposed to clients. A recent content analysis of sex industry research indicated the threat of HIV/AIDS is emphasised in a quarter of articles on female prostitution and almost 60% of articles on male prostitution (Dennis, 2008). With higher rates of HIV and STIs among men who have sex with men, much research has focused on describing the prevalence of HIV and STIs among male sex workers and their clients as well as ways in which safer sex messages can be disseminated and absorbed by these men. Morse, Simon, Osofsky, Balson and Gaumer (1991) suggested that male sex workers act as 'vectors of transmission' of HIV into the heterosexual community through clients who are married heterosexual men. Prevalence studies have shown that male sex workers have higher rates of HIV and STIs than female sex workers. Katsulis and Durfee (2012), in their research on Mexican sex workers, found male sex workers were still 10 times more likely than female sex workers to engage in sex without a condom during their most recent encounter with a client. Phua et al. (2009) found that health-related behaviours among online male sex workers are linked to masculinity, including the adoption or preference for 'active' or 'passive' sex roles in the commercial encounter or a gay or straight identity. Portrayals of hypermasculinity and concern with STIs were negatively correlated. And, although female sex workers were significantly more likely than males to have used a condom with a client, they were significantly less likely than males to have used a condom with their regular partner. Findings from this research, however, tend to be geographically diverse and contradictory. Compared to the general population of men who have sex with men, for example, male sex workers have been found to have comparable or slightly higher rates of overall condom use (Bimbi & Parsons, 2005).

Nonetheless, male sex workers have been identified as at greater risk of HIV and STIs because: fewer work in brothels, where they can be accessed by outreach workers; they are a more transient population; the nature of their work is clandestine and opportunistic; many do not identify as gay and, as such, may be dislocated from peer supports; and many do not identify as sex workers because of the temporary nature of the work, or they receive payment in kind. However, increased risk is likely related to structural factors, such as the criminalisation of sex work or same-sex relations (Oosthuizen, 2000; Ross et al., 2012). It also seems that while public-health strategies have been effective in many developed nations, male sex workers still present as a high-risk group in developing nations (Meng et al., 2010; Okal et al., 2009). While epidemiological research has included many non-western sites, it has tended to ignore local cultural contexts, reproducing paradigms from the Global North and paying little attention to how local configurations of masculinity influencer risk behaviours.

Concluding comments

Despite playing a significant role in sex-work encounters, men and masculinity have been largely absent in the research literature. Much research has been directed at solving 'problems' associated with sex work, these being defined largely in criminal and public health terms. And while masculinity, in terms of violence and risk taking, is strongly implicated in harms associated with sex work, the focus has mostly been on the practices of female sex workers and not the group who dominate involvement in all varieties of sex work: male clients. Men have also become increasingly visible as sex workers, with international research suggesting that changing social mores, technological change, migration and economic restructuring (including increased materialism and consumption) may give greater visibility to male sex workers, if not increase supply and demand for male sex workers on a global scale (Kong, 2014; Niccolai, 2014).

References

Aggleton, P. (Ed.). (1999). *Men who sell sex: International perspectives on male prostitution and HIV/AIDS*. London: UCL Press.

Aggleton, P., & Parker, R. (Eds.). (2015). *Men who sell sex: Global perspectives*. London: Routledge.

Alcano, M. (2011). 'Slaves of our own making': The fabrication of masculine identities between Java and Bali. *Indonesia and the Malay World, 39*(115), 373–389.

Allman, D., & Bozhinov, B. (2015). Sex work at the crossroads: Men who sell sex to men in Macedonia. In P. Aggleton & R. Parker (Eds.), *Men who sell sex: Global perspectives* (pp. 66–73). London: Routledge.

Bimbi, D. S., & Parsons, J. T. (2005). Barebacking among Internet based male sex workers. *Journal of Gay and Lesbian Psychotherapy, 9*(3/4), 89–110.

Boyce, P., & Isaacs, G. (2014). Male sex work in Southern and Eastern Africa. In V. Minichiello & J. Scott (Eds.), *Male sex work and society* (pp. 288–313). New York: Harrington Park Press.

Brooks-Gordon, B. (2006). *The price of sex*. New York: Taylor and Francis.

Caldwell, H. (2014). *Long-term clients who access commercial sex services in Australia* (MA thesis) University of Sydney, Sydney. https://ses.library.usyd.edu.au/handle/2123/8197.

Carael, M., Slaymaker, E., Lyerla, R., & Sarkar, S. (2006). Clients of sex workers in different regions of the world: Hard to count. *Sexually Transmitted Infections, 82*(s3), iii26–iii33.

Cunningham, S, & Kendall, T. D. (2011). Prostitution 2.0: The changing face of sex work. *Journal of Urban Economics, 69*(3), 273–287.

Dennis, J. (2008). Women are victims, men make choices: The invisibility of men and boys in the global sex trade. *Gender Issues, 25*(1), 11–25.

Earle, S., & Sharp, K. (2008). Intimacy, pleasure and the men who pay for sex. In G. Letherby, K. Williams, P. Birch & M. Cain (Eds.), *Sex as crime?* (pp. 63–79). London: Willan.

Edlund, L., & Korn, E. (2002). A theory of prostitution. *Journal of Political Economy, 110*(1), 181–214.

Farley, M., Schuckman, E., Golding, J. M., Houser, K., Jarrett, L., Qualliotine, P., & Decker, M. (2011). *Comparing sex buyers with men who don't buy sex: 'You can have a good time with the servitude' vs. 'You're supporting a system of degradation'*. Paper presented at the Psychologists for Social Responsibility Annual Meeting, Boston, MA.

Friedman, M. (2014). Male sex work from ancient times to the near present. In V. Minichiello & J. Scott (Eds.), *Male sex work and society* (pp. 3–33). New York: Harrington Park Press.

Gaffney, J., & Beverley, K. (2001). Contextualizing the construction and social organization of the commercial male sex industry in London at the beginning of the twenty-first century. *Feminist Review, 67*(1), 133–141.

Hodge, D. (2005). *Colonization of the Cuban body: Nationalism, economy, and masculinity of male sex work in Havana* (Doctoral dissertation). The City University of New York.
Holt, T., & Blevins, K. (2007). Examining sex work from the client's perspective: Assessing Johns using online data. *Deviant Behavior, 28*(4), 333–354.
Horswill, A., & Weitzer, R. (2018). Becoming the client: The socialization of novice buyers of sexual services. *Deviant Behavior, 39*(2), 148–158.
Hubbard, P. (1999). *Sex and the city: Geographies of prostitution in the urban west.* Aldershot: Ashgate.
Huysamen, M., & Boonzaier, F. (2015). Men's constructions of masculinity and male sexuality through talk of buying sex. *Culture, Health & Sexuality, 17*(5), 541–554.
Jamel, J. (2011). An investigation of the incidence of client-perpetrated sexual violence against male sex workers. *International Journal of Sexual Health, 23*(1), 63–78.
Jeffreys, E. (2007). Querying queer theory: Debating male-male prostitution in the Chinese media. *Critical Asian Studies, 39*(1), 151–175.
Katsulis, Y., & Durfee, A. (2012). Prevalence and correlates of sexual health among male and female sex workers in Tijuana, Mexico. *Global Public Health*, 7(4), 367–383.
Kinnell, H. (2008). *Violence and sex work in Britain.* London: Willan.
Koken, J., Bimbi, D., Parsons, J., & Halkitis, P. (2004). The experience of stigma in the lives of male Internet escorts. *Journal of Psychology and Human Sexuality, 16*(1), 13–32.
Kong, T. (2014). Male sex work in China. In V. Minichiello & J. Scott (Eds.), *Male sex work and society* (pp. 314–341). New York: Harrington Park Press.
Liguori, L., & Aggleton, P. (1999). Aspects of male sex work in Mexico City. In P. Aggleton (Ed.), *Men who sell sex: International perspectives on male prostitution and HIV/AIDS* (pp. 103–126). London: UCL Press.
MacPhail, C., Scott, J., & Minichiello, V. (2015). Technology, normalisation and male sex work. *Culture, Health and Sexuality, 17*(4), 483–495.
Meng, X., Anderson, A., Wang, L., Li, Z., Guo, W., Lee, Z., Jin, H., & Cai, Y. (2010). An exploratory survey of money boys and HIV transmission risk in Jilin Province, PR China. *AIDS Research and Therapy*, 7(1), 17.
Minichiello, V., Dune, T., Disogra, C., & Mariño, R. (2014). Male sex work from Latin American perspectives. In V. Minichiello & J. Scott (Eds.), *Male sex work and society* (pp. 362–397). New York: Harrington Park Press.
Minichiello, V., Mariño, R, Browne, J., Jamieson, M., Peterson, K., Reuter, B., & Robinson, K. (1999). A profile of the clients of male sex workers in three Australian cities. *Australian and New Zealand Journal of Public Health, 23*(5), 511–518.
Minichiello, V., & Scott, J. (Eds.). (2014). *Male sex work and society.* New York: Harrington Park Press.
Minichiello, V., Scott, J., & Callander, D. (2013). New pleasures and old dangers: Re-inventing male sex work. *Journal of Sex Research, 50*(3/4), 263–275.
Mitchell, G. (2010). Fare tales and fairy tails: How gay sex tourism is shaping the Brazilian dream. *Wagadu, 8*, 93–114.
Monto, M. A. (2004). Female prostitution, customers, and violence. *Violence Against Women, 10*(2), 160–188.
Monto, M. A., & Hotaling, N. (2001). Predictors of rape myth acceptance among male clients of female street prostitutes. *Violence Against Women*, 7(3), 275–293.
Morse, E., Simon, P., Osofsky, H., Balson, P., & Gaumer, H. (1991). The male prostitute: A vector for transmission of HIV infection into the heterosexual world. *Social Science Medicine, 32*(5), 535–539.
Moscheta, M., McNamee, S., & Santos, M. (2013). Sex trade among men: Negotiating sex, bodies and identity categories. *Psicologica and Sociedade, 25*, 44–53.
Niccolai, L. (2014). Male sex work in post-soviet Russia. In V. Minichiello & J. Scott (Eds.), *Male sex work and society* (pp. 343–361). New York: Harrington Park Press.
Okal, J., Luchters, S., Geibel, S., Chersich, M. F., Lango, D., & Temmerman, M. (2009). Social context, sexual risk perceptions and stigma: HIV vulnerability among male sex workers in Mombasa, Kenya. *Culture, Health & Sexuality, 11*(8), 811–826.
Oosthuizen, A. (2000). *Male prostitution and HIV/AIDS in Durban* (MA Thesis). Durban: University of Natal.
Ozbay, C. (2015). 'Straight' rent boys and the gays who sell sex in Istanbul. In P. Aggleton & R. Parker (Eds.), *Men who sell sex: Global perspectives* (pp. 74–87). London: Routledge.
Padila, M. (2007). 'Western Union Daddies' and their quest for authenticity: An ethnographic study of the Dominican gay sex tourism industry. *Journal of Homosexuality, 53*(1), 241–275.

Parsons, J., Koken, J., & Bimbi, D. (2007). Looking beyond HIV: Eliciting individual and community needs of male internet escorts. *Journal of Homosexuality, 53*(1/2), 219–240.

Phua, V. C., Ciambrone, D., & Vazquez, O. (2009). Advertising health status in male sex workers' online ads. *The Journal of Men's Studies, 17*(3), 251–258.

Reiss, A. J. (1961). The social integration of peers and queers. *Social Problems, 9*(2), 102–120.

Richter, M., & Isaacs, G. (2015). 'Cape Town is free': Reflections on male sex work in Cape Town, South Africa. In P. Aggleton & R. Parker (Eds.), *Men who sell sex: Global perspectives* (pp. 120–130). London: Routledge.

Rissel, C. E., Richters, J., Grulich, A. E., de Visser, R. O., & Smith, A. M. A. (2003). Sex in Australia: Experiences of commercial sex in a representative sample of adults. *Australian and New Zealand Journal of Public Health, 27*(2), 191–197.

Ross, M. W., Crisp, B. R., Månsson, S. A., & Hawkes, S. (2012). Occupational health and safety among commercial sex workers. *Scandinavian Journal of Work Environment Health, 38*(2), 105–119.

Ryan, J. (2006). Transgender sex workers. In M. Ditmore (Ed.), *Encyclopedia of prostitution and sex work, vol. 2* (pp. 499–506). Westport, CT: Greenwood Press.

Salamon, E. (1989). The homosexual escort agency: Deviance disavowal. *British Journal of Sociology, 40*(1), 1–21.

Sanders, T. (2008). Male sexual scripts. *Sociology, 42*(3), 400–417.

Scott, J. (2003a). A prostitute's progress: Male prostitution in scientific discourse. *Social Semiotics, 13*(2), 179–201.

Scott, J. (2003b). Prostitution and public health in New South Wales. *Culture, Health & Sexuality, 5*(3), 277–293.

Scott, J. (2011). Governing prostitution: Differentiating the bad from the bad. *Current Issues in Criminal Justice, 23*(1), 53–72.

Uy, J., Parsons, J., Bimbi, D., Koken, J., & Halkitis, P. (2004). Gay and bisexual male escorts who advertise on the internet: Understanding reasons for and effects of involvement in commercial sex. *International Journal of Men's Health, 3*(1), 11–26.

van Winjingaarden, J., & Iqbal, Q. (2015). Male sex work in urban Pakistan: Experiences from Lahore and Karachi. In P. Aggleton & R. Parker (Eds.), *Men who sell sex: Global perspectives* (pp. 146–158). London: Routledge.

Vanwesenbeeck, I., de Graaf, R., Van Zessen, G., & Straver, C. J. (1993). Protection styles of prostitute clients: Intentions, behavior and considerations in relation to AIDS. *Journal of Sex Education Therapy, 19*(2), 79–92.

Weitzer, R. (2000). *Sex for sale: Prostitution, pornography, and the sex industry*. New York: Routledge.

Weitzer, R. (2009). Sociology of sex work. *Annual Review of Sociology, 35*, 213–234.

Part 4

Spaces, movements and technologies

27

Men and masculinities in migration processes

Katarzyna Wojnicka

Introduction

Migration processes, understood as physical movements of people from one place to another in transnational, national and local contexts, are deeply gendered phenomena, and the experiences of actors involved in these processes are shaped by their genders (Donaldson, Hibbins, Howson & Pease, 2009). Therefore, this chapter focuses on the intersections between migration processes and men and masculinities. The first part of the chapter outlines the most influential trends and studies on men, masculinities and migration processes from both historical and contemporary perspectives. The second part is dedicated to the analysis of transnational male migrant experiences and their positioning in host societies from an intersectional perspective (Christensen & Qvotrup Jensen, this volume; Hearn, Blagojević & Harrison, 2013). This discussion is necessary to demonstrate that transnational male migrants are not a homogeneous group. The status of certain migrants can differ tremendously, as can be seen in the starkly different situations of male refugees compared to so-called 'international expats', for example. Hence, considerations of race, class, ethnicity, religion, sexualities and age are at the core of this analysis. The overall aim of here is to analyse interdisciplinary discussions of men and migration centred on the multidimensional and intersectional aspects of male experiences and identities, migrant men's practices and perceptions of migrant men and their masculinities in host societies.

Men and masculinities in migration studies

Despite the fact that a gendered perspective has been present in migration studies for several decades, men and masculinities issues are still rarely discussed as a separate research theme. The majority of gendered migration scholarship focuses predominantly on women's issues (Charsley & Wray, 2015). This is perhaps one of the greater paradoxes of the contemporary social sciences (Wojnicka & Pustułka, 2017), as throughout the centuries, men have consistently travelled more often, and further distances, than women (Transgen, 2007). Therefore, in the majority of classic migration studies, migrant men are usually the main subjects of analysis. One of the most explicit exemplifications of such a study is *The Polish Peasant in*

Europe and America: Monograph of an Immigrant Group by William I. Thomas and Florian Znaniecki (1918), widely considered to be one of the most influential 20th-century sociological works. Central to this study is the analysis of letters sent by Polish migrants in the United States to their relatives who remained in the homeland. The authors focused on four sets of letters written by the families Wróblewski, Markiewicz, Raczkowski and Borkowski, which at first glance suggests that the collective experiences of all family members are at the heart of the study. In fact, the vast majority of migration experiences described by Thomas and Znaniecki are male experiences. In the first case study, the narrative focuses on the father of the family and his desire to remarry. The second case study is concentrated on two brothers who migrated to the United States and the differing ways in which their migration experiences shaped their identities and life choices. Male migration is also the main theme in the Borkowski case, even though the analysed letters are authored by the wife of migrant Władysław, who stayed in her homeland and 'waited the rest of her life for his summons' (Zaretsky, 1996, p. 24). The only exception is the Raczkowski case study, as it is concentrated equally on the experiences of two siblings, Adam and Helena. However, despite the dominance of masculine perspectives in this study, *The Polish Peasant* lacks any kind of gendered reflection. This particular approach results in the above-mentioned paradox: migrant men are over-researched as 'normative' migrants, and yet persistently understudied due to the universalisation and presupposed singularity of male migrant experience. This trend can be found across the majority of later migration literature. For decades, this literature has thus been marked by a lack of research into the ways in which the male experience of migration processes influences the re/construction and performance of masculine identities.

This situation changed slightly at the beginning of the 21st century, when a handful of scholars, mostly those inspired by feminist scholarship, began conducting research that took masculinities into consideration as an important variable. According to Charsley and Wray (2015, p. 405), these early 'masculinity conscious' analyses mostly consisted of studies of men working in construction sites (Walter, Bourgois & Loinaz, 2004), male migrants working in households as 'handymen' (Perrons, Plomien & Kilkey, 2010) and migrant men employed in the (feminised) care sector, mostly as nurses or care workers (Batnitzky, McDowell & Dyer, 2008, 2009; McGregor, 2007). Furthermore, a number of scholars have contributed with important reflections to the study of migrant masculinities through their utilisation of postcolonial approaches. Among these works are Daniel Colemans' *Masculine migrations: Reading the Postcolonial Male in 'New Canadian' Narrations* (1998) and *South Asian Masculinities* (Chopra, Osella & Osella, 2004), as well as several works where migration is explored as a masculine rite of passage (e.g., Cohen, 2005; Monsutti, 2007; Osella & Osella, 2000). However, the most significant turning point for gendered reflections on men and migration occurred with the publication of the edited volume entitled *Migrant Men: Critical Studies of Masculinities and the Migration Experience* (Donaldson et al., 2009) in which the editors undertook the first specific attempt to bring together work on men and migration using approaches from critical men and masculinities studies (hereafter CSMM). This particular publication was a milestone not only for migration scholarship but also for CSMM, which until this point had not considered migration processes as important factors influencing men's lives and their performances of masculinity. According to Hearn,

> [m]any studies of men and masculinities focused on more immediate aspects of sociological life (even if paradoxically bodies are often not foregrounded), ethnographic moment, methodological nationalism [dominant analysis were concentrated around Katarzyna Wojnicka, thereafter K.W.] family, health, interpersonal violence, sexuality,

> workplace, welfarist approaches, rather than large-scale, international, comparative, transnational [approaches K.W.]. Questions of migration, men's migration and its effects was somewhat muted in CSMM and politics until recently.
>
> *(2016, p. 37)*

The intersectional character of *Migrant Men* is reflected in the diversity of male migrant groups portrayed in its particular chapters. Despite the work's Australian context, issues of class, race, ethnicity and citizenship are pivotal in almost all case studies and are not restricted to a national lens. Moreover, the main question in all analyses is how 'immigrant men renegotiate their gender identity as they relate their own cultural understandings of masculinity to the meanings and practices in the dominant culture' (Donaldson et al., 2009, p. 15). The added value of the book stems from its attention to the relationships between migrant and non-migrant (white) men and the implications these relationships have for power relations, hierarchies of masculinities and male privilege. Since then, more authors have produced scholarship linking CSMM and migration scholarship, resulting in the publication of several valuable books and an even larger number of scientific articles addressing men and migration. Of the former, special attention should be paid to those works that analyse migration as part of larger, transnational social processes (e.g., Hearn, 2015; Hearn et al., 2013; Vasquez del Aquila, 2014).

In recent years, scholars have continued to develop gendered approaches to studying male migrants, resulting in a number of publications concerned with the experiences of various migrant groups and diasporas. These include studies of Pakistani husbands and fiancés in the UK (Charsley, 2005; Charsley & Liversage, 2015), Polish workers in Western European countries (Kilkey, Plomien & Perrons, 2014; Pustułka & Ślusarczyk, 2016; Pustułka, Struzik & Ślusarczyk, 2015), documented and undocumented Mexican migrants in the USA (Broughton, 2008; Cantu, Naples & Vidal-Ortiz, 2009; Hondagneu-Sotelo & Messner, 1999; Golash-Boza & Hondagneu-Sotelo, 2013; Ramirez & Hondagneu-Sotelo, 2013; Schmalzbauer, 2013; Trouille, 2013), Chinese rural-urban migrants and their family arrangements (Lin, 2017) and Turkish 'Gästarbeiters' in Germany and Austria (Ewing, 2008; Scheibelhofer, 2012; Spindler, 2007; Spohn, 2002; Toprak, 2007), to name just a few. Nevertheless, many researchers focus on a small number of issues, such as the role of migrant men in the labour force, or on more negative aspects of their mobility as migrant men. These negative aspects are often associated with criminality and sexism (Griffiths, 2015) and linked with social problems such as domestic and sexual violence, youth criminality (Flores, 2014) or culturally specific crimes such as honour murders, forced marriages and female genital mutilation (Korteweg, 2012; Razack, 2004; Yurdakul & Korteweg, 2013). This approach draws a picture of migrant men as a rather homogeneous group who cause or (occasionally) deal with similar problems. As a result, migrant men in these studies are rarely seen as part of a complex and diverse social category, and their masculinities are seldom framed as intersectional and multidimensional social phenomena. Recognition of this multidimensionality might include consideration of masculinity as, for example, family and intimate relationships driven (Bell & Pustułka, 2017; Nobles, 2011; Parreñas, 2008; Pribilsky, 2012; Pustułka, Struzik & Ślusarczyk, 2015; Ramphele & Richter, 2006; Sinatti, 2014; Souralova & Fialova, 2017; Waters, 2010; Żadkowska, Kosakowska-Berezecka & Ryndyk, 2017), non-normative and non-heterosexual (Manalansan, 2006), racialised (Golash-Boza & Hondagneu-Sotelo, 2013) or connected to power and privilege (Connell & Wood, 2005; Hearn, 2015; Trąbka & Wojnicka, 2017).

Who are migrant men?

According to Hearn, '[w]omen, men, and further genders are likely to experience migration, emigration and immigration in different ways' (2015, p. 163). This statement is incontestable, although it must also be extended in order to recognise that diverse groups of men, women and other genders experience migration in different ways. Migrants' experiences are influenced not only by gender but also by other demographic and societal factors such as race, ethnicity, religious background, class, age, sexuality, nationality and primary geographical emplacement. Following this line of argumentation, male migrants cannot be seen as a homogeneous group, and their varied experiences and positioning in host societies are linked to a range of factors. There are profound differences between the perceptions and experiences of, for example, young male refugees from the Middle East applying for asylum in Europe and North America, older Eastern European male labour migrants residing in Western and northern Europe, middle-aged Mexican undocumented agricultural workers in the USA, and finally, so-called 'expats', that is, white male professionals from the Global North working in developing countries. Moreover, men who happen to be migrants may perform different kinds of male identities in their private and professional lives, have differing relationships to gender hierarchies and may variously represent hegemonic, complicit, hybrid and/or marginalised/subordinated types of masculinities (Connell, 1995; Trąbka & Wojnicka, 2017). Finally, within certain groups of male migrants there may be a variety of perceptions regarding gender roles and gender equality, and men within these groups may react differently to the gender-focused social norms they encounter in host countries. Therefore, the recognition of heterogeneity and the incorporation of intersectional approaches (Collins Hill & Bilge, 2016; see also Christensen & Qvotrup Jensen, this volume) are the most important starting points for analyses of men and migration. Neglecting these approaches results in the emergence of general (discursive) categories that attempt to capture and restrict male migrants to a singular identity. A powerful and vivid way of defining migrant men, and one that has been popular in recent public and media discourses, is the concept of 'foreign masculinity' (Scheibelhofer, 2017; Spindler, 2007). This portrayal of migrant men has strong negative connotations, as it defines migrants as dangerous, uncivilised men who break the norms of the host country. They are seen as potential perpetrators, particularly of sexual crimes, and a threat to local women, children, private property and the welfare state (Scheibelhofer, 2017). Such discourses represent migrants as almost exclusively non-white, low-class, non-Western, heterosexual men – for example criminal and sexually threatening Eastern European men or drug dealers from northern Africa (Scheibelhofer, 2017). Such men can be also described in the category of 'dangerous bachelors' (e.g., Gardner, 2010) that threatens local heteronormative power relations.

The multitude of male migrant masculinities

Asylum seekers

As already noted, the concept of 'foreign masculinity' has gained traction in European media discussions around the so-called 'migration crisis'. In the last three years, Europe has seen unprecedented waves of asylum seekers from the Middle East, North Africa and South Asia. According to data from Sweden and Germany, more than 2 million people applied for asylum between 2015 and 2018 in these two countries alone (Bundesamt für Migration und Flüchtlinge, 2018; Migrationsverket, 2018). Significantly, more than 60% of people seeking asylum were men. Their countries of origin, mainly Syria, Afghanistan and Iraq, have religious and cultural legacies that are rather distinct to those of the West. Global public-opinion research has depicted the values of these nations as potentially clashing with Western values, particularly with respect to gender equality and sexual liberalisation (Inglehart & Norris, 2003). As a result, in some cases, the recent influx of Muslim refugees to Europe has led to the emergence of public discourses referring to these men as potential threats to European values and host societies in general. Critical discussions have been to a large extent focused on migrant masculinity and the gender values of refugees. Indeed, the typical refugee referred to in much of this discourse is commonly portrayed as male and, in many cases, as a person lacking an appropriate (European) system of values with regard to gender and gender equality. Such perceptions, however, have not been based on any strong evidence and are the consequence of prejudice and the tendency to portray these men as dangerous 'others'. This particular group of migrants are often seen as homogeneous and are accused of being (potential) sexual perpetrators who do not recognise or understand the dynamics of European gender relations and the concept of gender equality as such. There remains a lack of analysis of this particular social group. However, by drawing on research conducted in migrants' countries of origin (e.g., UN Women Promundo – US, 2017), it is clear that, in reality, ideas of masculinity and femininity are framed in a variety of ways and depend on a particular subject's class, sexuality, religion or region of origin. Moreover, researchers describe a multiplicity of perceptions regarding gender equality, ranging from unfamiliarity or even rejection, to curiosity and acceptance (UN Women Promundo – US, 2017). This implies that male refugees are a heterogeneous group, and it demonstrates that their masculinity cannot be reduced to the simple (dangerous) 'foreign' type. Nevertheless, it may be that some migrants represent values and norms that align with this stereotype, as has been observed by Muchoki in his research on refugees from the Horn of Africa residing in Australia (2016). In his qualitative analysis on perceptions of gender roles, gender equality and sexual rights, he suggests that there is a great divide between the norms of this particular group of migrants and the norms of their host society. The majority of Muchoki's research participants represent radically conservative views regarding gender relations, do not recognise the concept of gender equality and perform the most traditional vision of masculinity. However, despite the differences among male refugees' attitudes and values, host societies tend to see all refugee men as 'other' and define them through the lens of hypermasculinity. At the same time, these men are, in fact, placed at the bottom of social hierarchies and often represent the most typical form of marginalised masculinity (Connell, 1995).

EU labour migrants

Male labour migrants are another distinctive and visible group of migrants in Europe. Polish men are a particularly good example of such migrants, as the size and intensity of migration flow from Poland to other EU countries is unprecedented. According to Polish authorities, more than 2 million people have relocated from Poland to countries such as the UK, Germany, the Netherlands, Ireland, Norway and others since 2004. Indeed, Polish people constitute one of the largest migrant groups within these EU countries. However, despite their Eastern European origin, Polish people are largely characterised as 'desirable' labour migrants: they are white, have European citizenship, share (to some extent) European values and, last but not least, they are presumed to be hard-working (Grabowska, 2016). Their position within host society gender hierarchies is significantly higher than that of non-European refugees. Nevertheless, their masculinity is still perceived through rather traditional lenses. Such men are predominantly seen as blue-collar workers, and thus their masculinity is often linked to their role as breadwinners. In many cases this results in a re-traditionalisation of gender roles and relationships within men's families and their country of origin, and a strengthening of their hegemonic position within these particular settings. At the same time, their position in host societies cannot be compared with that occupied by local men, as they are still perceived as less valuable, and so are subject to various forms of discrimination. Therefore, in the case of Polish male migrants, a specific form of ambivalence can be observed in relation to their privilege. They are better positioned than many other migrants as they possess the rights and legal status of EU citizens, but at the same time, as Eastern Europeans, they are subordinated in relation to locals (Ciupijus, 2011). As a consequence, their masculinities can be simultaneously hegemonic (within internal, family contexts) and marginalised (in external, host society contexts).

Expats

So-called 'expatriates' or 'expats' represent another category of labour migrants and can be described as cosmopolitan commuters who tend to be 'Western' and professional 'Eurostars' (Favell, 2008). They are usually white men, with prestigious professional positions, who relocate to places perceived as less developed than their countries of origin. Unlike the Polish men described above, they enjoy a set of privileges in their host societies that often extend beyond those afforded to local men (Maher & Lafferty, 2014). Expats include 'third-culture kids', that is,

> a specific category of serial migrants: people who have experienced multiple international migrations in their childhood and/or youth due to their parents' international career. They are often portrayed as growing up in a multicultural environment and are well-educated and privileged in terms of socioeconomic status.
>
> *(Trąbka & Wojnicka, 2017, p. 5)*

The gender identities of 'third-culture kids' are often strongly influenced by their mobility and their access to privileged positions in host societies, linked to their class, race, ethnicity and citizenship status. According to the authors, this results in the development of hegemonic (Connell, 1995) or hybrid (Arxer, 2011; Bridges & Pascoe, 2014) forms of masculinity. Moreover, unlike male refugees, they are rarely perceived through the lens of dangerous 'foreign' masculinity and in many cases are not even defined as migrants, as their social status is simply too high (Leinonen, 2012).

Conclusions

Taking into account the variety of male migrant experiences and the differentiations in how migrants are positioned in the social structures and gender hierarchies of host countries, it is clear that this particular social category is highly heterogeneous and influenced by a constellation of social factors. Hence, the only appropriate analytical and methodological framework for feminist analysis regarding men, masculinities and migration processes is an intersectional approach. However, analyses that address interconnections between gender, class, race, ethnicity and sexuality in migration processes must also be supplemented by the application of a geographical dimension. Spatiality plays a crucial role in positioning migrant men in the social structure of both host and sending societies. Geographical belonging is an important component of social embodiment and class status, and including it within an intersectional analysis can result in a more in-depth interpretation of gender hierarchies. A spatially intersectional perspective that underlines the pivotal role of a migrant's place of origin is especially useful because migrants' socio-locations 'are tied to the ever-important notion of hegemonic masculinity' (Wojnicka & Pustułka, 2017, p. 87) and its relationship to other types of masculinities. Intersectional approaches are closely linked to power relations dynamics analysis and thus enable scholars to explore in greater depth the diversity of male migrant experiences in terms of marginalisation and/or privilege. As has been demonstrated above, mobility can be either downward or upward, augmenting or decreasing the status of particular groups of migrant men. This not only shapes the type of gender identity imposed on migrants by others in their local society but also affects their own attitudes towards masculinities and the ways they are performed.

References

Arxer, S. L. (2011). Hybrid masculine power: Reconceptualizing the relationship between homosociality and hegemonic masculinity. *Humanity & Society*, *35*(4), 390–422.

Batnitzky, A., McDowell, L. & Dyer, S. (2008). A middle-class global mobility? The working lives of Indian men in a West London hotel. *Global Networks*, *8*(1), 51–70.

Batnitzky, A., McDowell, L., & Dyer, S. (2009). Flexible and strategic masculinities: The working lives and gendered identities of male migrants in London. *Journal of Ethnic and Migration Studies*, *35*(8), 1275–1293.

Bell, J., & Pustułka, P. (2017). Multiple masculinities of Polish migrant men. *NORMA: International Journal for Masculinity Studies*, *12*(2), 127–143.

Bridges, T., & Pascoe, C. J. (2014). Hybrid masculinities: New directions in the sociology of men and masculinities. *Sociology Compass*, *8*(3), 246–258.

Broughton, C. (2008). Migration as engendered practice: Mexican men, masculinity, and northward migration. *Gender & Society*, *22*(5), 568–589.

Bundesamt für Migration und Flüchtlinge. (2018). Asylzahlen. www.bamf.de/DE/Infothek/Statistiken/Asylzahlen/asylzahlen-node.html.

Cantu, L., Naples, N., & Vidal-Ortiz, S. (2009). *The sexuality of migration: Border crossings and Mexican immigrant men*. New York: New York University Press.

Charsley, K. (2005). Unhappy husbands: Masculinity and migration in transnational Pakistani marriages. *Journal of the Royal Anthropological Institute*, *11*(1), 85–105.

Charsley, K., & Liversage, A. (2015). Silenced husbands: Muslim marriage migration and masculinity. *Men and Masculinities*, *18*(4), 489–508.

Charsley, K., & Wray, H. (2015). Introduction: The invisible (migrant) man. *Men and Masculinities*, *18*(4), 403–423.

Chopra, R., Osella, C. & Osella, F. (Eds.). (2004). *South Asian masculinities: Context of change, sites of continuity*. New Delhi: Kali for Women and Women Unlimited.

Ciupijus, Z. (2011). Mobile Central Eastern Europeans in Britain: Successful European Union citizens and disadvantaged labour migrants? *Work, Employment and Society*, *25*(3), 540–550.

Cohen, D. (2005). Masculinity and social visibility: Migration, state spectacle and the making of the Mexican nation. *Estudios interdisciplinarios de America Latina y el Caribe*, *16*(1), 119–132.

Coleman, D. (1998). *Masculine migrations: Reading the postcolonial male in 'new Canadian' narrations*. Toronto: University of Toronto Press.

Collins Hill, P., & Bilge, S. (2016). *Intersectionality*. Cambridge: Polity Press.

Connell, R. W. (1995). *Masculinities*. Cambridge: Polity Press.

Connell, R. W., & Wood, J. (2005). Globalization and business masculinities. *Men and Masculinities*, 7(4), 347–364.

Donaldson, M., Hibbins, R., Howson, R., & Pease, B. (Eds.). (2009). *Migrant men: Critical studies of masculinities and the migration experience*. New York: Routledge.

Ewing, K. (2008). *Stolen honor: Stigmatizing Muslim men in Berlin*. Palo Alto, CA: Stanford University Press.

Favell, A. (2008). *Eurostars and eurocities: Free movement and mobility in an integrating Europe*. Malden, MA: Blackwell.

Flores, E. (2014). *God's gangs: Barrio ministry, masculinity and gang recovery*. New York: New York University Press.

Gardner, A. (2010). *City of strangers: Gulf migration and the Indian community in Bahrain*. Ithaca, NY: Cornell University Press.

Golash-Boza, T., & Hondagneu-Sotelo, P. (2013). Latino immigrant men and the deportation crisis: A gendered racial removal program. *Latino Studies, 11*(3), 271–292.

Grabowska, I. (2016). *Movers and stayers: Social mobility, migration and skills*. Frankfurt am Main: Lang.

Griffiths, M. (2015). 'Here, man is nothing!' Gender and policy in an asylum context. *Men and Masculinities, 18*(4), 468–488.

Hearn, J. (2015). *Men of the world: Genders, globalisations, transnational times*. London: Sage.

Hearn, J. (2016). *Where have the men gone? The understated history and significance of migration in critical studies/politics of men and masculinities*. Paper presented during International Workshop 'Men and Migration in Contemporary Europe', Centre for European Research at the University of Gothenburg, June 9–10, 2016.

Hearn, J., Blagojević, M., & Harrison, K. (Eds.). (2013). *Rethinking transnational men: Beyond, between and within nations*. New York: Routledge.

Hondagneu-Sotelo, P., & Messner, M. (1999). Gender displays and men's power: The 'new man' and the Mexican immigrant man. In S. Coontz, M. Parson, & G. Raley (Eds.), *American families: A multicultural reader* (pp. 342–358). New York: Routledge.

Inglehart, R., Norris, P. (2003). *Rising tide: Gender equality and cultural change around the world*. Cambridge: Cambridge University Press.

Kilkey, M., Plomien, A., & Perrons, D. (2014). Migrant men's fathering practices and projects in national and transnational spaces: Recent Polish male migrants to London. *International Migration, 52*(1), 178–191.

Korteweg, A. (2012). Understanding honour killing and honour-related violence in the immigration context: Implications for the legal profession and beyond. *Canadian Criminal Law Review, 16*(2), 33–58.

Leinonen, J. (2012). Invisible immigrants, visible expats? Americans in Finnish discourses on immigration and internationalization. *Nordic Journal of Migration Research, 2*(3), 213–223.

Lin, X. (2017). *Gender, modernity and male migrant workers in China: Becoming a 'modern' man*. New York: Routledge.

Maher, K. H., & Lafferty, M. (2014). White migrant masculinities in Thailand and the paradoxes of Western privilege. *Social & Cultural Geography, 15*(4), 427–448.

Manalansan, F. M. (2006). Queer intersections: Sexuality and gender in migration studies. *International Migration Review, 40*(1), 224–249.

McGregor, J. (2007). 'Joining the BBC (British Bottom Cleaners)': Zimbabwean migrants and the UK care industry. *Journal of Ethnic and Migration Studies, 33*(5), 801–824.

Migrationsverket. (2018). Asyl. www.migrationsverket.se/Om-Migrationsverket/Statistik/Asyl.html.

Monsutti, A. (2007). Migration as a rite of passage: Young Afghans building masculinity and adulthood in Iran. *Iranian Studies, 40*(2), 167–185.

Muchoki, S. (2016). *Intimacies, citizenship and refugee men*. London: Palgrave Macmillan.

Nobles, J. (2011). Parenting from abroad: Migration, nonresident father involvement and children's education in Mexico. *Journal of Marriage and Family, 73*(4), 729–746.

Osella, F., & Osella, C. (2000). Migration, money and masculinity in Kerala. *Journal of the Royal Anthropological Institute, 6*(1), 117–133.

Parreñas, R. (2008). Transnational fathering: Gendered conflicts, distant disciplining and emotional gaps. *Journal of Ethnic and Migration Studies, 34*(7), 1057–1072.

Perrons, D., Plomien, A., & Kilkey, M. (2010). Migration and uneven development within an enlarged European Union: Fathering, gender divisions and male migrant domestic services. *European Urban and Regional Studies, 17*(2), 197–215.

Pribilsky, J. (2012). Consumption dilemmas: Tracking masculinity, money, and transnational fatherhood between the Ecuadorian Andes and New York City. *Journal of Ethnic and Migration Studies, 38*(2), 323–343.

Pustułka, P., & Ślusarczyk, M. (2016). Work-life balance in the Polish migrant families settled in Norway. *Miscellanea Anthropologica et Sociologica, 17*(3), 71–91.

Pustułka, P., Struzik, J., & Ślusarczyk, M. (2015). Caught between breadwinning and emotional provisions: The case of Polish migrant fathers in Norway. *Studia Humanistyczne AGH, 14*(2), 117–140.

Ramirez, H., & Hondagneu-Sotelo, P. (2013). Mexican gardeners in the U.S. In M. Kilkey, D. Perrons, A. Plomien, P. Hondagneu-Sotelo & H. Ramirez (Eds.), *Gender, migration and domestic work: Masculinities, male labour and fathering in the UK and USA* (pp. 122–148). London: Palgrave Macmillan.

Ramphele, M., & Richter, L. (2006). Migrancy, family dissolution and fatherhood. In L. Richter & R. Morrell, *Baba: Men and fatherhood in South Africa* (pp. 73–82). Cape Town: HSRC Press.

Razack, S. (2004). Imperilled Muslim women, dangerous Muslim men and civilised Europeans: Legal and social Responses to forced marriages. *Feminist Legal Studies, 12*(2), 129–174.

Scheibelhofer, P. (2012). From health check to Muslim test: The shifting politics of governing migrant masculinity. *Journal of Intercultural Studies, 33*(3), 319–332.

Scheibelhofer, P. (2017). 'It won't work without ugly pictures': Images of othered masculinities and the legitimisation of restrictive refugee-politics in Austria. *NORMA: International Journal for Masculinity Studies, 12*(2), 96–111.

Schmalzbauer, L. (2013). Temporary and transnational: Gender and emotion in the lives of Mexican guest worker fathers. *Ethnic and Racial Studies Review, 38*(2), 211–226.

Sinatti, G. (2014). Masculinities and intersectionality in migration: Transnational Wolof migrants negotiating manhood and gendered family roles. In T.-D. Truong, D. Gasper, J. Handmaker & S. I. Bergh (Eds.), *Migration, gender and social justice* (pp. 215–226). Berlin: Springer.

Souralova, A., & Fialova, H. (2017). Where have all the fathers gone? Remarks on feminist research on transnational fatherhood. *NORMA: International Journal for Masculinity Studies, 12*(2), 159–174.

Spindler, S. (2007). Im Netz hegemonialer Männlichkeit: Männlichkeitskontruktionen junger Migranten. In M. Bereswill, M. Meuser & S. Scholz (Eds.), *Dimensionen der Kategorie Geschlecht: Der Fall Männlichkeit* (pp. 119–135). Munster: Westfälisches Dampfboot.

Spohn, M. (2002). *Turkische Männer in Deutschland: Familie und Identität: Migranten der ersten Generation erzählen ihre Geschichte.* Bielefeld: Transcript.

Thomas, W. I., Znaniecki, F. (1918). *The Polish peasant in Europe and America: Monograph of an immigrant group.* Urbana and Chicago, IL: University of Illinois Press.

Toprak, A. (2007). *Das schwache Geschlecht: Die turkischen Männer: Zwangsheirat, häusliche Gewalt, Doppelmoral der Ehre.* Freiburg: Lambertus.

Trąbka, A., & Wojnicka, K. (2017). Self-positioning as a man in transnational contexts: Constructing and managing hybrid masculinity. *NORMA: International Journal for Masculinity Studies, 12*(2), 144–158.

Transgen. (2007). *Gender mainstreaming European transport research and policies.* Copenhagen: University of Copenhagen.

Trouille, D. (2013). Neighborhood outsiders, field insiders: Latino immigrant men and the control of public space. *Qualitative Sociology, 36*(1), 1–22.

UN Women Promundo – US. (2017). Understanding masculinities: Results from the International Men and Gender Equality Survey (IMAGES) – Middle East and North Africa. www.unwomen.org/en/digital-library/publications/2017/5/understanding-masculinities-results-from-the-images-in-the-middle-east-and-north-africa.

Vasquez del Aquila, E. (2014). *Being a Man in a transnational world: The masculinity and sexuality of migration.* New York: Routledge.

Walter, N., Bourgois, P., & Loinaz, H. M. (2004). Masculinity and undocumented labor migration: Injured Latino day laborers in San Francisco. *Social Science and Medicine, 59*(6), 1159–1168.

Waters, J. L. (2010). Becoming a father, missing a wife: Chinese transnational families and the male experience of lone parenting in Canada. *Population, Space and Place, 16*(1), 63–74.

Wojnicka, K., & Pustułka, P. (2017). Migrant men in the nexus of space and (dis)empowerment. *NORMA: International Journal for Masculinity Studies, 12*(2), 89–95.

Yurdakul, G., & Korteweg, A. (2013). Gender equality and immigrant integration: Honor killing and forced marriage debates in the Netherlands, Germany, and Britain. *Women's Studies International Forum, 41*(1), 204–214.

Żadkowska, M., Kosakowska-Berezecka, N., & Ryndyk, O. (2017). Two worlds of fatherhood: Comparing the use of parental leave among Polish fathers in Poland and in Norway. In K. Slany, M. Ślusarczyk, P. Pustułka & E. Guribye (Eds.), *Transnational Polish families in Norway: Social capital, integration, institutions and care* (pp. 173–197). Frankfurt am Main: Peter Lang.

Zaretsky, E. (Ed.). (1996). *The Polish peasant in Europe and America: A classic work in immigration history.* Urbana and Chicago, IL: University of Illinois Press.

28

Locating critical masculinities theory

Masculinities in space and place

Madhura Lohokare

This chapter highlights research on the conceptual articulations between masculinities and spatiality, illustrating how these interlinkages constitute a productive site for deepening our understanding of masculinities as plural and situated. From the late 20th century onwards, the question of spatial organization has been foregrounded in social sciences' attempts to understand the radically reconfigured relations between people, places, identity and economic and political activity in an increasingly globalized world, giving rise to the *spatial turn* in social sciences (Appadurai, 1996; Lefebvre, 1991; Massey, 1994). It comes as no surprise, then, that spatiality is now considered to be central to the construction of gendered identities.

This review chapter covers geographical literature focusing on masculinity and literature within critical masculinity studies centred on specific geopolitical regions. Both these perspectives provide insights into ways in which locations, spaces and scales structure masculinities and the diverse methodologies to research them.

Masculinities and spatiality: the geographical imperative

Articulating geography and masculinity

Within the social sciences, pioneering research on gender and space needs to be credited to geography, especially scholarship in feminist geography, which highlighted how gender relations are organized and sustained in accordance with fundamentally spatial binaries, of the private and public, or the inside and outside (Bondi & Rose, 2003; Massey, 1994; McDowell, 1999). Thus, asking the question 'where?' is central to feminist geography, allowing it to incorporate power-laden intersections between social, political and economic processes that constitute a place, into the analysis of multiple identities (Nelson & Seager, 2005). The imperative to study masculinities as spatialized, emplaced and located in particular contexts has to be attributed to the above analytical framework (see also Gorman-Murray & Hopkins, 2014).

Jackson (1991), while acknowledging feminist theorizing in gendered geographies, presents an agenda for cultural geography to study masculinities as historically and geographically contingent, as well as to elucidate the spatial structures that sustain patriarchal gender relations. Hopkins and Noble (2009), in analyzing the shifting foci in research on masculinity in the last two decades, contend that there has been a movement from a largely sociological focus on questions of masculine power and resistance to gendered relations of power to a more cultural one, which is concerned with discursive constructions of masculine gendered identities and their intersections with other vectors of identity such as class, race and sexuality (p. 813). This shift is significant on account of it's centring of the question of context and located-ness: the lived experiences of masculine gendered identities is fundamentally seen to be shaped by the intersecting local, regional and global contexts and how these intersections materialize in a place. Place, in its broadest connotation here, is deemed not merely as a backdrop against which multiple masculinities are enacted, but becomes an entity which *renders* masculinities as multiple, moulding the construction, experience and performance of masculinities in diverse ways. Bringing in a geographical dimension to the production of masculinity thus enables its conceptualization as essentially plural.

Emergent research

Berg and Longhurst (2003) present a useful review of the burgeoning of geographical focus on masculinities in the 1990s and 2000s by focusing on the variety of research published in *Gender, Space and Culture*, a leading feminist geography journal. These decades saw the beginning of geographical explorations of the various cultural sites where masculinities are played out in socio-spatial arenas as varied as advertising (Jackson, 1994), queer spaces (Knopp, 1998), discourses of the city (Sommers, 1998) and gyms (Johnston, 1998).[1]

In 2005, van Hoven and Hörschelmann published their edited volume *Spaces of Masculinities*, which brought together research on masculinities in diverse cultural spaces and geographical locations, gesturing towards possibilities of future research arenas around space, place and masculinities. The volume covers excellent research on embodied practices of masculinities as being embedded in spaces as varied as changing dynamics of labour market of advanced capitalism (McDowell, 2005), industrial capitalism and its intersections with region (Dunk & Bartol, 2005) and the 'rural' in its discursive and material settings (Cloke, 2005; Evans, 2005). In a crucial shift of scale, the volume focuses on the 'body' as a spatial field and explores how institutional settings of prison (Janssen, 2005) and sports (Hall, 2005) constitute an arena of masculine assertion as well as contestation through the bodily practices of its members, while themselves getting shaped as male spaces. In the section titled, 'Sexuality and relationships', Skelton and Valentine (2005) and Aitken (2005) provide us with remarkable accounts of geographies of fathering, as practices of fatherhood, so central to defining masculinity, are negotiated within the dynamic spaces of family and community, thus illustrating how masculinities are essentially relational: constructed via complex interactions between men, women and children in the deeply 'private' spatial context demarcated as home/family. This volume represents a significant milestone in research on space and masculinities for bringing together a coherent framework which consolidated the conceptualizations of space to include *scale* (bodily, familial, regional, institutional, urban) and contexts (work, conflict, migration, relationships) and for grounding geographical research on masculine gendered identities *within* these intersecting contexts and scales.

In the last decade, research on negotiations of masculine gendered identities within cultural geography has burgeoned rapidly in arenas as diverse as leisure (Bull, 2009;

Evers, 2009; Kenway & Hickey-Moody, 2009), institutional setting of the school (O Donoghue, 2007; Curtin & Linehan, 2002), migration and diasporic settings (Snider, 2017; Tang, 2017; Ye, 2014) and in geographical areas which are moving away from the Euro-American and Australian context, where earlier research tended to be concentrated (Jackson & Balaji, 2011). In the following sections, I focus on geographical research on masculinities in the realm of work and domestic spaces. Since these crucial spatial binaries of private/public, home/work have had a definitive impact on constructions of gendered identities in the wake of modernity across global contexts, it will be productive to review how geographical research has enabled a shift in our understandings of how masculinities are re/imagined along these spatial binaries in the process rendering the latter as uncertain and fluid.

Spaces of work and masculinities in geography

Geographers have contributed in definitive ways in the arena of work as constitutive of masculinity, effectively exploring the aforesaid intersections between scales and contexts in the making of emplaced and plural masculinities. In her work examining spaces of merchant and finance banking, for instance, feminist geographer McDowell (2001, 1997) straddles the multiple scales of the body, organization and the city to illustrate the ways in which the social and material spaces of merchant and finance banking in London produce particular, embodied versions of masculinities and femininities. In doing so, this research signals a crucial shift from a concern with how women are excluded from masculine workspaces to a closer investigation of the processes through which workspaces are masculinized and how they shape gendered identities of men in multiple ways. Aspects such as emotional labour and expression of homosocial intimacy, hitherto only associated with the domestic sphere, are also brought to bear upon the realm of masculine identities through McDowell's (2001) research. Shifting the focus to the white working-class context of post-industrial Britain, wherein labour was being casualized and feminized on a large scale, McDowell (2005, 2003) and Nayak (2006) illustrate how achievement of masculinity for this particular class of men has been rendered precarious and elaborate upon the wide range of recuperative responses by white working-class men.

In the context of South Africa and Fiji, Meth (2009) and Presterudstuen (2014), respectively, complicate the centrality of employment to masculinity by documenting the affective responses of men to their lack of employment in the form of feelings of powerlessness and in narratives of moral decay as men negotiate the contradictions of their everyday reality and the expectations from their masculine roles.

Some more notable geographical research on masculinities in the arena of work includes the construction of migrant workers' masculinities in London, with a focus on the worksites as a place of othering of different ethno-national masculinities (Datta, 2009; Datta et al., 2009), the simultaneously hegemonic and subversive embodied performances of manhood in the surfboard-making workshops in Hawai'i, Australia and California (Warren, 2014) and the inscribing of miners' bodies with discursive meanings of heterosexuality, rurality and masculinity (Pini & Mayes, 2014). In their study of men in (the overwhelmingly feminized) care-giving roles, England and Dyck (2014) fill an important gap in the literature of care work and men by illustrating how men challenge the normative gendered expectations through formal and informal care work in the domestic spaces of home, the demands of which they negotiate in profoundly bodily terms.

'Placing' men in domestic and familial spaces

In the last decade, geographers have made an important contribution in disrupting the naturalized coupling of masculinity with work spaces: in placing men within their domestic and familial contexts, geographers have illustrated these spaces as important sites of masculine gender work. Considering the fact that 'the construction of masculinity is spatially manifest in the separation between home and work …' (Smith & Winchester, 1998, p. 328), geographical research on domestic spaces and masculinity has enabled a crucial shift in paradigmatic understandings of 'home' (as a deeply masculine space) and 'masculinity' (as also shaped by and performed via domesticity).

In one of the earliest geographical engagement with masculinities and work/home boundary, Smith and Winchester (1998) concluded that while workspaces continued to be the site of hegemonic masculine identity, men invariably dealt with the stress related to work pressure by negotiating their contribution to labour on the domestic front. However, even while men continued to benefit from the conventional gendered division of labour, Smith and Winchester (1998) claim that 'the very process of negotiation created the possibility of more fluid alternative masculine identities …' (p. 338). Contending that masculinity and domesticity are mutually co-constitutive, Gorman-Murray (2008, 2013) focuses on research in the past decade which has examined the emergent home-making, domestic labour and parenting practices of heterosexual, gay[2] and 'bachelor' men in Euro-American and Australian contexts and how shifting performances of masculinity in the space of home disrupts hegemonic constructions of masculinities. In his theoretical formulations around 'domestic masculinities' and 'masculine domesticities', Gorman-Murray (2008) argues that emergent home-making practices have reconfigured masculine identities and also that men's changing relationship with the home has led to newer insights into the gendered definitions of home.

Some of the more recent work centred on 'critical geographies of home' focus on men's active participation in interior design of their homes (Gorman-Murray, 2014; Walsh, 2011), gendered implications of men's DIY practices as care in New Zealand (Cox, 2013, 2014), men's participation in domestic food work in the UK (Meah, 2014) and on the ways in which ex-servicemen reimagine their masculinities within the context of their home and family (Atherton, 2009) to provide rich illustrations of how material practices of home making are becoming crucial sites of constitution and embodied expression of masculine gendered identities, in the wake of the gradual democratization of the traditional gendered roles associated with the twentieth-century domestic sphere.

In a stark departure from research on domestic masculinities centred largely on white men, May's (2014) research on experiences of homelessness amongst men of colour in Toronto investigates the strategies through which homeless men of colour construct a sense of home and a sense of the masculine self at multiple scales, including on the streets, within gangs of friends and within the larger neighbourhoods. Similarly, Meth (2014) illustrates the contradictory ways in which the discursive and material constructions of 'home' mediate poor urban men's experiences of violence in Durban, South Africa, and provides a much-needed geographical perspective on non-white/non-global North masculine identities.[3]

Apart from the materiality of domestic life, research on domestic masculinities has also started paying attention to how interrelationships which are circumscribed within the socio-spatial boundaries of home/family shape masculinity. In this context, Aitken (2005) stresses the need for research on fathering practices, not as monolithic but as contingent and contested across different spaces. This point is illustrated well in Skelton and Valentine's (2005) case studies of fathers' responses to the coming out of their gay sons, wherein heterosexual men negotiate fatherhood and masculinity in response to homosexuality along a spectrum: ranging from an aggressively homophobic masculine response to a more nurturing father-son relationship. In a similar vein, Tarrant (2013, 2014) examines the ways in which older men alleviate their anxieties about loss of masculine power on account of being confined to home by constructing home as a space of providing activity-based care to their grandchildren and as a site of their practical activities (like fixing things).

The above review hardly exhausts the repertoire of geographical research on this theme; however, it has tried to highlight instances which illustrate how geographical research has enabled the investigation of masculinities as emplaced and embedded within particular spaces, contexts and scales, ranging from the body to the nation, from institutions to home.

Local, regional vs. global masculinities: a question of scale?

The objective of this section is not so much to describe the range of literature on masculinities outside of Anglo-American spaces as much as it is to highlight the ways in which this literature has raised pertinent questions about the politics and the utility of theorizing masculinities in terms of scale and space. This is also related to the spatialized politics of knowledge production in this field, which has tended to establish a subtle hierarchy of research on masculinities: Berg and Longhurst (2003) spell out this hierarchy in their review of geographical research on masculinity, claiming that there is, 'a scaling of knowledge produced in metropolitan Anglo-America as universal (read: "theory"); while work produced in the non-metropolitan "peripheries" is scaled as local (read: "case study")' (pp. 355–356). This section highlights scholarly work on masculinities beyond the metropolitan locations, primarily to examine the implications of spatialized and scalar understandings of masculinity, as well to point towards literature on masculinities outside the Anglo-American contexts.

Referring to the skewed nature of production of hitherto scholarship on masculinities in geography, Jackson and Balaji (2011) point out that the range of research which explores masculinity outside the Anglo-American world has not gained the critical mass necessary to counterbalance the long legacy of research which has, 'concretized a White masculinity as the prototypical masculinity ...' (p. 21). Jackson and Balaji (2011) raise uncomfortable questions about the racist and imperial legacies which have shaped theoretical frames of research on masculinity, contending that the field of masculinity studies is dominated by a 'Eurocentric paradigm of Whiteness and its Others' (p. 21). While conceding that their own edited volume predominantly focuses on the Anglo-American world, Ruspini, Hearn, Pease and Pringle (2011) admit that that the choice of contributions from the Anglo-American world is determined largely by the geographical locations of the editors (generally in metropolitan centres of knowledge production in the global North), their respective academic circuits, the question of language and economic factors (p. 6). The irony of the possibility of the field of critical masculinity studies replicating a hegemonic masculinist pattern in the way knowledge on masculinities is produced at the global level should provide an impetus for this field to engage far more directly with the questions of *where* research on masculinities is produced and *who* produces this research.

Related to, but also in ways disparate from, the above concerns, the other framing context for this section is Connell's (2005, p. 72) conceptualization of a 'world gender order' which connects local gender regimes across the world via historical processes of colonialism, imperialism and, recently, globalization and transnational labour migration. For Connell, hegemonic masculinity within the world gender order implies that it operates at a multi-scalar level, with each level mutually influencing the other (Ford & Lyons, 2012).[4] This emphasis on the idea of a globalized hegemonic masculinity has been critiqued on several counts: Kenway, Kraack and Hickey-Moody (2006) question the very crux of this formulation by posing a very basic question, 'what constitutes the global frontier? Where is it? And if we are unsure where it is, what is the masculinity that it inscribes?' (p. 30). In raising these questions, the authors suggest that what is proposed as the globalized version of hegemonic masculinity still continues to be embedded in metropolitan economic and cultural centres of the Euro-American (white) world.

Kenway et al.'s (2006) edited volume *Masculinity Beyond the Metropolis* seeks to challenge this urban-centric research within the Anglo-American world, making a strong case for research which studies how male-gendered identities are shaped by locality/place and processes of globalization in non-metropolitan places (rural Australia) but also taking care to avoid a simplistic binary opposition between *local* and the *global*, in which the local is invariably acted upon the global. In doing this, Kenway et al. (2006) rely on cultural geographical perspective, propounded by Massey (1994), in which place is constituted out of the interaction of multiple social relationships which operate across spatial scales ranging from the most immediate (the household, the neighbourhood or the workplace) to the more distant (city policies, national political power, global finance), thus imbuing it with an inherent dynamism.

Ouzgane and Morrell's (2005) edited volume *African Masculinities* exemplifies this dynamic notion of region and its relevance for understanding masculinities, by elaborating upon Africa as heterogeneous, yet a geopolitical reality, shaped by conditions of post-coloniality and contemporary processes of globalization. The authors contend that, given this context, research on masculinities in Africa cannot neglect the implications of men in Africa being defined in terms of the imperial and racial 'Other' through the colonial and post-colonial period. Also, the ways in which African feminist scholarship has critiqued the basic assumptions of first-world feminism (of gender as a central organizing structure of society, of the primacy of the individual vis-à-vis community/kinship networks) and a long legacy of research in gender and development have affected the engagement of feminist research with masculinities in the continent, leading to uneven coverage of masculinities in research. In their conscious articulation of Africa as a historical and political space, Ouzgane and Morrell (2005) thus set the stage for examination of distinctly *African* masculinities as being embedded within these historical, political and social imperatives that make up the space; they assert that understanding masculinities as situated within a specific space/scale contributes in important ways to a generalized understanding of masculinity instead of remaining merely a 'variation'.[5]

The edited volume *South Asian Masculinities* (Chopra, Osella and Osella, 2004) provides us with similar framing of masculine identities specific to the region, in this case, within the spatio-temporalities of modernity. The editors assert that modernity within South Asia mediates masculine identities, manifested most clearly in the arena of nationalism and in the practices of consumer capitalism. While agreeing that South Asian masculinities are, 'rooted in local paths of a global modernity ...' (p. 17), the editors contend that academic research on masculinities reveals a gap in insights vis-a-vis relationships between modernity and practices of masculinity in non-Western contexts. In arguing that masculinities are located in peculiar relationships to statuses of caste, class and ethnicity in the South Asian context, the authors foreground the concept of intersectionality in theorizing masculinities. While intersectionality is hardly novel in research on masculinities, this volume alerts us to the fact that theoretical framings have to accommodate different axes contingent upon the specific contexts in which the latter operate, including race, caste, ethnicity, religion, region and sexuality.

Louie (2003), in an edited volume on *Asian Masculinities*, contends that Connell's idea of a world gender order is still premature, given the limited theoretical tools that researchers have to analyze non-Western masculinities in the latter's *own terms*. Louie (2003) illustrates how the majority of earlier research on Asian masculinities merely implied studying Chinese and Japanese men as minorities and as men of colour in white North America. However, he argues, if ethnic minorities in white America have to be researched as 'men of colour', they would invariably be researched using Euro-American notions of gender and sexuality, given the fact that minorities need to always seek to measure up to the cultures to which they are migrating. In order to avoid this fallacy, Louie (2003) proposes an investigation of, 'an archaeology of indigenous East Asian masculinities' (p. 2), which would enable research to arrive at an understanding of masculinities that derives its analytical frames from indigenous repertoires of gendered behaviours and norms, like the *wen-wu* dyad in China and Japan.[6]

Gutmann (2003), while introducing the edited volume *Changing Men and Masculinities in Latin America*, points to a concern that is inversely related to Louie's: of attributing traits of masculinity to an essentialized understanding of a particular region. Gutmann (2003) refers to certain clichéd tropes (like *machismo*, fatherhood as being tied to proving one's virility) through which masculine identity continues to be described academically in Latin America, leading to masculinity being uncritically tied to a regional space in essential terms. He challenges these generalized depictions, arguing that instead of exoticizing masculinities from a certain region, it is crucial to see how gendered identities in this region are enmeshed with global transformations in tandem with region-specific contexts, including the strong feminist movements across Latin America and social movements which have led to an unprecedented presence of women in the public sphere and fundamental changes in gendered equations in the private sphere. At the same time, Gutmann is aware of the dangers of a perspective which might merely put in place instead 'Latin versions of global trends and transformations' (p. 16). The case of masculinities in Latin America thus points towards the delicate balance that theorizing masculinities at regional or local scale has to achieve: of not losing sight of the particularity of gendered identities on the one hand, while on the other hand ensuring that our understanding of these identities are not trapped within a rigidly imagined particularity which does not accommodate the porosity and fluidity of boundaries that characterize contemporary spaces and territories.

Clearly, the above-mentioned scholarship on masculinity in regions outside the Anglo-American context is well aware of how transformations entailed in globalization are central to theorizing discourses and practices of masculinity in specific locations. And yet, each of these sets of scholarship emphasize the political imperative to understand masculinities in their specific locations as shaped by *their* specific idioms and their historical trajectories, in order to make theorizing on masculinities more robust. This scholarship contributes in destabilizing the simplistic binary of 'global' versus 'local' masculinities, by precisely showing how the two are inextricably enmeshed in a diverse range of contexts including representations of men in popular culture/literature (Chopra, Osella & Osella, 2004; Ouzgane & Morrell, 2005), international labour flows (Ford & Lyons, 2012), commodity consumption (Chopra, Osella & Osella, 2004; Jackson & Balaji, 2011), queer masculinities and desire (Gutmann, 2003; Louie & Low, 2003; Ouzgane & Morrell, 2005), sports (Jackson & Balaji, 2011; Louie & Low, 2003) and intersections between ethnicity, race and masculinities (Louie & Low, 2003; Ouzgane & Morrell, 2005). Collectively, this set of literature represents an important attempt to shift the concentration of research on masculinities away from Anglo-American contexts; importantly, it also challenges the use of the Anglo-American context as an implicit yardstick to understand masculinities across the non-Anglo-American life worlds.

The geographical as well as the critical masculinities perspectives, while by no means comprehensive, highlight the centrality of locating masculine-gendered performances and discourse within their particular contexts. Foregrounding the spatiality of masculinities is not just an imperative for arriving at more robust understandings of plural masculinities; it is also a political choice, in that it cautions us to the unequal geographies of production of knowledge on masculinities.

Notes

1 For a similar review of the imminent field, also see Longhurst (2000).
2 See Gorman-Murray (2007a, 2007b).
3 See also Meth (2009).
4 For a detailed trajectory of literature on globalization and masculinities and its theoretical assumptions, see Kenway et al. (2006, pp. 27–31).
5 See also Morrell and Swart (2005) for an elaboration upon post-coloniality within which they establish frames of analysis for studying masculinities in the 'Third World', including Africa.
6 See Ford and Lyons (2012) for a similar critique of Connell's critique of global hegemonic masculinity, via an elaboration upon the gendered identities of men in Southeast Asia.

References

Aitken, S. C. (2005). The awkward spaces of fathering. In B. van Hoven & K. Hörschelmann (Eds.), *Spaces of masculinities* (pp. 206–218). London: Routledge.

Appadurai, A. (1996). *Modernity at large: Cultural dimensions of globalization*. Minneapolis, MN: University of Minnesota Press.

Atherton, S. (2009). Domesticating military masculinities: Home, performance and the negotiation of identity. *Social & Cultural Geography, 10*(8), 821–836.

Berg, L. D., & Longhurst, R. (2003). Placing masculinities and geography. *Gender, Place & Culture, 10*(4), 351–360.

Bondi, L., & Rose, D. (2003). Constructing gender, constructing the urban: A review of Anglo-American feminist urban geography. *Gender, Place and Culture, 10*(3), 229–245.

Bull, J. (2009). Watery masculinities: Fly-fishing and the angling male in the South West of England. *Gender, Place and Culture, 16*(4), 445–465.

Chopra, R., Osella, C., & Osella, F. (Eds.). (2004). *South Asian masculinities: Context of change, sites of continuity*. New Delhi: Kali for Women and Women Unlimited.

Cloke, P. (2005). Masculinity and rurality. In B. van Hoven & K. Hörschelmann (Eds.), *Spaces of masculinities* (pp. 41–57). London: Routledge.

Connell, R. W. (2005). Globalization, imperialism, and masculinities. In M. S. Kimmel, J. Hearn & R. W. Connell (Eds.), *Handbook of studies on men and masculinities* (pp. 71–89). Thousand Oaks, CA: Sage.

Cox, R. (2013). The complications of 'hiring a hubby': Gender relations and the commoditisation of home maintenance in New Zealand. *Social and Cultural Geography, 14*(5), 575–590.

Cox, R. (2014). Working on masculinity at home. In A. Gorman-Murray & P. Hopkins (Eds.), *Masculinities and place* (pp. 227–238). Farnham: Ashgate.

Curtin, A., & Linehan, D. (2002). Where the boys are: Teenagers, masculinity and a sense of place. *Irish Geography, 35*(1), 63–74.

Datta, A. (2009). This is special humour: Visual narratives of Polish masculinities in London's building sites. In K. Burrell (Ed.), *After 2004: Polish migration to the UK in the 'new' European Union* (pp. 189–210). London: Ashgate.

Datta, K., McIlwaine, C., Herbert, J, Evans, Y, May, J., & Wills, J. (2009). Men on the move: Narratives of migration and work among low-paid migrant men in London. *Social & Cultural Geography, 10*(8), 853–873.

Dunk, T., & Bartol, D. (2005). The logic and limitations of male working-class culture in a resource hinterland. In B. van Hoven & K. Hörschelmann (Eds.), *Spaces of masculinities* (pp. 28–40). London: Routledge.

England, K., & Dyck, I. (2014). Masculinities, embodiment and care. In A. Gorman-Murray & P. Hopkins (Eds.), *Masculinities and place* (pp. 285–298). Farnham: Ashgate.

Evans, R. (2005). 'You questioning my manhood, boy?' Using work to play with gender roles in regime of male skilled-labour. In B. van Hoven & K. Hörschelmann (Eds.), *Spaces of masculinities* (pp. 179–190). London: Routledge.

Evers, C. (2009). 'The Point': Surfing, geography and a sensual life of men and masculinity on the Gold Coast, Australia. *Social and Cultural Geography, 10*(8), 893–908.

Ford, M., & Lyons, L. (2012). Introduction: Men and masculinities in Southeast Asia. In M. Ford & L. Lyons (Eds.), *Men and masculinities in Southeast Asia* (pp. 1–19). London: Routledge.

Gorman-Murray, A. (2007a). Contesting domestic ideals: Queering the Australian home. *Australian Geographer, 38*(2), 195–213.

Gorman-Murray, A. (2007b). Reconfiguring domestic values: Meanings of home for gay men and lesbians. *Housing, Theory and Society, 24*(3), 229–246.

Gorman-Murray, A. (2008). Masculinity and the home: A critical review and conceptual framework. *Australian Geographer, 39*(3), 367–379.

Gorman-Murray, A. (2013). Urban homebodies: Embodiment, masculinity, and domesticity in inner Sydney. *Geographical Research, 51*(2), 137–144.

Gorman-Murray, A. (2014). Materiality, masculinity and the home: Men and interior design. In A. Gorman-Murray & P. Hopkins (Eds.), *Masculinities and place* (pp. 209–226). Farnham: Ashgate.

Gorman-Murray, A., & Hopkins, P. (Eds.). (2014). *Masculinities in place*. Farnham: Ashgate.

Gutmann, M. (2003). Introduction: Discarding manly dichotomies in Latin America. In M. Gutmann (Ed.), *Changing men and masculinities in Latin America* (pp. 2–26). Durham, NC: Duke University Press.

Hall, M. C. (2005). Shifting spaces of masculinity: From Carisbrook to the MCG. In B. van Hoven & K. Hörschelmann (Eds.), *Spaces of masculinities* (pp. 143–151). London: Routledge.

Hopkins, P., & Noble, G. (2009). Masculinities in place: Situated identities, relations and intersectionality. *Social & Cultural Geography, 10*(8), 811–819.

Jackson, P. (1991). The cultural politics of masculinity: Towards a social geography. *Transactions of the Institute of British Geographers, 16*(2), 199–213.

Jackson, P. (1994). Black male: Advertising and the cultural politics of masculinity. *Gender, Place and Culture, 1*(1), 49–59.

Jackson, R. L. II, & Balaji, M. (Eds.). (2011). *Global masculinities and manhood*. Urbana-Champaign, IL: University of Illinois Press.

Janssen, J. (2005). Tattoos in prison: Men and their pictures on the edge of society. In B. van Hoven & K. Hörschelmann (Eds.), *Spaces of masculinities* (pp. 166–178). London: Routledge.

Johnston, L. (1998). Reading the sexed bodies and spaces of gyms. In H. Nast & S. Pile (Eds.), *Places through the body* (pp. 244–262). London: Routledge.

Kenway, J., & Hickey-Moody, A. (2009). Spatialized leisure-pleasures, global flows and masculine distinctions. *Social and Cultural Geography, 10*(8), 837–852.

Kenway, J., Kraack, A., & Hickey-Moody, A. (2006). *Masculinities beyond the metropolis*. New York: Palgrave Macmillan.

Knopp, L. (1998). Sexuality and space: Gay male identity politics in the United States, the United Kingdom, and Australia. In R. Fincher & J. M. Jacobs (Eds.), *Cities of difference* (pp. 149–176). New York: Guilford Press.

Lefebvre, H. (1991). *The production of space*. Oxford: Blackwell.

Longhurst, R. (2000). Geography and gender: Masculinities, male identity and men. *Progress in Human Geography, 24*(3), 439–444.

Louie, K. (2003). Chinese, Japanese and global masculine identities. In L. Kam & M. Low (Eds.), *Asian masculinities: The meaning and practice of manhood in China and Japan* (pp. 1–16). London: Routledge Curzon.

Louie, K., & Low, M. (Eds.). (2003). *Asian masculinities: The meaning and practice of manhood in China and Japan*. London: Routledge.

Massey, D. (1994). *Space, place and gender*. Minneapolis, MN: University of Minnesota Press.

May, J. (2014). "My place of residence": Home and homelessness in the greater Toronto area. In A. Gorman-Murray & P. Hopkins (Eds.), *Masculinities and place* (pp. 173–190). Farnham: Ashgate.

McDowell, L. (1997). *Capital culture: Gender at work in the city*. Malden, MA: Blackwell.

McDowell, L. (1999). *Gender, identity and place: Understanding feminist geographies*. Minneapoli, MN: University of Minnesota Press.

McDowell, L. (2001). Men, management and multiple masculinities in organisations. *Geoforum, 32*(2), 181–198.

McDowell, L. (2003). *Redundant masculinities: Employment change and white working-class youth*. Oxford: Blackwell.

McDowell, L. (2005). The men and the boys: Bankers, burger makers and bar men. In B. van Hoven & K. Hörschelmann (Eds.), *Spaces of masculinities* (pp. 19–30). London: Routledge.

Meah, A. (2014). Reconceptualising 'masculinity' through men's contributions to domestic foodwork. In A. Gorman-Murray & P. Hopkins (Eds.), *Masculinities and place* (pp. 191–208). Farnham: Ashgate.

Meth, P. (2009). Marginalised men's emotions: Politics and place. *Geoforum, 40*, 853–863.

Meth, P. (2014). Violence and men in urban South Africa: The significance of 'home'. In A. Gorman-Murray & P. Hopkins (Eds.), *Masculinities and place* (pp. 159–172). Farnham: Ashgate.

Morrell, R., & Swart, S. (2005). Men in the third world. In M. S. Kimmel, J. Hearn & R. W. Connell (Eds.), *Handbook of studies on men and masculinities* (pp. 90–113). Thousand Oaks, CA: Sage.

Nayak, A. (2006). Displaced masculinities: Chavs, youth and class in the post-industrial city. *Sociology, 40* (5), 813–831.

Nelson, J., & Seager, J. (2005). Introduction. In J. Nelson & J. Seager (Eds.). *A companion to feminist geography* (pp. 1–11). Oxford: Blackwell.

O Donoghue, D. (2007). 'James always hangs out here': Making space for place in studying masculinities at school. *Visual Studies, 22*(1), 62–73.

Ouzgane, L., & Morrell, R. (Eds.). (2005). *African masculinities: Men in Africa from the late nineteenth century to the present*. New York: Palgrave Macmillan.

Pini, B., & Mayes, R. (2014). Performing rural masculinities: A case study of diggers and dealers. In A. Gorman-Murray & P. Hopkins (Eds.), *Masculinities and place* (pp. 431–442). Farnham: Ashgate.

Presterudstuen, G. H. (2014). Masculinity in the marketplace: Geographies of post-colonial gender work in modern Fiji. In A. Gorman-Murray & P. Hopkins (Eds.), *Masculinities and place* (pp. 401–414). Farnham: Ashgate.

Ruspini, E., Hearn, J., Pease, B., & Pringle, K. (Eds.). (2011). *Men and masculinities around the world: Transforming men's practices*. New York: Palgrave Macmillan.

Skelton, T., & Valentine, G. (2005). Exploring notions of masculinity and fatherhood: When gay sons 'come out' to heterosexual fathers. In B. van Hoven & K. Hörschelmann (Eds.), *Spaces of masculinities* (pp. 143–151). London: Routledge.

Smith, G., & Winchester, H. H. (1998). Negotiating space: Alternative masculinities at the work/home boundary. *Australian Geographer, 29*(3), 327–339.

Snider, M. (2017). Being a man in the horse capital: Mexican farmworkers' masculinities in Kentucky. *Gender, Place and Culture, 24*(3), 343–361.

Sommers, J. (1998). Men at the margin: Masculinity and space in downtown Vancouver, 1950–1986. *Urban Geography, 19*(4), 287–310.

Tang, W. M. (2017). Migration, marginalization and metropolitaneity: Negotiation of masculinities of Nepali drug users in Hong Kong. *Gender, Place and Culture, 24*(2), 213–224.

Tarrant, A. (2013). Grandfathering as spatio-temporal practice: Conceptualizing performances of ageing masculinities in contemporary familial carescapes. *Social and Cultural Geography, 14*(2), 192–210.

Tarrant, A. (2014). Domestic ageing, masculinities and grandfathering. In A. Gorman-Murray & P. Hopkins (Eds.), *Masculinities and place* (pp. 241–254). Farnham: Ashgate.

van Hoven, B., & Hörschelmann, K. (Eds.). (2005). *Spaces of masculinities*. London: Routledge.

Walsh, K. (2011). Migrant masculinities and domestic space: British home-making practices in Dubai. *Transactions of the Institute of British Geographers, 36*(4), 516–529.

Warren, A. (2014). Crafting masculinities: A cultural economy of surfboard-making. In A. Gorman-Murray & P. Hopkins (Eds.), *Masculinities and place* (pp. 415–430). Farnham: Ashgate.

Ye, J. (2014). Migrant masculinities: Bangladeshi men in Singapore's labour force. *Gender, Place and Culture, 21*(8), 1012–1028.

29

Rural masculinities

Barbara Pini and Robyn Mayes

Beginnings

As with other fields of masculinity studies, those focused on rural spaces grew out of feminist scholarship. Writing in 1995 in the *Journal of Rural Studies*, Brandth (1995) was at the forefront of bringing the newly developing theorizing on men and masculinities to rural studies. This writing emerged out of her previous research exposing the previously unremarked tractor as a potent symbol of masculinity, which served to exclude women from farming (Brandth, 1994). In following up these research findings, Brandth (1995) undertook an analysis of representations of masculinity in farming advertisements over a ten-year period. Her findings revealed the dynamic nature of rural masculinities in that the dominant image of the farmer as a strong manual worker engaged in dirty labor was now sitting alongside, or perhaps was evolving into, a business-like masculinity that aligned with new agricultural technologies. Most critically, Brandth (1995) concluded her study by noting that this new variation may encode a reconstruction of hegemonic masculinity precisely in light of feminist challenges to dominant farming masculinities.

In the decades since Brandth's (1995) research, the scholarship on rural masculinities has grown exponentially; this is evident across a range of disciplinary fields, including anthropology, history, sociology, geography, film studies, literature, education, business, health and criminology. In this chapter we offer a selective overview of this research with an emphasis on the sociological and geographic approaches to rural masculinity. We do so through a focus on four of the key themes in scholarship to date: rural masculinities as relational, contextual, multi-faceted and multi-scalar. In the concluding section of the chapter we highlight the need to maintain the political imperative of rural masculinity research.

Rural masculinities as relational

From Brandth's (1995) pioneering work, feminist scholars further theorized the construction of rural masculinities as occurring, crucially, at the expense and exclusion of "others." They recognized that masculinities are constituted not in isolation but in relationship to other social categories, particularly femininity, and that this is key to understanding asymmetrical power relations. This issue is at the center of ethnographic research by Michael Leyshon on young men's actions in pubs in rural Ireland. In this environment, young men strongly guarded codes and norms govern who may drink, where they may drink and how much they can drink. Most obviously, Leyshon (2005, p. 166) writes, the rural pub is "no place for a girl," but also marginalized in this space are youth who are non-locals, young men who do not want to drink copious amounts and young men who do not want to engage in obscenities.

How rural men's understanding and enactment of masculinities shapes gender equality has been a key theme in a number of studies on rural masculinities from the developing world. Skovdal, Campbell, Nyamukapa and Gregson (2011), for example, have examined how rural Zimbabwean men's denial of HIV/Aids affects their female partner's capacity to access and adhere to antiretroviral therapy (ART). Using interviews and focus groups with health professionals, as well as male and female ART users, the authors argue that men view HIV/Aids as a threat to their masculinity and thus refuse to allow their women partners to seek treatment. They assert that health practitioners need to develop intervention strategies that seek to challenge and change definitions of HIV/Aids and rural masculinity. An equivalent caution to "consider gender scripts while planning or delivering" programs is offered by Izugbara (2008, p. 273) in research on masculinity scripts and abstinence-related beliefs of rural Nigerian male youth, as well as by Cole, Ranjitha, Surendran and Festus (2015) in research on rural Zambian masculinities and women's access to natural resources. Importantly, Dworkin, Hatcher, Colvin and Peacock (2012) demonstrate the efficacy of such an emphasis in reporting on an intervention program with rural South African men designed to address gender equality, definitions of masculinity, violence and HIV/Aids. While the authors acknowledge some limitations of the program and its evaluation, including that they do not have data on how men's masculine performances changed at a community level, they nevertheless highlight its successes in terms of shifting men's views at individual and group levels. Ultimately, their research emphasizes the importance of seeing rural men as potential partners in advancing gender equality and of recognizing the fluidity and malleability of rural masculinities.

In constructing themselves as rural and masculine, men position themselves in relation not only to women but also to urban men. This theme is at the center of research undertaken by Bye (2003, 2009). Drawing on data from rural Norway, Bye (2003, 2009) finds considerable evidence of rural young men adopting conventional discourses of masculinity which emphasize their physicality, expertise with technology, competence in the natural environment and having practical and manual skills. A recurring reference point is the urban young man. For example, while the rural young men view themselves as authentic hunters, patient, focused and skillful, they position the young city men who visit rural areas to hunt as incompetent, uncontrolled and self-indulgent (see also Trell, van Hoven & Huigen, 2012, 2014a, 2014b).

In research on rural masculinities, scholars have advanced ideas of relationality by noting that the identities of "rural" and "masculine" are themselves co-constitutive. The crossover between rurality and masculinity was elucidated early on in the literature in a study of military texts by Woodward (1998, 2000). She explained that it did not matter that most British military operations are undertaken in locations far removed from the countryside featured so prominently in depictions of the military, for these rural images powerfully convey a masculinity of independence, strength and adventure. Similar conclusions about the interconnectedness of masculinity and rurality have been identified in a wide range of studies, including a study of Western wear (Gibson, 2016), an analysis of a documentary program about at-risk youth in outback Australia (Pini & Mills, 2015) and in a project on agricultural training organizations (Bryant, 2006).

Rural masculinities as contextual

A growing body of research has situated rural masculinities in the context of changing economic and political conditions, drawing attention to the affective dimensions of these changes. Representative is Bryant and Garnham's (2014) study of farm suicide in times of economic stress. Their analysis of interviews with 42 male farmers highlights how the withdrawal of financial support and subsidies in times of crisis, a key feature of the political economy of neoliberalism, not only undermines farm viability but also undermines the masculine subjectivities of Australian farmers. In Australia, the identity of the male farmer is deeply intertwined with masculine pride attached to food production "for the common good of the nation" (Bryant & Garnham, 2014, p. 78). According to this moral economy, failure is the antithesis of the "good farmer" and entails substantial shame as well as a diminution of moral worth, which renders suicide a possibility. In this way, Bryant and Garnham (2014) powerfully demonstrate the significance of social, cultural, political and emotional contexts in shaping rural masculine subjectivities. Other work highlights the complexity and importance of transnational contexts. Of note is Kim's (2014) work on international marriage migration to rural South Korea. Her research examines South Korean rural men's negotiations of local masculine ideals upon marriage to Japanese or Filipina migrants. She links the growing prevalence of transnational marriage (and the rural "bachelor crisis") to contemporary economic neoliberalization, industrialization and urbanization at play in South Korea. In particular, Kim (2014) elucidates the way these husbands' assertions of dominance in the home is attuned to and shaped by the global political and economic rankings of their wives' countries of origin.

A focus on rural masculinities as entangled in wider socio-cultural and/or political/economic change has also been of interest to Silberschmidt (2001) and Perry (2005), who, in respective research on rural Uganda and rural Senegal, take up what has been referred to in the broader critical masculinities studies literature as the "crisis in masculinity." Each project is framed by a sensitivity to changes in the gender order or what Perry (2005, p. 209) labels a "post-colonial shift in patriarchal power." In both case-study sites, women have increased their role as producers and consumers while men's unemployment or employment in low-level work has increased. The authors posit that men's masculine identities have been undermined as a result. Further, as Perry (2005, p. 209) concludes, this has seen the emergence of new domestic tensions "around issues of labor, financial control, mobility, space and sexuality."

Importantly, research has shown that rural masculinities are not reshaped by political, economic, social and cultural contexts in a singular way. Indeed, they may not be reshaped at all, as Broughton (2008) demonstrates in a study of rural Mexican men's responses to the pressure to emigrate. Broughton (2008) asserts that rural men adopt different masculine stances in relation to migration, which she labels traditionalist, adventurer and breadwinner. All are imbued with masculinity but construct the experience of migration and the role of father differently. Maycock (2017) furthers this analysis in a case study of a rural Kamaiyan man named Ram, whose migrant trajectory from Nepal to India and back, over varying lengths of time, is marked by differently performed transnational migrant masculinities. Being a mobile laborer has different meanings in Ram's home compared to abroad in India. At home he is viewed as successful, as mobility offers adventure and the chance to be a breadwinner. However, the work Ram undertakes in India is hard, low-paid and gives him limited opportunity for consumption. In this respect Maycock (2017, p. 820) observes that "Ram's performance of masculinity can alternatively be viewed as subaltern while in India, and hegemonic (or in many ways desirable) when he is back in Kampur."

A further emerging body of work has sought to understand generational contexts in the recreation of rural masculinities. In recent work, Brandth (2016, p. 435) explores rural farm masculinities across two generations—that is, across "two socio-historical contexts"—in relation to practices of fatherhood. Her research demonstrates the ways in which rural masculinity is shaped by wider social changes, including women's off-farm work, just as it at the same time exhibits "stable features" (Brandth, 2016, p. 446). Similarly, Riley and Sangster (2017, p. 198), in pursuing the "contextual, fluid and interpersonal ways in which masculinities are achieved and performed," note the multiple intersections of masculinities between generations. At the same time, they demonstrate how aging farmers can avoid the subordinate masculinities often experienced by aging men. By virtue of the continuing valorization of hard work in farming masculinities, older farmers (who remain on the farm) can draw on their past efforts and attendant social capital to maintain their standing as farming men (see also Richardson, 2015; Riley, 2014).

Beyond a focus on farmers and farms, scholars have begun to examine other forms of rural work, and also sexuality, as significant and fluid contexts shaping the experience and performance of masculinity. Eckers' (2013) research examining the organization and worker experience of the tree-planting industry in British Columbia takes up both of these themes. Drawing on queer theory, this work challenges traditional assumptions underpinning scholarship addressing rural masculinity through demonstrating the inherent instability of the categories of heterosexuality and homosexuality. His research demonstrates how the conventional "binary understanding of sexuality as homo- and hetero-directed" limits understandings of the homosocial and homoerotic dimensions of rural masculinities in the context of tree-planting work (Eckers, 2013, p. 891). In both drawing attention to and problematizing heterosexuality as a stable and binary categorical context, Eckers (2013) advances a nuanced understanding of rural masculinity as highly contextual—not only in relation to place but also in regard to interrelationships between the organization of work and sexuality.

Rural masculinities as intersectional

Research on rural masculinities commenced with scholarship on farming men, and to a great extent it is this population that has continued to be the main focus for analysis to date. However, within this body of writing there is growing recognition of the need to understand not just how rurality and masculinity shape what it means to be a farmer but also how this occupational identity is inflected by other social categories. In illustrative work, Little (2003, 2007) and Little and Panelli (2007) take as their focus rural masculine heterosexualities. They show that rural masculine heterosexualities are inextricably linked to the reproduction of farm and community, traditional gender identities and ideas about nature.

Outside of the occupational realm of agriculture, a rich body of writing has emerged that further interrogates how rurality and masculinity intersect with other identities to create inclusions and exclusions. This work encompasses studies of mining-town men and sex workers (Pini, Mayes & Boyer, 2013), Dalit young men in rural India (Jeffrey, Jeffery & Jeffery, 2005) and gay men living in rural France and the United States (Annes & Redlin, 2012). Elsewhere, Francis (2014) and Abelson (2016) have contributed to a still nascent literature on transgender men in rural areas. In the former, Francis (2014, p. 550) details the life of Thatho, a transgender teacher in rural South Africa whose narrative, while "showing glimpses of transphobia and sexism, points to more negotiated, flexible gender relations" in the rural community of which he is part. Abelson (2016) also challenges the conflation of urban space and transgender lives in an intersectional analysis of 45 interviews with transgender men living in the Southeast and Midwest United States. Importantly, Abelson (2016) reports that the men's inclusion in rural communities is articulated through identifications with whiteness, rurality, heterosexuality and class. Interviewees deploy masculinities associated with these categories in order to claim sameness with non-transgender men in rural communities.

A key consideration in the literature on queer rural masculinities has been critiquing the metro-normativity of much queer scholarship, that is, the assumption that a successful queer life requires living in the city and that rural queers must therefore relocate to urban spaces to be fulfilled (see Halberstam, 2005; Jerke, 2010). Illustrative of research that has highlighted the varied ways in which queer lives can be lived is a study by Waitt and Gorman-Murray (2011), who detail the story of Harry, a 16-year-old Anglo-Australian working-class gay man living in a remote mining town in Western Queensland with his father. Harry moves from his small town to Sydney, where he has both positive and negative experiences, and then later to a regional community in North Queensland, where he experiences a sense of home and community. What Harry's story demonstrates is summarized by Lewis (2013, p. 305), who—reporting on findings from a study of gay men in Ottawa, Ontario, Canada—counsels that coming out needs to be understood as a "complex interplay of individuals' needs and desires and the networks and institutions they occupy *in* place (i.e., the social dynamics of places)" and not simply an incompatibility between one's sexuality and a singular, coherent place.

Despite the exciting developments in the literature as evidenced by the above scholarship, there is still much to be done in terms of illuminating intersectional differences in the practices of rural masculinity. There is a dearth of literature, for example, on disability and rural masculinities, as Pini and Conway (2017) highlight in presenting research about how the subject position "rural man" is navigated by men in the context of an acquired disability. Also lacking, as Stordal (2017) notes in a recent study of young boys in rural Norway, are detailed explorations of how childhood mediates rurality and masculinity. Another pressing gap in the literature is that of Indigenous men and rural masculinities.

As scholars continue to build knowledge about how rurality and masculinity intersect with other social identities, the focus needs to move beyond that of only the male body. This is highlighted in Sullivan's (2009) fascinating examination of the lives of queer women living in rural northern Ontario. Sullivan's (2009) work is notable in that it untethers the conflation of masculinity and the male body. She examines how some straight rural women are (mis)read as queer because of their investment in masculinity, while some queer women in the same space are (mis)read as heterosexual. Importantly, she asserts that that masculine femininity is a "highly valued quality within the 'macho' landscape" of the rural area of her study, so it is understandable why some women have considerable investment in such a gender performance (Sullivan, 2009, p. 3).

Rural masculinities as multi-scalar

A further foundational contribution of the early work on rural masculinities was to attend to the complexity of how rural masculinities are articulated across different scales. Feminists mapped the ways in which rural masculinity is constituted at the scale of the body (Brandth, 2016; Bryant, 2006), the workplace (Pini, 2008; Power, 2005), the local community (Little & Jones, 2000; Pini, 2006) and the nation (Hogan & Pursell, 2008). In doing so, they showed that, within as well as across scales, intersecting meanings afforded to rural masculinity involve a complex web of practices, beliefs and discourses pertaining to survival, control, self-reliance, strength, endeavor, independence and connection to the land.

New research continues to highlight the dynamism and malleability of rural masculinities at various intersecting scales. At the level of the body, Gibson (2016) analyzes the historical development and role of "western wear" in signifying a frontier masculinity widely appropriated in urban cultures. His analysis suggests the complex interconnections between bodily performances of frontier masculinity, including in non-rural spaces, and also its continuing power for the nation state. In her more recent work in Norway, Brandth (2016) has sought to understand not only the social but also the spatial reinvention of rural masculinity across generations. In doing so, she has shown how spaces of the farm are, over generations, reconfigured as sites of fathering. For example, whereas an older generation performed fathering in the "physical spaces of work," the new generation has sought to separate farm work and fathering, instead performing fathering more so in the domestic space of the farm house. Attention to the micro layers constituting the family farm advances our understanding of the scalar underpinnings of masculinity, in particular the fluid production of masculinity as linked to specific local sites and systems.

While such performances indicate fluidity in the constitution of rural masculinity and the incorporation of broader social and cultural shifts, rural masculinity is often presented in popular culture as fixed, if not "backward." Stenbacka (2011, p. 242) has explored this through analysis of three Swedish "docusoaps," which she argues construct the rural man as "unequal, incapable and deviant" while promoting the urban man as "equal, capable and constituting the norm." In this way, Stenbacka's work illuminates how urban-centric commercialized representations at the national scale position rural masculinity as "other." Rural masculinity thus continues to be bound up in hierarchical national representations of the rural and the urban. As Gottzén (2014) demonstrates, this positioning of the rural has been given impetus with the rise of right-wing extremist groups across the Western world as such groups (and the masculinities associated with them) are imagined as belonging to rural spaces (see also Jansson, 2005).

The multi-scalar nature of rural masculinities and the connections between the different scalar enactments of rural masculinities are also embedded in studies of queer sexualities outside the urban. Gorman-Murray, Waitt and Gibson (2008, p. 182), despite demonstrating positive change in terms of acceptance and belonging, also report that "everyday homophobia still exists" in non-metropolitan spaces. Such a conclusion is reached following an analysis of letters to an Australian country newspaper about the flying of the gay-identified rainbow flag on the Town Hall during a festival. The authors argue that the circulation of homophobia is embedded in multi-scalar and intersecting notions of rurality and heterosexuality tied to "family" and "nation."

Elsewhere, Kitiarsa (2005) and Rydstrøm (2006) show how embodied and localized performances of rural masculinity are connected to historically embedded nationally specific discourses of masculinity in their respective studies of young rural Thai boxers and punishment of sons by fathers in rural Vietnam. Kitiarsa (2005, p. 61) explains that "*Muai Thai*, or Thai-style boxing," is "a core part of modern Thailand's national identity" and, more particularly, national discourses of masculinity. She reveals the ways in which this discursive hegemony is reproduced at a village level with boxing competitions organized by key male leaders and positioned as integral to village life. At an individual level, rural male boxers privilege traditionally masculinized traits of dignity, pride, wit, skill and competitiveness. In her research, Rydstrøm (2006) reveals that the disciplining practices of fathers in rural Vietnam, which include brutal beatings, are entwined in the country's history of violence, Confucianism and associated notions of honor and morality and the patrilineal ancestor worship. She shows that a personal, embodied rural masculine practice, that of punishment, needs to be understood in terms of how masculinity is imagined and enacted across other contexts.

Conclusion

In rural studies where gender is often not on the agenda, it is exciting to witness the proliferation of scholarship on rural masculinities. The research canvassed here indicates a rich and dynamic scholarly engagement with the relations, intersections, contexts and multiple scales evident in the co-constructions of rurality and masculinity. This work uncovers dynamic localized performances and the ways these are shaped by and inform broader gender asymmetries. At the same time there is cause for caution. In particular, as work has flourished, much of it has also tended to become further and further removed from its feminist beginnings so that concerns with gender inequality, power relations and social change are often muted or overlooked (Pini, Brandth & Little, 2014). It is critical that research on rural masculinities question the broader gender order, rather than simply document performances of rural masculinity as an unproblematic social identity and sets of experience that simply require acknowledgement. Such a focus renders systemic power invisible, defuses the critical power of theory and limits the subject of enquiry. It is thus timely to re-politicize the study of rural masculinities. This is urgent given that rural people and places throughout the world continue to be negatively affected by factors such as globalization, agricultural restructuring, service depletion and out-migration.

References

Abelson, M. J. (2016). "You aren't from around here": Race, masculinity, and rural transgender men. *Gender, Place and Culture, 23*(11), 1535–1546.

Annes, A., & Redlin, M. (2012). The careful balance of gender and sexuality: Rural gay men, the heterosexual matrix, and 'effeminophobia. *Journal of Homosexuality, 59*(20), 256–288.

Brandth, B. (1994). Changing femininity: The social construction of women farmers in Norway. *Sociologia Ruralis, 34*(2/3), 127–149.

Brandth, B. (1995). Rural masculinity in transition: Gender images in tractor advertisements. *Journal of Rural Studies, 11*(2), 123–133.

Brandth, B. (2016). Rural masculinities and fathering practices. *Gender, Place and Culture, 23*(3), 435–450.

Broughton, C. (2008). Migration as engendered practice: Mexican men, masculinity and northward migration. *Gender & Society, 22*(5), 568–589.

Bryant, L. (2006). Marking the occupational body: Young women and men seeking careers in agriculture. *Rural Society, 16*(1), 62–79.

Bryant L., & Garnham B. (2014). The fallen hero: Masculinity, shame and farmer suicide in Australia. *Gender, Place and Culture, 22*(1), 67–82.

Bye, L. M. (2003). Masculinity and rurality at play in stories about hunting. *Norwegian Journal of Geography, 57*(3), 145–153.

Bye, L. M. (2009). "How to be a rural man": Young men's performances and negotiations of rural masculinities. *Journal of Rural Studies, 25*(3), 278–288.

Cole, S. M., Ranjitha, P., Surendran, R., & Festus, Z. (2015). Exploring the intricate relationship between poverty, gender inequality and rural masculinity: A case study from an aquatic agricultural system in Zambia. *Culture, Society and Masculinities*, 7(2), 154–170.

Dworkin, S. L., Hatcher, A. M., Colvin, C., & Peacock, D. (2012). Impact of a gender-transformative HIV and antiviolence program on gender ideologies and masculinities in two rural, South African communities. *Men and Masculinities, 16*(2), 181–202.

Eckers, M. (2013). "Pounding dirt all day": Labour, sexuality and gender in the British Columbia reforestation sector. *Gender, Place and Culture, 20*(7), 876–895.

Francis, D. (2014). "You must be thinking what a lesbian man teacher is doing in a nice place like Dipane Letsie School?" Enacting, negotiating and reproducing dominant understandings of gender in a rural school in the Free State, South Africa. *Gender and Education, 26*(5), 539–552.

Gibson, C. (2016). How clothing design and cultural industries refashioned frontier masculinities: A historical geography of Western wear. *Gender, Place and Culture, 23*(5), 733–752.

Gorman-Murray, A., Waitt, G., & Gibson, C. (2008). A queer country? A case study of the politics of gay/lesbian belonging in an Australian country town. *Australian Geographer, 39*(1), 171–191.
Gottzén, L. (2014). Racist hicks and the promise of world-centred masculinity studies. *NORMA: International Journal for Masculinity Studies, 9*(4), 213–216.
Halberstam, J. (2005). *In a queer time and place: Transgender bodies, subcultural lives.* New York: New York University Press.
Hogan, M. P., & Pursell, T. (2008). The real Alaskan: Nostalgia and rural masculinity in the last frontier. *Men and Masculinities, 11*(1), 63–85.
Izugbara, C. O. (2008). Masculinity scripts and abstinence-related beliefs of rural Nigerian male youth. *Journal of Sex Research, 45*(3), 262–276.
Jansson, D. R. (2005). A geography of racism: Internal orientalism and the construction of American national identity in the film *Mississippi Burning. National Identities,* 7(3), 265–285.
Jeffrey, C., Jeffery, P., & Jeffery, R. (2005). When schooling fails: Young men, education and low-caste politics in rural north India.. *Contributions to Indian Sociology, 39*(1), 1–38.
Jerke, B. W. (2010). Queer ruralism. *Harvard Journal of Law and Gender, 34,* 260–312.
Kim, M. (2014). South Korean rural husbands, compensatory masculinity, and international marriage. *The Journal of Korean Studies, 19*(2), 291–325.
Kitiarsa, P. (2005). "Lives of hunting dogs": Muai Thai and the politics of Thai masculinities. *South East Asia Research, 13*(1), 57–90.
Lewis, N. M. (2013). Beyond binary places: The social and spatial dynamics of coming out in Canada. *ACME: An International E-Journal for Critical Geographies, 12*(2), 305–330.
Leyshon, M. (2005). No place for a girl: Rural youth, pubs and the performance of masculinity. In J. Little & C. Morris (Eds.), *Critical studies in rural gender issues* (pp. 104–122). Aldershot: Ashgate.
Little, J. (2003). Riding the rural love train: Heterosexual and the rural community. *Sociologia Ruralis, 43*(4), 410–417.
Little, J. (2007). Constructing nature in the performance of rural heterosexualities. *Environment and Planning D: Society and Space, 25*(5), 851–866.
Little, J., & Jones, O. (2000). Masculinity, gender, and rural policy. *Rural Sociology, 65*(4), 621–639.
Little, J., & Panelli, R. (2007). "Outback romance?" A reading of nature and heterosexuality in rural Australia. *Sociologia Ruralis, 47*(1), 3–19.
Maycock, M. W. (2017). Hegemonic at home and subaltern abroad: Kamaiya masculinities and changing mobility in Nepal. *Gender, Place and Culture, 24*(6), 812–822.
Perry, D. L. (2005). Wolof women, economic liberalization, and the crisis of masculinity in rural Senegal. *Ethnology, 44*(3), 207–226.
Pini, B. (2006). A critique of "new" rural local governance: The case of gender in a rural Australian setting. *Journal of Rural Studies, 22*(4), 396–408.
Pini, B. (2008). *Rural masculinities and agricultural organizations worldwide.* Aldershot: Ashgate.
Pini, B., & Conway, M. (2017). Masculinity and fathering in the lives of rural men with a disability. *Journal of Rural Studies, 51,* 267–274.
Pini, B., Brandth, B. & Little, R. (Eds.) (2014). *Feminisms and Ruralities.* Lanham, MD: Lexington Books.
Pini, B., Mayes, R., & Boyer, K. (2013). "Scary" heterosexualities in a rural Australian mining town. *Journal of Rural Studies, 32,* 168–176.
Pini, B., & Mills, M. (2015). Constructing the rural in education: The case of *Outback Kids* in Australia. *British Journal of Sociology of Education, 36*(4), 577–594.
Power, N. (2005). The "modern fisherman": Masculinity in crisis or resilient masculinity? *Canadian Women's Studies, 24*(4), 102–108.
Richardson, M. J. (2015). Embodied intergenerationality: Family position, place and masculinity. *Gender, Pace and Culture, 22*(2), 157–171.
Riley, M. (2014). Still being the "good farmer": (Non-)retirement and the preservation of farming identities in older age. *Sociologia Ruralis, 56*(1), 96–115.
Riley, M., & Sangster, H. (2017). Merging masculinities: Exploring intersecting masculine identities on family farms. In B. B. Bock & S. Shortall (Eds.), *Gender and rural globalization: International perspectives on gender and rural development* (pp. 198–210). Wallingford: CAB International.
Rydstrøm, H. (2006). Masculinity and punishment: Men's upbringing of boys in rural Vietnam. *Childhood, 13*(3), 329–348.
Silberschmidt, M. (2001). Disempowerment of men in rural and urban East Africa: Implications for male identity and sexual behaviour. *World Development, 29*(4), 657–671.

Skovdal, M., Campbell, C., Nyamukapa, C., & Gregson, S. (2011). When masculinity interferes with women's treatment of HIV infection: A qualitative study about adherence to antiretroviral therapy in Zimbabwe. *Journal of the International AIDS society, 14*(29), 1–7.

Stenbacka, S. (2011). Othering the rural: About the construction of rural masculinities and the unspoken urban hegemonic ideal in Swedish media. *Journal of Rural Studies, 17*(3), 235–244.

Stordal, G. (2017). "We wouldn't be boys if we weren't clever with our hands": Childhood masculinity in a rural community in Norway. *NORMA: International Journal for Masculinity Studies, 12*(1), 65–79.

Sullivan, R. E. (2009). The (mis)translation of masculine femininity in rural space: (Re)reading 'queer' women in Northern Ontario, Canada. *Thirdspace: A Journal of Feminist Theory and Culture, 8*(2), 1–19.

Trell, E., van Hoven, B., & Huigen, P. (2012). "It's good to live in Järva-Jaani but we can't stay here": Youth and belonging in rural Estonia. *Journal of Rural Studies, 28*(2), 139–148.

Trell, E., van Hoven, B., & Huigen, P. (2014a). "In summer we go and drink at the lake": Young men and the geographies of alcohol and drinking in rural Estonia. *Children's Geographies, 12*(4), 447–463.

Trell, E., van Hoven, B., & Huigen, P. (2014b). Youth negotiation and performance of masculine identities in rural Estonia. *Journal of Rural Studies, 34*, 15–25.

Waitt, G., & Gorman-Murray, A. (2011). "It's about time you came out": Sexualities, mobility and home. *Antipode, 43*(3), 1380–1403.

Woodward, R. (1998). "It's a man's life": Soldiers, masculinity and the countryside. *Gender, Place and Culture, 5*(3), 277–300.

Woodward, R. (2000). Warrior heroes and little green men: Soldiers, military training and the construction of rural masculinities. *Rural Sociology, 65*(4), 640–657.

30

Men in caring occupations and the postfeminist gender regime

Ruth Simpson and Patricia Lewis

Introduction

Evidence of persistent horizontal occupational segregation in the form of gender-based distribution of occupations across sectors in the UK shows that approximately two-thirds of jobs are undertaken mainly by women or mainly by men. A recent report by the European Commission (2014) has highlighted the extent of this gendered occupational segregation by presenting statistics showing that two of the most important sectors for female employment (Wholesale and Retail; Health and Social Work) make up almost 40% of women's total employment but only 7% for men. However, evidence also suggests that men and women are moving into non-traditional roles: one in ten nurses are now men, and men make up 14% of students on training courses (Nursing and Midwifery Council, 2015), raising issues about their experiences and the extent to which this trend may be challenging gender based norms at work.

This chapter explores some of the practices of masculinity in the context of non-traditional, caring occupations (nursing, primary school teaching) in terms of how and to what extent traditional understandings of masculinity are challenged. Work in this field has tended to assume in a singular manner that men recoup masculinity in these occupations by distancing themselves from the feminine and reinforcing through various strategies a masculine identity. However, more recent work has problematised this positioning of 'distance' and has suggested that men often embrace the feminine (Huppatz & Goodwin, 2013; Pullen & Simpson, 2009) and move with ease between practices and understandings that may be identified as 'masculine' and 'feminine' in terms of how they undertake a caring role. In this chapter, we interrogate such arguments and contextualise these trends towards 'hybrid' masculinities (Bridges, 2014; Bridges & Pascoe, 2014) within a postfeminist cultural terrain.

Whilst a contested term, postfeminism is generally seen as a Western-based gender regime and 'cultural discourse' (Gill, 2007; Lewis, 2014) that shapes our attitudes and behaviour towards women's changing position in society (though, as Dosekun (2015) argues, its discourses and practices also 'circulate' influentially into non-Western contexts). Women's greater participation in the world of work and contemporary meanings around 'girl power' have led to a widespread assumption that equality in the workplace has been achieved (Gill, 2007; Gill & Scharff, 2011; Lewis, 2014; McRobbie, 2009), despite evidence of ongoing gender-based disadvantage within this sphere. Postfeminism is accordingly based on the assumed 'success' of feminism and of equal opportunities and the assumption that, with individual effort and agency, women can 'have-it-all' both in work and in the domestic/private domains (Gill, 2007; Gill & Scharff, 2011; Lewis, 2014). Celebrated as an asset through taken-for-granted and essentialist assumptions that they bring newly valued 'feminine' and relational skills into the workplace (Lewis, Benschop & Simpson, 2018), women are exhorted to reach their full potential, regardless of detrimental personal circumstances and/or of structural constraints, to be ambitious and to have self-belief. Against this background, while a body of work has explored the experiences and subjectivities of women within this postfeminist regime (e.g., Gill, 2007; McRobbie, 2009), literature has yet to systematically explore the implications of postfeminism for men. We trace in this chapter some of the potential responses on the part of men to postfeminism in the wider context of work as well as, more specifically, in non-traditional roles, e.g., in terms of male crisis and the mobilisation of traditional masculinity as well as in terms of the incorporation of the feminine into work values and practices. In so doing, we argue for the need to set new understandings of a 'caring' or more 'inclusive' masculinity within this socio-cultural context, highlighting the uneven nature of progress towards equality as well as new tensions relating to how masculinity is practised and performed.

Doing gender and non-traditional occupations

Much of the work on the experiences of men in non-traditional roles has adopted notion of gender as a social practice (Gherardi & Poggio, 2002) or as a situated 'doing' (Kelan, 2010; West & Zimmerman, 1987/2002). This conceives of gender not as the property of the individual or as a simple, unambiguous category but as (re)produced in its performance and, hence, fluid, dynamic and likely to take on multiple forms. Here, masculinity and femininity are actively produced as part of the work of gender in everyday interactions which are accountable in the light of normative and localised conceptions of what it means to be a woman or a man. In other words, the doing or practising of gender is assessed on the basis of 'commonsensical and normative knowledge' of the existence of two genders and the appropriate behaviour for each (Kelan, 2010, p. 180).

This 'doing' also takes place in particular institutional contexts, so that these contexts are implicated in how gender is performed. Looking at the institutional contexts of teaching and nursing in Australia and the UK, Pullen and Simpson (2009) show how men 'do' masculinity in that they are often called upon to be the disciplinarian within schools, while male nurses are expected to do heavy lifting work and to manage angry or abusive patients. Doing gender accordingly involves the (re)creation, negotiation and maintenance of difference in specific social and institutional contexts, providing a 'repertoire of practices' (Martin, 2003, p. 344) concerning what it means to perform a particular gender position – where failure to do gender appropriately will call individuals (their character, motives, predispositions) rather than institutions to account.

As Kelan (2010, p. 178) points out, 'Studies of doing gender in organizations tend to focus on how gender differentiation, hierarchy and asymmetry are maintained' through hegemonic performances of achievement and completeness, rather than on how gender, in different contexts, may be dismantled or challenged. Doing gender may be also be tied up with processes of *undoing* at levels of identity, self and practice, where undoing refers to those social interactions and associated discourses that reduce, dismantle and challenge gender difference (Deutsch, 2007). In the context of men working in non-traditional occupations, this leads to a consideration of how men construct, maintain, resist and subvert difference through their gender performances as well as how dominant discourses of heterosexual masculinity form the basis for the 'doing of difference' at work. Some masculinities may be given priority over others, and they may overlap or contradict one another (Connell, 2000; Kerfoot & Knights, 1998). From this perspective, masculinity is never complete and is the product of performances in specific situations involving the doing as well as the undoing of gender and of difference at work.

Work on men's 'doing' of gender in non-traditional contexts has largely focused on their career trajectories, some of the challenges they face and responses to those challenges. In terms of the former, men have often been found to benefit from moving into a non-traditional career, mainly by being fast-tracked into senior roles through what is known as the 'glass escalator' effect (Simpson, 2009; Williams, 1995). Male nurses, for example, often ascend the hierarchy more quickly than female counterparts or gravitate to career-enhancing specialist areas and away from general nursing care (Simpson, 2004; Williams, 1995), while male primary-school teachers can quickly move out of the classroom into senior management roles (Sargent, 2001; Simpson, 2004).

Despite these advantages, men also face challenges in their non-traditional careers. Many non-traditional roles rely on particular relational capacities that are associated with women rather than with men (Lewis & Simpson, 2007). This can create problems for men whose competence and suitability can be called into question if traditional forms of masculinity are displayed. Sargent (2001, p. 132), for example, refers to how male primary-school teachers are in a 'double bind': their presumed masculine interests in sport and male bonding give them an initial hiring advantage, but these same characteristics can alienate them from female staff. Harding, North and Perkins (2008), in a New Zealand study, highlight the challenges associated with the 'sexualisation of men's touch' in the intimate care of nursing and some of the vulnerabilities men face. Here Lupton (2000) notes a fear of 'feminisation' and stigmatisation on the part of men in these and other non-traditional occupations.

Much of the earlier research on men in these occupations has highlighted how responses to these challenges are oriented around 'doing' masculinity, i.e., by maintaining and creating *distance* from 'feminine' practices and values. Men have been found to reconstruct the job so as to minimise its non-masculine associations (Lupton, 2000; Simpson, 2004, 2009) and engage in compensatory gendered practices to restore a dominant or privileged position. One strategy, as referred to above, is 'careerism', where men aspire to management or supervisory posts (Simpson, 2009; Williams, 1995). They may move into what are seen as more 'masculine' specialisms. In nursing, for example, men often gravitate towards mental health, with historic links to custodialism, or to accident and emergency, seen as more technologically oriented and 'adrenalin charged' than standard nursing care. Other work has highlighted how men differentiate their relational skills from those seemingly possessed by women by presenting their skills as more 'rational' and 'cool-headed' (Pullen & Simpson, 2009). Davies and Eagle (2010), in a South African study, show how young male peer counsellors placed emphasis on their masculine 'credit', prioritising the importance of 'masculine' courage in their accounts of the work over 'feminine' care. The creation of such distance by men and the 'undoing' of femininity can be seen as necessary for the management and reinforcement of masculinity.

Hybridity and masculinity in non-traditional occupations

Other work has suggested, however, that rather than creating distance from the feminine as a way of 'doing' masculinity, men also 'undo' gender by embracing femininity within the role. Thus Pullen and Simpson (2009) refer to how men in Australia and the UK draw on feminine discourses (e.g., around caring; around motherhood), engaging comfortably with the feminine as 'New Men' to promote and celebrate difference from the masculine norm. Roberts (2012, p. 671) refers to how young men working in retail enacted a 'softened' masculinity which incorporated aspects of femininity such as pride and satisfaction from interaction and customer care. As Pullen and Simpson (2009) argue, men's emotional labour can be celebrated as an asset, whilst care performed by women is often devalued as a 'natural' part of femininity. Men can therefore claim special status within the discursive spaces of femininity, undoing masculinity through the uptake and co-option of the feminine.

This understanding of the doing and undoing of gender coincides with recent accounts of 'hybrid' masculinities, seen as part of a 'transformation' in men's behaviours (Bridges, 2014; Bridges & Pascoe, 2014; Demetriou, 2001). These forms of masculinity have been defined as the 'selective incorporation of elements of identity typically associated with various marginalised and subordinated masculinities and – at times – femininities into privileged men's performances and identities' (Bridges & Pascoe, 2014, p. 246). In a similar vein, Demetriou (2001) refers to hybridity as gender projects that incorporate 'bits and pieces' (p. 350) of masculinities, as well as femininities (Bridges, 2014). From this perspective, men are distancing themselves from hegemonic masculinity and are incorporating 'Others' into their identity projects and practices. Thus Anderson (2009) refers to a new 'inclusive' masculinity which incorporates values and performances seen as 'Other' and which is based on a more variable conception of gender, namely, one which is no longer dependent upon constrained and exclusionary understandings of hegemonic masculinity (such as those based on compulsory heterosexuality and homophobia). Elliott (2016) points to a 'caring masculinity' based on the integration of values of care – such as positive emotion, interdependence and relationality – into masculine identities. As Bridges (2014) contends, hybrid masculinities rely in part on a 'softer' and more 'sensitive' style of manhood, and he refers here to how heterosexual men are increasingly borrowing from 'gay aesthetics' (e.g., groomed, emotionally aware) to present themselves in favourable terms. From Anderson's optimistic perspective, this signals an erosion of patriarchy and a challenge to existing systems of gendered power.

While accepting changes have occurred in how masculinity is practised, some authors question the extent of the transformation that has supposedly taken place. For example, Connell and Messerschmidt (2005) argue that hybridity is simply a localised sub-cultural variation of how masculinity is performed. Bridges (2014) similarly refers to how the flexibility of identity associated with hybridity is not universally shared and may pertain mainly to young, white heterosexual men. Others suggest (e.g., Bridges, 2014; Bridges & Pascoe, 2014; Messner, 2007) that hybrid masculinities work in ways that perpetuate rather than diminish gendered power, blurring boundaries whilst underpinning existing power relations. As Bridges and Pascoe (2014) point out, by rejecting hegemony from a position of advantage (e.g., by signalling emotional expressiveness and progressive commitment to feminist ideals), men at the same time subtly align themselves with dominant forms, claiming a space of exceptionality and distinction through their mobilisation of difference from the norm. Accordingly, as Messerschmidt (2010) argues, masculinities can incorporate elements of femininity to obscure gender boundaries whilst reproducing existing systems of authority and power.

Postfeminism and hybrid masculinities

From our earlier discussion, the theoretical position of doing gender positions the enactments of masculinity or femininity within particular institutional contexts which prompt appropriate gendered performances. Doing and undoing are therefore to some extent contextually contingent at this institutional level, in that some work environments may encourage particular gendered displays. However, we suggest that this contingency overlooks the significance of the wider socio-cultural terrain and that this wider contextual level both explains and influences how gender is performed in non-traditional roles. In this regard, we suggest that postfeminism as a cultural discourse and contemporary 'gender regime' (Gill, 2007; Lewis, 2014) is fundamentally implicated in how men mobilise and co-opt femininity. In other words, values and practices of hybridity need to be set within this broader socio-cultural context.

As we have seen, this regime is organised primarily around the belief that feminism as a political movement has been successful and is no longer needed. Against this backdrop of so-called equality, Gill (2007) highlights key features of postfeminism: a focus on individual choice and agency; a resurgence in ideas of natural sexual difference and the marked re-sexualisation of women's bodies; an emphasis on self-surveillance, self-monitoring and discipline; and a shift from objectification to subjectification in how women are represented. Young women in particular are presented as freely choosing, empowered and agentic subjects, no matter how constrained their lives might be and where choice is seen as a substitute for feminism. In other words, the choices women make around work and home (e.g., to retreat to the domestic sphere; to work part-time) or in terms of self-presentation and style (e.g., as sexualised, excessively feminine) are seen as 'feminist' because they have been freely chosen. Despite some feminist gains in the world of work, this is to overlook ongoing inequalities and gender-based disadvantage where, as McRobbie (2009) argues, the denial of feminism as a political movement and the focus on the individual as the driver for change can serve to re-instate a new form of patriarchal power.

The implications of this gendered cultural regime on the experiences and subjectivities of women have been a focus of inquiry in cultural and media studies (e.g., Gill, 2007; Gill & Scharff, 2011; McRobbie, 2009) as well as, more recently, in the context of work (e.g., Lewis, 2014; Lewis et al., 2018) where these subjectivities seemingly allow greater agency in the individualised pursuit of success, whilst at the same time reinforcing traditional gender-based norms. Less documented in the literature has been the effects of postfeminism as a contemporary cultural regime on men and how postfeminist masculinities are discursively constructed. Exceptions include Rumens's (2017) account of how men variously perform postfeminist masculinities and the implications for gendered inequalities within the workplace, where feminism is often 'taken into account'. In a modern postfeminist culture, men must negotiate the demands made upon them by feminism: treating women as equals; sharing childrearing and domestic responsibilities; and caring for their female partners who may be more empowered, autonomous and successful in and outside work. Men's lives have accordingly changed in the wake of some feminist gains and in the context of wider changes in economic and social life including, pertinent to this chapter, moves away from traditionally masculine occupations in manufacturing and construction towards a greater reliance on the service sector, traditionally the domain of women.

How have men responded to these socio-economic and cultural pressures? Here, Lewis et al. (2018) identify two possible outcomes. Firstly, men can be seen to 'lose out' from the gains made by women, where contemporary accounts of women's success (captured in media representations that 'The Future is Female'), often based on their supposedly more advanced relational skills valued within leadership and in the growing service sector, are seen to exclude men. As Gill (2014) suggests, this has led to perceptions of men's vulnerability, anxiety and crisis with men presented as the victim of female success. In response, as she suggests, some men have retreated to a traditional masculinity as a form of 'backlash' (Faludi,

1992) that can be seen in a 'new lad' culture, particularly among younger men, based on a hedonistic celebration of manhood through heavy drinking and often predatory attitudes towards women. A second response is the potential uptake of 'New Man' attitudes and practices, identified above, based on the rejection of sexist attitudes and a traditional male role and which draws on a 're-constitution' of masculinity through the incorporation of 'feminine' skills – skills which have become increasingly valued as a 'cultural resource' in the context of work. From this perspective, a postfeminist gender regime affords men a new mobility and fluidity in terms of how gender can be done (Lewis et al., 2018), with men doing masculinity in ways that conform to understandings of the feminine. These 'New Man' practices and values (i.e., sensitive, caring, non-aggressive) are seen to be beneficial to women and to men, offering the potential for social change.

This suggests that understandings of hybrid masculinities in the context of work need to be located within a particular cultural terrain. This terrain is characterised by postfeminism and perceptions of female success, the importance of which has been overlooked in much of the literature on contemporary masculinity and its changing forms. The tendency, discussed above, for men to take up feminine practices within non-traditional roles may accordingly 'speak to' and reflect this contemporary postfeminist gender regime where, against newly valued 'feminine' skills, men can draw on both masculinity and femininity to gain advantage and where a more 'inclusive' (Anderson, 2009) masculinity may be seen to have emerged.

In support, O'Neill (2015) persuasively argues that optimistic accounts of contemporary masculinities and social change need to be interrogated in the context of postfeminism, where sexual politics are 'erased' through a denial of structural conditions and constraints, reflective of the postfeminist focus on individual agency and the assumption that equality has been achieved. Within a postfeminist context, the familiar dynamics of male oppression and female subordination are 'reworked' and 'patriarchal gender relations are upheld in new and apparently novel forms' (O'Neill, 2015, p. 104). These may include more expansive, tactile, expressive and non-hegemonic masculinities and a willingness for men to 'take up' more feminine practices and roles. However, as O'Neill argues and as referred to above, these accounts fail to challenge and disavow men's interests in unequal gender relations and patriarchal power, discussed further below.

Hybrid masculinities and changing gender relations

Earlier in this chapter we presented some interpretations of men's experiences in non-traditional occupations as separation or distance from the feminine, where men seek to recapture a masculine identity by 'doing' masculinity that is threatened in a 'feminised' role. Men accordingly colonise the feminine in their practices of care by calling up discourses of rationality, cool-headedness and detachment and bringing them into the masculine domain. As Deutsch (2007) suggests, studies of men and women in unconventional occupations tend, accordingly, to draw conclusions in terms of the preservation of the gender order rather than how it is disrupted or challenged.

Other work, however, has highlighted the significance of men's uptake of the feminine as well as the masculine (e.g., Huppatz & Goodwin, 2013; Pullen & Simpson, 2009), as men comfortably engage with behaviours and practices culturally coded feminine and through projects of femininity that seek to partly 'undo' masculinity as they minimise difference from women – a hybridity we have positioned within a postfeminist cultural regime. While some work (e.g., Anderson, 2009) suggests in an optimistic vein that a more 'inclusive' masculinity signals a breakdown of patriarchal power, much of the literature suggests that this 'expansion' into femininity represents a reconfiguration of hierarchical gendered relations and a flexibility of identity that is only afforded to privileged groups. Thus, as we have seen from accounts of men in non-traditional roles, any gender 'undoing' is incomplete in that 'New Man' identities both subvert and build on traditional notions of gender, through which (mainly young, white, heterosexual) men create value by simultaneously resisting and reifying hegemonic notions of masculinity. As Knights (2001) contends, discourses of 'New Manhood' that claim difference from and privilege over other 'masculine' men reject traditional masculinity, but in so doing they acknowledge and reinforce its dominant status. By doing masculinity and by appropriating femininity, masculinity is challenged and yet also sustained; it hangs suspended when men attempt to contest and resist it whilst simultaneously they accommodate and reinforce it. In other words, men claim special status within the discursive spaces of femininity and care because they are men and carry 'traces' of privilege and power. This resonates with Huppatz's (2012) contention concerning the existence of strong pressures towards hegemonic performances of gender as being symbolically legitimated and the most rewarded. Thus, in Bridges's (2014) terms, men capitalise on symbolic gender-based and sexual boundaries whilst obscuring, rather than weakening, gendered privilege and perpetuating inequality in new and less easily identifiable ways.

Set against a contemporary, postfeminist gender regime, this suggests a complicated terrain of uneven progress in terms of gender relations, with some traditional values and practices around gender being challenged, as evidenced in the uptake by men of some newly valued 'feminine' practices and roles, whilst others are further entrenched and/or simultaneously transformed into new manifestations of hierarchical gendered power. As Lewis et al. (2018) note, this suggests a diversity of experience where, in the context of postfeminism, traditional gender-based norms are both repudiated and reinforced and where normative understandings, practices and subjectivities re-emerge and take on new (non-traditional) forms. Resonant with Elliott's (2016) contention that *actual practices* of care work have some potential to change men and gender, Pullen and Simpson (2009), drawing on their empirical research on men in non-traditional occupations, capture the cross-currents of changing hierarchical relations and gendered power where any progress towards equality is likely to be incremental and uneven, showing how some behaviours in the form of daily, lived practices may be seen to be transformative while others may become more deeply embedded:

> … subversion, disruption and challenge can be seen to work in complex ways to partly overturn the dominant order of organizations but also to partly support it – working relationally in the dispersion of gendered relations per se. Men call up discourses of rationality and detachment and so bring emotionality into the masculine domain while at the same time they engage comfortably with 'feminine' practices of care: teachers listen patiently to their children in the classroom and mop up spilt paint; nurses change dressings and attach babies to the breast. In other words, some elements of gender relations may be questioned, others may become further entrenched and still others quietly transformed in day to activities of teaching and nursing care.
>
> *(Pullen & Simpson, 2009, p. 585)*

Conclusion

In this chapter we have located much of the theoretical work on the experiences of men in non-traditional occupations within conceptualisations of the 'doing' and 'undoing' of gender – highlighting how recent work has pointed to a new 'hybridity' as men draw on both masculinity and femininity, doing both simultaneously. We have positioned this gender mobility within the socio-cultural context of postfeminism as a gender regime based, in part, on assumptions of feminist gains and that equality has been achieved. De-industrialisation and the feminisation of local labour markets, exemplified in the erosion of 'masculine' jobs and a greater reliance on services for employment, have provided opportunities for men to move into non-traditional occupations, signifying, from a postfeminist perspective, a new gendered flexibility for men and a possible distancing from traditional, hegemonic masculinity. While this hybridity and a 'softer' more inclusive masculinity may herald a new cultural era of gender relations, we have seen how patriarchy may simply reassemble and take on new, less identifiable forms as men co-opt the feminine – a cultural resource that is increasingly valued inside and outside of work. As some of the research on men in non-traditional occupations has shown, this highlights, potentially, the uneven nature of change and how – in the context of small, localised daily practices (e.g., of service and of care) – gender relations may be transformed whilst other manifestations become more entrenched. Taken together, however, against a gender-based occupational segregation that remains stubbornly intact and whilst evidence suggesting a trend towards its erosion is a welcome development as men and women move into non-traditional roles, this indicates a complicated terrain where gender advantage and disadvantage are reconstructed in the context of wider economic and socio-cultural change.

References

Anderson, E. (2009). *Inclusive masculinities: The changing nature of masculinities*. London: Routledge.

Bridges, T. (2014). A very 'gay' straight? Hybrid masculinities, sexual aesthetics and the changing relationship between masculinity and homophobia. *Gender and Society, 28*(1), 58–82.

Bridges, T., & Pascoe, C. (2014). Hybrid masculinities: New directions in the sociology of men and masculinities. *Sociology Compass, 8*(3), 246–258.

Connell, R. (2000). *The men and the boys*. Cambridge: Polity Press.

Connell, R., & Messerschmidt, W. (2005). Hegemonic masculinity: Rethinking the concept. *Gender & Society, 19*(6), 829–859.

Davies, N., & Eagle, G. (2010). Boys as peer counsellors: What's under the overcoat. *Journal of Psychology in South Africa, 20*(4), 569–580.

Demetriou, D. (2001). Connell's concept of hegemonic masculinity: A critique. *Theory and Society, 30*(3), 337–361.

Deutsch, F. (2007). Undoing gender. *Gender and Society, 21*(1), 106–127.

Dosekun, S. (2015). For western girls only? Postfeminism as transnational culture. *Feminist Media Studies, 15*(6), 960–975.

Elliott, K. (2016). Caring masculinities: Theorizing an emerging concept. *Men and Masculinities, 19*(3), 240–259.

European Commission. (2014). The current situation of gender equality in the United Kingdom – Country Profile. Retrieved from http://ec.europa.eu/justice/gender-equality/files/epo_campaign/130911_country-profile_united_kingdom.pdf.

Faludi, S. (1992). *Backlash: The undeclared war against women*. New York: Broadway Books.

Gherardi, S., & Poggio, B. (2002). Creating and recreating gender order in organizations. *Journal of World Business, 36*(3), 245–259.

Gill, R. (2007). Postfeminist media culture: Elements of a sensibility. *European Journal of Cultural Studies, 10*(2), 146–166.

Gill, R. (2014). Powerful women, vulnerable men and postfeminist masculinity in men's popular fiction. *Gender & Language, 8*(2), 185–204.

Gill, R., & Scharff, C. (2011). *New femininities: Postfeminism, neoliberalism and subjectivity*. Basingstoke: Palgrave Macmillan.

Harding, T., North, N., & Perkins, P. (2008). Sexualising men's touch: Male nurses and the use of intimate touch in clinical practice. *Research and Theory for Nursing Practice: An International Journal, 22*(2), 88–102.

Huppatz, K. (2012). *Gender capital at work: Intersections of femininity, masculinity, class and occupation.* Houndsmills: Palgrave Macmillan.

Huppatz, K., & Goodwin, S. (2013). Masculinised jobs, feminised jobs and men's 'gender capital' experiences: Understanding occupational segregation in Australia. *Journal of Sociology, 49*(2–3), 291–308.

Kelan, E. K. (2010). Gender logic and (un)doing gender at work. *Gender, Work & Organization, 17*(2), 174–194.

Kerfoot, D., & Knights, D. (1998). Managing masculinity in contemporary organizational life: A man-(agerial) project. *Organization, 5*(1), 7–26.

Knights, D. (2001). *The 'new economy' and the 'new man': Virtual transitions or transitional virtualities.* Keynote address to Asia-Pacific Researchers in Organization Studies conference, Baptist University, Hong Kong, December.

Lewis, P. (2014). Postfeminism, femininities and organization studies: Exploring a new agenda. *Organization Studies, 35*(12), 1845–1866.

Lewis, P., Benschop, Y., & Simpson, R. (2018). *Postfeminism and organization.* London: Routledge.

Lewis, P., & Simpson, R. (Eds.). (2007). *Gendering emotions in organizations.* Basingstoke: Palgrave Macmillan.

Lupton, B. (2000). Maintaining masculinity: Men who do women's work. *British Journal of Management, 11*, S33–48.

Martin, P. Y. (2003). 'Said and done' versus 'saying and doing': Gendering practices, practicing gender at work. *Gender and Society, 17*(3), 42–366.

McRobbie, A. (2009). *The aftermath of feminism.* London: Sage.

Messerschmidt, J. (2010). *Hegemonic masculinities and camouflaged politics.* Boulder, CO: Paradigm.

Messner, M. (2007). The masculinity of the governator: Muscle and compassion in American politics. *Gender and Society, 21*(4), 461–480.

Nursing and Midwifery Council. (2015). *Equality and diversity annual report: 1 April 2013–31 March 2014.* Retrieved from www.nmc.org.uk/about-us/reports-and-accounts/equality-and-diversity-reports/.

O'Neill, R. (2015). Whither critical masculinity studies? Notes on inclusive masculinity theory, postfeminism and sexual politics. *Men and Masculinities, 18*(1), 100–120.

Pullen, A., & Simpson, R. (2009). Managing difference in feminized work: Men, otherness and social practice. *Human Relations, 62*(4), 561–587.

Roberts, S. (2012). Boys will be boys ... won't they? Change and continuities in contemporary young working-class masculinities. *Sociology, 47*(4), 671–686.

Rumens, N. (2017). Postfeminism, men, masculinities and work: A research agenda for gender and organization studies scholars. *Gender, Work and Organization, 24*(3), 245–259.

Sargent, P. (2001). *Real men or real teachers? Contradictions in the lives of men elementary school teachers.* Harriman, TN: Men's Studies Press.

Simpson, R. (2004). Masculinity at work: The experiences of men in female dominated occupations. *Work, Employment and Society, 18*(2), 349–368.

Simpson, R. (2009). *Men in caring occupations: Doing gender differently.* Basingstoke: Palgrave Macmillan.

West, C., & Zimmerman, D. (1987/2002). Doing gender. In S. Fenstermaker & C. West (Eds.), *Doing gender, doing difference* (pp. 3–23). London: Routledge.

Williams, C. (1995). *Still in a man's world: Men who do women's work.* Berkeley, CA: University of California Press.

31
Exploring fatherhood in critical gender research

Helena Wahlström Henriksson

> From the 1990s on, fatherhood as an institution, practice, and responsibility has generated unprecedented consideration in cultural, political, economic, legal, and medical arenas.
>
> (Podnieks, 2016, p. 2)

> Debates about fathers and fatherhood need to be more explicitly gendered and more explicitly about power.
>
> (Hearn, 2002, p. 245)

Introduction

How does one begin to speak about fathers, fatherhood, and fathering? Fathers are ubiquitous in 'actual' terms, since most men procreate during their lifetime. But they are also ubiquitous in cultural representations. Father figures, from 'God the father' in major world religions to the 'founding fathers' of nations, to paternalistic saviors of women and children in popular movies create webs of signification that impact upon our understanding of fathers, but even more on our understanding of the ideational centrality of fatherhood. If 'the father' is an upheld figure across many cultures in the world, this becomes especially interesting when juxtaposed with the complex, diverse, and not necessarily central ways that fathers figure in the actual everyday lives of children (and mothers). 'Fatherhood is, on the one hand, privileged in all patriarchal societies [...] on the other hand, fatherhood is also secondary to motherhood when it comes to actual parental care, nurture, and responsibility' (Wahlström, 2010, pp. 9–10). This paradox is one of the driving forces behind explorations of fathers in critical gender research.

This chapter offers an introduction to critical fatherhood studies. This is a vast field of research – or perhaps rather several fields – that has developed parallel with masculinity studies as such, and thus fatherhood studies emerge in various critical spaces, resulting in the current multifariousness of the scholarship. For this reason, the chapter does not comprise a comprehensive state-of-the-art but, rather, presents a selective presentation of exciting, sometimes contradictory focal points in this field as it stands in the present. As a literary and cultural studies scholar, I have been researching representations of fathers for several decades, at first in the context of the United States and later in that of Sweden. Here I will mainly draw upon English-language sources from these contexts, but to a lesser degree also upon work from other geopolitical locations. The discussion focuses on three strands of scholarship: social studies on men and masculinities; feminist cultural studies; and critical kinship studies. I link these, respectively, to three issues that are especially salient in contemporary research: the notion of father presence; the symbolic meanings of the father figure; and questions regarding the parental legitimacy of fathers. Finally, I raise some questions for the future of fatherhood studies.

Fathers, presence, and provision: social studies on men and masculinities

Fatherhood is a very prevalent experience among men. Statistically, 75% of men reproduce in their lifetime (one-third of these men are 'overrepresented' as fathers, that is, fewer men than women reproduce). It follows that critical studies of men and masculinities takes a keen interest in fatherhood. The field has been successful in raising the issue of fatherhood as gendered experience but has also been critiqued for losing sight of issues of power and for retaining homosocial perspectives on fathers, both tendencies that speak against the (pro)feminist stance of critical studies of men and masculinities (CSMM). The second epigraph to this chapter is a call for further attention to how fatherhood is 'gendered and [...] about power' (Hearn, 2002, p. 245), which can be read as a reaction to such tendencies.

Given the predominant social studies orientation of the field, fathers and fatherhood have been analyzed in terms of problems to be solved; problems such as father absence or fathering under difficult circumstances. Social fatherhood studies has done much to foreground the centrality of fatherhood in men's lives (Coltrane, 1996; Morgan, 2004) and to explore the diversity of fathers and fathering. Although often defined as central, it has also repeatedly been observed that fatherhood is not to masculinity as motherhood is to femininity (Dermott, 2008; Rotundo, 1993; Segal, 1990; cf. Morrel, 2006).

Perhaps in part to foreground good examples and counter problem discourses, social studies on fathers have been interested in exploring the meanings of 'good fatherhood'. In many locations, (good) fatherhood is increasingly understood not just in terms of provision but also in terms of 'stepping into' domesticity; as spending time with one's children, and as offering care and nurture (Forsberg, 2007; Johansson & Andreasson, 2017; United Nations, 2011). In the words of legal scholar Nancy Dowd, 'the redefinition of fatherhood must center around the nurture of children' (2000, p. 157; cf. Chodorow, 1978). The 'progress narrative' – the notion that fatherhood is changing for the better in late modernity – has been crucial in studies on fatherhood and masculinities, which are often invested in social change towards gender equality.

Understanding 'new' fatherhood in terms of presence, care, and involvement and foregrounding the potential for change away from 'old' fatherhood (and masculinities) that at times are perceived as toxic has also been central to much policy work, legislation, and changes in parenting practices in the past few decades. In some national settings, state regulation, including parental leave policies (notably in the Nordic countries) and regulation of working hours (for example, in the EU), has led to fathers spending more time with young children. In Sweden the notion of the 'gender-equal' or 'new' father has been the focus of much research (Bekkengen, 2002; Bergman & Hobson, 2002; Forsberg, 2007; Johansson & Andreasson, 2017; Klinth, 2002). 'New fatherhood' has also been promoted in the US and Australia (Lupton & Barclay, 1997; Wahlström, 2010).

However, there has also been critique against this understanding of contemporary fatherhood as marked by progress. While fatherhood may change over generations, historians have shown that, due to poor historical memory, 'old' fathers sometimes figure as monoliths in the research, in ways that have little to do with how fatherhood was 'done' in previous eras (Broughton & Rogers, 2007; Griswold, 1993; Johansen, 2001; King, 2015; LaRossa, 1997; Tosh, 1999). Against the progress narrative also stands research on the violence of fathers (Eriksson, 2002; Hearn, 2002; Pringle, 2016).

Furthermore, there are great discrepancies between ideals and practices of fatherhood, and questions have been raised regarding the actual impact of the 'new father' ideal on how fatherhood is lived or understood (Wahlström Henriksson, 2016a; Wall & Arnold, 2007). Studies consistently confirm that men spend substantially less time with their children compared to women. Male parents in the US spend on average 50% of the time female parents spend with their (joint) children. Where paternal leave is an option, fathers tend to use a fraction of the parental leave time used by mothers (Björk, 2017; Klinth, 2002). After divorce, fewer than 10% of children reside full time with their fathers (Sweden and UK); and single-parent families are predominantly single-mother families. Such figures point to discrepancies between, on the one hand, 'new fatherhood' discourses and, on the other hand, the actual presence of fathers in their children's lives. Judging by the literature, there is, on the whole, little symmetry between mothering and fathering. Father presence, furthermore, may be linked to various dimensions of power, such as youth (Siedler, 2006) or race (Coles, 2009; Connor & White, 2006; hooks, 2003), fathers' single parenting (Coles, 2015), or non-residency (Poole, Speight, O'Brien, Connolly & Aldrich, 2013; cf. Arendell, 1995; Marsiglio & Pleck, 2005).

It has also been observed that men may indeed take an interest in their children without being interested in gender equality, so father presence or involved fatherhood does not necessarily lead to equality between men and women (Bekkengen, 2002; Featherstone, 2009). Nor is there only one way to interpret state intervention to regulate 'father presence' in children's lives after divorce or separation, for it can be understood either as a progressive move towards father involvement or as a rather conservative re-inscription of men's power over women and children (Bergman & Hobson, 2002). Hence, meanings of fathers' involvement or presence are not unambiguous.

What also serves to temper the progress narrative about fathers, or the impact of the new father ideal as such, is the international research that confirms the provider function as a relentlessly central component of fatherhood throughout the world (Schwalb, Schwalb & Lamb, 2013). This centrality of the provider function has a variety of far-reaching effects on how fatherhood is lived. As Hearn notes, in late-capitalist societies such as the UK, the links between fatherhood, masculinity, and the provider role results in a 'strange alliance between employers' pressure on extracting full value and male employees' apparent preference for the (male) world of work to that of family' (Hearn, 2002, p. 269). However, for men who stand outside the world of salaried work or live in poverty, this father function may never be within reach, and this may lead to (a sense of) disqualification as a father and other negative effects for men as well as families. For others, living up to the provider function entails migrating to work and leaving families in other regions or countries, which in turn makes domestic presence in the everyday lives of their families impossible and in fact encodes 'father absence' as responsible fathering (Townsend, 2013).

The question of what the provider function means, then, varies across cultures. In welfare-state societies such as Sweden, with explicit goals of gender equality, policy has promoted a model where both men and women provide both 'cash and care' to sustain children materially and emotionally. In societies such as Australia, this 'dual-earner, dual-carer' model is less promoted (Smyth, Baxter, Fletcher & Moloney, 2013), and in societies lacking a welfare state, the model is less applicable. In South Africa, men's provision of cash and care for children may be divided between fathers who are migrant workers and 'other-fathers', that is, socially defined fathers who provide care and presence in the community (Morrel, 2006; Townsend, 2013). This emphasizes the impact of class, race, and local histories as well as the impact of the state and the market on practices of fathering (Hearn, 2002; Lewis, 2013).

The links between fathers and presence, between fathers and provision, are regulated by, for example, family law (Collier, 1995) and social policy (Curran & Abrams, 2000; Featherstone, 2009; Lewis, 2013; Morgan, 2002). But meanings of fathers, fatherhood, and fathering are also affected by mediated representations in literature, media, and the arts.

Father figures and symbolic power: feminist cultural studies

In terms of symbolic representations, fathers are central and upheld figures. This is logical in a world marked by male domination, in which narratives of origin, development, or achievement often circle around homosocial (family) relations. From 'fathers of the nation' to the father-son plots that proliferate throughout literary and cinematic history (Jeffords, 1988; Wahlström, 2010; cf. Devlin, 2005), cultural representations of fathers are privileged sites of meaning. Not least, they establish an ideational – and ideological – centrality of fatherhood that, by repetition, does 'pedagogical work' on us as humans (hooks, 2008).

In feminist research, fatherhood has typically been understood as linking paternity to patriarchy, and thus suspect and potentially harmful. Therefore, it has been central for feminist scholars to investigate the links between fathers or fatherhood and power and their effects on women and children. Authoritative and harmful father figures, as well as the violence of fathers, have been foregrounded (Bueno, Caesar & Hummel, 2000; hooks, 2003).

Indeed, much recent research establishes the connection between patriarchy, authoritarianism, and the figure of the father, not least in contexts of nationalism or nationalist struggle. In Zimbabwean literature, authoritarian fatherhood has been shown to be linked to masculinist nationalism after independence (Muponde, 2007; Musiyiwa & Chirere, 2007; Ndlovu-Gatsheni, 2007). This research is clear about how nationalism in the present hinders the reformulation of masculinities towards nurture and how the emphasis on symbolic 'fathers of the nation' rather than on participant male parenthood poses a serious threat to the life chances of women and girls – but also of men and boys (Richter & Morrell, 2006; Muchemwa & Muponde, 2007).

This reminds us that the family, and familial relations, often function as metaphors for the nation (Collins, 1998). In research on fatherhood and masculinities, links between fatherhood and the nation have been much discussed and problematized (Armengol, 2008; Figueroa, Jiménez & Tena, 2006; Gavanas, 2004; Leverenz, 2003; Muchemwa & Muponde, 2007; Morrel, 2006; Prinsloo, 2006; Wahlström, 2010). At the time of writing this chapter, in northern as well as southern locations, there is a resurgent desire for father figures on macro levels, as illustrated by the ways that 'strong men' speak to the masculinism and paternalism of national(ist) imaginaries (Smith, 2017; Yuval-Davis, 1997). Hence it continues to be a crucial task for scholarship to unpack these metaphors and their effects.

Popular film is a mainstream cultural expression that has consistently cast fathers as heroes in ways that uphold the ideal of the male savior. In fact, Hollywood has been demonstrated to take an ever greater interest in fathers since the late twentieth century (Bruzzi, 2005).

The focus on heroic fathers, or 'paternal protectionism' – personified by actors like Bruce Willis in the later *Die Hard* movies and Tom Cruise in *The War of the Worlds* – has been analyzed as part of the backlash against feminism commonly termed 'post-feminism' (Hamad, 2011, 2014). It has also been seen as a development strengthened by the close connections between US politics and Hollywood in the aftermath of the terrorist attacks in 2001 (Faludi, 2007). But even in films that focus on fatherhood and vulnerability linked to class, sexuality, or race – such as *The Full Monty* and *Priscilla, Queen of the Desert* (Tincknell & Chambers, 2002) or *The Pursuit of Happyness* (Hamad, 2014) – the centrality of fathers in cultural representation typically comes at the cost of erasing mothers/women. Because of this, some feminist scholars express skepticism regarding the progressive potentialities of the contemporary rise of interest in fatherhood (Bueno et al., 2000; Featherstone, 2009; Modleski, 1991; Podnieks, 2016; Wahlström, 2010; Åström, 2017; cf. Yeager & Kowaleski-Wallace, 1989).

Research shows that in 'gender-equal' Sweden, fathers are more likely to be praised for being active, 'involved' parents than are women (Björk, 2017). In Hollywood film, it has been noted, the 'good father is idealized in a way that the good mother never has been' (Bruzzi, 2005, p. xv). Such observations, although taken from disparate geopolitical contexts, suggest that while values and attitudes regarding men as parents are upheld, internalized, and reproduced in relation to motherhood, this happens in social reality as well as in mediated representations. Cultural representations are part of the social fabric within which understandings of fatherhood take shape. From a cultural studies perspective, the kinds of representations discussed in this section constitute a layer of meaning with/in and against which lived experience becomes meaningful or comprehensible. In the case of fatherhood, then, we live our realities also in relation to these symbolic meanings.

Language itself can provide insights into how parenthood is 'cultured' in ways that are predicated on gendered difference. In English, lexical differences between the verbs 'to father' and 'to mother' point to the non-symmetry between these two terms. To mother somebody is to birth, to care and nurture; to father somebody may mean to 'spawn' somebody. That is, fathering is quickly done and biological/genetic; mothering is a long-term experience, social in orientation (cf. Doucet, 2006; Laqueur, 1992; Ruddick, 1992). This linguistic non-symmetry illustrates that language as such harbors gendered differences concerning men and women as parents; a difference also illustrated by reference to mothers as primary and fathers as secondary parents in some contexts. However, it also illustrates a basic conceptual question in fatherhood studies: is 'spawning' children enough to claim 'fatherhood'? Or, to rephrase, how is legitimacy as a 'father' achieved?

Fathers, legitimacy, and access: critical kinship studies

The equation of procreation, or 'paternity', with fatherhood has long been questioned in the social research on men and masculinities, where scholars have distanced themselves from genetic/biological definitions, arguing that 'siring' is not the same as 'fathering' and suggesting instead that fathers be defined by their 'doing' of responsibility and care (Morgan, 2002). Fathers who are genetically unrelated to their children – heterosexual and homosexual fathers who achieve parenthood via ARTs, donor procedures, and/or surrogacy as well as adoptive fathers and stepfathers – also question procreation as the basis for recognition as fathers. Procreation as such is nevertheless central for understandings of fatherhood and fathering throughout the world. Spawning children is understood both as 'fathering' and as central to masculinity in many locations (Schwalb et al., 2013); research on men and reproductive health demonstrates that fertility is strongly associated with virility (Bodin, 2018). Scholarship on how the perceived necessity of producing genetic offspring plays out in particular settings shows that effects range from blaming men's infertility on women (Löwy, 2006) to shaming infertile men (Throsby & Gill, 2004). Thus, relationships among the procreative potentialities of male bodies, masculinity, and understandings of legitimate fatherhood and fathering are far from simple.

Critical kinship studies, often building on both anthropological and queer/feminist theorizing of kinship, explicitly questions and problematizes the ways that 'substance' – blood or genes – and law are taken to define family/kinship (Cutas & Chan, 2012; Kroløkke, Myong, Adrian & Tjornhoj-Thomsen, 2016). Reproduction as such is scrutinized, as are the ways that norms and power play out in reproductive practices. Much research has focused on ARTs, not least donor procedures and donor-conceived children. In recent years, single and/or lesbian motherhood via sperm donation and insemination has figured as a contested practice where the place of men and/as fathers is put in question; in donor discourses fathers can often be said to be reduced to sperm (Andreassen, 2019; Moore, 2007; cf. Faria, 2016; Mohr, 2015). This raises the question whether women reproducing without heterosex also entails 'getting rid of' fathers. Research results are ambiguous. While single and/or lesbian mothers via donor procedure do parent without fathers, fatherhood is not seldom assigned to donors by these women, who think of them as 'donor dads', and by donor-conceived children, who at times desire to establish contact with their 'real dad' or with 'donor siblings', that is, others conceived via sperm from the same donor (Andreassen, 2019). Furthermore, as some court cases in the UK have demonstrated, the law is at times ready to recognize donors as fathers, with, for example, legal visitation rights (*The Guardian*, 2015). ARTs do sever sexuality from procreation – and donors from parenting – in ways that certainly put pressure on social as well as juridical understandings of fatherhood. This disjuncture of genetic from social parenthood also puts the cultural ideal of involved fatherhood in new light, as amply illustrated in the Hollywood film *The Kids Are Alright*.

However, critical kinship studies also addresses fatherhood as lived experience; this is explored in the context of gay and single fathers, queer or trans* fathers (Ziv in Saar, 2013; Volcano 2016). The effects of family law on (the possibilities for) fathers' legitimacy are a central concern (Bremner, 2017). Gay men's access to parenthood has shifted a great deal over the past few decades in locations such as the US, the UK, and Scandinavia (Lewin, 2009; Mallon, 2004; Malmquist, forthcoming). While adoption is possible in some locations, surrogacy is increasingly the reproductive technology used to achieve parenthood for gay couples as well as single men (Carone, Biaocco & Lingiardi, 2017; Malmquist, forthcoming). Notably, while the place of fathers is 'diminished' in the context of single mothers via donor insemination, so is the place of genetic and gestational mothers in the context of men who parent via surrogacy (Nebeling Petersen, 2015), which brings us back to questions around parental power and the erasure of the 'other parent' discussed in the previous section.

Although critical kinship studies are positioned against the typically heterosexual focus of critical studies of men and masculinities, these strands of research nevertheless share an interest in issues like access to, and legitimacy for, fatherhood and fathering. While critical kinship studies explores the links between male bodies and fatherhood in diverse contexts, from sperm donor-conceived children to gay and queer parenthood, crucially, they also emphasize the real sexed differences concerning possibilities for reproduction and/or parenthood. Hence, in the instance of critical kinship studies, fatherhood studies today can be seen to loop back in interesting ways to the specificities of sexed and gendered bodies, issues of procreation, and involvement. Needless to say, whereas the rights of trans*fathers and queer fathers are voiced and promoted in some geographical locations, in other locations heterosexual men's right to reproduce stands unquestioned, and LGBTQ parenthood is taboo.

Conclusion

As I hope to have demonstrated, fatherhood is diverse and complex. Fatherhood is defined and regulated in multiple arenas including, *inter alia*, law, medicine, social policy, economy, politics, mediated representations, and language itself. Furthermore, fatherhood is contextual, embedded in temporal, spatial, and cultural specificities. Fatherhood is 'done' in various familial situations, and inflected by dimensions of power such as class, race, nationality, sexuality, age, and ability. Like masculinity as such, fatherhood is relational (Connell, 1995; Wahlström Henriksson, 2016b). Fathers, fatherhood, and fathering matter – in cultural representations in media, film, literature, or art as well as in the lived experiences of humans – in ways that affect the lives of particular families and individuals but also the understandings of 'peoples' and 'nations'.

Fatherhood research is also complex. This brief presentation of research on fathers in (feminist) masculinity studies and critical kinship studies illustrates that while much is at stake when fatherhood is placed front and center, critical perspectives and emphases vary a great deal. The extent to which these strands of research can cross-germinate in the future remains to be seen.

Many areas and issues are in need of further analyses. Questions about age and differences in fathering over the life course certainly warrant further study, as do the ways that social and genetic/biological meanings of fatherhood intertwine or collide. The same is true of investigations of transnational fatherhood, whether linked to the (relatively major) phenomenon of migration or the (relatively minor) phenomenon of fatherhood via commercial surrogacy. Certainly, as scholars on fatherhood, we need to engage in continuous, open-minded, interdisciplinary, and international dialogue. Researchers need to be clear about conceptual assumptions and as clear-eyed as possible about critical alliances and choices, whether these be, for example, homosocial and transnational (and if they are, why is this?) or heterosocial and nation-specific (and if they are, why is this?). As fatherhood studies continue to develop and thrive across geographical and academic locations, scholars will likely continue to highlight the multifarious ways in which fathering is done, how fatherhood and masculinity are co-constituted within the framework of variously male-dominated societies, and how fatherhood is conceptualized and experienced relationally with (for example) motherhood, non-fatherhood, and childhood. As ever, issues around gendered meanings of parenting need to be explored, explained, and understood in their given context, especially if the goal is to clarify how power operates in gendered ways in societies and human lives.

References

Andreassen, R. (2019). *Mediated kinship: Gender, race and sexuality in donor families*. London: Routledge.

Arendell, T. (1995). *Fathers and divorce*. Thousand Oaks, CA: Sage.

Armengol, J. C. (2008). Where are the fathers in American literature? Re-visiting fatherhood in U.S. literary history. *The Journal of Men's Studies, 16*(2), 211–226.

Åström, B. (2017). Marginalizing motherhood: Postfeminist fathers and dead mothers in animated film. In B. Åström (Ed.), *The absent mother in the cultural imagination: Missing, presumed dead* (pp. 241–258). Basingstoke: Palgrave Macmillan.

Bekkengen, L. (2002). *Man får välja: Om föräldraskap och föräldraledighet i arbetsliv och familjeliv*. Malmö: Liber.

Bergman, H., & Hobson, B. (2002). Compulsory fatherhood: The coding of fatherhood in the Swedish welfare state. In Hobson, B. (Ed.), *Making men into fathers: Men, masculinities, and the social politics of fatherhood* (pp. 92–124). New York: Cambridge University Press.

Björk, S. (2017). *Gender and emotions in family care: Understanding masculinity and gender equality in Sweden* (Doctoral dissertation). University of Gothenburg, Gothenburg.

Bodin, M. (2018). *To plan or not to plan: Gender perspectives on pregnancy planning, fertility awareness and preconception health care* (Doctoral dissertation). Uppsala University, Uppsala.

Bremner, P. (2017). Collaborative co-parenting and heteronormativity: Recognising the interests of gay fathers. *Child and Family Law Quarterly, 29*(4), 293–312.

Broughton, T. L., & Rogers, H. (Eds.). (2007). *Gender and fatherhood in the nineteenth century*. Basingstoke: Palgrave Mcmillan.

Bruzzi, S. (2005). *Bringing up daddy: Fatherhood and masculinity in post-war Hollywood*. London: British Film Institute.

Bueno, E. P., Caesar, T., & Hummel, W. (Eds.). (2000). *Naming the father: Legacies, genealogies, and explorations of fatherhood in modern and contemporary literature*. Lanham, MD: Lexington Books.

Carone, N., Biaocco, R., & Lingiardi, V. (2017). Single fathers by choice using surrogacy: Why men decide to have a child as a single parent. *Human Reproduction, 32*(9), 1871–1879.

Chodorow, N. (1978). *The reproduction of mothering*. Berkeley, CA: University of California Press.

Coles, R. L. (2009). *The best kept secret: Single black fathers*. Lanham, MD: Rowman & Littlefield.

Coles, R. L. (2015). Single-father families: A review of the literature. *Journal of Family Theory and Review, 7*(2), 144–166.

Collier, R. (1995). *Masculinity, law and the family*. New York: Routledge.

Collins, P. H. (1998). It's all in the family: Intersections of gender, race, and nation. *Hypatia, 13*(3), 62–82.

Coltrane, S. (1996). *Family man: Fatherhood, housework, and gender equity*. New York: Oxford University Press.

Connell, R. (1995). *Masculinities*. London: Routledge.

Connor, M., & White, J. (2006). *Black fathers: An invisible presence in America*. Mahwah, NJ: Lawrence Erlbaum.

Curran, L., & Abrams, L. S. (2000). Making men into dads: Fatherhood, the state, and welfare reform. *Gender & Society, 14*(5), 662–678.

Cutas, D., & Chan, S. (Eds.). (2012). *Families: Beyond the nuclear ideal*. London: Bloomsbury.

Dermott, E. (2008). *Intimate fatherhood: A sociological analysis*. London: Routledge.

Devlin, R. (2005). *Relative intimacy: Fathers, adolescent daughters, and postwar American culture*. Chapel Hill, NC: University of North Carolina Press.

Doucet, A. (2006). *Do men mother? Fathering, care, and domestic responsibility*. Toronto: University of Toronto Press.

Dowd, N. (2000). *Redefining fatherhood*. New York: New York University Press.

Eriksson, M. (2002). Men's violence, men's parenting and gender politics in Sweden. *NORA: Nordic Journal of Women's Studies, 10*(1), 10–15.

Faludi, S. (2007). *The terror dream: What 9/11 revealed about America*. London: Atlantic.

Faria, I. (2016). Family reimagined: Assisted reproduction and parenthood in Mozambique. In C. Kroløkke, L. Myong, S. W. Adrian & T. Tjornhoj-Thomsen (Eds.), *Critical kinship studies* (pp. 133–148). London: Rowman & Littlefield.

Featherstone, B. (2009). *Contemporary fathering: Theory, policy and practice*. Bristol: Policy Press.

Figueroa, J. G., Jiménez, L., & Tena, O. (Eds.). (2006). *Ser padres, esposos e hijos: prácticas y valoraciones de varones mexicanos*. Mexico City: El Colegio de Mexico.

Forsberg, L. (2007). Negotiating involved fatherhood: Household work, childcare and spending time with children. *NORMA: Nordic Journal for Masculinity Studies, 2*(2), 110–126.

Gavanas, A. (2004). Domesticating masculinity and masculinizing domesticity in contemporary U.S. fatherhood politics. *Social Politics, 11*(2), 247–266.

Griswold, R. (1993). *Fatherhood in America: A history*. New York: Basic Books.

The Guardian (2015, October 15). Court orders girl with two mothers to stay in touch with two fathers. Retrieved on January 17, 2019 from www.theguardian.com/law/2015/oct/15/court-girl-two-mothers-stay-in-touch-two-fathers.

Hamad, H. (2011). Extreme parenting: Recuperating fatherhood in Steven Spielberg's *War of the Worlds*. In H. Radner & R. Stringer (Eds.), *Feminism at the movies: Understanding gender in contemporary popular cinema* (pp. 241–254). New York: Routledge.

Hamad, H. (2014). *Postfeminism and paternity in contemporary U.S. film: Framing fatherhood*. New York: Routledge.

Hearn, J. (2002). Men, fathers and the state: National and global relations. In B. Hobson (Ed.), *Making men into fathers: Men, masculinities, and the social politics of fatherhood* (pp. 245–272). Cambridge: Cambridge University Press.

hooks, b. (2003). *We real cool: Black men and masculinity*. New York: Routledge.

hooks, b. (2008). *Reel to real: Race, sex, and class at the movies*. New York: Routledge.

Jeffords, S. (1988). Masculinity as excess in Vietnam films: The father-son dynamic of American culture. *Genre, 21*(4), 487–515.

Johansen, S. (2001). *Family men: Middle-class fatherhood in early industrializing America*. New York: Routledge.

Johansson, T., & Andreasson, J. (2017). *Fatherhood in transition: Masculinity, identity, and everyday life*. New York: Palgrave Macmillan.

King, L. (2015). *Family men: Fatherhood and masculinity in Britain, c. 1914–1960*. Oxford: Oxford University Press.

Klinth, R. (2002). *Göra pappa med barn: Den svenska pappapolitiken 1960–1995*. Umeå: Boréa.

Kroløkke, C., Myong, L., Adrian, S. W., & Tjornhoj-Thomsen, T. (Eds.). (2016). *Critical kinship studies*. London: Rowman & Littlefield.

Laqueur, T. (1992). The facts of fatherhood. In B. Thorne & M. Yalom (Eds.), *Rethinking the family: Some feminist questions* (pp. 155–175). Boston, MA: Northeastern University Press.

LaRossa, R. (1997). *The modernization of fatherhood: A social and political history*. Chicago, IL: University of Chicago Press.

Leverenz, D. (2003). *Paternalism incorporated: Fables of American fatherhood 1865–1940*. Ithaca, NY: Cornell University Press.

Lewin, E. (2009). *Gay fatherhood: Narratives of family and citizenship in America*. Chicago, IL: University of Chicago Press.

Lewis, C. (2013). Fatherhood and fathering research in the UK: Cultural change and diversity. In D. Schwalb, B. J. Schwalb & M. E. Lamb (Eds.), *Fathers in cultural context* (pp. 332–357). New York: Routledge.

Löwy, I. (2006). La fabrication du naturel: L'assistance médicale a la procréation dans une perspective comparée. *Tumultes, 26*(1), 35–55.

Lupton, D., & Barclay, L. (1997). *Constructing fatherhood: Discourses and experiences*. London: Sage.

Mallon, G. (2004). *Gay men choosing parenthood*. New York: Columbia University Press.

Malmquist, A. (forthcoming). Swedish gay men's pursuit of fatherhood: Legal obstacles and strategies for coping with them. *Lambda Nordica*.

Marsiglio, W., & Pleck, J. H. (2005). Fatherhood and masculinities. In R. Connell, J. Hearn & M. Kimmel (Eds.), *Handbook on men and masculinities* (pp. 249–269). New York: Routledge.

Modleski, T. (1991). *Feminism without women: Culture and criticism in a postfeminist age*. New York: Routledge.

Mohr, S. (2015). Living kinship trouble: Danish sperm donors' narratives of relatedness. *Medical Anthropology, 34*(5), 470–484.

Moore, L. J. (2007). *Sperm counts: Overcome by man's most precious fluid*. New York: New York University Press.

Morgan, D. (2002). Epilogue. In B. Hobson (Ed.), *Making men into fathers: Men, masculinities, and the social politics of fatherhood* (pp. 273–286). Cambridge: Cambridge University Press.

Morgan, D. (2004). Men in families and households. In J. Scott, J. Treas & M. Richards (Eds.), *The Blackwell companion to the sociology of families* (pp. 374–393). London: Blackwell.

Morrel, R. (2006). Fathers, fatherhood and masculinity in South Africa. In L. Richter & R. Morrell (Eds.), *Baba: Men and fatherhood in South Africa* (pp. 13–25). Cape Town: HSRC.

Muchemwa, K., & Muponde, R. (Eds.). (2007). *Manning the nation: Father figures in Zimbabwean literature and society*. Harare: Weaver Press.

Muponde, R. (2007). Killing fathers. In K. Muchemwa & R. Muponde (Eds.), *Manning the nation: Father figures in Zimbabwean literature and society* (pp. 17–30). Harare: Weaver Press.

Musiyiwa, M., & Chirere, M. (2007). The nature of fatherhood and manhood in Zimbabwean texts of pre-colonial and colonial settings. In K. Muchemwa & R. Muponde (Eds.), *Manning the nation: Father figures in Zimbabwean literature and society* (pp. 156–169). Harare: Weaver Press.

Ndlovu-Gatsheni, S. J. (2007). Fatherhood and nationhood: Joshua Nkomo and the re-imagination of the Zimbabwe nation. In K. Muchemwa & R. Muponde (Eds.), *Manning the nation: Father figures in Zimbabwean literature and society* (pp. 73–87). Harare: Weaver Press.

Nebeling Petersen, M. (2015). 'Between precarity and privilege: Claiming motherhood as gay fathers through transnational surrogacy.' In V. Kantsa, G. Zanini, L. Papadopoulou (Eds.), *Fertile citizens: Anthropological and Legal Challenges of Assisted Reproduction Technologies* (pp. 93-100). Athens: Alexandria Publications.

Podnieks, E. (Ed.). (2016). *Pops in pop culture: Fatherhood, masculinity, and the new man.* New York: Palgrave Macmillan.

Poole, E., Speight, S., O'Brien, M., Connolly, S., & Aldrich, M. (2013). What do we know about non-resident fathers? Retrieved from www.modernfatherhood.org/publications/what-do-we-know-about-non-resident-fathers/.

Pringle, K. (2016). Doing (oppressive) gender via men's relations with children. In A. Häyrén & H. Wahlström Henriksson (Eds.), *Critical perspectives on masculinities and relationalities: In relation to what?* (pp. 23–34). Cham: Springer.

Prinsloo, J. (2006). Where have all the fathers gone? Media(ted) representations of fatherhood. In L. Richter & R. Morrell (Eds.), *Baba: Men and fatherhood in South Africa* (pp. 132–146). Cape Town: HSRC.

Richter, L., & Morrell, R. (Eds.). (2006). *Baba: Men and fatherhood in South Africa.* Cape Town: HSRC.

Rotundo, E. A. (1993). *American manhood: Transformations in masculinity to the modern era.* New York: Basic Books.

Ruddick, S. (1992). Thinking about fathers. In B. Thorne & M. Yalom (Eds.), *Rethinking the family: Some feminist questions* (pp. 176–190). Boston, MA: Northeastern University Press.

Saar, T. (2013, February 23). Fifty shades of gay: Amalia Ziv explains why her son calls her 'dad'. *Haaretz* online. Retrieved on January 15, 2019 from www.haaretz.com/.premium-fifty-shades-of-gay-amalia-ziv-explains-why-her-son-calls-her-dad-1.5230870.

Schwalb, D. W., Schwalb, B. J., & Lamb, M. E. (Eds.). (2013). *Fathers in cultural context.* New York: Routledge.

Segal, L. (1990). *Slow motion: Changing masculinities, changing men.* New Brunswick, NJ: Rutgers University Press.

Siedler, V. (2006). *Young men and masculinities: Global cultures and intimate lives.* London: Zed.

Smith, D. J. (2017). *To be a man is not a one-day job: Masculinity, money, and intimacy in Nigeria.* Chicago, IL: University of Chicago Press.

Smyth, B. M., Baxter, J. A., Fletcher, R. J., & Moloney, L. (2013). Fathers in Australia: A contemporary snapshot. In D. Schwalb, B. J. Schwalb & M. E. Lamb (Eds.), *Fathers in cultural context* (pp. 361–382). New York: Routledge.

Throsby, K., & Gill, R. (2004). It's different for men: Masculinity and IVF. *Men and Masculinities, 6*(4), 330–348.

Tincknell, E., & Chambers, D. (2002). Performing the crisis: Fathering, gender, and representation in two 1990s Films. *Journal of Popular Film and Television, 29*(4), 146–155.

Tosh, J. (1999). *A man's place: Masculinity and the middle-class home in Victorian England.* New Haven, CT: Yale University Press.

Townsend, N. W. (2013). The complications of fathering in Southern Africa: Separation, uncertainty, and multiple responsibilities. In D. Schwalb, B. J. Schwalb & M. E. Lamb (Eds.), *Fathers in cultural context* (pp. 173–200). New York: Routledge.

United Nations. (2011). *Men in families and family policy in a changing world.* New York, NY: United Nations Department of Economic and Social Affairs, Division for Social Policy and Development. Retrieved on February 19, 2019 from www.un.org/esa/socdev/family/docs/men-in-families.pdf.

Volcano, D. L. (2016). Motstånd är fruktbart. *Tidskrift för genusvetenskap 37*(4), 15–27. Retrieved from http://ojs.ub.gu.se/ojs/index.php/tgv/article/viewFile/3821/3135.

Wahlström, H. (2010). *New fathers? Contemporary American stories of masculinity, domesticity, and kinship.* Newcastle-Upon-Tyne: Cambridge Scholars Publishing.

Wahlström Henriksson, H. (2016a). Pappahandbooks: Guidebooks for dads in twenty-first century Sweden. In E. Podnieks (Ed.), *Pops in pop culture: Fatherhood, masculinity, and the new man* (pp. 31–50). New York: Palgrave MacMillan.

Wahlström Henriksson, H. (2016b). Exploring the relationality of fatherhood: John Irving's *The Cider House Rules*. In A. Häyrén & H. Wahlström Henriksson (Eds.), *Critical perspectives on masculinities and relationalities: In relation to what?* (pp. 9–21). Cham: Springer.

Wall, G., & Arnold, S. (2007). How involved is involved fathering? An exploration of the contemporary culture of fatherhood. *Gender & Society*, *21*(4), 508–527.

Yeager, P., & Kowaleski-Wallace, B. (Eds.). (1989). *Refiguring the father: New feminist readings of patriarchy*. Carbondale, IL: Southern Illinois University Press.

Yuval-Davis, N. (1997). *Gender and nation*. London: Sage.

32

Reconfiguring masculinities and education

Interconnecting local and global identities

Máirtín Mac an Ghaill

Introduction

'They are turning our boys into girls.' Fifteen years ago this comment from an elderly woman captured the intense anxiety of the public response reported in Parliament and the media to the introduction of a Social, Personal and Health Education module, entitled *Negotiating Masculinities*, offered to boys in Irish schools (Mac an Ghaill, Hanafin & Conway, 2004). At a broader level, it illustrates that schooling systems traditionally have functioned as a social and cultural refuge for the projection of a society's social anxieties, particularly heightened and made visible at times of rapid change accompanied by discourses of crisis.

This chapter is written from within a British location, and it is acknowledged that masculinity and education have their own national specificities in terms of socio-economic, political and policy developments. Within this context, from an historical perspective masculinity appears as a most recent (late modern) concept in terms of providing an explanatory framework for boys' practices, behaviours and attitudes in the old institutions of (modern) schooling. The chapter begins with a critical engagement with research that helped to establish the field of inquiry, with, for example, a significant increase during the late 1980s and 1990s of educational literature on masculinities, particularly emanating from Australia and the UK (Davison & Frank, 2007). The second section examines contemporary international studies of masculinity and education, with the final section outlining a more radical departure in identifying how masculinity is being conceptually reconfigured in educational research (Onegubuzie, Leech & Collins, 2011). A re-reading of the literature over the last few decades enables us to trace the similarities and differences of how masculinity has and has not travelled across (inter)national spaces of educational institutions. Davison and Frank (2007), in the Preface to their edited collection *Masculinities and Schooling: International Practices and Perspectives*, productively suggest a critical analysis of masculinity and schooling in their text aiming 'to problematize the ordinary ways in which masculinities often escape the critical eye .... Highlighting some of the ways masculinities are practiced in different contexts and from varied cultural perspectives, this collection encourages more than simple, quick-fix solutions' (pp. xi–xii).

Critical engagement with research that established the field of inquiry

In early research, diverse strands of feminism have been of major intellectual importance with respect to making sense of schooling, masculinity and boys and highlighting that in the formation of gender identities, the social structures that reproduce social inequality are of central significance. Of specific importance was the use of patriarchy – as a complex and multi-levelled distribution of automatic power and as a conceptual framework to explain gender relations. For example, innovative feminist work stressed the importance of examining how school life, including internal geography, the form and content of the curriculum materials and relationships between teachers and students contributed to the reproduction of gender inequalities (Stanworth, 1981). In other words, the arrangement of the curriculum, pedagogy and assessment linked masculinity with a patriarchal dividend (Connell, 1987). Other research identified how boys' attitudes and behaviours systematically harmed girls' schooling experiences, as well as how boys also physically and emotionally harmed other boys (Arnot, 2002; Reay, 2001).

Also of major importance to early research on the education of working-class students was the use of class analysis. Within the context of industrial-based classed societies, materialist analyses of the social and cultural reproduction functions of schooling highlighting notions of power, hierarchy, subordination and exclusion provided important critiques of the more optimistic social democratic views of education as the central instrument of attaining social equality. One of the most insightful analytical and empirical accounts of masculinity and education, that of Willis's (1997) *Learning to Labour*, achieved its continuing resonance by capturing (white) working-class male students' lives at the end of this industrial period, which had provided a world-view central in the making of men and masculinities. Simultaneously, his work attracted international interest in terms of his intellectual exploration of key concepts including: boyness, working-class schooling and the gendering of paid labour. More recent materialist analyses of education and masculinity that critically build on this earlier work are located within the context of significant transformations in terms of globalisation, post-industrialisation, migration, neoliberalism and consumerism. For example, Garth, Nelson and Wallace (2017) in an edited collection address masculinity and aspiration in an era of neoliberal education, bringing together an international range of texts that provide a detailed exploration of emerging responses to the re-masculinisation of highly varied schooling systems and an accompanying diverse production of late modern male student identifications.

Connell's (1995) concept of hegemonic masculinity and its attendant relationships of marginalisation, complicity and subordination with other men have made a significant impact on early education research. In particular, cross-cultural studies in education have developed innovative texts by positioning multiple masculinities within the frames of hegemony, compulsory heterosexuality and homophobia (Mac an Ghaill, 1994a; Martino, 1999). Such concepts continue to be used but are reworked within a range of theoretical frameworks, including poststructuralism, suggesting a more complex relationship between hegemonic masculinities and other masculinities informed by an understanding of power relations as more fragmented. For example, Bender's (2001) ethnographic study exploring young men's lives in a US high school illustrates this more complex approach. He argues that, though they were positioned as marginalised within the broader school hegemony, they continued to use practices characteristic of hegemonic masculinities, such as the objectification of women and violence to other men, to stabilise their claims to authentic maleness. Significantly, the study by Redman, Epstein, Kehily and Mac an Ghaill (2002) of students in a UK primary school points to a means of understanding masculinity potentially outside a patriarchal dividend.

Contemporary diverse international studies of masculinity and education

This early critical literature challenged the default position of conventional schooling that often appeared to be a 'boys will be boys' approach, in which the biological category of male sex erased that of gender and the more specific notion of boys as a gendered cohort at an analytical level. Critical research also challenged conventional schooling's tendency to have a relatively local focus, beginning with a reductionist definitional conflation of education with schooling. In turn, in practice this often strategically led to adopting a national(ist) framework within which to address local policy and professional issues. This earlier critical research was carried out within a specific period of late industrial society.

From a contemporary perspective, one way of building on this earlier work in the field is to move away from the tendency, found in much of the research in the global North, to focus on the local and to frame our analysis through the concept of globalisation. Over the last few decades, we find the field opened up with a move from a *local* to a *global* perspective, and an awareness of the complex interconnection between them, in which education and masculinities and femininities are situated within shifting histories and geographies across borders, embedded within the intersectionality of multiple social categories that are researched in a wide range of empirical studies. These studies include examples that examine how the making and re-making of embodied masculinities (and femininities) are being produced through diverse (masculine) processes of neoliberalism, militarisation and securitisation that serve to illustrate the complexity of the theoretical, methodological and substantive questions and accompanying policy implications in the field at this time.

Earlier research on men within an international context adopted a cross-cultural analysis focusing on the local arrangements of the meaning of masculinity, and within this frame there was a wide range of theoretical and conceptual cross-cultural analyses of masculinities (Cornwall & Lindisfarne, 1994). A more recent postmodern approach shifts from examining men and masculinities in specific international locations to analyse gender relations as articulated through global processes. Globalisation can be understood as the unparalleled transfer of social, cultural, economic and political processes, procedures and technologies across national boundaries. Such movements are produced through a compression of time and space and the generation of a sense of immediacy and simultaneity about the world (Brah, Hickman & Mac an Ghaill, 1999). Research on globalisation, masculinities and education have developed innovative work in attempting to understand the impact of these transformations and the potential (re)configuration of local, national and transnational subjectivities and identities.

A key theme in contemporary empirical studies of the globalization of education is the centrality of neoliberal discourses in shaping institutional policies and professional practices, including the opening up of educational spaces beyond the school (Torres, 2009). Lindisfarne and Neale (2016, p. 30) usefully identify three kinds of change to indicate how neoliberalism works: 'The first concerns the materialization of inequality. The second is increased gender marking and the third requires a consideration of the increasing physical and cultural differences between the elite and ordinary people.' Illustrating the pervasiveness of neoliberalism as both an economic and political force imposed over the last 40 years, they finely display the reconfiguration of gender relations across (local) national spaces resulting from migration and its attendant experiences of economic reserve armies of the poor, political refugees and sex trafficking. Neoliberalism has been influential in promoting and implementing policies that facilitate the values of competitive individualism and a reduction in the role of the state and at the same time facilitate the shaping of individual subjectivities based on the cultivation of knowledge and skills that are seen to be in global market demand (Rizvi & Engel, 2009). In turn, a major impact on the development of gender equality, as an effect of neoliberalism's individualising process, is that it is helping to forge forms of masculinities and femininities. More specifically, from an educational perspective across the globe there is evidence of neoliberalism framing the re-masculinisation of schooling systems and the emergence of diverse neoliberal subjects among management, teachers and students.

For example, Liu (2017), in her research carried out in Beijing with 25 upper secondary school students, explores the significance of *chenggong*, meaning outstanding accomplishment, in the construction of their masculinities. She notes that the students claimed that *chenggong* was a prerequisite to live the 'good life', to be the 'good person' and, more particularly here, to be the 'good man.' Liu provides a complex picture of the young men's lives, and while acknowledging a range of differences among them, the overriding centrality of *cheggong* within the context of their schooling suggests to her that it has hegemonic status. Hence their schooling is strategically experienced as achieving this most prestigious form of masculinity. Liu captures very well the cost that these young men – a relatively advantaged cohort of the post-1990s only-child generation, often of urban middle class background – pay in a neoliberal educational system that is marked by intense competitive individualism in which they share the ideological belief that they are personally responsible for whether they become 'winners' or 'losers.' In contrast to the dynamics of male middle-class trajectories, Lin's (2017) study focuses upon single rural–urban male migrant workers, illustrating the value of educational credentials as an important form of capital for these working-class men to perform their 'capable' masculinity within the marriage market. Furthermore, Lin illustrates how the working-class migrant men negotiate their masculinity through claiming alternative cultural masculine values, such as being a filial son. In so doing, they were able to demonstrate masculine ideals as a capable man within a neoliberal context.

In a further example, Mannon and Kemp (2010) have provided insight into how neoliberalism has impacted upon Costa Rican society. Drawing upon ethnographic work in Heredia and interviews with twenty men aged 15–35 years, they identify how men are renegotiating manhood in light of neoliberal processes. The shift in the Costa Rican economy, with the erosion of the welfare state and secure middle-class careers alongside the reduction of high employment industries, has resulted in a predominance of the service sector and low-paid manufacturing work. This labour market restructuring has been accompanied by a gender occupational restructuring, with more women entering the workplace. While they experience low pay and poor conditions, their financial independence has been enhanced. Mannon and Kemp (2010) contrasts the women's experiences of these changes with those of working-class men, with the latter feeling marginalised and emasculated as a result of neoliberalism. In contrast, for middle-class young men, the neoliberal influence on education appears to be in continuity with the development of their masculinities that brings together educational qualifications, the values of entrepreneurialism and wealth generation. Hence education becomes a constitutive element of a competitive individualism, with the latter becoming central to the re-fashioning of young masculinities, shifting from traditional masculinity-making resources associated with family life, marriage and children to a neoliberal ideal of competitive individualism.

Empirical studies focusing on militarisation, securitisation and education is a second theme through which to explore the making and re-remaking of masculinity across contemporary international research. The militarisation and securitisation of schools is part of a broader aspect of the militarisation and securitisation of global society. Significantly, Via (2010) suggests that the interconnection between masculinity and the military can be found in themes of protection, aggression, bravery, courage and physical strength. From a research perspective, a major impact of globalisation on education is its central institutional significance as a space in which issues of risk and security are given increased priority. For Davies (2008), this has resulted in an increasing sense of militarisation in schools, which has in itself promoted particular forms of masculinity through its normalisation of male violence. This normalisation of violence and how it was challenged is captured in De Silva's (2005) ethnographic research on a high school in Sri Lanka, which helps us to understand how processes of globalisation impact upon the formation of masculinity in such local contexts. She provides a detailed qualitative account, describing an episode in which twenty-two male students were abducted and killed by the Sri Lankan army. One of the main findings of this research emerged in response to De Silva asking the boys whether, if they were abducted, they would inform on their friends who were activists. The boys said that they would but that they believed that their shared sense of *machan* (designating friendships that were equal, close and mutually supportive) would not diminish and that reporting their friends as activists would not affect their friendships. Therefore, in the context of brutal militarisation, boys were able to maintain a deeply intimate sense of friendship. De Silva claims that in the process, traditional masculinities that were based on deference to authority and older people were displaced by a masculinity based on a sense of injustice and activism. She locates these events within the context of the wider societal emergence of the discourses of terrorism that enabled the military involvement within the school and that were associated with particular modes of masculinity perceived as disruptive and disrespectful. As a consequence, terrorism became a justificatory cause to detain, interrogate, torture and sometimes murder particular kinds of young men.

Postcolonial analysis has been of central significance in highlighting the importance of the response to the complex colonial legacies across the global North, which is currently reporting an assumed crisis of multiculturalism and an accompanying emergence of the militarisation of schools, with discourses of securitisation now the central logic informing educational policies and practices, as wider geo-political transformations have reshaped the relationship between the local and the global. Within a British context, Shain (2011, p. 35) presents a postcolonial analysis of the contradictions of the government's appeals to Britishness and empire, arguing that

> Britishness tests, citizenship ceremonies, and Britishness taught on the school curriculum, could be read from this perspective as offering one way of hanging onto a sense of national identity in the face of pressure to compete as a global player.

The 'Muslim Question' is currently projected as a major international political, social and security problem across government, media and civil society discourses. Central to this anxiety is the schooling of Muslim boys and girls. In response, Mac an Ghaill and Haywood (2017) in an edited collection explore the intersection of masculinity, religion and nation-making, highlighting diverse narratives of a late modern reflexive generation of young men and women within a wide range of international educational contexts.

The conceptual reconfiguration of masculinity in educational research

This final section of this chapter outlines how masculinity is being conceptually reconfigured in educational research. A major danger of work in this field is that girls and young women are written out. Hence of major significance was the publication of Judith Halberstam's *Female Masculinity* (1998). This has been a key source for educational researchers who focus on the disconnection of masculinity from physiology, thus highlighting the assumed relationship between gender and sexuality, that is, the formation of masculinities through heterosexuality and links to power and potentially empowerment. Lobel, Slone and Winch's (1997) call for future educational research to explore the nature of female masculinity has only partially been answered. Ma'ayan's (2003) fieldwork with girls who take up masculine styles found that being masculine was aligned with norms of maturity. Therefore, in order to gain institutional and peer group approval, femininity was rejected and aligned with immaturity. Alongside this, the experience of these young women highlighted the disconnect between gender and sexuality in that the take-up of masculine styles did not determine particular erotic attachments. Embedded in this approach is the sense that adopting masculinity provides the possibility of empowerment. The notion resonates with Bhana (2008, p. 412), who suggests:

> The possibility of a conjunction between female and masculinity that challenges the pathology associated with transgressive women and applied to young girls in this study makes it possible to argue that African women are not waiting to be victims – that female masculinity can be empowering and suggests the multiple forms of power and domination – not the exclusive preserve of boys and men.

Similarly, Renold (2009), in her ethnographic research with 10–11-year-olds in two UK primary schools, suggests that girls 'queer' and contest the implicit relationship between masculinity and heterosexuality through the adoption of a tomboy positionality that included the rejection of all things deemed feminine, including associating with their peers.

In this research, the focus on the rejection of hegemonic masculine forms through the adoption of masculinity by girls leads to the possibility of a transgressive stance, offering a productive understanding of how masculinity may emerge. However, the disconnect between sex and gender does not always lead to transgressiveness, as Tong (2008) found in her discussion with girls who aligned themselves with masculine practices and held same-sex desires, while articulating strong homophobic attitudes towards men, especially men who demonstrated traditional feminine styles.

A post-masculinity position shifts the focus from an emphasis on the relationship between gender and sex to the relationship between gender and masculinity. This means that gender identities, subjectivities and identifications may be understood without reducing them to a notion of masculinity. Butler (2004) discusses the apparatus that underpins the notion of gender as being read through binaries such as male/female and masculine/feminine. As suggested by Frank, Davison and Lovell (2003), the strategy therefore in 'undoing gender' is to theoretically distance gender from masculinity (and femininity) across educational spaces to enable gender to be constituted through alternative social and cultural forms.

Educational researchers have used Butler's (1995) suggestion of the centrality of the heterosexual matrix in making sense of masculinity to explore teaching and learning interactions in which if there is little recognition or identifications with the heterosexual matrix, and hence the cultural forms of masculinity and femininity may be more ambiguous. Thorne (1993) illustrated this in her research, where she identifies how younger children 'cross genders', particularly in the absence of a developed heterosexual meaning system, and suggests the importance of recalibrating the relationship between gendered subjectivities and (hetero) sexual structures. For example, there is often a tendency to use adult-led (heterosexual) masculinities to explain boys' schooling experiences. Bronwyn Davies (2006) is also interested in the dynamics of category maintenance by children who transgress masculine and feminine orientated discourses and practices, suggesting the possibility of a third category of gender to ensure the 'breaking up the gender binary' (p. 88). For Haywood (2008), the gendered meaning systems of 8–12-year-old boys in his research in a UK state school were not located within easily definable heterosexual and homosexual binaries. Hence erotically charged behaviours between boys and between boys and girls were not collapsed within a logic of (homo/hetero) sexuality. With the structures of normative heterosexuality that underpin the articulation of masculinity (and femininity) being less salient, a masculinity identity that 'Othered' femininity, employed homophobia and celebrated heterosexuality was not taken up by these boys.

Finally, a critical response to a queering of gender and masculinity questions the marginalisation of structuring processes that produce social and cultural inequality. In other words, by letting go of masculinity, there is a risk that we lose the analytical purchase on the structuring processes that support inequalities. Work that has tried to combine both structuralist and post-structuralist approaches to the study of masculinity suggests the importance of re-reading masculinity through other social categories (see Flood, 2002). More specifically, rather than identify the articulation between cultural resources and maleness to constitute a masculinity or male gender, a recalibration of interpretive strategies opens up the possibility of understanding the dynamics of gender through other social categories. An example of this can be found in early work by Mac an Ghaill (1994b, p. 156), who attempts to understand the complex interplay between 'schooling, masculine cultural formations and sexual/racial identities.' In his consideration of black gay students in English schools, Mac an Ghaill (1994b) identifies how racial identities are spoken through sexual and gender codes that are also embedded by generation. This case study reveals the racial/ethnic hierarchies that were ascribed by teachers in their administration and pedagogy:

> So for example, in working class schools where there was a majority Asian student population with a mainly white minority, the dominant representations of Asian youth tended to be negative with caricatures of them as sly and 'not real men.' However, in working class schools which included significant numbers of African-Caribbeans, the students felt that the Asians were caricatured in a more positive way in relation to the African-Caribbeans, who were perceived as of 'low ability', 'aggressive' and 'anti-authority.'
>
> *(Mac an Ghaill, 1994b, p. 158)*

As a consequence, racial/ethnic categories are immediately gendered, classed and sexualised, with social relations of ethnicity simultaneously 'speaking' gender and sexuality. The result is a process of subjectification, where masculinity becomes an articulation of multiple differences and power and powerlessness exist in simultaneous positions or, as Butler (1997, p. 116) has argued, 'submission and mastery take place simultaneously, and it is this paradoxical simultaneity that constitutes the ambivalence of subjection.' Therefore the argument is not to reify 'masculinity' and deselect other social categories but to return to sites of gendered experience and theorise out of them, as 'situated knowledge' (Stoetzler & Yuval-

Davis, 2002). Importantly, research suggests that a focus on the simultaneity of categories requires analyses to understand how social relations do not articulate *with* one another but rather how social categories articulate *as* one another (Holvino, 2008, p. 15). As a result, we need to think not about the ways social categories accumulate but about the ways that they speak to each other at the same time. This method also provides the opportunity to re-read earlier research texts and imagine a synthesis of these positions between early feminist structuralist-based accounts of patriarchy alongside a deconstructionist emphasis on identities, subjectivities and identifications in the schooling of masculinity.

Conclusion: globally-inflected educational masculinities and femininities across borders

I opened this chapter with reference to research carried out in Ireland 15 years ago, identifying the public anxieties about the assumed changing societal sex/gender order as illustrated by assumptions about the feminisation of the school curriculum. As illustrative of the impact of the global changes in late modernity by 2018, Ireland, having passed legislation on same-sex marriage and addressing earlier discourses of crisis masculinity, now seems a different country (Inglis, 2014). Interestingly, in November 2017, Australia voted for same-sex marriage, which was the major theme of the 2018 Sydney New Year celebrations. A main argument of the campaign against a yes vote was that it would lead to the 'changing of our boys into girls.' Educational institutions continue to be a key site were these imagined changing gender orders that are often read as the inversion of hegemonic masculinity are been played out within national spaces. A comparative international research perspective on masculinity and education, as explored above, enables us to address globally-inflected shifting masculinities and femininities across borders. This chapter has set out to document some of these important conceptual shifts and modifications that may have a significant impact on the future use of masculinity in educational research, teaching and policy.

References

Arnot, M. (2002). *Reproducing gender? Critical essays on educational theory and feminist politics.* London: RoutledgeFalmer.

Bender, G. (2001). Resisting dominance? The study of a marginalized masculinity and its construction within high school walls. In J. N. Burstyn (Ed.), *Preventing violence in schools: A challenge to American democracy* (pp. 61–78). Mahwah, NJ: L. Erlbaum Associates.

Bhana, D. (2008). 'Girls hit!' Constructing and negotiating violent African femininities in a working-class primary school. *Discourse: Studies in the Cultural Politics of Education, 29*(3), 401–415.

Brah, A., Hickman, M. J., & Mac an Ghaill, M. (Eds.). (1999). *Global futures: Migration, environment and globalization.* Basingstoke: Palgrave.

Butler, J. (1995). Subjection, resistance, resignification: Between Freud and Foucault. In J. Rajchman (Ed.), *The identity in question* (pp. 229–249). London: Routledge.

Butler, J. (1997). *The psychic life of power: Theories in subjection.* Stanford, CA: Stanford University Press.

Butler, J. (2004). *Undoing gender.* Oxon: Routledge.

Connell, R. W. (1987). *Gender and power.* Cambridge: Polity Press.

Connell, R. W. (1995). *Masculinities.* Berkeley, CA: University of California Press.

Cornwall, A., & Lindisfarne, N. (1994). Dislocating masculinity: Gender, power and anthropology. In A. Cornwall & N. Lindisfarne (Eds.), *Dislocating masculinity: Contemporary ethnographies* (pp. 11–47). London: Routledge.

Davies, B. (2006). Identity, abjection and otherness: Creating the self, creating difference. In M. Arnot & M. Mac an Ghaill (Eds.), *The Routledge Falmer reader in gender and education* (pp. 72–90). London: Routledge.

Davies, L. (2008). Gender, education, extremism and security. *Compare: A Journal of Comparative and International Education, 38*(5), 611–625.

Davison, K. G., & Frank, B. W. (2007). Preface. In B. W. Frank & K. G. Davison (Eds.), *Masculinities and schooling: International practices and perspectives* (pp. ix–xv). Ontario: The Althouse Press.

De Silva, J. (2005). *Globalization, terror and the shaming of the nation: Constructing local masculinities in a Sinhala village*. Victoria: Trafford.

Flood, M. (2002). Between men and masculinity: An assessment of the term 'masculinity' in recent scholarship on men. In S. Pearce & V. Muller (Eds.), *Manning the next millennium: Studies in masculinities* (pp. 203–213). Bentley, WA: Black Swan.

Frank, B., Davison, K., & Lovell, T. (2003). Tangle of trouble: Boys, masculinity and schooling, future directions. *Educational Review, 55*(2), 119–133.

Garth, S., Nelson, J. S., & Wallace. D. O. (Eds.). (2017). *Masculinity and aspiration in an era of neoliberal education: International perspectives*. New York: Routledge.

Halberstam, J. (1998). *Female masculinity*. Durham, NC: Duke University Press.

Haywood, C. (2008). Genders and sexualities: Exploring the conceptual limits of contemporary educational research. *International Studies in Sociology of Education, 18*(1), 1–14.

Holvino, E. (2008). Intersections: The simultaneity of race, gender, and class in organization studies. *Gender, Work and Organization, 15*(5), 968–993.

Inglis, T. (2014). *Are the Irish different?* Manchester: Manchester University Press.

Lin, X. (2017) Singleness, masculinity and heteronormativity: Male migrant workers in China. In X. Lin, C. Haywood & M. Mac an Ghaill (Eds.), *East Asian men: Masculinity, sexuality and desire* (pp. 13–30). London: Palgrave Macmillan.

Lindisfarne, N., & Neale, J. (2016). Masculinities and the lived experiences of neoliberalism. In A. Cornwall., F. G. Karioris & N. Lindisfarne (Eds.), *Masculinities under neoliberalism* (pp. 29–50). London: Zed Books.

Liu, F. (2019). Chinese young men's construction of exemplary masculinity: The hegemony of chenggong. *Men and Masculinities, 22*(2), 294–316.

Lobel, T. E., Slone, M., & Winch, G. (1997). Masculinity, popularity, and self-esteem among Israeli preadolescent girls. *Sex Roles, 36*(5–6), 395–408.

Ma'ayan, H. D. (2003). Masculine female adolescents at school. *Equity & Excellence in Education, 36*(2), 125–135.

Mac an Ghaill, M. (1994a). *The making of men: Masculinities, sexualities and schooling*. Buckingham: Open University Press.

Mac an Ghaill, M. (1994b). (In)visiblity: sexuality, masculinity and 'race' in the school context. In D. Epstein (Ed.), *Challenging lesbian and gay inequalities in education* (pp. 152–176). Buckingham: Open University Press.

Mac an Ghaill, M., Hanafin, J., & Conway, P. F. (2004). *Exploring masculinities in Irish education: Teachers, materials and the media*. Dublin: National Council for Curriculum and Assessment.

Mac an Ghaill, M., & Haywood, C. (Eds.). (2017). *Muslim students, education and neoliberalism: Schooling a 'suspect community'*. London: Palgrave Macmillan.

Mannon, S. E., & Kemp, E. (2010). Pampered sons, (wo)manly men, or do-nothing machos? Costa Rican men coming of age under neoliberalism. *Bulletin of Latin American Research, 29*(4), 477–491.

Martino, W. (1999). 'Cool boys,' 'party animals,' 'squids' and 'poofters': Interrogating the dynamics and politics of adolescent masculinities in school. *British Journal of Sociology of Education, 20*(2), 39–63.

Onegubuzie, A. J., Leech, N. L., & Collins, K. M. T. (2011). Innovative qualitative data collection techniques for conducting literature reviews. In M. Williams & W. P. Vogt (Eds.), *The Sage handbook of innovation on social research methods* (pp. 182–204). Thousand Oaks, CA: Sage.

Reay, D. (2001). Spice girls, 'nice girls', 'girlies' and tomboys: Gender discourses, girls' cultures and femininities in the primary classroom. *Gender and Education, 13*(2), 153–166.

Redman, P., Epstein, D., Kehily, M. J., & Mac an Ghaill, M. (2002). Boys bonding: Same-sex friendship, the unconscious and heterosexual masculinities. *Discourse, 23*(2), 179–191.

Renold, E. (2009). Tomboys and 'female masculinity': (Dis)embodying hegemonic masculinity, queering gender identities and relations. In W. Martino, M. Kehler & M. Weaver-Hightower (Eds.), *The problem with boys: Beyond recuperative masculinity politics in boys' education* (pp. 224–242). New York: Routledge.

Rizvi, F., & Engel, L. C. (2009). Neo-liberal globalization, educational policy, and the struggle for social justice. In W. Ayers, T. Quinn & D. Stovall (Eds.), *The handbook of social justice in education* (pp. 529–541). Lanham, MD: Rowman & Littlefield.

Shain, F. (2011). *The new folk devils: Muslim boys and education in England*. Stoke-on-Trent: Trentham Books.

Stanworth, M. (1981). *Gender and schooling*. London: Women's Research and Resources Centre.

Stoetzler, M., & Yuval-Davis, N. (2002). Standpoint theory, situated knowledge and the situated imagination. *Feminist Theory*, *3*(3), 315–334.

Thorne, B. (1993). *Gender play: Girls and boys in school*. Buckingham: Open University Press.

Tong, C. K. M. (2008). Being a young tomboy in Hong Kong: The life and identity construction of lesbian schoolgirls. In P. A. Jackson, M. McLelland & A. Yue (Eds.), *AsiaPacifiQueer: Rethinking genders and sexualities* (pp. 117–131). Urbana, IL: University of Illinois Press.

Torres, C. A. (2009). *Education and neoliberal globalization*. New York: Routledge.

Via, S. (2010). Gender, militarism, and globalization: Soldiers for hire and hegemonic masculinity. In L. Sjoberg & S. Via (Eds.), *Gender, war, and militarism: Feminist perspectives* (pp. 42–57). Santa Barbara, CA: ABC Clio.

Willis, P. (1997). *Learning to labour: How working class boys get working class jobs*. Farnborough: Saxon House.

33

The coproduction of masculinity and technology

Problems and prospects

Andreas Ottemo

Both culturally and materially, technology plays an increasingly central role in contemporary society. Further, recent feminist new materialist research has demonstrated how boundaries between the symbolic/material, machinic/somatic and nature/culture are becoming ever more blurred (Dolphijn & van der Tuin, 2012). Technology – conceived broadly as everything from artefacts that extend our bodies and capacities to knowledge systems and ways of reasoning central to modernity – occupies a critical position in this process. We can understand it both as "integral to the constitution of subjectivity" (Wajcman, 2010, p. 145) and as providing stability to social formations and, hence, as the missing masses that make society durable (Latour, 1991). Of particular importance to the field of men and masculinity studies is the fact that "there is a materially and symbolically powerful relationship between men and technology" (Mellström, 2003, p. 18), central both to the masculinization of power in society at large and to what it means to be masculine. It is somewhat surprising, therefore, that the relationship between masculinity and technology has been, as Judy Wajcman (2004) puts it, "routinely overlooked in the field of men's studies" (p. 116). Mirroring this lack of attention to technology in masculinity studies, questions of gender and masculinity have traditionally not taken centre stage in the field of science and technology studies (STS) (Wajcman, 2010). Even at the intersection between these fields, within feminist scholarship on technology and in the subfield sometimes referred to as gender and technology research, questions of masculinity and technology have traditionally not been focused on explicitly. Often transcending but still emanating out of a concern for women's underrepresentation in science and technology, much gender and technology research has instead been "exclusion-focused" (Corneliussen, 2012, p. 210) and preoccupied with the problematic/non-existent link between women and technology (Faulkner, 2001; Sørensen, Faulkner & Rommes, 2011).

Questions of masculinity and technology are, however, not unchartered terrain. Since the early 1980s there has been a strand of initially mostly sociological research focused explicitly on masculinity and technology. This chapter begins by mapping these early developments. It then introduces the conceptual landscape that structures the field and illustrates theoretical points using empirical examples that also work to demonstrate how masculinity and technology research is relevant to masculinity studies in general. With the same ambition, a discussion of theoretical and methodological challenges follows. The chapter then concludes by pointing out some promising ways forward for this strand of research.

Intersecting genealogies

Examining the intersection of gender and technology is a highly cross-disciplinary endeavour. Consequently, mapping any singular starting point for research on masculinity and technology is problematic. First, there are at least two genealogies to consider: masculinity studies that focus on technology; and STS research that highlights masculinity. Not surprisingly, the first strand of research adheres mainly to the trajectory of gender and masculinity research, while the second strand follows and borrows from developments in STS. Second, substantial overlaps with a number of other research areas – such as new media studies, history of technology, cultural studies, anthropology, psychology and education – further complicate any notion of singular origin.

Recognizing that the field's genealogy is complex should not, however, hinder us from acknowledging that a particularly important early influence was that of sociological research on labour relations and technological change (cf. Lagesen, 2015). Here we find a whole range of studies describing how men have been able to defend privileged positions in a patriarchal capitalist workplace by monopolizing the use of certain technologies (e.g., Horowitz, 2001; Rothschild, 1983). Classical studies include Cynthia Cockburn's *Machinery of Dominance* from 1985. As the title reveals, dominance is a strong theme, and this is symptomatic of early analyses in the field, often highlighting a certain homology between men's domination of women and technology as a way of dominating and controlling nature.

Reflecting on these early studies, Wajcman (2000) notes that many of them suffered from technological determinism (which would later be challenged) and conceived of technology as a given, while examining the effects of its introduction in the workplace on men and women. Nevertheless, this research was able to open up Marxist critique of labour relations and technological change to gender analysis. As Wajcman recalls:

> Time and time again, gender was shown to be an important factor in shaping the organization of work that resulted from technological change. In sum, we argued that the relations of production are constructed as much out of gender divisions as out of class divisions.
>
> *(2000, p. 449)*

The focus on women's inferior status at work is also a strong theme in Sally Hacker's *Pleasure, Power and Technology* from 1989. Here Hacker explores the masculinization of technology by tracing its history from military institutions into engineering education and then into management of huge tech corporations as well as by discussing more subjective and psychic investments in men's relationship to technology. Hacker is particularly early in pointing out how passion, pleasure and even erotic dimensions are constitutive of men's relationship to technology.

An important insight from this early research, beyond putting gender on the agenda in research on technology, was that the question is not only how men design and control technology (and by extension women and nature). Rather, it was realized that the very category of technology was imbued with masculinity and that consequently, technology that was under women's control or primarily used by women was excluded from the category of technology. This insight pointed in the direction of thinking about gender and technology as mutually shaping, which later developed into the notion of gender and technology as co-constructed or co-produced (Schyfter, 2009).

While the focus on technologies of production was initially strong, technologies not as central to the workplace have also received attention. Military technology is perhaps the most striking example, where early studies such as Brian Easlea's *Fathering the Unthinkable* (1983) pointed out how representations of gender and sexuality play into the masculinization of weapon technology. While his interpretation that men give birth to new technologies to compensate for a form of "womb-envy" might be more suggestive than analytical, research on masculinity and military technology has repeatedly shown how a strongly gendered and sexualized imaginary operates in this domain (Gray, 1993; Wajcman, 1991).

Moreover, more mundane technologies such as the bicycle (Pinch & Bijker, 1984), the microwave oven (Cockburn & Ormrod, 1993) and the telephone (Martin, 1991), to name but a few, have received attention. Following Haraway's efforts (1991) to destabilize the border between nature/culture and body/machine using notions of the cyborg, attention has also been paid to the prosthetic aspects of technology and how technology reconfigures bodies and corporeal capacities. A case in point is Chris Hable Gray's (2000, 2003) studies of the male cyborg and the reconfiguration of gender that follows when the male body is fused with technology, be it in the military, medicine or popular culture. More concretely, masculinity and technology researchers have also investigated technologies that explicitly intervene with the gendered aspects of the body, such as male contraceptives (Oudshoorn, 2004), IVF technologies (Throsby & Gill, 2004) and Viagra (Loe, 2001). Some of these studies are primarily STS oriented and include gender only as an aspect, while others make gender the central focus. In the latter case, particular technological artefacts are sometimes not as central, and the focus has instead been on technology as "masculine culture" (Wajcman, 2010, p. 145). Such a broadening of scope has enabled researchers to both challenge received notions of technology and produce important knowledge about the technological cultures surrounding, for instance, engineering (Faulkner, 2000) and engineering education (Berner, 1996; Ottemo, 2015; Tonso, 2007), geek communities (Bell, 2013; Kendall, 1999) and cars (Balkmar, 2012; Landström, 2006a).

Conceptual landscape and developments

The idea of the mutual shaping of gender and technology – today often formulated using more post-structuralist language, as the coproduction of gender and technology – has already been alluded to above. This perspective has become paradigmatic in gender and technology studies during the past decades (Faulkner, 2001; Landström, 2007). Its basic idea is that instead of accepting received notions of technology and femininity and masculinity as categories with distinct meanings, these categories should be viewed as mutually constituting each other.

The fact that household technology tends to be relegated to the margins of the category of technology can be understood through such a lens (Cockburn & Ormrod, 1993). Given that this is technology traditionally used by women, its status as technology tends to be invisible, illustrating how gender shapes what we recognize as technology. And vice versa: engaging with technology is in many contexts a way of performing masculinity, so much so that women who do so sometimes qualify as "one of the guys" (Hacker, 1989, p. xvii), exemplifying how notions of technology shape how subjects are gendered.

Theorizing the relationship between masculinity and technology as one of coproduction does not entail suggesting that this relationship is stable, singular and uniform. Paralleling the pluralizing trend in masculinity studies more broadly, masculinity and technology researchers have paid attention to the manifold types of masculinities enacted in relation to technology. Wajcman (1991) was early and broadly sketched two types, differently positioned in the class structure. *The mechanical man* takes pride in his body, in being practical, strong and not afraid of dirt, grease or oil. *The engineer* is also practical, but ultimately is characterized more by his instrumental rationality and calculative approach to everything that gets in his way. He is in many ways a man of modernity. Wajcman argues that the engineer is a particularly fascinating configuration of masculinity, because engineering "cuts across the boundaries between physical and intellectual work and yet maintains strong elements of mind/body dualism" (p. 145). It is also a paradoxical position insofar as it represents a man who takes pride in being rational, controlled and instrumental, while also being very passionate and emotionally committed to technology (Holth, 2014).

With an even greater emphasis on being passionate and all but consumed by his relationship to technology, we have "the geek", also briefly discussed by Wajcman.[1] The geek is a good illustration of the coproduction thesis and the historically shifting and contingent relationship between masculinity and technology. When computers were first introduced, women played an important role, and up until the 1970s or even early 1980s, computing had no univocal gender connotations (Corneliussen, 2012). Given that computer technology lacked many of the material attributes connecting mechanical technology to masculine bodies, it seemed reasonable to suggest that the computer is "sex-blind and colour-blind" (Williams quoted in Griffiths, 1988, p. 145). Such "techno-optimism" was also discernible in relation to internet technology far into the 1990s, where writers such as Sadie Plant argued that this could be considered feminine technology and quoted cyberfeminist slogans suggesting that "The clitoris is a direct line to the matrix" (Plant, 1997, p. 59). Such cyber-utopianism has largely faded today (Wajcman, 2004). Instead, it is obvious that computer technology bears strong masculine connotations in the West and that the industry is heavily dominated by men.

Geek masculinity epitomizes this development and can be considered a configuration of masculinity that is deeply involved in the masculinization of digital technology. Through notions of the geek and the articulation of a form of incorporeal masculinity characterized not by strength or muscles but, rather, by a privileging of the brain and a certain contempt for "the flesh" (Turkle, 1984/2005, p. 201), historically well-established gender dichotomies such as mind/body and transcendence/immanence could be activated in relation to digital technology. Illustrating the notion of coproduction, such representations of masculinity resonated very well with digital technology conceived of as immaterial and as having the capacity to allow users to transcend bodily differences and limitations (Wajcman, 2004).

Given the increasingly central position of such technology in society, it is not surprising that, from a position in the margins, geek masculinity has today been "rehabilitated and partially incorporated into hegemonic masculinity" (Kendall, 1999, p. 261). David Bell (2013) has shown how the visibility of geek masculinity is today growing in both popular culture and society at large, and he has discussed how it is an intriguingly ambivalent configuration of masculinity insofar as it provides "a way of doing masculinities that at once resists, reaffirms, *and* ironizes hegemonic masculinity" (p. 77). Arguably, it poses both a challenge to and coincides (in the form of entrepreneurs like Mark Zuckerberg or Elon Musk) with a form of transnational business masculinity often described as hegemonic today (Connell & Wood, 2005). Research on geek masculinity can hence be considered important to everyone trying to understand contemporary transformations of masculinity, and thus it exemplifies how masculinity and technology research speaks not only to scholars interested in the gender/technology relationship but also to others.

To this triad of technomasculinities investigated in masculinity and technology research could be added a whole range of masculinities, defined more or less in relation to different forms of technology. For the present discussion, however, it may be enough to recognize that there are both stark differences and salient similarities between different configurations of technomasculinities. Stratified by class and race and different in their relationship to the body, one common feature, however, is a passionate relationship to technology. From the motor enthusiast to the passionate programmer or the geeky gamer, articulating passion for technology is a strong signifier. This is an almost universal finding across research on masculinity and technology and has held over time (Griffiths, 1988; Holth & Mellström, 2012).

It is therefore regrettable that this passion has not been more thoroughly theorized and deconstructed in masculinity and technology research. As Linda Vigdor (2011) argues, a gendered notion of passion for technology is often assumed rather than investigated when researchers explain "women's reticence and men's overindulgence" (p. 6) in relation to technology. This shortcoming connects to a broader reluctance to problematize (hetero) sexuality in gender and technology research. As Linda Stepulevage (1997) argued early, studies "tend to be grounded in a perspective of gender that implicitly assumes heterosexuality" (p. 197). Catharina Landström (2007) has levelled a similar critique, suggesting that "the unquestioned assumption that all relationships between women and men are heterosexually structured, and that this precedes and organizes everybody's relationships with technology, produces an analytical problem" (p. 13f).

In line with this critique, however, we have seen more masculinity and technology research that thematizes sexuality. Ulf Mellström (2004) has shown how a form of "technoeroticism" shapes masculine relationships to technology and described how men "attribute their machinery with the qualities they want to see in their partner as a form of a heterosexual relationship" (p. 379). Landström (2006a) has shown similarly how the expression and enactment of "love for cars in present day western culture is also a way to perform heterosexual masculinity" (p. 46), while Pablo Schyfter's (2009) research on motorcycles in Latin America suggests that it is an aspect of the motorcycle's ontology to be "constituted as a submissive partner" and that "romantic tropes employed in characterizing the agent-artefact relationship are constituted in relation to an ideal of heterosexual love" (2009, p. 95f; see also Balkmar, 2012; Ottemo, 2015). By shedding new light on the specific logics and semiotics involved in articulating masculinity with technology, such studies open the door to deconstructing monolithic understandings of masculinity and femininity in relation to technology, as well as deconstructing and rethinking desire and sexuality itself (e.g., Landström, 2007; Vigdor, 2011).

Moving in-between: theoretical and methodological concerns

Although theoretically symmetric in approaching both gender and technology from a constructivist angle, one challenge associated with the coproduction thesis is that, for most empirical researchers, it is hard to deliver the symmetry promised by the concept (Lagesen, 2012). STS researchers usually do a better job theorizing and analyzing technology than gender, and for gender/masculinity researchers the case is often the reversed. A connected problem is that being radically anti-essentialist in relation to both gender and technology, at the same time, ultimately leaves empirical researchers with few reference points to which they can anchor their analysis empirically. If we assume very little about the category of technology and very little about masculinity and femininity, there is a risk that their intersection will appear entirely empty. This may be one reason why many studies either take technology for granted and explore more in depth how particular masculinities and femininities are articulated in a given technological context – or, vice versa, accept received notions of "men" and "women" as given and focus unidirectionally on how gender shapes technology (Landström, 2007; Lohan, 2000).

This problem with the coproduction thesis was highlighted by Keith Grint and Steve Woolgar (1995) in an early critique of constructivist gender and technology research. They suggest that gender and technology researchers are not radical enough in their constructivism and that a lingering essentialism underpins many analyses. By virtue of some mechanism, not attended to empirically, one assumes, rather than shows, how the gender of a designer is built into the technological artefact being designed. Grint and Woolgar argue that this demonstrates a "failure of nerve" on the part of feminist technology researchers, suggesting instead that "The gender of a technology does not lie encased in the fabric of the material. It is instead the temporary contingent upshot of ongoing interpretation by designers, sellers, and users" (1995, p. 305).

This critique resonates well with Maria Lohan's (2000) writings some years later. She discusses how she and other feminist technology researchers are unwilling to accept the prescription of STS to "avoid all *a priori* assumptions" and accept that gender "will emerge if relevant" (p. 901) in the analysis. Lohan instead aligns with the view that "gender needs to be operationalized as an analytic category in order to be seen" (2000, p. 901). This does not, however, itself address the problem of black-boxing a subject's gender and positing it as a cause of the gendering of technology. As Landström has shown, it is instead a recurrent problem in masculinity and technology studies that researchers revert to an expressive understanding of gender, treating either the pre-discursive "sex" or inner stable gender identity of subjects as that which qualifies particular practices or technologies as masculine or feminine. Landström writes: "This 'black-boxing' of gender undermines the aim to understand the coproduction of gender and technology. If gender is already there, as a fixed element it can only function as a cause in relation to the socially constructed technology" (2007, p. 10). She underscores this critique by questioning the assumption that "what men do in homosocial contexts is masculine" (Landström, 2006b, p. 108, my translation) and suggests that, with such an approach, research can only teach us what we already know, i.e., that technology is masculine – and do so through a circular explanatory logic positing that the masculine coding of technology is a result of men's greater presence in technology, which is a consequence of its masculine coding. Landström (2007) breaks up this circularity by demonstrating how it draws intelligibility from the heterosexual matrix (as conceived by Judith Butler) and is underpinned by heteronormative assumptions present *both* in the empirical contexts investigated *and* in the conceptual frameworks deployed in such investigations. Further, in a more methodological vein, she suggests that an analyst working with, for example, interviews could stay "on the surface" (2007, p. 19) and concentrate on how gender is performed in the interview situation rather than probe for "deeper" meanings. In such a move she draws on an ethnomethodological push in STS research, acknowledging that it is an approach that "in itself points to description rather than critique" (2007, p. 17).

Sharing many of Landström's concerns, Monica Obreja (2012) takes quite the opposite stance in addressing these problems. Instead of assuming less and less about gender and technology, she turns to sexual difference theory and philosophical discourse to critique masculinist technology and find ground to think technology differently. She questions "a prosaic that characterizes as commonsensically masculine any field predominated by men [...] voiding gender of any content other than whatever certain sexed bodies do" (2012, pp. 194f). She insists instead that the relationship between masculinity and technology is *not* arbitrary and merely the result of historical association but, rather, a necessary consequence of more fundamental ontological divisions run through by sexual difference. She argues for an understanding of technology not as artefacts but as a mode of thinking, and she uses readings of Luce Irigaray and Martin Heidegger to explicate how this thinking is masculine in its forgetfulness of matter and the maternal as well as in its hunger for transcendence, control, dominance and instrumental use of nature.

Adopting something of a middle ground by refusing to empty gender and technology of any content but still avoiding essentializing and universalizing assumptions, Mellström (2009) advocates paying increased attention to the "cultural embeddeness" (p. 886) of gender and technology relations. Whether and how masculinity and technology are coproduced then becomes a contextual empirical question. He demonstrates the fruitfulness of this approach by focusing on the case of computer technology in Malaysia, illustrating a context where computing is considered a perfectly appropriate domain for women (see also Lagesen, 2008). To further exemplify, research by Namrata Gupta (2015) shows how a myriad of contextual factors relating to class, caste, patriarchy, family and labour relations shape gender/technology relations in India. The mind/body split, often taken as an aspect explaining masculine connotations of science and (digital) technology in the West, here appears to have more pluralizing effects. As Gupta argues, "jobs associated with computers are considered 'safe' for women, as they are office-based and require only mental and not physical strength" (pp. 666f). While not denying that there are also similarities with previously found patterns in the West, Gupta thus "questions the application of universal assumptions based on Western examples to countries in the east" and argues that "the economic and socio-cultural context has a substantial role in defining the relationship between technology and masculinity" (p. 661). This increased attention to the cultural embeddedness of gender/technology relations thus enables us to push beyond a privileging of Western assumptions when theorizing gender and technology. We can understand it as an approach informed by postcolonial critique and as a way of nuancing and making more complex our understanding of how masculinity and technology are or are not connected.

Conclusion and a look to the future

As has hopefully become clear from the above, research on masculinity and technology is both empirically diverse and a field that is struggling with theoretical and methodological challenges it shares with much of masculinity research. Notwithstanding its empirical diversity, however, there are relatively few studies from the Global South. A closer engagement with postcolonial research and an increased emphasis on technology's (post)colonial (and not only masculinist) logics would seem to be warranted. This could contribute to studies that deepen analysis of the complex enmeshment of gender, race, class and other intersectionalities with technology.

On a similar note, but related to the field of masculinity studies more broadly, Chris Beasley (2012) has argued that masculinity research would have a great deal to gain by engaging more closely with the developments in feminist theory, and this could be said of masculinity and technology research as well. Given that technology, much like gender, occupies a contested position right on the border between the material and the symbolic, the natural and the human-made, nature and culture, it could prove valuable to integrate more thoroughly the conceptual developments following the post-human turn in social theory broadly, and in feminist new materialist theory particularly. One challenge in this regard, for a field that understands itself as being concerned with masculinity and technology, is that the post-humanist push in new materialist approaches also de-centres gender as a primary interest. To some degree, this also challenges the viability of the concept of masculinity itself. Combining this "external" push with ongoing attempts to rearticulate masculinity studies from within by rethinking masculinity in less humanistic terms (Gottzén, 2011) and questioning (over)reliance on the concept of masculinity itself (Haywood, Johansson, Hammarén, Herz & Ottemo, 2017) could, however, provide fertile ground for reinvigorating masculinity and technology research and pushing the field's theoretical base forward.

Such a development could also benefit the entire field of masculinity studies. Masculinity and technology research has a long tradition of empirically investigating technology and materiality in relation to gender and corporeality. Through its roots in STS, it is also well acquainted with some of the methodological and theoretical thinking that animates current discussions in feminist (new materialist) theory. Thus, masculinity and technology research is well positioned, both empirically and theoretically, to enable an intensified dialogue between feminist theory and masculinity research.

Note

1 While under renegotiation today, the term traditionally signifies "mainly white, middle-class heterosexual (but desexualized) males, lacking in social and interpersonal skills and obsessed with arcane and specialist knowledges and skills" (Bell, 2013, p. 78; see also Gansmo, Lagesen & Sørensen, 2003).

References

Balkmar, D. (2012). *On men and cars: An ethnographic study of gendered, risky and dangerous relations* (Doctoral dissertation). Linköping University, Linköping.

Beasley, C. (2012). Problematizing contemporary men/masculinities theorizing: The contribution of Raewyn Connell and conceptual-terminological tensions today. *The British Journal of Sociology, 63*(4), 747–765.

Bell, D. (2013). Geek myths: Technologies, masculinities, globalizations. In J. Hearn, M. Blagojević & K. Harrison (Eds.), *Rethinking transnational men: Beyond, between and within nations* (76–90). New York: Routledge.

Berner, B. (1996). *Sakernas tillstånd: Kön, klass, teknisk expertis*. Stockholm: Carlsson.

Cockburn, C. (1985). *Machinery of dominance*. London: Pluto.

Cockburn, C., & Ormrod, S. (1993). *Gender and technology in the making*. London: Sage.

Connell, R. W., & Wood, J. (2005). Globalization and business masculinities. *Men and Masculinities*, 7(4), 347–364.

Corneliussen, H. G. (2012). *Gender-technology relations: Exploring stability and change*. Basingstoke: Palgrave Macmillan.

Dolphijn, R., & van der Tuin, I. (2012). *New materialism: Interviews & cartographies*. Ann Arbor, MI: Open Humanities Press.

Easlea, B. (1983). *Fathering the unthinkable*. London: Pluto.

Faulkner, W. (2000). Dualisms, hierarchies and gender in engineering. *Social Studies of Science, 30*(5), 759–792.

Faulkner, W. (2001). The technology question in feminism: A view from feminist technology studies. *Women's Studies International Forum, 24*(1), 79–95.

Gansmo, H. J., Lagesen, V. A., & Sørensen, K. H. (2003). Out of the boy's room? A critical analysis of the understanding of gender and ICT in Norway. *NORA: Nordic Journal of Women's Studies, 11*(3), 130–139.

Gottzén, L. (2011). Metaphors of masculinity: Hierarchies and assemblages. In A. Biricik & J. Hearn (Eds.), *GEXcel work in progress report volume XV, theme 9: Gendered sexualed transnationalisations, deconstructing the dominant: Transforming men, 'centres' and knowledge/policy/practice* (229–239). Linköping: GEXcel.

Gray, C. H. (1993). The culture of war cyborgs: Technoscience, gender, and postmodern war. *Research in Philosophy and Technology, 13*, 141–163.
Gray, C. H. (2000). MAN PLUS: Enhanced cyborgs and the construction of the future masculine. *Science as Culture, 9*(3), 277–299.
Gray, C. H. (2003). Posthuman soldiers in postmodern war. *Body & Society, 9*(4), 215–226.
Griffiths, M. (1988). Strong feelings about computers. *Women's Studies International Forum, 11*(2), 145–154.
Grint, K., & Woolgar, S. (1995). On some failures of nerve in constructivist and feminist analyses of technology. *Science, Technology, & Human Values, 20*(3), 286–310.
Gupta, N. (2015). Rethinking the relationship between gender and technology: A study of the Indian example. *Work, Employment and Society, 29*(4), 661–672.
Hacker, S. (1989). *Pleasure, power and technology: Some tales of gender, engineering, and the cooperative workplace.* Boston, MA: Unwin Hyman.
Haraway, D. (1991). A cyborg manifesto: Science, technology, and socialist-feminism in the late twentieth century. In D. Haraway (Ed.), *Simians, cyborgs and women: The reinvention of nature* (149–181). New York: Routledge.
Haywood, C., Johansson, T., Hammarén, N., Herz, M., & Ottemo, A. (2017). *The conundrum of masculinity: Hegemony, homosociality, homophobia and heteronormativity.* New York: Routledge.
Holth, L. (2014). Passionate men and rational women: gender contradictions in engineering. *NORMA: International Journal for Masculinity Studies, 9*(2), 97–110.
Holth, L., & Mellström, U. (2012). Revisiting engineering, masculinity and technology studies: Old structures with new openings. *International Journal of Gender, Science and Technology, 3*(2), 313–329.
Horowitz, R. (Ed.). (2001). *Boys and their toys? Masculinity, class, and technology in America.* New York: Routledge.
Kendall, L. (1999). Nerd nation: Images of nerds in US popular culture. *International Journal of Cultural Studies, 2*(2), 260–283.
Lagesen, V. A. (2008). A cyberfeminist utopia: Perceptions of gender and computer science among Malaysian women computer science students. *Science, Technology & Human Values, 33*(1), 5–27.
Lagesen, V. A. (2012). Reassembling gender: Actor-network theory (ANT) and the making of the technology in gender. *Social Studies of Science, 42*(3), 442–448.
Lagesen, V. A. (2015). Gender and technology: From exclusion to inclusion? In J. D. Wright *International encyclopedia of the social & behavioral sciences* (2nd ed., Vol. 9, 723–728). Amsterdam: Elsevier.
Landström, C. (2006a). A gendered economy of pleasure: Representations of cars and humans in motoring magazines. *Science Studies, 19*(2), 31–53.
Landström, C. (2006b). Rhizomatiska reflektioner om kön och teknik. In K. Sandell & D. Mulinari (Eds.), *Feministiska interventioner: Berättelser om och från en annan värld* (94–127). Stockholm: Atlas akademi.
Landström, C. (2007). Queering feminist technology studies. *Feminist Theory, 8*(1), 7–26.
Latour, B. (1991). Technology is society made durable. In J. Law (Ed.), *A sociology of monsters: Essays on power, technology, and domination* (103–131). London: Routledge.
Loe, M. (2001). Fixing broken masculinity: Viagra as a technology for the production of gender and sexuality. *Sexuality and Culture, 5*(3), 97–125.
Lohan, M. (2000). Constructive tensions in feminist technology studies. *Social Studies of Science, 30*(6), 895–916.
Martin, M. (1991). *"Hello, central?" Gender, technology, and culture in the formation of telephone systems.* Montreal: McGill-Queen's University Press.
Mellström, U. (2003). *Masculinity, power and technology: A Malaysian ethnography.* Aldershot: Ashgate.
Mellström, U. (2004). Machines and masculine subjectivity: technology as an integral part of men's life experiences. *Men and Masculinities, 6*(4), 368–382.
Mellström, U. (2009). The intersection of gender, race and cultural boundaries, or why is computer science in Malaysia dominated by women? *Social Studies of Science, 39*(6), 885–907.
Obreja, M. (2012). *Technology and sexual difference* (Doctoral dissertation) Linköping University, Linköping.
Ottemo, A. (2015). *Kön, kropp, begär och teknik: Passion och instrumentalitet på två tekniska högskoleprogram* [Gender, body, desire, and technology: Passion and instrumentality in two technical university programmes] (Doctoral dissertation). University of Gothenburg, Gothenburg.
Oudshoorn, N. (2004). "Astronauts in the sperm world": The renegotiation of masculine identities in discourses on male contraceptives. *Men and Masculinities, 6*(4), 349–367.

Pinch, T. J., & Bijker, W. E. (1984). The social construction of facts and artifacts: Or how the sociology of science and the sociology of technology might benefit each other. *Social Studies of Science, 14*(3), 399–441.

Plant, S. (1997). *Zeros + ones*. London: Fourth Estate.

Rothschild, J. (Ed.). (1983). *Machina ex dea: Feminist perspectives on technology*. New York: Pergamon.

Schyfter, P. (2009). *Entangled ontologies: A sociophilosophical analysis of technological artefacts, subjects, and bodies* (Doctoral dissertation). University of Edinburgh, Edinburgh.

Sørensen, K. H., Faulkner, W., & Rommes, E. (Eds.). (2011). *Technologies of inclusion: Gender in the information society*. Trondheim: Tapir Academic Press.

Stepulevage, L. (1997). Sexuality and computing: Transparent relations. In G. Griffin & S. Andermahr (Eds.), *Straight studies modified: Lesbian interventions in the academy* (197–211). London: Cassell.

Throsby, K., & Gill, R. (2004). "It's different for men": Masculinity and IVF. *Men and Masculinities, 6*(4), 330–348.

Tonso, K. L. (2007). *On the outskirts of engineering: Learning identity, gender, and power via engineering practice*. Rotterdam: Sense Publishers.

Turkle, S. (1984/2005). *The second self: Computers and the human spirit*. Cambridge, MA: MIT Press.

Vigdor, L. (2011). A techno-passion that is not one: Rethinking marginality, exclusion, and difference. *International Journal of Gender, Science and Technology, 3*(1), 4–32.

Wajcman, J. (1991). *Feminism confronts technology*. Cambridge: Polity Press.

Wajcman, J. (2000). Reflections on gender and technology studies: In what state is the art? *Social Studies of Science, 30*(3), 447–464.

Wajcman, J. (2004). *TechnoFeminism*. Cambridge: Polity Press.

Wajcman, J. (2010). Feminist theories of technology. *Cambridge Journal of Economics, 34*(1), 143–152.

34

Men on the move

Masculinities, (auto)mobility and car cultures

Dag Balkmar

Introduction

Feminist scholarship has long argued that mobility is gendered, that women and men are not equally able or likely to move on equal terms (Clarsen, 2014, pp. 96–97). Differences related to gender, race, sexuality, class, body, disability and nationality all matter "in determining who moves, how, at what speed, and with what degree of autonomy" (Oswin, 2014, p. 85). Mobility is gendered and strongly intertwined with gendered norms. As an example, it is only recently that Saudi Arabia has agreed to let women drive, and thereby also put an end to a longstanding policy that symbolized the oppression of women and control over their mobility in the country (Hubbard, 2017). In contrast, the relationship between men, masculinity and cars is often taken for granted as a more or less "natural" association (Balkmar, 2012). As Clarsen (2014) notes, compared to women, men have more often been associated and engaged with technologies of movement and their infrastructures, including, as will be the focus of this chapter, automobility and the automobile.

While the field of men and masculinities has studied many areas related to movement – including workplace mobilities, transnational masculinities, men's movements and migration – issues related to masculinities, automobility and transport have only recently begun to attract scholarly attention (Balkmar, 2012; Dahl, Henriksson & Levin, 2012; Hultman, 2013; Joelsson, 2013; Mellström, 2003; Redshaw, 2008; Walker, Butland & Connell, 2000). For example, these studies explore constructions of careless masculinities (Joelsson, 2013), combustion and hydraulic masculinities (Redshaw, 2008), ecomodern masculinity (Hultman, 2013) and modifier masculinity (Balkmar, 2012). These studies show how car cultures, car driving and identity formation through motor vehicles can be related to constructions of masculinity in many different ways, all intertwined with issues of embodiment, movement, space, risk-taking, power and control (Uteng & Cresswell, 2008). These relationships are also of central concern for environmental sustainability. However, even though transport and mobility issues stand at the very core of ecological damage and environmental concerns, these issues have only to a limited extent been part of critical debates in studies on men and masculinities (for exceptions see Balkmar & Hearn, 2018; Dahl, Henriksson & Levin, 2012; Hultman, 2013; Hultman & Pulé, 2018).

In this chapter, I argue that masculinity studies has much to contribute to mobility and transport issues. Against this background, it seems urgent to consider how the need for more sustainable mobilities also includes critical considerations of the many ways in which transport technologies are intertwined with the (re)production and contestation of masculinities and men's mobility practices. The chapter begins with a brief note on gendered mobilities and transport more generally, then moves on to discuss relationships between men, masculinity and automobility. This will include just a few examples of car cultures in the Global South; most examples will be from the Global North, where the majority of research has been conducted. This is followed by a section that focuses on driving, emotions and risk-taking. The chapter ends with a discussion on the implications of a transport future populated with increasingly automated vehicles, including what the implications for men and masculinities may be.

Brief notes on gendered mobilities and transport

Gender and mobility are inseparable concepts (Hanson, 2010). Feminist geographers have, for instance, developed the potential of gender, feminism and movement, including how mobilities and gender relate in intersectional ways (Hanson, 2010; Uteng & Cresswell, 2008). This feminist interest in gendered mobilities has not only documented intersections between sexual difference and mobility at different scales and across different modalities but has also paved the way for the transdisciplinary field of mobilities research (Clarsen, 2014).

The field of mobilities research includes "the spatial mobilities of humans, non-humans and objects; the circulation of information, images and capital", as well as critical considerations of the "affective and psycho-social implications of such mobility" (Sheller, 2014a, pp. 46–47). This includes considering not only the software systems, vehicles and infrastructures that enable or disable communication and travel (Sheller, 2014a) but also "gendered, racialized, and differently embodied (im)mobilities of inequality" (Büscher, Sheller & Tyfield, 2016, p. 485). As Mimi Sheller (2014a, p. 47) argues, mobility research as a field brings together dimensions such as the

> "social" concerns of sociology (inequality, power, hierarchies) with the "spatial" concerns of geography (territory, borders, scale) and the "cultural" concerns of anthropology and media studies (discourses, representations, schemas), while inflecting each with a relational ontology of the co-constitution of subjects, spaces and meanings.

Hence, mobility is not to be reduced to a matter of transport from A to B, but it provides grounds for further studying how power relationships shape mobility and immobility for different bodies, subjects and spatio-temporal forms (Sheller, 2014a, 2014b). One approach is to consider how certain dominant mobilities produce the subordination of other forms of mobility, which may limit the mobility of certain groupings or categories of people. In car-dominated societies, drivers tend to be positioned as "insiders" while pedestrians, cyclists and non-car drivers remain on the "outside" of such a system (McCarthy, 2011). Previous studies on daily travel patterns in the EU, the USA, Canada and Australia show that men's mobility is more car-dependent than women's; and men travel further than women (Transgen, 2007). These differences are intertwined with inequalities in urban infrastructure and gendered inequalities in the household and labour market, with the implication that "men and women make different uses of a shared system of transport" (Transgen, 2007, p. 5), including the related energy and oil consumption.

In the context of oil and energy consumption, geopolitical location is an important factor to consider. The world's top three oil producers in 2016 were Russia, Saudi Arabia and the USA. The USA is by far the largest user of oil in the world, in 2016 consuming 20% of the world total (USEIA, 2019). More specifically, "(b)y the mid-2000s, the US and Canada, with 5% of the global population, accounted for 27% of oil consumption, and Europe, with around 10% of the world's population, accounted for 24%" (Hearn, 2015, p. 156). These figures should be compared with the oil consumption of countries in the Global South. Africa, for example, "[...] has about 15% of the world's population, [but] it consumes only 3% of global commercial energy. The paradox is that Africa's share in global energy production is about 12%, and trending upwards" (African Development Bank, 2009, p. xxvi).

There are also great variations by gender and class to consider, particularly in relation to transport. Men expend more energy on transport than women in both the lowest income groups (160% more energy than women) and the highest income category (48% more energy than women) (Schiebinger, 2013, drawing on Räty & Carlsson-Kanyama, 2009). Schiebinger (2013) notes that, even though these differences decrease as income increases, they are still there. Hence oil and energy consumption related to transport must be considered in the context of geopolitical variations, including variations related to gender and class (Balkmar & Hearn, 2018). To a great extent, this is a matter of people using private cars. The following section takes a closer look at studies on car cultures more particularly, including their links to masculinity and masculine identity.

Men, masculinities and car cultures

Studies of car cultures have received attention within cultural studies, criminology, sociology, history, anthropology, geography, urban studies and gender studies (Corbett, 2003; Lumsden, 2009, 2010; Miller, 2001; Redshaw, 2008). Many aspects of automobility have been studied, including how mobilities are experienced (Balkmar & Joelsson, 2010, 2012; Dant, 2004; Lupton, 1999; Thrift, 2004), gendered (Jain, 2005; Scharff, 1991), classed (Seiler, 2008) and racialized (Gilroy, 2001; Nicholson, 2016). Below I focus on some of the ways in which automobility and car cultures are intertwined with constructions of men and masculinities, including the many layers of gendered identity, status and risk-taking.

In studies that explicitly discuss men's associations with the car, age and gender stand out; namely, young men's consumption of the car. This includes but is not limited to their performative car-related practices, such as when the car is used as a medium for self-presentation and communication (Hatton, 2007), as a subcultural expression (Carrabine & Longhurst, 2002) or when the focus is on social problems of youth, driving and risk-taking with motor vehicles (Collin-Lange, 2013; Dawes, 2002; Falconer & Kingham, 2007; Joelsson, 2013; Lumsden, 2009, 2010, 2013, 2015; O'Connor & Kelly, 2006; O'Dell, 2001; Redshaw, 2008; Vaaranen, 2004; Walker, Butland & Connell, 2000).

Many car cultures have existed in parallel with the more mainstream motoring culture (Lumsden, 2015). A common feature of these car cultures is their participants' engagement in the practice of car modification (Graham & White, 2007; Lumsden, 2015). In studies from Australia, Canada, Finland, Iceland, New Zealand, Norway, Sweden, the USA and the UK, links between primarily (rural) working-class masculinity and participation in car culture via activities such as "racer" culture, car modification and cruising have been studied (Balkmar, 2012; Bengry-Howell & Griffin, 2007; Best, 2006; Bjurström, 1995; Collin-Lange, 2013; Joelsson, 2013; Redshaw, 2008). Walker, Butland and Connell (2000, p. 159) note that

> Motor vehicles and their use offer boys and youth engaged in the construction of masculinity a number of experiences that many of them very much want: a sense of technical mastery, a realm that is symbolically masculine, a forum for friendship and peer recognition, thrills, laughter, and a certain amount of danger.

According to this quote, and many other studies on the topic, dangerous driving can be perceived as a quest for masculine prowess, status and power (Graham & White, 2007). Amy Best's (2006) ethnographic study of the car scene in San Jose, California, USA, focuses on, among other aspects, the meaning that young Chicanos invest in cruising, including intersections between race, risk and masculinity in both illegal and organized car-racing scenes. Anne-Sofie Lægran (2003, p. 142) notes, on the role of cars in young Norwegian men's lives, the centrality of speed for the driving experience and the ability to display "control in commanding authority over one's fate." From Finland, Heli Vaaranen's (2004) ethnographic account of the street-racing scene in Helsinki provides insights into how risk-taking intersects with class-based inequalities and emotions. The so-called "boy racer" scene in the UK has been examined in several studies, mainly in relation to car modification, risk-taking and moral fears (Bengry-Howell & Griffin, 2007; Hatton, 2007; Lumsden, 2009, 2010, 2013, 2015). Risk-taking with motor vehicles is also a central theme in Tanja Joelsson's (2013) study on young Volvo greasers in a Swedish peri-urban community. Her study considers risk-taking as a spatial phenomenon, intertwined with how personhood and social relationships matter through the risky activities engaged in by the young male greasers.

What connects these studies is how cars, car modification and various forms of risk-taking are understood as a way for young men to use cars to perform gender and class identity in specific sociocultural contexts. They reflect specific class relationships to cars and driving, which are traditionally associated with and manifested as rural working-class masculinity (Bjurström, 1995; Joelsson, 2013). Conceptions of rural areas stand out when car-related youth cultures are discussed, for example in Lægran's (2007) study of the "råners" in Norway or the greasers in Joelsson's study, both associated with (stagnating) rural areas. Risk-taking with cars and car modification becomes a way for young working-class men to display their masculinity despite being unemployed or stuck in low-paid jobs (Hatton, 2007). Along this way of reasoning, the modified car can be used to outpace men driving more expensive brands and, by doing so, can allow young men to reformulate working-class masculinity as more "authentic" compared to middle- and upper-class masculinities (Vaaranen, 2004).

Apart from deepening our knowledge about how risk-taking intersects with constructions of men and masculinities, these studies add perspectives that diversify the image of young(er) men, who tend in traffic safety discourse to be constructed as the (only) problematic category of drivers (Graham & White, 2007). As Redshaw (2008, p. 121) argues, speed and speeding need to be viewed as a much broader societal problem, related to "a broader culture in which increased speed has clearly been regarded as a positive gain and expectations of continual increases in speed are prevalent, particularly amongst motor vehicle manufacturers." In fact, the representation and promotion of car culture more generally – in sports, popular culture and advertisements – associate car culture with freedom, excitement and adrenaline, with very few restrictions (Redshaw, 2007). While the links between younger men, masculinity and various forms of risks and risk-taking have received attention in many different cultural contexts (Joelsson, 2013; Redshaw, 2008; Vaaranen, 2004), the practices of "unproblematic young drivers" remain much less thoroughly studied (Collin-Lange, 2013, p. 189).

In many respects, in both popular culture and historical accounts, the automobile has been associated with a particular configuration of masculinity, usually straight, white male drivers. Against this background, there is an absence of studies focusing on the relationship between automobility and the gay driver, a theme that has been addressed in Chris Lezotte's (2015) study on Lambda Car Club International. This study provides alternative constructions of masculinity, examining gay car culture and the role of cars in creating community among gay drivers. Other studies take up the intersections of (auto)mobility and race in particular car cultures. For example, race is discussed in the interpretation of "African-American auto-consumerism" (Gilroy, 2001, p. 83) and "the racialization of urban space in the auto age" (Hutchinson, 2003, p. 79), including a focus on how African-Americans from the 1930s to the 1960s used specific guide books to help them avoid dangerous towns and racist establishments in the USA (Pesses, 2017; Seiler, 2008). These studies illustrate how discrimination contributes to immobilizing racialized subjects, captured in the phrase "Driving While Black" (DWB). DWB originates from African-American communities and describes the risks associated with being a black driver and "being racially profiled by [the] police" (Nicholson, 2016, p. 553). Such discrimination is also gendered, as it is primarily black male drivers who are stopped, questioned, searched and immobilized by the police (Nicholson, 2016).

Driving, emotions and risk-taking

Over the history of automobility, amid the wide repertoire of emotions connected with car use, passion and eroticism have been fundamental elements in car cultures, especially with regards to men, masculinities, power and risk-taking (Balkmar & Joelsson, 2012; Redshaw, 2008; Sheller, 2004). For example, motor vehicles extend users' range of movement in ways that have been described as a symbiotic fusion of man and machine, where corporeal experiences of embodied control and power are continuously consolidated (Lohan & Faulkner, 2004; Lupton, 1999). This also includes its emotional dimensions. In a number of studies set in the Global South, more particularly among male motor mechanics in the Chinese diaspora, Mellström (2003, 2004) considers how emotions, intimacy and the love of technology and machines constitute central dimensions in many men's lives. From a cross-cultural perspective, drawing upon anthropological work in Malaysia and Sweden, he suggests that the pleasure found in handling, controlling and being with machines is central to the reproduction of gender orders, including hegemonic forms of masculinity. In her study of the representation of cars and humans in motoring magazines, Landström (2006, p. 26) notes that men and women are constructed as opposites: men's relationships with cars are "premised on passion and pleasure while women are figured as rational and unable to attach emotionally to cars" (i.e., as inadequate). This research exemplifies how the car is culturally and symbolically produced as masculine technology even though both men and women drive, care for and "love" cars across the world (Landström, 2006, p. 26). Together, these studies suggest that a more in-depth understanding of mobile culture's attractiveness and persistence needs to encompass the intense passions and embodied experiences associated with how men (and women) engage with motor vehicles in different ways and the potential risky and damaging effects that may follow from such practices.

Risk-taking remain a typically "male" problem, "done" through everyday practices related to transport and mobility (Redshaw, 2008). The World Health Organization (WHO) argues that road-traffic injuries need to be considered a global health problem. Each year there are 1.3 million road traffic deaths worldwide, and three out of four of these are among men:

> From a young age, males are more likely to be involved in road traffic crashes than females. About three quarters (73%) of all road traffic deaths occur among young males under the age of 25 years who are almost 3 times as likely to be killed in a road traffic crash as young females.
>
> *(WHO, 2017)*

Identified risk factors are speeding, driving under the influence of alcohol and non-use of seat belts (WHO, 2017). At least partly, these can be seen as material effects of gendered social norms that reproduce an investment of masculinity in risk-taking with motor vehicles (Redshaw, 2008).

So far, studies of automobility have only explored its violent effects and its gendered and emotional dimensions to a limited extent, even less so with an explicit focus on men and masculinities (Balkmar & Joelsson, 2010; Joelsson, 2013). However, several studies identify hybridized embodiment between human bodies and car bodies as of particular importance for understanding risk-taking and aggression in traffic (Katz, 1999; Lupton, 1999; Nixon, 2014). Studies in psychology and criminology suggest that aggressive driving needs to be analyzed as a gendered problem with regards to men's stronger sense of entitlement (Shreer, 2002) and men's inclination to status defence (Harding, Morgan, Indermaur, Ferrante & Blagg, 1998).

Towards safer and more sustainable transport futures?

The critical consideration of how automobility is gendered and reproduced is one thing; another important aspect is to consider how it is changing. This is a crucial dimension today, when safer and more energy-efficient forms of mobility are needed. Some studies illustrate how, in some parts of the world, car ownership is changing. In her study on Swedish-born men's views on sustainable travel, Dahl notes that especially younger generations living in urban areas in Sweden emphasize the need for car-sharing for the sake of the environment and that some men adopted what she calls "'new' masculine car-free subject positions" (Dahl, 2014, p. 351).

While the automobile and automobility changed the world during the 20th century, so-called self-driving cars and related automations are imagined to be the next major revolution in transportation technology. In the not-too-distant future, networked technologies may take away drivers' control over their vehicles and reassign it to the car designers, engineers and computers (Laurier & Dant, 2012). Based on how studies imagine this future transport system, self-driving cars are often constructed as being a way to solve many of the problems associated with the current automobility system, such as congestion, pollution and road-traffic crashes (Balkmar & Mellström, 2018). With the advent of fully autonomous cars, programmed to follow traffic regulations, many of the core values related to how masculinity, risk, power and control are performed by single car users are at stake as cars become more autonomous (Berscheid, 2016; Laurier & Dant, 2012). Based on Berscheid's (2016) work on masculinity in the German media discourse on automated driving, autonomous cars might put masculinity under threat, especially when we consider that self-determination and driving passion are key aspects of car-driving as a masculine practice. With such a redistribution of agency, self-driving vehicles may profoundly shift men's relationships with cars, with implications not only for individual drivers' "loss" of driving pleasure and control but also, and more importantly, with great implications for future employment and the potential loss of skilled jobs in the transport business (Balkmar & Mellström, 2018).

In conclusion, automated transport futures constitute one field of research where masculinity studies have much to offer in analyzing whether – and, if so, how – autonomous vehicles may challenge the foundations of current and future automobility systems, including their associations with and formations around masculinity, speed, pleasure, embodiment and sustainability. Critical studies of men and masculinities can provide insights for further understanding the importance of considering technology's complex role in (re-)shaping gender, including its embodiments, social relations, cultural formations and risks.

References

African Development Bank. (2009). *Oil and gas in Africa.* Oxford: Oxford University Press.

Balkmar, D. (2012). *On men and cars: An ethnographic study of gendered, risky and dangerous relations* (Doctoral dissertation). Linköping: Linköping University.

Balkmar, D., & Hearn, J. (2018). Men, automobility, movements, and the environment: Imagining (un) sustainable, automated transport futures. In J. Hearn, E. Vasquez del Aguila, & M. Blagojević (Eds.), *Unsustainable institutions of men: Transnational dispersed centres, gender power, contradictions* (pp. 227–254). New York: Routledge.

Balkmar, D., & Joelsson, T. (2010). Den bioniske mannen på autoerotiska äventyr – Mäns risktagande i trafikrummet [The bionic man on autoerotic adventures: Men's risk-taking in traffic space]. *NORMA: Nordic Journal for Masculinity Studies*, *5*(1), 27–44.

Balkmar, D., & Joelsson, T. (2012). Feeling the speed: The social and emotional investments in dangerous road practices. In M. Jansdotter Samuelsson, C. Krekula, & M. Åberg (Eds.), *Gender and change* (pp. 37–52). Karlstad: Karlstad University Press.

Balkmar, D., & Mellström, U. (2018). Masculinity and autonomous vehicles: De-gendering or re-segregating the relation between men, masculinity and cars? *Transfers: Interdisciplinary Journal of Mobility Studies*, *8*(1), 44–63.

Bengry-Howell, A., & Griffin, C. (2007). Self-made motormen: The material construction of working-class masculine identities through car modification. *Journal of Youth Studies*, *10*(4), 439–458.

Berscheid, A.-L. (2016, September). Masculinity in danger? The autonomous car as game changer, 1-9. Paper presented at the *Cars on/of culture: Mobility, materiality, representation conference*, Oxford, UK. Retrieved from www.inter-disciplinary.net/critical-issues/wp-content/uploads/2016/08/AnnaLena Berscheid-dpaper-cars1.pdf.

Best, A. L. (2006). *Fast cars, cool rides: The accelerating world of youth and their cars.* New York: New York University Press.

Bjurström, E. (1995). Baby you can drive my car: Bilen och motorcykeln som könskultur. In G. Bolin & K. Lövgren (Eds.), *Om unga män* (pp. 217–239). Lund: Studentlitteratur.

Büscher, M., Sheller, M., & Tyfield, D. (Eds.), (2016). Mobility intersections: Social research, social futures. [special Issue] *Mobilities*, *11*(4), 485–497.

Carrabine, E., & Longhurst, B. (2002). Consuming the car: Anticipation, use and meaning in contemporary youth culture. *Sociological Review*, *50*(2), 181–197.

Clarsen, G. (2014). Feminism and gender. In P. Adey, D. Bissell, K. Hannam, P. Merriman, & M. Sheller (Eds.), *The Routledge handbook of mobilities* (pp. 114–122). New York: Routledge.

Collin-Lange, V. (2013). Socialities in motion: Automobility and car cruising in Iceland. *Mobilities*, *8*(3), 406–423.

Corbett, C. (2003). *Car crime.* Cullompton: Willan.

Dahl, E. (2014). *Om miljöproblemen hänger på mig: Individer förhandlar sitt ansvar för miljön.* (Doctoral dissertation). Linköping: Linköping University.

Dahl, E., Henriksson, M., & Levin, L. (2012). Constructions of masculinities in conversations about public transport. *NORMA: Nordic Journal for Masculinity Studies*, 7(2), 160–181.

Dant, T. (2004). The driver-car. *Theory, Culture and Society*, *21*(4/5), 61–79.

Dawes, G. (2002). Figure eights, spin outs and power slides: Aboriginal and Torres Strait Islander youth and the culture of joyriding. *Journal of Youth Studies*, *5*(2), 195–208.

Falconer, R., & Kingham, S. (2007). Driving people crazy: A geography of boy racers in Christchurch, New Zealand. *New Zealand Geographer*, *6383*, 181–191.

Gilroy, P. (2001). Driving while black. In D. Miller (Ed.), *Car cultures* (pp. 81–104). New York: Berg.

Graham, H., & White, R. (2007). Young people, dangerous driving and car culture. *Youth Studies Australia, 26*(3), 28–35.

Hanson, S. (2010). Gender and mobility: New approaches for informing sustainability. *Gender Place and Culture, 17*(1), 5–23.

Harding, R., Morgan, F., Indermaur, D., Ferrante, A., & Blagg, H. (1998). Road rage and the epidemiology of violence: Something old, something new. *Studies on Crime and Crime Prevention,* 7(2), 221–238.

Hatton, Z. (2007). *The tarmac cowboys: An ethnographic study of the cultural world of boy racers.* (Unpublished doctoral dissertation). University of Plymouth.

Hearn, J. (2015). *Men of the world: Genders, globalizations, transnational times.* London: Sage.

Hubbard, B. (2017, September 26). Saudi Arabia agrees to let women drive. *The New York Times.* www.nytimes.com/2017/09/26/world/middleeast/saudi-arabia-women-drive.html.

Hultman, M. (2013). The making of an environmental hero: A history of ecomodern masculinity, fuel cells and Arnold Schwarzenegger. *Environmental Humanities, 2*(1), 83–103.

Hultman, M. & Pulé, P. (2018). *Ecological masculinities: Theoretical foundations and practical guidance.* London: Routledge.

Hutchinson, S. (2003). *Imagining transit: Race, gender and transportation politics in Los Angeles.* New York: Peter Lang.

Jain, S. (2005). Violent submission: Gendered automobility. *Cultural Critique, 61*(1), 187–214.

Joelsson, T. (2013). *Space and sensibility: Young men's risk-taking with motor vehicles.* (Doctoral dissertation) Linköping: Linköping University.

Katz, J. (1999). *How emotions work.* Chicago, IL: University of Chicago Press.

Lægran, A. S. (2003). Escape vehicles? The Internet and the automobile in a local-global intersection. In N. Oudshoorn & T. Pinch (Eds.), *How users matter: The co-construction of users and technologies* (pp. 81–101). Cambridge, MA: MIT.

Lægran, A. S. (2007). Exploring masculinity, technology, and identity in rural Norway. In R. Panelli, S. Punch & E. Robson (Eds.), *Global perspectives on rural childhood and youth* (pp. 46–57). London: Routledge.

Landström, C. (2006). A gendered economy of pleasure: Representations of cars and humans in motoring magazines. *Science Studies, 19*(2), 31–53.

Laurier, E., & Dant, T. (2012). What else we do while driving: Towards the driverless car. In M. Grieco & J. Urry (Eds.), *Mobilities: New perspectives on transport and society* (pp. 223–244). Farnham: Ashgate.

Lezotte, C. (2015). Out on the highway: Cars, community, and the gay driver. *Culture, Society & Masculinities,* 7(2), 121–139.

Lohan, M., & Faulkner, W. (2004). Masculinities and technologies, some introductory remarks. *Men and Masculinities, 6*(4), 319–329.

Lumsden, K. (2009). "Do we look like boy racers?" The role of the folk devil in contemporary moral panics. *Sociological Research Online, 14*(1), 2.

Lumsden, K. (2010). Gendered performances in a male-dominated subculture: 'Girl racers', car modification and the quest for masculinity. *Sociological Research Online, 15*(3), 6.

Lumsden, K. (2013). *Boy racer culture: Youth, masculinity and deviance.* London: Routledge.

Lumsden, K. (2015). (Re)civilizing the young driver: Technization and emotive automobility. *Mobilities, 10*(1), 36–54.

Lupton, D. (1999). Monsters in metal cocoons: "Road rage" and cyborg bodies. *Body & Society, 5*(1), 57–72.

McCarthy, D. (2011). "I'm a normal person": An examination of how utilitarian cyclists in Charleston South Carolina use an insider/outsider framework to make sense of risks. *Urban Studies, 48*(7), 1439–1455.

Mellström, U. (2003). *Masculinity, power and technology: A Malaysian ethnography.* London: Routledge.

Mellström, U. (2004). Machines and masculine subjectivity: Technology as an integral part of men's life experiences. *Men and Masculinities, 6*(4), 368–382.

Miller, D. (2001). *Car cultures.* Oxford: Berg.

Nicholson, J. A. (2016). Don't shoot! Black mobilities in American gunscapes. *Mobilities, 11*(4), 553–563.

Nixon, D. (2014). Speeding capsules of alienation: Social (dis)connections amongst drivers, cyclists and pedestrians in Vancouver, BC. *Geoforum, 54,* 91–102.

O'Connor, C., & Kelly, K. (2006). Auto theft and youth culture: A nexus of masculinities, femininities and car culture. *Journal of Youth Studies, 9*(3), 247–267.

O'Dell, T. (2001). Raggare and the panic of mobility: Modernity and everyday life in Sweden. In D. Miller (Ed.), *Car cultures* (pp. 105–132). Oxford: Berg.

Oswin, N. (2014). Queer theory. In P. Adey, D. Bissell, K. Hannam, P. Merriman, & M. Sheller (Eds.), *The Routledge handbook of mobilities* (pp. 85–93). New York: Routledge.
Pesses, M. W. (2017). Road less traveled: Race and American automobility. *Mobilities, 12*(5), 677–691.
Räty, R., & Carlsson-Kanyama, A. (2009). *Comparing energy use by gender, age, and income in some European countries*. Stockholm: Totalförsvarets forskningsinstitut.
Redshaw, S. (2007). Articulation of the car: The dominant articulation of racing and rally driving. *Mobilities, 2*(1), 121–141.
Redshaw, S. (2008). *In the company of cars: Driving as a social and cultural practice*. Aldershot: Ashgate.
Scharff, V. (1991). *Taking the wheel: Women and the coming of the motor age*. Albuquerque, NM: University of New Mexico Press.
Schiebinger, L. (2013). Climate change: Analyzing gender, and factors intersecting with gender. Retrieved from http://genderedinnovations.stanford.edu/casestudies/climate.html#tabs-2.
Seiler, C. (2008). *Republic of drivers: A cultural history of automobility in America*. Chicago, IL: University of Chicago Press.
Sheller, M. (2004). Automotive emotions. In M. Featherstone, N. Thrift, & J. Urry (Eds.), *Theory, Culture and Society 21*(4/5), 221–242.
Sheller, M. (2014a). Sociology after the mobilities turn. In K. Hannam, P. Adey, M. Sheller, P. Merriman, & D. Bissell (Eds.), *The Routledge handbook of mobilities* (pp. 45–54). New York: Routledge.
Sheller, M. (2014b). The new mobilities paradigm for a live sociology. *Current Sociology, 62*(6), 789–811.
Shreer, G. (2002). Narcissism and aggression: Is inflated self-esteem related to aggressive driving? *North American Journal of Psychology, 4*(3), 333–342.
Thrift, N. (2004). Driving in the city. *Theory, Culture and Society, 21*(4/5), 41–59.
Transgen. (2007). *Gender mainstreaming European transport research and policies*. Copenhagen: University of Copenhagen.
USEIA (US Energy Information Administration). (2019). What countries are the top producers and consumers of oil? Retrieved from: https://www.eia.gov/tools/faqs/faq.php?id=709&t=6.
Uteng, T. P., & Cresswell, T. (Eds.), (2008). *Gendered mobilities*. Aldershot: Ashgate.
Vaaranen, H. (2004). The emotional experience of class: Interpreting working-class kids' street racing in Helsinki. *Annals of the American Academy of Political and Social Science, 595*(1), 91–107.
Walker, L., Butland, D., & Connell, R. (2000). Boys on the road: Masculinities, car culture, and road safety education. *Journal of Men's Studies, 8*(2), 153–169.
WHO. (2017). Road traffic injuries. Fact sheet, www.who.int/mediacentre/factsheets/fs358/en/.

35

Men, health and medicalization

An overview

Steve Robertson and Tim Shand

Introduction

The concept of medicalization has been present within medical sociology for well over fifty years. Its historical development demonstrates a range of definitions[1] and the contested nature of the relationship of medicalization to technologies, globalization and modernity/post-modernity (Bell & Figert, 2012a; Rosenfield & Faircloth, 2006). Early feminist work soon highlighted links between gender and medicalization, and quickly progressed to extended its work through an emphasis on intersectionality (particularly around social class and ethnicity) and on agentic acts of compliance and resistance to medicalization processes. However, it was not until the early 2000s that work began to scrutinize relationships between men, masculinities and medicalization (Conrad, 2007; Rosenfield & Faircloth, 2006). Such work builds on this earlier feminist-inspired work, which provided an appropriate conceptual framework for critically considering where men and masculinities may fit with medicalization.

This chapter traces the historical roots of medicalization and where gender has been considered. It then provides a critical consideration of men, masculinity and medicalization through specific emphasis on two cases: coronary heart disease; and HIV in Sub-Saharan Africa.

A brief history of gender and medicalization

Early work on medicalization can be traced back to Parsons' (1951) consideration of the medical profession's role in controlling social deviance and Freidson's (1970) subsequent challenge to this view. Rather than accepting Parson's view of medicine as a positive force in maintaining equilibrium within the social system and as being politically neutral, Freidson recognized medicine as a collective force seeking to monopolize the production and control of health knowledge in its pursuit of professional autonomy and dominance (Rosenfield & Faircloth, 2006). Zola (1972) expanded this view, exploring and highlighting how the medical profession redefined social issues (such as childbirth, menopause and alcoholism) as medical problems rather than natural or social concerns.

Within this conceptual framework, deviant behaviour was no longer recognized as a moral or social deficit but became constructed as a diagnosed medical deficit (or illness) amenable only to treatment by professionally licenced (and internally policed) clinical practitioners (Conrad & Schneider, 1980). An important point for Zola (1972) was how medicalization linked with broader cultural shifts (well beyond medical domination) to individualize social problems and look for technical (often medical) solutions. In doing so, interventions beyond the level of the individual, such as addressing social inequalities, become closed off (Riska, 2003).

This work on medicalization, completed in the 1970s, rarely considered issues of gender within the conceptual frameworks developed (Bell & Figert, 2012a; Riska, 2003). This is surprising, given the emphasis on power dynamics, the control of bodies and medical (patriarchal) domination. It is even more surprising when early empirical studies primarily involved boys and men, such as hyperactive children (Conrad, 1975) and alcoholism (Schneider, 1978).

However, during this period, pioneering feminists were exploring the scrutiny of women's bodies by the medical profession, highlighting how natural aspects of women's life – menstruation, pregnancy/childbirth, the menopause/aging – all became cast as issues for medical concern, examination and intervention. Although such work did not directly utilize the concept of medicalization (Rosenfield & Faircloth, 2006), it nevertheless mapped how traditional roles of women as lay healers and birth assistants became superseded by scientific knowledge and interventions led by male physicians (Ehrenreich & English, 1973/2010). In this way, it is linked to notions of medicalization through an emphasis on professional dominance: medicalization could be understood as another process for achieving and maintaining patriarchy.

There was a common view among feminists during this period that women were particular (and deliberate) subjects of medicalization – attested to by high rates of surgery on female anatomy (hysterectomies, mastectomies) and high rates of prescriptions for psychosocial concerns such as anxiety and depression (Riska, 2003). Women were therefore mainly presented as 'victims and unwitting accomplices of a frequently hostile, paternalistic, and contemptuous male-defined medical system …' (Sandelowski, 1981, p. 139).[2]

This view of women as passive victims of a patriarchal medical profession became questioned when Riessman (1983) overtly linked feminist discussions to concepts of medicalization. In a seminal text, she considers how and why women actively participated (with physicians) in the construction of new medical definitions of natural bodily process. Using cases of the medicalization of childbirth and reproductive control, she demonstrates how this collaboration was rooted in class interests – the desire to be free from pain during labour and of unwanted and dangerous pregnancies, amongst 'well-to-do' women (in the 19th and early 20th centuries) generated a 'fit' between their interests and those of the expanding medical profession.[3] As she concludes: 'As women have tried to free themselves from the control that biological processes have had over their lives, they simultaneously strengthened the control of a biomedical view of their experience' (Riessman, 1983, p. 59).

Excellent feminist-inspired work in this same vein – exploring tensions and alliances that form around processes of medicalization and linking them to wider socio-political processes – continues. Neasbitt (2018), for example, examines medicalization with regard to female genital cosmetic surgery and shows how increasing rates of such surgery are situated historically and culturally within practices of neoliberal capitalism, new surgical technologies and increased bodily surveillance.

Such nuanced feminist work not only linked medicalization with gender but also contributed to understanding its links to technology and pharmaceuticalization (Bell & Figert, 2012b) and to patient empowerment and processes of compliance and resistance (Bell & Figert, 2012a). Medicalization has thus become recognized as more complex, as partial and contested with various groups, including the pharmaceutical industry and citizens themselves, being in conflict or alliance with medical claim-makers (Gabe & Monaghan, 2013).

Much of this recent work on medicalization draws on feminist work around intersectionality, neoliberal consumerism and globalization, and this creates fertile terrain for considering the relationships between men, masculinities and medicalization.

Men, masculinities and medicalization

Despite this excellent feminist work linking gender and medicalization, there was a surprising lack of theoretical or empirical work considering the relationships between men, masculinities and medicalization until the 2000s (Conrad, 2007; Rosenfield & Faircloth, 2006). Two main explanations for this have been proffered. First, there is an historical view that men and male (White European) bodies are the prototype, the norm, to which others are compared – supported by studies demonstrating how the male body has been overrepresented within anatomy textbooks (Petersen & de Bere, 2006; Riska, 2003). An implicit message is then promulgated that, if men's bodies are normative, then women's must be exceptional, abnormal and therefore prone to being pathologized and more readily medicalized (Giacomini, Rozée-Koker & Pepitone-Arreola-Rockwell, 1986).

This relates to a second explanation, widely recognized in the critical studies of men, where, by remaining fully in the foreground and representing the normative, men's gender can remain invisible and thus avoid critical scrutiny (Hearn & Morgan, 1990). As Petersen and de Bere (2006, p. 131) note, 'the medicalization of men's bodies and lives have remained largely hidden behind the cloak of neutrality ...' This stands in contrast to women, who, Riessman (1983) argues, are more vulnerable to medicalization because their natural bodily processes (menstruation, pregnancy, birth) are clearly visible while men's 'routine experiences' remain in the shadows.

Whilst these explanations might account for the lack of a gendered lens in early work relating to men and medicalization, Conrad (2007) notes that the same cannot be said of work since the start of the 21st century. Indeed, Bell and Figert (2012a) call work on men and medicalization a 'burgeoning field' (p. 110). Work on the medicalization of 'erectile dysfunction' (ED) has made clear links to how the 'normalcy' of male bodies and sexuality are reframed as the pharmaceutical industry looks to promote consumption of new 'treatments' (Baglia, 2005; Conrad, 2007). However, in line with Riessman's (1983) work, men are not passive victims in this process but can collaborate with female partners and physicians to frame ED as a medical issue (Loe, 2006) or reject such moves and see 'decreased erectile function as the embodiment of a shift to respectable older age' (Wentzell, 2013, p. 163). Similarly, work on male aging highlights how this has become medically constructed as the 'andropause' (and therefore treatable), as pharmacology and technology collude with a consumerist driven cultural desire for men to exude youth, health and fitness in a way previously only experienced by women (Conrad, 2007; Rohden, 2015; Szymczak & Conrad, 2006). Finally, work on the medicalization of hyperactivity has taken a gendered lens to explain sex-differences in educational achievement (Hart, Grand & Riley, 2006) and has expanded critical work on the 'diagnosis' of ADHD to adult men (Conrad, 2007).

These are just a few examples, and there are many more. We now consider two cases in more detail in order to highlight the complexity of the issues involved in work on men, masculinities and medicalization.

Men, medicalization and coronary heart disease

In pioneering work on the medicalization of masculinity, Riska (2000) considers how, in late 1950s America, high rates of stress and Coronary Heart Disease (CHD) became linked through the medical construction of a 'Type A personality'. Those presenting with specific behaviours (rapid body movements, tense facial expressions, excessive gesturing, general impatience) were more at risk of CHD. These Type A personality traits, however, were not distributed evenly through society; they were primarily noted to be present in white middle-class men. Furthermore, Riska (2002) draws attention to the fact that this Type A man aligns well with cultural (hegemonic) ideals of masculinity in the U.S. at this time and thereby suggests that 'Type A man was constructed by medicalizing masculinity' (p. 350). This heralded the start of seeing the hard-working, driven, responsible male breadwinner role as having a health cost attached to it (Harrison, 1978).

The story continues. Riska (2002) maps, from the late 1970s, the demise and replacement of Type A personality with a new construct, 'hardiness' (and we suggest its successor, 'resilience'), based around characteristics of control, commitment and a sense of change as a personal challenge. This new concept allowed middle-class men to square the circle between fulfilling their (stereotypical) expected role and staying well, as hardiness can 'protect men from the deleterious effect of stress on their health [...] men can be real men, succeed, and still be healthy' (Riska, 2002, p. 350). Whilst both Type A and hardy personalities are linked to medicalized masculinities,[4] it could be said that, mediated through CHD, one personality type dies whilst the other thrives in terms of health outcomes.

While Riska (2000, 2002) suggests that the construction of these two personality types, and the medicalization of masculinity, are linked to the capitalist enterprise and social class, we would expand this analysis further by considering two areas debated within medicalization. First, we think Riska's work can be expanded by considering how this shift in medicalized masculinities is informed by the rise of neoliberalism. As outlined elsewhere (Robertson, Gough & Robinson, 2018), neoliberal policies and the gig economy, including a rise in service-sector rather than manufacturing work, demand a new kind of worker – one flexible and adaptable, adept at social aspects of work relationships and with a self-reflexive work-identity that can be aware and responsive to the needs of consumer and employer alike. These changing work practices implicitly necessitated a concomitant incorporation of previously non-hegemonic masculine working practices. Connell and Wood's (2005) research on globalized business masculinities notes the incorporation of such practices – increased body awareness, emotion management and an endorsement of gender equality – among international executives. A move away from Type A personality to the construction of 'hardiness' (and resilience), we argue, was a necessary precursor to ensure the development of this more flexible (male) worker who is able to deal positively with the challenges of a fluid, people-oriented, neoliberal employment environment that relies heavily on emotion management and coping with rapid change: the old, medicalized Type A stereotype did not fit this new employment system requirement. However, such 'softer' masculinity practices (like reflexivity and emotion management) do not replace, but run alongside, traditional practices such as control, competitiveness and a fierce mutual scrutiny (Connell & Wood, 2005; Robertson et al., 2018). Masculinity then is hybridized in ways that give the impression of positive change toward libertarian gender practices while simultaneously maintaining men's historical privilege within underlying patriarchal structures (Bridges & Pascoe, 2014).

The ability (or not) to evolve into this new neoliberal worker is not dependent on personality but is itself embedded within the class structure. Robertson et al. (2018) highlight the difficulties faced by working-class men in shifting from manufacturing to service industry work and suggest that middle-class men have greater cultural and material resources to cope with this change: they are more likely to be 'hardy' or resilient. In constructing Type A personality and hardiness as individualized risk factors in CHD causation or protection (Riska, 2002, p. 354), the ability to link CHD to the wider (working) environment and social class is lost. As health inequalities persist, including those linked to CHD (McCartney, Scarborough, Webster & Rayner, 2012), work on medicalization needs to maintain a focus on materiality as well as social construction.

Second, medicalization, with its emphasis on the social construction of disease categorization, often neglects the role that materiality and corporeality might play in processes of medicalization. As Conrad (2007) states, such perspectives 'focus on the emergence of medical categories and how problems entered the medical domain, bracketing whether a phenomenon is "really" a medical problem' (p. 10). Whilst it is possible and acceptable to do such bracketing, we suggest that in doing so, medicalization can miss the role that corporeal experiences can play in processes of collusion and resistance in medicalization.

Riska (2003) notes that there was little or no opposition among men to medical discourses of Type A personality and CHD causation but says little about why. Thinking about Riessman's (1983) work exploring how pain experiences led middle-class women to collude in the medicalization of childbirth, we suggest something similar in relation to men and CHD. Whilst partly driven by the medical profession, middle-class executive men in 1950s America (and elsewhere) also noted themselves as being susceptible to CHD and thereby aligned with medicine (and pharmaceutical and biotechnology sectors) in demanding early diagnosis and treatment. If this meant accepting a medicalization of masculinity under a Type A personality umbrella, this seems small price to pay to stay alive. Just as early middle-class, liberal, feminists focused on access to good care as an equal-rights issue for women (Riska, 2003), so middle-class men colluded to ensure good quality CHD services.

We further suggest that moves to demedicalize masculinity with regard to CHD through the construction of hardiness (and resilience) also act to reintroduce a class-related pejorative view of masculinity within the neoliberal context. In recasting causes of CHD as matters of individualized lifestyle choice (smoking, drinking, exercise and diet), rather than being linked to socioeconomic context, high rates of CHD are reframed as issues of social irresponsibility: a real, corporeal issue, CHD, becomes partly (re)constructed (and demedicalized) as being the result of morally poor choices. Masculinity is implicated, and men constructed as irresponsible, through their higher rates of smoking, drinking and poorer diet. Yet these are not class-free discourses. Higher rates of, and mortality from, CHD among certain groups of men – particularly those from areas of social deprivation and men from certain ethnic groups – can be explained by their greater (irresponsible masculine) engagement in unhealthy activities and lower rates among White middle-class men explained by their superior hardiness or resilience: non-White ethnic and working-class White masculinities are viewed as health destructive and middle-class masculinities as health-enhancing. The underpinning discourse, therefore, is that some groups of men (White, middle-class) are more worthy of access to CHD services and treatment than others – this is reflected in health disparities in access to CHD services and in CHD outcomes (Leigh, Alvarez & Rodriguez, 2016; Psaltopoulou et al., 2017).

Corporeal experiences, then, rather than being bracketed, should form part of the context for understanding the contested processes of medicalization.

Men, medicalization and HIV in the global south

The biomedical response to HIV and AIDS, the disproportionate burden of which is experienced in sub-Saharan Africa (SSA) (Gayle & Hill, 2001), has seen huge advancements since the first reported cases in 1981. Despite this, treatment remains unavailable to many – only 59% of the 36.9 million people living with HIV globally are accessing antiretroviral therapy, ART (UNAIDS, 2018) – and efforts to prevent new HIV infections remain a poor relation compared to treatment (Poku, 2016). In 2017, an estimated additional 1.8 million people became newly infected with HIV, most being in the global South (UNAIDS, 2018).

Part of the challenge is that the field of HIV prevention has been mired in competing approaches, often with biomedicalized 'quick fix' approaches taking precedence over social, cultural and behavioural change approaches. In mapping transformations in HIV prevention strategies from the 1980s onwards, Giami and Perrey (2012) draw on medicalization to highlight shifts from behavioural (pre-2007) to biomedical and surgical prevention techniques (post-2007) – a shift they believe is symbolic of a general trend toward the biomedicalization of sexuality. Early work using behavioural approaches required the medicalization of sexuality – previously private matters of intimacy became matters for public discussion and debate often led by public health professionals. Yet, because of the demographics of HIV/AIDS, the focus of such discussions was not gender neutral but focused on male sexuality and sexual practices. New normative meanings of (male) sexuality – in terms of risk of infection, risk behaviour, safe sex practices, at-risk groups – with primarily health (rather than pleasure) connotations, were constructed, and sex and sexuality moved centre stage in the health professional arena.

Despite this medicalization of male sexuality and practices, as shifts from behavioural to biomedicalized and pharmaceuticalized approaches emerged, it was women (infected pregnant women) who became some of the first to receive early antiretroviral drugs (Bayer, 2014), and such focus continues today in SSA (Gitome et al., 2014). As with other aspects of gender and medicalization, this could be interpreted in two ways: one is that women are passive victims of early pharmaceutical experimentation; the other is that there is an appropriate focus on the health of future generations. For more than 15 years, an insufficient focus on men within the context of HIV in SSA has been highlighted by critical South African gender scholars (Morrell, 2001; Ratele et al., 2007), leading to a proliferation of research on masculinities, sexualities and HIV in the region. This bias simultaneously renders women and girls responsible for male sexuality (Bhana & Pattman, 2009). Despite a growth in the body of knowledge on men and HIV in the global South, and the ground-breaking work of local organizations around HIV behavioural change with men,[5] broader HIV practice has largely focused on women and girls. Although this has been for important reasons, it neglects the role of men and boys, particularly heterosexual men. This is reflected in the recent UNAIDS World AIDS Day report (UNAIDS, 2017), which shows that men are less likely than women to know their HIV status, to access and adhere to ART and are more likely to die of AIDS-related illnesses.

Shifting from behavioural approaches that might address cultural male gender norms (around sex, help-seeking etc.) to biomedicalized approaches in the SSA context may partly generate these HIV gender health disparities. Giami and Perrey (2012) highlight how, within biomedicalized approaches, external treatment for the consequences of behaviours takes precedence, thereby making changes in sexual behaviour less necessary. As an example, it is estimated that only 10 condoms are available to every man in SSA over his lifetime (UNAIDS, 2015), yet significant funding has been invested in research and provision of biomedical interventions to reduce HIV transmission, such as vaginal microbicides (for women) and voluntary male circumcision (VMMC). This despite evidence that condom use decreases the probability of male-to-female transmission of HIV by around 80–95% (Pinkerton & Abramson, 1997; Weller & Davis-Beaty, 2002). Indeed, as medicalized approaches increase, international funding for condom procurement is stagnating (UNFPA, 2015), and opportunities to promote condoms as a critical complement to these are missed (UNFPA, 2015).

Few programmes adequately address gender-based, socio-cultural norms that hinder effective condom use, such as men's desire to mix bodily fluids, that real sex requires ejaculation inside someone and that condomized sex is not pleasurable sex (Shand, forthcoming). Arguably, medical and pharmaceutical companies have led a drive to introduce newer medicalized responses, which eclipse existing efficacious methods. For example, VMMC can reduce the risk of HIV acquisition by men by 70% yet has no protective effects for women (Qiang, Lu, Xiao & Ping, 2015). Despite this, 11.7 million circumcisions were performed in SSA by 2015 (WHO, 2016) yet such service provision rarely integrates VMMC with discussions around the aforementioned gender norms.

Similarly, vaginal microbicides, a protective gel applied inside the vagina, were hailed as a huge step forward for women in HIV prevention. However, subsequent studies failed to demonstrate their effectiveness (Obiero, Mwethera, Hussey & Wiysonge, 2012). In addition, despite significant investment, only a few countries in the global South undertook acceptability studies which included the male partners of women (Abdulai et al., 2012). Given the unequal power dynamics between men and women, a lack of male partner acceptability for using microbicides has proved an important barrier to their use (Abdulai et al., 2012). Addressing these gendered contexts has remained peripheral to the priorities of those advancing medicalized approaches.

Treatment as prevention (TasP) studies show that early initiation of ART significantly reduces onward HIV transmission (Cohen et al., 2011; WHO, 2016). TasP is therefore widely used as a public health intervention but is not without limitations. First, the costs attached to maintaining an expanding pool of people reliant on daily medication in the SSA context is unlikely to be sustainable (Poku, 2016). Second, for TasP to work with men relies on persuading them to test, take and adhere to treatment, which, as noted above, remains a challenge. The rollout of TasP has not been met with a concomitant focus on addressing the blind spot around men and HIV, or in shifting gendered sexual practices (Venkatesh, Flanigan & Mayer, 2011). Biomedicalized approaches to HIV, which do not address broader contextual and policy issues, can thereby be completely ineffective, and treatment alone cannot be the sole solution for successful HIV intervention. As Venkatesh et al. (2011) note, it must be part of a comprehensive package of prevention approaches including shifting sexual practices and promoting condom use to reduce the number of new infections.

Recently there has been a resurgence of discussion about an HIV vaccine or cure.[6] While such developments should be encouraged, the roll-out of such new technologies should be combined with strategies which address health-damaging gender norms. There is good evidence that, particularly in the resource-constrained SSA context, approaches focusing on family and community system strengthening are a vital component of successful intervention which might be complemented by biomedicalized approaches (Gitome et al., 2014).

Summary

Early work developing the concept of medicalization made few links to gender dynamics and even fewer attempts to link men, masculinities and gender to medicalization processes. It is likely that this slow start was due to the 'normalcy' attached to the (White, European) male body, rendering it invisible, while women and their bodily processes become constructed as atypical and, therefore, a more visible and pathologized focus of concern. However, processes of medicalization soon came to be seen as more than efforts to extend medical domination; situated within the wider socioeconomic context, processes of medicalization could be seen as serving the system requirement of capitalism, or at least aligning with it for mutual benefit. Important feminist work in the 1970s and 1980s made links between medicalization and systems of patriarchy and also began to highlight that people, women, were not passive victims but could also collaborate or resist medicalization processes.

Despite this, it was not until the start of the 21st century that a critical gendered lens began to focus on aspects of men, masculinities and medicalization. Since then, work has explored the medicalization of male aging (the andropause, baldness, erectile dysfunction), of male expression and coping (hyperactivity disorder, alcoholic dependence), but also the medicalization of masculinity itself (for example, in relation to CHD) and of male sexuality (for example, in relation to HIV).

Within all of this work, the complexity of understanding medicalization has become apparent. Well beyond attempts at medical domination, medicalization has been expanded to incorporate pharmaceuticalization, biotechnologicalization and globalization. Work around gender and medicalization has not only engaged with these newer concepts but has also extended work through its emphasis on intersectionality (particularly around social class and ethnicity) and on agentic acts of compliance and resistance to medicalization processes. Much of this latter work has been feminist inspired, and this set the scene for subsequent work on men, masculinities and medicalization which would not otherwise have had an adequate conceptual framework to take work forward.

There is much still to be done. Work around men and medicalization, despite being a growing area of work, is still in its infancy and limited to some quite specific subjects. It is exciting to think how this might expand over the coming years.

Notes

1 We use the following broad definition of medicalization: '[medicalization] consists of defining a problem in medical terms, using medical language to describe a problem, adopting a medical framework to understand a problem or using a medical intervention to "treat" it' (Conrad, 2000, p. 322).
2 Although, as Riska (2003) points out, it important to note that liberal feminists at this time offered a more optimistic view, focussing on demands for more women doctors and more medical information to revert previous gender-biased care and medical knowledge.
3 Though it should be clearly noted that Riessman (1983) recognized that this 'fit' was not an easy one but was 'tension-filled and fraught with contradictions for women, who have both gained and lost with each intrusion medicine has made' (p. 57).
4 Riska (2002, p. 355) suggests that whilst Type A personality medicalizes masculinity, hardiness demedicalizes it.

5 See the work of Sonke: Gender Justice (www.genderjustice.org.za), AMSHeR (www.amsher.org) and GrassRoot Soccer (www.grassrootsoccer.org).
6 See www.avert.org.

References

Abdulai, M. A., Baiden, F., Adjei, G., Afari-Asiedu, S., Adjei, K., Tawiah, C., & Newton, S. (2012). An assessment of the likely acceptability of vaginal microbicides for HIV prevention among women in rural Ghana. *BMC Women's Health, 12*(1), 40.

Baglia, J. (2005). *The Viagra AdVenture: Masculinity, media, and the performance of sexual health.* New York: Lang Publishing.

Bayer, R. (2014). The medicalization of HIV prevention: New opportunities beset by old challenges. *The Milbank Quarterly, 92*(3), 434–437.

Bell, S. E., & Figert, A. E. (2012a). Gender and the medicalization of healthcare. In E. Kuhlmann & E. Annandale (Eds.), *The Palgrave handbook of gender and healthcare* (pp. 127–142). Basingstoke: Palgrave Macmillan.

Bell, S. E., & Figert, A. E. (2012b). Medicalization and pharmaceuticalization at the intersections: Looking backward, sideways and forward. *Social Science & Medicine, 75*(5), 775–783.

Bhana D., & Pattman R. (2009). Researching South African youth, gender and sexuality within the context of HIV/Aids. *Development, 52*(1), 68–74.

Bridges, T., & Pascoe, C. J. (2014). Hybrid masculinities: New directions in the sociology of men and masculinities. *Sociology Compass, 8*(3), 246–258.

Cohen, M. S., Chen, Y. Q., McCauley, M., Gamble, T., Hosseinipour, M. C., Kumarasamy, N., … Pilotto, J. H. (2011). Prevention of HIV-1 infection with early antiretroviral therapy. *New England Journal of Medicine, 365*(6), 493–505.

Connell, R. W., & Wood, J. (2005). Globalization and business masculinities. *Men and Masculinities*, 7(4), 347–364.

Conrad, P. (1975). The discovery of hyperkinesis: Notes on the medicalization of deviant behavior. *Social Problems, 23*(1), 12–21.

Conrad, P. (2000). Medicalization, genetics, and human problems. In C. E. Bird, P. Conrad & A. M. Freemont, *Handbook of medical sociology* (5th ed., pp. 322–333). Upper Saddle River, NJ: Prentice Hall.

Conrad, P. (2007). *The medicalization of society.* Baltimore, MD: Johns Hopkins University Press.

Conrad, P., & Schneider, J. W. (1980). *Deviance and medicalization: From badness to sickness.* St. Louis, MO: Mosby.

Ehrenreich, B., & English, D. (1973/2010). *Witches, midwives, & nurses: A history of women healers.* New York: The Feminist Press at CUNY.

Freidson, E. (1970). *The profession of medicine.* New York: Dodd Mead & Co.

Gabe, J., & Monaghan, L. (2013). *Key concepts in medical sociology.* London: Sage.

Gayle, H. D., & Hill, G. L. (2001). Global impact of human immunodeficiency virus and AIDS. *Clinical Microbiology Reviews, 14*(2), 327–335.

Giacomini, M., Rozée-Koker, P., & Pepitone-Arreola-Rockwell, F. (1986). Gender bias in human anatomy textbook illustrations. *Psychology of Women Quarterly, 10*(4), 413–420.

Giami, A., & Perrey, C. (2012). Transformations in the medicalization of sex: HIV prevention between discipline and biopolitics. *Journal of Sex Research, 49*(4), 353–361.

Gitome, S., Njuguna, S., Kwena, Z., Ombati, E., Njoroge, B., & Bukusi, E. A. (2014). Perspectives paper: Medicalization of HIV and the African Response. *African Journal of Reproductive Health, 18*(3), 25–33.

Harrison, J. (1978). Warning: The male sex role may be dangerous to your health. *Journal of Social Issues, 34*(1), 65–86.

Hart, N., Grand, N., & Riley, K. (2006). Making the grade: The gender gap, ADHD, and the medicalization of boyhood. In D. Rosenfeld & C. Faircloth (Eds.), *Medicalized masculinities* (pp. 132–165). Philadelphia, PA: Temple University Press.

Hearn, J., & Morgan, D. (Eds.). (1990). *Men, masculinities and social theory.* London: Unwin Hyman.

Leigh, J. A., Alvarez, M., & Rodriguez, C. J. (2016). Ethnic minorities and coronary heart disease: An update and future directions. *Current Atherosclerosis Reports, 18*(2), 9.

Loe, M. (2006). The Viagra blues: Embracing or resisting the Viagra body. In D. Rosenfeld & C. Faircloth (Eds.), *Medicalized masculinities* (pp. 21–44). Philadelphia, PA: Temple University Press.

McCartney, D., Scarborough, P., Webster, P., & Rayner, M. (2012). Trends in social inequalities for premature coronary heart disease mortality in Great Britain, 1994–2008: A time trend ecological study. *BMJ Open*, *2*(3), e000737.

Morrell, R. (2001). *Changing men in Southern Africa*. London: Zed Books.

Neasbitt, J. Y. (2018). *Female genital cosmetic surgery: Neoliberalism, medicalization, and the pathologization of embodiment* (PhD dissertation). University of California, Santa Cruz.

Obiero, J., Mwethera, P. G., Hussey, G. D., & Wiysonge, C. S. (2012). Vaginal microbicides for reducing the risk of sexual acquisition of HIV infection in women: Systematic review and meta-analysis. *BMC Infectious Diseases*, *12*(1), 289.

Parsons, T. (1951). *Social structure and dynamic process: The case of modern medical practice*. New York: Free Press.

Petersen, A., & de Bere, S. R. (2006). Dissecting medicine: Gender biases in the discourses and practices of medical anatomy. In D. Rosenfeld & C. Faircloth (Eds.), *Medicalized masculinities* (pp. 112–131). Philadelphia, PA: Temple University Press.

Pinkerton, S. D., & Abramson, P. R. (1997). Effectiveness of condoms in preventing HIV transmission. *Social Science & Medicine*, *44*(9), 1303–1312.

Poku, N. K. (2016). HIV prevention: The key to ending AIDS by 2030. *The Open AIDS Journal*, *10*, 65.

Psaltopoulou, T., Hatzis, G., Papageorgiou, N., Androulakis, E., Briasoulis, A., & Tousoulis, D. (2017). Socioeconomic status and risk factors for cardiovascular disease: Impact of dietary mediators. *Hellenic Journal of Cardiology*, *58*(1), 32–42.

Qiang, W., Lu, Y., Xiao, L., & Ping, H. (2015). Circumcision status and risk of HIV acquisition during heterosexual intercourse for both males and females: A meta-analysis. *PLoS One*, *10*(5), e0125436.

Ratele, K., Fouten, E., Shefer, T., Strebel, A., Shabalala, N., & Buikema, R. (2007). 'Moffies, jocks and cool guys': Boys' accounts of masculinity and their resistance in context. In T. Shefer, K. Ratele, A. Strebel, N. Shabalala & R. Buikema (Eds.), *From boys to men: Social constructions of masculinity in contemporary society* (pp. 112–127). Cape Town: University of Capetown Press.

Riessman, C. K. (1983). Women and medicalization: A new perspective. *Social Policy*, *14*(1), 3–18.

Riska, E. (2000). The rise and fall of Type A man. *Social Science & Medicine*, *51*(11), 1665–1674.

Riska, E. (2002). From Type A man to the hardy man: Masculinity and health. *Sociology of Health & Illness*, *24*(3), 347–358.

Riska, E. (2003). Gendering the medicalization thesis. In M. T. Segal, V. Demos & J. J. Kronfeld (Eds.), *Gender perspectives on health and medicine* (pp. 59–87). Bingley: Emerald.

Robertson, S., Gough, B., & Robinson, M. (2018). Masculinities and health inequalities within neoliberal economies. In C. Walker & S. Roberts (Eds.), *Masculinity, labour, and neoliberalism* (pp. 311–334). Switzerland: Springer.

Rohden, F. (2015). Promotion of andropause in Brazil: A case of male medicalization. In C. Smith-Morris (Ed.), *Diagnostic controversy* (pp. 89–116). London: Routledge.

Rosenfield, D., & Faircloth, C. (2006). Medicalized masculinities: The missing link. In D. Rosenfeld & C. Faircloth (Eds.), *Medicalized masculinities* (pp. 1–20). Philadelphia, PA: Temple University Press.

Sandelowski, M. (1981). *Women, health, and choice*. Upper Saddle River, NJ:Prentice Hall.

Schneider, J. W. (1978). Deviant drinking as disease: Alcoholism as a social accomplishment. *Social Problems*, *25*(4), 361–372.

Shand, T. (forthcoming).

Szymczak, J., & Conrad, P. (2006). Medicalizing the aging male body: Andropause and baldness. In D. Rosenfeld & C. Faircloth (Eds.), *Medicalized masculinities* (pp. 89–111). Philadelphia, PA: Temple University Press.

UNAIDS. (2017). *Blind Spot: Reaching out to men and boys: Addressing a blind spot in the response to HIV*. Geneva: Joint United Nations Programme on HIV/AIDS (UNAIDS).

UNAIDS. (2018). *Data, 2018*. Joint United Nations Programme on HIV/AIDS (UNAIDS), Geneva.

UNAIDS. (2015, July 7). *UNFPA, WHO and UNAIDS: Position statement on condoms and the prevention of HIV, other sexually transmitted infections and unintended pregnancy*. Joint United Nations Programme on HIV/AIDS (UNAIDS). Retrieved December 9, 2018 from www.unaids.org/en/resources/presscentre/featurestories/2015/july/20150702_condoms_prevention.

UNFPA. (2015). *Contraceptives and condoms for family planning and STI & HIV prevention. External procurement support report 2014*. New York: UNFPA.

Venkatesh, K. K., Flanigan, T. P., & Mayer, K. H. (2011). Is expanded HIV treatment preventing new infections? Impact of antiretroviral therapy on sexual risk behaviors in the developing world. *Aids, 25*(16), 1939–1949.

Weller, S. C., & Davis-Beaty, K. (2002). Condom effectiveness in reducing heterosexual HIV transmission. *Cochrane Database of Systematic Reviews*, 1.

Wentzell, E. A. (2013). *Maturing masculinities: Aging, chronic illness, and Viagra in Mexico*. Durham, NC: Duke University Press.

WHO. (2016). *Voluntary medical make circumcision for HIV prevention in 14 priority countries in East and Southern Africa*. Geneva: WHO.

Zola, I. K. (1972). Medicine as an institution of social control. *The Sociological Review, 20*(4), 487–504.

Part 5
Cultures and aesthetics

36

The 'male preserve' thesis, sporting culture, and men's power

Christopher R. Matthews and Alex Channon

Introduction: studying sport and gender

Since the mid-19th century, when the modern Westernised form of competition sport took shape, there has been a shifting yet robustly gendered structure to the experience of playing, consuming, managing, teaching and marketing sport. In this regard, save for a number of important examples, sports in various forms were created by men, for men (and boys). In light of this, critical studies of men, masculinity and sport culture have emerged as a major area of research in the sociology of sport (e.g., Dunning, 1986; Messner, 1992; Messner & Sabo, 1990; Pronger, 1990). Drawing on various feminist, social constructionist, or poststructuralist theories of gender, these scholars argued that sport served to sustain symbolic idealisations of male power, normalise the marginality of women and reinforce rigid status hierarchies among men themselves. In exposing the inequalities enshrined within sports culture, along with the manifold dangers endured by boys and men in the stakes of 'proving' masculinity[1] in and through sport, this body of scholarship placed the potentially harmful nature of the masculinity–sport relationship firmly into the academic discourse on sport and society.

Furthering recommendations for positive change, scholars of men, masculinity and sport joined wider feminist activism challenging the established male hegemony in sport. Coupled with shifting social attitudes towards women's athleticism (Cahn, 1994; Heywood & Dworkin, 2003; Theberge, 1987) and growing, yet somewhat limited, public enfranchisement of sexual minority groups (Anderson, 2009; Pronger, 2000) from the mid-1990s onwards, the activist ambitions of pro-feminist scholars have begun, in part, to be realised. Nevertheless, the long-standing relationship between men, narratives about masculinity and certain sporting spaces has been maintained, recast and in some places reinforced (Aitchison, 2006; Matthews, 2014, 2016a; McKay, Messner, & Sabo, 2000; Wellard, 2012).

In this chapter we explore these social processes by turning attention to the concept of sport as a 'male preserve'. With this notion as our starting point, we outline in turn how sport has historically constituted male power in both structural and symbolic ways; how its role in doing so has begun to be challenged from without as well as within; and how those at the centre of this relationship have managed to 'hold back the tide' of change in several important respects. Throughout, we explore the dynamics of gender relations, rather than simply focusing on 'masculinity', as it is within the detailed unfolding of such social processes that we argue scholars are able to more adequately evidence, conceptualise and theorise the lives of men. Although our focus is necessarily limited due to the constraints of space, we argue that these dynamics represent a key analytical problem for academics interested in sport and critical studies of men, as they point to pertinent questions around social change, gender relations, and the operation and preservation of power.

Sport as a male preserve

Against the general trend of a lack of early interest in gender within the scholarship on men's sports, Kenneth Sheard and Eric Dunning published one of the first sociological research papers about sport in which gender was explicitly explored as the central theme. 'The Rugby Football Club as a Type of "Male Preserve"' (Sheard & Dunning, 1973) placed their account of rugby subcultures within historically shifting patterns of gender relations in England. They argue that such spaces serve to insulate men from wider social changes threatening to undermine their traditional, taken-for-granted, superior social status. Dunning's (1986) later work developed this reasoning further, suggesting that technological innovation, modern state formation and the general pacification of day-to-day life in Western societies had exerted an equalising force on the balance of power between the sexes, removing several structural bases of men's social power. In the face of widespread cultural and institutional change, sport provided men a site where the formal exclusion of women, and the overt celebration of powerful and aggressive visions of masculinity, enabled them to continue to construct idealised versions of themselves as rightfully dominant. Sporting spaces thereby 'preserved' notions of masculinity which would support – through pervasive and powerful symbolism – the continuation of male supremacy.[2]

As scholarly attention to gender, sport and masculinity began to accelerate, the notion of sport as a male preserve quickly gained conceptual purchase (Birrell, 1984; Bryson, 1987; Dunning, 1986; Theberge, 1985). In highlighting the gendered dimensions of the historical development, ideological underpinnings, participation levels and administration of sport, critical scholars effectively demonstrated that such social enclaves can provide 'dramatic symbolic proof' (Messner, 1990, p. 204) of (heterosexual) men's physical and psychological superiority over women and 'other' (that is, effeminate or gay) men. Increasing focus on such issues continued through the 1990s, with research on women, sport and gender highlighting the manner in which sports served to exclude, control, disempower and/or sexualise women (e.g., Greendorfer & Rubinson, 1997; Hargreaves, 1994; Kane & Lenskyj, 1998). If women had any place in sports at all, it was shown to be one that was subordinate to men, and particularly one that served the interests of an assumed all-heterosexual male audience; an imaginary construct that nevertheless served as the de facto authority on sporting consumers' taste.

Meanwhile, critical attention to men in sport turned to the irony of how sport's symbolism empowered men as a group, but unevenly so, and often at the cost of mental and physical damage in the lives of those men whose efforts produced such symbolism (Connell, 2005; Messner, 1990; Messner & Sabo, 1990; Whitson, 1990; Young, 1993). Messner (1990) captured this process with his pithy notion of the 'body-as-weapon'. Here, in learning to consider their bodies as machine-like objects of ritualised violence, male athletes not only caused acute and chronic damage to their opponents/colleagues[3] but similarly caused physical and mental harm to themselves. This 'maim-or-be-maimed' (Hoch, 1972) mentality is regularly taken as a given 'part of the game' in men's sports (Hughes & Coakley, 1991; Matthews

& Channon, 2016; Messner & Sabo, 1990), such that this mechanism for sustaining men's social superiority also works against the interests of those whose labour underpins it. By the mid to late 1990s then, scholarship exposing the operation of sport as a male preserve had developed a number of critical trajectories revealing the harmful, exclusionary, sexist and exploitative nature of this enterprise.

In more recent years, gender-focused research on men and women in sport has proliferated, covering many different and intersecting topics, although themes pertinent to the role of sport in constructing and confirming male power remain central to many – if not most – analyses. With particular respect to men and sport, research has revealed several phenomena which are instructive in this regard. Among many others, these include the mediating role of race relations in men's power chances within sport, largely evidencing the favourable experiences of whites (Anderson & McCormack, 2010; Carrington, 1998; Lawrence, 2016); the intersection of sport, masculinity and (dis)ability, suggesting sport serves as a vehicle of masculine recuperation for disabled men, although often in ways which may reproduce sexism (Lindemann & Cherney, 2008; Sparkes & Smith, 2002); the increasing commodification of men's body image in sport and fitness cultures, which has led, among other things, to the proliferation of various pathological behaviours among men (Atkinson, 2007; White & Gillett, 1994); but also the gradual – if partial – 'softening' of narratives about masculinity in sport, creating new possibilities for identity construction and gender performance for both gay and straight men within sporting spaces (Anderson, 2009; Anderson, McGrath & Bullingham, 2016; Channon & Matthews, 2015a; Pronger, 2000).

Collectively, this research has done much to describe and critique the masculine archetypes that are (or at least, historically have been) normative in sports worlds and which underpin the social significance of sport as a male preserve. Such an ideology usually draws on constructions of 'real' men as 'naturally' strong, tough, competitive, muscular and aggressive, visibly expressed through dramatic performances of the male body. Perhaps, above all else, such performances highlight men's ability to dominate others, which is arguably a central characteristic in constructions of 'hegemonic' forms of masculinity (Connell, 2005).

Indeed, Connell's (2005) hegemonic masculinity thesis has become something of a lingua franca for those wishing to theorise men's power, bodies and relationships with women and each other within sport. This 'hegemony' can involve instances of direct physical domination through acts of violence[4] (Connell, 2005; Messner, 2002) but also through the symbolic capital which embodied images of masculinity-as-power invest in the majority of men, as part of what Connell (2005) terms the 'patriarchal dividend'. This conflation of (usually) heterosexual men with physical power – relative to the construction of homosexual men as effeminate and weak (Pronger, 1990; Wellard, 2012) and all women as the inevitably weaker and inferior sex – has long been seen to lend support to the power relations at work in a gender order centred on heterosexual male privilege (e.g., McKay et al., 2000; Messner & Sabo, 1990).

As such, exclusion from sport, and/or trivialisation and ridicule within or through it, have often been the experience of women, gay men, and various others who sit outside of the narrowly defined norms of gender built around such spaces. Meanwhile, generating and maintaining such symbolism means that some men – who would superficially appear to benefit from this system the most – may ultimately pay a costly price for their efforts. When presented in this light, the role of sport as a male preserve has been criticised for its role in perpetuating social injustice. In many respects, such challenges have led to previously male-dominated sporting spaces undergoing significant change. In the following section, we discuss two such changes to sport that have gone some way in undermining the role it can play in constructing notions of male supremacy, drawing on case studies from our research into combat sports to do so.

Challenge and change

As noted above, a defining feature of sport's sociological utility as a male preserve has been its exclusion of women and gay men, along with any others who do not conform to masculine archetypes. The work of evidencing heterosexual men's 'natural'[5] pre-eminence in the spheres of bravery, competitiveness, strength, toughness and so on cannot proceed very effectively if women and gay men can appear alongside them, demonstrating those same attributes (Bryson, 1990; Cahn, 1994; Channon & Matthews, 2015b; Matthews & Channon, 2016; Theberge, 1987). Yet, throughout the 20th century, women's gradual inclusion in sport ate away at the exclusive male territory it represented, with all but a tiny minority of elite-level sports now open to women competitors, and participation figures at the Olympic Games now at near-equal levels (International Olympic Committee, 2016). LGBT people, meanwhile, have similarly become far more visible in sports, with a series of high-profile athletes 'coming out' over the past few years, along with the establishment of LGBT sports clubs and movements such as the Gay Games (Krane & Waldron, 2000; Pronger, 2000; Waitt, 2003). Together these have constituted important shifts in sport's potential role in constituting structures of gender and power.

These changes have perhaps been most striking in the field of combat sports, given the symbolic proximity these hold to those characteristics most central to the ideals of masculinity noted above (Channon, 2018; Matthews, 2014, 2016a). With this in mind, it is not surprising to find that, of all sports on the programme of the Summer Olympic Games, boxing was the last to continue the formal exclusion of female competition, with the International Olympic Committee taking until 2009 to stipulate that women should be included in Olympic boxing competitions. Regarding professional combat sports, the *Ultimate Fighting Championship* likewise took until 2012 to introduce women to its roster of professional fighters. Public reception of these athletes has, however, been largely positive – both within subcultural spaces built around the sports and in more mainstream media coverage (Godoy-Pressland, 2015; Jakubowska, Channon & Matthews, 2016; Woodward, 2014). The high-profile exploits of women fighting have provided ample opportunity for the construction of discourses challenging orthodox ideals of gender, arguably weakening the symbolic value of these sports as male preserves.

A similar story can be told of sexual minority men who have, until very recently, been a near-invisible group within combat sports.[6] The coming-out of highly-ranked boxer Orlando Cruz in 2012, as well as the outing of mixed martial artist and former gay porn actor Dakota Cochrane[7] in the same year, were met with broadly positive responses in the press (Channon & Matthews, 2015a; Channon, Matthews & Wagner, 2013). The opportunity these athletes presented to open dialogue about homophobia in combat sports, as well as to provide journalists the chance to reflect on the progressive ethos that seemed to be at work in wider sporting spaces, further revealed a shift away from the exclusionary and overtly hostile climates identified in earlier work on heavily masculinised sports worlds. Around the same time, the rising visibility of 'gay' or LGBT-friendly boxing clubs in several major Western cities (e.g., Brighton, Glasgow, London, Paris, New York) reveals shifting perceptions within both boxing and sexual minority communities as to the possibility of sexual diversity in combat sports.

However, while much (if, admittedly, not all) media coverage and fan response towards these athletes was positive, reception of transgender woman and mixed martial artist Fallon Fox has been far less so, often replicating transphobic and essentialist assumptions about immutable, binary and hierarchal sex difference. Typically constructing Fox as a 'man in disguise', whose performances would amount to 'violence against women' (Felt, 2014), such hostility reveals one of the limits of the changes undergone in this particular male preserve. Despite wider inclusion of participants, there remains an ideological commitment to a binary model of sex and a normalised assumption of inevitable male pre-eminence. Interestingly, this observation opens conceptual space to discuss the second aspect of our analysis here – the impact of sex integration in sport on constructions of gender – for while Fox's example indicates the continuation of transphobic sentiment in sport, rationalised through discourses of fairness or (in combat sports particularly) anti-violence, such notions also pertain to debates around mixed-sex competition.

A typical refrain from proponents of sex segregation in sport – an historical norm so pervasive that few ever challenge it (McDonagh & Pappano, 2008) – is that physiological differences between males and females make fair competition in athletic contests impossible. Sweeping generalisations and reductive simplifications notwithstanding, it is true that physiological differences affecting sports performance can very often be observed between sex categories. Yet, this does not necessarily preclude the possibility of fair competition between men and women in all aspects of sport; nor does it mean that men and women have not tried to play sports together at all (see Channon, Dashper, Fletcher & Lake, 2017). This begs the sociological question of what happens *vis-à-vis* sport's operation as a male preserve when it becomes sex-integrated.

With respect to martial arts and combat sports, several studies have examined sex integration in training and competition (e.g., Channon & Jennings, 2013; Guérandel & Mennesson, 2007; Maclean, 2017). Here, the prospect of cross-sex competition dramatically departs from orthodox gendered logic stressing inevitable male supremacy in the realm of physical contests. From the point of view of such normalised assumptions, the supposition that men might be able to learn something from training with women, and furthermore that a woman might stand any chance of defeating a man in a fight seem highly improbable. And yet, empirical evidence reveals that such exchanges do take place in many martial arts and combat sports – most often with respect to training, but occasionally also in competition (Channon, 2013; Fields, 2005; McNaughton, 2012; Miller, 2010). That women might be accorded respect as men's training partners, or legitimate competitors, reveals a profound change in the conceptualisation of sex difference and gender propriety in sporting cultures ostensibly coded as masculine. This, alongside the symbolic meaning of women defeating men (although relatively rare, such instances are reported in the literature), emerge as key outcomes of sex-integrated training vis-à-vis gender.

Analysing the impact of male-female touch in such settings, Channon and Jennings (2013) argued that such experiences challenged normalised conceptions of female inferiority among both male and female practitioners. By training together and gaining first-hand experience of each other's physical potential, martial artists in various disciplines were shown to change both perceptions of sex differences and their behaviour in sex-integrated environments. Such work therefore 'became a lived-out "undoing" of gender, impacting upon the practitioners' understandings and embodied performances of sex difference' (Channon & Jennings, 2013, p. 500). Maclean (2017) argued, meanwhile, that joint training experiences helped build meaningful, mutually respectful relationships between young men and women training in karate. She notes that 'the sex-integrated practice of karate elevates the respect given to women by … disrupting ideas of women's bodies as primarily sexual objects subordinate in ability to men' (2017, p. 271).

Both observations, supported in other studies that have examined sex integrated sporting spaces (Channon et al., 2017), reveal significant departures from the homosocial, often misogynistic and homophobic, male-dominated subcultures revealed in earlier studies of 'masculine' sports. Women and homosexual men taking part in activities that had previously operated as 'male preserves' represent an important challenge to men's exclusive access to the socialisation opportunities, skill development and embodied symbolic capital these sports represent. Yet sex-integrated sport goes a step further, challenging the often taken-for-granted assumption that (all) male bodies possess insurmountable advantages over (all) females, a doctrine that has long been (and for the most part, continues to be) enshrined within segregationist sports policies (Pieper, 2017). However, neither of these types of challenges have resulted in the complete destruction of sport's role as a male preserve. In the following section we outline some of the ongoing ways in which apparently inclusive, and even integrated, sports can continue to shore up ideological notions of male supremacy.

Residual patriarchy: the preserve in pieces

While it is clear from the preceding comments that the often-simplistic associations between men, masculinity and sport have been undermined and subverted in important ways, evidence from various sources highlights how social power, and with it inequality, is often reworked, renegotiated and, despite some symbolically important evidence to the contrary, maintained (Atkinson, 2011; Connell, 2005; Matthews, 2016b; Pease, 2000). So while clear shifts in what Connell (2005) calls the 'gender order' have undermined structural components upon which patriarchal social relations have been built, it is still possible to evidence the manner in which many men are able to lay claim to influence and power by virtue of their performances of masculinity. This is as true in sports worlds (Atkinson, 2011; Matthews, 2014, 2016a) as it is in society more broadly (Matthews, 2016b).

Recognising the enduring character of sport's role as a male preserve through times of change, Matthews (2016a) reconsidered the thesis in relation to his ethnographic work on boxing. Within a weightlifting and boxing gym, where women occupied a marginalised and minimised position, Matthews (2014) draws attention to the manner in which narratives about masculinity had to be expressed and lived out in carefully considered and contextually negotiated ways in order to fit with wider social proprieties. While the men in his study believed that their 'natural' male biology justified some level of violent and aggressive behaviour, they were acutely aware of shifting social pressures that made such expressions largely illegitimate. As such, they crafted contextually appropriate performances of manhood which drew on pugilistic codes to frame relatively controlled 'ritual violence' in sparring, and 'self-bullying' in the form of risky training practices, as somehow 'naturally' masculine. By interpreting such action as contextually appropriate releases of their innate male tendencies, these men were able to explain, justify and legitimate the relative preservation of this space for men and their 'masculine' behaviours (Matthews, 2014, 2016a).

In this sense, Matthews argues that while the straightforward structural organisation of sport as a homosocial space for heterosexual men has significantly diminished, thanks to the opening up of such spaces to those previously excluded from them, 'we can [now] think of the male preserve as a site for the dramatic representation and reification of behaviours symbolically linked to patriarchal narrations of manhood' (Matthews, 2016a, p. 329). In weaving narratives about manhood, sport and violence together with routine performances that are common within such spaces, this work helps shed light on the manner in which 'male preserves' are maintained, recast and reproduced via discursive meaning-making, even at the same time as they seem to be diminishing in other respects.

Furthermore, this illustrates the micro-sociological and symbolic interactions that underpin the reproduction and reification of a 'male preserve' (Matthews, 2014, 2016a). In empirically and theoretically exploring some of these details it is possible to more adequately describe the means by which sports worlds perpetuate what might be described as a form of 'residual' patriarchal relations. Aside from the continuation of narratives reifying the naturalisation of masculinity through combat sports, this effect is also achieved through various ways in which women's growing presence within them remains subordinated to men's in several respects. These include challenges to the authority of female officials; the relative lack of female (head) coaches in combat sports; the continuing disparity between professional male and female athletes' financial rewards or access to training facilities; and the sexualisation of female combat athletes in the media (see Channon, Quinney, Khomutova & Matthews, 2018; Jennings, 2015; Kavoura, Chroni, Kokkonen & Ryba, 2015; McCree, 2015). Each of these phenomena serve as a not-so-subtle reminder that men remain central, in both symbolic and tangible ways, to the social world of combat sports.

Perhaps unsurprisingly, similar resistances also emerge when considering the social organisation and lived experience of sex integration in sport. Many men and women may initially struggle to grasp the concept of integrated training or competition – specifically in sports involving fighting – as this falls very far outside of everyday gender propriety (Channon, 2013). Discursive constructions of male-to-female hitting, in particular, as 'violence against women' create a moral imperative to avoid mixed sparring among men, who may also struggle to come to terms with the potential embarrassment of 'losing' to a woman in an activity at which they are assumed to possess an inevitable advantage. Indeed, with respect to mixed competition, in many countries'/states' laws and in many combat sports authorities' rules, sex-integrated competitions are illegal, even if mixed-sex training might be a norm. Meanwhile, sexualised connotations of touching others' bodies (particularly in grappling-based sports) create additional hesitations over concerns of sexual impropriety (Channon & Jennings, 2013; Mierzwinski, Velija & Malcolm, 2014). As such, the inability to step away from orthodox gender constructions may eventually become a major obstacle to successful training, making for awkward and unproductive encounters that frustrate, rather than facilitate, progressive social development through sport.

The consequences of these (and other) problems are varied, but perhaps most pertinent to the present chapter is the effect they may have on women's ability to access the benefits of participating equally in sports that have historically constituted male preserves. At the interactional level, both well-intentioned hesitation and dismissive hostility from male training partners can lead to women's place within sporting clubs being compromised; unchallenged sexist assumptions derived from orthodox gender expectations can create unwelcoming or off-putting social environments, ensuring that few women enter or stay within clubs that are ostensibly open to them; while bans on women competing against men in their respective weight categories leaves women's skills underdeveloped if few female opponents can be found in regional or local competitions (Channon, 2013; Channon & Jennings, 2013; Owton, 2015). Together, such factors operate to perpetuate old systems of male privilege, effectively reducing the symbolic impact of women's entry into male preserves.

Concluding thoughts

Within the limited space available to us, we have mapped key developments in the sociological study of sport as both reflective of, and symbolically constitutive of, men's domination elsewhere in society. A variety of evidence can be used to unpick simplistic conceptions of sport as purely a male or masculine social endeavour. The argument we have presented here is that, notwithstanding such challenges and social shifts, it is essential to still continue to critically explore the ways in which sport can operate as a male preserve. Indeed, it is incumbent on scholars to move beyond some of the more obvious, headline-grabbing examples of the progressive inroads that women and girls, along with various LGBT people, have made into the traditionally heterosexist and masculine world of sport, in order to explore the subtle ways that the male preserve might be reinvented and recreated. And by centring a focus on such shifting dynamics, scholars interested in exploring the lives of men can produce more nuanced and robust accounts of sport and gender-based power.

Notes

1 In the sense of both asserting one's own status a man but also in so doing, serving the political project of proving men's power in a more generalised sense.
2 Paul Hoch's (1972) polemic neo-Marxist treatise, *Rip off the Big Game*, explores associated themes in American professional sport, although with a stronger focus on their pertinence to capitalist labour relations.
3 Somewhat ironically, athletes on opposing sides in professional sport should probably be considered as work colleagues. It is, after all, their collective labour which produces the marketable commodity of sporting spectacle, although this often involves the mutual destruction of each other's bodies.
4 Although there is little space to unpack this problematic and complex term here, in Matthews and Channon (2017) we discuss how various forms of 'violence' in sport might be understood.
5 See Matthews (2014) for a relatively recent examination of how this process of naturalising men's performances of masculinity takes place.
6 With a focus on men and masculinities here, we omit discussion of lesbians in the interests of space. Needless to say, because of the typical conflation of combat sports with masculinity, and female masculinity with lesbianism, the presence of lesbians or bisexual women in these sports is not so troubling to the typical gendered norms constructed around it as is the presence of gay or bisexual men.
7 Despite appearing in a number of gay porn films Cochrane always rejected his public 'outing' and instead claimed to be 'gay for pay' while in a long-term heterosexual relationship.

References

Aitchison, C. (2006). *Sport and gender identities: Masculinities, femininities and sexualities*. London: Routledge.

Anderson, E. (2009). *Inclusive masculinity: The changing nature of masculinities*. Abingdon: Routledge.

Anderson, E., & McCormack, M. (2010). Intersectionality, critical race theory, and American sporting oppression: Examining black and gay male athletes. *Journal of Homosexuality, 57*(8), 949–967.

Anderson, E., McGrath, R., & Bullingham, R. (2016). *Out in sport: The experiences of openly gay and lesbian athletes in competitive sport*. Abingdon: Routledge.

Atkinson, M. (2007). Playing with fire: Masculinity, health, and sports supplements. *Sociology of Sport Journal, 24*(2), 165–186.

Atkinson, M. (2011). *Deconstructing men and masculinity*. Oxford: Oxford University Press.

Birrell, S. (1984). Studying gender in sport: A feminist perspective. In N. Theberge & P. Donnelly (Eds.), *Sport and the sociological imagination* (pp. 125–135). Fort Worth, TX: Texas Christian University Press.

Bryson, L. (1987). Sport and the maintenance of masculine hegemony. *Women's Studies International Forum, 10*(4), 349–360.

Bryson, L. (1990). Challenges to male hegemony in sport. In M. Messner & D. Sabo (Eds.), *Sport, men, and the gender order: Critical feminist perspectives* (pp. 173–184). Champaign, IL: Human Kinetics.

Cahn, S. K. (1994). *Coming on strong: Gender and sexuality in twentieth century women's sport*. New York: Free Press.

Carrington, B. (1998). Sport, masculinity and black cultural resistance. *Journal of Sport and Social Issues*, *22*(3), 275–298.

Channon, A. (2013). Enter the discourse: Exploring the discursive roots of inclusivity in mixed-sex martial arts. *Sport in Society*, *16*(10), 1293–1308.

Channon, A. (2018). Martial arts studies and the sociology of gender: Theory, research and pedagogical application. In P. Bowman (Ed.), *The martial arts studies reader* (pp. 155–170). London: Rowman & Littlefield.

Channon, A., Dashper, K., Fletcher, T., & Lake, R. J. (Eds.). (2017). *Sex integration in sport and physical culture: Promises and pitfalls*. Abingdon: Routledge.

Channon, A., & Jennings, G. (2013). The rules of engagement: Negotiating painful and 'intimate' touch in mixed-sex martial arts. *Sociology of Sport Journal*, *30*(4), 487–503.

Channon, A., & Matthews, C. R. (2015a). 'It is what it is': Masculinity, homosexuality, and inclusive discourse in mixed martial arts. *Journal of Homosexuality*, *62*(7), 936–956.

Channon, A., & Matthews, C. R. (Eds.). (2015b). *Global perspectives on women in combat sports: Women warriors around the world*. Basingstoke: Palgrave Macmillan.

Channon, A., Matthews, C. R., & Wagner, H. (2013, April). *Coming out fighting: Discursive constructions of masculinity and homosexuality in online combat sports media*. Paper presented at Discourse, Power, Resistance 13, University of Greenwich, London.

Channon, A., Quinney, A., Khomutova, A., & Matthews, C. R. (2018). Sexualisation of the fighter's body: Some reflections on women's mixed martial arts. *Corps*, *16*(1), 383–391.

Connell, R. W. (2005). *Masculinities*. Cambridge: Polity Press.

Dunning, E. (1986). Sport as a male preserve: Notes on the social sources of masculine identity and its transformations. *Theory, Culture and Society*, *3*(1), 79–90.

Felt, H. (2014, November 14). Transgender MMA fighter Fallon Fox faces toughest opponent yet: Prejudice. *The Guardian*. Retrieved from www.theguardian.com/sport/2014/nov/14/transgender-mma-fighter-fallon-fox-joe-rogan.

Fields, S. K. (2005). *Female gladiators: Gender, law and contact sport in America*. Chicago, IL: University of Illinois Press.

Godoy-Pressland, A. (2015). Moral guardians, miniskirts and Nicola Adams: The changing media discourse on women's boxing. In A. Channon & C. R. Matthews (Eds.), *Global perspectives on women in combat sports: Women warriors around the world* (pp. 25–40). Basingstoke: Palgrave Macmillan.

Greendorfer, S. L., & Rubinson, L. (1997). Homophobia and heterosexism in women's sport and physical education: A review. *Women in Sport and Physical Activity Journal*, *6*(2), 189–210.

Guérandel, C., & Mennesson, C. (2007). Gender construction in judo interactions. *International Review for the Sociology of Sport*, *42*(2), 167–186.

Hargreaves, J. (1994). *Sporting females: Critical issues in the history and sociology of women's sports*. London: Routledge.

Heywood, L., & Dworkin, S. L. (2003). *Built to win: The female athlete as cultural icon*. Minneapolis, MN: University of Minnesota Press.

Hoch, P. (1972). *Rip off the big game*. Garden City, NY: Doubleday.

Hughes, R., & Coakley, J. (1991). Positive deviance among athletes: The implications of overconformity to the sport ethic. *Sociology of Sport Journal*, *8*(4), 307–325.

International Olympic Committee. (2016). *Women in the Olympic movement: Update –January 2016*. Lausanne: Olympic Studies Centre.

Jakubowska, H., Channon, A., & Matthews, C. R. (2016). Gender, media, and mixed martial arts in Poland: The case of Joanna Jędrzejczyk. *Journal of Sport and Social Issues*, *40*(5), 410–431.

Jennings, L. A. (2015). *She's a knockout! A history of women's fighting sports*. London: Rowman & Littlefield.

Kane, M. J., & Lenskyj, H. (1998). Media treatment of female athletes: Issues of gender and sexuality. In L. Wenner (Ed.), *MediaSport: Cultural sensibilities and sport in the media age* (pp. 186–201). Boston, MA: Routledge & Kegan Paul.

Kavoura, A., Chroni, S., Kokkonen, M., & Ryba, T. V. (2015). Women fighters as agents of change: A Brazilian jiu jitsu case study from Finland. In A. Channon & C. R. Matthews (Eds.), *Global perspectives on women in combat sports: Women warriors around the world* (pp. 135–152). Basingstoke: Palgrave Macmillan.

Krane, V., & Waldron, J. (2000). The gay games: Creating our own sports culture. In K. Schaffer & S. Smith (Eds.), *The Olympics at the millennium: Power, politics and the games* (pp. 147–166). New Brunswick, NJ: Rutgers University Press.

Lawrence, S. (2016). Racialising the 'great man': A critical race study of idealised male athletic bodies in *Men's Health* magazine. *International Review for the Sociology of Sport, 51*(7), 777–799.

Lindemann, K., & Cherney, J. L. (2008). Communicating in and through 'Murderball': Masculinity and disability in wheelchair rugby. *Western Journal of Communication, 72*(2), 107–125.

Maclean, C. (2017). Friendships worth fighting for: Bonds between women and men karate practitioners as sites for deconstructing gender inequality. In A. Channon, K. Dashper, T. Fletcher & R. J. Lake (Eds.), *Sex integration in sport and physical culture: Promises and pitfalls* (pp. 264–274). Abingdon: Routledge.

Matthews, C. R. (2014). Biology ideology and pastiche hegemony. *Men and Masculinities, 17*(2), 99–119.

Matthews, C. R. (2016a). The tyranny of the male preserve. *Gender & Society, 30*(2), 312–333.

Matthews, C. R. (2016b). Exploring the pastiche hegemony of men. *Palgrave Communications, 2*(1), 1–9.

Matthews, C. R., & Channon, A. (2016). 'It's only sport': The symbolic neutralisation of 'violence'. *Symbolic Interaction, 39*(4), 557–576.

Matthews, C. R., & Channon, A. (2017). Understanding sports violence: Revisiting foundational explorations. *Sport in Society, 20*(7), 751–767.

McCree, R. (2015). The fight outside the ring: Female boxing officials in Trinidad and Tobago. In A. Channon & C. R. Matthews (Eds.), *Global perspectives on women in combat sports: Women warriors around the world* (pp. 104–118). Basingstoke: Palgrave Macmillan.

McDonagh, E., & Pappano, L. (2008). *Playing with the boys: Why separate is not equal in sports*. New York: Oxford University Press.

McKay, J., Messner, M. A., & Sabo, D. (Eds.). (2000). *Masculinities, gender relations and sport*. London: Sage.

McNaughton, M. J. (2012). Insurrectionary womanliness: Gender and the (boxing) ring. *The Qualitative Report, 17*, 1–13.

Messner, M. A. (1992). *Power at play: Sports and the problem of masculinity*. Boston, MA: Beason Press.

Messner, M. A. (2002). *Taking the field: Women, men, and sports*. Minneapolis, MN: University of Minnesota Press.

Messner, M. A., & Sabo, D. (Eds.). (1990). *Sport, men and the gender order: Critical feminist perspectives*. Champaign, IL: Human Kinetics.

Mierzwinski, M., Velija, P., & Malcolm, D. (2014). Women's experiences in the mixed martial arts: A quest for excitement? *Sociology of Sport Journal, 31*(1), 66–84.

Miller, S. A. (2010). Making the boys cry: The performative dimensions of fluid gender. *Text and Performance Quarterly, 30*(2), 163–182.

Owton, H. (2015). Reinventing the body-self: Intense, gendered and heightened sensorial experiences of women's boxing embodiment. In A. Channon & C. R. Matthews (Eds.), *Global perspectives on women in combat sports: Women warriors around the world* (pp. 221–236). Basingstoke: Palgrave Macmillan.

Pease, B. (2000). *Recreating men: Postmodern masculinity politics*. London: Sage.

Pieper, L. P. (2017). Preserving la differencé: The elusiveness of sex-segregated sport. In A. Channon, K. Dashper, T. Fletcher & R. J. Lake (Eds.), *Sex integration in sport and physical culture: Promises and pitfalls* (pp. 28–45). Abingdon: Routledge.

Pronger, B. (1990). *The arena of masculinity: Sport, homosexuality, and the meaning of sex*. New York: St. Martin's Press.

Pronger, B. (2000). Homosexuality and sport: Who's winning? In J. McKay, M. A. Messner & D. Sabo (Eds.), *Masculinities, gender relations and sport* (pp. 222–244). London: Sage.

Sheard, K. G., & Dunning, E. G. (1973). The rugby football club as a type of 'male preserve': Some sociological notes. *International Review of Sport Sociology, 8*(3), 5–24.

Sparkes, A. C., & Smith, B. (2002). Sport, spinal cord injury, embodied masculinities, and the dilemmas of narrative identity. *Men and Masculinities, 4*(3), 258–285.

Theberge, N. (1985). Towards a feminist alternative to sport as a male preserve. *Quest, 37*(2), 193–202.

Theberge, N. (1987). Sport and women's empowerment. *Women's Studies International Forum, 10*(4), 387–393.

Waitt, G. (2003). Gay game: Performing 'community' out of the closet of the locker room. *Social and Cultural Geography, 4*(2), 167–183.

Wellard, I. (2012). *Sport, masculinities and the body*. London: Routledge.

White, P., & Gillett, J. (1994). Reading the muscular body: A critical decoding of advertisements in flex magazine. *Sociology of Sport, 11*(1), 18–39.

Whitson, D. (1990). Sport in the social construction of masculinity. In M. Messner & D. Sabo (Eds.), *Sport, men and the gender order: Critical feminist perspectives* (pp. 19–29). Champaign, IL: Human Kinetics.

Woodward, K. (2014). Legacy of 2012: Putting women's boxing into discourse. *Contemporary Social Science, 9*(2), 242–252.

Young, K. (1993). Violence, risk, and liability in male sports culture. *Sociology of Sport Journal, 10*(4), 373–396.

37

Masculinity never plays itself

From representations to forms in American cinema and media studies

Terrance H. McDonald

From gangsters flaunting guns to cowboys fighting outlaws to muscular heroes delivering catchphrases, moving images generate many opportunities to analyze masculinities, especially the stereotypes and ideals they project. However, examining representations of masculinity through characters, dialogue, and narrative events are far from the only methods for examining masculinities within cinema and media studies. While reading representations of masculinities is a popular practice in the field, there is also the potential to investigate a number of other issues. For example, scholars can investigate how patriarchy structures visual pleasure (Mulvey, 1975/2009) or how masculinities are conveyed through film style (Bruzzi, 2013). Furthermore, as I will map at the end of this chapter, moving images also create the capacity to speculate about masculinities as forms. With so much written on masculinities in the field of cinema and media studies, it would be impossible to engage with every work that contributes to the discourse. In place of an insuperable task, this chapter identifies significant methodologies for the study of masculinities and moving images, and it highlights key contributions that shaped or augmented the theory and praxis of the field. While this chapter emphasizes important theoretical concepts and critical debates that focus on American cinema, it also references important international work in English that extends this discourse into discussions of European and World cinemas to reveal the nuances and specificities of international masculinities.

Beginnings: representation and spectatorship

Joan Mellen (1977) was one of the first scholars to engage in a book-length study of masculinities in American cinema. Before a discussion of dominant trends displayed by Hollywood masculinities within each decade, Mellen's (1977) introduction outlines how there is a "fabrication in American films of a male superior to women, defiant, assertive, and utterly fearless" (p. 3). This recognition by Mellen occurs during an important shift within cinema studies, which is propelled by a psychoanalytic turn that meets an increasing focus on feminist perspectives. Highlighting the gender inequality present in Hollywood films, Mellen's work connects to a feminist challenge to a patriarchal hierarchy that seeks to demonstrate the structures of oppression that maintain systemic sexism in popular narrative cinema.

However, Mellen (1977) also notes the impact that these cinematic ideals of masculinity have on the lives of men (p. 5). Rather than simply articulating a critique, she takes the time to engage with the specific nuances of each decade and considers the motivations as well as the outcomes of these images. In addition, Mellen (1977) does not take popular narrative cinema as a monolith with a singular representation of masculinity, and she points to nuances that differentiate the "Big Bad Wolves" of different decades and to other representations (i.e., the films of Chaplin and Keaton) that embrace a shared "human vulnerability" (pp. 4–5). Although there are few references to Mellen's book made by other works in the field, her work should be noted as making key observations that have remained primary concerns for scholars working at the intersections of masculinities and moving images. Within her readings of popular films, Mellen outlines the detrimental socio-cultural effects that are caused by the unrealistic masculine ideals of Hollywood. What is now a common observation from various perspectives of cultural studies, Mellen (1977) acknowledges that popular media can leave us, as viewers, with "an overwhelming sense of our own inadequacy" (p. 5). This initial work by Mellen seizes on the potential of popular film and other media to have a harmful impact on society if the unrealistic masculinities represented become consumed as models to emulate.

Laura Mulvey's 1975 journal article "Visual Pleasure and Narrative Cinema" provided a theoretical foundation for making connections between socio-cultural conditions and moving images. Far more influential than Mellen's book, Mulvey provided a set of concepts that could be mobilized to study representations of gender within cinema studies. In addition, beyond a discussion of representations, Mulvey's focus on film form launched an interrogation of cinematic style and spectatorship, which had been taken as universal (Metz, 1982). "In a world ordered by sexual imbalance," states Mulvey (1975/2009), "pleasure in looking has been split between active/male and passive/female" (p. 19). While Mulvey's objective is to deconstruct the framework of popular narrative cinema in order to advocate for a feminist avant-garde style of filmmaking that re-structures practices of cinematic viewing, the concepts she developed out of psychoanalytic theory for critiquing this gendered split in visual pleasure remain central to the field. For examining representations of masculinities within cinema studies, the notion of "active" male characters driving the narrative action and taking control of the look, or the gaze, remains a key issue. Although she is focused on classical Hollywood (approximately 1915 to 1960), many of the scholars referenced in this chapter still use Mulvey's concepts. Mulvey (1975/2009) notes that there are three looks that combine to sustain visual pleasure: the look of the male character, the look of the camera, and the look of the spectator. For example, in Alfred Hitchcock's *Vertigo* (1958), when Scottie follows Madeleine into a flower shop, viewers are aligned with his gaze through a cut from his looking to her as the object of his looking. Mulvey's theory is important because it provides tools for breaking down the codified structure of moving images, especially popular narrative cinema. Moreover, her work launches a conversation about how sexual difference impacts visual pleasure, which leads to challenges and augmentations of her theory (e.g., Kaplan, 2000a).

For Mulvey (1975/2009), a sexual imbalance occurs through the construction of a male gaze – the three looks – that objectifies women, which reflects the patriarchal structure of society as well as a means for culturally maintaining this inequality (p. 20). The passive female characters of popular narrative cinema are framed as a striking display for male characters as well as male spectators (the theory is problematically heteronormative), hence her conceptualization of the male gaze that is so often employed in studies of gender and cinema. Mulvey notes that women are a spectacle as well as a perceived danger for the male unconscious, which is steeped in psychoanalytic theory. Her reading of Freud and Lacan has been critiqued, but it is still recognized as generative (see Rodowick, 1991). By sparking castration anxiety that threatens and overwhelms those in control of the gaze, female characters within popular films receive two responses motivated by the male unconscious: an investigation of the feminine threat and demystification of her, which leads to saving or punishing (common in film noir, as Mulvey notes); or a fetishization that breaks female characters down into individual parts through close-up and other visual strategies (Mulvey, 1975/2009, p. 22). "Man is reluctant to gaze at his exhibitionist self," states Mulvey (1975/2009), which explains why the look concentrates on woman as spectacle (p. 20). Kaplan (2000b), among others, would question if the gaze is always male or if it is possible to explore alternative processes of looking in relation to popular narrative cinema. Despite many critiques, Mulvey's theory remains an important reference point, or counterpoint, for work on gender within cinema and media studies. For works that challenge this heteronormative perspective, see de Lauretis (1991), Greven (2009, 2016), and Waugh (1996, 2000). Diawara (1988) and hooks (1996) interrogate Mulvey's concepts in relation to Black spectatorship. Also, emerging work on Latin American cinema and masculinities incorporates Mulvey's theory, but scholars also demonstrate the shortcomings of this perspective for analyzing films made outside of the United States (e.g., de la Mora, 2006; Rocha, 2012; Subero, 2014, 2016; Venkatesh, 2016).

Steve Neale's 1983 journal article is a response to Mulvey, and it remains a key reference for analyzing masculinities and moving images. Neale (1983/1993) begins by acknowledging the importance of Mulvey's work, but he also notes that few works analyze "how heterosexual masculinity is inscribed and the mechanisms, pressures, and contradictions that inscription may involve" (p. 9). Neale does not seek to counter Mulvey's claim regarding women as spectacle, but instead he outlines how a patriarchal structure displaces an erotic looking away from male bodies. While critiques of Mulvey's theory offer instances of women spectators experiencing visual pleasure by looking at male bodies, Neale accepts the parameters of Mulvey's theory and probes what tendencies keep spectators from looking at and objectifying male bodies. In particular, Neale notes that if male bodies within popular narrative films are active, such as being engaged in combat or chasing after a criminal, then these activities offer moments when male bodies are on display. "All of which implies that male figures on the screen are subject to voyeuristic looking," states Neale, "both on the part of the spectator and on the part of other male characters" (p. 16). Therefore, what prevents the gaze of a spectator from eroticizing male bodies in battle or on horseback or at work in uniform? In short, nothing stops any viewer from looking where and how they want to look. Nonetheless, for Neale, there is a visual structure, as identified by Mulvey, which displaces or obscures many of the possibilities for this type of looking.

While spectators may find male bodies visually pleasurable, the composition of popular narrative films (especially from classical Hollywood) tends to foreclose opportunities for us to directly access these moments through the looks of characters and the camera. "We are offered the spectacle of male bodies," states Neale (1983/1993), "but bodies unmarked as objects of erotic display" (p. 18). Consequently, Mulvey's point about the reluctance of men to stare at their exhibitionist selves holds, but the male body is still very much on display within popular narrative films. Where the female body, within this patriarchal structure, is objectified by the looks of characters and spectators, something different is occurring in relation to male bodies, according to Neale. "We see male bodies stylized and fragmented by close-ups," argues Neale, "but our look is not direct, it is heavily mediated by the looks of the characters involved" (p. 18). Therefore, given that male characters drive the action as well as the heteronormative predisposition of the patriarchal system, male characters look at other male characters with different feelings and, by extension, so do spectators who submit to the visual patterns of a film suturing (Silverman, 1983) them into this perspective. For Neale (1983/1993), these "looks are marked not by desire, but rather by fear, or hatred, or aggression" (p. 18). Neale reads the looks of other male characters as informing the dominant viewing position of spectators, which is rarely one of erotic desire and, instead, becomes informed by the type of action within the scene. Overall, Neale highlights the tendency of popular narrative cinema to repress male homosexuality by functioning to deny or obfuscate moments where the male body is an "object of investigation" (p. 19). Furthermore, Neale's work is important because it outlines the fragility of patriarchy and heterosexuality, which must be consistently maintained through the denial of any alternative subjectivities or pleasures.

A crisis of masculinity?

Similar to a masculinities studies discourse that emerged in the 1980s and 1990s, the construction of masculinities becomes a central focus for analysis within cinema studies, which aims to decenter the male subject and reveal the default tendency to conflate masculinity as universal. However, this methodology can veer into readings of masculinity in crisis. For example, Pam Cook (1982) asks this question in reference to Martin Scorsese's *Raging Bull* (1980). This trend motivates scholars to return to previous periods of cinema to interrogate representations of masculinities in order to reveal a crisis, such as Frank Krutnik's (1991) work on film noir. "The displacement of the narratively organised process of masculine consolidation, and the prevalence of traumatised or castrated males," argues Krutnik, "can be taken as signs of a disjunction between, on the one hand, the contemporary representational possibilities of the masculine self-image and, on the other, the traditional cultural codifications of masculine identity" (p. 91). Analyzing the hard-boiled detective films of the 1940s, Krutnik connects the dominant male character types as well as the typical narrative structure to a socio-cultural issue related to changing gender definitions. Therefore, the masculine traits and male characters that frequent film noir during this period become a symptom of "some kind of crisis of confidence within the contemporary regimentation of male-dominated culture" (Krutnik, 1991, p. 91). Through this approach, the failures of tough-talking male characters found in films such as Billy Wilder's *Double Indemnity* (1944) or Jacques Tourneur's *Out of the Past* (1947) are shown to speak to, if not replicate, the angst of men within America in the wake of World War II.

Representations of masculinity in postwar American films have generated a lot of scholarship, such as Kaja Silverman's (1992) psychoanalytic investigation of alternative masculinities. Her *Male Subjectivity at the Margins* examines both literary and cinematic texts, with a large section of the text devoted to postwar masculinity. Overall, Silverman states, "the masculinities which this book will interrogate, and even in certain instances work to eroticize or privilege, are those which not only acknowledge but embrace castration, alterity, and specularity" (p. 3). Therefore, she builds on the initial observations made by Neale and pushes the boundaries of masculinities studies beyond the framework set by Mulvey's initial journal article. Despite attributes of castration, alterity, and specularity being a condition for all subjectivities, Silverman demonstrates that conceptions of masculinities deny this reality and leave these attributes connected primarily to the female subject (p. 3). Therefore, she probes instances where representations of male subjectivity are found at the margins, or beyond dominant regimes of representation. Through psychoanalytic theory, Silverman outlines how dominant or essentialist notions of the male subject are undermined as well as how "the paternal function" fails within these films (p. 52). Furthermore, for Silverman, these postwar Hollywood films that feature male soldiers who return "with a physical or psychic wound" and that explore this condition "dramatize the vulnerability of conventional masculinity" (p. 53). While concerned with non-conventional masculinity, Silverman's work also highlights the acceptance of a crisis discourse. For example, Silverman argues that *It's a Wonderful Life* "addresses the crisis in postwar male subjectivity" (p. 120). Therefore, within these readings we can recognize how postwar America is often determined to be a period when masculinity is in crisis (Lawrence, 1997).

Mike Chopra-Gant (2006) confronts the notion of postwar masculinity in crisis through a discussion of genre films from the 1940s. Nevertheless, assumption of masculine crisis remains a popular perspective within cinema studies scholarship. For Chris Robé (2013), "it has become something of a mantra to proclaim white heterosexual American masculinity in 'crisis'" (p. 101). This "mantra" extends into various decades of American cinema. "Since the 1980s," argue Susanne Kord and Elisabeth Krimmer (2011), "there has been a broad consensus in literature, albeit written from varying perspectives and with different agendas, that masculinity is in 'crisis'" (p. 37). Discussions of masculine crisis can be found within many contexts and in relation to distinct periods and regions of filmmaking (e.g., Chopra-Gant, 2013; Davies, 1995; Ging, 2013; Harwood, 1997; Holmlund, 2008; Ly, 2012; Mizejewski, 2008; Pang, 2002; Powrie, 1997; Rigoletto, 2014; Robinson, 2000; Stringer, 1997). However, there is a challenge to this masculine crisis discourse. Tania Modleski (1991) makes an important intervention to argue that "we need to consider the extent to which male power is actually consolidated through cycles of crisis and resolution, whereby men ultimately deal with the threat of female power by incorporating it" (p. 7). By projecting a crisis in response to challenges from social justice movements striving for equality, Modleski views masculinity, supported by a patriarchal framework, as projecting white, heterosexual men as victims to undercut these movements.

The recent work of Philippa Gates (2006) and Barry Keith Grant (2011) push back against this masculine crisis discourse. For Grant, it is more appropriate to view masculinities as part of ongoing negotiations. Reading any period from American film history as representing a masculine crisis, according to Grant, "is both inappropriate hyperbole and a serious misunderstanding of Hollywood cinema" (2011, p. 6). By dedicating chapters to individual periods in American cinema, Grant argues that popular narrative cinema is part of "an ongoing dialogue with audiences about ceaseless challenges to and valorization of heteronormative ideals" (2011, p. 6). Therefore, Grant's work provides an important pathway for returning to individual moments within history of cinema to read individual films, cycles, and genres to investigate the relationship between representations of masculinities in film and socio-cultural concerns regarding socio-cultural definitions of gender in any given moment. This trend of focusing on a specific period of American cinema to examine the way in which masculinities are represented is a common approach (see Cohan, 1997; Combe & Boyle, 2013; Holmlund, 2008; Jeffords, 1994; Shary, 2013; Studlar, 1996), as is reading individual genres in a given moment or the evolution of representations in a given genre, such as the horror film (Clover, 2015; Grant, 1996), the bromance (Alberti, 2013; DeAngelis, 2014), the action adventure film (Gallagher, 2006; Purse, 2011; Tasker, 1993), and the war film (Donald & MacDonald, 2011; Eberwein, 2007; Mann, 2014). In addition, scholars have interrogated representations of Black masculinities in American cinema and beyond (e.g., Boylorn, 2017; Gillespie, 2016; O'Brien, 2017; Reid, 1993; Sexton, 2017; Watkins, 1998). Moreover, the approach to periods and genres is also popular beyond American cinema scholarship, including work on martial arts cinema from Hong Kong (Teo, 2009; Yip, 2017), Hong Kong cinema more generally (Pang

& Wong, 2005; Sandell, 1996; Stringer, 1997), Korean cinema (Jung, 2011; Kim, 2004), Japanese cinema (Standish, 2000), Latin American cinema (de la Mora, 2006; Rocha, 2012; Subero, 2016), and Spanish cinema (Hartson, 2017).

Gates' (2006) challenge to the masculine crisis discourse is similar to Grant's, but she offers a more substantial reading of masculinities studies scholarship as well as the prevailing views within cinema studies before reading periods of the Hollywood detective film. Furthermore, by conceptualizing masculinities as in continuous fluctuation (p. 49), Gates offers a pathway for reading representations of masculinities within established methodologies of the field. "The aim of popular film is not to record reality," states Gates (2006), "but to process it through idealized characters, narratives, and themes into a fantasy that will bring pleasure to its audience" (p. 48). Therefore, whether films offer viewers the hard bodies of 1980s action films, or men undergoing existential crisis as was popular in the 1990s, there is no evidence to support the notion that men in society are experiencing a crisis (Gates, 2006, p. 49). Gates situates her analysis within a lineage of cinema studies that privileges bodies (e.g., Holmlund, 2002; Lehman, 1993, 2001; Tasker, 1993) and the notion, developed through a reading of Judith Butler, that masculinity is a performance or a masquerade. Gates challenges the connection of masculinity to male bodies, which is more thoroughly addressed by scholars investigating female characters within roles usually aligned with masculinity (i.e., Modleski, 1999; Tasker, 1998).

Masculinities and form

Following Gates and many of the other scholars discussed here, moving images are routinely analyzed for how masculinities are represented and the possible socio-cultural implications of these representations. When analyzing representations of masculinities, the focal point is the characters and narrative events that connect to socio-cultural notions of masculinity – whether the film is seen as addressing a concern of viewers or if the film is understood as influencing audiences to adopt a specific point of view. For example, Susan Jeffords (1994) demonstrates how the hard bodies of action heroes during the Reagan era reflected American concerns related to the domestic and foreign perceptions of the nation. Hollywood action of films of the 1980s, according to Jeffords, "offered narratives against which American men and women could test, revise, affirm, or negate images of their own conceptions of masculinity" (1994, pp. 11–12). Beyond the methodologies that read representations, new movements within the field are emerging. Stella Bruzzi (2013) puts forth a new approach through her claim that "spectacular, 'men's cinema' uses style and *mise en scène* to convey masculinity, not merely represent it" (p. 5). In a reading of Brad Bird's *Mission: Impossible – Ghost Protocol* (2011), Bruzzi argues, "[t]he spectator is placed here, as in many other examples of 'men's cinema', in a position of quasi-identification, not so much with the hero as with the film's visual style" (2013, p. 5). This approach opens up new potentialities for masculinities studies and moving images because it challenges scholars to investigate how visual style mediates our conceptualizations and experiences of masculinities. There is also a direct connection here to the initial points raised by Mulvey, which returns to an interrogation of film form as intimately intertwined with gendered meanings.

With the title to this chapters as a nod to Thom Andersen's *Los Angeles Plays Itself* (2003), thinking about masculinities and moving images often intermingles with words familiar to Hollywood: looking, performance, masquerade, crisis, persona, illusion, constructed, and fabricated. However, unlike the Los Angeles explored cinematically by Andersen, masculinities have no physical referent. Even if Los Angeles, and Hollywood, change over time and the city can perform as other places, there remains a space connected by streets that has existed as long as the movies. Masculinities have no such physical referent – even if essentialist discourses attempt to persuade us with pseudo-science and myths. What becomes apparent in a survey of work on masculinities and moving images is that masculinity can never play itself. From Mulvey's theoretical work that outlines how images of women are the bearers of meaning, to Neale's notion of masculinity as a spectacle consistently displaced from male bodies, to Gates' understanding of masculinity in constant fluctuation, masculinities remain ever fleeting. Constructed in a given moment by socio-cultural opinions or briefly glimpsed in the fading persona portrayed by an icon, masculinities remain traced in borrowed time only ever possible because we imagine them to be. Codes or qualities or characteristics or tendencies or conditions, masculinities are predisposed to being read as images because images are all they can become. However, this feature does not impede masculinities from having a tangible impact on people, environments, societies, culture, and, all too relevant in our given moment, politics. Like any fiction, it is tempting to believe, especially if it offers others to blame for circumstances that are unfavourable or disappointing. Therefore, identifying and critiquing problematic representations and highlighting alternative images are vital tasks – as much of the works discussed in this chapter do.

While harnessing the potential to be destructive, masculinity never playing itself can also be quite generative. If masculinity is so codified and lacking an essential or natural set of characteristics, then there is the potential to always already think masculinities in new ways. Consequently, beyond analyzing representations of masculinity, a turn to a radical formalism (Brinkema, 2014) and the affordances of form (Levine, 2015) can open up a reading of masculinities as forms that can launch creative speculation. This approach embraces a film philosophy methodology that seizes moving images as a vibrant force for creative thinking as opposed to recognizing static signs contained by images. Furthermore, this approach mobilizes developments in formalism that, as Brinkema (2014) notes, involves the slow, close reading of "montage, camera movement, mise-en-scène, color, sound" as well as "more ephemeral problematics such as duration, rhythm, absences, elisions, ruptures, gaps, and points of contradiction (ideological, aesthetic, structural, and formal)" (p. 37). Through a close reading of masculinities as forms, masculinities are conceptualized as taking shape through moving images, which exposes their capacity to materialize via structures as well as transform in relation to forces (McDonald, 2018). Therefore, even if masculinity never plays itself, readings masculinities as forms continuously fractures transcendent ideals and essentialist views that attempt to anchor masculinity within toxic and oppressive systems. In place of such problematic renditions, tired proclamations, and unjust hierarchies, the forms of masculinities that take shape through a close reading of moving images and creative speculation unceasingly push us to conceptualize masculinities through the unexpected and astonishing potential of what has yet to come.

References

Alberti, J. (2013). *Masculinity in the contemporary romantic comedy: Gender as genre.* London: Routledge.

Boylorn, R. M. (2017). From boys to men: Hip-hop, hood films, and the performance of contemporary Black masculinity. *Black Camera, 8*(20), 146–164.

Brinkema, E. (2014). *The forms of the affects.* Durham, NC: Duke University Press.

Bruzzi, S. (2013). *Men's cinema: Masculinity and mise en scène in Hollywood.* Edinburgh: Edinburgh University Press.

Chopra-Gant, M. (2013). "I'd fight my dad": Absent fathers and mediated masculinities in *Fight club*. In T. Shary (Ed.), *Millennial masculinity: Men in contemporary American cinema* (pp. 85–100). Detroit, MI: Wayne State University Press.

Chopra-Gant, M. (2006). *Hollywood genres and postwar America: Masculinity, family and nation in popular movies and film noir*. London: I. B. Tauris.

Clover, C. J. (2015). *Men, women, and chainsaws: Gender in the modern horror film*. Princeton, NJ: Princeton University Press.

Cohan, S. (1997). *Masked men: Masculinity and the movies in the fifties*. Bloomington, IN: Indiana University Press.

Combe, K., & Boyle, B. (2013). *Masculinity and monstrosity in contemporary Hollywood films*. New York: Palgrave Macmillan.

Cook, P. (1982). Masculinity in crisis? *Screen, 23*(3/4), 39–46.

Davies, J. (1995). Gender, ethnicity and cultural crisis in *Falling down* and *Groundhog day*. *Screen, 36*(3), 214–232.

de la Mora, S. (2006). *Cinemachismo: Masculinities and sexuality in Mexican film*. Austin, TX: University of Texas Press.

de Lauretis, T. (1991). Queer theory: Lesbian and gay sexualities: An introduction. *Differences, 3*(2), iii–xviii.

DeAngelis, M. (Ed.). (2014). *Reading the bromance: Homosocial relationships in film and television*. Detroit, MI: Wayne State University Press.

Diawara, M. (1988). Black spectatorship: Problems of identification and resistance. *Screen, 29*(4), 66–79.

Donald, R., & MacDonald, K. (2011). *Reel men at war: Masculinity and the American war film*. Lanham, MD: The Scarecrow Press.

Eberwein, R. (2007). *Armed forces: Masculinity and sexuality in the American war film*. New Brunswick, NJ: Rutgers University Press.

Gallagher, M. (2006). *Action figures: Men, action films, and contemporary adventure narratives*. New York: Palgrave Macmillan.

Gates, P. (2006). *Detecting men: Masculinity and the Hollywood detective film*. Albany, NY: State University of New York Press.

Gillespie, M. B. (2016). *Film Blackness: American cinema and the idea of Black film*. Durham, NC: Duke University Press.

Ging, D. (2013). *Men and masculinities in Irish cinema*. New York: Palgrave Macmillan.

Grant, B. K. (Ed.). (1996). *The dread of difference: Gender and the horror film*. Austin, TX: University of Texas Press.

Grant, B. K. (2011). *Shadows of doubt: Negotiations of masculinity in American genre films*. Detroit, MI: Wayne State University Press.

Greven, D. (2009). *Manhood in Hollywood: From Bush to Bush*. Austin, TX: University of Texas Press.

Greven, D. (2016). *Ghost faces: Hollywood and post-millennial masculinity*. Albany, NY: State University of New York Press.

Hartson, M. T. (2017). *Casting masculinity in Spanish film: Negotiating identity in a consumer age*. Lanham, MD: Lexington Books.

Harwood, S. (1997). *Family fictions: Representations of the family in 1980s Hollywood cinema*. New York: St. Martin's Press.

Holmlund, C. (2002). *Impossible bodies: Femininity and masculinity at the movies*. London: Routledge.

Holmlund, C. (2008). Movies and millennial masculinity. In C. Holmlund (Ed.), *American cinema of the 1990s: Themes and variations* (pp. 225–248). New Brunswick, NJ: Rutgers University Press.

hooks, b. (1996). *Reel to real: Race, class and sex at the movies*. London: Routledge.

Jeffords, S. (1994). *Hard bodies: Hollywood masculinity in the Reagan era*. New Brunswick, NJ: Rutgers University Press.

Jung, S. (2011). *Korean masculinities and transnational consumption*. Hong Kong: Hong Kong University Press.

Kaplan, E. A. (Ed.).(2000a). *Feminism and film*. Oxford: Oxford University Press.

Kaplan, E. A. (2000b). Is the gaze male? In E. A. Kaplan (Ed.), *Feminism and film* (pp. 119–138). Oxford: Oxford University Press.

Kim, K. H. (2004). *The remasculinization of Korean cinema*. Durham, NC: Duke University Press.

Kord, S., & Krimmer, E. (2011). *Contemporary Hollywood masculinities: Gender, genre, and politics*. New York: Palgrave Macmillan.

Krutnik, F. (1991). *In a lonely street: Film noir, genre, masculinity*. London: Routledge.

Lawrence, A. (1997). Jimmy Stewart is being beaten: Rope and the postwar crisis in American masculinity. *Quarterly Review of Film & Video, 16*(1), 41–58.

Lehman, P. (1993). *Running scared: Masculinity and the representation of the male body*. Philadelphia, PA: Temple University Press.

Lehman, P. (Ed.). (2001). *Masculinity: Bodies, movies, culture*. London: Routledge.

Levine, C. (2015). *Forms: Whole, rhythm, hierarchy, network*. Princeton, NJ: Princeton University Press.

Ly, B. (2012). Screening the crisis of monetary masculinity in Rithy Panh's *One night after the war* and *Burnt theatre*. In D. C. L. Lim & H. Yamamoto (Eds.), *Film in contemporary Southeast Asia: Cultural interpretation and social intervention* (pp. 53–72). London: Routledge.

Mann, B. (2014). *Sovereign masculinity: Gender lessons from the war on terror*. Oxford: Oxford University Press.

McDonald, T. H. (2018). *Mediated masculinities: The forms of masculinity in American genre film, 1990–1999*. (Doctoral dissertation). Brock University, Canada. Retrieved from http://hdl.handle.net/10464/13355

Mellen, J. (1977). *Big bad wolves: Masculinity in the American film*. London: Elm Tree Books.

Metz, C. (1982). *The imaginary signifier: Psychoanalysis and the cinema*. Bloomington, IN: Indiana University Press.

Mizejewski, L. (2008). Movies and the off-white gangster. In C. Holmlund (Ed.), *American cinema of the 1990s: Themes and variations* (pp. 24–44). New Brunswick, NJ: Rutgers University Press.

Modleski, T. (1991). *Feminism without women: Culture and criticism in a 'postfeminist' age*. London: Routledge.

Modleski, T. (1999). *Old wives' tales: Feminist revisions of film and other fictions*. New York: I. B. Tauris.

Mulvey, L. (1975/2009). Visual pleasure and narrative cinema. In *Visual and other pleasures* (2nd ed., pp. 14–27). New York: Palgrave Macmillan.

Neale, S. (1983/1993). Masculinity as spectacle: Reflections on men and mainstream cinema. In S. Cohen & I. R. Hark (Eds.), *Screening the male: Exploring masculinities in Hollywood cinema* (pp. 9–20). London: Routledge.

O'Brien, D. (Ed.). (2017). *Black masculinity on film: Native sons and white lies*. New York: Palgrave Macmillan.

Pang, L. (2002). Masculinity in crisis: Films of milkyway image and post-1997 Hong Kong cinema. *Feminist Media Studies, 2*(3), 325–340.

Pang, L., & Wong, D. (2005). *Masculinities and Hong Kong cinema*. Hong Kong: Hong Kong University Press.

Powrie, P. (1997). *French cinema in the 1980s: Nostalgia and the crisis of masculinity*. Oxford: Oxford University Press.

Purse, L. (2011). *Contemporary action cinema*. Edinburgh: Edinburgh University Press.

Reid, M. A. (1993). *Redefining Black film*. Berkeley, CA: University of California Press.

Rigoletto, S. (2014). *Masculinity and Italian cinema: Sexual politics, social conflict and male crisis in the 1970s*. Edinburgh: Edinburgh University Press.

Robé, C. (2013). "Because I hate fathers, and I never wanted to be one": Wes Anderson, entitled masculinity, and the "crisis" of the patriarch. In T. Shary (Ed.), *Millennial masculinity: Men in contemporary American cinema* (pp. 101–121). Detroit, MI: Wayne State University Press.

Robinson, S. (2000). *Marked men: White masculinity in crisis*. New York: Columbia University Press.

Rocha, C. (2012). *Masculinities in contemporary Argentine popular cinema*. New York: Palgrave Macmillan.

Rodowick, D. N. (1991). *The difficulty of difference: Psychoanalysis, sexual difference, and film theory*. London: Routledge.

Sandell, J. (1996). Reinventing masculinity: The spectacle of male intimacy in the films of John Woo. *Film Quarterly, 49*(4), 23–34.

Sexton, J. (2017). *Black masculinity and the cinema of policing*. New York: Palgrave Macmillan.

Shary, T. (Ed.). (2013). *Millennial masculinity: Men in contemporary American cinema*. Detroit, MI: Wayne State University Press.

Silverman, K. (1983). Suture. In K. Silverman (Ed.), *The subject of semiotics* (pp. 194–236). Oxford: Oxford University Press.

Silverman, K. (1992). *Male subjectivity at the margins*. London: Routledge.

Standish, I. (2000). *Myth and masculinity in the Japanese cinema: Towards a political reading of the 'tragic hero'*. London: Routledge.

Stringer, J. (1997). "Your tender smiles give me strength": Paradigms of masculinity in John Woo's *A better tomorrow* and *The killer*. *Screen, 38*(1), 25–41.

Studlar, G. (1996). *This mad masquerade: Stardom and masculinity in the jazz age*. New York: Columbia University Press.

Subero, G. (2014). *Queer masculinities in Latin American cinema: Male bodies and narrative representations*. London: I. B. Tauris.

Subero, G. (2016). *Gender and sexuality in Latin American horror cinema: Embodiments of evil*. New York: Palgrave Macmillan.

Tasker, Y. (1993). *Spectacular bodies: Gender, genre and the action cinema*. London: Routledge.

Tasker, Y. (Ed.).(1998). *Working girls: Gender and sexuality in popular cinema*. London: Routledge.

Teo, S. (2009). *Chinese martial arts cinema: The wuxia tradition*. Edinburgh: Edinburgh University Press.

Venkatesh, V. (2016). *New Maricón cinema: Outing Latin American film*. Austin, TX: University of Texas Press.

Watkins, S. C. (1998). *Representing: Hip hop culture and the production of Black cinema*. Chicago, IL: University of Chicago Press.

Waugh, T. (1996). *Hard to imagine: Gay male eroticism in photography and film from their beginnings to Stonewall*. New York: Columbia University Press.

Waugh, T. (2000). *The fruit machine: Twenty years of writings on queer cinema*. Durham, NC: Duke University Press.

Yip, M. F. (2017). *Martial arts cinema and Hong Kong modernity: Aesthetics, representation, circulation*. Hong Kong: Hong Kong University Press.

38

Masculinities in fashion and dress

Andrew Reilly and José Blanco F.

Introduction to fashion, dress, and masculinities

Dressing the body is not only a daily practice but also a meaningful cultural phenomenon. Through the centuries, men have been engaged in appearance management practices just as complex and elaborate as those performed by women—yet the concept of fashion remains one that is mostly discussed within a frame of female practice. Colin Campbell (2012) insists that monitoring and discovering fashion styles and evaluating and selecting clothing pieces is a practice central to the development of identity. Dressing the male body on a daily basis is indeed about managing and performing identity in general and masculinity or masculinities in particular. Through a number of modifications and supplementations to the body, men choose to reinforce or minimize both biological and societal notions of masculinity. Fashion, a concept related to the use of appearance management, and clothing that is 'of the moment', 'of the place', or 'of the moment and place', allow men to negotiate identity and difference by using objects and processes that are codified as communicating shared meanings of masculinity at a given time and place. Additionally, fashion as in subcultural, countercultural, or anti-fashion practices allows men to challenge and resist those notions via the highly visual means of clothing and appearance management.

The field of fashion studies per se is relatively new, with origins traceable to the mid-twentieth century. Writers have addressed men's fashion, dress and appearance management practices throughout history either by pointing out or criticizing styles and trends that appear at a given time and place; by analyzing the creation, use, and significance of specific objects; or by studying how those objects reflect or help create a specific social, cultural, or geopolitical context. The number of studies on the connection between fashion and masculinity has increased in the last few decades. A *Men's Fashion Reader*—edited by Andrew Reilly and Sarah Cosbey—was published in 2008 and was followed by a similar volume edited by Peter McNeill and Vicki Karaminas, published just one year later, in 2009. While both tomes collect some classical writing related to men's clothing, the anthologies offered an opportunity to also present recent research coming from a variety of methods and perspectives such as the use of fashion as a tool to define identity or as a tool for resistance and defiance. Besides those two primary perspectives, the field of men's fashion studies also emphasizes questions related to the creation and consumption of apparel products and to the male body in itself within the context of changing beauty and body image parameters. Shaun Cole pioneered research on gay men's apparel (2000) and men's underwear (2010) while Christopher Breward has looked into historic British masculinities (2004) and the significance of the suit on men's wardrobes (2016). Paul Jobling has examined connections between masculinity and fashion advertising (2005, 2014), and Jennifer Craik (2005) has looked into the use of uniforms in a variety of settings including military, education and sports. Adam Geczy and Vicki Karaminas (2017) explored connections between fashion, masculinity and popular culture by examining a number of male types such as dandies, sailors, cowboys, hipsters, and superheroes. The appearance of the journal *Critical Studies in Men's Fashion* (Reilly, 2014) signaled the growth of the field providing researchers with an opportunity to publish their work from a number of perspectives including queer and gay fashion, global and subcultural masculinities, menswear in fashion exhibitions, and fashion consumption.

This chapter introduces the reader to basic concepts in fashion and its connection to masculinity by first discussing examples of how men manage their identity by adopting pieces such as business suits and by explaining how this 'managed self' can also be contested via fashion. We present a narrative of fashion in modern historical Euro-American societies to establish the slow change from fashion as a reflection of dominant hegemonic masculinities to the more fluid and complex masculinities appearing in fashion since the 1960s. The last section of the essay reviews a few examples of global geopolitical masculinities to illustrate that, although male fashion is fairly globalized, men around the world use fashion and appearance management to either comply with or rebel against notions of localized masculinities.

The business suit is, perhaps, the best example of a negotiated masculine identity—that of the 'career man'. Joanne Entwistle (1997) argues that the 'managed self' appears when external—in this case corporate—forces control the body and the clothes it wears. The suit, in this context, is considered a symbol of adherence to the code of businessmen attire. Wilbur Zelinsky (2004) actually describes the business suit as a crucial element of globalized male attire and believes that, historically, the adoption of business suits indicated the level of modernity in a society. The uniformity created by the business suit, however, has been constantly challenged by women who adopted the 'most masculine' of garments for their own use and by men who have subdued its meaning by either challenging uniform dress codes associated with the suit or by incorporating parts of it as part as their casual attire. This autonomy is what Entwistle (1997) calls the 'enterprising self', where, in opposition to the managed self, an individual produces an appearance developed through a regime of individual decisions and practices.

Fashion is, then, not only a reflection of social and cultural constructs but also a site of cultural production and identity negotiation; a tool for the construction of multiple performed and intersectional identities that are relational and fluid, changeable, and not fully stable. Recent research on men's fashion emphasizes plural masculinities (e.g., Beaule, 2015; Reddy-Best & Howell, 2014; Roberts, 2015). Observing global construction of masculinities, as discussed later in this chapter, also evidences how fashion and appearance management practices are used to question hegemonic masculinity stereotypes. Closer observation of localized fashion masculinities suggests that, although male attire is increasingly globalized, men around the world continue to challenge normative notions of dress, particularly notions that arose from European and American geographical and cultural colonization. Furthermore, masculinities in a given country can hardly be classified under one or even a few parameters. Local masculinities are performed via fashion and appearance management in different ways in urban and rural settings. Ken Moffatt (2012) argues that urban masculinities are hybrid, resulting from the complex social and cultural interplay of race, ethnicity, gender, class, and sexuality provided by the city landscape. Fashioned masculinities, thus, are as different as are the places men inhabit, since certain fashion codes are applied to locations such as bars, sports and music venues, domestic settings, office spaces, etc.

Racial, ethnic, and national masculine identities, then, are also negotiated through the consumption of fashion. In the hands of African-American men, pieces of African garb worn since the 1960s have signified rebellion against racial oppression in the United States, while articles of clothing long considered feminine are used by men to challenge Western concepts of masculinity and highlight other interpretations of maleness. Masculinity as an expression of gender can be reinforced through generally accepted codes of masculine appearance management and fashion. Those same codes can be easily challenged via appearance management—a skirt, a wig, a little bit of make-up—to construct alternative and non-conformist identities. Fashion can even be used to communicate an alternative class identity that operates, at least momentarily and superficially, when a man transforms himself into a member of a different class by 'dressing the part'. Fashion is essential to the creation, performance, and questioning of cultural constructs about masculinity. The selection of clothing is not only central to the development of specific notions about masculinity; fashion, indeed, is often a signifier for specific types of masculinity.

Modern historical Euro-American masculinities and fashion

Men's fashion and appearance management practices have always reflected the zeitgeist. Male fashion, however, became more diverse as an identity marker (age, status, social class) towards the end of the Middle Ages. In the centuries to follow, male fashion would remain as elaborate, complex, and changing as female fashion. The first step towards any type of standardization of men's fashion was the introduction in England in 1666 of the three-piece suit by King Charles II. The suit consisted of a coat, a vest or waistcoat, and breeches made in similar material and colors. During the eighteenth century, the three-piece suit worn by men of the upper classes was heavily decorated, embroidered, even trimmed in fur. Men wore white stockings and padded devices to create artificial calves. Their heads were adorned with powdered wigs—often arranged in ponytails and braids. All of the above were signs of a type of sartorial masculinity far from the more subdued styles that emerged in the nineteenth century. J. C. Flügel (1930) dubbed the sudden change in style and, by extension, in perception of color and pattern in connection to masculinity during the 1800s as the 'great masculine renunciation' (p. 110).

This transition was due mainly to a change in taste from the Baroque and Rococo aesthetic to an interest in neoclassical aesthetics, in part as a reflection of Napoleon's own inclinations. Furthermore, the change was propelled by the French Revolution, when sartorial excess was seen as a sign of the decadent aristocracy that the uprising aimed to eliminate. The 'Empire' man of the early nineteenth century discarded embroidery, satin, and lace in favor of plain fabrics and basic colors (i.e., black pants, blue coats, white waistcoats). The masculine silhouette also changed to a slightly more revealing fit, with pantaloons hugging the legs more closely, coats cinched at the waist, and garments—occasionally supported by corsets—cut to create a full-chested figure. This fashionable dandy, as these men were known in England, evolved not just from an interest in self-presentation but as a result of social, political, and economic changes in London during the period 1790 to 1840. The dandy look, originally adopted by wealthy and well-connected men, was eventually imitated by many and evolved into street style (Breward, 2009).

This masculine silhouette, seen as modern and glamorous, remained in place with slight variations during most of the nineteenth century for middle- and upper-class men in most urban centers. Urban men also managed their appearance to sport a clean-shaven look with short hair, although long sideburns and curly side locks became trendy by mid-century. Neckwear was considered a staple of masculine style, and men wore a variety of pieces including cravats, bowties, and four-in-hand ties—which became popular towards the end of the nineteenth century. Victorian etiquette in clothing was followed in different parts of the world, including, for instance, large Latin American cities where an understanding of European style was seen as an indication of proper upbringing and social status. Etiquette manuals indicated the proper type of neckwear, hat, textile, color, and coat shape for different occasions. As such, a tailcoat was considered *de rigueur* for formal evening wear, while a frock coat—with a flared skirt portion—was reserved for daytime. The 'sack' jacket was introduced as an alternative for less formal occasions and today is still the basic shape of any business suit. The sack is not the only piece of the male wardrobe that was introduced as an informal alternative and later became a staple of formal masculinity; the tuxedo jacket also made its appearance towards the end of the century as a less formal alternative to the tailcoat. The interplay of formality–informality in historic masculinities is also obvious with the introduction of sports clothing by the late nineteenth century, when pieces such as the Norfolk jacket and knee-length pants (knickers) became part of the daily wardrobe for active men.

'Traditional' historic gender binaries were fully established in the nineteenth century as clothing preferences for both genders closely followed cultural and societal standards. Although there were some deviations from the norm, masculine sartorial rebellion became more common in the twentieth century. Edwardian men favored a narrower silhouette, well-pressed clothes, and careful grooming. This dominant style, however, was challenged by several groups, including avant-garde artists such as the futurists, who not only wore bright colors and garments constructed in uncharacteristic shapes but also advocated for the creation of a unisex style. Into the 1920s, the students at Oxford University became known not only for the low laced shoes they wore but also for wider leg trousers known as 'Oxford Bags'. Other changes in men's attire came as a result of the rising popularity of automobiles and the need for 'motoring garments' and as result of World War I, which increased the use of pieces such as trench coats, wristwatches, and sweaters. The world of sports was also partially responsible for the appearance of more casual staples in the men's wardrobe. as the legend of the soft shirt introduced by tennis player Rene Lacoste attests. There were even organized efforts to challenge norms of masculine attire. The Men's Dress Reform Party opposed what they considered the 'feminine' look of fitted and curvy suits while advocating the use of more comfortable versions including shorter pants and strap sandals.

Sartorial challenges to masculine codes increased exponentially in the years leading up to and following World War II. In London, the Teddy Boys, a predominantly working-class group, revived Edwardian styles that were markedly different from the dominant fashion trends of the period. In the United States, Zoot Suits worn by African-American and Latino men were in direct defiance of government-issued restrictions to conserve textiles during World War II. The Zoot Suit style, discussed again later in this essay, incorporated high waist pants, large jackets with broad shoulders and wide lapels, large bow ties, and extremely long pocket watch chains. In the postwar years, sartorial rebellion also came in the hands of teenagers who decidedly embraced styles that visually separated them from their parents' generation. Teen culture, influenced by rock 'n' roll music, was stereotypically defined by the use of jeans, t-shirts, leather jackets, and built-up hairstyles.

By the middle of the twentieth century, men's fashion and appearance management changed dramatically, due to cultural and social shifts. The postmodern ethos began to question social expectations of age, gender, class, and race. The Youthquake heralded a new era of young people's fashion influence, as teenagers and adolescents started working part-time jobs and used their extra money on their own aesthetic creations. Jeans, once the domain of the working class, were adopted by young men and created a sartorial style based on movie starts and the rebellious anti-hero film characters played James Dean and Marlon Brando, among others. Films like *The Wild One* (1953) and *Rebel Without a Cause* (1955) featured lead characters in jeans and, in the case of the former, black leather jackets. Black leather jackets were particularly attractive to young men due to their multi-symbolic messages of hero, antihero, revel, protector, and survivor (DeLong & Park, 2008).

The 'Peacock Revolution' is the term used for the radical shift in masculine aesthetics in the 1960s. Whereas menswear prior was mostly sedate, sober, and embraced stereotypical masculinity, the new style of dressing in the 1960s encompassed bright colors, patterns, a plethora of fabrications; in general, men were experimenting with visual aesthetics. Musical artists such as the Beatles, Elvis Presley, and David Bowie ushered in 'long' hair, tailored glamour, and androgyny, respectively. Unisex and androgynous clothing represented masculinity in the middle of the twentieth century, as young people started to question the authenticity of the Western binary gender system. Designers like Rudi Gernreich offered unisex designs while artists like David Bowie and Prince made exploration of feminine qualities acceptable. The androgynous look blended both masculine and feminine elements into one unified ensemble. In the beginning of the twenty-first century, a new form of androgyny emerged, where masculine and feminine elements were juxtaposed to each other as if to reinforce one's status as a man but one who also has feminine attributes (Barry & Reilly, 2020).

By the later twentieth century, the male body became highly sexualized, and men turned to highlighting their bodies through working out, bodybuilding, and revealing clothing. The era of free love in the 1960s ushered in the hippy look of psychedelic colors, bold patterns, and natural fibers. By the 1970s this had changed to the disco look of low-rise pants and matching jacket with tight shirts—with exposed chests and a gold chain—as exemplified by John Travolta in *Saturday Night Fever* (1977). Sexualization of men continued in the 1980s and 1990s with attention turned towards a muscular and toned body, dropped waistlines on pants, and exposed designer underwear. The terms 'metrosexual' (straight men interested in fashion and taste), 'lumbersexual' (men with perfect thick beards, tight pants, plaid shirts, and work boots), and 'spornosexual' (men with defined athletic physiques typical of sportsmen and pornography) were all appellations of various men's styles in the late twentieth century and early twenty-first centuries where attention to one's appearance and body were important.

In the early twenty-first century, hipsters redefined masculine aesthetic again. Vázquez-López (2015) explains that the term was used broadly and therefore escapes precise definition and illustration. The author, however, states that in general, 'the subculture was characterized for its consumer behavior and eagerness to rediscover old techniques, practices, and styles while demonstrating a strong interest in do-it-yourself construction as well as bespoke fashions and accessories' (pp. 157–158). At the turn of the twenty-first century, hipster males embraced body hair, full beards, a plethora of conspicuous old school tattoos, vintage clothing, and out-of-style glasses. Their look matured into more slick styles, incorporating fitted clothes such as skinny jeans and formal attire including skinny ties as well as hair and grooming practices such as full beards and handlebar mustaches.

In addition to the expansion of forms mainstream masculinity, gay masculinity and aesthetics began to emerge in the latter half of the twentieth century. One of the first subcultural aesthetic styles to emerge was the Leatherman look of the 1950s, which was a reaction to the stereotype that gay men were effeminate. Leathermen donned working-class clothes of denim jeans and leather boots paired with leather vests to give a distinctively strong, stereotypically masculine aesthetics. Clones emerge in the 1960s and 1970s as perfections of traditional, working-class masculinity, replete with tight jeans, plaid shirts, and—most importantly—thick mustaches. These subcultural aesthetics were termed the 'butch shift' to highlight gay men as masculine rather than as feminine (Fernbach, cited in Humphries, 1985).

Geopolitical masculinities and fashion

In this section, we offer examples of geopolitical masculinities and fashion that highlight differences from masculinity and dress in a Euro-American context. While we cannot offer a comprehensive review of all forms of geopolitical masculinities, fashion, and dress, we share examples that exhibit ideas about masculinity in different ethnic cultures. We selected African-American, Latino, Japanese, and Korean males' dress because they demonstrate both how ethnic masculinities developed within a Euro-American context (as in the cases of African-American and Latino men's dress) and how fashioned masculinities have developed independent of Euro-American Westernized concepts of masculinity (as in the cases of Japanese and Korean men's dress).

African-American masculine aesthetics

African-American masculine dress has its roots mainly in West and Central Africa and is the result of the Atlantic slave trade (also called *Maafa* or 'great disaster' in Swahili) in the sixteenth through eighteenth centuries. During the Antebellum era in the southern United States, slaves either wore clothing supplied by the slave-owners or made do with rags; and after emancipation, assimilation into the dominant white American culture was status quo. An early form of African-American dress to appear was the Zoot Suit, which first appeared around 1935 and was worn in Harlem by jazz musicians and African-American youth who enjoyed dancing and bebop music (McClendon, 2015). 'As a subcultural gesture, these oversized and stylistically outrageous suits symbolized a statement of defiance—a refusal to be subservient to the white majority' (English, 2013, p. 74). The suit represented an affluent lifestyle and was especially controversial during and after WWII, when fabric was in short supply and austerity was *de rigueur*. The Zoot Suit would later be adopted by Mexican-American, Filipino-American, and white youth as a stylish representation of their own definition of masculinity.

By the 1960 and 1970s, masculinities in African-American dress was represented by reclamation of ethnic identity via references to African aesthetics and was promoted by advocates under the 'Black is Beautiful' movement. African-American men were encouraged to shed white cultural practices and highlight their own cultural backgrounds by wearing *dashikis* (a colorful tunic common in West Africa), the West African *grand boubou* (a sleeveless robe worn over a long-sleeve shirt and trousers pegged at the ankle of the same color), the Senegalese kaftan, and Ghanaian kente cloth. Other examples of African-American masculine aesthetics included donning the uniforms and symbols of African-American political groups such as the Black Panther Party. Men also shed hair-straightening products that produced the conk, a straight hairstyle, and opted to wear afros, cornrows, and dreadlocks, which were visual references to slavery and African ethnic groups.

African-American masculinity changed in the 1980s with the advent of hip-hop music and influences from musical artists. Various aesthetic styles emerged coincident with the emerging musical styles of hip-hop. According to Rebecca Robinson (2008), Old School, as personified by Run-DMC, included dark colors of Kangol hats or fedoras, denim, gold rope chain necklaces, and Adidas sneakers or Doc Marten boots. New School incorporated more colorful and flamboyant styles, including Adidas, Puma, or Converse shoes; branded clothing such as Tommy Hilfiger; and African aesthetics such as the 'motherland medallion', a silhouette of African in Rastafarian colors of red, yellow, and green. Gangsta style included gang-based looks of darkly colored parkas, flannel shirts, baseball caps worn backwards, oversized jeans, colorful bandannas, and Timberland work boots or black Palladium Army boots. And the Playa style featured business suits to evoke 'luxury, economic success, sexual promiscuity, and conspicuous consumption' (p. 259).

Today no one look captures African-American masculinity; rather, there are a plethora of styles, including contemporary hip-hop variations, dapper dandified style, and glitter make-up, which allows African-American men to explore masculinity outside of stereotypes (Street, 2017).

Latino and Latin American masculinities

Males belonging to other minority groups living in the United States have also utilized dress and appearance to both affirm and confront their status as 'the other'. Similar practices appear at the hands of minorities and immigrants in most parts of the world. The Latino population in the United States has adopted styles such as the aforementioned Zoot Suit as a form of protest. Just like the Black Panthers, the Young Lords Organization—a Latino group formed in Chicago and New York in the 1970s—adopted a clearly militant dress code that incorporated a number of military pieces such as US Army-issued field jackets, fatigue pants, combat boots, and purple berets. Their attire was also inspired by revolutionary movements in Latin America and the clothing worn by Che Guevara. A more recent example is found in Puerto Rican groups both in the island and in the diaspora who have adopted imagery from the native Puerto Rican Taíno culture. Tattoos, t-shirts, baseball hats, and several other pieces are used as part of an effort aimed at recovering native Puerto Rican identities and turning them into cultural capital to promote a sense of belonging that is particularly important in a country which remains a colony in the twenty-first century.

Latin American males living outside their country of origin may be more inclined to adopt garments associated with the concept of 'traditional' or 'national' dress, particularly in celebrations of their culture or country of origin. A salient example is the Cuban *guayabera*, a man's shirt which became one of the most important symbols of cultural heritage among Cuban expatriates around the world. The guayabera is a button-front, light-weight dress shirt usually manufactured in white or pastel-colored cotton or linen with a traditional collar and either long or short sleeves. The shirt features a straight hem with side slits and is usually worn un-tucked. Pride in Cuban heritage is expressed by wearing the guayabera for special occasions, particularly weddings, as well as for social and cultural gatherings. Other pieces in the male Latin American wardrobe that carry similar meanings include the Andean poncho, the garb of the Argentine *gaucho* or cowherd; the Mexican *charro* or mariachi suit, costumes worn by Mexican dancers inspired by ancient Aztec dress; and a number of national 'peasant' costumes created in the nineteenth century as representations of the nascent Latin American nations but heavily influenced by European peasant clothing.

Latin American men are confronted with the burden of stereotypes such as 'machismo' and 'Latin Lover'. The burden of such labels is evident in over-sexualized descriptions of Latin American men, particularly descriptions of fashion choices for male pop starts and athletes that emphasize the fact that their clothes may fit the body and be more revealing than elsewhere in the world. Machismo in itself is a contested term decidedly based on impressionistic evidence and assumptions, and no connection can be made between the way a man dresses and this stereotype. For the sake of argument, some generalizations can be made about Latin American men, perhaps including a more open interest in appearance management and garment selection as well as certain openness to colorful apparel. Urbanites care about well-ironed clothes, shined shoes, and the perception of their ability to discern between trends, colors, and brands. Discussing gender identity among Peruvian men, Norma Fuller (1996) argues that in Latin America, appearance management—particularly of the face—is associated with inner qualities, and therefore people perceive body appearance as an indicator of a man's social worth.

Talking about Latin American and Latino men as a monolithic group, however, is problematic, since there are great differences among men and their choices of clothing depending not only on the climate of different regions but also particularly in a number of cultural differences in the region that arose as part of the process of colonization and decolonization, continuous immigration, permanence of native groups, and globalization. Just like a range of masculinities exists worldwide, a number of fashioned masculinities appear in the region. Urbanites mostly follow global fashion trends, while taste in music, sports, or hobbies often implies the adoption of other styles such as surf and skate and urban wear. Caribbean masculinities, in contrast, although often discussed along with Latin American ones, are drastically different and denote clear influences from African masculinities as a result of the racial and ethnic composition in the region by the arrival of enslaved Africans in the eighteenth and nineteenth centuries.

Masculinity in contemporary Japan and Korea

Whereas the Euro-American tradition of masculinity included inflexible adherence to gender norms, Japanese and Korean contemporary males are moving away from such rigidity and exploring feminine aspects of masculinity via dress. Both Japan and Korea were collectivist cultures for many centuries, where uniformity was expected. Traditional Japanese (*kimono*) and Korean (*hanbok*) menswear were generally a robe-type garment made of natural fibers such as silk, cotton, wool, flax, or raime, both worn with loose-fitting pants (*hakama* and *baji*, respectively) in generally subdued colors. Both contained crests that signified the wearer's family. One could argue that the relative sameness of the clothing echoed the principles of a collectivist society. However, due to the introduction of Western principles and ideas, Western-style clothing was slowly adopted as symbolic of modernity (Slade, 2009). While the Euro-American man's suit is still worn in both countries, as are jeans, t-shirts, etc., the contemporary styling of them or the use of make-up is divergent from the traditional Euro-American concept of masculinity.

Kawaii is a contemporary aesthetic common among Japanese men. *Kawaii* translates as cute, and in Japan *kawaii* abounds everywhere, from technology to food to clothes (Richie, 2003). According to Slade (in press), contemporary *kawaii* men's fashion emerged in the

1970s and was a result of social unrest and cultural tensions between older and newer generations: 'It emerged, however, not as an acquiescence to the sociocultural mainstream but as an ironic form of disassociation and resistance … that undermines the seriousness of the dominant cultural values.' The *kawaii* aesthetic is manifested by a youthful expression, including a lithe, smooth, hairless body and head hair that is natural in color or dyed in pastel colors. Clothing can include *kigurumi* (adult-sized child's hooded animal costume/pajamas) or clothing ensembles can also reference childhood innocence and can feature kittens, unicorns, emoji symbols, and accessories suck as Hello Kitty buttons or *randoseru* (classic Japanese children's backpacks). Thus, in this example, masculinity is represented by cuteness.

Korean men's fashion also differs drastically from the Euro-American tradition of masculinity. Idols are extremely popular musical artists (K-pop) who sign and perform under a talent agency's label and are considered to be the pinnacle of male masculinity. Whereas Japanese *kawaii* is predicated on cuteness, Korean idols are beautifully feminine in appearance. Idols may dye their hair, wear fitted clothes made of clingy knits, and typically wear makeup to create a flawless face, shape eyebrows, and apply pink lipstick. Outside of the Idol career, other professional men follow suit in their own use of makeup. Miller (2014) notes, 'Make-up and what it can achieve in terms of refinement of the male body has come to equate to personal and professional success' (p. 248), and that makeup is not applied to color the face, as it is generally used by women, but to create a healthy face through enhancing one's natural features and covering flaws. Thus, in this example, masculinity is represented by unblemished perfection.

Conclusion

Masculinity is a multi-dimensional experience both in historic and current contexts. Fashion, as a reflection of the zeitgeist, evidences in a visual way the tastes and concerns of each period as well as different experiences of masculinity. Male fashion has mirrored normative practices such as the use of uniforms and business suits; but it has also challenged notions of masculinity in every period. Appearance management and clothing choices are intrinsically tied to the construction of performed masculine identities, and fashion is one of the most important mechanisms by which maleness is conveyed.

What defines masculinity via dress has shifted with each era. During the Renaissance, men's attire was colorful, flamboyant, and luxurious and associated with the higher classes. After the Industrial Revolution, which altered society in terms of gender and class, menswear became more utilitarian and somber. Clothing was indeed a visual aspect of the seriousness of men's work; anything feminine was viewed as frivolous and suspect. This uniformity has since been challenged by many segments of society who found masculine expression in areas long ignored by the dominant idea of Western, white masculinity. Thus masculine expression in fashion today is not a fixed notion but one that highlights the splintered identities and intersections of gender, class, race, and sexual orientation, among others.

References

Barry, B., & Reilly, A. (2020). The new androgyny. In A. Reilly & B. Barry (Eds.), *Crossing gender boundaries: Fashion to create, disrupt and transcend.* Chicago: Chicago University Press.

Beaule, C. (2015). Andean clothing, gender and indigeneity in Colonial Period Latin America. *Critical Studies in Men's Fashion, 2*(1), 55–73.

Breward, C. (2004). *Fashioning London: Clothing and the modern metropolis.* London: Berg.

Breward, C. (2009). Fashion and the man: From suburb to city street. In P. McNeil & V. Karaminas (Eds.), *The men's fashion reader* (pp. 409–428). London: Berg.
Breward, C. (2016). *The suit: Form, function and style*. London: Reaktion Books.
Campbell, C. (2012). The modern western fashion pattern, its functions and relationship to identity. In A. M. González & L. Bovone (Eds.), *Identities through fashion: A multidisciplinary approach* (pp. 9–22). New York: Berg.
Cole, S. (2000). *Don we now our gay apparel: Gay men's dress in the twentieth century*. New York: Berg.
Cole, S. (2010). *The story of men's underwear*. New York: Parkstone Press.
Craik, J. (2005). *Uniforms exposed: From conformity to transgression*. Oxford: Berg.
DeLong, M., & Park, J. (2008). From cool to hot to cool: The case of the black leather jacket. In A. Reilly & S. Cosbey (Eds.), *The men's fashion reader* (pp. 166–179). New York: Fairchild.
English, B. (2013). *A cultural history of fashion in the 20th and 21st centuries: From catwalk to sidewalk*. London: Bloomsbury.
Entwistle, J. (1997). Power dressing and the fashioning of the career woman. In M. Nava, I. MacRury & B. Richards (Eds.), *Buy this book: Studies in advertising and consumption* (pp. 311–323). London: Routledge.
Flügel, J. C. (1930). *The psychology of clothes*. London: Hogarth.
Fuller, N. (1996). Los estudios sobre masculinidad en Perú. In P. Ruiz-Bravo (Ed.), *Detrás de la puerta: Hombres y mujeres en el Perú de hoy* (pp. 39–57). Lima: Pontificia Universidad Católica del Perú.
Geczy, A, & Karaminas, V. (2017). *Fashion and masculinities in popular culture*. New York: Routledge.
Humphries, M. (1985). Gay machismo. In A. Metcalf & M. Humphries (Eds.), *The sexuality of men* (pp. 70–85). London: Pluto.
Jobling, P. (2005). *Man appeal: Advertising, modernism and menswear*. Oxford: Berg.
Jobling, P. (2014). *Advertising menswear: Masculinity and fashion in the British media since 1945*. London: Bloomsbury.
McClendon, A. D. (2015). *Fashion and jazz: Dress, identity, and subcultural improvisation*. London: Bloomsbury.
McNeil, P., & Karaminas, V. (Eds.). (2009). *The men's fashion reader*. Oxford: Berg.
Miller, J. (2014). Making up is masculine: The increasing cultural connections between masculinity and make-up. *Critical Studies in Men's Fashion, 1*(3), 241–253.
Moffatt, K. (2012). *Troubled masculinities: Reimagining urban men*. Toronto: University of Toronto Press.
Reddy-Best, K., & Howell, A. (2014). Negotiations in masculine identities in the Utilitikilts brand community. *Critical Studies in Men's Fashion, 1*(3), 223–240.
Reilly, A. (Ed.). (2014). *Critical studies in men's fashion*. Bristol: Intellect Press.
Reilly, A., & Cosbey, S. (Eds.). (2008). *The men's fashion reader*. New York: Fairchild.
Richie, D. (2003). *The image factory: Fads and fashion in Japan*. London: Reaktion Books.
Roberts, J. H. (2015). 'Don't call me white': Fashioning Sami Zayn's Arabic and transnational identities. *Critical Studies in Men's Fashion, 2*(2/3), 213–223.
Robinson, R. J. (2008). It won't stop: The evolution of men's hip-hop gear. In A. Reilly & S. Cosbey (Eds.), *The men's fashion reader* (pp. 253–264). New York: Fairchild.
Slade, T. (2009). *Japanese fashion: A cultural history*. Oxford: Berg.
Slade, T. (2019). Cute men in contemporary Japan. In A. Reilly & B. Barry (Eds.), *Crossing gender boundaries: Fashion to create, disrupt and transcend* (pp. 78–90). Bristol: Intellect Books.
Street, M. (2017, May 26). Photographer reclaims black masculinity with #GlitterBoys. *NBC News*. Retrieved from www.nbcnews.com.
Vázquez-López, R. (2015). The hipster. In J. Blanco (Ed.), *Clothing and fashion: American fashion from head to toe, Vol. 4* (pp. 157–159). Santa Barbara, CA: ABC-CLIO.
Zelinsky, W. (2004). Globalization reconsidered: The historical geography of modern western male attire. *Journal of Cultural Geography, 22*(1), 83–134.

39

Masculinities, food and cooking

Michelle Szabo

Are you a meat eater or a vegetarian? Are you a fast food junkie or a foodie? Do you enjoy, tolerate or avoid cooking? The answers to these questions reveal a great deal about our identities. How we orient to food speaks volumes about how we see ourselves and how others see us.

Food choices tell particularly interesting stories about masculinity. These stories vary richly across space and time, as well as across social location. But there are also enough similarities that, within our own cultures and subcultures, we are able to recognize 'masculine' food behaviour. The present chapter focuses on food and masculinities in the 20th and early 21st centuries and is located primarily in the Global North. While there is a growing body of work on food and masculinities in the Global South and periphery countries (e.g., DeLessio-Parson, 2017; Gvion, 2011; Mager, 2010; Meah, 2014a, 2014b) and some of this work will be included here, it is not within the scope of this chapter to offer a comprehensive review of literature from across the globe.

What exactly is a 'masculine' approach to food? As foundational masculinities scholars point out, there are a multiplicity of behaviours and orientations that earn the label of 'masculine', depending on the context (Connell, 1995; Messerschmidt, 2018). For example, masculine norms around food might be quite different in a ranching community in Argentina than those on a First Nations reserve in Canada, in a Buddhist enclave in Korea or at a Norwegian gay fathers' support group. The interactional context is also important. Individuals enact masculinity differently depending on where and with whom they are eating (e.g., at home with children, at work with colleagues, at the gym) (Sobal, 2005; Messerschmidt, 2018). However, this does not mean 'anything goes'. People must negotiate gender norms as they move through their particular life contexts or risk social sanctions, from teasing to violence (Messerschmidt, 2018). There are mainstream cultural norms that are reinforced through prominent cultural discourses and the mainstream media. I will refer to these as 'dominant' masculine norms (Messerschmidt, 2015). There are also subcultural norms which may be less celebrated in the national or regional contexts but are still potent within the subcultures in question. Individuals may also take actions that challenge dominant norms but do not fit neatly into subcultural themes. I will refer to these latter two categories as 'exceptions' to dominant masculine norms.

The individuals who are expected to embody and thus co-construct masculine norms are usually boys and men. It is also cisgender males who have been the majority of research participants in empirical investigations of masculinities. Nevertheless, masculine behaviours are also sometimes enacted by women, intersex, trans and genderqueer people. Unfortunately, while research on female, intersex, trans and genderqueer masculinities is increasing (Halberstam, 1998; Messerschmidt, 2015; Noble, 2003), such investigations considering *food* are extremely rare. This chapter will sometimes refer to empirical research about how men act and are portrayed to shed light on what gets defined as 'masculine'. However, this does not mean that masculinities are *equivalent to* the practices of cisgender men.

The following are key findings from the social sciences and humanities literature on masculine expectations and approaches to food in the late 20th and early 21st centuries. I outline norms that have been identified, as well as exceptions to these norms, mainly but not exclusively in the Global North.

Food and masculinities: late 20th- & early 21st-century patterns

Meat eating

The first food behaviour that has been associated with dominant masculinity in the late 20th and early 21st centuries is meat consumption. One reason for this is the association of meat with hunting, a historically male-dominated subsistence activity and pastime. Although women have been involved in hunting to various degrees in different cultural groups, the strength, skill and violence involved in the hunt have typically been seen as the purview of men (Bates, 2013; Bidwewidam, 2013; Bye, 2003). In present-day settler cultures where hunting is less common, associations between animal protein and masculine virility nevertheless remain strong (Sobal, 2005). Men, who are on average (and idealized as) physiologically larger than women, are thought to need more protein for optimum health than women (McPhail, Beagan & Chapman, 2012), and the ingestion of animal muscle is seen to add to human brawn (Brady & Ventresca, 2014).

The meat-centred barbecue has also had particular gendered currency in many regions of the world. Whether at a North American or Oceanic backyard barbecue, a white South African *braai* or an Argentinian *asado*, barbecuing meat has often been culturally framed as a masculine practice (DeLessio-Parson, 2017; Dummit, 1998; Feldman, 2003). If 'feminine' cooking – comforting, predictable – is done indoors with implements that *contain* the actual or virtual fire (e.g., a stove), then 'masculine' cooking – adventurous, unpredictable – is done outdoors in a wilder space over more open flames. Barbecuing is also often done only occasionally (e.g., on weekends or special occasions), allowing it to be a leisure activity distanced from 'feminine' quotidian cooking (Szabo, 2013).

Whether a cultural group gets its meat primarily through hunting, trapping, fishing or farming, meat eating necessarily involves killing a sentient being. For many Indigenous and rural settler groups, this killing is a cultural good – an honoured tradition and a 'connection with creation' (Bidwewidam Indigenous Masculinities Research Team, 2013, p. 12). However, scholars have also highlighted the more nefarious links between masculinity, hunting/meat eating and violence, especially in colonial cultures (e.g., Adams & Donovan, 1995). One compelling example, also related to the practice of *barbecuing*, is described by Feldman (2003) in his ethnographic study of the apartheid-era '*braai* tortures' in South Africa. Under the guise of interrogating Black political dissidents, white South African policemen ritualistically combined the subjugation, butchering and burning of their captives with many of the practices of the white South African *braai* (e.g., alcohol consumption, male commensality and the barbecuing of meat). For Feldman, this symbolic 'beastialization' and 'consumption' of the Black captives was a symbolic re-creation of apartheid-era class, race and gender dominance.

Returning to regular meat consumption, meat is especially prioritized among the working class (Alkon et al., 2013). In his landmark study of taste and class in 1960s France, Bourdieu (1984) described working-class food practices as being 'chiefly distinguished by the inclusion of … meat' with 46% of farm workers, 17% of manual workers and only 6% of senior executives eating meat for breakfast (p. 382). Bourdieu (1984) accounted for these class differences by suggesting that the working class have 'tastes of necessity', wherein foods which supply the necessary caloric intake for physically demanding work are preferred. More recently, scholars suggest that, since working-class men have less access to economic capital, they may be more likely to value meat's traditional symbolic link to power and vitality (Maurer, 2002).

This is not to deny the significance of meatless diets for men in particular ethnocultural, class and spiritual communities. In India, many Hindus, Buddhists and Jains follow religious precepts of non-violence or oneness with all beings (Walters & Portmess, 2001) and 73%, 69% and 66% of men in the Indian states of Rajasthan, Haryana and Punjab, respectively, are vegetarians (Census India, 2014). Meat avoidance maintains its significance for many in the South Asian diaspora (Jagganath, 2017) and, as Nath (2010) demonstrates, is also practised by Hare Krishna, Seventh Day Adventists and Buddhist minority groups in the Global North. Outside of religious reasons, vegetarianism is largely practised for health reasons and as a contribution to sustainability and animal welfare (Ruby, 2012). Clark (2004) also describes the importance of meat avoidance for men in anarchist punk subcultures in the U.S. as a symbol of resistance against mainstream masculinity and violence. In keeping with Bourdieu (1984), in the Global North, meatless diets are more common among the middle and upper classes than among the working class (Gossard & York, 2003).

Despite pockets of vegetarianism around the globe, meat eating is the general norm among men. Vegetarians compromise less than 10% of the population in each of Canada, the U.S., the U.K., Ireland, Australia, New Zealand, Germany and Israel (Ruby, 2012). In many of these countries, vegetarian women vastly outnumber vegetarian men, and more women than men report positive attitudes toward vegetarianism (Ruby, 2012). Further, the censure and scrutiny encountered by men on meatless diets (DeLessio-Parson, 2017; Nath, 2011) suggests that meatlessness among men in most parts of the world is still far from normalized. In Tibet, where Buddhist precepts are interpreted along a continuum from requiring occasional meat to requiring complete avoidance of meat, these religious notions exist in tension with lay cultural norms associating meat consumption with a 'heroic masculine ideal' of strength and domination over animals (Barstow, 2017). In India, vegetarians make up only a minority (29%) of the total male population (Census India, 2014).

Unhealthy eating

The second food practice associated with dominant masculinity in the late 20th and early 21st centuries is a relatively carefree approach to nutrition – one which contrasts with the health and body image anxieties associated with femininity (Cairns & Johnston, 2015). This framing of a masculine approach to food as casual is notable in pop culture and advertising, where images of male gluttony and culinary ignorance abound (Parasecoli, 2005, 2008). In advertising, we see the heteronormative man blissfully devouring a bag of Doritos or a plate of KFC wings in front of the game, or ordering a pizza to feed the kids when his female partner is away. In Hollywood film, the culinary incompetence of the hypermasculine hero is the source of comic relief (Parasecoli, 2008). A too great concern with nutrition is largely associated with femininity and homosexuality – and thus a threat to dominant masculinity (Parasecoli, 2005, 2008).

Empirical studies confirm that these patterns are also replicated in households. Large-scale dietary studies in several countries demonstrate that men consume less fruit, fewer vegetables and less fibre than women, as well as more fat, salt and soft drinks (Beer-Borst et al., 2000; Li et al., 2000; PHAC, 2009). Qualitative studies show that participants tend to associate 'unhealthy eating' (junk food, fast food) with men and masculinity and 'healthy eating' (salads, vegetables, low-fat foods) with women and femininity (e.g., McPhail et al., 2012; Roos, Prattala & Koski, 2001).

These behaviours have serious health implications for men. The 'masculine' diet in the Global North has been linked to earlier mortality in men (Mroz, Chapman, Oliffe & Bottorff, 2011), greater likelihood of death from heart disease (PHAC, 2009) and the greater prevalence of diet-related diseases such as obesity and diabetes (Kanter & Caballero, 2012). Further, when men in heterosexual partnerships are diagnosed with a health condition requiring dietary change, it is often their female partners who lead this change (Mroz et al., 2011). In fact, women are frequently seen as the 'guardians of family health', whereas men are seen as 'uninterested' in nutrition or even a 'corrupting influence' on children (Beagan, Chapman, D'Sylva & Bassett, 2008; Tanner, Petersen & Fraser, 2014).

There are, however, particular subgroups in which health consciousness is more of a masculine norm. Among athletes and in the fitness and body building communities (queer and straight), a focus on nutrients is expected among men, as this is associated with athleticism, sexual attractiveness and self-control (Brady & Ventresca, 2014; Parasecoli, 2005). Some men in qualitative studies (e.g., foodies, fathers) also evince a focus on nutrition, including attention to the nutritional health of children (Owen, Metcalfe, Dryden & Shipton, 2010; Szabo, 2014a). Some male celebrity chefs, such as Jamie Oliver, are also taking up the mantle of health. As part of his 'Food Revolution' in the U.K. and U.S., Oliver claims to want to 'improve the health and happiness of future generations through the food they eat' (Jamie's Food Revolution, n.d.). While Oliver may be normalizing masculine interest in nutrition to some degree (Rodney, Johnston & Chong, 2017), some scholars argue that the campaign presents a middle-class framing of 'proper food'. In so doing, it is argued, Oliver participates in the common middle-class pathologization of working-class food practices, which are seen to be less healthy (Hollows & Jones, 2010). Overall, masculinity, especially working-class masculinity, is still largely associated with a carefree approach to nutrition.

Distance from household cooking

The third signifier of dominant masculinity around food is being the recipient, rather than the producer, of household meals (Szabo & Koch, 2017). There has been change in this area. For example, in the Global North, younger men spend more time cooking at home than older men, and men generally spend more time in home cooking than in the past (Bianchi, Milkie, Sayer & Robinson, 2000; Statistics Canada, 2010; US Bureau, 2017). Men in Scandinavia in particular seem to have embraced home cooking (Aarseth & Olsen, 2008; Neuman, Gottzén & Fjellström, 2017b), with men in Sweden, for example, spending almost as much time as women in food preparation (Statistics Sweden, 2016). However, in most other OECD countries, women spend at least twice as much time engaged in household cooking as men (Miranda, 2011).

A significant body of qualitative research discusses the reasons for this division of labour among cisgender heterosexual couples. In some ethno-cultural communities, such as the Punjabi, Goanese and African diasporas in Canada, cooking is often simply seen as 'women's work' (Beagan et al., 2008; D'Sylva & Beagan, 2011). In research with white Canadians, Americans, Australians, Britons and Israelis, participants give practical reasons for women's greater cooking responsibilities such as that women have 'more time' for food preparation because they have fewer paid work hours than men and that women 'enjoy' or are 'better at' cooking than men (e.g., Beagan et al., 2008; Gvion & Patkin, 2017).

But these practical reasons may be less important than the fact that providing meals for loved ones is associated with feminine nurture and care. Research since the 1980s has shown that catering to the preferences of family members and creating a sense of home, family and ethno-cultural identity through home-cooked meals is a way that women have traditionally 'done femininity', just as *receiving* these things is a way that men have 'done masculinity' (DeVault, 1991; Murcott, 1982). For some women, feeding the family is a meaningful and potentially empowering role, such as in diasporic communities in the Global North, where culinary traditions are key to cultural maintenance (e.g., D'Sylva & Beagan, 2011). In the Global South, women's feeding work may be a source of such benefits as public recognition, entrepreneurial opportunities and bonding with other women (Meah, 2014a, 2014b). Research in the Global North showing women's desire for greater gender equality vis-à-vis foodwork also shows that many women are still tied *emotionally* to the ideal of providing nutritious and appetizing meals to loved ones (Cairns & Johnston, 2015). While men seem to be engaging more in home cooking, in many cisgender heterosexual households this is often framed as 'helping' (e.g., picking up groceries from a list that their spouse has made) rather than taking on equal responsibility for feeding the household (Cairns & Johnston, 2015; Gvion & Patkin, 2017; Owen et al., 2010). Comical images of men failing at household cooking in popular culture help to mark the practice as out of the ordinary for (straight) men (Parasecoli, 2008, 2017), unless it is done for heterosexual seduction (Parasecoli, 2005). The association of masculine household cooking with leisure (e.g., barbecuing, hobby cooking) also supports a division of labour in heterosexual households where men can freely *choose* when they want to cook, while women shoulder the responsibility the rest of the time (Cairns & Johnston, 2015; Gvion & Patkin, 2017; Szabo, 2013). Research about transmen confirms that eating another's cooking helps to construct a recognizable masculinity. In her research with female partners of transmen in the U.S., Pfeffer (2010) found that these women helped to bolster the masculinities of their partners by doing more of the carework in their households, including cooking.

Particular groups of men seem to be bucking this trend, however, by taking on significant responsibility for home cooking. This is sometimes related to the necessities of contemporary household arrangements. For example, men living without women – such as single men, divorced or widowed men and men in gay partnerships – cook more often than men living with female partners (Cutler, Glaeser & Shapiro, 2003; Daniels & Glorieux, 2017), often approaching cooking as a necessary life skill (Sellaeg & Chapman, 2008; Williams & Germov, 2017). Having loved ones who *depend* on them for food (especially children) also seems to correlate with men investing more time and energy in household cooking (Aarseth & Olsen, 2008; Szabo, 2013, 2014a).

There is also evidence of some change in attitude toward cooking among men, especially those who are frequent home cooks. Some middle-class men in Scandinavia and Canada, for example, express a view of cooking as both a leisurely activity *and* a taken-for-granted (and sometimes tedious or frustrating) household responsibility (Aarseth & Olsen, 2008; Neuman, Gottzén & Fjellström, 2017a; Szabo, 2013, 2014a). For many of these men, home cooking is no longer a 'feminine' activity but a marker of a 'modern'/'egalitarian' masculinity that distinguishes them from 'macho' men or men in previous generations (Aarseth & Olsen, 2008; Neuman et al., 2017b; Szabo, 2014b).

The research in this section, while evidence of some exceptions to traditional masculine norms, does not show that home cooking has become a normalized masculine activity. Men who embrace home cooking are still often praised and rewarded for their 'progressive' behaviour (Sellaeg & Chapman, 2008; Szabo, 2014b) or questioned for their gender transgressions (Moldes, 2017).

Professional cooking

Although cooking in the domestic sphere has traditionally been marked as 'feminine', professional cooking has been marked as 'masculine', constructing what Harris and Giuffre (2015) call the 'haute/home split'. This is partly based on the ideology of 'separate spheres' in which, after the industrial revolution, women became associated with the private domain of the home and men with the public world of paid work (see Szabo & Koch, 2017). In line with this, early cooking schools in 19th-century France, the home of haute cuisine, did not accept women because they were thought to have a primal rather than intellectual relationship with food (Harris & Giuffre, 2015). This gender divide is still evident, as home cooking continues to be largely associated with the 'feminine' qualities of nurture and care (Cairns & Johnston, 2015) while the professional culinary world values the 'masculine' traits of stamina, artistry, and aggressive showmanship (Harris & Giuffre, 2015; Swenson, 2009). In 2014, 84% of the 160 esteemed head chef positions in the top fifteen U.S. restaurant groups were held by men (Sutton, 2014). Moreover, the female professional chefs that *do* make it into the spotlight are typically portrayed as domestic advisors or sex symbols rather than artists or professionals (Johnston, Rodney & Chong, 2014; Swenson, 2009).

There are notable exceptions to this 'haute/home' split. Celebrity chefs Jamie Oliver and Rocco Dispirito are portrayed in their cookbooks and TV shows cooking at home for their loved ones (Rodney et al., 2017). Female celebrity chefs like Nigella Lawson and Padma Lakshmi are portrayed in their books and shows embracing the self-oriented pleasures rather than the other-oriented responsibilities of food (Johnston et al., 2014). Cooking shows with male hosts that purport to teach men to cook at home have the potential to develop food skills and interest in the wider male population. As cooking instruction has historically revolved around 'bourgeois' tastes (de Solier, 2005), shows such as *The Naked Chef* in Britain and *Huey's Cooking Adventures* in Australia have been hailed as innovative for framing home cooking around more working-class masculine sensibilities (de Solier, 2005; Hollows, 2003). At the same time, there are also critiques that such shows still frame masculine cooking around the idea of self-oriented leisure rather than other-oriented responsibility, leaving men off the hook from mundane, everyday cooking for others (de Solier, 2005; Hollows, 2003). Moreover, as Cox (2017) argues, the recent prominence of masculine professional cooking in pop culture can give the public the illusion that men are participating equally in domestic food work, which is generally not the case, as detailed above.

The masculinity on display in the professional culinary world has implications not only for class and gender but also for race and sexuality. As studies of cookbooks and cooking shows demonstrate, the majority of well-known male chefs display a white heteronomative masculinity (Johnston et al., 2014). In addition, the few male chefs of colour who are featured as hosts are often typecast in 'rags-to-riches' narratives (Rodney et al., 2017) or shown cooking 'ethnic' food, creating a narrative of 'otherness' or exception.

In brief, images in the Global North of the professional chef have begun to incorporate elements of working-class masculinities, and to a lesser extent femininities and racialized masculinities. However, the professional chef is still largely imagined as a heterosexual, white man.

Conclusion

Food practices are related in fascinating and complex ways to masculinity norms. An overview of the social sciences and humanities literature located primarily in the Global North reveals four key food behaviours that have been framed as 'masculine' in the late 20th and early 21st centuries: meat eating, unhealthy eating, being the recipient of domestic cooking and professional cooking. In addition, dominant masculinity vis-à-vis food (just as dominant masculinity in general (Messerschmidt, 2015)) has largely been conceptualized in a dichotomous and opposing relationship with femininity. If meat avoidance and healthy eating are feminine, then meat eating and unhealthy foods are masculine. If home cooking is feminine, then being treated to home-cooked meals is masculine. If domestic cookery is feminine, then culinary artistry and performance is masculine. This framing of masculinity has been demonstrated in both cultural products and empirical trends.

These gender norms have implications not only for men's health, as detailed above, but also for equality between and among genders. Some feminists have argued that women's greater responsibilities for domestic food provision and family health can be seen as a privilege or form of power. In this line of thinking, feeding others, creating a sense of home, comfort and well-being and maintaining ethno-cultural food traditions are reframed as essential human goods for which women receive recognition, self-affirmation and cultural power (D'Sylva & Beagan, 2011; Meah, 2014a, 2014b). That these goods are less associated with masculinity may thus be seen as disadvantageous to masculine-identified people. However, it has been widely argued that a gendered division of food practices has significant negative consequences for the well-being of people of all genders (e.g., Szabo & Koch, 2017). If women continue to be seen as experts in the domestic (unpaid) realm and men in the professional realm, then this limits women's access to professional opportunities and economic independence. If women continue to have responsibility for the unnoticed mundane food-related work in households while men are praised for occasional weekend cooking, then men will continue to have disproportionate access to domestic leisure time, especially in heterosexual partnerships (Parker & Wang, 2013). Conversely, if masculine-identified people (including gay, straight, bi, queer, intersex and trans folks) continue to encounter condemnation when they embrace 'feminine' food practices, a hegemonic system will continue (Messerschmidt, 2018). We have also seen how dominant masculinity privileges white, cisgender, middle-class heterosexual men vis-à-vis food practices such as by framing as universal the experiences and sensibilities of these particular men.

On that note, this chapter runs the risk of also leaving out some important voices and issues because of the pervasiveness of research on white, cisgender, heterosexual, middle-class men and my identification as a white, cisgender, middle-class, heterosexual woman. I hope that future research will examine in greater detail the experiences of other masculinities around food including gay, working-class, racialized, trans and female masculinities. I also hope to see more comprehensive investigations of masculinities and food in the Global South.

References

Aarseth, H., & Olsen, B. M. (2008). Food and masculinity in dual-career couples. *Journal of Gender Studies, 17*(4), 277–287.

Adams, C., & Donovan, J. (Eds.). (1995). *Animals and women: Feminist theoretical explorations*. Durham, NC: Duke University Press.

Alkon, A. H., Block, D., Moore, K., Gillis, C., DiNuccio, N., & Chavez, N. (2013). Foodways of the urban poor. *Geoforum, 48*, 126–135.

Barstow, G. (2017). *Food of sinful demons: Meat, vegetarianism and the Limits of Buddhism in Tibet*. New York: Columbia University Press.

Bates, C. (2013). *Masculinity and the hunt: Wyatt to Spenser*. Oxford: Oxford University Press.

Beagan, B., Chapman, G.E., D'Sylva, A., & Bassett, B. R. (2008). 'It's just easier for me to do it': Rationalizing the family division of food work. *Sociology, 42*(4), 653–671.

Beer-Borst, S., Hercberg, S., Morabia, A., Bernstein, M. S., Galan, P., Galasso, R., … & Ribas, L. (2000). Dietary patterns in six European populations: Results from EURALIM, a collaborative European data harmonization and information campaign. *European Journal of Clinical Nutrition, 54*(3), 253–262.

Bianchi, S., Milkie, M., Sayer, L., & Robinson, J. (2000). Is anyone doing the housework? Trends in the gender division of household labor. *Social Forces, 79*(1), 191–228.

Bidwewidam Indigenous Masculinities Research Team. (2013). *Indigenous masculinities, identities and mino-bimaadiziwin*. Toronto: Ontario Federation of Indian Friendship Centres.

Bourdieu, P. (1984). *Distinction*. London: Routledge & Kegan Paul.

Brady, J., & Ventresca, M. (2014). 'Officially a vegan now': On meat and renaissance masculinity in pro football. *Food and Foodways, 22*(4), 300–321.

Bye, L. M. (2003). Masculinity and rurality at play in stories about hunting. *Norwegian Journal of Geography, 57*(3), 145–153.

Cairns, K., & Johnston, J. (2015). *Food and femininity*. New York: Bloomsbury.

Census India. (2014). Sample registration system baseline survey 2014. Retrieved from www.censusindia.gov.in/vital_statistics/BASELINE%20TABLES07062016.pdf.

Clark, D. (2004). The raw and the rotten. *Ethnology, 43*(1), 19–31.

Connell, R. W. (1995). *Masculinities*. Berkeley, CA: University of California Press.

Cox, E. (2017). 'Don't try this at home': Men on TV, women in the kitchen. In M. Szabo & S. Koch (Eds.), *Food, masculinities and home* (pp. 231–247). London: Bloomsbury.

Cutler, D. M., Glaeser, E. L., & Shapiro, J. M. (2003). Why have Americans become more obese? *Journal of Economic Perspectives, 17*(3), 93–118.

Daniels, S., & Glorieux, I. (2017). Cooking up manliness: A practice-based approach to men's at-home cooking and attitudes using time-use diary data. In M. Szabo & S. Koch (Eds.), *Food, masculinities and home* (pp. 31–58). London: Bloomsbury.

DeLessio-Parson, A. (2017). Doing vegetarianism to destabilize the meat-masculinity nexus in La Plata, Argentina. *Gender, Place & Culture, 24*(12), 1729–1748.

de Solier, I. (2005). TV dinners: Culinary television, education and distinction. *Continuum: Journal of Media & Cultural Studies, 19*(4), 465–481.

DeVault, M. L. (1991). *Feeding the family: The social organization of caring as gendered work*. Chicago, IL: University of Chicago Press.

D'Sylva, A., & Beagan, B. (2011). 'Food is culture, but it's also power': The role of food in ethnic and gender identity construction among Goan Canadian women. *Journal of Gender Studies, 20*(3), 279–289.

Dummit, C. (1998). Finding a place for father: Selling the barbecue in postwar Canada. *Journal of the Canadian Historical Association, 9*(1), 209–223.

Feldman, A. (2003). Strange fruit: The South African Truth Commission and the demonic economies of violence. In B. Kapferer (Ed.), *Beyond rationalism: Rethinking magic, witchcraft and sorcery* (pp. 234–265). New York & Oxford: Berghahn.

Gossard, M. H., & York, R. (2003). Social structural influences on meat consumption. *Human Ecology Review, 10*(1), 1–9.

Gvion, L. (2011). Cooking, food, and masculinity: Palestinian men in Israeli society. *Men and Masculinities, 14*(4), 408–429.

Gvion, L., & Patkin, D. (2017). 'Women have a gift for cooking': Israeli male teachers' view of domestic cookery. In M. Szabo & S. Koch (Eds.), *Food, masculinities and home* (pp. 59–74). London: Bloomsbury.

Halberstam, J. (1998). *Female masculinity*. Durham, NC: Duke University Press.

Harris, D., & Giuffre, P. (2015). *Taking the heat: Women chefs and gender inequality in the professional kitchen.* New Brunswick, NJ: Rutgers University Press.

Hollows, J. (2003). Oliver's twist: Leisure, labour and domestic masculinity in. *The Naked Chef. International Journal of Cultural Studies, 6*(2), 229–248.

Hollows, J., & Jones, S. (2010). 'At least he's doing something': Moral entrepreneurship and individual responsibility in *Jamie's Ministry of Food. European Journal of Cultural Studies, 13*(3), 307–322.

Jagganath, G. (2017). Foodways and culinary capital in the diaspora: Indian women expatriates in South Africa. *Nordic Journal of African Studies, 26*(2), 107–125.

Jamie's Food Revolution. (n.d.). What we do. Retrieved August 2017 from www.jamiesfoodrevolution.org/what-we-do.

Johnston, J., Rodney, A., & Chong, P. (2014). Making change in the kitchen? A study of celebrity cookbooks, culinary personas, and inequality. *Poetics, 47*, 1–22.

Kanter, R., & Caballero, B. (2012). Global gender disparities in obesity: A review. *Advances in Nutrition, 3* (4), 491–498.

Li, R., Serdula, M., Bland, S., Mokdad, A., Bowman, B., & Nelson, D. (2000). Trends in fruit and vegetable consumption among adults in 16 US states: Behavioral risk factor surveillance system, 1990–1996. *American Journal of Public Health, 90*(5), 777–781.

Mager, A. K. (2010). *Beer, sociability, and masculinity in South Africa.* Bloomington, IN: Indiana University Press.

Maurer, D. (2002). *Vegetarianism: Movement or moment?* Philadelphia, PA: Temple University Press.

McPhail, D., Beagan, B., & Chapman, G. E. (2012). 'I don't want to be sexist but …': Denying and re-inscribing gender through food. *Food, Culture and Society, 15*(3), 473–489.

Meah, A. (2014a). Reconceptualising 'masculinity' through men's contributions to domestic foodwork. In P. Hopkins & A. Gorman-Murray (Eds.), *Masculinities and place* (pp. 191–208). Farnham: Ashgate.

Meah, A. (2014b). Reconceptualizing power and gendered subjectivities in domestic cooking spaces. *Progress in Human Geography, 38*(5), 671–690.

Messerschmidt, J. W. (2015). *Masculinities in the making: From the local to the global.* Lanham, MD: Rowman & Littlefield.

Messerschmidt, J. W. (2018). *Hegemonic masculinity: Formulation, reformulation, and amplification.* Lanham, MD: Rowman & Littlefield.

Miranda, V. (2011). Cooking, caring and volunteering: Unpaid work around the world. *OECD Social, Employment and Migration Working Papers* (No. 116). OECD Publishing.

Moldes, M. D. (2017). Stumbling in the kitchen: Exploring masculinity, Latinicity, and belonging through performative cooking. In M. Szabo & S. Koch (Eds.), *Food, masculinities and home* (pp. 92–107). London: Bloomsbury.

Mroz, L., Chapman, G., Oliffe, J., & Bottorff, J. (2011). Gender relations, prostate cancer and diet: Re-inscribing hetero-normative food practices. *Social Science and Medicine, 72*(9), 1499–1506.

Murcott, A. (1982). 'It's a pleasure to cook for him': Food, meal times and gender in South Wales households. In E. Gamarnikow, D. Morgan, J. Purvis & D. Taylorson (Eds.), *The public and the private* (pp. 78–90). London: Heinemann.

Nath, J. (2010). 'God is a vegetarian': The food, health and bio-spirituality of Hare Krishna, Buddhist and Seventh-Day Adventist devotees. *Health Sociology Review, 19*(3), 356.

Nath, J. (2011). Gendered fare? A qualitative investigation of alternative food and masculinities. *Journal of Sociology, 47*(3), 261–278.

Neuman, N., Gottzén, L., & Fjellström, C. (2017a). Masculinity and the sociality of cooking in men's everyday lives. *The Sociological Review*, *65*(4), 816–831.

Neuman, N., Gottzén, L., & Fjellström, C. (2017b). Narratives of progress: Cooking and gender equality among Swedish men. *Journal of Gender Studies*, *26*(2), 151–163.

Noble, J. B. (2003). *Masculinities without men*. Vancouver: University of British Columbia Press.

Owen, J., Metcalfe, A., Dryden, C., & Shipton, G. (2010). 'If they don't eat it, it's not a proper meal': Images of risk and choice in fathers' accounts of family food practices. *Health, Risk and Society*, *12*(4), 395–406.

Parasecoli, F. (2005). Feeding hard bodies: Food and masculinities in men's fitness magazines. *Food and Foodways*, *13*(1), 17–37.

Parasecoli, F. (2008). *Bite me: Food in popular culture*. London: Berg.

Parasecoli, F. (2017). Kitchen mishaps: Performances of masculine domesticity in American comedy films. In M. Szabo & S. Koch (Eds.), *Food, masculinities and home* (pp. 197–212). London: Bloomsbury.

Parker, K., & Wang, W. (2013). *Modern parenthood: Roles of moms and dads converge as they balance work and family*. Washington, DC: Pew Research Center.

Pfeffer, C. A. (2010). 'Women's work'? Women partners of transgender men doing housework and emotion work. *Journal of Marriage and Family*, *72*(1), 165–183.

PHAC – Public Health Agency of Canada. (2009). *Tracking heart disease and stroke in Canada*. Ottawa: Public Health Agency of Canada.

Rodney, A., Johnston, J., & Chong, P. (2017). Chefs at home? Masculinities on offer in celebrity chef cookbooks. In M. Szabo & S. Koch (Eds.), *Food, masculinities and home* (pp. 213–230). London: Bloomsbury.

Roos, G., Prattala, R., & Koski, K. (2001). Men, masculinity and food: Interviews with Finnish carpenters and engineers. *Appetite*, *37*(1), 47–56.

Ruby, M. (2012). Vegetarianism: A blossoming field of study. *Appetite*, *58*(1), 141–150.

Sellaeg, K., & Chapman, G. E. (2008). Masculinity and food ideals of men who live alone. *Appetite*, *51*(1), 120–128.

Sobal, J. (2005). Men, meat and marriage: Models of masculinity. *Food & Foodways*, *13*(1), 135–158.

Statistics Canada. (2010). Overview of the time use of Canadians. General social survey. Minister of Industry. Catalogue no. 89-647-X.

Statistics Sweden. (2016). *Women and men in Sweden: Facts and figures*. Stockholm: Statistics Sweden.

Sutton, R. (2014, March 6). Women everywhere in food empires but no head chefs. *Bloomberg News*. Retrieved from www.bloomberg.com/news/articles/2014-03-06/women-everywhere-in-chang-colicchio-empires-but-no-head-chefs.

Swenson, R. (2009). Domestic divo? Televised treatments of masculinity, femininity and food. *Critical Studies in Media Communication*, *26*(1), 36–53.

Szabo, M. (2013). Foodwork or foodplay? Men's domestic cooking, privilege & leisure. *Sociology*, *47*(4), 623–638.

Szabo, M. (2014a). Men nurturing through food: Challenging gender dichotomies around domestic cooking. *Journal of Gender Studies*, *23*(1), 18–31.

Szabo, M. (2014b). 'I'm a real catch': The blurring of alternative and hegemonic masculinities in men's talk about home cooking. *Women's Studies International Forum*, *44*, 228–235.

Szabo, M., & Koch, S. (Eds.). (2017). *Food, masculinities and home: Interdisciplinary perspectives*. London: Bloomsbury.

Tanner, C., Petersen, A., & Fraser, S. (2014). Food, fat and family: Thinking fathers through mothers' words. *Women's Studies International Forum*, *44*, 209–219.

US Bureau of Labor Statistics. (2017). American time use survey: 2016. Results retrieved from www.bls.gov/news.release/pdf/atus.pdf.

Walters, K., & Portmess, L. (2001). *Religious vegetarianism: From Hesiod to the Dalai Lama*. Albany, NY: State University of New York Press.

Williams, L., & Germov, J. (2017). From 'The missus used to cook' to 'Get the recipe book and get stuck into it': Reconstructing masculinities in older men. In M. Szabo & S. Koch (Eds.), *Food, masculinities and home* (pp. 108–125). London: Bloomsbury.

40

Men, masculinities and music

Sam de Boise

Introduction

Men, masculinity and masculinit*ies* have been studied in different ways in relation to music. Musical texts and musical interpretation may be informed by societal notions of masculinity (singular) or masculinit*ies* (plural), whilst practices of listening, consumption and the global production of recorded music implicates transnational relations between and involving men. This chapter draws from literature from gender studies, social psychology, feminist musicology, cultural studies and sociology in order to detail how work on music implicates men, masculinity, masculinities and music in different ways. The aim of this chapter is thus to demonstrate how music can be understood both as: 1) a *cultural expression* or *representation of*; and 2) as *influenced by* relations concerning, men, masculinity and/or masculinit*ies*.

Moral panics and music's effect on men

Debates around music's potential for 'corrupting' men, or changing their behaviour, extend over thousands of years. In Plato's *Republic*, for instance, he argued that Ioanian and Lydian modes encouraged 'drunkenness, softness and idleness' (Plato, 2007, p. 94) in men and that particular rhythms could lead men to 'meanness and promiscuity or derangement' (Robinson, 2005, p. 381). Focusing on 9th-century Britain, Leach (2009) demonstrates that men in monasteries were banned from singing polyphony or chant, and particularly falsetto, which were seen to emulate 'womanly qualities' due to the high pitch. Nor were they allowed to indulge in listening for enjoyment, for fear that 'passively' listening to music might 'feminise them' (Leach, 2009, p. 24).

During the 16th and 17th centuries, across Europe, there was a concern that certain types of music actually produced the sickness of melancholia (Gibson, 2009), which was understood as a 'feminine' affliction. This suggested that 'inappropriate listening' or listening to the 'wrong' music could cause physiological symptoms which would compromise men's ability to act rationally and thus compel them to act in 'more feminine' ways. Debates on music's suitability for men were echoed in other parts of Europe, with Castiglione's *Book of the Courtier* (one of the first instructive manuals on how men ought to behave at court) too arguing that: '[...] music is indeed well suited to women, and perhaps also to others who have the appearance of men, but not to *real men*; for the latter ought not to render their minds effeminate and afraid of death' (Castiglione, 1959 [1561], p. 74, emphasis added). Even as late as 2004, parents who wanted to 'cure' their gay sons were offered the following tips by 'reparative therapists' in the US: 'avoid activities considered of interest to homosexuals, such [as] art museums, *opera, symphonies*' (Nicolosi cited in Bright, 2004, p. 73, emphasis added).

Masculine aesthetics

It is difficult to talk about music's impact on a historically stable sense of 'men' or masculinity, given that both 'masculinity' and 'maleness' are historically and culturally specific constructs (Petersen, 1998). Yet there are clear historical concerns around how music impacts on *behaviour* amongst those designated* male, as well as compromising normative judgements around what its critics feel it should mean to *be* a 'real' man in different places, at different points in time.

Notably, specific sonic textures have often been linked to gendered constructs across societies. For example, McClary (1991) demonstrates that, in the Western classical traditions, the codifying of sounds themselves operate alongside, are influenced by and help to reinforce idealised, discrete, binary-gender systems. In an exemplary instance, she notes that the 1970 *Harvard Dictionary of Music* defined a 'masculine ending' as finishing on a *strong* beat and a feminine ending ('preferred in more romantic styles') on a *weak* beat. In this case, these binaries (strong/masculine vs. weak/feminine) are not simply neutral descriptions but value-laden, *a*ppositional (rather than oppositional) terms whereby McClary observes that '[...] the "feminine" is [regarded as] weak, abnormal and subjective; the "masculine" is strong, normal and objective' (1991, p. 10). Here, different value systems are attached to certain music structures, parts or styles (romantic vs. modernist), with some regarded as of more or less value due to their gendered connotations (Maus, 1993).

It is possible to 'read' masculinity in Western classical pieces due to the fact that a number of compositions were constructed to represent ideas of harmony between 'masculine' and 'feminine' or 'male' and 'female' (Biddle & Gibson, 2009). However, different uses of pitch, harmony, tonality and instrumentation are still used in various ways, transnationally, to underscore images of men and masculinity in cinema and theatre. As Järviluoma, Moisala and Vilkko (2003) indicate, lower pitches and 'harsher', deeper tones, as well as different types of instrumentation (trumpets or distorted guitar), are used more often when men are on screen whereas, by contrast, major-harmonic, 'fluttering' melodies have historically been associated more with 'respectable' women. Furthermore, the sounds instruments make (timbre), as well as their pitch, their status and their physical size, frequently shape who is expected (or allowed) to play them in different contexts, in both global Northern and Southern nations (Basso, 1989; Green, 1997; Nannyonga-Tamusuza, 2015; Wych, 2012).

Genres themselves can also be coded as either more 'masculine' or 'feminine', depending on the particular aesthetic of the performers, with judgements around genre 'authenticity' heavily influenced by gendered connotations (Kruse, 2002). For instance, Frith and McRobbie's (1978) work showed how by analysing distinctions between the (aptly) colloquially termed 'cock rock' and 'teenybopper' music in the 1970s it is possible to see how 'masculinity' is, quite literally, *performed*. In addition to utilising sonic markers commonly associated with masculinity (loud, fast and heavy drumming, distorted guitars), they observed how 'cock rock' performers would embody more obvious masculine signifiers; these included standing with one's legs wide apart, holding the guitar between the legs like an extended phallus, exaggerating physical gestures and 'strutting' about the stage so as to occupy more space and thereby symbolically demonstrate dominance. Similar observations have been made in relation to metal, which has often been understood as advancing a particularly aggressive (white) heterosexual 'masculine' aesthetic, both sonically and through performance (Hill, 2016; Rafalovich, 2006; Walser, 1993).

With regard to rap, a focus on rhythmically driven, lower registers, with the beat taking a much more prominent focus, have also been interpreted as a manifestation of 'Black masculinity' (Djupvik, 2014). Whilst hip hop takes cues musically from African diasporic music traditions, it is often understood as an expression of, or used sonically to underscore, images of US Black men's bodies. McLeod (2009) observes how rap, especially, is used alongside images of Black athletes in the US. Yet, as he notes, the music in tandem with these representations feeds back into, or amplifies more general accusations of 'hypermasculinity' directed at African-American men. For instance, as he argues, US rapper Notorious B.I.G's *Things Done Changed* is often used when introducing predominantly African American football players in NFL coverage. This has the effect that 'The hypermasculine gangsta pose, which is often reinforced with aggressive beats, sinister sounding bass lines, and general production excess mirrors, or perhaps intentionally confronts, the stereotypical view of black athletes and masculinity in general' McLeod (2009, p. 210). Here the prominence of the beat and the staccato vocal delivery are regarded as sonically communicating 'aggression' and 'dominance', whilst the 'sinister' bass lines (the repetition of the same two quaver notes, occasionally pitched up semitone) are associated with particular understandings of 'masculinity' due to the depth of the register and refusal to conform to a discernible harmonic structure.

Listening to multiple masculinit*ies*

Across the world there are contrasting and relational configurations between masculinit*ies*, rather than one coherent set of contextually specific behavioural norms or practices, which constitute (a singular) masculin*ity* (Aboim, 2010). Crucially, then, when analysing music's relationship to men, it is important to be attentive to the way in which intersectional and geographic differences between men also affect way in which different musical aesthetics, and thus their appeal, are manifest.

Dynamics of class and masculinity have been most frequently implicated in an explanation of music's gendered appeal. For instance, Palmer (1997) details how Bruce Springsteen's popularity stemmed from his image as a 'working class hero' which involved his lyrical focus on issues of de-industrialisation, affecting manual-labour occupations in the US, references to New Jersey, as well as his embracing of 'traditional' notions of (white) 'breadwinner masculinity' and relationships between fathers and sons.

Worley (2017) similarly identifies that in the punk subgenre, Oi!'s appeal amongst UK working-class men can be explained by its stress on sonic markers associated with (white) working-class men's leisure activities (inspired by football chants) as well as a lyrical and subcultural stress on physical toughness, aggression and self-sufficiency. Punk and 'DIY culture' have more often been read through a lens which emphasises both the gender-subversive aspects of punk style and ethos, in the anti-establishment lyrical focus, whilst at the same time recognising the exclusionary, fraternal homosociality and masculinist performativity of the scenes themselves (Leblanc, 1999; Mullaney, 2007; O'Meara, 2003).

Others have suggested that music can be a way of identifying counter-hegemonic and perhaps even transformative patterns of behaviour associated with 'softer' or more 'inclusive' masculinities (see Roberts, 2014). For instance, the use of 'camp' and 'dandyish' aesthetics became a staple feature of British 'pop masculinities' from the 1970s onwards, challenging narratives around men's gendered performances as based on domination and power (Hawkins, 2009). Similarly, Houston (2012) observes how (predominantly white, middle-class, cis-male) musicians within indie scenes in the US directly position themselves in relation to overtly 'macho' or hegemonic forms of masculinity, whilst Korean 'K-Pop' (boy)bands have embraced aesthetically 'soft' gendered performances as a commercially successful strategy (Jung, 2011). These manifestations arguably reflect broader transnational shifts in how men have been encouraged to embrace emotional introspection and expression, reject sexist behaviour and demonstrate greater 'sensitivity' (see Bannister, 2006; King, 2013).

Most frequently, hip hop and rap have been read as gendered expressions of both class and race or as offering a raced understanding of class. Lyrically, rap has detailed racial profiling, police brutality and poverty endured particularly by young Black men across the US (Saddik, 2003). In Sweden too, hip hop's lyrical and aesthetic focus has often been concerned with questions of identity, outsidership ('*utanförskap*'), marginalisation and racism from the point of view of men of colour growing up in an ethnocentric society (Sernhede, 2007), with grime in the UK taking up similar issues (Charles, 2016). Music, therefore, can be a tool to understand masculinity and men as assemblages, or as hybridised, whilst contesting the idea of static ethnic and/or racialized identities (see also Bakrania, 2013).

Crucially, these perspectives complicate the dominant narrative that music 'belongs to', or should be read as a manifestation of, a singular, racialised masculine identity. Given that Western and global Northern popular and classical traditions are indebted to music from Eastern and global Southern diasporas (Gilroy, 1991; Peress, 2004; Reck, 1985), it is clear that cultural influence does not just 'flow' in one direction. Even music as seemingly 'white' as black metal is performed by Black men in South Africa and Arab men in Saudi Arabia (Caminero, 2016; Chester, 2015). Similarly, Black men and women were important in the development of punk, whose history is often rendered colour and gender blind (Reddington, 2007; Wadkins, 2012).

This contests the idea that race, ethnicity and gender explain either music's aesthetic appeal or origins. At the same time, however, it is vital to recognise that music consumption is frequently fetishised along racial and gendered lines. The masculine exoticism of 'world music' has been key to its marketed appeal amongst white audiences in the global North (Kheshti, 2015), whilst musical signifiers and symbols associated with 'Black masculinity' have been (and continue to be) appropriated in racist ways by white audiences and performers (Rodriquez, 2006; Yousman, 2003). Here, processes of othering and exotification in relation to music implicate complex transnationally gendered power relations in an understanding of race, class and masculinities (Bridges & Pascoe, 2014).

Music and men's behaviour

Whilst many of these examples emphasise some of the more positive, socially conscious aspects of music, social psychological research has detailed the impact of different types of music on men's *behaviour*, with a particular emphasis on anti-feminist and toxic outcomes. Research and media outlets particularly have linked overt misogyny, homophobia and status and respect through violence to hip hop and rap (Kistler & Lee, 2009; Oware, 2011) and metal particularly (see Lawrence & Joyner, 1991). Dancehall, which has been linked to the expression of 'Caribbean masculinity' (Brown, 1999), has even been named in British parliamentary politics as actively encouraging homophobia against gay men in other states (Johnson & Vanderbeck, 2014). Listening to dancehall, amongst other factors, has even been regarded as one of the most significant predictors of homophobic attitudes and opposition to gay rights (West & Cowell, 2015).

Research has also noted gendered correspondence between the type of values the music 'promotes' and (predominantly young) men's behavioural or psychological correlates (see Colley, 2008). Some have argued that young men – especially those who are more likely to feel (or report feeling) anger, depression and sadness – are attracted to corresponding types of music which express these values (Garrido & Schubert, 2013). Dynamics of age, too, are important here, however, in that age, in addition to gender, tends to play a larger role in *reported* emotions – particularly 'negative' ones such as anger or sadness – in relation to men's and boys' music preferences (de Boise, 2015).

Yet much of the research studying links between music and aggression, especially, do not question their own presumptions about how entire genres are categorised as 'aggressive', 'hypermasculine' or 'depressive' by researchers rather than by the listeners. Experimental studies in particular are often structured to elicit responses under artificial conditions amongst white, cis-male US college students, which do not necessarily interrogate a wide variety of understandings; nor do they necessarily prove a link between men or boys' listening and their *behaviour*.

Furthermore, lyrical and sonic content must be read through gendered colonial relations (Cooper, 2004; hooks, 2004) rather than through essentialist discourses about the relationship of music to homogenous ethnic or racial categories. Thus, attempts to 'prove' links between certain types of music and violence/sexism/misogyny are themselves shaped by gendered geopolitical, social and economic relations around men and masculinity/ies. There are particularly racist tropes in that attempts to demonstrate links between music associated with Black men and 'hypermasculinity', especially, fail to acknowledge the term's connotative roots in conservative fantasies of the 'hyper-sexualised,' violent 'Black male body' (hooks, 2004, p. 46). Certain types of music thus may generate more accusations of misogyny or homophobia because of their associations with 'Black masculinity' rather than a thorough attention to lyrical content within genre (Fried, 1996; Weitzer & Kubrin, 2009). Notably, within genres which supposedly embody 'softer' masculinities, misogynistic lyrics are still heavily visible but do not receive the same moral condemnation, due to their more common associations with white, middle-class men in the global North (de Boise, 2014).

Queering masculinity/queer masculinities

Importantly, there is not simply one way to 'read' or interpret performances of masculinity/ies in music. Music has always been a space for queer people and the expression of queer desires (Brett & Wood, 2006). Music acts as a focal point for expressions of Black queerness in Johannesburg in ways that are not easily explained by recourse to Northern-centred explanations of gender and sexuality (Livermon, 2014; Wilkinson, 2017) whilst gay men have also often occupied positions of authority within musical spaces in global Northern countries (Brett & Wood, 2006). Even in morally repressive, conservative cultures there have been consistently queer themes such as same-sex erotic intimacy between men, particularly in public operas (Koestenbaum, 1991), that have not been possible in other areas of social life.

Queer theorists have frequently, therefore, sought to subvert 'dominant' or linear readings of performers and texts, and neat associations between musical content and gendered interpretation. Even with regards to misogynistic and/or homophobic forms of music, it is possible to offer different interpretations which do not presume a simplistic analysis of 'hegemonic' or 'hyper' masculinity. Queer analyses of 'heterosexist hip-hop', for instance, detail how, despite strong heteronormative overtones, there are also clear instances of same-sex intimacy and homoeroticism evident in the lyrics (Jarman-Ivens, 2006; Oware, 2011).

Such approaches have also demonstrated how masculinity/ies is not an inherent property of the heterosexual, cis-gendered male body. For instance, Berggren (2014), exploring how 'female masculinities' (Halberstam, 2012) are performed in Swedish hip hop, notes how women adopt many of the same lyrical tropes present in 'gangsta' rap but invert them to provide a critique of hetero-patriarchal norms. Similarly, the simultaneous performance and subversion of cis-masculine tropes by queer, working-class country artists or trans* metal cover bands complicates the idea of an inherent correspondence between gender, genre, performance and aesthetics, as well as queering the gendered aesthetic assumptions themselves (Gregory, 2013; Hubbs, 2014). This destabilises the idea that heteronormative, cis-gendered masculinity is a function of, or pre-requisite to, music's aesthetic appeal.

More recently, Hawkins (2016) has shown how tropes around 'Black masculinity' are queered through the performance of queer hop and 'homo-hop'. Noting how these artists flirt with and disrupt the sonic cues associated with established notions of 'masculinity' in hip hop, he draws attention to their lyrical focus on queer relationships as well as their adoption of visual cues associated with queer cultures (vogueing and 'camp' aesthetics). These artists not only play with and subvert 'feminine' and 'masculine' signifiers but also challenge both the invisibility of queer men within hip hop as well as the exclusion of Black men's bodies from largely ethnocentric queer spaces in global Northern music cultures.

Gendering production: transnational men and the global music industries

Analysing musical texts and listening practices can help to understand social formations of men, masculinity and masculinities. Yet it is also important not to detach music creation from gendered global forces of production. Even though music can be a space for men and boys to challenge certain normative gendered expectations, either through aesthetic practice or performance, access to different music spaces are unevenly stratified and reinforced by differing forms of privilege.

Firstly, homosocial networks are key in corroborating men's and boys' gender performances through music, with particular emphases on competition as a means of developing particular music skills (Clawson, 1999); these are vital in reproducing and maintaining these quantitative imbalances more generally (Cameron, 2003). Homosocial networks therefore lead to the particular exclusion of young women from music learning environments and networks. Formal music education in global Northern countries is also heavily stratified by intersections of gender, class, race and ethnicity (Born & Devine, 2015), with elite conservatories failing to include people of colour, even if they admit more women to music programs than previously (de Boise, 2018).

In addition, there are clear similarities in cis-gendered men's behaviour toward people of other genders across various music spaces in different countries. This ranges from undermining women musicians' technical competence, to transphobia and sexual harassment (Gadir, 2017) in both 'classical' and 'popular' music spaces. Music written by cis-gendered men in the key geopolitical 'centres' is also far more likely to be canonised whilst there are comparably greater resources which go into marketing men as musicians (Donze, 2017).

A structural focus on who actually ends up working within the music industries also reveals that the industries themselves maintain fairly strict gendered divisions of labour. This is particularly the case with regards to music technicians and producers whereby producers and music technicians are overwhelmingly men from global Northern states. Given the increasingly important role of producers in shaping musical reception, as well as becoming 'stars' in their own right, this gendered division inevitably confers greater power on men in the global North. As an example, in *NME*'s list of the 50 'Greatest Music Producers Ever', not a single woman is named, and most are from Western Europe and the US. This is despite women being amongst the most influential pioneers in music technology (Hinkle-Turner, 2003) and the development of key production techniques in Caribbean nations (Bronfman, 2016).

Senior executives within the global music industries are also more likely to be men. Despite roughly even numbers of men and women in the industries overall, men made up 70% of senior executive industry positions in the UK (UK Music, 2017) and Sweden (Musiksverige, 2017). There are also divisions in the gendering of jobs within the industries, with women more likely to work in PR rather than artist management and development (Hesmondhalgh & Baker, 2015). Furthermore, in terms of musicians registered with the main royalty-paying organisations (and who thus are more likely to be paid for their labour), available data reveal that men account for anywhere between 80% to 91% of those registered in different countries (STIM, 2016; UBC, 2016).

Finally, gendered labour within the music industries is influenced by, and thrives on, gendered transnational, geopolitical inequalities, indicating a need to think about relations of centre and periphery in gendered analyses (Ratele, 2014). Whilst digitalisation has intensified the dislocation of music corporations from the nation state, the uneven distribution of influence by organisations with economic interests in different countries, within global music markets, is a long-standing trend. As Devine (2015) observes, when analysing the music industries, there is a tendency to ignore questions of how the physical goods are both manufactured and disposed. Yet these chains necessarily implicate transnational relations between men, given that those who are most likely to mine the components required for listening devices, those who assemble the goods, those who transport e-waste and those who dispose of it are likely to be men in poorer and developing countries. Thus, music consumer markets in global Northern countries directly impact on the health of men in developing nations through the generation and processing of music e-waste (see Grant & Oteng-Ababio, 2012).

Conclusion

This chapter has noted how music implicates men, masculinity and masculinit*ies* in different ways. There is considerable debate around the extent to which music itself is a *representation* or *expression* of the values held by particular groups of men, and the extent to which it actively *affects* men's understandings of how they should behave. Importantly, music, or debates around these perceived expressions and effects can be a means of exploring the way in which societies think about gendered norms as well as a means of deconstructing the very 'nature' of gender.

Sounds and individual pieces are often constructed with gendered relations in mind, and connotative associations are often made between sonic textures and men's bodies. Importantly, intersectional dynamics partially explain the aesthetic presentation of different types of music, as well as its appeal amongst different groups of men. Yet, whilst there is some evidence to indicate that music can also be used to support homophobic and/or misogynistic sentiments, cultural homophobia and misogyny play a role in musical interpretation. As such, musical interpretation may change depending on the listener or the performer as well as the historical and cultural context. Queer approaches, especially, have demonstrated that a number of different interpretations of genres or pieces of music are possible and that there is no necessary correspondence between the gendered aesthetic of the music and either the audience or performer's gender.

Yet, despite the queering of masculinity or normative expectations surrounding men's behaviour in music, it is important to note that the music industries themselves are still very much dominated by men and, especially, homosocial networks. Whilst alternatives clearly exist to global corporations, there is a clear disconnect between the often democratic, revolutionary and gender-subversive intentions and the often conservative gendered practices of the institutions themselves. Furthermore, given that the music industries rely on material relations of production, this necessarily implies unequal relationships between men on a global scale.

References

Aboim, S. (2010). *Plural masculinities: The remaking of self in private life*. Farnham: Ashgate.

Bakrania, F. (2013). *Bhangra and Asian underground: South Asian music and the politics of belonging in Britain*. Durham, NC: Duke University Press.

Bannister, M. (2006). *White boys, white noise: Masculinities and 1980s indie guitar rock*. Farnham: Ashgate.

Basso, E. (1989). Musical expression and gender identity in the myth and ritual of the Kalapalo of Central Brazil. In E. Koskoff (Ed.), *Women and music in cross cultural perspective* (pp. 163–176). Champaign, IL: University of Illinois Press.

Berggren, K. (2014). Hip hop feminism in Sweden: Intersectionality, feminist critique and female masculinity. *European Journal of Women's Studies*, *21* (3), 233–250.

Biddle, I., & Gibson, K. (2009). *Masculinity and western musical practice*. Farnham: Ashgate.

Born, G., & Devine, K. (2015). Music technology, gender, and class: Digitization, educational and social change in Britain. *Twentieth-Century Music*, *12* (2), 135–172.

Brett, P., & Wood, E. (2006). Lesbian and gay music. In P. Brett, E. Wood, & G. Thomas (Eds.), *Queering the pitch: The new lesbian and gay musicology* (pp. 351–378). Abingdon: Routledge.

Bridges, T., & Pascoe, C. J. (2014). Hybrid masculinities: New directions in the sociology of men and masculinities. *Sociology Compass*, *8* (3), 246–258.

Bright, C. (2004). Deconstructing reparative therapy: An examination of the processes involved when attempting to change sexual orientation. *Clinical Social Work Journal*, *32* (4), 471–481.

Bronfman, A. (2016). *Isles of noise: Sonic media in the Caribbean*. Chapel Hill, NC: University of North Carolina Press.

Brown, J. (1999). Masculinity and dancehall. *Caribbean Quarterly*, *45* (1), 1–16.

Cameron, S. (2003). The political economy of gender disparity in musical markets. *Cambridge Journal of Economics*, *27* (6), 905–917.

Caminero, K. (2016, October 16). 'Black black metal' takes South Africa. *The Daily Beast*. Retrieved from www.thedailybeast.com/black-black-metal-takes-south-africa.

Castiglione, B. (1959 [1561]). *The book of the courtier* (C. S. Singelton, Trans.). Garden City, NY: Anchor Books.

Charles, M. (2016). Grime central! Subterranean ground-in grit engulfing manicured mainstream spaces. In K. Andrews & L. A. Palmer (Eds.), *Blackness in Britain* (pp. 89–99). London: Routledge.

Chester, N. (2015, April 21). Meet the Saudi Arabian black metal band that's breaking Saudi law by being a black metal band. *Vice*. Retrieved from www.vice.com/en_us/article/zngeew/anti-religious-black-metal-band-in-saudi-arabia-666.

Clawson, M. A. (1999). When women play the bass: Instrument specialization and gender interpretation in alternative rock music. *Gender & Society, 13* (2), 193–210.
Colley, A. (2008). Young people's musical taste: Relationship with gender and gender-related traits. *Journal of Applied Social Psychology, 38* (8), 2039–2055.
Cooper, C. (2004). *Sound clash: Jamaican dancehall culture at large*. New York: Palgrave Macmillan.
de Boise, S. (2014). Cheer up emo kid: Rethinking the 'crisis of masculinity' in emo. *Popular Music, 33* (2), 225–242.
de Boise, S. (2015). *Men, masculinity, music and emotion*. London: Palgrave Macmillan.
de Boise, S. (2018). Gender inequalities and higher music education: Comparing the UK and Sweden. *British Journal of Music Education, 35* (1), 23–41.
Devine, K. (2015). Decomposed: A political ecology of music. *Popular Music, 34* (3), 367–389.
Djupvik, M. (2014). Welcome to the candy shop! Conflicting representations of black masculinity. *Popular Music, 33* (2), 209–224.
Donze, P. L. (2017). Gender and popular culture: A comparison of promoter and listener preferences for popular music artists. *Sociological Perspectives, 60* (2), 338–354.
Fried, C. B. (1996). Bad rap for rap: Bias in reactions to music lyrics. *Journal of Applied Social Psychology, 26* (23), 2135–2146.
Frith, S., & McRobbie, A. (1978). Rock and sexuality. *Screen Education, 29*, 3–19.
Gadir, T. (2017). Forty-seven DJs, four women: Meritocracy, talent and postfeminist politics. *Dancecult: Journal of Electronic Dance Music Culture, 9* (1), 50–72.
Garrido, S., & Schubert, E. (2013). Adaptive and maladaptive attraction to negative emotions in music. *Musicae Scientiae, 17* (2), 147–166.
Gibson, K. (2009). Music, melancholy and masculinity in early modern England. In I. Biddle & K. Gibson (Eds.), *Masculinity and western musical practice* (pp. 41–66). Farnham: Ashgate.
Gilroy, P. (1991). Sounds authentic: Black music, ethnicity, and the challenge of a 'changing' same. *Black Music Research Journal, 11* (2), 111–136.
Grant, R., & Oteng-Ababio, M. (2012). Mapping the invisible and real 'African' economy: Urban e-waste circuitry. *Urban Geography, 33* (1), 1–21.
Green, L. (1997). *Music, gender and education*. Cambridge: University of Cambridge Press.
Gregory, G. (2013). Transgender tribute bands and the subversion of male rites of passage through the performance of heavy metal music. *Journal for Cultural Research, 17* (1), 21–36.
Halberstam, J. (2012). Global female masculinities. *Sexualities, 15* (3/4), 336–354.
Hawkins, S. (2009). *The British pop dandy: Masculinity, popular music and culture*. Farnham: Ashgate.
Hawkins, S. (2016). *Queerness in pop music: Aesthetics, gender norms and temporality*. London: Routledge.
Hesmondhalgh, D., & Baker, S. (2015). Sex, gender and work segregation in the cultural industries. *The Sociological Review, 63* (s1), 23–36.
Hill, R. (2016). *Gender, metal and the media*. London: Palgrave Macmillan.
Hinkle-Turner, E. (2003). Women and music technology: Pioneers, precedents and issues in the United States. *Organised Sound, 8* (1), 31–47.
hooks, b. (2004). *We real cool: Black men and masculinity*. London: Routledge.
Houston, T. M. (2012). The homosocial construction of alternative masculinities: Men in indie rock bands. *The Journal of Men's Studies, 20* (2), 158–175.
Hubbs, N. (2014). *Rednecks, queers & country music*. Berkeley, CA: University of California Press.
Jarman-Ivens, F. (2006). Queering masculinities in heterosexist rap music. In S. Whitely & J. Rycenga (Eds.), *Queering the popular pitch* (pp. 199–219). London: Routledge.
Järviluoma, H., Moisala, P., & Vilkko, A. (2003). *Gender and qualitative methods*. London: Sage.
Johnson, P., & Vanderbeck, R. M. (2014). *Law, religion and homosexuality*. Abingdon: Routledge.
Jung, S. (2011). *Korean masculinities and transcultural consumption: Yonsama Rain, Old Boy, K-Pop idols*. Hong Kong: Hong Kong University Press.
Kheshti, R. (2015). *Modernity's ear: Listening to race and gender in world music*. New York: New York University Press.
King, M. (2013). *Men, masculinity and the Beatles*. Farnham: Ashgate.
Kistler, M. E., & Lee, M. J. (2009). Does exposure to sexual hip-hop music videos influence the sexual attitudes of college students? *Mass Communication and Society, 13* (1), 67–86.
Koestenbaum, W. (1991). The queen's throat: (Homo)sexuality and the art of singing. In D. Fuss (Ed.), *Inside/out: Lesbian theories, gay theories* (pp. 205–234). London: Routledge.

Kruse, H. (2002). Abandoning the absolute: Transcendence and gender in popular music discourse. In S. Jones (Ed.), *Pop music and the press* (pp. 134–155). Philadelphia, PA: Temple University Press.

Lawrence, J., & Joyner, D. (1991). The effect of sexually violent rock music on males' acceptance of violence against women. *Psychology of Women Quarterly, 15*, 49–63.

Leach, E. E. (2009). Music and masculinity in the middle ages. In I. Biddle & K. Gibson (Eds.), *Masculinity and western musical practices* (pp. 37–56). Farnham: Ashgate.

Leblanc, L. (1999). *Pretty in punk: Girls' gender resistance in a boys' subculture*. New Brunswick, NJ: Rutgers University Press.

Livermon, X. (2014). Soweto nights: Making black queer space in post-apartheid South Africa. *Gender, Place & Culture, 21* (4), 508–525.

Maus, F. E. (1993). Masculine discourse in music theory. *Perspectives of New Music, 31* (2), 264–293.

McClary, S. (1991). *Feminine endings: Music, gender and sexuality*. Minneapolis, MN: University of Minnesota Press.

McLeod, K. (2009). The construction of masculinity in African American music and sports. *American Music, 27* (2), 204–226.

Mullaney, J. L. (2007). 'Unity admirable but not necessarily heeded': Going rates and gender boundaries in the straight edge hardcore music scene. *Gender & Society, 21* (3), 384–408.

Musiksverige. (2017, October 25). Jämställdhet i Musikbranschen. Retrieved from www.musiksverige.org/blogg/2017/10/25/jmstlldhet-i-musikbranschen.

Nannyonga-Tamusuza, S. (2015). *Baakisimba: Gender in the music and dance of the Baganda people of Uganda*. London: Routledge.

O'Meara, C. (2003). The Raincoats: Breaking down punk rock's masculinities. *Popular Music, 22* (3), 299–313.

Oware, M. (2011). Brotherly love: Homosociality and black masculinity in gangsta rap music. *Journal of African American Studies, 15* (1), 22–39.

Palmer, G. (1997). Bruce Springsteen and masculinity. In S. Whitely (Ed.), *Sexing the groove: Popular music and gender* (pp. 100–117). London: Routledge.

Peress, M. (2004). *Dvořák to Duke Ellington*. Oxford: Oxford University Press.

Petersen, A. (1998). *Unmasking the masculine: 'Men' and 'identity' in a sceptical age*. London: Sage.

Plato. (2007). *The republic*. London: Penguin.

Rafalovich, A. (2006). Broken and becoming god-sized: Contemporary metal music and masculine individualism. *Symbolic Interaction, 29* (1), 19–32.

Ratele, K. (2014). Currents against gender transformation of South African men: Relocating marginality to the centre of research and theory of masculinities. *NORMA: International Journal for Masculinity Studies, 9* (1), 30–44.

Reck, D. R. (1985). Beatles orientalis: Influences from Asia in a popular song tradition. *Asian Music, 16* (1), 83–149.

Reddington, H. (2007). *The lost women of rock music: Female musicians of the punk era*. Aldershot: Ashgate.

Roberts, S. (Ed.). (2014). *Debating modern masculinities: Change, continuity, crisis?* Basingstoke: Palgrave Pivot.

Robinson, J. (2005). *Deeper than reason: Emotion and its role in literature, music, and art*. Oxford: Oxford University Press.

Rodriquez, J. (2006). Color-blind ideology and the cultural appropriation of hip-hop. *Journal of Contemporary Ethnography, 35* (6), 645–668.

Saddik, A. J. (2003). Rap's unruly body: The postmodern performance of black male identity on the American stage. *TDR/The Drama Review, 47* (4), 110–127.

Sernhede, O. (2007). *Alienation is my nation: Hiphop och unga mäns utanförskap i Det nya Sverige*. Stockholm: Ordfront.

STIM. (2016). *Annual report 2016*. Stockholm: STIM.

UBC. (2016). UBC annual report 2015. Retrieved from www.ubc.org.br/Hotsite/Relatorio_Anual/2015/eng/cap-4.html.

UK Music. (2017). *UK music diversity survey 2017*. London: UK Music.

Wadkins, K. E. (2012). 'Freakin' out': Remaking masculinity through punk rock in Detroit. *Women & Performance: A Journal of Feminist Theory, 22* (2/3), 239–260.

Walser, R. (1993). *Running with the devil: Power, gender and madness in heavy metal music*. Middletown, CT: Wesleyan University Press.

Weitzer, R., & Kubrin, C. (2009). Misogyny in rap music: A content analysis of prevalence and meanings. *Men and Masculinities, 12* (1), 1–27.

West, K., & Cowell, N. (2015). Predictors of prejudice against lesbians and gay men in Jamaica. *The Journal of Sex Research, 52*, 296–305.

Wilkinson, S. (2017, October 3). Out of this world: i-D meets mykki blanco. *i-D Vice*. Retrieved from https://i-d.vice.com/en_uk/article/43a57j/out-of-this-world-i-d-meets-mykki-blanco.

Worley, M. (2017). *No future: Punk, politics and British youth culture, 1976–1984*. Cambridge: Cambridge University Press.

Wych, G. (2012). Gender and instrument associations, stereotypes and stratification: A literature review. *National Association for Music Education, 30* (2), 22–31.

Yousman, B. (2003). Blackophilia and blackophobia: White youth, the consumption of rap music, and white supremacy. *Communication Theory, 13* (4), 366–391.

41

Masculinities and literary studies

Past, present, and future directions

Josep M. Armengol

This chapter offers an introduction to the field of study of literary masculinities. After tracing its origins and development within the broader field of masculinity studies, it continues by illustrating the field's applications to literary criticism, showing how literature may help question traditional notions of masculinity but also point to alternative ways of being man. The chapter finishes analyzing some of the latest debates within the field of literary masculinities. As in the case of masculinity studies in general, current studies of literary masculinities seem to be divided into identity-based and poststructuralist approaches, which this chapter illustrates through the concepts of "ethnic" and/vs. "female" masculinities, respectively.

Studies of literary masculinities: a short history

Even though David Leverenz's *Manhood and the American Renaissance* (1989), his seminal study on representations of masculinity in 1850s U.S. literature, is still considered the foundational text on literary masculinities, research had already begun in the early 1980s and has since continued to thrive. Thus, for example, Alfred Habegger's *Gender, Fantasy, and Realism in American Literature* (1982) had already explored representations of masculinity in the realist novels of Henry James and William Dean Howells, just as Peter Schwenger's *Phallic Critiques: Masculinity and Twentieth-Century Literature* (1984) had analyzed masculinity in the fiction of Mailer, Mishima, and Hemingway. In this latter text, Schwenger also pointed to the interface between sexuality and literary style, subversively claiming that "there is such a thing as a masculine style" (1984, p. 12). Two other influential early texts focusing on literature were Eve Kosofsky Sedgwick's *Between Men: English Literature and Male Homosocial Desire* (1985), which drew on (literary) erotic triangles to undermine the traditional binary between "homoerotic" and "homosocial" desire, and the anthology *Men in Feminism* (1987), edited by Alice Jardine and Paul Smith, which focused on (male) feminism in literature and culture. Equally influential were Wayne Koestenbaum's *Double Talk: The Erotics of Male Literary Collaboration* (1989) and Joseph

A. Boone and Michael Cadden's *Engendering Men: The Question of Male Feminist Criticism* (1990). If the former centered on literary collaboration between male authors,[1] Boone and Cadden's edition of *Engendering Men* signaled "several avenues" (1990, p. 4) from which a criticism by men doing feminism might emerge.[2] Andrew P. Williams (1999), for his part, centered on images of masculinity in early modern British literature, whereas David Rosen in *The Changing Fictions of Masculinity* (1993) had already sketched the first history of masculinity in British literature.

Of course, women made equally decisive contributions to the subject from the start. Like Boone and Cadden, Laura Claridge and Elizabeth Langland's *Out of Bounds: Male Writers and Gender(ed) Criticism* (1990), for instance, analyzed several male writers to begin to examine the feminist inclination of their works.[3] And, if most early studies of literary masculinities had focused on the dominant Anglo-American context, Michael Kane's *Modern Men: Mapping Masculinity in English and German Literature, 1880–1930* (1999) set out to re-read, from a comparative perspective, some of the canonical works of modernist literature in both English and German with reference to the issues of masculinity, homosociality, and nationalism, while Peter Murphy's *Fictions of Masculinity* (1994) used authors such as Kafka, Günter Grass, and the Egyptian Mahfouz to compare different constructions of literary masculinities across different cultures. Following in the steps of Hispanic social scientists and anthropologists (Mirande, 1997), some of the earliest texts on literary masculinities were also published in Spanish and/or focused on the Hispanic context, including *Nuevas masculinidades* (2000), and *Hombres escritos por mujeres* (2003), both edited by Àngels Carabí and Marta Segarra. While the former looked at different models of masculinity in literature and the media, Hispanic and international, the latter concentrated on representations of masculinities by women writers worldwide.

Since the 1990s, then, the field has just continued to rapidly develop and expand, ranging from Ben Knights' *Writing Masculinities* (1999), focused on male narratives in twentieth-century fictions, to Berthold Schoene's *Writing Men* (2000), a literary history of (British) masculinities from Frankenstein to "the New Man." The latter offered an important corrective to the field's recurrent heterosexist biases, incorporating several gay authors and fictions.[4] Amongst the latest additions to the field are Todd W. Reeser's *Masculinities in Theory* (2009), one of the first introductions to masculinities from a Humanities rather than literary angle, and two studies by Stefan Horlacher, *Constructions of Masculinity in British Literature from the Middle Ages to the Present* (2011) and *Configuring Masculinity in Theory and Literary Practice* (2015), both focused on British literature.[5] These have been recently complemented by *Alternative Masculinities for a Changing World* (2014), edited by Carabí and Armengol, which explores non-dominant models of masculinity in contemporary (U.S.) culture and literature, and *Masculinities and Literary Studies* (Armengol, Bosch-Vilarrubias, Carabí & Requena, 2017), which illustrates the intersections between masculinities and literary criticism as well as some of the latest advances ensuing thereof. Other recent texts include *Queering Iberia* (Armengol, 2012), centered on representations of queer masculinities from different Hispanic cultures; Rafael M. Mérida's *Hispanic (LGT) Masculinities in Transition* (2014), which explores representations of LGT masculinities in the Hispanic context right after Franco's death; and Juan Rey's *The Male Body as Advertisement* (2015), focused on images of masculinities in different Spanish and Latin American media. Such texts have all helped the field to move beyond its often heterosexist and Anglo-centric biases. Given the growing number of publications on cultural representations of masculinities, it is no wonder, then, that Michael Kimmel (2009) has defined this (sub)field as "probably the center" (p. 16) of current masculinity research, which, in his view, has since the 1990s privileged cultural studies of masculinities *vis-à-vis* the hegemony of psychological, anthropological, and sociological studies of the two previous decades.

A masculinity studies approach to literature: aims and methods

Despite the growing body of texts on literary masculinities, the field remains largely unexplored in academia, especially in comparison to literary studies on women. While the feminist analysis of literary women has already become part of the academic curriculum and is quite familiar to both female and male students, the analysis of literary masculinities remains largely unpracticed and unknown. As literary critic Berthold Schoene complained:

> Ask any discerning male student to write an essay on Jane Austen's representation of women, or the straitjacketing impact of patriarchal gender politics on the women in Shakespeare's comedies, and the result is often clearly and cogently argued. However, ask them to comment on the representation of men and the response is often a mixture of discomfort, nervous agitation and silence.
>
> *(2000, p. viii)*

There are several reasons for this. On the one hand, the analysis of the images of women in literature has a fairly long history within feminist literary criticism, while the feminist study of literary masculinities is a relatively recent and, by comparison, small addition to academia. Except for a few critics such as Leslie Fiedler (1960) and David Leverenz (1989), scholars have only just begun to analyze masculinity in contemporary culture and literature. As Peter Murphy indicates, "more recent, and sometimes more radical, books have been written by sociologists, psychologists, and historians, not literary or cultural critics" (1994, p. 4). Furthermore, there are few texts that suggest how an analysis of literary masculinities could proceed. And, no matter how well-intentioned, it does not seem to be enough for masculinity scholars simply to adopt and start imitating feminist perspectives, aims, and resolutions. In order to deal with the specific dilemma of their masculine condition, men, as Schoene (2000) elaborates in this respect, must try to develop their own counter-discourse against patriarchy.

Despite the fact that we still lack a critical vocabulary pertinent to the analysis of literary masculinities, however, a masculinity studies re-reading of literature may be and has been proven beneficial for several reasons. First of all, just as the erroneous assumption that male experience equals human experience affected literary criticism's treatment of women as characters and authors, so has it limited our perceptions about men in literature. Therefore, studies of literary masculinities entail a radical re-vision of the way we read literature and of the way we perceive men and masculine ideals therein. In James Riemer's words, masculinity studies explore "our culturally defined ideals of masculinity and how they" affect "men's lives, transforming universal human experiences into ones that are distinctly masculine" (1987, p. 289). Thus this approach has shifted the focus of criticism from the manner in which men's lives reflect abstract, universal issues to a more intimate, personal concern with how cultural values, particularly those related to ideals of masculinity, affect men's lives on a personal level (Riemer, 1987). Re-reading supposedly universal and genderless issues such as emotions and violence from the perspective of masculinity, for example, may help illustrate how masculine ideals affect, and often restrict and complicate, men's lives in culture and literature.[6]

Another implication of re-reading literature from this angle is the possibility of analyzing a significant part of literary works as social documents reflecting different cultural conceptions of masculinity. Since cultures are varying and plural, rather than monolithic, studies of literary masculinities, as Riemer (1987) indicates, are centrally concerned with showing the multiple conceptions and representations of masculinities in fiction. For example, Ernest Hemingway's representations of stoic, tough, violent, and apparently unemotional male characters in *In Our Time* (1925) differ substantially from John Steinbeck's portrait of the close, affectionate, and atypically nurturing male friendship between George and Lennie in *Of Mice and Men* (1937).

If, as it seems, a writer's concepts of masculinity may differ from those of his contemporaries, the difference tends to be even greater when we contrast representations of masculinity from disparate historical epochs. One need only compare, for example, the representations of masculinity in James Fenimore Cooper's *Leatherstocking Novels* (1823–1841), focused on the celebration of a heavily masculine warrior mentality in nineteenth-century America, and Edmund White's *Chaos* (2010), on contemporary gay male identity, to see how manhood ideals have been radically transformed over the years in the United States.[7] Yet a masculinity approach to literature analyzes how men and masculinities change over time and also what aspects of masculinity remain unchanged. Thus one can find some commonalities, for example, between the fiction of Ernest Hemingway and the contemporary American writer Richard Ford, both of whom deal with the connections between masculinities and hunting, albeit from radically different perspectives. While Hemingway tends to celebrate trophy-hunting as a proof of manhood, Ford subverts this classic Hemingwayesque vision, repeatedly portraying animal killings by men as (failed) attempts to compensate for their inner vulnerability.[8]

Like social concepts of masculinity, then, literary concepts of masculinity are culture-specific. Thus, for example, scholars have increasingly been paying attention to literary representations of masculinity from the global South and/or outside the Anglophone world by authors such as Ken Lipenga from Malawi, Pumla Dineo Gqola from South Africa, and Nedim Gürsel from Turkey (Alkan, 2017), to name but a few, all of whom deconstruct hegemonic (i.e., white) concepts of masculinity through their works, showing how notions of masculinity are not universal but context-bound, as they vary across cultures and over time. No wonder the relationship between studies of literary masculinities and the larger field of masculinity studies has been described as a "reciprocal" one (Riemer, 1987, p. 291), as cultural and literary constructions of masculinity feed off one another. Just as re-reading literature for what it says about social conceptions of masculinity widens the base of masculinity studies knowledge, information obtained from other fields, such as sociology or psychology, can illuminate our re-readings of literature in new and interesting ways by affecting the shape of literary criticism itself.

Despite the undeniable value of literature as a social document reflecting our masculine ideals, however, such literary analyses cannot be taken as literal sociological, psychological, or anthropological studies on masculinity. As James D. Riemer insists, studies of literary masculinities "cannot be expected to give the whole 'truth' about manhood in relation to a particular social, economic, racial-ethnic environment," although "they can offer valuable insights into areas for further, potentially corroborating research by sociologists, psychologists, and social anthropologists" (1987, p. 291).[9] If, as Teresa De Lauretis (1987) argued, "gender is (a) representation" and "the representation of gender *is* its construction" (p. 3), then it follows that cultural representations of gender are crucial to understand, and rethink, its social constructions. While literature is neither "a case study" nor "a recipe," literary works, as the Nobel Prize-winning author Toni Morrison insisted, usually have something in them that "enlightens," something that "opens the door and points the way. Something ... that suggests what the conflicts are" (Evans, 1984, p. 341), thus providing valuable insights into a myriad of social issues, including the social construction of masculinities.

Notwithstanding the social and historical value of "classic" (i.e., white, male-authored) literary texts, one should avoid, in any event, restricting the analysis of masculinity to literary works that focus on the values of the white, middle-class, heterosexual male, which James D. Riemer identifies as a "limitation characteristic of a majority of the research and scholarship" on masculinities (1987, p. 291). By studying literary works which depict men's lives beyond the bourgeois experience, we can see how masculinity varies according to class, as the working-class male characters in novels such as Pietro Di Donato's *Christ in Concrete* or Jack London's *People of the Abyss* illustrate, as well as ethnic (e.g., Toni Morrison's *Song of Solomon*) and/or sexual (e.g., Edmund White's *Chaos*) specificities. Hence the growing number of publications on literary representations of African-American (Awkward, 2002; Reid-Pharr, 2001), Arab (Bosch-Vilarrubias, 2016), Asian (Eng, 2001), Jewish (Rosenberg, 2001), or Indian (Sinha, 1995), amongst other ethnicities,[10] as well as on gay characters, by critics such as Schoene (2000) and Knights (1999), to name but a few.

From what has been pointed out so far, one could conclude, then, that the aim of a masculinity studies approach to literature is "re-vision," which the writer and essayist Adrienne Rich beautifully defined as "the act of looking back, of seeing with fresh eyes, of entering an old text from a new critical direction" (1975, pp. 90–91). In studies of fictional masculinities, this re-vision entails analyzing both traditional and alternative literary models of manhood. In Riemer's words: "To change men's lives [one needs] more than recognition of the limitations and negative effects of our present ideals of manhood. There also must be a recognition and reinforcement of positive alternatives to traditional masculine ideals and behaviors" (1987, p. 298).

Admittedly, there are not many "positive" or "alternative" images of masculinity in literature. The Western literary tradition has provided us with men who embody a number of traditional masculine ideals, and men who fight the burden and limitations of those ideals. Seldom are we provided with positive images of men who represent alternatives to those traditional ideals (Riemer, 1987). There are, however, some "positive" images of masculinity in fiction. For example, in John Steinbeck's *Of Mice and Men* (1937), George and Lennie fight economic hardship and social isolation by developing a close friendship pattern that is unusually intimate, supportive, and generous. Similarly, in Toni Morrison's *Song of Solomon* (1977), Milkman Dead, who becomes more and more relational and other-directed as the novel advances, moves beyond his father Macon's individualistic, self-centered, and competitive masculine values. Likewise Tayo, the protagonist of Leslie Silko's *Ceremony* (1977), returns to his Native-American origins to reshape his masculinity. Moving away from violence and War in the Pacific, Tayo chooses to re(dis)cover his ancestral heritage and the communal values of his culture. In so doing, he finally becomes a much more relational, caring, and nurturing male character. In Richard Ford's *Independence Day* (1995), Frank Bascombe gradually abandons the manly code of individualism and emotional disengagement, and he finally becomes a more relational, nurturing, and supportive father and lover. Similarly, in Ford's *Rock Springs* (1987) and *A Multitude of Sins* (2001), several male characters move away from their violent fathers or their equally aggressive male friends to embrace a new, alternative, non-violent model of manhood.[11] Making us aware of these innovative literary texts might thus be one of the most significant contributions that a masculinity studies approach to literature can make. "For, in the end, it will be easier for men to revise the way they live their lives if," as Riemer (1987, p. 299) suggests, "we can help them recognize the possibilities of what they might become."[12]

Masculinities and literary studies: current debates and future directions

As in the case of masculinity studies in general, many recent studies of men in literature seem to be characterized by their growing specificity, moving away from previous literary "histories" of masculinity into more specialized topics and case studies. Thus, for example, if *Embodying Masculinities* (2013), edited by Josep M. Armengol, deals with literary representations of the male body in U.S. culture and literature, Greg Forter's *Murdering Masculinities* (2000) focuses on the issue of fantasies of gender and violence in the contemporary American crime novel, just as most of the chapters in *Masculinities and Literary Studies* (Armengol et al., 2017) deal with literary representations of the relationship between masculinities and specific topics like transnationalism, affect, fatherhood, ageing, and neoliberalism, amongst others. Moreover, there exists, as has already been noted, an increasing number of specific texts on ethnic literary masculinities, which offers an important corrective to the field's historical tendency to center on hegemonic (*read* white) masculinity as the norm. Yet, despite the continued academic interest in "ethnic" (*read* non-white) masculinities, one must not forget the growing focus on the study of white masculinity as a specific gendered and ethnic construct, with the intersections of masculinity and whiteness studies constituting one of the field's latest advances and innovations.[13]

While intersectionality has increasingly become one of the main axes around which much current scholarship on (literary) masculinities revolves, it seems relevant to note, though, that most of these recent works are divided between, on the one hand, their emphasis on gendered and ethnic identities and, on the other, the poststructuralist theories, on which they often rely, which insist that are our identities are far from stable and fixed. As in the social sciences, the most innovative approaches to the discussion in literary and cultural theory are those, I believe, that have been able to synthesize sexual politics and poststructuralist theories in new productive ways. The work by David L. Eng (2001) may be considered a case in point. In the introduction, he insists that his project attempts to interrogate "the commonalities that support, as well as the dissonances that qualify, coalitions among American men" (2001, p. 4). Insisting further, Eng argues that precisely because the feminization of the Asian male in the Western cultural landscape often results in his figuration as feminized or homosexualized, we must take care to explore the theoretical links between queer studies, with its focus on (homo)sexuality and desire, and women's studies, with its focus on gender and identity, in relation to the production of Asian American male subjectivity (p. 16). Thus Eng combines (feminist) sexual politics and queer theory in highly innovative ways. Equally innovative is Jean Bobby Noble's *Masculinities Without Men?* (2004), which applies Judith (now Jack) Halberstam's concept of "female masculinity" (1998) to literary texts. While challenging the exclusive association of (literary) masculinity with maleness, however, Noble (2004) both draws on and moves beyond Halberstam's classic study in highly subversive ways. Where Halberstam (1998) had established a close connection between female masculinity and lesbian/butch masculinity, Noble avoids it throughout, seeking a fully "post-identity politic and, at times, post-queer, anti-heteronormative but trans-ed materialization of masculinity" (2004, p. xxxix). And, if Halberstam had distinguished between male and female masculinities, positing them as radically separate, Noble defends their interdependence, redefining them as dialogic rather than opposite concepts. Even though Noble avoids presenting male masculinity as the original and female masculinity as a derivative, she proves her inextricability, insisting that "the argument that female masculinity does not notice, or is not influenced by, or does not reciprocate or return the gaze to male masculinity cannot be supported" (2004, p. xli). By analyzing the interconnections between male and female masculinity, and by applying these to literary texts such as Radclyffe Hall's *The Well of Loneliness* and Leslie Feinberg's *Stone Butch Blues*, amongst others, Noble (2004) has thus managed to radically innovate the study of literary masculinities, pointing to female masculinity as no doubt one of the field's most promising present and future research venues.

From this one may conclude, then, that social and literary constructions go hand in hand. In fact, some of the most relevant contributions to masculinity studies have come from literary studies like Sedgwick's *Between Men* (1985) or Halberstam's *Female Masculinity* (1998), which also makes ample use of cultural and film representations, to name but a few. Similarly, originally "sociological" concepts like Connell's (1995) "hegemonic masculinity" are constantly applied to cultural and literary criticism. Moreover, revisiting literature from a masculinity studies perspective has contributed to shedding new light on literary works but also on masculinity studies in general and, indeed, on the social construction of masculinity itself. Rather than pit literary against psychosocial studies of masculinities, it may be much more fruitful, then, to start looking at them as mutually informative. Literary works are "imagined," indeed. Yet it is imagination, above all, that is most needed in our current societies if we are all to live better, happier lives.

Notes

1 More specifically, Koestenbaum argued that when two men write together, they engage in double talk, "they rapidly patter to obscure their erotic burden, but the ambiguities of their discourse give the taboo subject some liberty to roam" (1989, p. 3).

2 Boone and Cadden (1990) argued that, by the 1990s, men had already begun to redefine themselves as men and, therefore, as critics of the literary and cultural texts that they had inherited and were in the process of recreating. "In engendering ourselves, in making visible our textual/sexual bodies," they concluded, "we thus acknowledge our part in a movement whose time, we hope, has come" (1990, p. 7).

3 Thus Claridge and Langland (1990) proved the subversive, feminist potential of several texts written by male writers, such as Hawthorne's *The Scarlet Letter* (1850) and Henry James's *The Bostonians* (1886), to name but a few.

4 It is important to recognize, however, that some critics, like Peter F. Murphy (1994), had already done so.

5 See also Armengol (2010), which shows the applicability of masculinity studies to literary criticism through an in-depth analysis of the fiction of contemporary U.S. writer Richard Ford.

6 Armengol's study (2010) on Richard Ford's fictional re-visions of masculinity may serve as an illustration of this.

7 Social historians such as Michael Kimmel, Joe Dubbert, and Peter Filene have already made such a sociological use of literature, although "on a limited scale" (Riemer, 1987, p. 290).

8 See Armengol (2010, pp. 100–120).

9 Besides shedding light on the social construction of masculinity, a masculinity studies approach to literature is also valuable in re-reading works by authors who have been often associated with defining and perpetuating manly ideals (Riemer, 1987). Such a re-reading entails not only questioning patriarchal masculinities in literary texts but also challenging former traditional critical readings of these texts. Just as male characters' lives are often limited by ideals of masculinity, so does the acceptance of traditional patriarchal values influence and limit the ways criticism has analyzed the works of writers clearly identified with traditional manly ideals. For example, critics such as Mark Spilka (1990) have argued that in Hemingway's *The Sun Also Rises* (1926), Jake Barnes betrays the manly code and fails the test of masculinity. Spilka (1990) claims that, being sexually impotent, Jake cannot seduce Brett Ashley and so is not a "real" man. For Spilka (1990), Jake fails

the manly code as he delivers Brett into the hands, or, rather, the bed, of Romero, who, in Spilka's view, is more of a man than Jakes. However, a different approach to the novel will show how Jake is not a failure as a man. Rather, he is considered as such by a patriarchal code which links masculinity to sexual possession through penetration. It is not Jake who fails the code but the code and other male ideals that have failed the man. As James D. Riemer concludes in this respect, "ideals of manhood are the source of Jake's problem and often the reason he is unable to deal with it in any manner but escape" (1987, p. 297).

10 Of course the list of texts that explore literary representations of ethnic masculinities is enormous and far too long to include here. For a more complete list, see Michael Flood's annotated bibliography on gender and masculinities under the sections "Literature and literary theory" and "Race and ethnicity" (www.xyonline.net/bibliography).

11 See Armengol (2010).

12 For a full-length study of alternative masculinities in (U.S.) culture and literature, see Carabí and Armengol (2014).

13 See, for example, Babb (1998), Robinson (2000), and Armengol (2014).

References

Alkan, B. (2017). Formation of masculinity in Nedim Gürsel's *Yüzbaşının Oğlu*. *NORMA: International Journal for Masculinity Studies*, *12*(1), 23–37.

Armengol, J. (2010). *Richard Ford and the fiction of masculinities*. New York: Peter Lang.

Armengol, J. (Ed.). (2012). *Queering Iberia: Iberian masculinities at the margins*. New York: Peter Lang.

Armengol, J. (Ed.). (2013). *Embodying masculinities: Towards a history of the male body in U.S. culture and literature*. New York: Peter Lang.

Armengol, J. (2014). *Masculinities in black and white: Manliness and whiteness in (African) American literature*. New York: Palgrave Macmillan.

Armengol, J., Bosch-Vilarrubias, M., Carabí, A., & Requena, T. (Eds.). (2017). *Masculinities and literary studies: Intersections and new directions*. New York: Routledge.

Awkward, M. (2002). Black male trouble: The challenges of rethinking masculine differences. In J. K. Gardiner (Ed.), *Masculinity studies and feminist theory: New directions* (pp. 290–304). New York: Columbia University Press.

Babb, V. (1998). *Whiteness visible: The meaning of whiteness in American literature and culture*. New York: New York University Press.

Boone, J. A., & Cadden, M. (Eds.). (1990). *Engendering men: The question of male feminist criticism*. New York: Routledge.

Bosch-Vilarrubias, M. (2016). *Post-9/11 representations of Arab men by Arab American women writers: Affirmation and resistance*. New York: Peter Lang.

Carabí, À., & Armengol, J. (Eds.). (2014). *Alternative masculinities for a changing world*. New York: Palgrave Macmillan.

Carabí, À., & Segarra, M. (Eds.). (2000). *Nuevas masculinidades*. Barcelona: Icaria.

Carabí, À., & Segarra, M. (Eds.). (2003). *Hombres escritos por mujeres*. Barcelona: Icaria.

Claridge, L., & Langland, E. (Eds.). (1990). *Out of bounds: Male writers and gender(ed) criticism*. Amherst, MA: University of Massachusetts Press.

Connell, R. (1995). *Masculinities*. Berkeley, CA: University of California Press.

De Lauretis, T. (1987). *Technologies of gender*. Bloomington, IN: Indiana University Press.

Eng, D. L. (2001). *Racial castration: Managing masculinity in Asian America*. Durham, NC: Duke University Press.

Evans, M. (Ed.). (1984). *Black women writers (1950–1980): A critical evaluation*. New York: Anchor.

Fiedler, L. (1960). *Love and death in the American novel*. New York: Criterion Books.

Forter, G. (2000). *Murdering masculinities*. New York: New York University Press.

Habegger, A. (1982). *Gender, fantasy, and realism in American literature*. New York: Columbia University Press.

Halberstam, J. (1998). *Female masculinity*. Durham, NC: Duke University Press.

Horlacher, S. (2011). *Constructions of masculinity in British literature from the middle ages to the present*. New York: Palgrave Macmillan.

Horlacher, S. (Ed.). (2015). *Configuring masculinity in theory and literary practice*. Leiden: Brill.

Jardine, A., & Smith, P. (Eds.). (1987). *Men in feminism*. New York: Methuen.

Kane, M. (1999). *Modern men: Mapping masculinity in English and German literature, 1880–1930*. London & New York: Cassell.

Kimmel, M. (2009). Masculinity studies: An introduction. In J. Armengol & A. Carabí (Eds.), *Debating masculinity* (pp. 16–30). Harriman, TN: Men's Studies Press.

Knights, B. (1999). *Writing masculinities: Male narratives in twentieth-century fiction*. London: Macmillan.

Koestenbaum, W. (1989). *Double talk: The erotics of male literary collaboration*. New York: Routledge.

Leverenz, D. (1989). *Manhood and the American renaissance*. Ithaca, NY: Cornell University Press.

Mérida, R. M. (Ed.). (2014). *Hispanic (LGT) masculinities in transition*. New York: Peter Lang.

Mirande, A. (1997). *Hombres y machos: Masculinity and Latino culture*. Boulder, CO: Westview Press.

Murphy, P. (Ed.). (1994). *Fictions of masculinity: Crossing cultures, crossing sexualities*. New York: New York University Press.

Noble, J. B. (2004). *Masculinities without men? Female masculinity in twentieth-century fictions*. Vancouver: British Columbia University Press.

Reeser, T. W. (2009). *Masculinities in theory: An introduction*. New York: Wiley.

Reid-Pharr, R. (2001). *Black gay man: Essays*. New York: New York University Press.

Rey, J. (Ed.). (2015). *The male body as advertisement: Masculinities in Hispanic media*. New York: Peter Lang.

Rich, A. (1975). When the dead awaken: Writing as re-vision. In B. Charlesworth-Gelpi & A. Gelpi (Eds.), *Adrienne Rich's poetry* (pp. 90–91). New York: Norton.

Riemer, J. D. (1987). Rereading American literature from a men's studies perspective: Some implications. In H. Brod (Ed.), *The making of masculinities: The new men's studies* (pp. 289–300). Boston, MA: Allen & Unwin.

Robinson, S. (2000). *Marked men: White masculinity in crisis*. New York: Columbia University Press.

Rosen, D. (1993). *The changing fictions of masculinity*. Urbana & Chicago, IL: University of Illinois Press.

Rosenberg, W. (2001). *Legacy of rage: Jewish masculinity, violence, and culture*. Amherst, MA: University of Massachusetts Press.

Schoene, B. (2000). *Writing men: Literary masculinities from Frankenstein to the new man*. Edinburgh: Edinburgh University Press.

Schwenger, P. (1984). *Phallic critiques: Masculinity and twentieth-century literature*. New York: Routledge and Kegan Paul.

Sedgwick, E. K. (1985). *Between men: English literature and male homosocial desire*. New York: Columbia University Press.

Sinha, M. (1995). *Colonial masculinity: The "manly Englishman" and the "effeminate Bengali" in the late nineteenth century*. Manchester: Manchester University Press.

Spilka, M. (1990). *Hemingway's quarrel with androgyny*. Lincoln, NB: University of Nebraska Press.

Williams, A. P. (Ed.). (1999). *The image of manhood in early modern literature: Viewing the male*. Westport, CT: Greenwood.

42

Men and masculinity in art and art history

Bettina Uppenkamp

In both art and art history, masculinity, as a historically contingent and socially constructed category, only came into focus through the feminist critique by female artists and art historians during the 1970s, both of whom contested the art historical 'canon' – one of the most hierarchical and masculinist (Salomon, 1993). Difficulties surrounding recognition for female artists in an art world dominated by men – that is, the sheer invisibility of works by women while images of femininity are omnipresent in the very same museums and galleries – were understood as a systematic form of discrimination that expressed patriarchal relationships and androcentric values. Feminist scholars questioned male-dominated views of women and representations of the female body, while female artists attempted to re-evaluate femininity and experimented with a new *picture language*. From the mid-1980s there was a shift away from an exclusive focus on those female artists and views of women excluded from art history. Instead, scholars spoke of *constructions of masculinity and femininity in art and art history* (Lindner, Schade, Wenk & Werner, 1989), where the representational effects of gender, the semantic implications of the concept of gender differences and their productivity in the visual field were emphasised. These methodological shifts, from feminist research of women to gender studies of art, were founded in discourse analysis, psychoanalysis and postmodern deconstruction (Broude & Garrard, 1992; Schade & Wenk, 1995; Söntgen, 1996a; Zimmermann, 2006).

While masculinity in art was first thematised as a relatively monolithic and normative construction, it soon became clear that the concept in the history of art is exceedingly complex. This chapter presents scholarship on art and art history and discusses how men and masculinity have become the subject of research in various forms. It focuses on the feminist critique of the cult of the genius; questions regarding the artist and his (self)portraits; the iconographical investigation into the context of presentation and the staging of the male or female body; questions animated from the biography and sexual orientation of the artist and its meaning for the work; the deployment of theories of the 'male gaze'; and the role of art in racist and other exclusionary practices.

Authorship and the genius of the artist

The artist as creator is a central trope in the history of art, and its exaggerated importance has long been dealt with in the field (Schade & Wenk, 1995). Part of the work undertaken by gender art history scholars is to deconstruct masculinity and the authority tied to this mythical figure (Hoffmann-Curtius & Wenk, 1997), in the writing of art history as well as in forms of artistic self-expression. At the heart of this critique stands a founding text for the discipline of art history: Giorgio Vasari's (1550/1568) *Le vite de' più eccellenti pittori, scultori ed architettori*. Vasari's historiographic narrative was organised around the chronological biographies of famous male artists, in accordance with the value-impregnated categories of 'influence' and 'innovation'. Here a close connection between life and work was forged – a model that proved to be formative for how the history of art was subsequently written. The relationships between masters and their apprentices amounted to a history of fathers and their sons, progressing toward a perfected state of art. At the pinnacle of this historical development, Vasari placed Michelangelo, so that Florence could be claimed as the cultural epicentre. With Vasari, many of the stereotypes are already present that still continue to structure discussions about, and support the idea of, the masculinity of the artist. For instance, the artist is conceived as a spirit transcending nature and operating out of the sphere of the pure idea, while the female gender is banished to the sphere of reproduction. This opposition serves to accentuate the masculine power to create, which no longer solely imitates but controls and transcends nature (Christadler, 2006). The close connection between the artist's personality and the character of the work paves the way for the cult of the genius of the 18th and 19th centuries. This mythical image of the artist remains current to this day and operates within art criticism and is often served by the artists themselves. The exceptional position of the artist and the high esteem of artistic practice goes hand in hand with 'the license for eccentric behavior' (Schade & Wenk, 1995, p. 346).

The prevailing image of the modern artist coheres around terms such as freedom, individualism, originality, progress – terms that go hand in hand with the concept of masculinity (Halbertsma, 1995). According to Lisa Tickner (1994), changes to the economic conditions for artistic practice, which began no later than the 19th century, ran parallel with changes in how the artist was regarded as a role model. The modern shift in the conditions of production for art meant the loss of traditional ways for the artist to be commissioned by, for instance, the parish, the public or individuals. With respect to this, there was now a necessity to prove oneself on the market. One of the characteristics of modern industrialised society is the fact that women have increasingly moved into positions of employment and also artistic professions; by the 1900s, academies were gradually opening to women. However, the fear of a feminisation and an effeminacy of art soon spread; the artists of the avant-garde responded with 'new kinds of harsh, procreative, and virile masculinities' (Tickner, 1994, p. 47). Dominant figures of the artist from the 19th century, such as the Dandy, were obsolete. Avant-garde art seemed to be often indelibly marked by anti-bourgeois sentiments and therefore advanced an especially virile, aggressive, but apparently authentic 'masculine' ideal, appropriating codes of proletarian masculinity as well as romanticising ethnic minorities. The figure of the 'primitive' – living in promiscuity, overbearing of women and violating the norms of middle-class decorum – was a potent source of inspiration. Even so, under the sway of the first-wave women's movement, Dadaists and Surrealists used their own (heterosexual) masculinity as an object for artistic reflexion in rather playful ways before WWII. This was especially the case within the circle surrounding Marcel Duchamp (Hopkins, 2008; Jones, 2002). It was not simply a dressing-up game with gendered attributes and masquerades (Zapperi, 2012); masculinity was, rather, thematised with respect to its physiological functions, its bodily secretions, obsessions, perversions and rituals. Such 'queer' strategies of negotiating masculinity and dissolving its boundaries can also be observed in art after WWII up to the present (e.g., pop art, Matthew Barney), while contending notions of virile men are repeatedly renewed, for instance in the drastic gestures of abstract expressionism or the 'new wild'.

(Self) portraits of men

In art history, the portrait is considered to display something of the subjectivity and the concrete psychosocial situation of the depicted individual. Commonly, self-portraits are understood as the processing of biographical experience as well as a form of expression for introspective self-understanding. Portraits are furthermore considered as a medium for 'self-fashioning' (Greenblatt, 1980/2005) – and increasingly so, since the so-called *performative turn* (Fischer-Lichte, 2008).

Traditionally, the individual portrait is considered an achievement of the Renaissance, often associated with the 'discovery of the individual'. Since Jacob Burckhardt's (1860/2004) influential book on Renaissance culture, the subject has been connected with ideas surrounding autonomy and sovereignty – a view that more recent critical historiography has relinquished – but nonetheless an 'increased visibility of the idea of an individual self' equally applies to the early modern age (Koos, 2006, p. 19). In the Renaissance, most male portraits showed a connection between the image of a masculine self and power, between sovereignty and strength. Portraits of rulers and statues of commanders sitting upright on their horses, self-confident and dutiful pictures of businessmen and intellectuals, all indicate this.

Today there are surprisingly few gendered and historically informed analyses of the specific means and visual codes through which masculinity is presented. One notable exception is Patricia Simons' (1997) discussion of how different representations of the masculine self were accentuated during the 15th and 16th centuries. Drawing on Eve Kosovsky Sedgwick's (1985) concept of homosociality, she argued that the male portraits are not simply the likenesses of individuals but contain references to relationships with other men. This could entail relationships between those depicted in the portrait and the image's addressee or between the artist and his client. Such relationships were forged through friendship or patronage or could even be of a pedagogical or erotic nature.

In her ground-breaking work on early modern art, Marianne Koos (2004, 2006) explores the special case of the lyrical portraits of men in Venetian painting from the early part of the 16th century. Koos traces out a variegated image of masculinities that were in conflict with the norms of upper-class masculinity. According to Koos, an alternative ideal of masculinity is developed in the portraits that was connected to both introspection and emotional attunement: the images show a sensitive, sensuous and luxuriously adorned masculinity, borrowing their imagery from representational conventions of feminine portraits. Such stylised subjectivity indicates a withdrawal from, and a critique of, those societal roles forced upon men.

The inherent plurality and contradictory nature of masculinity is also indicated in the way artists represented themselves. The topic of modern self-portraiture is thematised by Irit Rogoff (1989), who was one of the first to question how artistic self-understanding is produced through configurations of masculinity. Rogoff examines how artists legitimise the position they claim for themselves through pictorial references to the artistic tradition and the cultural authority attached to it. The forms of masculinity raised by such references are in no way consistent. Max Liebermann, for example, portrays himself intentionally unemotional, working at the easel or in his upper-middle-class living environment. Through this, the values of a patriarchal-bourgeois work ethic enter the scene. In contrast, Kirchner's expressive self-stylisation as an injured soldier is interpreted by Rogoff (1989) as 'an expression of the marginality of the Self' (p. 36), endowed with the pathos of a heroic outsider-masculinity cultivated by the avant-garde of the early 20th century. In Europe, the experiences of the world wars shook the bourgeois and military forms of 19th-century masculinity to its very core. In art, masculinity was articulated along a continuum between the poles of the damaged and the assertive self, with even infirmity becoming, in the self-portrayal of some artists, a sign of self-confidence. (McCallum, 2018; Söll, 2016). How strongly war challenges the image of man in art can be indexed internationally (Fitzpatrick, 2015). Rogoff (1989), however interprets Liebermann's self-staging as a strategic response to anti-Semitic hostility and as an argument for the right to social belonging.

The male nude figure

'The male nude figure is a forgotten matter' (Walters, 1978, p. 9). With this statement, Margaret Walters introduces her study that traces the transformed meanings and significance of the undressed male body in art from antiquity to the 20th century. Today the nude figure as art form (Clark, 1957) invokes associations with the spectacle of a more or less erotically staged undressed female figure. This development only started during the late 18th century in the context of the visual economy of the culture of the bourgeoisie and its rigid gender ideologies, which principally projected ideas of the sensual and the erotic onto the female body. In previous centuries, the gender of beauty was in fact male, particularly in genres of art considered 'classical'. During the 5th and 6th centuries BCE, the preferred nude figure in Greek art was male. During antiquity, three ideal types of the male nude figure developed: muscular, hypermasculine bodies, associated with the heroic strength of Heracles (Bischoff, 1998; Kimmich, 1997); athletic-masculine and yet adolescently graceful bodies, typified by Apollo; and finally, the fragile, pretty, but graceful body of the adolescent, embodied in the figure of Narcissus. Not until the 4th century BCE did the figure of the female nude appear, finding its classical expression in Praxiteles' sculpture of Venus. Yet the figure of the nude male (as well as the female nude) has been associated with sensuality since antiquity. It was invested with an abundance of political, religious and moral meanings and took also the position of the desired body – a fact often denied in traditional art history. For instance, the canonical realisation of a combination of aesthetic, ethical and epistemological ideals, the so-called Doryphoros ('Spear-Bearer') was subject to several Roman imitations of the original by Polykleitos (around 440 BCE). The classic contrapposto of this athlete is a visualisation of the right measure through the balancing of opposites; his inner sense of harmony as well as his tense calm expressed autonomy and self-control and thus the embodiment of male virtue. Similarly, Michelangelo's marble 'David' (1502), arguably the most famous sculpture in the history of art, is a prototypical representation of the young, heroic stylised male nude figure. This figure condenses grounded military discipline and bourgeois notions of virtue (Verspohl, 1981). This *virtus* of the Florentine citizen represents an ideal masculinity harmonising young grace and virility with the gravity and authoritarian severity of an antique colossus statue.

The confrontation with the neoclassical nude male figure, which emerged around the 1800s, has become particularly productive for art history research on masculinity (Crow, 1995; Fend, 2003; Solomon-Godeau, 1997a). French neoclassical art has to be seen as closely related to the social changes wrought by the French Revolution (Crow, 1995). The nude figure, which since the Renaissance had served as an 'embodiment of universal human values', 'once again acquired new meaning in the art of neoclassicism' (Fend, 2003, p. 9, author's translation). The artistic forms of masculinity, however, present themselves as clearly contradictory and multifaceted, but were partly linked to redefinitions of gender relations and a 'noisy scientification' of sex differences (Honegger, 1991, p. 2), which began during the time of the enlightenment and lasted until the middle of the 19th century, culminating in the production of a rigid, essentialising polarity between women and men.

A seminal text for art historical masculinity research is Abigail Solomon-Godeau's (1997a) *Male Trouble: A Crisis in Representation*. Focusing on the period between the French Revolution and the July Monarchy, Solomon-Godeau explores the homosocial character of the revolutionary culture and its artistic contexts of production. Contrasting models of masculinity can be observed in the official, representative art of the time: a heroic-masculine, active masculinity, on the one hand, and, on the other, a feminised and passively eroticised masculinity, often in the form of a naked sleeping or dying youth. These contending models were already formed in antiquity and constituted an inner binarism, which periodically characterises the artistically idealised images of masculinity, even if their social recognition by no means follows such symmetry (Solomon-Godeau, 1997b). For Solomon-Godeau, this strategy of transferring female characteristics to the male body so that concerns about gender difference can be avoided amounts to the 'internalisation and simultaneous colonisation of femininity' (1997b, p. 235).

However, the effeminate male nude figures of the late 18th century were almost completely supplanted by the female nude figure in the 19th century. There was thus a clear displacement of gender positions (Solomon-Godeau, 2004). In Modernist art, the naked male body no longer served public concerns, becoming more an expression of emotions as well as mental and physical limit states (Callen, 2018). At the beginning of the 20th century, artists such as Edward Munch, Eugène Jansson and J. A. G. Acke could garner much attention in Scandinavia with their pictures of nude masculinity (Körber, 2013). Fascism reactivated the classical, public male nude figure, turning the Greek athletes into terrifying violent fighters and warriors and putting them into the service of the ideal of the Aryan race (Barbanera, 2016; Frietsch, 2012).

The more recent presence of the male nude figure in the exhibition landscape indicates that interest in representations of the male naked body and masculinity has returned. This new attention is certainly due to the broadening thematisation of masculinity in art, which seeks to relate to sociologically oriented masculinity studies (Bühler, 2013; Natter, 2012).

Homosexuality and art

The thematisation of homosexual masculinity plays an important role in art historical research on masculinity, increasingly in dialogue with gay and queer studies. This applies as much to the question of the artists' sexuality and the (blurred) traces of their sexuality in the works themselves, as well as to the question of how masculinity can or must be represented in order to be appropriate objects of homosexual identification or desire (Härle, Popp & Runte, 1997). Solomon-Godeau (1997a) has partly been attacked as homophobic from gay theory, not least because she does not speak of homosexuality as an already established category of identity for the period around 1800, preferring instead the concept of homosociality (Sedgwick, 1985; see also Longstaff, this volume). The notion of homosociality is oriented more towards social interaction than identity. The problem, according to Solomon-Godeau's critics, is that this gesture is analogous to the suppression and denial to which both homosexuality and homosexual artists were subject at all times. The current discussion of homosexuality in the discipline of art history reveals an internal dispute: a conflict between, on the one hand, an interest in the identities of gay subjects, practices and representations and, on the other, accounts of homosexuality as an identity category as a 19th-century invention without denying the existence of homosexual practices in past eras. It was not until the 19th century that depictions of St. Sebastian became icons and the early Christian martyr became a gay 'patron saint' (Castro-Gómez, 1997; Eekhoud, 1909). A further motif from antiquity, invested with homosexual content and prominent in art from the early modern age (e.g., Michelangelo, Correggio and Rembrandt), was the abduction of the boy Ganymede by his godfather Jupiter in the form of an eagle (Saslow, 1986).

Research on homosexual masculinity in older art refers to both the lives and work of the 'master artists', who might be considered homosexual on the basis of biographical details and archival material. Such Renaissance and Baroque figures include Donatello, Leonardo da Vinci, Michelangelo, Benvenuto Cellini and Michelangelo da Caravaggio. An exemplary text in this regard was Sigmund Freud's (1910/1969) much-discussed study of Leonardo (see Herding, 2000). It is regarded as indisputable fact that many of these and also less prominent artists – for example, Giovanni Antonio Bazzi, known as Sodoma – came into conflict with anti-sodomy laws based on denunciations that were usually anonymous (Wittkower & Wittkower, 1963). Less malicious sources also include references to love for other men, without this corroborating any particular sexual orientation. It remains controversial whether Donatello's bronze 'David' (c. 1444), the Genius of Victory by Michelangelo (1505–1524) and the Amor Victorious by Caravaggio (1601) can all be regarded as evidence of a distinctive iconology of homosexuality in Italian culture during the early modern period, as Andreas Sternweiler (1993) sought to demonstrate in his pioneering work. Even if both the sensual qualities and the erotic appeal of these works of art may be part of a culture in which sexual contact among men was widespread, the methodological challenges remain rife, as they are linked to an anachronistic retrospective projection of modern identitarian concepts on pre-modern artistic material (Rubin, 2018).

The ideals of male beauty, defined during antiquity and then later revived in the Renaissance and passed on via the academic tradition, still dominate the body aesthetic circulating in homosexual worlds in the 20th century. The flawless and seemingly invulnerable strength of these ideal male bodies, also and especially in their nakedness, is understood by Reinhard Biederbeck and Bernd Kalusche (1987) as a response to the threat to homosexual life. In accepting this masculine ideal of beauty, the authors explore how a form of homosexual desire is often dissimulated, hiding behind the official images of masculinity, which are invested with the authority of tradition.

However, any notion of a specific gay aesthetic must be denied. This does not mean that sexual and aesthetic preferences, alongside visual codes of subcultural milieus, do not leave visible traces in art. Homosexuality in art becomes especially visible when homosexual desire uses art as a means for both self-inquiry and self-expression, as has been stated with greater regularity since the 1980s. In the second half of the 20th century, the LGBTQ movement has led to the removing of taboos about homosexuality.

Gazes and signs

The regulation and gender-specific hierarchisation of visual relationships, in particular the question of the male gaze and the way in which the female body functions in the picture as a sign of male sexuality and power, has become an important research topic in art-historical gender studies from the late 1970s and onwards (Broude & Garrard, 1992; Schade & Wenk, 1995; Söntgen, 1996b). Decisively, the theoretical and methodological springboard for this was film studies. In particular, Laura Mulvey's (1975) 'Visual Pleasure and Narrative Cinema' has been frequently adopted, though controversially, in the field of art history. With reference to psychoanalysis, Mulvey analyses the gaze between the genders in the illusionistic narratives of Hollywood cinema, according to which woman is the passive image and the spectacle while man is the active bearer of the look. Here cinema provides a double fulfilment: namely, the *scopophilic* desire to look at another person (normally the female star) as an erotic object, as well as the satisfaction of the ego libido through narcissistic identification with the omnipotent male protagonist (see McDonald, this volume). In transposing these thoughts from film to art, and thus to the still image, one has to contend with the absence of illusionistic narration (Söntgen, 1996b). Nonetheless, even the medium of film continuously operates by interrupting the narrative in favour of the fetishising close-up of the face or body of the female star.

Griselda Pollock (1988) has, with reference to Mulvey, deciphered the images of women by the pre-Raphaelite painter Dante Gabriel Rossetti, where not femininity but, rather, masculinity is negotiated as a sexual position. According to Pollock, Rossetti abstracts the naturalistic characteristics of the human face, such as plasticity and proportion, in favour of an accentuation of the eyes and especially the mouth as eroticised zones in an otherwise less defined area; he amplifies symbolic attributes with erotic connotations, along with ostentatious investment in attractive strong colours, thereby obscuring unrealistic representations. Male sexuality had to redefine itself in the Victorian era (see also Yeates & Trowbridge, 2014), and for Pollock (1988), love and loss, desire and death were split apart and projected onto the radical other, represented in visions of the female.

The genesis of the voyeuristic gaze as a specific gender-coded formation of seeing dates back to the early modern period (Schade & Wenk, 1995). The paradigmatic relationship between the gazing male artist and the female body as the object of the gaze is evident, for example, in Albrecht Dürer's famous woodcut of a draughtsman drawing a reclining woman (included in 'Instruction in Measurement with Compass and Ruler,' 1538). Daniela Hammer-Tugendhat (1997) has shown that in the early modern period, under the influence of Aristotelianism, a metaphysics of the sexes identifies masculinity with both form and intellect, whereas femininity is the formed body. Specifically, the absence of the male body (and thus the invisibility of male desire along with the concomitant sexualisation of femininity), expresses and stabilises the male-defined position. Thus Hammer-Tugendhat's thesis is that masculinity is not represented in the image but shows itself in the form of the relation of the gaze between a quasi-bodiless (because imageless) male and the embodied female.

Masculinity and racism

In 1975, dressed as a man in the 'typical' bodily habitus of a black male, the US-American, black female concept artist Adrian Piper took a walk along the street. During this experiment, Piper saw herself as liberated from the female role, and yet at the same time she was confronted with the racist anxieties of her surroundings (Spector, 1997). This performance, *Mythic Being: Getting Back no. 1*, is documented in a series of photographs, one of which bears the title: 'I embody everything you most hate and fear'. Kobena Mercer has spoken of equally violent and sexist fantasies that link to racist white representations of the black male body (Mercer, 1994). Further, bell hooks (1995) has discussed images of black men constituting racist/sexist iconography, where the use of a terrifying as well as a fascinating arsenal of hypermasculine stereotypes imagines the male black body to be animalistic, violent and frighteningly potent. In their attempts to produce positive and reassuring images of black masculinity, the imagery of the abolitionist movement remained the counter image to this iconography. For example, the central emblem of liberation from slavery and equal human dignity shows a black person on his knees, asking to be released from his chains; an image of helpless, castrated masculinity (Schmidt-Linsenhoff, 1997). The contradictory image of black masculinity in the arts, which has gone through several transformations since the Black Power movement, has been the theme of a big show in the Whitney Museum in 1994/95 (Golden, 1994).

In the field of gender and art history, the categories of race, class and gender are recognised as increasingly interdependent. Anne Lafont (2019), for example, provides a gender-informed revision of the visual culture and arts in the Age of Enlightenment in the context of colonial history, slavery and the resistance to colonial exploitation. In the context of ongoing processes of globalisation and the hybridisation of artistic means and forms of expression, art scholars are challenged to critically analyse as well as discuss the role of art and the entanglements of art history in exclusionary and racist practices (Paul, 2008). Images of non-white men, be it black or oriental men, are analogous to forms of exoticised femininity, a permanent part of the European world view. The form and implications of the visual construction of masculinity is seldom questioned, but such questions are crucial in view of current political developments.

Conclusion

Gender studies approaches to art history are based on the premise that gender difference is embedded in the whole area of artistic production and reception. If art and life are no longer understood as separate spheres, without the relationship between artistic representation and social reality ever appearing as pure and immediate, then this is especially politically explosive: images of masculinity and femininity are understood not only as expressions and images of gendered ideological constructions but also as both active and formative in conveying norms, inviting modes of identification, offering models as well as undermining stereotypes, revealing (im)possibilities, creating desire and inciting hate. Masculinity in art is subject to great variation. As a category of difference, with implications and effects, masculinity has been long embedded in the dominant image of artistic creativity and has silently provided the norms by which art has been judged.

Over the centuries, the male body was the standard of beauty and meaning. Historically changing and sometimes conflicting concepts of masculinity between authority and marginality have influenced the social position of artists and have determined the concrete forms images of men take. Thus far, studies on masculinity in art have for the most part focused on the early modern period, the 19th century, as well as Modernist and contemporary art. In contrast, the Middle Ages or the early 18th century have barely been examined in light of representations of masculinity. Numerous themes still lurk here, including the elements of a historically hegemonic masculinity manifested in art. Studies on masculinity have preferred to focus on its so-called crisis. Beyond the problematic implications of the concept of crisis and its inflationary use, this suggests that it is not only artists who are continuously trying to liberate masculinity from its corset.

References

Barbanera, M. (2016). *Il corpo fascista: Idea del virile fra arte, architettura e disciplina.* Perugia: Aguaplano.

Biederbeck, R., & Kalusche, B. (1987). *Motiv Mann: Der männliche Körper in der modernen Kunst.* Gießen: Anabas.

Bischoff, C. (1998). Die Schwäche des starken Geschlechts: Herkules und Omphale und die Liebe in bildlichen Darstellungen des 16. bis 18. Jahrhunderts. In M. Dinges (Ed.), *Hausväter, Priester, Kastraten: Zur Konstruktion von Männlichkeit in Spätmittelalter und Früher Neuzeit* (pp. 153–181). Göttingen: Vandenhoeck & Ruprecht.

Broude, N., & Garrard, M. D. (Eds.). (1992). *The expanding discourse: Feminism and art history.* New York: Icon Editions.

Bühler, K. (Ed.). (2013). *Das schwache Geschlecht: Neue Mannsbilder in der Kunst.* Bern: Kunstmuseum.

Burckhardt, J. (1860/2004). *Die Kultur der Renaissance in Italien: Ein Versuch.* Hamburg: Nicol.

Callen, A. (2018). *Looking at men: Art, anatomy and the modern male body.* New Haven, CT: Yale University Press.

Castro-Gómez, V. R. (1997). Eros und Gewalt: Die Figur Sebastians als Leitmotiv homoerotischer Ikonographie. In G. Härle, W. Popp & A. Runte (Eds.), *Ikonen des Begehrens* (pp. 177–189). Stuttgart: M. & P. Verlag für Wissenschaft und Forschung.

Christadler, M. (2006). Kreativität und Genie: Legenden der Kunstgeschichte. In A. Zimmermann (Ed.), *Kunstgeschichte und Gender: Eine Einführung* (pp. 253–272). Berlin: Reimer.

Clark, K. (1957). *The nude: A study in ideal form.* London: Murray.

Crow, T. E. (1995). *Emulation: Making artists for revolutionary France.* New Haven, CT: Yale University Press.

Eekhoud, G. (1909). Saint Sébastien dans la peinture. *Akademos: Revue Mensuelle D'Art Libre et de Critique, 1*(1), 171–175.

Fend, M. (2003). *Grenzen der Männlichkeit: Der Androgyn in der französischen Kunst und Kunsttheorie 1750–1830.* Berlin: Reimer.

Fischer-Lichte, E. (2008). *The transformative power of performance. A new aesthetics.* London & New York: Routledge.

Fitzpatrick, A. (2015). Veiled Iranian identities in the photographic art of Sadegh Tirafkan. In Ä. Söll & G. Schroder (Eds.), *Der Mann in der Krise? Visualisierungen von Männlichkeit im 20. und 21. Jahrhundert* (pp. 182–198). Köln: Böhlau.

Freud, S. (1910/1969). Eine Kindheitserinnerung des Leonardo da Vinci. In S. Freud (Ed.), *Studienausgabe, Vol. X* (pp. 87–159). Frankfurt: Fischer.

Frietsch, E. (2012). Nackte Männlichkeit als Repräsentation des Staates: Aktdarstellung in der Zeit des Nationalsozialismus. In T. G. Natter (Ed.), *Nackte Männer von 1800 bis heute* (pp. 98–105). München: Hirmer.

Golden, T. (Ed.). (1994). *Black male: Representations of masculinity in contemporary American art.* New York: Whitney Museum of American Art.

Greenblatt, S. (1980/2005). *Renaissance self-fashioning: From More to Shakespeare.* Chicago, IL: University of Chicago Press.

Halbertsma, M. (1995). Feministische Kunstgeschichte. In M. Halbertsma & K. Zijlmans (Eds.), *Gesichtspunkte: Kunstgeschichte heute* (pp. 173–195). Berlin: Reimer.

Hammer-Tugendhat, D. (1997). Zur Repräsentation des Liebesaktes in der Kunst der Frühen Neuzeit. In G. Völger (Ed.), *Sie und Er: Frauenmacht und Männerherrschaft im Kulturvergleich vol. 2* (pp. 192–198). Köln: Rautenstrauch-Joest-Museum.

Härle, G., Popp, W., & Runte, A. (Eds.). (1997). *Ikonen des Begehrens.* Stuttgart: M. & P. Verlag für Wissenschaft und Forschung.

Herding, K. (2000). Freud's *Leonardo*: A discussion of recent psychoanalytic theories. *American Imago, 57*(4), 339–368.

Hoffmann-Curtius, K., & Wenk, S. (Eds.). (1997). *Mythen von Autorschaft und Weiblichkeit im 20. Jahrhundert.* Marburg: Jonas.

Honegger, C. (1991). *Die Ordnung der Geschlechter: Die Wissenschaften vom Menschen und das Weib.* Frankfurt: Campus.

hooks, b. (1995). *Art on my mind: Visual politics.* New York: New Press.

Hopkins, D. (2008). *Dada's boys: Masculinity after Duchamp.* New Haven, CT: Yale University Press.

Jones, A. (2002). Equivocal masculinity: New York Dada in the context of World War I. *Art History, 25*(2), 162–205.

Kimmich, D. (1997). Herakles: Heldenposen und Narrenpossen: Stationen eines Männermythos? In W. Erhart & B. Herrmann (Eds.), *Wann ist der Mann ein Mann? Zur Geschichte der Männlichkeit* (pp. 173–191). Stuttgart & Weimar: Metzler.

Koos, M. (2004). Identität und Begehren: Bildnisse effeminierter Männlichkeit in der venezianischen Malerei des frühen 16. Jahrhunderts. In M. Fend & M. Koos (Eds.), *Männlichkeit im Blick: Visuelle Inszenierungen in der Kunst seit der Frühen Neuzeit* (pp. 53–77). Köln: Böhlau.

Koos, M. (2006). *Bildnisse des Begehrens: Das lyrische Männerporträt in der venezianischen Malerei des frühen 16. Jahrhunderts – Giorgione, Tizian und Umkreis*. Emsdetten & Berlin: Edition Imorde.

Körber, L. A. (2013). *Badende Männer: Der nackte männliche Körper in der skandinavischen Malerei und Fotografie des frühen 20. Jahrhunderts*. Berlin & Bielefeld: De Gruyter.

Lafont, A. (2019). *L'art et la race: L'africain (tout) contre l'oeil des Lumières*. Dijon: Les Presses du réel.

Lindner, I., Schade, S, Wenk, S., & Werner, G. (Eds.). (1989). *Blick-Wechsel: Konstruktionen von Männlichkeit und Weiblichkeit in Kunst und Kunstgeschichte*. Berlin: Reimer.

McCallum, C. (2018). *The fate of the new man: Representing and reconstructing masculinity in Soviet visual culture, 1945–1965*. DeKalb, IL: Northern Illinois University Press.

Mercer, K. (1994). Fear of a black penis. *Art Forum International, 32*(8), 80–81, 122.

Mulvey, L. (1975). Visual pleasure and narrative cinema. *Screen, 16*(3), 6–18.

Natter, T. G. (Ed.). (2012). *Nackte Männer von 1800 bis heute*. München: Hirmer.

Paul, B. (2008). Kunstgeschichte, Feminismus und Gender Studies. In H. Belting, H. Dilly, W. Kemp, W. Sauerländer & M. Warnke (Eds.), *Kunstgeschichte: Eine Einführung* (pp. 297–336). Berlin: Reimer.

Pollock, G. (1988). *Vision and difference: Femininity, feminism and the histories of art*. London: Routledge.

Rogoff, I. (1989). Er selbst: Konfigurationen von Männlichkeit und Autorität in der deutschen Moderne. In I. Lindner, S. Schade, S. Wenk & G. Werner (Eds.), *Blick-Wechsel: Konstruktionen von Männlichkeit und Weiblichkeit in Kunst und Kunstgeschichte* (pp. 21–40). Berlin: Reimer.

Rubin, P. L. (2018). *Perspectives on the male body and Renaissance art*. New Haven, CT: Yale University Press.

Salomon, N. (1993). Der kunsthistorische Kanon: Unterlassungssünden. *Kritische Berichte, 21*(4), 27–40.

Saslow, J. M. (1986). *Ganymede in the Renaissance: Homosexuality in art and society*. New Haven, CT: Yale University Press.

Schade, S., & Wenk, S. (1995). Inszenierungen des Sehens. Kunst, Geschichte und Geschlechterdifferenz. In H. Bußmann & R. Hof (Eds.), *Genus: Zur Geschlechterdifferenz in den Kulturwissenschaften* (pp. 340–407). Stuttgart: Kröner.

Schmidt-Linsenhoff, V. (1997). Sklaverei und Männlichkeit um 1800. In A. Friedrich, B. Haehnel, V. Schmidt-Linsenhoff & C. Treuther (Eds.), *Projektionen: Rassismus und Sexismus in der visuellen Kultur* (pp. 96–111). Marburg: Jonas.

Sedgwick, E. K. (1985). *Between men. English literature and homosocial desire*. New York: Columbia University Press.

Simons, P. (1997). Homosociality and erotics in Italian Renaissance portraiture. In J. Woodall (Ed.), *Portraiture: Facing the subject* (pp. 29–51). Manchester: Manchester University Press.

Söll, Ä. (2016). *Der neue Mann? Männerporträts von Otto Dix, Christian Schad und Anton Räderscheidt 1914–1930*. Paderborn: Fink.

Solomon-Godeau, A. (1997a). *Male trouble: A crisis in representation*. London: Thames and Hudson.

Solomon-Godeau, A. (1997b). Irritierte Männlichkeit: Repräsentation in der Krise. In C. Kravagna (Ed.), *Privileg Blick: Kritik der visuellen Kultur* (pp. 223–239). Berlin: id-Verlag.

Solomon-Godeau, A. (2004). Ist Endymion schwul? Spannungsgeladene Fragen zwischen Feminismus, Gay und Queer Studies. In M. Fend & M. Koos (Eds.), *Männlichkeit im Blick: Visuelle Inszenierungen in der Kunst seit der Frühen Neuzeit* (pp. 15–34). Köln: Böhlau.

Söntgen, B. (Ed.). (1996a). *Rahmenwechsel: Kunstgeschichte als feministische Kulturwissenschaft*. Berlin: Akademie Verlag.

Söntgen, B. (1996b). Den Rahmen wechseln: Von der Kunstgeschichte zur feministischen Kulturwissenschaft. In B. Söntgen (Ed.), *Rahmenwechsel: Kunstgeschichte als feministische Kulturwissenschaft* (pp. 7–23). Berlin: Akademie Verlag.

Spector, N. (1997). Performing the body in the 1970s. In J. Blessing (Ed.), *Rrose is a rrose is a rrose: Gender performance in photography* (pp. 156–175). New York: Guggenheim Museum.

Sternweiler, A. (1993). *Die Lust der Götter. Homosexualität in der italienischen Kunst: Von Donatello zu Caravaggio*. Berlin: Verlag Rosa Winkel.

Tickner, L. (1994). Men's work? Masculinity and modernism. In N. Bryson, M. Holley & K. Moxey (Eds.), *Visual culture: Images and interpretations* (pp. 42–82). Middletown, CT: Wesleyan University Press.

Verspohl, J. (1981). Michelangelo und Macchiavelli: Der David auf der Piazza della Signoria in Florenz. *Städel-Jahrbuch, 8*, 204–246.

Walters, M. (1978). *The nude male: A new perspective*. Harmondsworth: Penguin.

Wittkower, M., & Wittkower, R. (1963). *Born under Saturn: The character and conduct of artists: A documented history from antiquity to the French revolution*. New York: Random House.

Yeates, A., & Trowbridge, S. (Eds.). (2014). *Pre-Raphaelite masculinities: Constructions of masculinities in art and literature*. Farnham: Ashgate.

Zapperi, G. (2012). *L'artiste est une femme: La modernité de Marcel Duchamp: Stratégies artistiques et masculinité*. Paris: Presses Université de France.

Zimmermann, A. (Ed.). (2006). *Kunstgeschichte und Gender: Eine Einführung*. Berlin: Reimer.

Part 6

Problems, challenges and ways forward

43

Masculinities, law and crime

Socio-legal studies and the 'man question'

Richard Collier

Introduction

This chapter presents a brief overview of the history and development of masculinity theorising and research on men and masculinities within the context of the related disciplines of law and criminology. In each field, it considers how masculinity has been conceptualised and approached, identifying key themes and concerns and drawing on examples from masculinities scholarship in law/legal studies and crime. The chapter pays particular attention to the *way* masculinity has been studied in these disciplines, identifying differences between jurisdictions (for example, common law and civil law) and emerging ideas that, within an international frame such as this collection, cast new light on the interconnections between men, gender, law and crime. Considering men *as men*, as gendered subjects and not 'taken for granted' genderless figures, the chapter suggests that recent work seeking to ask the law's 'man question' has much to offer the study of men and masculinities; at the same time, legal scholarship itself has much to gain from a closer engagement with the study of masculinities, leading to new ways of thinking about men, power and dominance within a global frame.

The first and second sections trace the development of the study of masculinities in the disciplines of law and criminology respectively, considering key differences, shared concerns and providing examples of studies in the field. Section three unpacks the conceptualisation of masculinity in this work looking especially at recent developments that have sought to ask new questions about the relationship between men, law and crime. Concluding remarks consider the politics, potential and limitations of studying masculinity within the contexts of law and crime, reviewing the literature within the context of a reconfiguration of gender relations in a global context that, it is argued, sheds light on the interconnections between masculinities, power, law and crime.

Legal studies, masculinities and the 'man' of law

The interrogation of the relationship between law and gender constitutes a distinctive and well-established sub-field of legal studies internationally; a body of work that has, albeit often implicitly, sought to address an array of questions about men and masculinities. Within scholarship on women, gender equality and the world's legal professions, for example, we find a recurring concern with how questions about men and gender intersect with aspects of women's legal careers and, more specifically, how associations between the law, men and masculinities and related ideas about the gendered (masculine) nature of many legal workplace cultures, organizational practices and values and so forth have historically shaped the socially structured world of the law – in ways, importantly, that have had deleterious consequences for women that they do not have for men. These gendered cultures, contemporary research suggests, remain entrenched across many professional fields associated with law; a form of masculine domination profoundly difficult to dislodge, evidenced by continued male labour market dominance at senior levels across the world's legal professions and the persistence of (in some accounts growing) gendered divisions in the law (see, e.g., Schultz & Shaw, 2008; Sommerlad, 2016).

At a disciplinary level, I have argued in more detail elsewhere that law was – compared to other fields such as social sciences, arts and humanities – something of a latecomer to the study of men and masculinities (Collier 2015b, 2010). Within the academic study of law, however, on closer examination, a set of ideas *about* masculinity have in fact long been a central feature of the feminist legal scholarship that developed during the 1970s and 1980s. Law libraries and the legal and criminological canons alike have historically been, in Carol Smart's (1976) evocative words, full of books *by* men, *on* men and written *for* men. The vast international literature on university legal education; numerous legal biographies of the 'great figures' of the law across jurisdictions; the images of the famous judges that still decorate the walls of many university law schools and the institutions of law globally; work on what it means to be inculcated into the law's cultural practices and values; each, historically at least, have been very much about *men's* lives and men's careers. Recent studies of women legal academics and women's legal biographies (cf., for example, Cownie, 2015; Mossman, 2006; Wells, 2001), alongside an array of international feminist judgements projects (e.g., Hunter, McGlynn & Rackley, 2010), archival historical work on women in law (First Hundred Years, 2015) and inspirational women of the law events serve, in part, as a corrective to this history of the lives of men. It is work that also challenges assumptions about the connections between masculinity and law with which this history has been associated.

It was a taken for granted 'way of thinking' about law, therefore, that feminist legal scholarship over the past thirty years or so has, across countries and in different ways, sought to challenge by positioning men as, precisely, contingent, social and politically accountable gendered subjects. This is the backdrop against which, by the late 1980s and early 1990s, the study of masculinities emerged as a distinctive topic within legal studies internationally (see, for examples of this earlier work, Collier 1995, 1991; Thornton, 1989). These engagements with masculinity, drawing on developments in feminist legal theory and the growing critical study of men and masculinity literature, the latter influenced notably by the work of Raewyn Connell, tended to deploy various ideas about men and gender; for example, the masculinism and homosociality of law's institutions; the contingent nature of the 'man of law' (Naffine, 1990); the complex interconnections between masculinities and the 'making of men' as legal professional subjects (e.g., Collier, 1998a); the correlation between masculinity and the idea of a 'bleached out', embodied and benchmark legal worker; how assumptions about legal professional*ism* connect, on closer examination, to culturally normative ideas about men and masculinity (see, e.g., Collier, 2015a; Sommerlad & Sanderson, 1998; Thornton, 2016). Masculinity was here deployed in such a way as to capture aspects of the dominant cultures, practices and values of the legal discipline, a set of ideas about men and masculinity enmeshed with understandings of the way, say, professional legal identities become mediated, formed and transformed within particular workplace contexts – what it meant, that is, to both 'do law' and 'do masculinity' (Smart, 1989).

Meanwhile, a rather different strand of scholarship sought to deploy the concept of masculinity in exploration of the gendered nature of legal methods and reasoning; to unpack, that is, the (gendered) nature of 'malestream' jurisprudential traditions, ways of *thinking about* the law and gender (see generally Conaghan, 2013). This was a marked feature of feminist legal scholarship during the 1980s and 1990s concerned with the way legal concepts, methods and foundational assumptions were each inflected by assumptions about men's lives and the normative nature of masculinity. Later feminist-inflected work influenced by postmodernism, in contrast, sought to explore the discursive construction of this 'man', 'men' and 'masculinities' of law set within situated social and legal contexts. This approach mirrored wider themes within the sociological study of masculinity at the time regarding the need to better recognise, and draw out more precisely than earlier work had done, the idea of complexity, fragmentation and differentiation within the lives of men; and, related to this, the need to challenge not just the 'woman of law' (Smart, 1989) but also the very idea of a unitary masculine subject in seeking to ask the law's 'man question' (Dowd, 2010). An engagement with masculinity, in short, far from being marginal in legal studies, can itself be read as a marked feature of scholarship on gender within this disciplinary field. What therefore of criminology?

Masculinities, crime and criminology

Feminist criminological work has challenged a positivist model of crime and emphasis on individual pathology – a model that has dominated, and in many respects still dominates, the discipline of criminology and allied subjects. In so doing it has brought into the criminological gaze new ways of thinking about masculinity, power and dominance. Over the past three decades this exploration of the relationship between men, masculinities and crime has itself assumed an increased prominence within criminology, exemplified by the sheer number of articles, reports, conferences, seminars and books on the topic of masculinities and crime. Indeed, as in the case of law, by the early to 1990s, masculinities had also emerged as a distinctive sub-field within the discipline of criminology internationally (see, e.g., Collier, 1998b; Jefferson, 1997; Messerschmidt, 1993; Newburn & Stanko, 1994); and, today, an engagement with masculinities is a well-established feature of the criminological terrain; a marked presence within criminological monographs (e.g., Ellis, 2016), journals and textbooks alike. Masculinity is a feature of several disciplinary overviews of criminology and encyclopaedias and handbooks (see, e.g., Carlen & Jefferson, 1996; Lander & Ravn, 2014; Maguire, Morgan & Reiner, 1997; Tierney, 2010; Tomsen, 2008; Winlow, 2001).

The starting point for this engagement can be tracked to what was seen as a paradox at the heart of the discipline. For earlier feminist scholars (e.g., Smart, 1976) the historical problem for criminology was not so much that it had failed to recognise that the object of study had been, largely, the relationship between men and crime. Rather, the target of the feminist critique concerned *the way in which* this sex-specificity of crime was conceptualised, flawed in (at least) two senses. First, criminology had failed to account in anything like an adequate manner for the nature of women's offending; to understand, for example, women as victims/survivors of crime, the treatment of women within criminal justice systems and the scale of men's violence to women and girls. Second, criminology had failed more generally to address the gender of crime at a theoretical level; that is, to tackle the masculinity or maleness of crime itself, to divert the analytic gaze from questions of female conformity *to* male criminality and how this reframing of the relationship between gender of crime raised questions about masculinity (Heidensohn, 1996). This aligns to arguments made within the critical study of men and masculinities literature regarding the need to consider the actions of men as gendered beings across diverse fields of social life (see, e.g., Connell, 1987, 2005). Criminological theories thus had historically held out to be general explanations of crime; they were, in fact, about men/male crime, with women all too often seen in negative/gendered terms (Smart, 1976, 1990).

A now rich and vast body of feminist criminological scholarship internationally has, of course, sought to redress this balance and better understand the crimes of women (see, e.g., Gelsthorpe & Hedderman, 2018; Mallicoat, 2018; Mukherjee & Scutt, 2015). Explicitly addressing the interconnections between men, masculinity and crime, however, took a rather different trajectory. Heralded initially as a 'new direction' or 'new frontier' for criminology to discover (Maguire et al., 1997), something without which, it was argued, there would be no progress for the discipline (Walklate, 1995), the question was asked: if criminology could not explain the gender-ratio of crime (why do men commit so much more crime than women?), or its own 'generalizability problem' (Daly & Chesney-Lind, 1988), what was the social and political significance of such a 'gender blindness'? (Gelsthorpe & Morris, 1988). What, in short, did a historical failure to engage with the gender of men tell us about the relative success(es) or failure(s) of criminology itself in seeking to account for and/or control crime more generally?

Over the years this debate about masculinities and crime has become emblematic of far wider concerns and anxieties around social, economic, cultural and political change; debates in which questions long familiar to criminology – around, say, the intersections of class, poverty, race, ethnicity and/or disadvantage in relation to crime – have frequently coalesced in a concern with some specific issues about 'the problem of men' and masculinity, not least via the recurring trope of 'masculinity in crisis'. I argue elsewhere that, notwithstanding the heterogeneity of the concerns addressed and diversity of methodological approaches and epistemological assumptions contained within the work, certain sociological and social-psychological approaches have been particularly significant in shaping this field of study, especially within Anglo-American criminology, from the 1990s to the present day (Collier, 2003). Of particular influence is what has been termed the 'accomplishing masculinities' approach, associated most closely perhaps with James Messerschmidt (1993); and, in a rather different engagement with masculinity and crime, the psycho-social perspective advanced by the British criminologist Tony Jefferson (e.g., 1997, 1998, 2002), either writing alone or with others (Gadd, 2000; Gadd & Jefferson, 2007); what John Hood-Williams usefully described as a turn from 'structures to psyches' in criminological thinking about men (Hood-Williams, 2001). Intriguingly, and with regard to subsequent developments in criminology, Lander and Ravn (2014) suggest that research on gendered norms and the construction and enactment of masculinities within criminology has itself not kept up with developments in gender research, and issue I return to below (see also Messerschmidt, 2018).

The former 'accomplishing masculinities' approach draws on the concept of hegemonic masculinity, the critique of which having itself become the focus of a distinctive sub-field of scholarship within masculinities literature (Connell & Messerschmidt, 2005). What is brought into the criminological frame is an attempt to integrate more precisely the complexities of race, class, gender and sexuality in understanding the power of men and the gender of men's crimes; to take, that is, structural patterns of inequality seriously. From the outset, however, problems were identified: the argument, for example, that this 'structured action' perspective failed to account for or theorise the subjectivity of individual men; why, that is, some men 'turn to' crime and others do not, given that most crime is committed by highly specific sub-groups of the category 'men' (see, e.g., Collier, 1998b; Hood-Williams, 2001; Jefferson, 1997). For others, the very idea of hegemonic masculinity, and much of the critical sociology of masculinity literature, rested on a set of problematic, class-based assumptions about men, crime and power (Hall, 2002; see further below). The existence of a supposedly dominant masculine cultural form appeared to frame an account of (biological) men's endeavours to become (real) 'men'; to accomplish their masculinity. Yet not only could such an argument be read as tautological (Walklate, 1995); it was also, some argued, inflected by a kind of universalism and form of theorising that was, in criminology by the end of the 1980s, associated with a discipline that was somehow enmeshed with a set of masculinist values and assumptions and a distinctly problematic relationship to feminism (Smart, 1990).

In contrast to this approach, therefore, writers adopting what became known as a psychosocial approach to masculinities and crime argued that what was needed was a closer engagement with the interrelationship between the individual and the social (Gadd & Jefferson, 2007); more specifically, the social-structural and psychic processes which inform men's experience of masculinity (see, e.g., Jefferson, 1994, 1997). What was missing was the complexity of male subjectivity, the contradictions and difficulties that men can experience in 'becoming masculine' (whatever that may involve). This work questioned the idea of an (always, already) empowered masculine subject (Jefferson, 1997), and the focus of analysis shifted to the way in which a non-unitary and inherently contradictory subject came to invest – whether consciously and unconsciously – in empowering social discourses (Jefferson, 1997, 1998; Gadd, 2000).

Once again, however, problems were identified, not least a tendency to assume that masculinity itself had an irreducible core with regard to which particular psychological/psychoanalytic processes resulted in distinctive (masculine/feminine) gendered identities (see Hood-Williams, 2001). For Hall (2002), meanwhile, these kinds of engagements with masculinity side-stepped analysis of the interconnections between masculinity, crime and questions of political economy and class power; how, for example, the crimes of young, economically marginalised males must be located in the context of capitalism's global socioeconomic processes. Further, it was argued, this approach was as equally androcentric as the social structure theories it claimed to supersede, presenting in effect a kind of positivistic notion of criminological progression, yet another 'grand theory' of the crimes of men. What was absent was precisely the structural and political dimensions of gendered desires, projections, aspirations, fears and so forth, as well as, politically, how they might then be addressed and challenged in any meaningful way. And, perhaps most tellingly, this work was charged with reflecting a deeply problematic relationship to feminism. For Adrian Howe, for example, in her book *Sex Violence and Crime: Foucault and the Man Question*, this strand of work was inflected with 'an extraordinary anti-feminist animus' in its rejection of feminist work as 'simplistic, theoretically naïve and not as "advanced" as it should be' (Howe, 2009, p. 139).

What was lost here, it was argued, in the evocation of a general problem of 'masculinity', was the very questions of power and accountability that had been central to earlier feminist work on law and crime. Far from engaging with issues of power, violence and structure, criminology had framed these questions about men, gender and crime via various readings of 'weak and inadequate men', in so doing ascribing attributes to feminism and viewpoints that have 'rarely been voiced since the 1970s' (Howe, 2009, p. 141). As in the field of law, meanwhile, critics noted how the resulting call for dominant ideas of masculinity to be challenged, transcended, changed and so forth co-existed with a tendency for masculinity itself to 'float free' from questions of what men actually *do*; a cultural debate about men 'wrestling with the meaning of masculinity' running alongside an effacing of arguments derived from feminist scholarship about men's social power relative to women and men's individual and collective interest in maintaining present gender relations. 'Changing men', as Connell (1987, 2005) had long argued, could not be reduced to individual or collective projects of self-actualisation.

Making the connections: recent developments, questions and concerns

In recent years, legal scholarship has, internationally, to an arguably greater degree than criminology, seen something of a resurgence of interest in masculinity theorising. This is evidenced by the number of books, articles, special issues of journals, conferences and other events on the topic (see, e.g., Collier, 2010; Dowd, 2010; Fineman & Thomson, 2014; Harvard Journal of Law and Gender, 2010; Nevada Law Journal, 2013). This work is raising new questions about masculinity and law, marked by a heightened focus on questions of intersectionality and the attempt to engage with what has been termed the multidimensional nature of masculinit*ies*. This is a notable feature of recent legal masculinities scholarship in the United States, where the development of a 'multidimensional masculinity theory' has sought to bring together themes within feminist legal work, perspectives derived from the men and masculinities literature and critical race theory (Rudy Cooper & McGinley, 2012). Other work in law, meanwhile, reflects the growing interest in transnational dimensions of contemporary masculinity (Connell & Messerschmidt, 2005; Connell & Wood, 2005) and the idea of transnational men more generally (Hearn, 2015; Hearn, Bragojević & Harrison, 2012), interrogating the implications of this transnational frame for understandings of diverse aspects of legal practice and legal professionalism (e.g., Collier, 2013, 2015a). Shifts within masculinity in the legal sphere are here linked to broader social, political and economic transformations associated, in particular, with neoliberalism.

Underscoring these developments, meanwhile, the well-documented diversification and expansion of the legal profession's 'supply side' internationally over recent decades, rise of formal commitments to gender equity across legal institutions and cultural shifts associated with the entry of traditionally non-normative lawyers to the world's legal professions have each served to challenge earlier understandings of the 'naturalness' of law's masculinity and gendered forms of legal professionalism. Yet at the same time, research suggests that traditional gender cultures in law persist and formal commitments to gender equity can themselves co-exist with entrenched gender divisions, not least regarding who constitutes an 'ideal' legal worker (Sommerlad, 2007). Links between masculinity and legal professionalism, far from being archaic relics of a bygone age, continue to shape the processes of social closure in the law and the gendering of commitment in this field (Sommerlad, 2016; Thornton, 2016); and questions of gender and race, ethnicity and social class still mediate in far-reaching ways dominant understandings of such professionalism and progression in legal careers.

In looking to theoretical connections between law and criminology, meanwhile, I argue elsewhere that there is no one approach to or conceptualization of masculinity to be found

(Collier, 2015a, 2015b). Rather, masculinity has been used to encompass some diverse attributes such as, for example, the psychological characteristics of men within crimino-legal arenas; various ideas about the gendered (that is, masculine) nature of experiences and identities in relation to legal institutions; notions of masculine organisational cultures (say, in the legal professions, policing and so forth); and, particularly in criminology, a range of psychoanalytic inflected and structural-power-based readings of men's gendered practices, alongside analyses of men's gendered behaviour within specific organisational settings linking to law and crime. There is, in short, no one model of masculinity underscoring this literature; rather, we find an array of engagements with the interconnections between law, crime and gender in relation to learning processes, cultural notions of manhood, ideas about masculine identities, power and control frameworks and so forth.

In relation to law and crime it is also possible to detect the influence of another strand of scholarship on men and gender over the past decade, that has sought to critique and complicate the concept of masculinity/masculinities itself. In both disciplines, as noted above, the dominant frame of analysis has been one in which what is constituted discursively as a political 'problem' tends, all too often, to be a set of often contradictory, contingent ideas around masculinity. Yet this is a debate routinely framed in such a way that the focus of analysis then becomes a set of questions about, and an analytic engagement with, the abstract concept of *masculinities* rather than *men* (Hearn, 2004, 2014). That is, in seeking to 'name men as men' in relation to a discussion of, say, gender and legal careers, the social category of 'men' is actually more hegemonic than any model of masculinities, whether they are deemed to be hegemonic or not. For writers such as Jeff Hearn (2014), therefore, the problem is not necessarily 'masculinity' per se. It is *men* and the very questions of gender and power, accountability and attribution raised within feminist scholarship; questions that can be easily sidestepped if the analytic and political problem is identified as an abstract, ill-defined gender concept and not those individuals empowered in distinctive ways by contemporary social and legal arrangements and power relations.

Related to this point, and of particular significance in a comparative context such as this collection of essays, it is important to question whether there has been a distinct Western-centric focus to much scholarship on masculinities and law to date (Collier, 2015a). Legal masculinities work, for example, has been shaped to a significant degree, if not exclusively, by scholars writing from within common law traditions (notably North America, Australia and the UK). At a methodological level, this work has approached legal systems, the role of the state and so on via an exploration of the ideas about masculinity found within a set of legal texts and, especially, a body of (judge-made) case law (Collier, 2015b). This deconstructive unpacking or revealing of (say) hegemonic masculinity in law, however, does not necessarily play out in the same way across other jurisdictions and civil law legal systems, with different traditions, legal professions, cultures and histories. At the same time, it is important to remember that the organisational structures of legal education and scholarship have evolved across countries in ways that reflect varying degrees of sympathy, or otherwise, with the kinds of critical, contextual, socio-legal analysis that shapes masculinities work. In some contexts, indeed, it may appear unusual, if not transgressive, simply to speak *of* a relationship between law and masculinity in the context of legal studies.

Meanwhile, as Connell (2007) asks, what happens if we were to look beyond the 'Anglosphere'? In the case of law, what new questions about masculinities, states and legal systems, legal methods and sources might arise? (Collier, 2015b; see also Büchler, Cottier & Holz, 2012). It is necessary to recognise, that is, how different inflections within and between jurisdictions around legal cultures, relationships between law and state, the structuring of the legal profession, role of the judiciary and so forth shape these engagements with masculinity. This draws attention to the need for cultural specificity in discussing law and masculinity; at the very least, a need to be more *precise* about what is meant by masculinity as it is deployed across these legal contexts.

Concluding remarks

Law and criminology illustrate how specific disciplines, in different ways and at different moments, have sought to divert their analytic gaze towards men and masculinities and ask the 'man question' (Dowd, 2010). In each, informed by themes within both feminist scholarship and the critical study of men and masculinities, recent work has sought to posit a more complex and nuanced conception of power and engage with a reconfiguration of gender relations, including dominant forms of masculinity, within a global context. This takes on particular importance in the context of a masculinist political revival across different parts of the world aligned to the rise of openly sexist and male chauvinistic political agendas (Kimmel, 2013; Mellström, 2016). In looking to the study of law and masculinity in this international frame, it is important, I have suggested, that critical analysis of men's practices address both these transnational political-economic shifts in gender relations and regional-local legal cultures and practices set within specific national-legal contexts; cognisant throughout of how questions of individual biography/background, the intersectional, multidimensional nature of masculinities mediate experiences of, say, legal workplaces and interactions therein. Contemporary economic, political and cultural imperatives are redrawing a global gender order in ways that have reframed but still privilege notions of masculinity. Indeed, the resurgent masculinist rhetoric of the Alt-Right, growing social divisions and endurance of white, hetero-patriarchy across diverse cultural and political contexts suggests, if anything, a renewal of patriarchy. Masculinity studies, including in the contexts of law and crime, as above, have a vital contribution to make at a time of such backlash to progressive gender politics.

Far from depicting the law in terms of a narrative of feminisation, it may be more accurate, therefore, to trace a realignment of gender relations involving new formations of masculinity, if not a 'remasculinisation' of law itself; a reshaping of ideas of legal professional*ism*, noting how such an appeal to 'professionalism', and the institutional, disciplinary framework of law, has historically been a gendered project enmeshed with assumptions about masculinity (Hearn, Biese, Choroszewicz & Husu, 2016). With regard to the contemporary legal profession, Thornton and Bagust (2007) argue that women's acceptance as equals within the jurisprudential community continues to come against one seemingly intractable problem; the limited success there has been in 'encouraging men to focus less on their careers in order to take greater responsibility for caring for children and elderly relatives'; and how the 'centrality of the normative worker as both full-time and male still seems to be almost impossible to dislodge' (Thornton & Bagust, 2007, p. 805). This is the context in which recent debates about inclusivity and diversity among lawyers and legal professionals play out, one in which the intersections of gender and ethnicity, race, social class, sexual orientation, dis/ability, language and others retain an all too forceful relevance.

References

Büchler, A., Cottier, M., & Holz, S. (Eds.). (2012). *Legal gender studies = Rechtliche Geschlechterstudien: Konzepte, Entwicklungen und Perspektiven – eine kommentierte Quellensammlung*. Basel: Helbing & Lichtenhahn.

Carlen, P., & Jefferson, J. (1996). Masculinities and crime [Special issue]. *British Journal of Criminology, 33*(6), entire issue.
Collier, R. (1991). Masculinism, law and law teaching. *International Journal of the Sociology of Law, 19*(4), 427–451.
Collier, R. (1995). *Masculinity, law and the family*. London: Routledge.
Collier, R. (1998a). Nutty professors, men in suits and new entrepreneurs: Corporeality, subjectivity and change in the law school and legal practice. *Social and Legal Studies*, 7(1), 27–53.
Collier, R. (1998b). *Masculinities, crime and criminology*. London: Sage.
Collier, R. (2003). Men, masculinities and crime. In C. Sumner (Ed.), *The Blackwell international companion to criminology* (pp. 285–308). Oxford: Blackwell.
Collier, R. (2010). *Men, law and gender: Essays on the 'man' of law*. London: Routledge.
Collier, R. (2013). Rethinking men and masculinities in the contemporary legal profession: The example of fatherhood, transnational business masculinities and work-life balance in large law firms. *Nevada Law Journal, 13*(2), 101–130.
Collier, R. (2015a). Naming men as men in corporate legal practice: Gender and the idea of 'virtually 24/7 commitment' in law. *Fordham Law Review, 83*(5), 2387–2406.
Collier, R. (2015b). Sources, methods and the man question. *Legal Information Management, 15*(1), 19–24.
Conaghan, J. (2013). *Law and gender*. Oxford: Oxford University Press.
Connell, R. W. (1987). *Gender and power*. Cambridge: Polity.
Connell, R. W. (2005). *Masculinities* (2nd ed.). Cambridge: Polity.
Connell, R. W. (2007). *Southern theory*. Cambridge: Polity.
Connell, R. W., & Messerschmidt, J. (2005). Hegemonic masculinity: Rethinking the concept. *Gender and Society, 19*(6), 829–859.
Connell, R. W., & Wood, J. (2005). Globalization and business masculinities. *Men and Masculinities*, 7(4), 347–364.
Cownie, F. (2015). The United Kingdom's first woman law professor: An Archerian analysis. *Journal of Law and Society, 42*(1), 127–149.
Daly, K., & Chesney-Lind, M. (1988). Feminism and criminology. *Justice Quarterly, 5*(4), 498–538.
Dowd, N. (2010). *The man question: Male subordination and privilege*. New York: New York University Press.
Ellis, A. (2016). *Men, masculinities and violence: An ethnographic study*. Abingdon: Routledge.
Fineman, M., & Thomson, M.. (Eds.). (2014). *Exploring masculinities: Feminist theory reflections*. Farnham: Ashgate.
First Hundred Years Project. (2015). Retrieved from https://first100years.org.uk.
Gadd, D. (2000). Masculinities, violence and defended psycho-social subjects. *Theoretical Criminology, 4*(4), 429–449.
Gadd, D., & Jefferson, T. (2007). *Psychosocial criminology: An introduction*. London: Sage.
Gelsthorpe, L., & Hedderman, C. (2018). *Women, crime and criminal justice*. Bristol: Policy Press.
Gelsthorpe, L., & Morris, A. (1988). Feminism and criminology in Britain. *British Journal of Criminology, 28*(2), 93–110.
Hall, S. (2002). Daubing the drudges of fury: Men, violence and the piety of the 'hegemonic masculinity thesis'. *Theoretical Criminology, 6*(1), 35–61.
Harvard Journal of Law and Gender. (2010). Law and masculinities [Special issue], *33*(2), entire issue.
Hearn, J. (2004). From hegemonic masculinity to the hegemony of men. *Feminist Theory, 5*(1), 49–72.
Hearn, J. (2014). Men, masculinities and the material(-)discursive. *NORMA: International Journal for Masculinity Studies, 9*(1), 5–17.
Hearn, J. (2015). *Men of the world: Genders, globalizations, transnational times*. London: Sage.
Hearn, J., Biese, I., Choroszewicz, M., & Husu, L. (2016). Gender, diversity and intersectionality in professions and potential professions. In M. Dent, I. Lynn Bourgeault, J. L. Denis & E. Kuhlmann (Eds.), *The Routledge companion to the professions and professionalism* (pp. 75–88). London: Routledge.
Hearn, J., Bragojević, M., & Harrison, K. (Eds.). (2012). *Rethinking transnational men*. London: Routledge.
Heidensohn, F. (1996). *Women and crime*. Basingstoke: Macmillan.
Hood-Williams, J. (2001). Gender, masculinities and crime: From structure to psyches. *Theoretical Criminology, 5*(1), 37–60.
Howe, A. (2009). *Sex, violence and crime: Foucault and the 'man' question*. Abingdon: Routledge-Cavendish.
Hunter, R., McGlynn, C., & Rackley, E. (Eds.). (2010). *Feminist judgements: From theory to practice*. Oxford: Hart.

Jefferson, T. (1994). Theorizing masculine subjectivity. In T. Newburn & E. E. Stanko (Eds.), *Just boys doing business? Men, masculinities and crime* (pp. 10–31). London: Routledge.

Jefferson, T. (1997). Masculinities and crime. In M. Maguire, R. Morgan & R. Reiner (Eds.), *The Oxford handbook of criminology* (2nd ed., pp. 535–557). Oxford: Clarendon Press.

Jefferson, T. (1998). Muscle, 'hard men' and 'iron' Mike Tyson: Reflections on desire, anxiety and the embodiment of masculinity. *Body & Society, 4*(1), 77–98.

Jefferson, T. (2002). Subordinating hegemonic masculinity. *Theoretical Criminology, 5*(1), 63–88.

Kimmel, M. S. (2013). *Angry white men: American masculinity at the end of an era.* New York: Nation Books.

Lander, I., & Ravn, S. (2014). *Masculinities in the criminological field: Control vulnerability and risk taking.* London: Routledge.

Maguire, M., Morgan, R., & Reiner, R. (Eds.). (1997). *The Oxford handbook of criminology.* (2nd ed.). Oxford: Clarendon Press.

Mallicoat, S. L. (2018). *Women, gender, and crime: Core concepts.* London: Sage.

Mellström, U. (2016). In the time of masculinist political revival. *NORMA: International Journal for Masculinity Studies, 11*(3), 135–138.

Messerschmidt, J. W. (1993). *Masculinities and crime: Critique, and reconceptualization of theory.* Lanham, MD: Rowman & Littlefield.

Messerschmidt, J. W. (2018). *Masculinities and crime: A quarter century of theory and research.* Lanham, MD: Rowman & Littlefield.

Mossman, M. J. (2006). *The first women lawyers: A comparative study of gender, law and the legal professions.* Oxford: Hart.

Mukherjee, S. K., & Scutt, J. A. (Eds.). (2015). *Women and crime.* London: Routledge.

Naffine, N. (1990). *Law and the sexes: Explorations in feminist jurisprudence.* Sydney: Allen & Unwin.

Nevada Law Journal. (2013). Men, masculinities and law: A symposium on multidimensional masculinities theory [Special issue], *13*(2), entire issue.

Newburn, T., & Stanko, E. A. (Eds.). (1994). *Just boys doing business? Men, masculinities and crime.* London: Routledge.

Rudy Cooper, F., & McGinley, A. C. (Eds.). (2012). *Masculinities and the law: A mutlidimensional approach.* New York: New York University Press.

Schultz, U., & Shaw, G. (2008). Editorial: Gender and judging. *International Journal of the Legal Profession, 15*(1–2), 1–5.

Smart, C. (1976). *Women, crime and criminology.* London: Routledge & Kegan Paul.

Smart, C. (1989). *Feminism and the power of law.* London: Routledge.

Smart, C. (1990). Feminist approaches to criminology or postmodern woman meets atavistic man. In L. Gelsthorpe & A. Morris (Eds.), *Feminist perspectives in criminology* (pp. 70–84). Buckingham: Open University Press.

Sommerlad, H. (2007). Researching and theorizing the processes of professional identity formation. *Journal of Law and Society, 34*(2), 190–217.

Sommerlad, H. (2016). "A pit to put women in": Professionalism, work intensification, sexualisation and work–life balance in the legal profession in England and Wales. *International Journal of the Legal Profession, 23*(1), 61–82.

Sommerlad, H., & Sanderson, P. (1998). *Gender choice and commitment: Women solicitors in England and Wales and the struggle for equal status.* Aldershot: Ashgate.

Thornton, M. (1989). Hegemonic masculinity and the academy. *International Journal of the Sociology of Law, 17*(2), 115–130.

Thornton, M. (2016). The flexible cyborg: Work-life balance in legal practice. *Sydney Law Review, 38*(1), 1–21.

Thornton, M., & Bagust, J. (2007). The gender trap: Flexible work in corporate legal practice. *Osgoode Hall Law Journal, 45*(4), 773–811.

Tierney, J. (2010). *Criminology: Theory and context.* Harlow: Longman.

Tomsen, S. (Ed.). (2008). *Crime, criminal justice and masculinities.* Aldershot: Ashgate.

Walklate, S. (1995). *Gender and crime: An introduction.* Hemel Hempstead: Prentice Hall/Harvester Wheatsheaf.

Wells, C. (2001). Working out women in law schools. *Legal Studies, 21*(1), 116–138.

Winlow, S. (2001). *Badfellas: Crime, tradition and new masculinities.* Oxford: Berg.

44

Discursive trends in research on masculinities and interpersonal violence

Floretta Boonzaier and Taryn van Niekerk

Globally, interpersonal violence has been ranked among the top 30 leading causes of premature death amongst 264 causes, resulting in 1.2 million deaths in 2016 (Wang et al., 2017). Compared to women, men are disproportionally represented, with 5.2% of male deaths and 1.6% of female deaths being attributed to interpersonal violence in 2010. Men between the ages of 15 and 35 years are more likely to suffer fatal injuries as a result of interpersonal violence and are additionally positioned as 'at risk' for becoming perpetrators of interpersonal violence, both against other men and against women (Lozano et al., 2012). At the same time, it is estimated that more than one-third of women worldwide have been victims of intimate partner violence perpetrated by men (World Health Organisation, 2013). It is fair to say that violence is explicitly gendered and implicates the question of masculinities whether we are talking about violence against women, children or against other men (McCarry, 2007).

The disproportionate representation of young black men in the data on interpersonal violence has been interrogated in public health and psychological research across a range of contexts. For example, in South Africa, homicide and interpersonal violence were the leading cause of fatal injury for young men between the ages of 15 and 29, at 184 per 100 000 and rated at nine times the global average (Norman, Matzopoulos, Groenewald & Bradshaw, 2007; Pillay-van Wyk et al., 2016), with young black[1] men as the most common victims of this violence (Ratele, 2013b). Similarly, in the US, higher rates of fatal and non-fatal violence has been found amongst young black men than amongst any other group, with homicide being the leading cause of death for black men between the ages of 15 to 24 (Centers for Disease Control, 2009, cited in Rich, 2009). Across geopolitical contexts such as South Africa (Mathews et al., 2016) and the US (Rich & Grey, 2005) were also parallels in the 'risk profiles' for men's violence victimisation and perpetration to include: individual and household poverty, lower levels of educational attainment, abuse suffered as a child, higher traumatic experiences, greater control in relationships, personal beliefs about inequitable gender relationships, personal views on rape, alcohol abuse and having multiple concurrent sexual partners. In addition, in the US, repeat victims of violence are more likely to be black, male, poor, have used or are currently using drugs, unemployed, living in poor neighbourhoods, have had prior arrests and were carrying a weapon (Cooper et al., 2000, cited in Rich, 2009).

We argue that central to the ongoing development of violence scholarship is the critical engagement with discourses manifest in the public and academic sphere that mark black men and masculinities as inherently violent, criminals and figures to be feared (Boonzaier, 2018; Langa, Kirsten, Bowman, Eagle & Kiguwa, 2018) and that position them as *a risk* and *at risk* (see Rosenkrantz Lindegaard, 2009). Toward a call for more complex theorisations on interpersonal violence, we suggest that studies on violence take a contextual, historical and intersectional perspective to generate greater insight into the complex ways in which violent moments are produced. We interrogate key issues on masculinities and interpersonal violence, paying attention to the intersections between 'race', class, sexuality, age and location.

In this chapter, we begin by providing an overview of key mainstream approaches to men, masculinities and interpersonal violence studies. We then draw specifically on global southern literature with a particular focus on Africa by way of example, although the arguments we make about the ways in which masculinities and interpersonal violence have been theorised and the 'effects' of such work have reach across geopolitical contexts. We reflect on three emerging discourses on men and masculinities and the meanings of interpersonal violence. These are: 1) historical traumas and colonial patriarchy; 2) neoliberalism and masculinities; and 3) transforming (African) masculinities. We focus specifically on gender-based violence (GBV), violence between men, homophobic violence and homicide as forms of interpersonal violence that have been predominantly located in the literature as the 'violence of black men'. Additionally, we take a critical decolonial feminist reading (Lugones, 2010; Rutherford, 2018) of this literature to show how, in times that may be considered 'post' colonial, representations of black and African men, black families and black communities continue to be racialised and resonate strongly with colonial tropes on Africa and African people.

Mainstream approaches to men, masculinities and interpersonal violence studies

Decades of research have theorised the connections between masculinities and interpersonal violence, predominantly emerging in global Northern contexts such as the United States and United Kingdom. According to Berggren, Gottzén and Bornäs (2020, in press), these historical and contemporary studies on men, masculinities and interpersonal violence have had global influence and have been shaped by a range of theoretical approaches and niche areas of research. These include, but are not limited to, socialist feminist research, social network approaches, accounts research and psychosocial criminological approaches, amongst others. These approaches are not mutually exclusive but have been intricately shaped by or in response to each other, at times, even overlapping.

Some of the major contributions emerging from socialist feminist research include the seminal body of scholarship by Raewyn Connell and Jeff Hearn, which has been paramount to theorising gendered relationships (Connell, 1987; Hearn, 1998). This includes Connell's formulation of hegemonic masculinity that draws on Gramsci's notion of hegemony and is defined as the 'configuration of gender practice which embodies the currently accepted answer to the problem of legitimacy of patriarchy, which guarantees (or is taken to guarantee) the dominant position of men and the subordination of women' (p. 77). Also central to this feminist theorising tradition of masculinity is the work by Messerschmidt (1993) and West and Zimmerman (1987) that foregrounds gender as an ongoing, repetitive practice and accomplishment. Furthermore, social network research and relationality have occurred across various feminist traditions and include male peer support theory (see Schwartz & DeKeseredy, 1997) and the work of Hearn, Kimmel and Whitehead, who place a strong focus on the power men exercise over other men (homosocial power relations) in the context of patriarchal relations to more intricately understand the motivations behind men's violence against women (Hearn & Whitehead, 2006; Kimmel, 2008). In theorising about the accomplishment of masculinity as strongly influenced by men's social networks, Kimmel's (2008) book, *Guyland*, highlights the collective culture of masculine entitlement and protection and how it makes various forms of violence against women possible.

Other important approaches to studying masculinity and violence include that of accounts research as well as those emerging from psychosocial criminology (Berggren et al., 2020, in press). Largely predicated by radical feminist discourse, accounts research refers to the dynamic body of scholarship tracing men's discourses of violence on a micro level that centres the notion of accountability, justifications, victim-blaming and minimisations that allow violent men to neutralise – and at times, mutualise – their acts of violence and to obscure the dominant-submissive relations between themselves and their partners (e.g., Adams, Towns & Gavey, 1995). In contrast, psychosocial theories in criminological studies on men and masculinities have been central to addressing some of the critiques levelled against accounts research that has been argued to decontextualise men's lives, and has been illustrated through the seminal psychoanalytical, psycho-discursive and poststructuralist work by Jefferson, Hollway and Gadd (Gadd & Jefferson, 2007; Hollway, 2004; Jefferson, 1996).

The above approaches illustrate how feminist theorising, predominantly situated in northern contexts, has been central to bringing home the point of men's violence as specifically *gendered* and perpetrated predominantly by men. However, as much of this body of scholarship is located within the global North and framed within mainstream Western feminist discourse, we have also seen massive shifts in theorising unilaterally about patriarchy. The shifts in feminist theorising on men's violence have occurred alongside critiques by black, postcolonial, decolonial, African, indigenous and other marginalised forms of feminist theorising in response to narrow Western feminist preoccupations with patriarchy as the only form of women's oppression and men's domination and violence (Collins, 1990; Kiguwa, 2004; Lugones, 2010). Intersectional, decolonial and African feminist theorising, for example, has foregrounded multiplicity and entanglement in the recognition of other sites of power that include, as a starting point, race, class, sexuality, religion, culture, coloniality, disability, age and location – recognising that these intersect in complex ways with gender to produce historical, social, cultural, political, economic and spatial experiences and dynamics. In the sections that follow, we take the above advancements in theorising as our starting point for a critical review of theorising on men, masculinities and interpersonal violence with a focus on global southern literature and, more particularly, on Africa by way of example.

Historical traumas and colonial patriarchy

African scholarship on masculinities and interpersonal violence centres a discourse of hegemonic masculinity that manifests in the perpetration of interpersonal violence between men, as well as by men against women. Different forms of masculinity (e.g., subordinate, complicit, hegemonic) are argued to exist within any given context while exercising varying degrees of power over women, and other men (Connell & Messerschmidt, 2005), and are shaped by both 'race' and class politics that are central to expressions of masculinity (see Langa & Kiguwa, 2013). Intersectional investigations into men who perpetrate violence have contributed to the dismantling of binaries illustrating, for example, how young black men – marginalised at the intersection of their 'race' and class – who find themselves on the peripheries of matrices of oppression experience extreme pressures and limited opportunities to enact a 'thriving' masculinity that may be considered to be hegemonic (Langa & Kiguwa, 2013; Ratele, 2013b). The argument has been made that masculine dominance may then be expressed with and through the body through activities such as gang membership allowing for some status gain and the taking up of forms of masculinities considered to be dominant (Ragnarsson, Townsend, Thorson, Chopra & Ekström, 2009; Rich & Grey, 2005; Salo, 2007). Scholarship has shown the ways in which violence against men and women is an encouraged expression of masculinity in its capacity to attract 'respect' from peers and other community members in contexts such as Kenya (Goodman, Serag, Raimer-Goodman, Keiser & Gitari, 2017), the Democratic Republic of Congo (Hollander, 2014) and South Africa (Brittijn, 2013; Langa & Kiguwa, 2013; Mathews, Jewkes & Abrahams, 2014; Wechsberg et al., 2013). In contrast, men's departures from masculine subjectivities that may be considered hegemonic have been shown to make them vulnerable to ridicule by community members, peers and family (Van Niekerk & Boonzaier, 2016), while men who have sex with men (MSM) have found themselves vulnerable to physical and sexual violence in Tanzania (Anderson, Ross, Nyoni & McCurdy, 2015), Namibia (Stephenson, Hast, Finneran & Sineath, 2014) and South Africa (Judge & Nel, 2008; Reygan & Lynette, 2014).

Although we suggest that it has not gone far enough, this strand of literature has assisted with countering reductionist and deterministic discourses that uncritically position black men and masculinities as the embodiment of hegemonic masculinity, marking men by their youth, levels of education and unemployment status, for example, and decontextualising experiences of masculinity in relation to men's racialised histories (Morrell, Jewkes & Lindegger, 2012; Shefer, Ratele, Strebel, Shabalala & Buikema, 2007). In referring to multiple hegemonic masculinities in the African context, the interplay of social identities of race, class, urban and rural are foregrounded in their capacity to locate and position masculinities relative to their social, political and historical contexts. Although not sufficiently engaged in the literature, there has been some recognition that we need to attend to the effect of the unprocessed traumas from the histories of colonialism, apartheid and other continuing oppressions faced by black men (and others) that shapes the masculine subjectivities they take up (Ratele, 2013a). Ratele (this volume) continues this argument by calling attention to the effects of slavery and colonisation on black men's lives. By engaging in research on black masculinities and interpersonal violence, feminist intersectional and decolonial analyses are required to understand black men's racialisation and gender-making projects in tandem with an awareness of the complex entanglements of these various forms of power, privilege and oppressions and how they are implicated in the perpetration of interpersonal violence.

Critical studies of men and masculinities have acknowledged the interplay between men's racial and gendered subjectivities; insights that are strongly influenced by black feminist teachings. An important area of work emerging from this school of thought includes a focus on black masculinities and emotions (Biko, 2004; Ratele, 2013b) as well as the scholarship related to intergenerational violence, highlighting the continuities of violence through generations (Mathews, Jewkes & Abrahams, 2011). We see trends in scholarship on critical men, masculinities and violence studies that interrogate the fundamentals of how to humanise research participants (see Paris & Winn, 2014) whose lives have been powerfully shaped by the epistemic and material violences of colonialism, slavery and apartheid but who have simultaneously benefitted from patriarchal domination and have perpetrated violence against men and women during the course of their lives (Boonzaier & van Niekerk, 2018). Some of this work that pays attention to historical trauma has been carried through into South African scholarship interrogating how the emotions of men – marginalised through their race and social class – might be implicated in the perpetration of interpersonal violence and crime (Biko, 2004; Ratele, 2013b). This scholarship aims to gain a deeper understanding of the interplay of emotions of anger, rage, hatred and fear, alongside historical, structural and symbolic analyses and the destructive impact of these emotions on black masculinities (Ratele, 2013b). The emerging scholarship in this area also engages colonial patriarchy through recognition of the continuities of colonialism and how it continues to shape the lives and experiences of the formerly colonised and their descendants, through structural violence and ongoing political, social and economic exclusions and marginalisations (Irwin & Umemoto, 2016) – specifically with respect to understanding men's violence.

Although we are sketching important advances in the theorising on men and masculinities in global southern contexts, the African context in particular, we suggest that this work has transnational implications and a strong potential for growth; for the holding together of an understanding of the links between masculinity and men's perpetration of violence, on the one hand, and the oppressive histories and contemporary contexts of men's lives on the other. The development of this work is absolutely vital, especially as we continue to see, in work that attempts to understand violence perpetrated by black men, stereotypical representations of black masculinities as 'essentially violent'.

Neoliberalism and masculinities

Neoliberal contexts have become increasingly important for understanding the desires and practices of men, including their perpetration of interpersonal violence. Described as an economic system and ideology shaped by globalisation and capitalism, neoliberalism 'enshrines the values of competition, entrepreneurialism, market participation [...], (and) individual responsibility (e.g., employability)' (Phoenix, 2004, p. 228). Through its potential to protect some citizens and significantly benefit others, the neoliberalist ideology foregrounds assumptions around choice, individualism and people as free rational agents; what Gavey (2012) has called the 'neoliberal deceit', the deceptive assurance that we have choice. The neoliberal matrix also produces cumulative disadvantage for those already on the margins, producing circuits of dispossession and showing how the historical and continuing 'overdevelopment of whites relies directly upon the underdevelopment and sustained dispossession of black (people) ...' (Fine & Ruglis, 2009, p. 31). This framing of neoliberal subjectification has important implications for the production of gendered (masculine) subjectivities as neoliberal values intrude into and shape personal and private spaces (Gavey, 2012).

Studies undertaken in South Africa, Congo and Kenya, for example, have noted the extent to which a lack of financial resources and the inability to survive financially is linked to men's perpetration of interpersonal violence. More specifically, gender-based and intimate-partner violence have been shown to be entangled with reported feelings of emasculation, loss of social standing and insecurities linked to fears that intimate partners will leave (Brittijn, 2013; Goodman et al., 2017; Hollander, 2014; Langa & Kiguwa, 2013; Mathews et al., 2014). A shortage of employment is argued to propel South African men into seeking income through illegal means, often involving gang membership and violence against other men and women (Brittijn, 2013; Mathews et al., 2014), with violence overall being seen as a way for men to 'accomplish' and 'perform' masculinity (Messerschmidt, 1993). In neoliberal transnational contexts that continue to perpetuate ideas around free choice and responsibility, on the one hand, and individualised notions of failure linked to shame, on the other, marginalised, indigenous and black men's lives become sites for the enactment of global neoliberalist philosophies – and therefore an understanding of men's desires and forms of masculinity requires interrogation in its local context.

In Africa, a history of colonialism, enslavement, dispossession and decimation, the denial of education, job opportunities and land to black communities means that the burden of poverty and unemployment fall largely within these communities today (Seedat, Van Niekerk, Jewkes, Suffla & Ratele, 2009). The normative nature of neoliberalism has meant that policies and other mechanisms continue to contribute to the marginalisation and dispossession of those who already marginalised. These conditions make it virtually impossible for individual men to break from this cycle of dispossession. Studies highlight how notions of economic power and masculinity are intertwined (Brittijn, 2013; Langa & Kiguwa, 2013), with work showing how, on the one hand, 'respectable' masculinity is constructed as involving financial security and access to secure employment while, on the other, very few men actually have access to these forms of economic security in increasingly 'insecure' times. In the absence of these means to achieve 'successful' masculinity, men are argued to adopt alternate methods of gaining 'respect' – through the perpetration of violence, for example.

Scholars have problematised the normalisation and hegemony of neoliberalist ideology, its naturalisation of oppression and victim-blaming discourses of those who already find themselves marginalised, silenced and subjugated, reducing their lack of participation in 'social competition' to a sign of 'weakness' and 'poor education' (Phoenix, 2004, p. 229). Thus ideas around autonomy are dependent on an individual's positioning; those who find themselves in powerful positions in the social hierarchy are suggested to have greater access to the autonomy, agency and choice idealised in the neoliberal age, as they already receive the necessary supports from various societal structures and have the existing support structures that may buffer them in moments of setback (Fine & Ruglis, 2009; Rutherford, 2018). What this emerging discursive strand in the current literatures shows is that African and other marginalised masculinities (especially in the global South) cannot be understood outside of the legacies and continuities of colonialism, and apart from global northern values and ideas around 'choice' that are projected onto 'subjects' in the global South. As Ratele (2013a) argues, the colonialist, '"white authority male voice" from the rich West' serves to silence and 'other' African men thus contributing towards a global 'blindness to the geopolitics of masculinities' (p. 262).

Transforming (African) masculinities

A third strand we see in work on masculinities and interpersonal violence is work that draws on the two discursive trends above but more explicitly aims to challenge the ways in which marginalised, black or African masculinities are represented, usually as 'the problem'. Research has dealt with the ways in which black masculinities – constructed as *a* risk and *at* risk (see Rosenkrantz Lindegaard, 2009) – may find ways to negotiate social change and counter hegemonic narratives that demonise black, indigenous masculinities. Studies have paid attention to the resistance expressed by African men against hegemonic representations of black masculinities as well as how they go about reshaping these discourses of violence in ways that have meaning to them and that foreground resistance to a struggle, solidarity and empowerment (Langa & Eagle, 2008; Langa & Kiguwa, 2013; Rosenkrantz Lindegaard, 2009). In this volume, Farahani and Thapar-Björkert, for example, show how postcolonial masculinities are rearticulated, contested and negotiated across spatial and socio-political contexts through examples of research on Iranian born men in Stockholm, Sydney and London.

In Johannesburg, South Africa, Langa and Eagle (2008), for example, illustrate how black men took on subject positions as 'militarised men' as a form of resistance to the violence carried out against them by the Apartheid government. They believed that it was their duty 'as men' to be brave and courageous in the face of violence, as a means to achieving justice, and to fight for what was rightfully theirs (Langa & Eagle, 2008). In other work by Langa and Kiguwa (2013), violence perpetrated during service delivery protests by black men were viewed as the only way to 'dethrone' others from their assumed positions of power. Disempowered young black men used violence as a means to reassert their power and drew on militarised discourses of masculinity that were historically rooted in practices such as 'toyi toyi', burning of public property, and singing anti-apartheid struggle songs (Langa & Kiguwa, 2013). It is suggested that militarised masculinities are constantly being reinvented and shaped by the past, indicating that meanings of violence require a historical lens. Violence and protests are furthermore shown to act as a form of solidary-building and empowerment, to create a sense of unity amongst economically disempowered young men (Langa & Kiguwa, 2013). Similar discourses around the legitimacy of violence as political strategy were debated from 2015 onwards in South Africa within large-scale student movements to tackle coloniality and racism in the higher education system (Fairbanks, 2015; Xaba, 2017).

These representations that construct violence as a positive means to an end can be interpreted through the work of Fanon, who writes about colonialism as a powerful form of violence and a structure that will only be destroyed when threatened with greater violence. As Fanon (1963, p. 27) stated, 'decolonization is always a violent phenomenon,' and this notion is important for contextualising the meaning behind violence in post-colonial contexts. Furthermore, this idea shows how violence might be seen as a force of solidarity and resistance; how it might mobilise the masses and their struggle for liberation; and how violence might create a common consciousness – a notion which we consider important in our conceptualisation of interpersonal violence and masculinities in Africa, a continent in which the vestiges of colonialism and enslavement are deeply felt. The literature emerging from African scholarship on men and masculinities then indicates that the meanings of interpersonal violence – through an historical lens – are key to understanding and addressing interpersonal violence.

Concluding remarks

In this chapter we offered a feminist decolonial reading of the literatures on men and masculinity and interpersonal violence, specifically focusing on the work produced on the African continent. We did so by illuminating three interlinked discursive trends that together, if further developed, hold possibilities for breaking the assumed links between (black) masculinity and violence and for reimagining new forms of masculinity. A few years ago, a renowned critical scholar of men and masculinities wrote about the 'problems boys and men create' and 'the problems boys and men experience' (Hearn, 2007, p. 13). In this chapter we contend that the global focus with respect to interpersonal violence has been on the former. We argue that more recently we are able to locate shifts in the discourse that might enable us to see, understand and work with the relationality between these two positions toward advancing non-violence and non-violent forms of masculinity.

We close this chapter with our more general considerations around decolonising the ways in which we do research and how our scholarship might go about 'unsettling' colonial ways of *doing* research. We are reminded of how our work, as researchers, in the academy is determined by colonial tropes and neoliberalist ideologies that urgently requires our critical engagement. This work requires urgent disruption. We additionally note the ways in which research approaches within studies on masculinities and interpersonal violence dominated by northern models appear to be increasingly challenged by decolonial, feminist and indigenous researchers in favour of developing models that are more relevant to the values and worldviews cultivated in local transnational contexts. This chapter critically engages with opportunities for indigenous and other marginalised researchers to foreground research methods, approaches and models that are based on their own values, priorities and worldviews and that continue to 'work to change the nature of what "counts" as research, how it is undertaken, and with what aims' (Rutherford, 2018, p. 637), thereby undoing some of the epistemic violences of colonisation and the continuing colonial research endeavour in the ways in which it retells and packages the stories of the colonised and their descendants (Tuck & Wayne Yang, 2014). This work is ever more pressing for the scholarship on masculinities and interpersonal violence.

Note

1 We speak inclusively to the experiences of black groups, thereby referring to all people marginalised and oppressed under white capitalist patriarchy. We acknowledge the importance of resisting essentialist racial categorisations imposed by colonial discourse and, more specifically, the apartheid government in the South African context, yet also recognise the sense of solidarity and shared experiences amongst the oppressed.

References

Adams, P. J., Towns, A., & Gavey, N. (1995). Dominance and entitlement: The rhetoric men use to discuss their violence towards women. *Discourse & Society, 6*(3), 387–406.

Anderson, A. M., Ross, M. W., Nyoni, J. E., & McCurdy, S. A. (2015). High prevalence of stigma-related abuse among a sample of men who have sex with men in Tanzania: Implications for HIV prevention. *AIDS Care, 27*(1), 63–70.

Berggren, K., Gottzén, L., & Bornäs, H. (2020), in press. Theorizing masculinity and intimate partner violence. In L. Gottzén, M. Bjornholt & F. Boonzaier (Eds.), *Men, masculinities and intimate partner violence.* Routledge.

Biko, S. (2004). *I write what I like: A selection of his writings.* Johannesburg: Picador Africa.

Boonzaier, F. (2018). Challenging risk: The production of knowledge on gendered violence in South Africa. In Fitz-Gibbon, K., Walklate, S., McCulloch, J., & Maree Maher, J. (Eds.), *Intimate partner violence, risk and security: Securing women's lives in a global world* (pp. 71–87). London: Routledge.

Boonzaier, F., & van Niekerk, T. (2018). 'I'm here for abusing my wife': South African men constructing intersectional subjectivities through narratives of their own violence. *African Safety Promotion: A Journal of Injury and Violence Prevention, 16*(1), 2–19.

Brittijn, M. (2013). 'We're not boys anymore, we need to be courageous': Towards an understanding of what it means to be a man in Lavender Hill. *Agenda, 27*(1), 49–60.

Collins, P. H. (1990). *Black feminist thought: Knowledge, consciousness, and the politics of empowerment.* Boston, MA: Unwyn Hyman.

Connell, R. W. (1987). *Gender and power: Society, the person, and sexual politics.* Stanford, CA: Stanford University Press.

Connell, R. W., & Messerschmidt, J. W. (2005). Hegemonic masculinity: Rethinking the concept. *Gender & Society, 19*(6), 829–859.

Fairbanks, E. (2015, November 18). Why South African students have turned on their parents' generation. *The Guardian.* Retrieved from www.theguardian.com/news/2015/nov/18/why-south-african-students-have-turned-on-their-parents-generation.

Fanon, F. (1963). *The wretched of the earth.* New York: Grove.

Fine, M., & Ruglis, J. (2009). Circuits and consequences of dispossession: The racialized realignment of the public sphere for U.S. youth. *Transforming Anthropology, 17*(1), 20–33.

Gadd, D., & Jefferson, T. (2007). *Psychosocial criminology*. Los Angeles, CA: Sage.

Gavey, N. (2012). *Intimate intrusions of the neoliberal deceit*. Keynote address presented at the International Congress of Psychology, 22 – 27 July, Cape Town International Convention Centre, Cape Town, South Africa.

Goodman, M. L., Serag, H., Raimer-Goodman, L., Keiser, P., & Gitari, S. (2017). Subjective social standing and conflict tactics among young Kenyan men. *American Journal of Community Psychology, 60*(1–2), 257–266.

Hearn, J. (1998). *The violences of men: How men talk about and how agencies respond to men's violence to women*. London: Sage.

Hearn, J. (2007). The problems boys and men create, the problems boys and men experience. In T. Shefer, K. Ratele, A. Strebel, N. Shabalala & R., Buikema (Eds.), *From boys to men: Social constructions of masculinity in contemporary society* (pp. 13–32). Cape Town: University of Capetown Press.

Hearn, J., & Whitehead, A. (2006). Collateral damage: Men's 'domestic' violence to women seen through men's relations with men. *Probation Journal, 53*(1), 38–56.

Hollander, T. (2014). Men, masculinities, and the demise of a state: Examining masculinities in the context of economic, political, and social crisis in a small town in the Democratic Republic of the Congo. *Men and Masculinities, 17*(4), 417–439.

Hollway, W. (2004). *Psycho-social research*. London: Lawrence & Wishart.

Irwin, K., & Umemoto, K. (2016). *Jacked up and unjust: Pacific Islander teens confront violent legacies*. Berkeley, CA: University of California Press.

Jefferson, T. (1996). From 'little fairy boy' to 'the complete destroyer': Subjectivity and transformation in the biography of Mike Tyson. In M. Mac an Ghaill (Ed.), *Understanding masculinities* (pp. 153–167). Philadelphia, PA: Open University Press.

Judge, M., & Nel, J. (2008). Exploring homophobic victimisation in Gauteng, South Africa: Issues, impacts and responses. *Acta Criminologica: Southern African Journal of Criminology, 21*(3), 19–36.

Kiguwa, P. (2004). Feminist critical psychology in South Africa. In D. Hook, N. Mkhize, P. Kiguwa, A. Collins, E. Burman & I. Parker (Eds.), *Critical psychology* (pp. 187–209). Lansdowne: UCT Press.

Kimmel, M. (2008). *Guyland: The perilous world where boys become men*. New York: Harper.

Langa, M., & Eagle, G. (2008). The intractability of militarised masculinity: A case study of former self-defence unit members in the Kathorus area, South Africa. *South African Journal of Psychology, 38*(1), 152–175.

Langa, M., & Kiguwa, P. (2013). Violent masculinities and service delivery protests in post-apartheid South Africa: A case study of two communities in Mpumalanga. *Agenda, 27*(1), 20–31.

Langa, M., Kirsten, A., Bowman, B., Eagle, G., & Kiguwa, P. (2018). Black masculinities on trial *in absentia*: The case of Oscar Pistorius in South Africa. *Men and Masculinities*, 10.1177% 2F1097184X18762523.

Lozano, R., Naghavi, M., Foreman, K., Lim, S., Shibuya, K., Aboyans, V., … Ahn, S. Y. (2012). Global and regional mortality from 235 causes of death for 20 age groups in 1990 and 2010: A systematic analysis for the global burden of disease study 2010. *The Lancet, 380*(9859), 2095–2128.

Lugones, M. (2010). Toward a decolonial feminism. *Hypatia, 25*(4), 742–759.

Mathews, S., Govender, R., Lamb, G., Boonzaier, F., Dawes, A., Ward, C., … & Röhrs, S. (2016). *Towards a more comprehensive understanding of the direct and indirect determinants of violence against women and children in South Africa with a view to enhancing violence prevention*. Cape Town: Safety and Violence Initiative, University of Cape Town.

Mathews, S., Jewkes, R., & Abrahams, N. (2011). 'I had a hard life': Exploring childhood adversity in the shaping of masculinities among men who killed an intimate partner in South Africa. *The British Journal of Criminology, 51*(6), 960–977.

Mathews, S., Jewkes, R., & Abrahams, N. (2014). 'So now I'm the man': Intimate partner femicide and its interconnections with expressions of masculinities in South Africa. *The British Journal of Criminology, 55*(1), 107–124.

McCarry, M. (2007). Masculinity studies and male violence: Critique or collusion? *Women's Studies International Forum, 30*(5), 404–415.

Messerschmidt, J. W. (1993). *Masculinities and crime: Critique and reconceptualization of theory*. Lanham, MA: Rowan & Littlefield.

Morrell, R., Jewkes, R., & Lindegger, G. (2012). Hegemonic masculinity/masculinities in South Africa: Culture, power, and gender politics. *Men and Masculinities, 15*(1), 11–30.

Norman, R., Matzopoulos, R., Groenewald, P., & Bradshaw, D. (2007). The high burden of injuries in South Africa. *Bulletin of the World Health Organization, 85*, 695–702.

Paris, D., & Winn, M. T. (Eds.). (2014). Preface: To humanize research. In *Humanizing research: Decolonizing qualitative inquiry with youth and communities* (pp. xiii–xx). London: Sage.

Phoenix, A. (2004). Neoliberalism and masculinity: Racialization and the contradictions of schooling for 11 to 14-year-olds. *Youth & Society, 36*(2), 227–246.

Pillay-van Wyk, V., Msemburi, W., Laubscher, R., Dorrington, R. E., Groenewald, P., Glass, T., ... & Nannan, N. (2016). Mortality trends and differentials in South Africa from 1997 to 2012: Second National Burden of Disease Study. *The Lancet Global Health, 4*(9), e642–e653.

Ragnarsson, A., Townsend, L., Thorson, A., Chopra, M., & Ekström, A. M. (2009). Social networks and concurrent sexual relationships: A qualitative study among men in an urban South African community. *AIDS Care, 21*(10), 1253–1258.

Ratele, K. (2013a). Of what value is feminism to black men? *Communicatio, 39*(2), 256–270.

Ratele, K. (2013b). Subordinate black South African men without fear. *Cahiers d'Études africaines, LIII*(1–2), 247–268.

Reygan, F., & Lynette, A. (2014). Heteronormativity, homophobia and 'culture' arguments in KwaZulu-Natal, South Africa. *Sexualities, 17*(5–6), 707–723.

Rich, J. A. (2009). *Wrong place, wrong time: Trauma and violence in the lives of young black men*. Baltimore, MD: Johns Hopkins University Press.

Rich, J. A., & Grey, C. M. (2005). Pathways to recurrent trauma among young black men: traumatic stress, substance use, and the 'code of the street'. *Public Health Matters, 95*(5), 816–826.

Rosenkrantz Lindegaard, M. (2009). Navigating terrains of violence: How South African male youngsters negotiate social change. *Social Dynamics: A Journal of African Studies, 35*(1), 19–35.

Rutherford, A. (2018). Feminism, psychology, and the gendering of neoliberal subjectivity: From critique to disruption. *Theory & Psychology, 28*(5), 619–644.

Salo, E. (2007). Social construction of masculinity on the racial and gendered margins of Cape Town. In T. Shefer, K. Ratele, A. Strebel, N. Shabalala & R., Buikema (Eds.), *From boys to men: Social constructions of masculinity in contemporary society* (pp. 160–180). Cape Town: University of Capetown Press.

Schwartz, M. D., & DeKeseredy, W. S. (1997). *Sexual assault on the college campus: The role of male peer support*. Thousand Oaks, CA: Sage.

Seedat, M., Van Niekerk, A., Jewkes, R., Suffla, S., & Ratele, K. (2009). Violence and injuries in South Africa: Prioritising an agenda for prevention. *The Lancet, 374*(9694), 1011–1022.

Shefer, T., Ratele, K., Strebel, A., Shabalala, N., & Buikema, R. (Eds.). (2007). From boys to men: An overview. In *From boys to men: Social constructions of masculinity in contemporary society* (pp. 1–12). Cape Town: University of Capetown Press.

Stephenson, R., Hast, M., Finneran, C., & Sineath, C. R. (2014). Intimate partner, familial and community violence among men who have sex with men in Namibia. *Culture, Health & Sexuality, 16*(5), 473–487.

Tuck, E., & Wayne Yang, K. (2014). R-words: Refusing research. In D. Paris & M. T. Winn (Eds.), *Humanizing research: Decolonizing qualitative inquiry with youth and communities* (pp. 223–247). London: Sage.

Van Niekerk, T. J., & Boonzaier, F. A. (2016). 'The only solution there is to fight': Discourses of masculinity among South African domestically violent men. *Violence Against Women, 22*(3), 271–291.

Wang, H., Abajobir, A., Abate, K., Abbafati, C., Abbas, K., Abd-Allah, F., ... Abu-Rmeileh, N. (2017). Global, regional, and national under-5 mortality, adult mortality, age-specific mortality, and life expectancy, 1970–2016: A systematic analysis for the Global Burden of Disease Study 2016. *Lancet, 390*(10100), 1084–1150.

Wechsberg, W. M., Myers, B., Reed, E., Carney, T., Emanuel, A. N., & Browne, F. A. (2013). Substance use, gender inequity, violence and sexual risk among couples in Cape Town. *Culture, Health & Sexuality, 15*(10), 1221–1236.

West, C., & Zimmerman, D. H. (1987). Doing gender. *Gender & Society, 1*(2), 125–151.

World Health Organization. (2013). *Global and regional estimates of violence against women: Prevalence and health effects of intimate partner violence and non-partner sexual violence*. Geneva: World Health Organization.

Xaba, W. (2017). Challenging Fanon: A black radical feminist perspective on violence and the Fees Must Fall movement. *Agenda: Empowering Women for Gender Equity, 31*(3–4), 96–104.

45

Masculinities, war and militarism

Claire Duncanson

Introduction

What is the connection between masculinities and militarism? Is the concept of masculinities a useful one for understanding militarism and war? How do we challenge and transform violent, militaristic or misogynist masculinities as part of a strategy for peace? This chapter starts by introducing the pioneering scholarship of feminists and other masculinities scholars who first drew attention to the connections between masculinities and militarism, many of whom argued that masculinities are causal in militarism and war (Cockburn, 2010). The second section discusses the work of scholars who complicated that original insight by drawing out attention to the multiplicity of masculinities at play in militarism and war, and their inherent contradictions and instabilities. The final section highlights the scholarship that concerns itself with the question of whether masculinities can change, and whether this facilitates peace.

Masculinities, war and militarism: making the connections

Numbers of female military personnel may be on the rise, but militaries remain dominated, as they have for centuries, by men. Few feminists or other scholars of masculinity argue that this male dominance of militaries is explained by biology. The idea that your biology determines your behaviour and that boys are just born more aggressive than girls is just not credible, as numerous studies now show (Fine, 2005; Jordan-Young, 2011). Men do not dominate in the world's militaries because they are naturally more violent, aggressive and tough, feminist scholars argue, but because in many cultures across time and space, proving oneself on the battlefield has been deemed an important way to prove oneself a man (Goldstein, 2003; Cockburn, 2007). This is evident in the clichés such as the military will "make a man of you" and "turn boys into men" (Hockey, 2003, p. 15). Boys and men are socialized into thinking that being tough, being aggressive, being in authority and in control are important markers of being a man. To different degrees, and in different ways in different parts of the world, many still bring up their children with the messages that "boys don't cry", that boys have to be brave and to learn to stand up for themselves in a fight (Connell, 2000).

To those who doubt that aggression is socially constructed, pioneer of feminist International Relations (IR) Cynthia Enloe points to the way that soldiers are trained in the military. "If masculinity in the raw were sufficient, there would be little need for the sweat, blisters and humiliations of basic training" (Enloe, 1993, p. 55). In his hefty volume on *Gender and War*, Goldstein concurs, arguing that the reality of combat is fear and confusion and that there is much evidence to show that men on the whole find combat horrible and unnatural. Why else, he writes, would we need conscription and harsh discipline in training, punishment for desertion and rewards (both material and non) for fighting? (Goldstein, 2003, p. 253). Masculinity is an "artificial status which is typically constructed around a culture's need for brave and disciplined soldiers" (Goldstein, 2003, p. 283).

As another pioneering feminist scholar of military masculinities, Sandra Whitworth, puts it: "Military training helps to nurture the exaggerated ideals of manhood and masculinity demanded by national militaries" (2004, pp. 242–243). The transformation of boys into men, for her, is

> accomplished through the denigration of everything marked by difference, whether that be women, people of colour, or homosexuality. It is not by coincidence that the insults most new recruits face are gendered, raced and homophobic insults: young soldiers are learning to deny, indeed to obliterate, the 'other' within themselves.
>
> *(Whitworth, 2004, pp. 242–243)*

Similar processes are found across a range of contexts, such as Turkey (Altinay, 2004), South Africa (Cock, 1994; Shefer & Mankayi, 2007) and the UK (Hockey, 2003; Woodward, 1998). Considering some of the violence experienced in war – the evidence that "women have been raped with penises, fists and miscellaneous weapons, their breasts cut off, their foetuses sliced out" (Cockburn, 2007, p. 248) and that battlefield accounts report the obvious sexual pleasure some men take in killing and in other forms of violent abuse directed against women, men and even children (Ruddick, 1983) – many feminists argue that to understand war and its perpetuation we need to bring into view some of the "uncomfortable *cultural* realities of training and fighting" (Cockburn, 2007, p. 248):

> War as institution is made up of, refreshed by and adaptively reproduced by violence as banal practice, in the everyday life of boot camp and battlefield. Masculinity in its various cultural forms is an important content of that cycle: masculinity shapes war and war shapes masculinity.
>
> *(Cockburn, 2007, p. 249)*

In addressing the connection between masculinities, militarism and war, it is not just the links between men and violence that feminists highlight. Other aspects of masculinity are important – military men are socialized into thinking that it is manly to protect women and children, that it is manly to take risks (not play safe), be active not passive, competitive not compromising, to be brave not cowardly and so on. These different aspects of militarized masculinity constitute one-half of an "elaborate gender ideology" (Enloe, 1983, p. 211) which encourages men to believe their role is to fight and protect and teaches women that theirs is to look after the "home front", the "Just Warrior and Beautiful Soul" of war's ongoing mythology (Elshtain, 1982, 1987; also see Tickner, 2001).

The results of this socialization of recruits into militarized masculinity are the routine workplace discrimination and harassment, the sexual exploitation and violence and the greater efforts required to be accepted that female military personnel report and researchers document (Carreiras, 2006; D'Amico & Weinstein, 1999; Herbert, 1998; Mathers, 2013; Woodward & Winter, 2007). The United States military has been shaken by a succession of sexual exploitation scandals, but these highly visible incidents are arguably just the tip of the iceberg (Enloe, 2007) – not just in the US but in many armed forces (Mathers, 2013; Obradovic, 2014). Studies of US military veterans since the 1970s found that 71% of the women said they were sexually assaulted or raped while serving and that some 80% of military sexual assaults are never reported (Benedict, 2009). As Congresswoman Jane Harman put it, "Women serving in the U.S. military are more likely to be raped by a fellow soldier than killed by enemy fire in Iraq" (cited in Benedict, 2009). High rates of domestic violence (see, e.g., Harrison, 2003); prostitution around military bases (see, e.g., Enloe, 2000); the widespread use of rape as a weapon of war (Leatherman, 2011); and the realization that soldiers serving as peacekeepers also have perpetrated sexual violence (Westendorf & Searle, 2017) consolidated the feminist case that militarized masculinities constitute a major barrier to feminist goals of gender equality and peace.

One of the reasons feminist and other scholars argued that militarized masculinities are so important is because of the evidence that ideas about masculinity forged through military training and culture also influence civilian men. From Samuel Johnson's 1778 assertion that "every man thinks meanly of himself for not having been a soldier," to ongoing valorizations of military culture in many societies today, there is much evidence for Morgan's (1994) view that constructions of masculinity and femininity in the military context shape the entire gender order (also see Connell, 1995; Segal, 1997). Constructions of gender within militaries shape masculinities in obvious places, for example other institutions in the security sector (such as the police, private security, and ministries of defence) but also in public life more broadly. The outcome is that it is hard for many men, particularly those in positions of authority and leadership, to be seen as too risk-averse, compromising or conciliatory. It becomes hard, in particular, for any man, especially leaders, to admit to vulnerability and interdependence, of either themselves or their state. Instead they are compelled to pursue weapons and policies that perpetuate the myth of the possibility of perfect security, perfect invulnerability (Cohn, 1987, 2013). President Trump and his sabre rattling might be the most extreme example, but ideals of masculinity arguably work in subtle ways to constrain leaders of all stripes.

Masculinities, militarism and war: complicating the connection

Feminists and other critical masculinities scholars have gone beyond *making the connections* between masculinities, militarism and war, however, and have sought to show how complex this relationship is. Some fear that in emphasizing the mutually reinforcing nature of masculinity and militarism – that war makes men and men make war – scholars can reify the very gendered dichotomies they aim to challenge (Dawson, 1994). Stern and Zalewski (2009, p. 616) call this the "sex/gender paradox" or "predicament", the way that feminist interventions end up reinvoking the "very grammars that initially incited them as narratives of resistance" and becoming complicit in the violences they seek to ameliorate.

Scholars have highlighted the huge variety in military masculinities (see, e.g., Enloe, 1983, 1993; Hooper, 2001). If we consider the masculinity of the officer class (authoritative, well-bred, well-educated, commanding), the masculinity of the infantry private (tough, aggressive, hard-drinking) and the masculinity of the engineer (skilled with machines, mechanics, technology), for example, we can see that they are all recognizably masculine, but all very different. As such, masculinities scholars have stressed the importance of recognizing that masculinity always intersects with other aspects of identity – class, nation and race in particular – in the construction of military identities (see Kirby & Henry, 2012; Woodward & Duncanson, 2017). Some scholars thus focus on teasing out the specificities of militarized masculinities in different national contexts (see, e.g., Ashe, 2012; Oxlund, Østergaard & Kayonde, 2010; Parpart, 2015; Rones, 2017; Sasson-Levy, 2002). Others have teased out the relationship between gender and sexuality (Bulmer, 2013; Herbert, 1998). Some have highlighted the ways in which male recruits, for example, are arguably active participants in the construction of masculinities, not just moulded from above by military commanders seeking to fill the ranks (Connell, 1995; Morgan, 1994). Men consciously act in certain ways, and this in part informs their masculinity – i.e., they pick their job specialization (though that choice of course is also in some ways mediated by class, race, age and so on); they choose how much to buy into cultures of aggression.

A thriving scholarship considers "masculinities at the margins", in recognition of the fact that it is not just militarized masculinities in state militaries that drive militarism and war, but militarized masculinities in all sorts of contexts. Recent work on military masculinities includes research on terrorism (Messerschmidt & Rohde, 2018) and rebel groups (Duriesmith, 2016; de Silva, 2014); drone operators (Heyns & Borden, 2017) and cyborgs (Masters, 2005); deserters (Maringa, 2017) and dissenters (Tidy, 2016). Paul Higate has been a pioneer in this development, first editing a volume challenging the idea that military masculinities could only be found where there was a formal military setting (2003) and then again with his work on Private Military and Security Companies (PMSCs) (2012b, 2012a). Indeed, militarized masculinities in PMSCs have attracted much feminist attention (Chisholm, 2014; Eichler, 2013; Stachowitsch, 2015). This research has highlighted, in Stachowitsch's (2015, p. 364) summary,

> that private security constitutes a variety of masculinities, which integrate business, humanitarian, and militarized characteristics; that masculinities are being redefined in and through new security regimes; that security contractors make sense of their practices through the framework of masculinity; that masculinities serve to devalue the labor of men from the Global South; that masculinist perceptions inform redefinitions of security; and that masculinities are used to legitimize the outsourcing of security functions.

Veterans have also become a popular subject of study, with Sarah Bulmer and Maya Eichler (2017, p. 175) persuasively arguing that they "illustrate that the unmaking of a militarized masculine identity is never complete, much as the archetype of militarized masculinity can never be fully achieved."

Indeed, something that is often pointed to in discussion of military masculinities is contradiction (see, e.g., Amar, 2011; Basham, 2012; Henry, 2015; Hynes, 1998; Morgan, 1994; Titunik, 2008). For example, in many ways the archetype of the masculine soldier is avoidance of emotion, holding one's fears inside, what is called in the UK "the stiff upper lip", but, at the same time, soldiers often cry at the death or injury of a comrade or express extreme anger, and when they do, this is rarely deemed inappropriate and chastised by other soldiers (Morgan, 1994). Similarly, we think of masculinity as involving authority, command and dominance – but soldiering involves more subservience, obedience and deference to authority than any other profession a young man could enter (Enloe, 1993). Attention to looking good, to ironing clothes, to keeping your room tidy – all things usually deemed the preserve of young women, not men – are demanded and respected in the military (Hooper, 2001). Belkin's (2011) study of US recruits found that they were routinely compelled to engage in behaviours that are supposedly disavowed by dominant forms of masculinity, such as military hazing rituals involving the penetration of other men, indicating that militarized masculinity is structured by contradictions deliberately designed to confuse recruits and ensure obedience.

The idea that masculinities are multiple, contradictory and involve agency has become widely accepted. However, as Charlotte Hooper has argued, it puts feminists in something of a conundrum:

> if men routinely exhibit so-called feminine characteristics, and if the similar activities and qualities can be labelled masculine or feminine depending on interpretation and a change of emphasis, and if the term *masculinity* has no stable ingredients, then why take the claims of feminists seriously at all?.
>
> *(2001, pp. 62–63)*

This is why many scholars have found Raewyn Connell's concept of hegemonic masculinity (see Carrigan, Connell & Lee, 1985) to be so useful, the idea that masculinities are not merely multiple and equal but rather exist in relations of hierarchy, dominated by a loosely coherent and evolving hegemonic form. As the Gramscian origins of the term "hegemony" suggest (see Gramsci, 1971), hegemonic masculinity dominates not through force but through consent. In other words, the majority of men (and women) respect and value this way of being a man, even if the majority of men do not enact it. It is context dependent, but in many militaries it is associated with the practices, skills and symbolic importance of combat (toughness, endurance, courage, action, risk-taking), often with hard-drinking, heterosexual prowess and disdain of homosexuality but also often with the authority and control of the commanding officer. It is a cultural ideal, but it has important material effects – certain ways of acting are privileged: competition over compromise, action over consultation, force over talking, etc. – and those men who most resemble the hegemonic model are privileged.

The concept of hegemonic masculinity is useful because it has enabled critical scholars to reconcile the multiple, dynamic and contradictory nature of masculinities with insights into the connection between masculinity and militarism (Hutchings, 2007). Specifically, it has helped them think through how the ideal of the combat-experienced commanding officer is not the only form of masculinity, but it is a very powerful model, which, through consent, has dominated as one form of "ideal man". The idea of hegemonic masculinity helps explain the way in which the ideal masculinity in any context may shift but is always valorized over that which is designated feminine. It is as a result of this ongoing privileging of the masculine over the feminine that certain advantages (wealth, respect, power) stay in the hands of men (some more than others), both within and beyond the military (Connell, 1987; Connell & Messerschmidt, 2005; Hooper, 2001).

That said, the concept of hegemonic masculinity may raise as many problems as it solves. If hegemonic masculinity is not a personality type, but rather *the way in which particular groups of men inhabit positions of power and wealth* (Carrigan et al., 1985) and how they make their dominance seem natural and legitimate, can there ever be change which challenges the power of hegemonic masculinity? A concept which does not allow for progressive change – for the dismantling of the idea that aggression, risk-taking, conquest and so on are some sort of ideal – is of limited use to critical scholars. Connell, however, always stressed that hegemony may fail, and several scholars have attempted to develop this strand in Connell's thinking in order to aid feminism's project of unravelling hegemonic masculinity (Christensen & Jensen, 2014; Duncanson, 2015).

Others think the concept is flawed because it fails to capture what is going on empirically: being a member of the military or a military-like institution is *not* necessarily the most accepted or most respected, let alone the most hegemonic, way of being a man, even in conflict-affected situations. The military or insurgents may be seen by affected communities as unwanted outsiders, while unarmed civilian community leaders are treated with far more respect (Myrttinen, Khattab & Naujoks, 2017). Indeed, scholars increasingly call for more attention to be given to the masculinities at play in militarism and war that are *not* associated with power, violence or heroic protectors of the weak and vulnerable (Chisholm & Tidy, 2017; Parpart & Partridge, 2014). In many conflict-affected areas, the concept which is perhaps more relevant is that of "thwarted masculinities," that is:

> masculinities of men who are bound by expectations of living up to dominant notions of masculinity in the face of realities which make it practically impossible to achieve these, leading to frustration and at times various forms of violence, against both others and oneself.
>
> *(Myrttinen et al., 2017, p. 108; also see Dolan, 2010)*

And, of course, many men and boys are simply vulnerable, more than anything else, in wartime; and dominant norms of masculine strength can, seemingly paradoxically, increase this vulnerability (Myrttinen et al., 2017).

Unravelling militarized masculinities for peace

Some of the scholarship which calls for attention to non-violent and non-hegemonic masculinities at play in militarism and war is explicitly focused on the normative project of dismantling violent masculinities and promoting more egalitarian models in the service of peace. The evidence that men predominate across the spectrum of violence led Connell to conclude that any "strategy for peace must concern itself with this fact, the reasons for it, and its implications for work to reduce violence" (2000, p. 22). The beginnings of such a strategy were fleshed out under the auspices of UNESCO in the late 1990s (see Breines, Connell & Eide, 2000). Many initiatives have followed, such as efforts to unravel the links between weapons, masculinities and violence as part of the disarmament, demobilization and reintegration (DDR) of ex-combatants after war (see Theidon, 2009) or to transform masculinities in war-affected contexts through group education or community outreach (see Myrttinen, Naujoks & El-Bushra, 2014; Wright & Welsh, 2014).

Several scholars have addressed the question of whether the post-Cold War shift in many Western militaries away from wars of territorial defense towards peace, humanitarian and stabilization operations changed militarized masculinities. Canadian peacekeepers in Somalia (Razack, 2004; Whitworth, 2004), American "humanitarian soldier-scholars" (Dyvik, 2016; Khalili, 2011; Niva, 1998) and British "forces for good" (Duncanson, 2013; Welland, 2015) in Iraq and Afghanistan have been presented (by themselves, their militaries and in national and international media and policy discourses) as "tough but tender" (Niva, 1998, p. 118); as skilled in such tasks as, for example, the provision of humanitarian aid, escorting children to school, negotiating ceasefires and communicating across cultural divides as fighting. In scholarship on all these cases, however, the authors caution to be wary of ascribing progress to these new masculinities. All too often, the masculinity of the altruistic, humanitarian soldier of the Western military is constructed through implicit or sometimes explicit comparison with those who are portrayed as the hypermasculine belligerents, the uncivilized barbaric hordes consumed by ancient hatreds or the feminized civilian population, the weak, passive victims of war. "Softer, kinder" masculinities thus appear always to entail new race or class oppressions. The reason these masculinities are so problematic is that this discourse, this "powerful and seductive story of the West bringing human rights and democracy to non-Western countries" (Razack, 2004, p. 47), distracts from the root causes of conflicts, which can be found firstly in the legacies of colonialism and cold-war superpower politics, including surplus armaments; and secondly in the neoliberal economic policies which have dominated the global political economy since the 1980s. Nonetheless, some scholars retain optimism that taking more seriously the masculinities of peacebuilders, including resisters and conscientious objectors (Conway, 2014; Duncanson, 2013; Myrttinen et al., 2017), may be a potential resource for peace.

The lesson from this scholarship on peacebuilder masculinities is perhaps threefold. First, to unravel hegemonic militarized masculinities in the service of peace, it cannot be enough for the military *practices* that are seen as manly to change. There also has to be change in *relations* between military personnel and both real and imagined others in order challenge the power relations at play in gender. Relations of hierarchy, oppression and exclusion must be replaced with relations of equality, empathy and mutual respect. Second, if there is insufficient attention to intersections of masculinity with other vectors of identity (such as race, class or sexuality), change in masculinity can reinforce oppressions along these other axes. This implies that a strategy for peace would need to include encouraging respect for multiple ways of being a man in military contexts and more fluid identities, recognizing similarities, interdependence and mutual vulnerabilities. Third, there is little to gain from military masculinities being redefined in less violent ways if broader social, political and economic forces – which drove the interventions into Somalia, Iraq and Afghanistan – are not simultaneously challenged.

Despite the introduction of complexity and dissenting voices over the years, feminist and other critical gender scholars continue to find the relationship between masculinities, militarism and war an important area of study. They tend to proceed mindful of the complexities, the contradiction and dynamism and the challenge of theorizing power relations without cementing them. But the original contention, that socially constructed gender norms which associate masculinity with power, violence and control play a role in driving conflict and insecurity, remains an important motivation and guiding insight for many scholars, and prompts research which is, few would contest, needed now more than ever.

References

Altinay, A. G. (2004). *The myth of the military nation: Militarism, gender, and education in Turkey*. New York: Palgrave Macmillan.

Amar, P. (2011). Middle East masculinity studies: Discourses of 'men in crisis', industries of gender in revolution. *Journal of Middle East Women's Studies*, 7(3), 36–70.

Ashe, F. (2012). Gendering war and peace: Militarized masculinities in Northern Ireland. *Men and Masculinities*, *15*(3), 230–248.

Basham, V. (2012). *War, identity and the liberal state*. London: Routledge.

Belkin, A. (2011). *Bring me men: Military masculinity and the benign facade of American empire, 1898–2001*. London: Hurst.

Benedict, H. (2009). *The lonely soldier: The private war of women serving in Iraq*. Boston, MA: Beacon Press.

Breines, I., Connell, R., & Eide, I. (Eds.). (2000). *Male roles, masculinities and violence: A culture of peace perspective*. Paris: UNESCO Publishing.
Bulmer, S. (2013). Patriarchal confusion? Making sense of gay and lesbian military identity. *International Feminist Journal of Politics, 15*(2), 137–156.
Bulmer, S., & Eichler, M. (2017). Unmaking militarized masculinity: Veterans and the project of military-to-civilian transition. *Critical Military Studies, 3*(2), 161–181.
Carreiras, H. (2006). *Gender and the military: Women in the armed forces of western democracies*. London: Routledge.
Carrigan, T., Connell, R. W., & Lee, J. (1985). Toward a new sociology of masculinity. *Theory and Society, 14*(5), 551–604.
Chisholm, A. (2014). The silenced and indispensible: Gurkhas in private military security companies. *International Feminist Journal of Politics, 16*(1), 26–47.
Chisholm, A., & Tidy, J. (2017). Beyond the hegemonic in the study of militaries, masculinities, and war. *Critical Military Studies, 3*(2), 99–102.
Christensen, A-D., & Jensen, S. Q. (2014). Combining hegemonic masculinity and intersectionality. *NORMA: International Journal for Masculinity Studies, 9*(1), 60–75.
Cock, J. (1994). Women and the military: Implications for demilitarization in the 1990s in South Africa. *Gender & Society, 8*(2), 152–169.
Cockburn, C. (2007). *From where we stand: War, women's activism and feminist analysis*. London: Zed Books.
Cockburn, C. (2010). Gender relations as causal in militarization and war. *International Feminist Journal of Politics, 12*(2), 139–157.
Cohn, C. (1987). Sex and death in the rational world of defence intellectuals. *Signs, 12*(4), 687–718.
Cohn, C. (2013). *Women and wars: Contested histories, uncertain futures*. Newark, NJ: Wiley.
Connell, R W. (1987). *Gender and power: Society, the person and sexual politics*. Cambridge: Polity Press.
Connell, R W. (1995). *Masculinities*. Cambridge: Polity Press.
Connell, R W. (2000). Arms and the man: Using the new research on masculinity to understand violence and promote peace in the contemporary world. In I. Breiness, R. Connell & I. Eide (Eds.), *Male roles, masculinities and violence: A culture of peace perspective* (pp. 21–33). Paris: UNESCO Publishing.
Connell, R. W., & Messerschmidt, J. W. (2005). Hegemonic masculinity: Rethinking the concept. *Gender & Society, 19*(6), 829–859.
Conway, D. (2014). *Masculinities, militarisation and the end conscription campaign*. Manchester: Manchester University Press.
D'Amico, F. J., & Weinstein, L. L. (1999). *Gender camouflage: Women and the US Military*. New York: New York University Press.
Dawson, G. (1994). *Soldier heroes: British adventure, empire and the imagining of masculinities*. London: Routledge.
de Silva, J. (2014). Valour, violence and the ethics of struggle: Constructing militant masculinities in Sri Lanka. *South Asian History and Culture, 5*(4), 438–456.
Dolan, C. (2010). *War is not yet over: Community perceptions of sexual violence and its underpinnings in eastern DRC*. London: International Alert.
Duncanson, C. (2013). *Forces for good? Military masculinities and peacebuilding in Afghanistan and Iraq*. Basingstoke: Palgrave Macmillan.
Duncanson, C. (2015). Hegemonic masculinity and the possibility of change in gender relations. *Men and Masculinities, 18*(2), 231–248.
Duriesmith, D. (2016). *Masculinity and new war: The gendered dynamics of contemporary armed conflict*. London: Routledge.
Dyvik, S. L. (2016). *Gendering counterinsurgency: Performativity, embodiment and experience in the Afghan "theatre of war"*. London: Routledge.
Eichler, M. (2013). Gender and the privatization of security: Neoliberal transformation of the militarized gender order. *Critical Studies on Security, 1*(3), 311–325.
Elshtain, J. B. (1982). On beautiful souls, just warriors and feminist consciousness. *Women's Studies International Forum, 5*(3/4), 341–348.
Elshtain, J. B. (1987). *Women and war*. Brighton: Harvester.
Enloe, C. (1983). *Does khaki become you? The militarisation of women's lives*. Boston, MA: South End Press.
Enloe, C. (1993). *The morning after: Sexual politics at the end of the Cold War*. Berkeley, CA: University of California Press.

Enloe, C. (2000). *Bananas, beaches and bases: Making feminist sense of international politics* (Updated ed.). Berkeley, CA: University of California Press.

Enloe, C. (2007). *Globalization and militarism: Feminists make the link.* Rowman & Littlefield [second edition published 2016].

Fine, C. (2005). *Delusions of gender: The real science behind sex differences.* London: Icon Books.

Goldstein, J. (2003). *War and gender: How gender shapes the war system and vice versa.* Cambridge: Cambridge University Press.

Gramsci, A. (1971). *Selections from the prison notebooks.* London: Lawrence & Wishart.

Harrison, D. (2003). Violence in the military community. In P. Higate (Ed.), *Military masculinities: Identity and the state* (pp. 71–90). Westport, CT: Praeger.

Henry, M. (2015). Parades, parties and pests: Contradictions of everyday life in peacekeeping economies. *Journal of Intervention and Statebuilding, 9*(3), 372–390.

Herbert, M. S. (1998). *Camouflage isn't only for combat: Gender, sexuality and women in the military.* New York: New York University Press.

Heyns, C., & Borden, T. (2017). Unmanned weapons: Looking for the gender dimensions. In F. N. Aoláin, N. Cahn, D. F. Haynes & N. Valji (Eds.), *The Oxford handbook of gender and conflict* (pp. 376–389). Oxford: Oxford University Press.

Higate, P. (2003). *Military masculinities: Identity and the state.* Westport, CT: Praeger.

Higate, P. (2012a). Drinking vodka from the "butt-crack": Men, masculinities and fratriarchy in the private militarized security company. *International Feminist Journal of Politics, 14*(4), 450–469.

Higate, P. (2012b). "Cowboys and professionals": The politics of identity work in the private and military security company. *Millennium, 40*(2), 321–341.

Hockey, J. (2003). No more heroes: Masculinity in the military. In P. Higate (Ed.), *Military masculinities: Identity and the state* (pp. 15–25). Westport, CT: Greenwood Publishing.

Hooper, C. (2001). *Manly states: Masculinities, international relations, and gender politics.* New York: Columbia University Press.

Hutchings, K. (2007). Making sense of masculinity and war. *Men and Masculinities, 10*(4), 389–404.

Hynes, S. (1998). *The soldiers' tale: Bearing witness to modern war.* London: Pimlico.

Jordan-Young, R. M. (2011). *Brain storm.* Harvard, MA: Harvard University Press.

Khalili, L. (2011). Gendered practices of counterinsurgency. *Review of International Studies, 37*(4), 1471–1491.

Kirby, P., & Henry, M. (2012). Rethinking masculinity and practices of violence in conflict settings. *International Feminist Journal of Politics, 14*(4), 445–449.

Leatherman, J. (2011). *Sexual violence and armed conflict.* Cambridge: Polity Press.

Maringa, G. (2017). Gendered military identities: Army deserters in exile. In R. Woodward & C. Duncanson (Eds.), *The Palgrave international handbook of gender and the military* (pp. 289–302). London: Palgrave Macmillan.

Masters, C. (2005). Bodies of technology. *International Feminist Journal of Politics,* 7(1), 112–132.

Mathers, J. (2013). Women in state militaries. In C. Cohn (Ed.), *Women and wars: Contested histories, uncertain futures* (pp. 124–145). Cambridge: Polity Press.

Messerschmidt, J. W., & Rohde, A. (2018). Osama Bin Laden and his jihadist global hegemonic masculinity. *Gender & Society, 32*(5), 663–685.

Morgan, D. (1994). Theatre of war: Combat, the military, and masculinities. In H. Brod & M. Kaufman (Eds.), *Theorising masculinities* (pp. 165–182). London: Sage.

Myrttinen, H., Khattab, L., & Naujoks, J. (2017). Re-thinking hegemonic masculinities in conflict-affected contexts. *Critical Military Studies, 3*(2), 103–119.

Myrttinen, H., Naujoks, J., & El-Bushra, J. (2014). *Re-thinking gender in peacebuilding.* London: International Alert.

Niva, S. (1998). Tough and tender: New world order, masculinity and the Gulf War. In M. Zalewski & J. Parpart (Eds.), *The 'man question' in international relations* (pp. 109–128). Boulder, CO: Westview.

Obradovic, L. (2014). *Gender integration in NATO military forces: Cross-national analysis.* Farnham: Ashgate.

Oxlund, B., Østergaard, L. R., & Kayonde, G. N. (2010). Men in uniforms: Masculinity, sexuality and HIV/AIDS in Western Rwanda. *Journal of Psychology in Africa, 20*(4), 601–611.

Parpart, J. (2015). Militarized masculinities: Heroes and gender inequality during and after the nationalist struggle in Zimbabwe. *NORMA: International Journal for Masculinity Studies, 10*(3–4), 312–325.

Parpart, J., & Partridge, K. (2014). Soldiering on: Pushing militarized masculinities into new territory. In M. Evans, C. Hemmings, M. Henry, H. Johnstone, S. Madhok, A. Plomien & S. Wearing (Eds.), *The SAGE handbook of feminist theory* (pp. 550–565). London: Sage.

Razack, S. (2004). *Dark threats and white knights: The Somalia affair, peacekeeping and the new imperialism*. Toronto: University of Toronto Press.

Rones, N. (2017). Theorizing military masculinities and national identities: The Norwegian experience. In R. Woodward & C. Duncanson (Eds.), *The Palgrave international handbook of gender and the military* (pp. 145–162). London: Palgrave Macmillan.

Ruddick, S. (1983). Pacifying the forces: Drafting women in the interests of peace. *Signs, 8*(3), 471–489.

Sasson-Levy, O. (2002). Constructing identities at the margins: Masculinities and citizenship in the Israeli army. *Sociological Quarterly, 43*(3), 357–383.

Segal, L. (1997). *Slow motion: Changing masculinities, changing men* (2nd ed.). London: Virago.

Shefer, T., & Mankayi, N. (2007). The (hetero)sexualisation of the military and the militarisation of (hetero)sex: Discourses on male (hetero)sexual practices among a group of young men in the South African military. *Sexualities, 10*(2), 189–207.

Stachowitsch, S. (2015). The reconstruction of masculinities in global politics: Gendering strategies in the field of private security. *Men and Masculinities, 18*(3), 363–386.

Stern, M., & Zalewski, M. (2009). Feminist fatigue(s): Reflections on feminism and familiar fables of militarisation. *Review of International Studies, 35*(3), 611–630.

Theidon, K. (2009). Reconstructing masculinities: The disarmament, demobilization, and reintegration of former combatants in Colombia. *Human Rights Quarterly, 31*, 1–34.

Tickner, J. A. (2001). *Gendering world politics: Issues and approaches in the post-Cold War era*. New York: Columbia University Press.

Tidy, J. (2016). The gender politics of "ground truth" in the military dissent movement: The power and limits of authenticity claims regarding war. *International Political Sociology, 10*(2), 99–114.

Titunik, R. F. (2008). The myth of the macho military. *Polity, 40*(2), 137–163.

Welland, J. (2015). Liberal warriors and the violent colonial logics of 'partnering and advising'. *International Feminist Journal of Politics, 17*(2), 289–307.

Westendorf, J-K., & Searle, L. (2017). Sexual exploitation and abuse in peace operations: Trends, policy responses and future directions. *International Affairs, 93*(2), 365–387.

Whitworth, S. (2004). *Men, militarism, and UN peacekeeping: A gendered analysis*. Boulder, CO: Lynne Rienner.

Woodward, R. (1998). "It's a man's life!" Soldiers, masculinity and the countryside. *Gender Place and Culture, 5*(3), 277–300.

Woodward, R., & Duncanson, C. (Eds.). (2017). *The Palgrave international handbook of gender and the military*. London: Palgrave Macmillan.

Woodward, R., & Winter, T. (2007). *Sexing the soldier: The politics of gender and the contemporary British Army*. London: Routledge.

Wright, H., & Welsh, P. (2014). *Masculinities, conflict and peacebuilding: Perspectives on men through a gender lens*. London: Saferworld.

46

Ecological masculinities

A response to the Manthropocene question?

Martin Hultman and Paul Pulé

Introduction

According to current global scientific debates, the human species has become a potent geological force that is destroying the living conditions of our own and many other species on Earth. This is tightly coupled with a new epoch broadly termed the 'Anthropocene', or human-induced changes in the climate and environment that scholars alternatively refer to as the 'Sociocene', 'Technocene', 'Homogenocene', 'Econocene', 'Plantationocene' and 'Capitalocene', to be replaced by a kin-inducing 'Chthulucene' (Angus, 2016; Haraway, 2015). Providing further resistance to human homogenisation and our alarming impact on the planet, others have pointed out that this epoch is also awash with gendered inequities (Di Chiro, 2017; Gibson-Graham, 2011; Haraway, 2007; Harcourt & Nelson, 2015; Raworth, 2014). Recently, Kate Raworth raised an important question: 'Must the Anthropocene be a Manthropocene?'. She suggested that we must not only name our present epoch the Anthropocene but also propose solutions to the pressing issues of our time by critically considering certain kinds of masculinities that socialise (mostly, but not exclusively) men to act in ways that are profoundly destructive towards the sovereignty of human and other-than-human others or 'otherised others' (Warren, 2000, p. 43). These destructive notions of masculinities might be considered 'industrial/breadwinner masculinities' (Hultman & Pulé, 2018). Unsurprisingly, it is the same fraternity of mostly men accompanied by masculinist notions of internalised superiority over otherised others that characterises climate change denial (Anshelm & Hultman, 2014) and has been identified recently as consistent with the core characteristics of a conservative and right-wing 'white male effect' (Krange et al., 2018). Sadly, these masculinist affronts to life-sustaining policies and practices are not isolated; they are finding purchase amongst those reformist leaders of governmental climate negotiations as well. This second group of (generally) well-intended global leaders are closely affiliated with the development of government policies and practices or hold top management positions in transnational corporations that shape those agendas. They prioritise the research, design and geo-engineering of planetary solutions to the world's social and environmental problems (Fleming, 2017; Hultman, 2013). Such individuals (again, mostly but not exclusively men) can be considered representatives of 'ecomodern masculinities'. Such an analysis aligns with ecological feminist research that has been cross-examining these and related concerns for more than 40 years (Buckingham, 2004).

Research across masculinities politics has, until now, focused on issues such as class, sexualities, violence, crime, education, family, popular media, militarism and justice (Connell & Pearse, 2015; Hultman & Pulé, 2018; Kimmel, 1994; Kimmel et al., 2005). One of the first studies to problematise and link 'hegemonic masculinities' with environmental issues was Raewyn Connell's (1990) sociological study of male rural environmental leaders, which we revisit in more detail momentarily. Beyond this and a growing number of recent publications on the topic (Allister, 2004; Enarson & Pease, 2016; Gaard, 2017; Hultman, 2013; Hultman & Pulé, 2018; MacGregor, 2017; MacGregor & Seymour, 2017; Pulé, 2013; Pease, 2014; Requena-Pelegrí, 2017; Salovaara, 2015), the specific intersection between environmental politics and masculinities studies has been comparably scant (Gaard, 2014).

In this chapter, we consider the notion of necessary configurations beyond the constraints of industrial/breadwinner and ecomodern masculinities, in support of a transition from hegemonisation to ecologisation. We suggest our notion of ecological masculinities as a constructive response to the roles of men and masculine identities in the Manthroprocene. The exit politics central to our notion of ecological masculinities represent a theoretical framework and plurality of practices reflective of what we see as a masculine ecologisation process (Hultman & Pulé, 2018). Before elucidating ecological masculinities, we provide a brief critical assessment of industrial/breadwinner and ecomodern masculinities, given their respective influential configurations on the social, economic, political and environmental conditions across the Global North. These two distinct masculine configurations represent 'unmarked' (i.e., normalised) categories whose social and environmental impact on the world is hidden by the systems that created and continue to maintain them (MacGregor, 2017). We follow this analysis by introducing ecological masculinities as a relational category, based on care for the glocal commons—a term highlighting the confluence of globalisation and localisation that has been in use since the 1980s—which stresses the benefits of simultaneously universalising and particularising our consideration of social and environmental problems. While the former two masculine socialisations continue to dominate, they both also exemplify constrained configurations of modern Western masculinities, exposing their mutually problematic contributions to global fecundity, not only in reference to human and otherised others, but for men and masculinities as well.

The violence of industrial/breadwinner masculinities

The most dauntless supporters (and beneficiaries) of Western industrial extractivism as well as climate change denial are men (Hultman, 2017). For our purposes, the term 'industrial/breadwinner masculinities' is used here interchangeably with Western 'patriarchal', 'hegemonic' and 'normative' masculinities (which we apply primarily to men, but also to the masculinities adopted by women and non-binary/genderqueer people). We use the term 'industrial' to refer primarily to those individuals who possess and manage the means of production and support service corporations at the highest levels of their control, and who are handsomely rewarded by the wealth-creating practices that these industries generate. Some of the most visible examples of these kinds of masculinities manifest in fossil fuel and mining executives, financial managers and bankers, corporate middle and senior level managers and administrators—the vast majority being Western, white and male (Connell, 2017). We also include shareholders in this category, since they reap the corporate profits of the companies that they have invested in, recognising that the demographics of this group can be quite variable and therefore levelling our critique primary at majority shareholders who also tend to be Western, white and male. The term 'industrial' also notes the ways that broader social and environmental implications of industrialisation are backgrounded for the sake of capital growth. The term 'breadwinner' refers to those workers who operate the means of production at the behest of those who possess and control industrial productivity. They include employees at the 'coalface' of primary extractive industries, the junior and middle-level managers of that productivity, as well as the workers and managers of support services that enable primary productivity to flourish; effectively bonding them to industrialists in a socio-economic co-dependency. These masculinities are comprehensively unmarked (their privileges, relative to those of women, non-binary/genderqueer people and otherised others, are so conspicuous and mainstreamed as to be invisible or normalised) and represent fraternities of men and masculine identities that are the most characteristic of modern Western malestream personae.

One of the planet's most pressing environmental concerns provides us with a clear example of the importance of developing a critical analysis of industrial/breadwinner masculinities: climate change denial. The link between industrial/breadwinner masculinities and climate change denialism exposes a rift between these unmarked renditions of modern Western malestreams and Earthcare. The mere suggestion that we live on a vulnerable planet that is being rapidly transformed by anthropogenic factors such as carbon emissions has sparked strong protests, particularly on the part of those who stand to gain the most from unfettered industrialisation, and whose gendered identities, unsurprisingly, are aligned most strongly with industrial/breadwinner masculinities as we define them here (Anshelm & Hultman, 2014; Hultman & Pulé, 2018; Supran & Oreskes, 2017). Previous studies demonstrate that climate denialism is created by small groups of (mostly white and Western) men who are intricately interwoven with socialisations of masculine hegemonisation, representing overt characterisations of malestream socio-economic and political mechanisms. As concerns for climate change have gained momentum, climate denialism, particularly from this cadre of corporate and industrial allies and beneficiaries, has been ramped up in response (Hultman & Anshelm, 2017). Consider the way that research within ExxonMobil confirmed already in the 1980s the severe consequences of emissions from coal, oil and gas, but was intentionally downplayed by the company's management in order to extend markets and preserve profits (Supran & Oreskes, 2017). Aligned with manipulative trends such as this, industrial/breadwinner masculinities advocate for the wholesale elimination of policies and practices that would otherwise regulate industrial productivity within sustainable limits, despite the fact that such regulation could pull us back from a perilous global climatic precipice by dispensing with fossil fuels in favour of renewables as one key strategy to prevent atmospheric run-away effects (Hultman & Anshelm, 2017). Many politicians and scholars in environmental politics thought this configuration was on its way out, but current political influences of fossil fuel lobbying in alignment with recent rises in nationalism, populism, white supremacy and neo-fascism throughout the Global North, has moved climate change denial and industrial/breadwinner masculinities to centre stage in the upper echelon of influential nations, most notably in the US under the Trump administration and Brazil under Bolsonaro (Hultman et al., forthcoming).

Greenwashed ecomodern masculinities

Ecomodern masculinities are co-joined with reformist responses to environmental concerns. They represent a category of masculinities that are distinguishable from industrial/breadwinner masculinities. These masculine identities pervade leadership roles in local, regional and international social and environmental policy reform as well as corporations engaged in techno-fixes and clean energy innovations that aim to engineer solutions to our pressing social and environmental problems.

Ecological modernisation can be considered an assemblage of organised responses that pay lip-service to the costs of industrialisation on human societies and the ecological integrity of Earth by offering watered-down pathways to protect and preserve economic growth while also offering measured care for society and environment (Adler et al., 2014; Hultman & Yaras, 2012). The movement has been championed in particular by men located in the highest positions of regulatory control and has remained beholden to the profit motif of corporate capitalism by placing too much attention on the machinations of production and trade while offering minimal mitigation for the woes of working families and the plethora of ecosystems that our survival and prosperity depend upon, regardless of wealth and standards of living (Hultman, 2013).

Ecomodern masculinities typically valorise sustainability in alignment with neoliberalism. While distinct from industrial/breadwinner masculinities in a willingness to seek compromise, ecomodern masculinities have emerged paradoxically: aligning with courage, global responsibility and determination, increased care for the glocal commons but also remaining adherent to market forces. In this sense, we consider ecomodern masculinities to be a masculinist bind of sorts. Consider the example of Elon Musk. Claiming pride of place as a popular visionary, Musk is broadly hailed as the 21st century's 'smartest entrepreneur' and a man with great passion for the radical and broad-scale implementation of socially and environmentally conscious innovations. He is renowned for a slew of pro-environmental strategies that aim to 'make the world a greener and better place' by using technology to extend the 'good life' to all (Fiegerman, 2017). But a profitable implementation of Musk's innovations as broad and comprehensive strategies for change expose a reliance on technofixes – such as electric cars, expanding demands for increased growth fed by social, economic and political enmeshments – all of which are fundamentally reliant upon industrial extractivism of Earth's natural resources. David Abraham (2015) is one of many who have noted that even solar panels are energy intensive and rare-earth-mineral dependent, as are many of the essential components of the Tesla vehicles. The marketing strategy used to sell the Tesla electric vehicles include ecomodern notions such as 'unparalleled performance', 'long range', 'safe', 'exhilarating', 'stress free', 'ludicrously fast', 'quick', 'ample', 'capable', 'uncompromised' and 'real' (Tesla, 2017). The hidden environmental costs come with individual costs alike, as Musk's health has taken a toll when choosing the company instead of wellbeing (Lyons, 2018).

To take a deeper, broader and wider approach to societal and self-care, we argue that we must push further than the greenwash of ecomodern masculinities. In the following sections, we introduce a third category of masculinities that accelerates a shift towards raised levels of care for the glocal commons. We discuss our four fields of inspiration that form the foundations of an ecologised masculinities theory and point to a plurality of associated practices that we refer to as ecological masculinities.

Ecological masculinities: combining knowledge from four traditions

As we work towards introducing ecological masculinities, we gather knowledge from four previous important research traditions. We recognise that they are not the only resources that lend relevance to masculine ecologisation, but they represent those that have been our greatest influences. They are masculinities politics, deep ecology, ecological feminism and feminist care theory.

Masculinities politics

The first stream that has significantly informed our formulation of ecological masculinities is research on masculinities across a politicised terrain broadly considered masculinities politics. This field of study represents a diverse set of perspectives that have emerged about men and masculinities along with their impacts on those who are otherised (Hultman & Pulé, 2018). We particularly acknowledge Australian sociologist Raewyn Connell, who not only examined the complexities and consequences of hegemonic masculinities through her publications (Connell, 1987, 1995) but also examined the impacts of hegemonic masculinities on the human/nature relationship in a pivotal paper titled 'A Whole New World: Remaking Masculinity in the Context of the Environmental Movement' (1990; see also, 2017). Connell has been key in arguing that men have legitimised male domination to such an extent that their positions of domination have been both institutionalised and embodied through hierarchical, heteronormative, aggressive, competitive and homosocial networks that advantage men and exclude women (and non-binary/genderqueer people as well) and are so pervasive that they persist in socially and environmental justice communities too (Connell, 2017). Her analysis of male domination holds true in reference to the human/nature relationship as well, where the social and environmental impacts of masculinist hegemonies become normalised within the context of the institutionalised systems that have created them. We bring three core tenets of Connell's work to our vision of ecological masculinities: the importance of plurality, an understanding of hegemony and frontal examinations of the ways that ecology can facilitate exit politics for men in particular as well as for humans in broader terms.

Deep ecology

Deep ecology was introduced by Arne Næss, who focused on raised self-awareness, nature reverence and care for Earth (1973). Næss strove to bring an end to anthropocentrism (or human-centeredness) and argued that humans should understand themselves as intrinsically part of nature. Deep ecology encourages us to consider personalised and intimate encounters with nature and our deep selves as guides in this discovery. Through a deep ecological lens, an ecosophy (or personalised Earth wisdom) amplifies the ways that Earth care emerges from phenomenologies of humans as unavoidable and unique Earthlings. Agreeing with Næss in bringing humanity onto a level playing field with the rest of life and its many complex processes, it is this deeper valuing of each other, otherised others and ourselves as inescapably interdependent with all life that we also subscribe to as a valuable component of ecological masculinities. Such ontological reasoning made a comeback in academic discussions in the beginning of the 21st century through traditions such as material feminisms, posthumanities and science and technology studies (Hultman & Pulé, 2018).

However, deep ecology has long been steeped in controversy. William Cronon (1995) criticised the assumptions of some deep ecologists that wilderness is the otherised out there. He exposed the deep ecological reflection of human power over nature (especially with the rise of agricultural innovations) as dependent on our own demise if equity amongst all life is to emerge. Implicit in such critiques of deep ecology was a lack of structural analyses, suggesting romanticised (even juvenile) understandings of the complexities that our species has manufactured and relied upon in order to assert our primacy over otherised humans and the planet (Cronon, 1995). In *Nature Ethics: An Ecofeminist Perspective*, Marti Kheel (2008) argued that the pervading gender myopia of male environmental leaders marked the need for ecological feminism to be positioned as a feminist-inspired environmental revolution, that deep ecology, beyond Næssian agility, failed to fully embrace. This is an important reflection that helps us to distinguish ecological masculinities from deep ecology. Where Næss was transcendent towards social constructivist views of the world that effectively skipped over structural (esp. gendered) analyses, we acknowledge and honour the presence of 'masculine', 'feminine' and 'other' identities within all humans, recognising that while these terms are in and of themselves problematic in pulling us towards gendered stereotypes, they also strongly influence the ways we self-identify and translate those identities into the human/nature engagements. They are, after all, laden with notions of masculinised 'asserting' juxtaposed against feminised and otherised (non-binary/genderqueer) notions of 'yielding'. We argue for a closer alignment with the core tenets of ecological feminism in ways that Næss's deep ecology did not (Diehm, 2003, p. 30). Ecological masculinities prioritise the structural significance of gender politics reflected in language as much as praxes, noting that these contributions to a deep green future are too great to be relegated to individual, gender-attuned ecosophies. It is our view that gendered analyses must remain central to any structural transformation towards a deep ecologically inspired praxes that prioritise social and environmental justice for all life.

Ecological feminism

As our third stream of influence, ecological feminism brings rich, diverse and foundational leadership to our understandings of the hubris of hegemonic masculinities. While peppered with an array of, at-times conflicting, ecofeminist views (i.e., various interpretations of ecological feminist theory), the metanarrative of ecological feminism created a bulwark against androcentrism (or male-centredness) further to the anthropocentrism catechised by deep ecology (Plumwood, 1993). Ecofeminists remind us that everyone is not treated equally. For example, those who are regionally and/or internationally wealthy are more complicit in generating (and benefitting from) social and environmental inequities. This is a notion that ecological feminism has been championing since the inception of the discourse in the early 1970s (Cuomo, 2017). From a plurality of ecofeminisms, we recognise acute (and understandably at-times impatient) views about the contemporary impacts of men's sexism and environmental mastery on otherised humans and others, the ways these mechanisms of domination have become institutionalised and what we might do about the resultant dire circumstances they have manifested. While we acknowledge the historical role of rebuttals of malestream masculinities such as this, we refute essentialist interpretations that characterise some binary ecofeminists who locked onto alleged notions of women as innately caring in ways that, biologically speaking, men are not, effectively cornering all men as bad and wrong socio-politically and ecologically speaking. Looking beyond these essentialist views as the vast majority of ecofeminist scholars do, we seek structural solutions to the problems we face that translate some of the core tenets of ecological feminism into discourses on men and masculinities. In doing so, we seek to accentuate the capacity of any and all men and masculinities to participate in exit politics towards a deep green future (MacGregor & Seymour, 2017).

Within the ecological feminist discourse, important developments of queering ecofeminisms pioneered by Catriona Sandilands (1994) and Greta Gaard (1997) (and some other queer ecologists) inspire us the most. Sandilands (1994) raised fresh questions about the roles of gays, lesbians, bisexual and queers in environmental movements, acknowledging the distinct voices that these various constituencies represent. Leveraging off Anne Cameron's call for a 'profound "queering"' of ecopolitics when it is subjected to 'poly sexual scrutiny', she proceeded to highlight the paradoxical everythingness and nothingness of queers as 'boundary-creatures' that problematises our addictive adherence to the dualistic hierarchies of gendered power and politics (Sandilands, 1994, pp. 21–22; also see Mortimer-Sandilands & Erickson, 2010). In doing so, Sandlilands made a strong case for understanding the queerness of nature. Gaard's (1997) 'Towards a Queer Ecofeminism' captured the important intersecting terrain between conceptualisations of ecofeminisms and queering of gendered terrains. Gaard's investigations of nature stood alongside her critical views of colonialism and logics of domination. In doing so, she identified the limits and stretched the bounds of the well-intended deconstructions of heterosexism that permeated ecofeminisms. Her analyses exhorted queers to become visible and in doing so to declare the rich texture of their lives and the unique views they bring forth about moving through the world (Gaard, 1997; also see Gaard 2017). In this sense, Gaard tilled the intersecting terrain between ecofeminist and queer theories, championing critical views of male domination through her consideration of the inward and erotic along with the expansive and diverse at the same time. Developments in queer ecologies, which find their foundations in such views, are now gathering renewed momentum.

Further and offering some of the freshest contributions to queer ecologies, Nicole Seymour challenged prejudices that frame trans people as '"unnatural"—not just generally against "Mother Nature's" plan, as lesbian, gay, and bisexual people [and others] are often considered, but also literally, physically constructed through medicine, technology, or even toxicity' (2017, p. 255). Seymour recognised the positive influence of material feminism but struggled with the troublesome tendency in that discourse to call us back to limited binary views of women's and men's 'real' bodies contrasted against the less prescriptive realities of trans people that pervade queer realities and interrogations of identity. She turned instead towards 'organic transgenderism' as a possibility which 'emerges from an expanded ecological consciousness and environmental ethics' (Seymour, 2017, p. 257).

These post-gendered threads influence the ontological base for masculine ecologisation and its plurality of emergent praxes as well. The grounded theories that emerged and gained momentum as ecological feminism (and the queer ecologies that arose from them) matured, help us anticipate levels of multiplicity, steering us away from essentialist/deterministic and towards social/structural understandings of ecological masculinities. Further and consistent with the wisdoms of ecological feminism, the conceptual and political implications of this insight must be accompanied by personalised and embodied practices as well.

Feminist care theory

Domestic and familial performances by women have been traditionally bolted t
notions of care. Feminist care theory has both troubled and sought solutions to thi
tion for some time and as a consequence is a fourth tradition that has shaped e
culinities. We touch on understandings of ethics of care drawn from broa
the concept. In our most recent work on ecological masculinities (H
we seek masculine applications for feminist care theory that reach
and (at times) essentialist views of feminist care theory that we
Gilligan (1982) and Nel Noddings (1984).

Maria Puig de la Bellacasa (2015) suggested that care is an embodied phenomenon constantly enacted with materialities. Care compels us to get involved in our lives and the environments we are steeped in, in very concrete ways. For example, we both care for (feel caringly towards someone or something) and care about (through the tangible expressions of our actions) our partner's needs, our children's education, our homes, our gardens, our pets etc. In doing so we are motivated to value others and behave accordingly. Care calls us to support others generously; to be of service to what we consider to be righteous and good. Care is present in all human beings in one way or another and was likely instrumental in the very survival of our species' and in this sense it is in fact not gendered. However, our socialisations shape the scope of our expressions of care and directly impact the ways we manifest it in our daily lives. Thom Van Dooren (2014) suggested that care emerges as an important concept shaping our interactions with our environment from global to local scales. Van Dooren (2014, p. 293) noted that 'care is a vital concept for an engaged environmental humanities.' In this sense, care can be a great motivator, driving us to act selflessly, at times beyond the limits of rational thinking towards selflessness as we encounter human and otherised others.

We need to not only re-direct masculine care broadly (which is evident considering the most toxic of structural institutions such as the Trump administration) but also ensure that the parameters of that care are broadened, deepened and widened (which is not characteristic of such overtly paternalistic institutions). In doing so, we proceed to bring men and masculinities to the very heart of a deep green future for all life. Such is our conceptualisation and praxis of ecological masculinities.

Ecological masculinities: from hegemonisation to ecologisation

While industrial/breadwinner masculinities have scathing impacts on people and the planet, and ecomodern efforts have delivered some limited (but far from transformative) successes across the globe, deprivations of Earth's fecundity persist. This calls for the need for continued creativity to seek truly effective solutions to the problems we face.

Throughout this chapter ... d that masculine hegemonisation thrives from the slow violence ... curing such a crucial piece in the puzzle of our ... es off the table—the broader care for the glocal ... modern Western standards of living (which ... enges to malestream primacy) and the internal- ... n, which have served Western white wealthy ... and environmental care as women's business. ... mistakes of the past? One key response to ... gical grounding of masculinities is plural, ... ised masculine frameworks and praxes, as ... nswer is to admit that masculine hegemo- ... gs regardless of the bodies and identities ... as relevant to the human/nature relation- ... ling and being willing to move beyond ... at the slow malestream ecocide towards ... heart of our social and ecological prob- ... me from elaborating on the ways we ... to normalise practices of social and

environmental justice as inherent to and substitutive for socialisations of men and masculinities.

Ecological masculinities is proposed as alternative to industrial/breadwinner hegemonies and ecomodern reforms. We have argued that the potential to expose and non-violently resolve the anthropocentric discord between Earth, others and ourselves is possible within our very constructs of manhood and masculine identities. For this reason, we consider the 'ecological' metaphor along with its literal meanings to be an appropriate term to use not only as a noun but also as a verb. In doing so, we have focused our attention on the need for men and masculinities to 'ecologise' relationally and create more caring encounters with self and others that bring us closer to a deep green future. Through the variable applications of this term, ecological masculinities prioritises relationality that recognises our material interconnectedness with humans and other-than-humans alike. In this chapter we have aimed to create a pathway for men and masculinities to break free from the magnetic binds of male domination and participate more fully in the task of caring for our common future. Doing so points us in the opposite direction of the alarming trajectories of a looming Manthropocene, acknowledging the costs of male domination and marking the currently unmarked implications of malestream masculinities that open us, in profound and deep ways, to the relational benefits for all life.

References

Abraham, D. (2015). *The elements of power: Gadgets, guns, and the struggle for a sustainable future in the rare metal age.* New Haven, CT: Yale University Press.

Adler, F., Beck, S., Brand, K., Brand, U., Graf, R., Huff, T., & Zeller, T. (2014). *Ökologische Modernisierung: zur Geschichte und Gegenwart eines Konzepts in Umweltpolitik und Sozialwissenschaften.* Frankfurt: Campus Verlag.

Allister, M. (Ed.). (2004). *Ecoman: New perspectives on masculinities and nature.* Charlottesville, VA: University of Virginia Press.

Angus, I. (2016). *Facing the Anthropocene: Fossil capitalism and the crisis of the earth system.* New York: Monthly Review Press.

Anshelm, J., & Hultman, M. (2014). A green fatwā? Climate change as a threat to the masculinity of industrial modernity. *NORMA: International Journal for Masculinity Studies, 9*(2), 84–96.

Buckingham, S. (2004). Ecofeminism in the twenty-first century. *The Geographical Journal, 170*(2), 146–154.

Connell, R. (1987). *Gender and power: Society, the person, and sexual politics.* Stanford, CA: Stanford University Press.

Connell, R. (1990). A whole new world: Remaking masculinity in the context of the environmental movement. *Gender & Society, 4*(4), 452–478.

Connell. R. (1995). *Masculinities* (2nd ed.). Cambridge: Polity Press.

Connell, R. (2017). Foreword: Masculinities in the Sociocene. In S. MacGregor & N. Seymour (Eds.), *Men and nature: Hegemonic masculinities and environmental change* (pp. 5–8). Munich: RCC Perspectives.

Connell, R., & Pearse, R. (2015). *Gender in world perspective* (3rd ed.). Cambridge: Polity Press.

Cronon, W. (1995). The trouble with wilderness: Or, getting back to the wrong nature. In W. Cronon (Ed.), *Uncommon ground: Rethinking the human place in nature* (pp. 69–90). New York: W. W. Norton & Co.

Cuomo, C. (2017). Sexual politics in environmental ethics: Impacts, causes, alternatives. In S. Gardiner & A. Thompson (Eds.), *The Oxford handbook of environmental ethics* (pp. 288–300). New York: Oxford University Press.

Di Chiro, G. (2017). Welcome to the white (m)Anthropocene? A feminist-environmentalist critique. In S. MacGregor (Ed.), *Routledge handbook of gender and environment* (pp. 487–505). Milton Park: Routledge.

Diehm, C. (2003). Natural disasters. In C. Brown & T. Toadvine (Eds.), *Eco-phenomenology: Back to the earth itself* (pp. 171–185). Albany, NY: State University of New York Press.

Enarson, E., & Pease, B. (Eds.). (2016). *Men, masculinities and disaster.* Milton Park: Routledge.

Fiegerman, S. (2017, October 4). Elon Musk to Quit Tesla, jumps on a Bitcoin tech startup. *CNN Tech*. Retrieved from http://cnn-newsreport.com/Elon-Mask-invests-72-million-on-a-bitcoin-tech-startup/.

Fleming, J. (2017). Excuse us, while we fix the sky: WEIRD supermen and climate engineering. In S. MacGregor & N. Seymour (Eds.), *Men and nature: Hegemonic masculinities and environmental change* (pp. 23–28). Munich: RCC Perspectives.

Gaard, G. (1997). Towards a queer ecofeminism. *Hypatia*, *12*(1), 114–137.

Gaard, G. (2014). Towards new ecomasculinities, ecogenders, and ecosexualities. In C. Adams & L. Gruen (Eds.), *Ecofeminism: Feminist intersections with other animals and the earth* (pp. 225–240). New York: Bloomsbury Publishing.

Gaard, G. (2017). *Critical ecofeminism*. Lanham, MD: Lexington Books.

Gibson-Graham, J. (2011). A feminist project of belonging for the Anthropocene. *Gender, Place and Culture*, *18*(1), 1–21.

Gilligan, C. (1982). *In a different voice: Psychological theory and women's development*. Cambridge, MA: Harvard University Press.

Haraway, D. (2007). *When species meet*. Minnesota, MN: University of Minnesota Press.

Haraway, D. (2015). Anthropocene, Capitalocene, Plantationocene, Chthulucene: Making kin. *Environmental Humanities*, *6*(1), 159–165.

Harcourt, W., & Nelson, I. (Eds.). (2015). *Practising feminist political ecologies: Beyond the 'green economy'*. London: Zed Books.

Hultman, M. (2013). The making of an environmental hero: A history of ecomodern masculinity, fuel cells and Arnold Schwarzenegger. *Environmental Humanities*, *2*(1), 79–99.

Hultman, M. (2017). Natures of masculinities: Conceptualising industrial, ecomodern and ecological masculinities. In S. Buckingham & V. le Masson (Eds.), *Understanding climate change through gender relations* (pp. 87–101). London: Routledge.

Hultman, M., & Anshelm, J. (2017). Masculinities of climate change. Exploring examples of industrial, ecomodern and ecological masculinities in the age of Anthropocene. In M. Cohen (Ed.), *Climate change and gender in rich countries* (pp. 19–34). London: Routledge.

Hultman, M., Björk, A., & Viinikka, T. (forthcoming). Far-right and climate change denial: Denouncing environmental challenges via anti-establishment rhetoric, marketing of doubts, industrial/breadwinner masculinities enactments and ethno-nationalism. In B. Forchtner, C. Kølvraa & R. Wodak (Eds.), *Contemporary environmental communication by the far right in Europe*. London: Routledge.

Hultman, M., & Pulé, P. (2018). *Ecological masculinities: Theoretical foundations and practical guidance*. Milton Park: Routledge.

Hultman, M., & Yaras, A. (2012). The socio-technological history of hydrogen and fuel cells in Sweden 1978–2005: Mapping the innovation trajectory. *International Journal of Hydrogen Energy*, *37*(17), 12043–12053.

Kheel, M. (2008). *Nature ethics: An ecofeminist perspective*. Lanham, MD: Rowman & Littlefield.

Kimmel, M. (1994). Masculinity as homophobia: Fear, shame, and silence in the construction of gender identity. In H. Brod & M. Kaufman (Eds.), *Theorizing masculinities* (pp. 119–141). London: Sage.

Kimmel, M., Hearn, J., & Connell, R. (Eds.). (2005). *Handbook of studies on men and masculinities*. Thousand Oaks, CA: Sage.

Krange, O., Kaltenborn, B. P., & Hultman, M. (2018). Cool dudes in Norway: Climate change denial among conservative Norwegian men. *Environmental Sociology*, *5*(1), 1–11.

Lyons, K. (2018, August 17). Tesla's stock falls sharply after Elon Musk reveals "excruciating" year. *The Guardian*. Retrieved from www.theguardian.com/technology/2018/aug/17/elon-musk-says-past-year-has-been-excruciating-and-worst-is-yet-to-come.

MacGregor, S. (Ed.). (2017). *Routledge handbook of gender and environment*. Milton Park: Routledge.

MacGregor, S., & Seymour, N. (Eds.). (2017). *Men and nature: Hegemonic masculinities and environmental change*. Munich: RCC Perspectives.

Mortimer-Sandilands, C., & Erickson, B. (Eds.). (2010). *Queer ecologies: Sex, nature, desire*. Bloomington, IN: Indiana University Press.

Næss, A. (1973). The shallow and the deep, long-range ecology movement: A summary. *Inquiry*, *16*(1/4), 95–100.

Noddings, N. (1984). *Caring: A feminine approach to ethics & moral education*. Berkeley, CA: University of California Press.

Pease, B. (2014). Reconstructing masculinity or ending manhood? The potential and limitations of transforming masculine subjectivities for gender equality. In A. Carabí & J. Armengol (Eds.), *Alternative masculinities for a changing world* (pp. 17–34). New York: Palgrave Macmillan.

Plumwood, V. (1993). *Feminism and the mastery of nature*. London: Routledge.

Puig de la Bellacasa, M. (2015). Making time for soil: Technoscientific futurity and the pace of care. *Social Studies of Science*, *45*(5), 691–716.

Pulé, P. 2013. *A declaration of caring: Towards ecological masculinism* (Doctoral dissertation). Murdoch University, Perth.

Raworth, K. (2014, October 20). Must the Anthropocene be a Manthropocene? *The Guardian*. Retrieved on October 5, 2017 from www.theguardian.com/commentisfree/2014/oct/20/anthropocene-working-group-science-gender-bias?CMP=Share_iOSApp_Other.

Requena-Pelegrí, T. (2017). Green intersections: Caring masculinities and the environmental crisis. In J. Armengol & M. Vilarrubias (Eds.), *Masculinities and literary studies: Intersections and new directions* (pp. 143–152). New York: Routledge.

Salovaara, H. (2015, October). Male adventure athletes and their relationships to nature. Poster presented at *The Seventh FINSSE Conference*, Vaasa, Finland. Retrieved from www.researchgate.net/publication/303234498_Male_Adventure_Athletes_and_Their_Relationship_to_Nature.

Sandilands, C. (1994). Lavender's green? Some thoughts on queer(y)ing environmental politics. *UnderCurrents: Journal of Critical Environmental Studies*, *6*, 20–25.

Seymour, N. (2017). *Strange natures: Futurity, empathy, and the queer ecological imagination*. Urbana, IL: University of Illinois Press.

Supran, G., & Oreskes, N. (2017). Assessing ExxonMobil's climate change communications (1977–2014). *Environmental Research Letters*, *12*(8), 1–18.

Tesla. (2017). Retrieved from http://tesla.com.

Van Dooren, T. (2014). Care: Living lexicon for the environmental humanities. *Environmental Humanities*, *5*(1), 291–294.

Warren, K. (2000). *Ecofeminist philosophy: A western perspective on what it is and why it matters*. Lanham, MD: Rowman & Littlefield.

47

Masculinity and/at risk

The social and political context of men's risk taking as embodied practices, performances and processes

Victoria Robinson

Introduction

Risk and risk taking have been particularly theorised in relation to hegemonic forms of masculinity. This has been in the context of symbolic and material behaviours, subjectivities, relationships and practices. Traditionally, 'real men' are, therefore, those who do not display fear or vulnerability when faced with risky situations such as scaling a rock face, engaging in armed combat or in other extreme and everyday situations where to lose face is to lose identity (Robinson, 2008). Nor do they want to appear 'out of control' or too emotional, if 'at risk' themselves from, for example, economic, social and political changes, shifts in ideological constructions of masculinity or challenges from feminism (Hearn, 1993). Therefore, risk must be 'masterfully' managed.

Besides being 'masterfully' managed, risk has been seen to be controlled, resisted and sometimes reformulated by men, across diverse contexts and sites (see Borden, 2001; Coleman, 2015; Dyck, 2000; Mellström & Ericson, 2014; Robinson & Hockey, 2011; Tulloch & Lupton, 2003). Theorists have discussed topics such as mental and physical health, sport, sexuality, violence, conflict, migration and occupational and financial risks, amongst others, in the light of these different ways of conceptualising how risk is both experienced and performed. Such discussions have raised some fundamental issues and questions about masculinity itself, gender relations, how risk is related to structures and structural constraints and how it may be negotiated differently across the life course, as well as in response to ever increasing and rapidly changing political, economic, social and cultural circumstances.

Further, a focus on men's risk and risk taking allows key concepts in critical masculinity studies to be investigated and expanded, including the so-called 'crisis' in masculinity, and it affords debates with feminism and gender relations to be more fully explored than hitherto. In addition, the focus on intersectionality necessary to theorising risk can illuminate it in relation to diverse masculinities in embodied practices. Theorising risk in these ways can also reveal that risk taking (or indeed, avoiding risk) can afford men agency, and this idea is brought into sharp relief when it is acknowledged that risk-taking behaviours can be seen as both involuntary and, in some specific activities and behaviours, voluntary.

Therefore the concept of 'voluntary risk taking' will also be utilised in in this chapter to examine this hegemonic 'mantra' for men, as the concept allows for a focus on men actively seeking out risk. Risk has been seen to be actively promoted in the performance of hegemonic masculinities in sporting and other diverse contexts, and there is research particularly on young men in this respect (see Curry & Strauss, 1994; Robinson, 2008, 2013; Summers, 2007). However, some embodied sites, such as extreme sports, allow for such risk taking to be problematised and to investigate if alternative masculinities are produced in such sporting contexts. That is, the very notion of risk taking itself allows for traditional masculine stereotypes to be reinvented.

The theoretical exploration of risk has been both conceptual and empirical across different sites and spheres. In addition, the theorising across different spheres and sites of masculinity and risk has altered over time and become more nuanced, across structural, individual and global levels. This can be seen across a number of substantive areas, discussed below, where risk is located in specific and rapidly changing historical and cultural locations. Moreover, research presented here on risk can be seen to support an argument that if risk and transition are linked together, then risk itself can be conceived of as a process. Therefore, the intensity of risky behaviours and practices are seen to vary across the life course and in connection to economic, political and social constraints, which can be explored in new ways than previously.

A focus on masculinity can also help interrogate the way in which the notion of risk itself previously has been imagined and conceptualised. For instance, it is important to consider a range of men's risk experiences; how research on men, masculinity and risk is increasingly (if not yet fully) informed by intersectionality; and how normative discourses of race, class, sexuality and age construct cultural imaginaries around masculinity and risk, as well as their impact on men's experiences and risk-taking behaviour.

Firstly, therefore, this chapter considers the wider theoretical context for risk and risk taking which has been established in recent times (Beck, 1999; Lyng, 2005; Tulloch & Lupton, 2003). It is important to initially acknowledge that feminist and other scholars, most notably critical studies of men and masculinity theorists, have seen men as a threat and risk to the wellbeing and safety of women and other non-hegemonic men. I then go on to explore some of the literature which has established the diverse economic, social, sexual and cultural links between men, masculinities and risk taking. The view that men themselves are at risk through their risk-taking attitudes, behaviours and identities will also be investigated. As Ulf Mellström and Mathias Ericson (2014, p. 147) cogently argue:

> Risk connotes a longstanding gendered 'leitmotif' in most, if not all societies, where risk taking and mastering fear are closely connected to masculine heroism and accompanying cultural imaginaries. In many ways, masculinity as a gendered configuration conflates with acts of courage, mastering fear, and risk 'management'. As such, the connection between masculinity and risk is multilayered, ranging from the becoming subject to structural organisation and global risk taking. Masculinity at risk is thus intentionally an ambiguous construction that points in various directions and raises many questions.

These interrelated strands – the traditional links between men, masculinity, risk and risk taking, men at risk to others as well as a critical exploration of the idea of men themselves being 'at' risk as a group and at risk to themselves – will form the overarching framework for my argument.

Contextualising risk and risk taking

A central premise at the heart of both theoretical and policy discussions has been the question of how modern societies both experience and respond to emerging social, economic, cultural, technological and natural challenges. Risk and risk taking have, in recent years, been a fundamental topic and area of debate within the disciplines and have informed global policy decisions on a range of (gendered) issues, ranging from health, the use and purpose of technology and the environment, to name but a few (Lash, 2000; Tulloch & Lupton, 2003). Furthermore, international political and economic uncertainty, increasing lack of trust in experts and institutions, climate change and associated natural disasters have increased the complexity of everyday life for individuals. The effects of this differ according to gender and other variables such as class, race and ethnicity, age, dis(ability) and sexuality. This complexity can be seen to manifest itself in an array of choices, which can bring ambiguity and confusion and the creation of an unnecessary risk society or, conversely, an antipathy to any forms of risk taking. However, it can also arguably be seen to increase (gendered) agency and reflexivity.

It has been argued by Åsa Boholm (2015) that risk itself is a construct which is shaped by social, economic, political and cultural contexts. According to her, this means that the perception, management and communication of risk is situated in relation to both culturally informed and socially embedded knowledge and experiences. She also acknowledges how risk (and for my purposes, gendered risk) is interpreted in society by men and women based on their identities, norms and values in relation to their everyday worlds, and how risk needs also to be seen in the context of globalization.

Meanwhile, John Tulloch and Deborah Lupton (2003) highlight the importance of Scott Lash's (1993, 2000) call to explore how diverse groups, including those of gender class, race and ethnicity, age and their intersections respond to risk in aesthetic and emotional ways. Thus I will draw attention here to a number of areas where men's relationships and different located experiences of risk have been seen as important to investigate. This, Tulloch and Lupton argue, affords more chances of fluid and interchanging ways of viewing risk, which also draw on men's embodied and affective judgements.

Of interest to any discussion of men, masculinity, risk and risk taking is Stephen Lyng's (2005) assertion that risk-taking experiences are engaged in to escape different and increasingly more complex aspects of contemporary life; or, as he puts it: as 'an especially pure expression of the central institutional and cultural imperatives of the emerging social order' (2005, p. 5). Elizabeth Silva and Tony Bennett (2004), moreover, note that in globalised, modern societies there exists both risk and choice. In their view, it is in the sphere of the everyday where these complexities are best able to be observed. Thus the structural constraints alongside men's agency in relation to risk and risk taking need to be discussed, through a number of substantive areas as raised below.

Men and risk

As I noted at the start, feminists clearly have a long and well-established theoretical and empirical tradition of seeing men as putting women and less hegemonic men, such as gay men, at risk. This has been theorised and data has been collected on topics such as violence, reproductive rights, inequality at work, family relationships, sexuality and migration, to name but a few (see Robinson & Richardson, 2015). As well, as already noted, risk taking has been connected to hegemonic forms of masculinity (see Connell, 2000; Messner, 1992; Robinson & Hockey, 2011). In a Western context, an early study by Stanley Cohen (1972/2011) utilised the concept of moral panic and looked at how British young male subcultures such as mods and rockers were viewed and defined by the media and those with political power as being dangerous to others through their subcultural activities. Cohen argued, using the concept of the deviancy amplification spiral, that those in authority exaggerated the risks these groups posed to others. The notion of moral panic has been used more recently in reference to marginalised groups of men, such as migrants, to explain people's fear and stereotypical beliefs that migrant men, in particular, are more likely to commit crime, bring drugs into the country and are constructed as potential rapists in comparison to local men (see Rumbaut, 2016; Wojnicka, this volume). Rubén Rumbaut provides data for the US context to show that, on the contrary, immigrants, including those who are undocumented, are less likely to commit crime or be imprisoned than those who are native born. He suggests that the prejudice inherent in this erroneous assumption can be explained by centuries-old and lingering colonialist attitudes.

More recently, and relating to another area, David Duriesmith (2016) in discussing masculinity, war and conflict argues that risk taking is seen as essential to forging men into being effective in combat. Further, in conflict situations this risk taking is accompanied by emotional detachment and aggressive performance. Masculinity is constructed on both institutional/structural levels, for example, through male bonding exercised during training and on a personal level. This risk taking extends to men risking their own wellbeing and lives but also the lives of others on the battlefield (see also Morgan, 1992). Lauren Jencik (2016), for example, researching traumatization and masculinity in conflict in Eastern Congo, maintains that men are trapped in a cycle of not seeking assistance when traumatised, due to a perceived stigma of not being seen as 'masculine' enough. She further argues that greater attention to men and women's different experiences of trauma needs to account for socio-demographic aspects of ethnicity, including age, ethnicity, education and income.

Another area which has received attention regarding masculinity and risk is the sexual sphere. In a study of young men, risk and sexuality in the Caribbean, David Plummer (2013) argues that taking risks serves to define youthful masculinity and is both sought out and experienced as a 'rite of passage'. He also found that risk was intimately connected to masculinity, but issues of safety were not. Being sexually active often meant not using condoms, with a risk of a female partner becoming pregnant or the attendant risks surrounding sexual health for both partners. Similarly, Alethea Jeftha's views (2006), concerned with how young men construct their masculinities and the interrelationship of this on adolescent male risk-taking behaviour and a macho culture in the context of South Africa's high HIV/AIDS rates, found that at least some notions of culturally specific hegemonic masculinities had power over their identity construction and everyday experiences.

Risk taking in the sexual sphere has also been theorised in relation to how structures such as the Church influence men's experiences dealing with the risk of contracting and living with of HIV and AIDS, as research in Botswana highlights. Muse Dube (2012) argues that the Church needs to engage with men more, in an effort to change ideas about manhood and sexual risk. Therefore, risk is seen here as constructed at the level of organizations, as well as through personal perceptions and the cultural imaginary.

Though there is a body of literature which has started to look at young men and risk, as the examples specifically in relation to sexuality above reveal, there does exist a growing body of work on older men and risk, even if this is not as prevalent. One area which has received recent attention is around midlife and older men's risk taking in relation to sexual performance and Viagra consumption. Barbara Marshall (2006) argues that the post-Viagra 'men's health' industry expands the medicalisation of masculinity and male sexuality into later life. Therefore the aging male body is seen, in this way, primarily in terms of disorder and dysfunction. Further, Raffaella Camoletto and Chiara Bertone (2012) argue that this medicalisation of male sexuality has the effect of renaturalising men and restoring their assumed biological virility within the discourse around Viagra taking. It does this by emphasising gendered scripts of both respectability and risk-taking predatory male behaviour. However, Annie Potts et al. (2004) complicate this by arguing that older men have diverse 'Viagra stories' and that these narratives have the potential to disrupt reductionist and mechanistic accounts of male bodies, sexuality and risk taking. So a focus on risk in this context allows for discussion of masculinity as ideologically constructed but also potentially fluid.

A different area where dominant constructions and enactments of masculinity have been critically linked to risk is in the world of finance and management. Early studies include, for example, Cliff Cheng's (1996) work on how masculinities are constructed in organisations where risk taking is celebrated if it brings the desired status and profits to individuals and organisations. Later studies such as Penny Griffin's (2013) have explored current economic contexts such as the global financial crisis and how men's power and privilege are bound up with their risk taking in ways which fundamentally underpin capitalism. The importance of seeing risk in this specific field in emerging technological contexts is noted by Devin Mills and Lia Nower (2019). Because men gamble more than women, according to them, advances in technology are important to note, as the concept of the male risk taker takes on new meanings in rapidly changing online environments.

The studies already referred to reveal that masculinities, risk and risk taking are interconnected, socially sanctioned, discursively constituted and individually embodied and experienced. Further, they can be seen to have been centrally concerned with exploring and critiquing hegemonic masculinity, the construction of sexual and other identities in both public and private spheres and the impact of different men's risk-taking behaviour on others. This includes not only the institutional forming of particular types of masculinity through encouraged stereotypical masculine traits and behaviours and the rewards but also the costs of men adhering to such scripts.

Attention therefore has turned more recently to the issue of men being 'at risk' themselves, due, in part, to how risk can be seen to be sutured in new ways into the very fabric of (hegemonic) masculinities in rapidly changing social, cultural, economic, political and ideological contexts. This potentially allows for a more nuanced exploration of men's ambiguity in relation to risk, incorporating more emphasis on men's reflexivity and agency, their vulnerability as well as power, the increased recognition of the importance of an intersectional perspective on these issues and an awareness of the interrelatedness of local and global sites. I will return to the topic of masculinity and sexuality in the next section, as it is frequently impossible to separate out when men are at risk to others or to themselves, as some of the examples referred to illustrate.

Men at risk

In this context, much recent theoretical debate and empirical research, worldwide, has been concerned with men's health and wellbeing, given that men traditionally visit a doctor less often than women and die on average earlier than women. Schlichthorst et al. (2016) argue that men's emphasis on self-reliance entails that their reticence to seek out medical help, even when they know they would benefit from doing so. Haider Warraich and Robert Califf (2017), for example, elaborate on 'toxic masculinity' and the effect of hegemonic masculinity on men's life expectancy. Indeed, an overarching view of researchers on the links between health and masculinity is that masculinity serves as a risk factor, not a buffer across diverse health contexts (Levant & Wimer, 2014).

Suicide is the single biggest killer of men under 45 in the UK – 84 take their own lives every week (Mackay, 2018). Other research has linked men to being three times more at risk of suicide than women in the UK (The Samaritans, 2017). A study on migrant men and mental health in Canada by Hilario et al. (2018) found that there were negative implications for their mental health among some of the young men interviewed. They spoke of the effects of the glass ceiling and discrimination at work and the depression that accompanied being seen as a 'perpetual foreigner' by others. More generally, previous studies in this area have offered views that socio-demographic factors, such as socio-economic position and employment status, are factors which influence men's suicide rates (Pirkis et al., 2017).

However, as Emma Cueto (2016) observes, though men have a higher suicide rate than women, the elderly, non-Hispanic white men have a higher rate of suicide than men from other racial and ethnic backgrounds. Cueto found that this is despite having greater economic resources than older men of colour, and better physical health than older women. In support of this view, Silvia Canetto (2017) argues that it is white, older men who may be seen to be psychologically less well equipped to cope with the normal challenges of aging, due to privileges they enjoy up until late adulthood. Arguably, therefore, they can be seen as at greater risk of suicide.

In another area, Haroon Siddique (2017) points to recent studies in the UK which argue that men in the most traditional 'masculine' jobs are at a greater risk of taking their own lives, such as construction workers. This is prompting new measures to overhaul workplace cultures and convince them to seek help. Thomas Thurnell-Read and Andrew Parker (2008), Hernan Ramirez (2011) and Ericson (2014) all take forward this idea of men and risk taking in occupational practices. Moreover, Nathan Blair's (2013) account of how white working-class stereotyped hegemonic masculinity is represented in reality TV programmes, which, for instance, have centred on men in high-risk occupations such as trawler men in the UK; Dag Balkmar's (2014) work on Swedish working-class men's conception of risk and class in a Swedish car community further expand debates in this sphere.

As indicated previously, risk and risk taking have been theorised in the context of masculinities and sexuality. Yet a renewed focus here on men *at* risk in this context allows for a complexity of issues such as ethnic differences, gender relations and men's reflexive understanding of theirs' and others' risk taking to be located in relation to challenging and shifting economic, political and (gendered) ideological discourses.

I have demonstrated that a wide range of literature exists that shows how imperatives to 'prove' masculinity, through the prevalence of the male 'sexual drive' discourse, is salient in shaping hegemonic masculinities – heterosexual prowess is also shown through men having multiple partners and the proliferation of cultural discourses which men draw on to legitimise such performances. In this respect, Shari Dworkin (2015) is concerned with the costs to men, not just their female partners, through the lens of heterosexuality. She sees this as shaping men's HIV risks through these heterosexual norms. Anders Ragnarsson et al.'s (2010) study sees men at high risk of HIV, where masculine norms and biologically essentialist discourses prevail despite a high risk of HIV transmission, fuelled by similar discourses and practices.

These examples of research on sexuality, ethnicity and risk reveal that men are sometimes simultaneously at risk to others *and* at risk to themselves. Moreover, Tamara Shefer et al. (2015) argue that it has been a largely deterministic discourse on men's sexuality and masculinity that informs cultural understandings of adolescent male sexuality, making assumptions that young women are vulnerable and therefore powerless, whilst young men are also viewed as inevitably powerful and the perpetrators of sexual violence. Thus they argue for more complex ways of understanding young men and risk, in that the situation of their precariousness and vulnerability needs to be acknowledged and addressed by scholars.

The issue of male violence against other men is also important to address, as men are themselves often at risk of violence, either death or injury, at the hands of other men. Much research on this issue focuses on men living in urban settings, but rural men also show a relatively high risk of causing harm to others and also to themselves (Carrington & Scott, 2008). In South Africa, the highest cause of mortality among poor young black men is violence and/or murder by other men, which is then manifested through crime, gang activity and endemic violence. Rebecca Davis (2017) documents that male perpetrators of violence attack women, children and men but that the victims are predominantly other men. She agrees that we need to 'disentangle masculinity' and that destructive stereotypes of what it means to be an 'authentic' man must be resisted. Instead, men have to be able to be viewed as vulnerable and as victims, if the reality that men in South Africa are five times more likely to be murdered than women is to be tackled. Further evidence of men's vulnerability can be seen in the context of male violence in prison. Sasha Gear (2010) found that the dominant male prison culture in South Africa endorses rape and long-term relationships of sexual abuse by legitimising violence and is informed by traditional ideologies of gender and sexuality.

Another area which has started to be engaged with in relation to masculinity and men at risk is the proliferation of new technology, for example, with studies of the effects of the increased availability of pornography and video games. Philip Zimbardo (2015) argues that that young men's brains and social skills are being drastically altered by excessive use of video games and that this then affects men's ambiguous sense of themselves, which he links to a 'crisis in masculinity'. Such studies, though able to be critiqued as being overly behaviouristic, reveal the need to have a renewed, interdisciplinary dialogue between the social sciences and STEM subjects, given such technological and scientific developments.

Indeed, it is this acknowledgement of the ambiguity of men's diverse and intersectional identities, along with their inherent contradictions, which this and other studies already referred to have revealed, that allows masculinity and risk to be explored in a more nuanced and reflexive way than previously. Such studies also reveal that men who either voluntarily and consciously, or not, transgress hetero normative masculinities, such as gay men, run the risk of facing physical and psychological violence in everyday contexts and in more extraordinary sites that have been mentioned, such as prisons (see Schultz, 2018, for discussion of violence against gay men and the transgender community in India).

How transgressing hetero normative masculinity entails risk taking that may be more positive, both for men themselves and for their partners and families, can be seen by viewing masculinity and risk as both a process and a transition. In relation to sport, Lyng's (2005) notion of voluntary risk taking affords new theoretical and empirical directions to be taken, when risk is seen as process and is situated/contextualised. Further, risk can be seen as transitional when sporting participants' experiences and attitudes to risk activities change over the life course – on having children, for example – as well as across historical time, when societies construct risk and gender differently (see Joelsson, 2014; Robinson, 2008, 2013).

It is also important to note that theorists are turning their attention to men and risk taking across different spheres in different cultural contexts and outside of the sporting sphere. Nur Radzi et al.'s (2018) study of Malaysian men found that being a risk taker, as well as being perceived as competitive and independent, were becoming a more important signifier of masculinity than more traditional aspects such as body size or being the family provider in both professional and personal lives.

Conclusion

With recognition of this conceptual shift from men at risk to others to men at risk themselves, Mellström and Ericson (2014) argue for the wider relevance of theorising men, masculinities and risk: 'we are also convinced that theorising risk and risk-taking and masculinity is a productive way to address questions of power, difference, vulnerability and agency in masculinity studies and beyond' (p.150).

This emphasis allows for new directions in the study of masculinities, risk and risk taking, some of which I have identified above. These include an increasing emphasis on intersectionality and the importance of investigating risk globally and cross culturally; an awareness of rapidly changing political international contexts, such as the rise of the alt-right in the US and the far right in general internationally; increasing public discussions of 'toxic masculinity' via social media; the effects of globalisation and the mass movement of peoples and its local effects; and the need to theorise risk as a process over both historical and biographical time. Furthermore, the interaction of cultural discourses and constructed narratives of men, risk and risk taking with rapid technological advances and use of social media, and the increasing influence of this on men's embodied practices and performances, is another area of concern.

Finally, how to balance and address the inherent contradictions and tensions in seeing men simultaneously as posing risks to women and other less hegemonic men, being at risk as men as a group and being a risk to themselves, is a pressing challenge.

References

Balkmar, D. (2014). Negotiating the 'plastic rocket': Masculinity, car styling and performance in the Swedish modified car community. *NORMA: International Journal for Masculinity Studies, 9*(3), 166–177.

Beck, U. (1999). *World risk society*. Cambridge: Polity.

Blair, N. (2013). The working class heroes: Analysing hegemonic masculinity in occupational reality TV. *The Plymouth Student Scientist, 6*(1), 137–160.

Boholm, A. (2015). *Anthropology and risk*. London: Routledge.

Borden, I. (2001). *Skateboarding, space and the city*. Oxford: Berg.

Camoletto, R. F., & Bertone, C. (2012). Italians (should) do it better? Medicalisation and the disempowering of intimacy. *Modern Italy, 17*(4), 433–448.

Canetto, S. S. (2017). Suicide: Why are older men so vulnerable? *Men and Masculinities, 20*(1), 49–70.

Carrington, K., & Scott, J. (2008). Masculinity, rurality and violence. *British Journal of Criminology, 48*(5), 641–666.

Cheng, C. (1996). *Masculinities in organizations*. London: Sage.

Cohen, S. (1972/2011). *Folk devils and moral panics*. London: Routledge.

Coleman, D. (2015). Traditional masculinity as a risk factor for suicidal ideation: Cross-sectional and prospective evidence from a study of young adults. *Archives of Suicide Research, 19*(3), 366–384.

Connell, R. W. (2000). *The men and the boys*. Cambridge: Polity.

Cueto, E. (2016, January 6). Older white men more at risk for suicide, and hyper masculinity could be a big part of that, research suggests. *Bustle*. Retrieved from www.bustle.com/articles/133895-older-white-men-more-at-risk-for-suicide-and-hyper-masculinity-could-be-a-big-part.

Curry, T. J., & Strauss, R. H. (1994). A little pain never hurt anybody: A photo-essay on the normalization of sport injuries. *Sociology of Sport Journal, 11*(2), 195–208.
Davis, R. (2017, May 10). Analysis: How South Africa's violent notion of masculinity harms us all. *Daily Maverick*. Retrieved from www.dailymaverick.co.za/article/2017-05-10-analysis-how-south-africas-violent-notion-of-masculinity-harms-us-all.
Dube, M. W. (2012). Masculinities and violence in a HIV and AIDS context: Sketches from Botswana cultures and Pentecostal churches. In E. Chitando & S. Chirongoma (Eds.), *Redemptive masculinities: Men, HIV and religion* (pp. 323–353). Geneva: World Council of Churches Publications.
Duriesmith, D. (2016). *Masculinity and new war: The gendered dynamics of contemporary armed conflict*. London: Routledge.
Dworkin S. L. (2015). *Men at risk: Masculinity, heterosexuality, and HIV/AIDS prevention*. New York: New York University Press.
Dyck, N. (Ed.). (2000). *Games, sports and cultures*. Oxford: Berg.
Ericson, M. (2014). Firefighters as exceptional: Heroism, nationalism and masculinity in times of suburban riots and anti-racist protests. *NORMA: International Journal for Masculinity Studies, 9*(3), 178–190.
Gear, S. (2010). Imprisoning men in violence: Masculinity and sexual abuse: A view from South African prisons. *South African Crime Quarterly, 33*, 25–32.
Griffin, P. (2013). Gendering global finance: Crisis, masculinity, and responsibility. *Men and Masculinities, 16*(1), 9–34.
Hearn, J. (1993). Emotive subjects: Organizational men, organizational masculinities and the (de) construction of 'emotions'. In S. Fineman (Ed.), *Emotion in organizations* (pp. 142–166). London: Sage.
Hilario, C. T., Oliffe, J. L., Wong, J. P., Browne, A. J., & Johnson, J. L. (2018). "Just as Canadian as anyone else"? Experiences of second-class citizenship and the mental health of young immigrant and refugee men in Canada. *American Journal of Men's Health, 12*(2), 210–220.
Jeftha, A. (2006). *The construction of masculinity and risk-taking behaviour among adolescent boys in seven schools in the Western Cape*. (Unpublished master's thesis). Department of Women and Gender Studies, University of the Western Cape, Cape Town.
Jencik, L. (2016). Traumatization and masculinity in conflict: Understanding individual causes of violence in Eastern Congo. Unpublished manuscript, Tufts University, USA. Retrieved from https://tufts.academia.edu/LaurenJencik.
Joelsson, T. (2014). Careless men, careless masculinities? Understanding young men's risk-taking with motor vehicles as violations. *NORMA: International Journal for Masculinity Studies, 9*(3), 191–204.
Lash, S. (1993). Reflexive modernization: The aesthetic dimension. *Theory, Culture & Society, 10*(1), 1–23.
Lash, S. (2000). Risk culture. In B. Adams, U. Beck & J. Van Loon (Eds.), *The risk society and beyond: Critical issues for social theory* (pp. 47–62). London: Sage.
Levant, R. F., & Wimer, D. J. (2014). Masculinity constructs as protective buffers and risk factors for men's health. *American Journal of Men's Health, 8*(2), 110–120.
Lyng, S. (Ed.). (2005). *Edgework: The sociology of risk-taking*. London: Routledge.
Mackay, H. (2018, March 28). Male suicide: 'His death was the missing piece of the jigsaw'. *BBC News Online*. Retrieved from www.bbc.co.uk/news/uk-43572779.
Marshall, B. L. (2006). The new virility: Viagra, male aging and sexual function. *Sexualities, 9*(3), 345–362.
Mellström, U., & Ericson, M. (2014). Introduction: Masculinity at risk. *NORMA: International Journal of Masculinity Studies, 9*(3), 147–150.
Messner, M. A. (1992). *Power at play: Sports and the problem of masculinity*. Boston, MA: Beacon Press.
Mills, D. J., & Nower, L. (2019). Preliminary findings on cryptocurrency trading among regular gamblers: A new risk for problem gambling? *Addictive Behaviors, 92*, 136–140.
Morgan, D. (1992). *Discovering men*. London: Routledge.
Pirkis, J., Currier, D., Butterworth, P., Milner, A., Kavanagh, A., Tibble, H., … Spittal, M. (2017). Socio-economic position and suicidal ideation in men. *International Journal of Environmental Research and Public Health, 14*(4), 365.
Plummer, D. C. (2013). Masculinity and risk: How gender constructs drive sexual risks in the Caribbean. *Sexuality Research and Social Policy, 10*(3), 165–174.
Potts, A., Grace, V., Gavey, N., & Vares, T. (2004). 'Viagra stories': Challenging 'erectile dysfunction'. *Social Science & Medicine, 59*(3), 489–499.

Radzi, N. S. M., Hamid, B. D. H. A., & Bakar, K. A. (2018). The discursive construction of modern masculine identities in contemporary Malaysia. *GEMA Online Journal of Language Studies, 18*(3), 36–56.

Ragnarsson, A., Townsend, L., Ekström, A. M., Chopra, M., & Thorson, A. (2010). The construction of an idealised urban masculinity among men with concurrent sexual partners in a South African township. *Global Health Action, 3*(1), 5092.

Ramirez, H. (2011). Masculinity in the workplace: The case of Mexican immigrant gardeners. *Men and Masculinities, 14*(1), 97–116.

Robinson, V. (2008). *Everyday masculinities and extreme sport: Male identity and rock climbing*. Oxford: Berg.

Robinson, V. (2013). *Rock climbing: The ultimate guide*. Westport, CT: Greenwood Press.

Robinson, V., & Hockey, J. (2011). *Masculinities in transition*. Basingstoke: Palgrave Macmillan.

Robinson, V., & Richardson, D. (Eds.). (2015). *Introducing gender and women's studies*. (5th ed.). Basingstoke: Palgrave Macmillan.

Rumbaut, R. G. (2016, November 2). Zombie ideas and moral panics: Framing immigrants as criminal and cultural threats. Russell Sage Foundation Blog Series. Retrieved from www.russellsage.org/zombie-ideas-and-moral-panics-framing-immigrants-criminal-and-cultural-threats.

Schlichthorst, M., Sanci, L. A., Pirkis, J., Spittal, M. J., & Hocking, J. S. (2016). Why do men go to the doctor? Socio-demographic and lifestyle factors associated with healthcare utilisation among a cohort of Australian men. *BMC Public Health, 16*(3), 1028.

Schultz, K. (2018, June 2). Gay in India, where progress has come only with risk. *The New York Times*. Retrieved from www.nytimes.com/2018/06/02/world/asia/gay-in-india-where-progress-has-come-only-with-risk.html.

Shefer, T., Kruger, L. M., & Schepers, Y. (2015). Masculinity, sexuality and vulnerability in 'working' with young men in South African contexts: 'You feel like a fool and an idiot ... a loser'. *Culture, Health & Sexuality, 17*(s2), 96–111.

Siddique, H. (2017, March 17). Male construction workers at greatest risk of suicide, study finds. *The Guardian*. Retrieved from www.theguardian.com/society/2017/mar/17/male-construction-workers-greatest-risk-suicide-england-study-finds.

Silva, E., & Bennett, T. (Eds.). (2004). *Contemporary culture and everyday life*. Durham: Sociologypress.

Summers, K. (2007) Unequal genders: Mothers and fathers on mountains. In V. Robinson, (Ed.), *Special Issue of Sheffield Online Papers in Social Research: "Gender and Extreme Sports: The Case of Climbing"*, August, Issue 10.

The Samaritans. (2017). Suicide facts and figures. Retrieved from www.samaritans.org/about-samaritans/research-policy/suicide-facts-and-figures.

Thurnell-Read, T., & Parker, A. (2008). Men, masculinities and firefighting: Occupational identity, shop-floor culture and organisational change. *Emotion, Space and Society, 1*(2), 127–134.

Tulloch, J., & Lupton, D. (2003). *Risk and everyday life*. London: Sage.

Warraich, H. J., & Califf, R. (2017, June 26). Men still die before women: Is toxic masculinity to blame? *The Guardian*. Retrieved from www.theguardian.com/commentisfree/2017/jun/26/men-die-before-women-toxic-masculinity-blame.

Zimbardo, P. (2015). *Man disconnected: How technology has sabotaged what it means to be male*. London: Rider.

48

Trends and trajectories in engaging men for gender justice

Tal Peretz

Men are engaged around the world, individually and in groups, in working towards gender justice by preventing and responding to men's violence against women, challenging and educating other men, and shifting masculinity norms to create more egalitarian ways of being a man. This is truly a global project, with well-established organizations on every continent, ranging from Promundo in Brazil to Sonke Gender Justice Network in South Africa. There are countless groups in the United States, India, and Sweden, campaigns by worldwide organizations such as the #HeForShe campaign by the United Nations, global networks such as the MenEngage Alliance and the White Ribbon Campaign, and regular worldwide events such as the 2014 Global Symposium on Engaging Men and Boys, in Delhi, and the 2015 International Conference on Masculinities: Engaging Men and Boys for Gender Equality, in New York City. Thanks to these organizations and networks, we have increasingly been able to communicate, evaluate, and compare these programs globally, to find trends, learn from each other, and improve local efforts.

In this chapter I review the current state of men's anti-violence and gender justice engagements globally, outlining some general themes and synthesizing overarching concerns. I begin with the broad theories that help us think about men's gendered activism, then move to a discussion of some of the many overlapping paradigms that underlie men's anti-violence and gender justice work. I then move to a discussion of some of the issues facing men's engagement projects right now, including issues of accountability, evaluation, collaboration, and constituencies. Finally, I outline some issues that seem likely to be inherent in the project of engaging men in ending violence against women and undermining men's unequal power and privilege, and I draw together a few final conclusions.

Overarching theories

As men's engagement in anti-violence and gender-justice efforts has been increasingly valued, a growing literature has developed around it. The body of work now includes a historical empirical analysis of men's engagement in the United States over the last 50 years (Messner, Greenberg & Peretz, 2015), a global comparative analysis of men's engagements in different countries and contexts (Ruspini, Hearn, Pease & Pringle, 2011), and a collection intended to bridge the conversation between scholars and practitioners (Flood & Howson, 2015). A global research network called Mobilizing Men for Violence Prevention has formed and published numerous research articles (e.g., Tolman et al., 2016, 2019), and multiple special editions of academic journals have collected related research articles (Gibbs, Vaughan & Aggleton, 2015; *Global Social Work*, forthcoming). While there are certainly still significant gaps in our knowledge about engaging men (discussed below), a discursive foundation exists, and some overarching themes have arisen.

A few different theoretical perspectives help us understand men's place in gendered social movements. Key themes across these perspectives include seeing masculinity as socially constructed, as opposed to unchanging and intrinsic to male bodies, and multiple, with many different ways of performing masculinity, shaped by different social contexts, ideologies, and intersecting racial, sexual, religious, and class-based identities. These are important because they allow us to see the possibility of challenging and changing problematic masculine norms and behaviors, as well as offering an array of possible masculinities to draw inspiration from in altering harmful masculine norms.

Connell's hegemonic masculinity theory, embedded in a larger structural theory of gender orders, is especially useful in understanding where men's power within the gender order is vulnerable to change (1987; see also Connell & Pearse, 2014). Hegemonic masculinity is the socially ascendant form of masculinity, understood as the 'common sense' about appropriate manhood in a given time and social context; in most gender orders, this understanding of masculinity is used to justify the oppression of women and the subordination of marginalized men. This helps us recognize the diversity of masculinities and femininities and draws attention to relations of power between them. To Connell, there is no stable, unitary masculinity; masculinities must be understood as historical projects that function as part of a gender order, always defined in relation to femininities, with dominant masculinities also defined in relation to subordinated masculinities. The goal of masculinity movements, then, is not to 'end' or 'destroy' hegemonic masculinity but to shift the hegemonic ideals in support of their own ends.

Historically, men have responded to women's calls for equality in three ways: antifeminist, profeminist, and masculinist (Kimmel, 1987). Where antifeminist movements explicitly push to maintain men's dominance over women and profeminists support gender equity, masculinist movements respond to perceived feminization with calls for separate spaces where men can pursue an imagined 'pure' masculinity. Masculinist movements in the United States have included the Boy Scouts of America, the mythopoetic men's movement of the 1980's, and, most recently, Men Going Their Own Way[1] and the constellation of associated online communities (Kimmel, 1996; Nicholas & Agius, 2017).

A separate, overlapping lens for understanding men's political and social movements is the Terrain of Masculinity Politics, a triangular field that illustrates the three primary points of focus for men's gender politics: men's privileges and the benefits they receive from sexist social structures; the challenges and harms men experience from masculinity; and the differences and inequalities among men (Messner, 1997). Increasing focus on one point necessarily draws away from the others. This helps explain why groups that focus overmuch on the costs to men, especially when they lose sight of the structural and institutional arrangement of gender inequality in favor of individual experiences (and falsely equate men's and women's harmful experiences), tend to lose sight of sexism, male privilege, and the differences between men, often sliding into antifeminist 'Men's Rights' arguments. Messner therefore suggests that movements and groups working to engage men in gender-justice activism must balance these three points but that the greatest emphasis should remain on critiquing sexism, both institutional and individual, and undermining male privilege.

This lens has been useful in considering overarching strategies for engaging men in gender-justice work. Flood (2007) transformed this lens into three principles for engaging men. He suggests that men's groups should 1) be guided by feminism and framed with a feminist political agenda, in partnership with and accountable to women and women's groups; 2) enhance boys' and men's lives; and 3) acknowledge both the commonalities and diversities among men. Markus Theunert, President of the Confederation Swiss Men's and Fathers' Organizations, revises this further for a 'triple advocacy' model. Under this model, men's groups support women's rights and movements, involve men's vulnerabilities and concerns, and build partnerships and alliances around a wider range of issues linked to masculinities (everything from sports teams to racial-justice movements to barbershops).

It is important to recognize that, even in social movements addressing gendered violence, men actually have multiple—sometimes overlapping—positions. While men are frequently discussed as the perpetrators of gendered violence (and indeed, for most types of gendered violence, regardless of the gender of the victim, the perpetrator is much more likely to be a man), scholars have increasingly been focusing on men as victims (e.g., Ferrales, Nyseth Brehm & Mcelrath, 2016; Rumney, 2009), as passive or active bystanders (e.g., Banyard, 2011; Katz, Heisterkamp & Fleming, 2011), and as potential allies (e.g., Messner et al., 2015; Tolman et al., 2016, 2019). The groups and organizations discussed in the next section focus on this perspective, aiming to engage men in ending violence against women and bringing about a more gender equitable world.

Organizations and paradigms on the ground

The ways that men have been working for gender justice have become both institutionalized and diversified over time. In the United States, for example, there is record of men supporting women's efforts as far back as W. E. B. DuBois and Frederick Douglass' support of women's suffrage at the Seneca Falls Convention in 1848. Men marched alongside (or behind) women during the mass movement days of the 1970s, and soon after began formalizing and institutionalizing organizations and groups of their own with the specific mission of supporting women's equality and ending men's violence against women (Messner et al., 2015). Today there are men's anti-sexist groups of many different kinds, working around the world on a wide range of issues related to gender inequality, directed towards many different populations of men, taking many different approaches to these issues, and in some cases connected to transnational networks; their strategies vary in part to address local contexts, capacity, and goals (Carlson et al., 2015). The following discussion of these groups and the paradigms that guide their work is necessarily incomplete and simplified, selective, and subjective, but it is intended to highlight some of this diversity.

Perhaps the most common programmatic tactic is education and skill-building. Many different programs create workshops and classes that teach audiences, sometimes co-ed but often all-male, various skills and knowledge that support anti-violence and gender-justice goals. Relationship skills – such as cooperative problem-solving, nonviolent communication, and equitable relationship norms – are a clear place where educating men can have a direct relationship on the safety of women in their lives; the same is true of sexual-consent education, which includes definitions of consent, practice asking for clear consent, and challenging consent myths. Empathy-building programs specifically work to make the pain and hardships of sexual violence real to men, by having men imagine the impacts on their lives if a woman close to them were raped, or in some cases by having them listen to the experiences of men who have experienced sexual violence (Langhinrichsen-Rohling, Foubert, Brasfield, Hill & Shelley-Tremblay, 2011).

One specific version of skill-building is bystander intervention. Bystander intervention trainings attempt to turn male audience members from passive onlookers into active sentries prepared to avert or interrupt sexual assaults (Banyard, 2011). Approaching men as bystanders offers these programs a way out of addressing men as only either victims or perpetrators of violence, both of which create difficulties for men's participation. These presentations train audience members to look for 'red flags', such as repeatedly or insistently providing someone alcohol or isolating someone from their friends, and teach audience members nonconfrontational strategies for intervening, such as distracting the perpetrator or joining their conversation. While many bystander-intervention models focus on interrupting acts of sexual violence, others also prioritize undermining the sense of peer support for gender inequality by intervening in cases of sexist joking, sexualization and gendered insults towards women, and any other behaviors that support rape culture. Groups such as Mentors in Violence Prevention (founded in the United States but now operating internationally) posit that these interventions are even more effective if they come from high-status men, such as athletes and officers of men's organizations (Katz, Heisterkamp & Fleming, 2011). The hope is that engaging these high-status men and interrupting rape-supportive cultural tropes can shift social norms about acceptable and rewarded masculine behaviors.

Social norming campaigns are based on the idea that people are more likely to act in ways supported by the norms of their peers and that most men mistakenly believe that their peers are more supportive of sexual violence than is the case. By making it clear that most of their peer group supports healthy masculinities, consensual sex, bystander intervention, etc., social norming campaigns reduce the sense of peer support for sexist and violent behavior and hope thereby to reduce the prevalence of the behavior itself. Many organizations that work on college campuses in the United States include this as a part of their efforts, including Mentors in Violence Prevention and Men Against Violence. Posters that declare the high percentage of students who agree with statements like 'I would stop sexual activity if my partner was not excited about it' and t-shirts with phrases like 'Consent Tip #11: Does this feel good to you?' and 'I love consensual sex' are used to make it clear that there is widespread support for these norms. This principle is also at play in the entertainment-education programs of groups such as Breakthrough in India and anti-sexual-assault radio shows in Africa (Lapsansky & Chatterjee, 2013). Clearly, skill-building, bystander, and social-norming models often overlap and are used synergistically. The most effective campaigns are often multimodal, using in-person presentations and discussions, fliers and advertisements, word-of-mouth, social networking, etc.

An underlying concern in all of these programs is whether to use existing masculine norms such as strength, responsibility, and paternal protection of partners to draw men in, like the 'My strength is not for hurting, so when she said no I said OK' posters of the MyStrength campaign (California, USA) do, or whether this in fact reinforces harmful masculine norms and contradicts or undermines the overarching goal of gender equity (Gibbs, Vaughan & Aggleton, 2015; McGann, 2009; Murphy, 2009). Because efforts to use existing masculine norms risk reinforcing essentialist notions of masculinity (and of gender more broadly), this brings up a related concern at the theoretical core of these issues: the reinforcement or deconstruction of binary understandings of gender. While some men's engagement programs rely, whether uncritically or strategically, on using the logic of gender binaries, other programs attempt to deconstruct this binary sense of gender. Programs such as Sweden's Machofabriken (The Macho Factory) are based on the theory that without a binary gender system, one gender (men) cannot have oppressive power over another (women) and would have no reason to enact gendered/sexual violence (Jewkes et al., 2015). The tension between these two perspectives can also be finessed by insisting that 'the long-term aim of gender transformative interventions must be the removal of gender binaries, but [...] the short-term objectives of discrete interventions may be much more limited' (Gibbs, Vaughan & Aggleton, 2015, p. 89).

Explicitly gender-transformative intervention programs have been found to have positive effects on men's attitudes, behaviors, and outcomes in multiple areas related not only to sexual violence but also to sexual health and gender equality more broadly (Barker, Ricardo, Nascimento, Olukoya & Santos, 2010). Gender-transformative programs are those which overtly aim to transform gender norms and promote gender-equitable attitudes and practices, as opposed to those which accommodate gender differences without attempting to alter gender norms (gender-sensitive) and those which do not address gender or take it into account (gender-neutral). By directly engaging participants in critical reflection on the social construction of masculinities and the impacts of gender norms in their lives, these programs undermine the common fallacies about masculinity and provide both room and encouragement for participants to redefine masculinity for themselves, with the intention that the new masculinities they ascribe be less sexist and less violence-supportive.

Theatre has been used to bring anti-sexist messages to audiences in creative ways. InterAct, an interactive, skill-building sexual assault prevention program based in Long Beach, California, has actors portray authentic scenes of scenarios that may lead to sexual and relationship violence and then invites audience members to take the stage, become a character in the scene, and practice intervening in ways that they hope will prevent the violent event (Rich, 2010). In Cape Town, South Africa, the Sonke Gender Justice Network has used 'ambush theatre' to engage unknowing audiences in public spaces such as bus stations (Sonke Gender Justice, 2013). A small group of actors create the scene without letting on that they know each other and have rehearsed the scene: one man harasses a woman, another man loudly challenges him, and they get into a fight. Once the mock fight has drawn a crowd, they abruptly stop fighting and explain that all three of them are actors, hand out fliers about the campaign, and engage their audience in a conversation about street harassment and how to intervene.

Public story-sharing similarly works to highlight examples of positive masculinity, shows men critiquing harmful masculine norms, and provides role models and peer support to audiences. The personal connection and dramatic impact of storytelling draws audiences in and engages their emotions in changing their beliefs and behaviors; the authenticity and openness of the storytellers invite audience members to engage in similarly authentic and vulnerable ways. The American organization Men Can Stop Rape, for example, hosts Healthy Masculinity Campus Conversations, where a few men share personal stories of the effects of healthy and harmful masculinities in their lives and then invite audience members into a guided discussion (Men Can Stop Rape, 2011). The international program The Men's Story Project (Peretz, Lehrer & Dworkin, 2018; Peretz & Lehrer, 2019) includes storytelling through diverse artistic modes such as slam poetry and dance and invites local community resources and organizations to be a part of the debriefing process.

Some groups have formed with the intent of addressing the ways sexism and gender-based violence occur in marginalized communities. Black Men for the Eradication of

Sexism, Muslim Men Against Domestic Violence, and the Sweet Tea Southern Queer Men's Collective all take an intersectional perspective (all in Atlanta, Georgia, USA), having their conversations in ways that recognize and respond to the marginalization they face while addressing the particular gendered challenges facing their communities, including how men in their communities are privileged in particular ways and how women in their communities face multiple marginalization (Peretz, 2017). Their efforts include making sure that discussions of police brutality against African Americans include women sexually assaulted and killed by police, speaking out against interpretations of the Quran that are used to justify men's violence against women, or writing public documents that name the ways that gay men still receive male privilege.

Current issues in engaging men

Globally, there are some ongoing concerns that mark the project of engaging men in reducing gender inequality and gender-based violence. Recent conversations among those engaged in this work have frequently centered around the problems of accountability, intersectionality, evaluation, collaboration, expanding constituencies, and compassionate critique. While many of these issues have been present for at least 50 years of men's activism, it remains to be seen whether they are inherent whenever men get involved in this work.

While accountability generally expresses the idea of doing anti-sexist work in a way that is responsible and justifiable, making sure to not reproduce systems of inequality or reinforce masculine privilege, what this specifically means and looks like is very much debated. For example, if you are a man giving presentations to other men or boys in order to reduce gendered inequalities, who are you accountable to: some general sense of egalitarian ethics and behavior? the specific men and boys in your audiences? the people or institutions who fund your work? women or the feminist movement? if you're accountable to women, which ones? (since women often disagree about how to do this work). Other accountability concerns include: men learning to challenge each other's sexism; understanding male privilege and doing the internal work to stop enacting it—that is, curtailing privilege-related microaggressions like interrupting and speaking over women, assuming leadership competence, and taking up disproportionate space; men's groups competing for funding and resources with women's groups and specifically with support services for survivors of men's violence; making decisions without taking women's perspectives into account; etc.

Based on the lives and thoughts of Black women, intersectionality is the idea that axes of oppression such as race, gender, class, and sexuality overlap, interact, and are experienced simultaneously (see Christensen & Jensen, this volume). The classic example is that Black women experience sexism differently than white women do, and they experience racism differently than Black men do—but these ideas apply to men as well, and must be considered in order to engage them effectively (Peretz, 2017). For example, one classic illustration of masculine privilege is feeling safe walking alone at night, but this does not match the experiences of marginalized men who have to fear state violence or of gay/queer men who might reasonably fear heterosexist or cissexual violence. How do we have conversations that recognize and make space for these men's experiences of violence and marginalization while still holding them accountable for their behaviors that uphold gender inequality?

Moreover, there is the intersectional issue of which men are understood as violent, dangerous, problematically hypermasculine, or 'at risk' of becoming abusive partners. Socially privileged groups often use claims of sexism, hypersexuality, and inappropriate violence to marginalize and ostracize groups of men already subordinated due to their race, class, religion, caste, etc. The myth of the Black rapist in the United States, Western stereotypes about Muslim men, and colonial constructions of the global South all illustrate how, by setting up men of color as a demonized, hypersexist 'other', privileged groups of men construct themselves by contrast as good, egalitarian, civilized, etc. without having to confront or challenge their own sexism and violent behaviors. Moreover, as Ratele, Shefer & Botha explain with regards to efforts to engage men in South Africa, this discourse sets up gender-justice work as 'a Western, white, middle-class, and foreign import that challenge[s] African culture', a perception which can be 'used to legitimate certain patriarchal practices and serves to diffuse and delegitimize gender activism' (2011, p. 254).

Due to both a shortage of funding resources and difficulty connecting with the knowledge and expertise necessary, many men's engagement projects struggle to meaningfully evaluate the effectiveness of their programs. Evaluation is crucial for gauging effectiveness, understanding challenges, improving programs, and securing funding, so it is clearly a major concern—but the kinds of changes that gender justice projects with men aim towards are notoriously difficult to evaluate meaningfully. Recently, a few different organizations have approached this issue directly: the White Ribbon Campaign, a global organization originally based in Canada, has worked towards crafting an evaluation model specific enough to be helpful but flexible enough to be used across Canada and possibly internationally as well; the research network Mobilizing Men for Violence Prevention created a shareable online tool for evaluating single events; and the Center for the Study of Men and Masculinities in New York, USA, has worked to connect researchers and practitioners in the hopes of increasing evaluation quality. Still, many organizations are caught in a catch-22, as funders often desire or require evaluations but rarely fund them or provide the expertise necessary to do them well, meaning that evaluation research often needs to be funded before funding can be secured.

Collaborations between practitioners and researchers illustrate both the difficulties and the importance of collaborations more generally. Collaborations with women and women's groups are clearly important. Collaborations with groups that organize around other issues that impact men's lives, from fatherhood to racial justice, can also increase the reach and effectiveness of groups that work to engage men. Creative collaborations can help connect violence-prevention projects with local communities, as in the case of the Buzz for Safety workshops run at local men's barbershops by the Center for Hope and Healing in Lowell, Massachusetts, USA. Of course, collaborations also magnify and multiply the concerns of accountability: if you collaborate with a group, how are you accountable to them? Do you become accountable for their actions if they do something problematic? Are there strategic possibilities for collaborations with groups that might otherwise function to protect male privilege and enforce domination, like sports teams or the military?

Getting more men involved in advocacy around issues previously seen as 'women's concerns' is already an expansion of the constituency involved in these issues. However, it is coming to also mean reaching new groups of men who have not previously been included (which brings back the idea of intersectionality), as well as getting men who are not directly involved in gender-justice organizations to change their beliefs and behaviors around gender. New men's engagement projects are beginning in Turkey, Tanzania, North Africa, and Arab countries, while others are expanding the age range at which we engage men, reaching into high school and junior high age groups.

Finding ways for men to open up about their own lives, discuss their pain and vulnerability, and feel listened to and recognized is an important step in getting them to engage and change their beliefs and behaviors (Gibbs, Vaughan & Aggleton, 2015). As masculinities scholar and philosopher Harry Brod put it at the International Conference on Masculinities in 2015, 'we never talk people into changing, we listen them into changing'. The idea of compassionate critique is key in thinking about how to engage men and address the harms they experience from masculinity and gender inequality while still maintaining accountability and a focus on the disproportionate impacts negative harms of gender inequality for women. Compassionate critique is also important in addressing the issue of anti-feminist men, some of whom are men with real wounds and legitimate grievances but who misdirect their feelings, blaming women or a misguided notion of feminism because they have not been provided with any other way of making sense of their lives. The challenges here include distinguishing the ideologues from the genuinely hurting, keeping systemic inequalities and social power in view, and figuring out how to make the crucial transition from discussing men's pain to feminist analyses of gender and power.

Inherent problems in engaging men

There are some problems in men's gender-justice organizing that do seem to be inherent and unchanging. Some of these are the same kinds of problems any social movement organization might face: funding, resources, membership, leadership, communication, connecting with audiences and keeping their interest, making a longstanding issue continue to feel relevant, and navigating push-back from counter-movements. Some of them, though, are specific to this movement. There is an inherent contradiction in using male privilege to undermine male privilege, which is at the heart of the project of engaging men. This shows up in the long, difficult, and imperfect process individual men must go through to examine and alter their own sexist socialization, as well as the microaggressions most men unknowingly enact in feminist spaces. It shows up in the difficulty many men have in reconciling the difficult realities women live with, exactly those things that gender-justice movements attempt to alter, with their own experiences. It is part of the pedestal effect, wherein men receive disproportionate attention, praise, gratitude, and respect for their efforts towards gender justice, even when only repeating what women have said or done for decades (Peretz, 2018). Even when the men themselves do everything they could do correctly, men's presence often still garners more media attention and can dilute the central messages of anti-sexist and anti-violence campaigns because of the way the wider society sees these issues (Kretschmer & Barber, 2016).

Conclusions

What can we expect as men increasingly become involved in gender-justice work? More men will mean more resources, reach, and positive impact, but they are likely to continue bringing the myriad problems of sexist social structures in with them. Men's engagement programs respond directly to the structures of the society around them (Carlson et al., 2015; Messner et al., 2015) and indeed seem to be more effective the more they are able to directly address local realities. Programs in Africa do best when they respond to the racial context and geographical distances (Dworkin, 2015; Gibbs, Vaughan & Aggleton, 2015); programs in India are shaped by literacy rates and development funding (Verma et al., 2006); programs in countries with high HIV rates productively collaborate with HIV education and prevention efforts (Barker et al., 2010; Dworkin, 2015; Gibbs, Vaughan & Aggleton, 2015; Verma et al., 2006); and programs in America struggle with the race, class, and religious segregation there (Peretz, 2017). One other local reality that is easy to overlook because of its ubiquity is that, in every society, there are local forms of gender inequality and sexist behaviors that will also shape the men's engagements. Because of this, as long as sexism is built into social structures, engaging men will be an imperfect endeavor.

There is no perfect approach to the work. Tensions are inherent in the project of engaging men, so it is important not to let perfect be the enemy of good. A key task for scholars and activists, therefore, is to better understand the limitations of men's engagements and strategize ways to maximize the benefits while minimizing the risks and harms.

Note

1 Boy Scouts of America was founded in 1910 among a wave of 'boy's lib' organizations, with the intention of getting boys together in the woods, among men and away from perceived feminizing influences, to learn 'manly' skills like fire building and archery (Kimmel, 1996). The mythopoetic men's movement, notably influenced by poet Robert Bly, brought groups of men together for spiritualist retreats to perform rituals and find a tribalistic 'deep masculine' and reclaim power they perceived to be lost to feminism, post-industrial capitalism, and modernity/post-modernity. An offshoot of the online Men's Rights/Men's Power Movement, Men Going Their Own Way focuses creating 'safe spaces' for men and encouraging them to defend their individual 'sovereignty' by avoiding relationships with women, who are seen as powerful, overbearing enemies who deceptively take advantage of men. All of these movements rely on essentialist ideas of gender and position women/femininity as weakening and harming men while necessarily ignoring the power imbalances, violence, and exploitation between men.

References

Banyard, V. L. (2011). Who will help prevent sexual violence: Creating an ecological model of bystander intervention. *Psychology of Violence, 1*(3), 216–229.

Barker, G., Ricardo, C., Nascimento, M., Olukoya, A., & Santos, C. (2010). Questioning gender norms with men to improve health outcomes: Evidence of impact. *Global Public Health, 5*(5), 539–553.

Carlson, J., Casey, E., Edleson, J. L., Tolman, R. M., Walsh, T. B., & Kimball, E. (2015). Strategies to engage men and boys in violence prevention: A global organizational perspective. *Violence Against Women, 21*(11), 1406–1425.

Connell, R. (1987). *Gender and power: Society, the person and sexual politics*. Cambridge: Polity.

Connell, R. W., & Pearse, R. (2014). *Gender: In world perspective* (3rd ed.). Cambridge: Polity.

Dworkin, S. L. (2015). *Men at risk: Masculinity, heterosexuality and HIV prevention*. New York: New York University Press.

Ferrales, G., Nyseth Brehm, H., & Mcelrath, S. (2016). Gender-based violence against men and boys in Darfur: The gender-genocide nexus. *Gender & Society, 30*(4), 565–589.

Flood, M. (2007). Involving men in gender policy and practice. *Critical Half: Bi-Annual Journal of Women for Women International, 5*(1), 9–13.

Flood, M., Howson, R. (2015). *Engaging men in building gender equality*. Newcastle upon Tyne: Cambridge Scholars.

Gibbs, A., Vaughan, C., & Aggleton, P. (Eds.). (2015). Beyond working with men and boys [special issue]. *Culture, Health & Sexuality*, 17(sup2), entire issue.

Jewkes, R., Morrell, R., Hearn, J., Lundqvist, E., Sikweyiya, Y., Blackbeard, D., Lindegger, G., Quayle, M. & Gottzén, L. (2015). Hegemonic masculinity: Combining theory and practice in gender interventions. *Culture, Health & Sexuality, 17*(s2), 112–127.

Katz, J., Heisterkamp, H. A., & Fleming, W. M. (2011). The social justice roots of the mentors in violence prevention model and its application in a high school setting. *Violence Against Women, 17*(6), 684–702.

Kimmel, M. (1996). *Manhood in America*. New York: Free Press.

Kimmel, M. S. (1987). Men's responses to feminism at the turn of the century. *Gender & Society, 1*(3), 261–283.

Kretschmer, K., & Barber, K. (2016). Men at the march: Feminist movement boundaries and men's participation in Take Back the Night and Slutwalk. *Mobilization: An International Quarterly, 21*(3), 283–300.

Langhinrichsen-Rohling, J., Foubert, J. D., Brasfield, H. M., Hill, B., & Shelley-Tremblay, S. (2011). The men's program: Does it impact college men's self-reported bystander efficacy and willingness to intervene? *Violence Against Women, 17*(6), 743–759.

Lapsansky, C., & Chatterjee, J. (2013). Masculinity matters: Using entertainment education to engage men in ending violence against women in India. *Critical Arts, 27*(1), 36–55.

McGann, P. (2009). A letter to Michael Murphy in response to 'Can "men" stop rape? Visualizing gender in the "My strength is not for hurting" rape prevention campaign'. *Men and Masculinities, 12*(1), 131134.

Men Can Stop Rape. 2011. Healthy masculinity campus conversations. Retrieved March 9, 2018, from www.mencanstoprape.org/Healthy-Masculinity-Campus-Conversations/.

Messner, M. A. (1997). *Politics of masculinities: Men in movements.* Lanham, MD: AltaMira Press.

Messner, M. A., Greenberg, M. A., & Peretz, T. (2015). *Some men: Feminist allies and the movement to end violence against women.* Oxford: Oxford University Press.

Murphy, M. J. (2009). Can 'men' stop rape? Visualizing gender in the 'My strength is not for hurting' rape prevention campaign. *Men and Masculinities, 12*(1), 113–130.

Nicholas, L. & Agius, C. (2017). *The persistence of global masculinism: Discourse, gender and neo-colonial re-articulations of violence.* Cham: Springer.

Peretz, T. (2017). Engaging diverse men: An intersectional analysis of men's pathways to antiviolence activism. *Gender & Society, 31*(4), 526–548.

Peretz, T. (2018). Seeing the invisible knapsack: Feminist men's strategic responses to the continuation of male privilege in feminist spaces. *Men and Masculinities.* doi:10.1177/1097184X18784990.

Peretz, T., Lehrer, J., & Dworkin, S. L. (2018). Impacts of men's gender-transformative personal narratives: A qualitative evaluation of the Men's Story project. *Men and Masculinities.* doi:10.1177/1097184X18780945.

Peretz, T., & Lehrer, J. (2019). The men's story project: Promoting healthy masculinities via men's public, personal narrative-sharing. *Global Social Welfare.* doi: 10.1007/s40609-018-00133-0.

Ratele, K., Shefer, T., & Botha, M. (2011). Navigating past 'the white man's agenda' in South Africa: Organising men for gendered transformation of society. In E. Ruspini, J. Hearn, B. Pease & K. Pringle (Eds.), *Men and masculinities around the world: Transforming men's practices* (pp. 247–260). New York: Palgrave Macmillan.

Rich, M. D. (2010). The interACT model: Considering rape prevention from a performance activism and social justice perspective. *Feminism & Psychology, 20*(4), 511–528.

Rumney, P. N. S. (2009). Gay male rape victims: Law enforcement, social attitudes and barriers to recognition. *The International Journal of Human Rights, 13*(2/3), 233–250.

Ruspini, E., Hearn, J., Pease, B., & Pringle, K. (Eds). (2011). *Men and masculinities around the world: Transforming men's practices.* New York: AIAA.

Sonke Gender Justice. (2013, April 25). About ambush theatre – YouTube. *About ambush theatre.* Retrieved from www.youtube.com/watch?v=9APzGdoQVOY.

Tolman, R. M., Casey, E. A., Allen, C. T., Carlson, J., Leek, C., & Storer, H. L. (2016). A global exploratory analysis of men participating in gender-based violence prevention. *Journal of Interpersonal Violence.* doi:10.1177/0886260516670181.

Tolman, R. M., Casey, E. A., Carlson, J. M., Allen, C.T., & Leek, C. (2019). Global efforts to engage men and boys in gender-based violence prevention [Special Issue], *Global Social Welfare. 6*(4), entire issue.

Verma, R. K., Pulerwitz, J., Mahendra, V., Khandekar, S., Barker, G., Fulpagare, P., & Singh, S. K. (2006). Challenging and changing gender attitudes among young men in Mumbai, India. *Reproductive Health Matters, 14*(28), 135–143.

Index

Made in the USA
Middletown, DE
24 October 2023